INTERACTIONAL
PSYCHOLOGY
AND
PERSONALITY

THE SERIES IN CLINICAL AND COMMUNITY PSYCHOLOGY

CONSULTING EDITORS:

CHARLES D. SPIELBERGER and IRWIN G. SARASON

Becker	● Depression: Theory and Research
Endler and Magnusson	● Interactional Psychology and Personality
Friedman and Katz	● The Psychology of Depression: Contemporary Theory and Research
Klopfer and Reed	● Problems in Psychotherapy: An Eclectic Approach
Reitan and Davison	● Clinical Neuropsychology: Current Status and Applications
Spielberger and Sarason	● Stress and Anxiety, volume 1
Sarason and Spielberger	● Stress and Anxiety, volume 2
Ulmer	● On the Development of a Token Economy Mental Hospital Treatment Program

IN PREPARATION

Averill	● Patterns in Psychological Thought: Readings in Historical and Contemporary Texts
Bermant, Kelman, and Warwick	● The Ethics of Social Intervention
Brehm	● The Application of Social Psychology to Clinical Practice
Cattell and Dreger	● Handbook of Modern Personality Theory
Cohen and Mirsky	● Biology and Psychopathology
Janisse	● A Psychological Survey of Pupillometry
Kissen	● From Group Dynamics to Group Psychoanalysis: Therapeutic Application of Group Dynamic Understanding
London	● Strategies of Personality Research
Olweus	● Aggression in the Schools
Sarason and Spielberger	● Stress and Anxiety, volume 3
Spielberger and Sarason	● Stress and Anxiety, volume 4
Spielberger and Diaz-Guerrero	● Crosscultural Research on Anxiety

INTERACTIONAL PSYCHOLOGY AND PERSONALITY

Edited with commentary by

Norman S. Endler
Department of Psychology
York University, Toronto

David Magnusson
Psychological Laboratories
University of Stockholm

HEMISPHERE PUBLISHING CORPORATION

Washington   London

A HALSTED PRESS BOOK
JOHN WILEY & SONS
New York   London   Sydney   Toronto

Hemisphere Publishing Corporation
1025 Vermont Ave., N.W., Washington, D.C. 20005

Distributed solely by Halsted Press, a Division of John Wiley & Sons, Inc., New York.

Library of Congress Cataloging in Publication Data

Main entry under title:

Interactional psychology and personality.

Includes indexes.
    1. Personality and situation. 2. Interpersonal relations.
I. Endler, Norman Solomon, 1931–   II. Magnusson,
David.
BF698.I48   155.2   75-15816
ISBN 0-470-24109-8

Printed in the United States of America

CONTENTS

CONTRIBUTORS

Henry A. Alker

Gordon W. Allport

Michael Argyle

Jean M. Arsenian

John Arsenian

Daryl J. Bem

Leonard Berkowitz

Doyle W. Bishop

Jack Block

Kenneth S. Bowers

Isidor Chein

Allen T. Dittmann

Bo Ekehammar

Norman S. Endler

Fred E. Fiedler

Norman Frederiksen

Russell G. Geen

Marianne Gerzén

Robert E. Grinder

J. McV. Hunt

Margaret I. Leggett

Brian R. Little

David Magnusson

Walter Mischel

Rudolf H. Moos

Marcia Mutterer

Edward A. Nelsen

Borje Nyman

Lawrence A. Pervin

Harold L. Raush

Rolf Gunnar Sandell

S. B. Sells

Ross Stagner

Thaddeus J. Taylor

Edison J. Trickett

Paul L. Wachtel

Michael A. Wallach

Peter A. Witt

PREFACE

Research and theory in the area of personality have been dominated by the trait model, which presumes latent predispositions that manifest themselves in terms of response consistencies across different situations. However, since the early 1960s the trait model has come under serious attack by situationists and interactionists. Although the theoretical basis for an interactionist approach to personality was proposed in the 1920s and 1930s, the systematic empirical research on this issue was not forthcoming until the 1960s. In fact, many of the empirical studies that have been published in the 1960s and early 1970s were developed almost independently of the theoretical bases proposed in the 1920s.

The first international conference on person by situation interactions took place in Stockholm, Sweden, during June 1975. The interest that this conference has generated among the active researchers in this field attests to the importance of the issue of person by situation interactions.

The specific aims of this book include presentation of the theoretical issues and empirical support for a person by situation interaction model of personality. When we originally started working on this book, we thought there would not be sufficient empirical material. Much to our (pleasant?) surprise we were faced with the task of selecting from a large number of articles those we thought most appropriate to our aims. Most of the 36 papers finally selected are contemporary in that 33 of them were originally published since 1963. In fact, over half (19) have been published since 1970. At least one of the editors has been involved in over one fourth (10) of the 36 papers selected. The research is based on data collected in both North America and Europe.

Chapter 1 (written by the editors) compares and contrasts four personality models (trait, psychodynamic, situationism, interactionism) in order to highlight the differences between the trait model and interactionism with respect to the determinants of actual behavior, the developmental aspects of actual behavior, and the research strategies and measurement of actual behavior. The four basic characteristics of interactionism (continuous process of interaction, intentional and active subjects, cognitive factors, and the psychological meaning of the situation) are discussed, and unidirectional causation and reciprocal causation in interaction are compared. Finally, in analyzing situations, a comparison is made between physical and psychological environments on the one hand and perception and reaction approaches to studying situations on the other. Chapter 1 also presents a table that highlights the differences among the four basic personality models.

Chapters 2–6 present empirical and theoretical studies that have relevance for the person–situation interaction model in personality. The results of many of the studies pertinent to interactionism are not readily available to undergraduate and graduate studies because they are widely dispersed in the scientific literature. A major aim has been to make most of the research in this area readily accessible to scholars and researchers, and an attempt has been made to integrate the various findings.

There are two sections to each of these chapters: (1) an introduction to and commentary on the readings (written by the editors), which discusses the issues, provides a theoretical and methodological background for them and, when appropriate, shows their relevance to other chapters and provides appropriate references; (2) a number of selected articles relevant to the issues discussed in the introduction and commentary section.

Chapter 2 discusses the basic issues in interactional psychology, while chap. 3 presents the results of relevant empirical studies. Chapter 4 is concerned with methodologies for analyzing person by situation interactions; chap. 5 focuses on the analyses of situations, studying the environment. Finally, chap. 6 is concerned with some recent controversies in the field of interactionism.

This book has been aimed primarily at advanced undergraduates and graduates. It may serve as a text or supplementary text for courses in personality research and in personality theory. Obviously it can be used as a sourcebook for researchers in the field of personality. We hope this book will raise more questions than it will answer and will therefore encourage readers to seek solutions to the issues discussed.

We would like to express our gratitude to the authors of the articles included in this book and to the various publishers for granting us permission to reproduce their papers. Specific acknowledgments are included on the first page of each article. Work on this book was partially supported by a John B. C. Watkins Canada Council Leave Fellowship to N.S.E., and by a grant from the Swedish Council for Social Science Research to D.M. Most of the editorial work on this book was done at the Psychological Laboratories, University of Stockholm, where N.S.E. was on sabbatical as a visiting professor (during 1973–1974) and D.M. was on sabbatical from his duties as director of the laboratories.

Valuable comments and suggestions have been made by Dr. Dan Olweus of the Department of Psychology at the University of Bergen, Dr. Daisy Schalling of the Department of Psychology at the University of Stockholm, Dr. Ross Stagner of Wayne State University, and Drs. Morris Eagle and David Reid of York University.

We wish to thank Barbro Svensson, Ann-Sofi Hedell, and Eva Hamilton for secretarial assistance and Håkan Stattin for assistance in preparing the index.

Much of our own research that is included in this book has been supported by research grants from the National Institute of Mental Health (NIMH), The

Ontario Mental Health Foundation (Canada), the Canada Council, and the Swedish Council for Social Science Research. Obviously this work has involved crosscultural collaboration.

Finally we would like to thank our wives and our children, who have helped in more ways than they are probably aware of!

Norman S. Endler
David Magnusson

INTERACTIONAL
PSYCHOLOGY
AND
PERSONALITY

CHAPTER ONE

PERSONALITY AND PERSON BY SITUATION INTERACTIONS

PERSONALITY MODELS

A prime concern in the area of personality is the issue of the determinants or sources of behavior. What initiates the behavioral manifestations of personality? What directs it? How does personality develop? How does one measure personality? Is behavior consistent across situations, or is it situation-specific? How do situations and persons interact in eliciting behavior? To put these problems in perspective it is useful to distinguish four main models in personality psychology: the trait model; the psychodynamic model, with its roots in psychoanalysis; the situationism model, with its roots in behaviorism; and the interactionism model.[1]

Historically, theory, research, and method in personality have been dominated primarily by the trait model and partially by its precursor, the type model. The trait model has played the dominant role in personality for many decades, both in terms of research on actual behavior, the construction and use of measuring instruments, and methods and models for data treatment, and with respect to the practical use of behavioral data. However, since about 1960, the opposing person–situation interaction model advocated earlier by a number of psychological theorists has been empirically tested by many investigators.

Obviously there are internal differences within each of the four basic personality models. However, it is possible to identify a core for each model that distinguishes it from the others on a number of parameters. In order to compare the trait and interactionistic models it is fruitful to describe the four basic models with respect to three essential parameters:

---

[1] A fifth model, phenomenology, initiated by Husserl (see Boring, 1950, p. 367) has also had an important impact on personality theory and research. Basically, this model is concerned with the individual's introspective and internal subjective states or experiences. This model has emphasized such variables as the self-concept (see Rogers, 1951, 1959), personal constructs (see Kelly, 1955), and psychological fields (see Lewin, 1935, 1936). It has important consequences for humanistic psychology, existential psychology, and psychotherapy. Since a basic aim of the present discussion is to compare and contrast the trait model and the interactionism model on certain fundamental issues, no further discussion of phenomenology will be presented. For a survey of phenomenological theories, the reader should consult Mischel (1971).

1

1. the determinants of actual behavior (i.e., the explanation of actual behavior in a situation);
2. the development aspects of actual behavior (i.e., how an individual's reaction pattern is determined ontogenetically); and
3. the consequences of (1) and (2) with respect to research strategy.

(1) The Determinants of Actual Behavior

The trait model (and its precursor, the type model) and the psychodynamic model regard actual behavior as determined by latent, stable dispositions.

Type model. The first *type* theorist was probably Hippocrates (ca. 400 B.C.E.) who suggested four basic types of temperament (choleric, melancholic, sanguine, and phlegmatic) and attributed these temperaments to different bodily humors (yellow bile, black bile, blood, and phlegm, respectively). In the last century, Kretschmer (1926), a German psychiatrist, postulated that schizophrenia was associated with an asthenic (thin) body build and manic depressive reactions with a pyknic (fat) body build. He then attempted to relate these body build types to different temperaments in the normal population. Sheldon (1949) attempted to dimensionalize the body build typology and related three dimensions of physique (endomorphy, mesomorphy, and ectomorphy) to three dimensions of temperament (viscerotonia, somatotonia, and cerebrotonia, respectively). Jung's (1923) classification of introversion and extroversion types is based purely on a psychological classification and does not concern itself with physique. Most of the typologies have a biological and constitutional emphasis and assume that the expression of personality (e.g., temperament) is caused by physique or body build. These typologies represent what might be called the "categorical" view of personality since they assume discrete categories of personality.

Trait and psychodynamic models. The *trait model* is a dimensional one and assumes that there are various continuous dimensions with individual differences on each of these dimensions. The trait theorists emphasize traits as the prime determinants of behavior, and psychodynamic theories, such as psychoanalysis, assume a basic personality core, which serves as a predispositional basis for behavior in different situations. The factors determining behavior are within the person himself, i.e., $B = f(P)$. In the description of individuals the interest for these two models lies in the relation between responses in different situations, and between responses and the latent dispositions for which the responses are supposed to be indicators. Traits are the main sources of behavioral differences, and furthermore, for the trait model, the rank order of individuals with respect to a certain behavior is consistent across different situations. This assumption of stable rank orders does not always hold for the psychodynamic model. However, in most cases and in the absence of the operation of defense mechanisms, the assumption of rank order stability is also valid for that model. Both the trait model and the psychodynamic model may be called response–response (R–R) models of behavior.

Situationism model. *Situationism*, which is the antithesis of the trait and psychodynamic models with respect to causality, regards situational factors, or the stimuli in the situation, as the main determinants of individual behavior, i.e., $B = f(S)$. Social psychologists and sociologists (Cooley, 1902; Cottrell, 1942a, 1942b; Mead, 1934) as well as social learning theorists (e.g., Bandura, 1971; Bandura & Walters, 1963; Skinner, 1953, 1960) believe that situations are the main sources of behavioral differences. This model is basically a stimulus–response (S–R) model.

Interactionism model. According to *interactionism*, actual behavior is the result of an indispensable, continuous interaction between the person and the situations he encounters (i.e., $B = f(P, S)$. This implies that the individual's behavior is influenced by significant features of the situations, but furthermore the individual chooses the situations in which he performs and selects significant situational aspects which then serve as cues for his activities in these situations. He subsequently affects the character of these situations. The interactional viewpoint will be further developed in this chapter.

Comparison of the models regarding causality. The most extreme trait position would postulate that individual behavior would be attributed solely to factors within the person, implying that no inter-individual differences in behavior would be due to the situations in which behavior occurs, nor to person–situation interactions. Similarly, the most extreme situationistic position would postulate that individual behavior is solely determined by situational factors and that person factors and interactions do not contribute at all to behavior variation. The most extreme interactionistic position would postulate that the systematic behavioral variation would be solely due to interactions and not at all to person or situation factors as main factors. Obviously *no one* is advocating any of these extreme positions, but the difference among these viewpoints is primarily a matter of the relative emphases placed on the various factors. For a trait or psychodynamic theorist the *personal* (inner directed) factors are most dominant and the ones of most interest for his research; for a situationist theorist, most of the variance is due to the *situational* (outer directed) factors, and his prime research interest is in such factors; and for an interactionist the *person by situation* interaction is the most important one to be studied.

(2) Developmental Aspects of Actual Behavior

Trait and psychodynamic models. The models differ markedly with respect to the emphasis they place on developmental aspects, and with respect to their views on the ontogenetic background for actual, present behavior. The trait model pays less attention to developmental aspects than the psychodynamic model. Basically, however, the traits are regarded as stable dispositions, which are affected to some degree by maturation, but not primarily by environmental factors. For the psychodynamic theorists the latent dispositions determining actual behavior have been formed on the basis of early interpersonal experiences modifying the expression of inherited instincts or motivational forces. Individual differences in adult behavior are a function of both genic and experiential determinants (see Dewald, 1969, regarding his discussion of Freud). The developmental aspect of psychodynamic theory is in a sense partially a stimulus-response (S–R) theory, because it assumes that early experiences (environmental factors) affect the expression of the basic instincts, and both these types of factors interact to influence the adult personality.

Situationism model. The developmental basis for adult behavior according to situationism is social learning (e.g., Bandura & Walters, 1963; Rotter, 1954), and little attention is paid to inherited factors. The actual reaction pattern in a situation is determined by social learning processes.

Interactionism model. For the person–situation interaction model, development involves a social learning process that emphasizes the interaction between person variables and meaningful situations. The focus on person variables is in terms of cognitive social learning and on the meanings that situations have for individuals. Not only do situations affect individuals but the person selects and subsequently influences the situations he interacts with (e.g., see Mischel, 1973a [8] [2]).

(3) Research Strategy and Measurement of
Individual Characteristics

Perhaps the most important differences between the models are their consequences for research strategies, for methods and models of data collection, and for data treatment.

Trait model. The greatest impact with respect to personality research has been made by the trait model. Tests and questionnaires, the most frequently used methods for collecting data, both in research and in applied psychology (e.g., classification, selection, and counselling), are intimately related to the trait model. Similarly, classical test theory (using true scores) and factor analysis (assuming stable personality factors), the most frequent models and methods for data treatment, are intimately related to the trait model. Thurstone (1947, p. 57), formulating the theoretical basis in personality for the use of factor analysis, stated ". . . that mental phenomena can be identified in terms of distinguishable functions, which do not participate equally in everything that mind does. It is

---

[2] Bold-face numbers in square brackets refer to the article number in this text.

these functional units that we are looking for with the aid of factorial methods. It is our scientific faith that such distinguishable mental functions can be identified. . . ." The interest of trait psychologists in the internal relationships among individual characteristics led to the frequent use of regression techniques. Trait psychology is the main exponent of what Cronbach (1957) has called "correlational psychology."

Psychodynamic model. Psychodynamic theorists have shown little interest in measurement problems and in formal techniques for data collection. This is natural since the psychodynamic model is primarily interested in idiographic description. Interviews and free association are the major methods for collecting information, and the case history (case descriptions) the appropriate method for presenting their results.

Situationism model. Situationism has not generated any methods of its own for data collection and data treatment, but has relied instead on the classical methods of experimental psychology. Researchers in this field have attempted to determine the effects of various experimental treatments (stimuli) on subsequent responses. The most frequently used method for data collection has been behavioral response counts, and the most common method for data treatment has been analysis of variance. However, in analyzing situations, factor analysis (Endler, Hunt, & Rosenstein, 1962) and psychophysical and scaling methods have been used (Magnusson, 1971 [28]).

Interactionism model. The model of interactionism has wide-ranging con-sequences for research strategy, for the construction of instruments for data collection, and for the choice of models for data treatment. Results of research during the 1960s and 1970s (which will be discussed later) on the person-situation issue, show clearly that the traditional methods and models used by trait psychology are inappropriate for many important purposes in personality research and applied psychology. The appropriate methods for data collection within the context of an interactional model should analyze information in the multidimensional patterns of reactions across situations for individuals. For many purposes, both in research and in applied settings, traditional questionnaires normally used for data collection should be replaced by the S–R (situation-response) type of inventories, developed by Endler, Hunt, and Rosenstein (1962). In the S–R inventories, individuals, responses, and situations are taken into account simultaneously. An interactional research strategy should also include, for example, new methods such as the Markov model for studying continuous interactional processes (see, for example Raush, 1972), and de-scriptive models for forming homogeneous groups of individuals on the basis of their distinctive patterns of reaction across situations (e.g., Mårdberg, 1973). Chapter four in this book includes methodological papers that are relevant to the interactionism model.

CRITIQUE OF THE TRAIT MODEL

The trait model has probably played the most dominant role in personality research and applied psychology. It is partially because of this that its inadequacies have become most obvious. Research methods and strategies are not independent of the theoretical bases of personality, and in criticizing the trait model one should focus on its theory as well as on its methods and research strategies.

According to the trait model, an individual can be described in terms of a combination of traits (e.g., dependency, anxiety, aggressiveness, achievement), which are supposed to be stable, latent dispositions. These latent dispositions determine a person's manifest behavior and account for consistency in individual behavior across different situations. Allport (1937) conceived of traits as tendencies or predispositions to respond and suggested that there are *"bona fide* mental structures in each personality that account for the consistency of its behavior" (p. 289). For Allport (1937), Cattell (1950, 1957, 1965), and Guilford (1959), traits are the basic units to be studied in personality. Wallace (1967) has suggested using skills, rather than dispositions, as the basic units. Although the various trait theorists do not agree as to the specific structure and content of traits, they do agree that traits are latent dispositions that account for consistencies in behavior across a wide variety of situations. Thus, behavior can be explained in terms of traits.

Given this point of view of the "classical" trait theory, it is sufficient to merely study the individual. Situations are taken into account, but the provoking and restricting effect of situational factors on behavior is not supposed to change the rank order of individuals for a given trait. This means that the rank order of individuals for any given trait is supposed to be the same for different situations independent of the situational characteristics, except for errors of measurement (see Argyle and Little, 1972 [1]). For example, this is the assumption underlying the construction and use of homogeneous scales that measure personality variables (see Magnusson, 1974a).

It should be clear that what has been called trait theory in the earlier discussion is not a unified theory about which all trait theorists would agree. Among other things, the theoretical formulations have changed from the earlier ones proposed by Allport (1937) and Thurstone (1947), for example, to later ones suggested by Cattell (1965) and Stagner (1974). Possibly, late advocates of a trait position would not agree about our description of the trait theory. For example, both Cattell (1965) and Stagner (1974) have proposed a modified trait position that is cognizant of situational factors. However, our description of the basic elements of the trait position is correct as a description of that position as it has been used as a basis for *measurement* in empirical personality research and application for many decades. The trait measurement model has influenced both the construction and use of methods for data collection, and the development and use of data models and methods for data treatment. Therefore, it is essential for further personality research and application that the crucial assumptions made in the trait theory, as described here, are tested empirically.

Consistency versus Situational Specificity

A crucial question for trait psychology as it was described here is: Does the rank order of individuals with respect to a specific variable (e.g., anxiousness) show the trans-situational stability which is assumed by trait theorists, or is behavior situation-specific? This question has been tested empirically in at least two major ways:

1. By investigating and comparing the variance due to individuals with the variance due to the main sources of situations and reactions (modes of response) and with the variance due to person–situation interactions and other two-way interactions. Most empirical studies of the transsituation stability hypothesis have been conducted using this approach, despite some of its limitations, for that purpose. These limitations have been discussed by Magnusson (1974a).

2. By studying the correlation of individual rank orders for a specific personality variable across different situations. Although the correlational approach provides a more direct test of the assumption of cross-situational stability, it has been less influential than the multidimensional variance components approach. This is probably because the multidimensional variance components approach provides an empirical basis for developing an alternative to the trait model.

(a) Multidimensional variance components research strategy. The first empirical studies on the consistency–specificity issue using the multidimensional variance approach were published by Raush, Dittmann, and Taylor (1959a; 1959b [9]), and by Raush, Farbman, and Llewellyn (1960). In a study of the behavior of delinquent boys in various settings, and using a multivariate information transmission analysis of ratings of observed behavior, they found that the person by situation interaction accounted for more behavioral variance than either persons or situations. In a study of anxiousness, Endler, Hunt, and Rosenstein (1962) introduced and developed an S-R Inventory of Anxiousness, a type of questionnaire that has been used in many later studies. In the S-R type of inventory the subjects rate their own reactions on a number of scales for each of a number of verbally described situations, thus yielding a three-dimensional (persons by reactions by situations) data matrix.

Endler and Hunt (1966 [10], 1969 [11]) using modified forms of the original anxiety inventory and employing a variance components technique (Endler, 1966b [21]) found that individual differences accounted for about 4 to 5 percent of the total variance, and situations about 4 percent for males and about 8 percent for females, but the person–situation interactions accounted for about 10 percent. In fact, all the simple two-way interactions accounted for about 30 percent of the variance, which was more than the sum of the contributions for individuals and situations. With respect to hostility, Endler and Hunt (1968 [13]) found that individual differences accounted for about 19 percent of the variance for males and about 15 percent for females, situations for about 5 percent of males and about 7 percent for females, and the person by situation interaction about 11 percent. All the simple two-way interactions accounted for about 30 percent of the variance.

In evaluating this data, it should be clear that the outcome of the analyses of variance is dependent to some degree on the choice of individuals, situations, and reactions that are studied. The specific choice of individuals, situations, and reactions affects the relative contribution of each of these sources of variance to the total variance. However, the data seriously question the trait position of trans-situational consistency of behavior. And other studies using different samples of individuals, different kinds of reaction variables, and different kinds of situations support the same conclusion.

Moos (1968 [17], 1969, 1970), using the Endler and Hunt variance components model, analyzed self ratings in the actual presence of situations and observations of subjects' overt behavior (smiling, smoking, talking). Moos used various types of ward settings as the situations, tested psychiatric patients and ward staff, and analyzed a number of different variables. Sandell (1968 [19]) studied choice behavior (type of drink preferred) in various situations; Nelson, Grinder, and Mutterer (1969 [12]) reported results from studies on honesty; and Bishop and Witt (1970 [18]), using an S-R Inventory for the study of leisure time activities, published data also invalidating the trait position. Fiedler (1971 [15]), in his review of empirical research, found that leadership effectiveness was dependent on situational characteristics. Using a variation of the Endler et al. (1962) S-R Inventory of Anxiousness, Endler (1973 [33]) and Ekehammar, Magnusson, and Ricklander (1974) obtained anxiety data pointing to the same conclusions, as was the case in the studies on conforming behavior by Endler (1966a); Endler and Hoy (1967); Endler, Wiesenthal, and Geller (1972); and Weisenthal, Endler, and Geller (1973). A study by Trickett and Moos (1970 [20]) of self ratings of feelings and initiatives, made by pupils at school, gave similar results, indicating a high degree of situational specificity of behavior in the classroom situation, as did earlier studies of other variables (Amidon and Flanders, 1961; Feather, 1961). Many of these studies have been summarized by Bowers (1973, [7]), Mischel (1973a [8]), and Ekehammar (1974).

(b) Correlational research strategy. The more direct test of the assumption of cross-situational stability or consistency of behavior, using the correlational approach, was conducted by Hartshorne and May (1928) in their classic study of honesty. Their results have been the focus of much debate, but it seems justified to conclude that their study does not support the trait theoretical assumption. Magnusson, Gerzén, and Nyman (1968 [16]) and Magnusson, Heffler, and Nyman (1969), using the same approach, investigated the cross-situational stability in ratings of cooperative ability, self-confidence, and leadership, and in objective measures of talking time. They did this by a systematic variation of the situation variables of group composition and task. They did not find any cross-situational stability. Actually, the correlations between ratings from situations that differed with respect to both situational variables were zero.

A further development of the correlational approach in studying the trait hypothesis about trans-situational consistency is to analyze by factor analysis a set of intercorrelations between different situational measures of the same main dependent variable. According to the trait hypothesis, most of the total variance will then be explained by one main factor. More than one factor was found in studies by Sakoda (1952), using data from the OSS situational tests; by Burton (1963), who reanalyzed the honesty data from Hartshorne and May (1928); and by Nelson, Grinder, and Mutterer (1969 [12]), who also studied honesty data.

Evaluation

Mischel (1968, 1969, 1971), Pervin (1968 [3]), Vernon (1964), Argyle and Little (1972 [1]), Endler (1973 [33]; 1975a, 1975b [2]), Endler and Magnusson (1974), and Argyle (1975), evaluating the trait position, have indicated that there is little empirical support for the belief in trans-situational consistencies of behavior. The results from the studies discussed here not only strongly support the inappropriateness of the trait model as a general basis for the use of personality data in description and prediction of behavior in actual situations, but also as a general basis for personality research. The effect of situational specificity varies, however, with the kinds of variables studied and, to some extent, with the kinds of subjects used (cf. Endler, 1973 [33], on psychiatric patients compared with normal subjects). These conclusions are based on results from studies on social behavior and noncognitive personality variables, such as aggression, anxiety, attitudes to authority, conformity, dependency, rigidity, self-confidence, and leadership. Hunt (1966), on the basis of empirical evidence, has questioned the belief in fixed intelligence, but there is some evidence for stability over time, and for trans-situational consistency with respect to intellectual and cognitive variables (see Mischel, 1968, 1969, 1973a [8] for a summary). Some personality variables bearing an affinity to "cognitive style," like impulsivensss (cf. Shapiro, 1965), may also belong to this latter group of variables.

THE PERSON–SITUATION INTERACTION MODEL IN PERSONALITY

The empirical studies referred to in the preceding section were basically planned to test the trait hypothesis about trans-situational consistency of behavior. As stated, the results were not congruent with a trait psychological model. Instead, the results of studies using the analysis of variance (variance components) approach supported the alternative interactionism model, stressing the interaction between the individual and the situations he encounters.

Early Formulations

The concept of interactionism is neither new nor unique to psychology. Aristotle was probably the first to formulate an interactionist view of behavior (see Shute, 1973). Philosophers' current interest in interactionism is attested to by a recent symposium on contextual interactionism (Smith, 1973). The seventeenth-century physicist Robert Hooke proposed that the elasticity of a substance is a function of the interaction of the nature of the material and the degree of situational stress (Bridgwater and Kurtz, 1963). Weiss (1969) has pointed to the importance of organism–environment interactions for biology.

Although there has been a proliferation of research on interactionism in psychology since about 1960, the theoretical basis for the interaction model of personality was discussed much earlier. In fact, the first empirical studies on person–situation interactions (in the 1960s) were conducted without any clear connection to the earlier theoretical bases. Kantor (1924, 1926), although not citing supporting empirical evidence, was one of the first to postulate a person–situation interaction theory of behavior. He stated that the unit of study for psychology was "the individual as he interacts with all of the various types of situations which constitute his behavior circumstances" (Kantor, 1924, p. 92). In 1935, in a behavioristic frame of reference, Tolman, in his formula for the determination of actual behavior, stressed the necessity of taking situational factors, as well as person factors, into account. "The independent variables S (an environmental stimulus set up), H (the heredity of the organism), T (the past training of the organism) and P (physiological appetite or aversion) are full causes for the final resulting behavior. And if we symbolize the latter by B, then a total equation of the form B = f(S, H, T, P) can be written" (cf. Tolman, 1951, p. 102).

Lewin, in his field theory and in his general thinking (1935, 1936, 1938, 1951), presented an interactionistic viewpoint which has influenced many later theorists. He stressed the interaction between personality and a meaningful environment, $B = f(P, E)$, and maintained the indispensable interdependency of personal and situational factors in eliciting behavior. According to Lewin, the individual is part of the situation. In these formulations, he actually fore-shadowed the main elements of modern interactionism.

The interaction between personal factors and situation factors was also an essential characteristic of Murray's (1938) need–press theory. "Since, at every moment, an organism is within an environment which largely determines its behavior, and since the environment changes—sometimes with radical abruptness—the conduct of an individual cannot be formulated without a characterization of each confronting situation, physical and social" (Murray, 1938, p. 39). The unit of analysis for the study of personality, according to Murray, is the organism–environment interaction, rather than either variable per se. Murray's theory uses parallel constructs for individuals and environments. *Need* refers to a characteristic of the individual, and *press*, which is concerned with need satisfaction and frustration, refers to a characteristic of the environment. Need–press combinations are called *themas* in Murray's theory. Since Murray uses parallel dimensions to describe needs and presses, his scheme may be useful for an examination of person–situation interactions.

Angyal (1941), using the construct of "biosphere," underlined the importance of the meaningful environment and maintained the Lewinian viewpoint that the individual-environment construct is a unit and cannot be decomposed into persons and environments. Sullivan's (1953) discussion of interpersonal relations belongs to the interactionistic tradition. Murphy's (1947) biosocial theory is basically an interactionist theory, and Rotter (1954), in his social learning approach to personality, clearly emphasizes the interactionist position. In his cognitive adaptation-level theory Helson (1959, 1964) clearly formulated an interactionistic view, stating that person variables ". . . can be studied and understood only as they interact with concrete situations, and operationally such concepts have no meaning apart from situational factors" (Helson, 1959, p. 610). Sakoda (1952), referring to Lewin, explicitly expressed his belief in the interactionistic approach, and Cronbach (1957) argued for a psychological description of behavior that considers the situations in which behavior is studied.

Recent Formulations

Concurrent with the first empirical studies on person by situation interaction, "modern" formulations of interactionism began to appear (for example, Endler & Hunt, 1966 [10], 1968 [13], 1969 [11]; Hunt, 1965; Magnusson, Gerzén, & Nyman, 1968 [16]; Raush, 1965 [22]; Sells, 1963a [27], 1963b). On the basis of summaries of empirical studies on trans-situational consistency of behavior, comprehensive discussions of modern interactionism have been provided by Pervin (1968 [3]), Argyle and Little (1972 [1]), Bowers (1973 [7]), Mischel (1973a [8], 1973b [36]), Endler (1973 [33], 1975b [2]), and Ekehammar (1974). Mischel has moved from a situationistic viewpoint in his earlier discussions (1968, 1969) to a clear interactionist position (1973a [8]). Sherif and Sherif (1969) in their discussion of social interaction, Carson (1969) in his development of Sullivan's interpersonal theory, Jones and Nisbett (1971) and Schneider (1973) in their reviews of the literature on person perception, and Olweus (1973, pp. 281–286) discussing his research on aggression, all operate within an interactionistic framework. Recent discussions of the person by situation interaction issue have also been provided by Wallace (1967), Block (1968 [4]), Magnusson and Heffler (1969), Vale and Vale (1969), Goldfried and Kent (1972), and Krasner and Ullmann (1973).

Conceptions of recent formulations of interactional psychology can be summarized by four main points:

1. Behavior is determined by a continuous process of interaction between the individual and the situation he encounters (feedback).
2. The individual is an intentional, active agent in this interaction process.
3. Cognitive factors are important in interaction.
4. The psychological meaning of the situation to the individual is an essential determinant of behavior.

(a) **Continuous process of interaction.** There is a continuous interdependency between persons and situational factors (*feedback*), and this interaction is a prime determinant of behavior (e.g., Lewin, 1935, 1936). This interaction provides a multivariate, two dimensional (situation by response reaction) pattern of behavioral variability across situations for each person. Furthermore, this interactive pattern is, to some extent, idiographic (see, e.g., Endler and Hunt, 1969 [11]; Magnusson, 1971 [28]; Raush, Farbman, & Llewellyn, 1960). One way of analyzing this pattern has been to obtain a three dimensional matrix (persons by reactions by situations) for individuals, and study the relative influence of each main source, each simple interaction, and the triple interaction. This is the basis for the empirical studies referred to in the presentation of the person by situation interaction issue. The implications of this approach will be discussed in this chapter (see section on uni-directional causation and reciprocal causation in interaction).

(b) **Intentional and active agents.** The person is an intentional and active agent in the interactional process. He interprets the situations and assigns meaning to them. To some extent, he selects his situational encounters and by his conscious and unconscious actions affects the character of the situations (see Bowers, 1973 [7]; Mischel, 1973a [8]; and Stagner, 1973 [6]). This implies that behavior is purposive (Tolman, 1951) and goal-directed (Arsenian and Arsenian, 1948 [24]).

(c) **Cognitive factors.** As a consequence, it is obvious that cognitive factors are an important determinant of behavior. The relevance of cognitive factors in the person by situation interaction was emphasized by Tolman (1949, p. 412). Bowers (1973 [7]) discusses a "biocognitive conception of behavior," and Mischel (1973a [8]) argues that the following five cognitive variables and their interactions are important in explaining individual differences: (a) construction competence (the ability to construct or generate particular cognitions and behaviors); (b) encoding strategies and personal constructs; (c) behavior-outcome and stimulus-outcome expectancies in particular situations; (d) subjective stimulus values; and (e) self-regulatory systems and plans, rules, and self-reactions for the performance and organization of complex behavior sequences. These cognitive person variables interact with situations in determining behavior. They develop ontogenetically in terms of a social learning process interacting with a given genetic disposition.

(d) **Psychological meaning of the situation.** In terms of situational variables the psychological meaning that a situation has for an individual is an essential determinant of his behavior (see Magnusson, 1971 [28]). The emphasis on psychologically investigating environmental factors (situations) and the psychological meanings of situations in person–situation interaction studies have important consequences for research strategy. The situation as a variable in interactionism will be discussed in more detail later in this chapter.

Unidirectional Causation and Reciprocal Causation in Interaction

The concept of interaction discussed here refers to the interaction of two independent variables (persons and situations), rather than to the interaction between independent and dependent (behavior) variables. Overton and Reese (1973) have made an important distinction between two models of man: the *mechanistic*, or reactive, model and the *organismic*, or organism, model. The organismic model could just as well be called a dynamic model of man. For the mechanistic model the interaction is between causes, rather than between chains of causes and effects. This model is concerned with unidirectional causality and assumes that independent variables affect dependent variables. The organismic model is concerned with a reciprocal action (feedback) between environmental events and behavior. It is concerned with reciprocal causation so that not only do events affect the behavior of organisms, but the organism is also an active agent in influencing environmental events. This last view is an essential element of the modern person–situation interaction view of behavior (Bowers, 1973 [7]; Mischel, 1973a [8]). Pervin (1968 [3]) clearly expresses the distinction between these two types of causality and suggests the term *interactional* for unidirectional causality, and the term *transactional* for reciprocal causation (see Endler, 1975b [2] for a further discussion of the Overton–Reese position).

Overton and Reese (1973) state that the analysis of variance approach to the treatment of data is tied to the mechanistic model of man and is therefore inappropriate for the study of behavioral processes as they are perceived by the organismic model. They advocate the use of methods for data treatment that are adjusted to the specific nature of the data that are obtained according to the reciprocal causation (feedback) model.

Ultimately, we have to be concerned with a model that examines the effects of person–situation interactions on behavior and the effect this behavior has on situational factors. However, we are not yet at the stage in psychology where we have isolated the basic parameters that affect behavior, nor do we know how they interact with each other. Furthermore, the methodology and technology to examine the nature of dynamic interaction have not yet been fully developed. In effect, we are suggesting that it is necessary to examine both types of interaction. Unfortunately, most of the research to date on interaction (as attested to by the research articles in this book) has been concerned with the reactive model of man and with the interaction of independent variables in affecting behavior. Hopefully, in the future there will be research that empirically examines dynamic interaction and investigates the bidirectional (feedback) nature of organismic interaction. A promising start has been made in this direction, as attested to by Raush's (1972) use of a Markov model for investigating the process of interaction and of change.

ANALYSES OF SITUATIONS: THE ENVIRONMENT IN INTERACTIONAL PSYCHOLOGY

Theoretical Distinctions

A great deal of effort has been expended in personality research in an attempt to dimensionalize personality constructs. However, although the S-R learning theorists have attested to the importance of situations as determinants of behavior, relatively little effort has been expended in dimensionalizing, defining, and determining the nature of situations. Environments can be distinguished in terms both of type and of level.

Objective and subjective (psychological) environments (type). According to interactional psychology, the environment plays an indispensable role in the determination of behavior. The early interactionists (see section on early formulations) recognized this fact and were concerned with and discussed the role of the environment in behavior. In those discussions a distinction was usually made between two types of environments, the physical and the psychological. The various theorists have used different terms (e.g., Kantor, 1924, 1926, *biological-psychological environment*; Koffka, 1935, *geographical-behavioral environment*; Murray, 1938, *alpha press-beta press*) with somewhat different meanings. However, the main conceptual distinction with respect to type of environment has been between the *objective* "outer world" (physical and social variables) as it affects the individual, and the *subjective* world (psychological variables), the environment as the individual perceives it and reacts to it (see Fiske, 1971, and Pervin, 1968 [3]).

Macro and micro environments (level). A further distinction of the "outer world" as an environment that affects individual behavior has been discussed by Magnusson, Dunér, and Zetterblom (1975). They distinguished between the *physical environment*, which can be described on a molar level (buildings, parks, lakes, homes, streets, etc.) or on a molecular level (that is, in terms of single objects or single stimulus variables), and the *social environment*, which also can be discussed on two levels: the macro-social environment defined by the laws, norms, values, etc., that are common to a whole society or a culture; and the micro-social environment defined by the norms, attitudes, habits, etc., of the specific groups and persons with whom an individual interacts directly, at school, at home, during leisure time, etc. The macro-social environment can be regarded as common to most members of a society, whereas the micro-social environment is, to some degree, unique for each individual. The importance of the macro-social environment for various aspects of people's behavior has been stressed by social psychologists, sociologists, and anthropologists (e.g., Arsenian & Arsenian, 1948 [24]).

The subset of the "outer world," which an individual encounters and acts upon in his daily life, including both physical and social environmental factors, can be conceptualized in Brunswik's (1952, 1956) term as the *ecology*. Actual behavior takes place in a *situation*, which is here defined as that part of the ecology that an individual can perceive and react upon immediately (Murray, 1938, p. 40), the "momentary situation" in Lewin's terminology (1936, p. 217).

Empirical Approaches to Systematic Analyses of the Environment

Though the environment has been the object of much interest for the interactionists, very few empirical studies of a psychological nature have been conducted. In connection with the growing research on the person by situation interaction during the sixties and the early seventies, the need for systematic analyses of the environment and especially of the situations in which behavior is studied became more obvious. This has been explicitly formulated from a number of viewpoints (e.g., Abelson, 1962; Endler, 1975b [2] ; Magnusson, 1971 [28] ; Miller, 1963; Moos, 1973; Pervin, 1968 [3] ; Schneider, 1973; Sells, 1963a [27]). An interest in situational analyses has also been indicated in recent formulations of psychodynamic theory (see Wachtel, 1973 [35]), and by modern trait theories (e.g., Allport, 1966 [5] ; Cattell, 1965; Stagner, 1973 [6]).

As indicated earlier, the environment can be described in two main ways (with different levels of generality for each one):

1. In terms of the objective "outer world," the environment "as it is," independent of the interpretations made by the individuals reacting to it.
2. In terms of psychological significance of the environment to the individual, the subjective world.

In terms of the objective "outer world," the description can be made in terms of physical factors, social factors, or a combination of physical and social factors. The psychological significance of the environment can be investigated by studying the individual's *perception* of the situation (the meaning he assigns to a situation) and *reaction* to a situation (a specific situation or the general environment).

Situational domains: perceptions and reactions. Since behaviors occur in situations, then logically much interest and effort should be devoted to empirical studies of situations. Magnusson (1971 [28]) has argued that in empirical studies of situational characteristics, the choice of situations should be made after a definition of situational domains. For example, he discussed sets of situations that were homogeneous with respect to such situational factors as interpersonal relationships, leisure activities, studies, work duties, job positions, etc. Homogeneous domains of situations can be defined in terms of objective characteristics (physical and/or social) and/or subjective characteristics (perceptions and/or reactions). With respect to subjective factors, this can be accomplished via factor analysis based on subjects' reactions (see Endler, Hunt, & Rosenstein, 1962) or via psychophysical scaling methods based on subjects' perceptions of situations (see Magnusson, 1971 [28]).

Situations can also differ in other respects. Some are weak; some are strong in terms of their effects on behavior. Some are relevant, others irrelevant for the behavior being investigated. Some are facilitating or provocative, others inhibitory (see Magnusson, 1974b; Mischel, 1973a [8]).

The objective approach. Some researchers have advocated the approach involving a description and classification of the "objective environment." Tolman's behavioristic equation for studying the person by situation interaction referred to the physical characteristics of the environment in his equation. The most comprehensive outline for a classification of situations in objective terms has been provided by Sells (1963a [27]). Gibson (1960) and Lazarus (1971) have discussed physical factors as determinants of behavior on a molar level, and Sherif and Sherif (1956, 1963, 1969) have stressed the social factors in the environment. Krause (1970) has suggested seven main aspects of social behavior settings that investigators should consider, and Moos (1973) has recently provided a schema for studying the psycho-social environment. Chein (1954 [25]) has proposed a schema for investigating the objective behavioral environment and has been concerned with both physical and social characteristics. Proponents of ecological psychology (see Barker, 1965, regarding "behavioral settings") and environmental psychology (Craik, 1973) clearly emphasize the physical characteristics of the environment.

The subjective approach. Most interactionists have underlined the importance of the psychological significance of situations as a determinant of behavior (Angyal, 1941; Cattell, 1965; Koffka, 1935; Lewin, 1935; Murphy, 1947; Murray, 1938; Raush, Farbman, & Llewellyn, 1960; Rotter, 1954). This line of research has recently been advocated by Magnusson (1971 [28]), Schneider (1973), Bowers (1973 [7]), Mischel (1973a [8]), and Endler (1975b [2]).

This approach stresses the meaning that a situation has for the individual, his perception of the situation. However, until recently no systematic studies have been conducted in terms of how individuals interpret situations and assign meaning to them. Magnusson (1971 [28]) has discussed this fact and has proposed an empirical method for studying the perception of situations (Eke-hammar & Magnusson, 1973; Magnusson & Ekehammar, 1973).

The approach using situation reaction data as the basis for analysis has been advocated by Rotter (1954), who suggested that situations could be classified in terms of the similarity of behavior they evoke in individuals. This approach has recently been discussed by Frederiksen (1972 [26]), and Endler, Hunt, and Rosenstein (1962) and Endler and Hunt (1968 [13]) have classified situations by factor analysis of anxiety and hostility data. (For a similar approach, see anxiety scales developed by Hodges & Felling, 1970, Magnusson and Ricklander, c.f. Ekehammar, Magnusson & Ricklander, 1974, and Schalling, 1971.) For example, Endler et al. (1962) have found three situational anxiety factors (interpersonal, physical danger, and ambiguous) using situation reaction data. Similarly, Eke-hammar, Magnusson, and Ricklander (1974) have also used anxiety reaction data for classifying situations.

Recently Magnusson and Ekehammar (1975b [30]), and Ekehammar, Schalling, and Magnusson (1974) have compared the situation perception approach and the situation reaction approach in the same study. The two approaches for studying situations produced essentially the same results, with some interesting discrepancies (see chap. 5).

THE PLAN OF THIS BOOK

Following this introductory chapter there are five chapters of theoretical and empirical papers.

Chapter 2, *Basic Issues*, contains eight papers. The paper by Argyle and Little (1972 [1]) discusses four types of behavioral variability and relates these to five personality models. Endler (1975b [2]) points to the need for examining situations psychologically and proposes an interaction model for personality research. Pervin (1968 [3]) discusses three important issues that are relevant for interactional psychology, and Block (1968 [4]) suggests four conceptual reasons for the apparent inconsistency of personality. Allport (1966 [5]) and Stagner (1973 [6]) defend the trait position, and Bowers (1973 [7]) criticizes the overemphasis on situationism and proposes an interactionist viewpoint as an alternative to both the trait and situationist viewpoint. Mischel (1973 [8]) proposes a cognitive social learning reconceptualization of personality that emphasizes interaction.

Chapter 3, *Empirical Studies*, includes a dozen papers that provide empirical support for person by situation interactions in personality. The variables studied include: social interaction of hyperaggressive boys (Raush, Dittmann, & Taylor, 1959 [9]); anxiety (Endler & Hunt, 1966, 1969 [10, 11]); honesty (Nelsen, Grinder, & Mutterer, 1969 [12]); hostility (Endler & Hunt, 1969 [13], Berkowitz & Geen, 1967 [14]); leadership (Fiedler, 1971 [15]); ratings of behavior in group situations (Magnusson, Gerzén, & Nyman, 1968 [16]); various variables in a therapeutic community (Moos, 1968 [17]); leisure time (Bishop & Witt, 1970 [18]); choice behavior (Sandell, 1968 [19]); and feelings and initiatives in classrooms (Trickett & Moos, 1970 [20]).

Chapter 4, *Methodologies for Analyzing Person by Situation Interactions*, contains three papers. Endler (1966 [21]) illustrates how a variance components technique can be used to study person–situation interactions, Raush (1965 [22]) demonstrates the use of multivariate transmission analysis in studying interactions, and Magnusson and Ekehammar (1975 [23]) show the use of latent profile analysis in studying interactions. All three papers provide concrete empirical examples illustrating the various methods.

Chapter 5, *The Analyses of Situations: Studying the Environment*, contains seven papers, which are concerned with analyzing situations, with respect to personality research. Arsenian and Arsenian (1948 [24]) propose a psychosocial model for investigating "tough" and "easy" cultures, Chein (1954 [25]) suggests a schema for investigating the objective behavioral environment, and Frederiksen (1972 [26]) proposes a taxonomy of situations and an approach that would facilitate the investigation of person–situation interactions. Sells (1963 [27]) attempts to classify situations, but focuses primarily on the objective (physical) environment, while Magnusson (1971 [28]) presents an empirical analysis of situational dimensions based on subjects' perceptions (psychological environment). The Moos (1972 [29]) paper assesses the psychosocial environments of community-oriented treatment programs. In the final paper in this chapter, Magnusson and Ekehammar (1975 [30]) compare the psychological significance of situations in terms of perceptions of and reactions to situations.

Chapter 6, the final chapter, includes six papers concerned with some recent *Controversies* in interactional psychology. Alker (1972 [31]) defends the importance of individual differences in personality and criticizes Mischel's emphasis on situations, while Bem (1972 [32]) defends Mischel and argues against cross-situational consistency. Endler (1973 [33]) rejects Alker's claims and proposes an interactional model for personality, while Wallach and Leggett (1972 [34]) criticize the moderator variable strategy and suggest that one should look for consistency in behavior and its products. The Wachtel (1973 [35]) and the Mischel (1973 [36]) papers are concerned with the person–situation controversy as it applies to psychodynamic theories. Wachtel defends the psychoanalytic viewpoint, and Mischel criticizes the psychodynamic approach and suggests some links between behavioral approaches and existential–phenomenological approaches.

SUMMARY

This chapter, in discussing the determinants of sources of behavior, has compared and contrasted four personality models: trait model, psychodynamic model, situationism, and interactionism. We have indicated that the models differ with respect to (a) the determinants of actual behavior, (b) the developmental

Table 1. A Schematic Comparison of Four Personality Models

Parameters of comparison	Models			
	Psychodynamic	Trait	Situationism	Interactionism
1. Actual behavior determinants	Inner directed	Inner directed	Outer directed	Inner–outer directed
2. Development				
a. Interest in development	a. Yes	a. No	a. Yes	a. Yes
b. Nativism–empiricism	b. Both	b. Nativism	b. Empiricism	b. Empiricism
c. Biological–psychological emphasis	c. Both	c. Biological	c. Psychological	c. Both
3. Research strategy (measurement and treatment of data)				
a. Methods of data collection	a. Interviews, case histories	a. Questionnaires, ratings, tests	a. Experiments	a. Observations, tests, questionnaires, experiments
b. Type of data	b. Verbal descriptions	b. Questionnaire scores, test scores, rating scores	b. Experimental data, frequency counts	b. Test scores, questionnaire scores, experimental data
c. Treatment of data	c. Interpretation of verbal descriptions	c. Correlation, factor analysis	c. Analysis of variance	c. Analysis of variance, factor analysis, patterns of correlations, Markov chains
4. Populations primarily focused on				
a. Age groups	a. Adults and children	a. Adults	a. Adults and children	a. Adults and children
b. Normal-abnormal	b. Abnormal	b. Both	b. Normal	b. Normal
5. Consistency-specificity issue	Consistency of behavior across situations	Consistency of behavior across situations	Inconsistency of behavior across situations (specificity)	Person–situation interactions and other interactions; Behavior varies across situations and subjects
6. Units of analysis	Dynamics (underlying motives and instincts; traits)	Traits	Situations	Person–situation interactions and other interactions
7. Type of laws sought	R–R and S–R	R–R	S–R	S–R–S–R–S–R ....

aspects of actual behavior, and (c) the research strategies and measurement of individual characteristics.

While criticizing the trait model, we have indicated its dominant role in personality theory and research. The empirical evidence does not support the trait model, and the correlational research strategy that it has used has precluded the determination of the relative contributions of various sources of behavior. The multidimensional variance components research strategy was discussed, and empirical results were presented that supported a person–situation interaction view of personality.

The person–situation interaction model in personality was presented in terms of both early and more recent formulations. Conceptions of recent formulations of interactional psychology make four main points: interaction is a continuous process, individuals are active and intentional agents, cognitive factors are important, and the psychological meaning of situations is an essential determinant of behavior. Unidirectional causation and reciprocal causation (feedback) were compared and contrasted with respect to interaction.

A distinction was made between the physical (objective) environment and the psychological environment. The need for studying situations psychologically was stressed and approaches emphasizing individuals' reactions to and perceptions of situations were discussed.

The plan of the book was outlined. After this initial chapter, there are five chapters containing theoretical and empirical papers: *Basic Issues* (chap. 2), *Empirical Studies* (chap. 3), *Methodologies for Analyzing Person by Situation Interactions* (chap. 4), *The Analyses of Situations: Studying the Environment* (chap. 5), and *Controversies* (chap. 6).

The four basic models were compared and contrasted on only a few parameters, as a means for providing a critique of the trait model and as a basis for providing theoretical and empirical support for the person by situation interaction model. A more detailed comparison of the four models is presented schematically in Table 1.

REFERENCES

Abelson, R. P. Situational variables in personality research. In S. Messick and J. Ross (Eds.), *Measurement in personality and cognition.* New York: Wiley, 1962.

Alker, H. A. Is personality situationally specific or intrapsychically consistent? *Journal of Personality,* 1973, *40,* 1–16.

Allport, G. W. *Personality: A psychological interpretation.* New York: Holt, 1937.

Allport, G. W. Traits revisited. *American Psychologist,* 1966, *21,* 1–10.

Amidon, E., & Flanders, N. A. The effects of direct and indirect teacher influence on dependent-prone students learning geometry. *Journal of Educational Psychology,* 1961, *52,* 286–291.

Angyal, A. *Foundations for a science of personality.* Cambridge, Mass.: Harvard University Press, 1941.

Argyle, M. Personality and social behaviour. In B. R. Little (Ed.), *New perspectives in personality.* Harmondsworth: Penguin Books, 1975 (in press).

Argyle, M., & Little, B. R. Do personality traits apply to social behaviour? *Journal for the Theory of Social Behaviour,* 1972, *2,* 1-35.

Arsenian, J., & Arsenian, J. M. Tough and easy cultures: A conceptual analysis. *Psychiatry,* 1948, *11,* 377-385.

Bandura, A. *Social learning theory.* New York: General Learning Press, 1971.

Bandura, A., & Walters, R. *Social learning and personality development.* New York: Holt, Rinehart and Winston, 1963.

Barker, R. G. Explorations in ecological psychology. *American Psychologist,* 1965, *20,* 1-14.

Bem, D. J. Constructing cross-situational consistencies in behaviour: Some thoughts on Alker's critique of Mischel. *Journal of Personality,* 1972, *40,* 17-26.

Berkowitz, L., & Geen, R. G. Stimulus qualities of the target of aggression: A further study. *Journal of Personality and Psychology,* 1967, *5,* 364-368.

Bishop, D. W., & Witt, P. A. Sources of behavioral variance during leisure time. *Journal of Personality and Social Psychology,* 1970, *16,* 352-360.

Block, J. Some reasons for the apparent inconsistency of personality. *Psychological Bulletin,* 1968, *70,* 210-212.

Boring, E. G. *A history of experimental psychology* (2nd Ed.). New York: Appleton-Century-Crofts, 1950.

Bowers, K. S. Situationism in psychology: An analysis and a critique. *Psychological Review,* 1973, *80,* 307-336.

Bridgwater, W., & Kurtz, S. *Columbia Encyclopedia* (3rd Ed.). New York: Columbia University Press, 1963.

Brunswik, E. *The conceptual framework of psychology.* Chicago: The University of Chicago Press, 1952.

Brunswik, E. *Perception and the representative design of psychological experiments.* Berkeley: University of California Press, 1956.

Burton, R. V. Generality of honesty reconsidered. *Psychological Review,* 1963, *70,* 481-499.

Carson, R. C. *Interaction concepts of personality.* Chicago: Aldine, 1969.

Cattell, R. B. *Personality: A systematic theoretical and factual study.* New York: McGraw-Hill, 1950.

Cattell, R. B. *Personality and motivation structure and measurement.* Yonkers-on-Hudson, N.Y.: World Book Co., 1957.

Cattell, R. B. *The scientific analysis of personality.* Chicago: Aldine, 1965.

Chein, I. The environment as a determinant of behavior. *Journal of Social Psychology,* 1954, *39,* 115-127.

Cooley, C. H. *Human nature and the social order.* New York: Scribner's, 1902.

Cottrell, L. S. Jr. The analysis of situational fields. *American Sociological Review,* 1942, *7,* 370-382. (a)

Cottrell, L. S. Jr. The adjustment of the individual to his age and sex roles. *American Sociological Review,* 1942, *7,* 618-625. (b)

Craik, K. Environmental psychology. In P. H. Mussen and M. R. Rosenzweig (Eds.), *Annual Review of Psychology,* 1973, *24,* 403-422. (Palo Alto: Annual Reviews, Inc.)

Cronbach, L. J. The two disciplines of scientific psychology. *American Psychologist,* 1957, *12,* 671-684.

Dewald, P. A. *Psychotherapy: A dynamic approach* (2nd Ed.). Oxford: Blackwell Scientific Publications, 1969.

Ekehammar, B. Interactionism in personality from a historical perspective. *Psychological Bulletin,* 1974, *81,* 1026-1048.

Ekehammar, B., & Magnusson, D. A method to study stressful situations. *Journal of Personality and Social Psychology,* 1973, *27,* 176-179.

Ekehammar, B., Magnusson, D., & Ricklander, L. An interactionist approach to the study of anxiety. *Scandinavian Journal of Psychology,* 1974, *15,* 4-14.

Ekehammar, B., Schalling, D., & Magnusson, D. Dimensions of stressful situations: A comparison between a response analytical and a stimulus analytical approach. *Reports from the Psychological Laboratories*, the University of Stockholm, 1974, No. 414.

Endler, N. S. Conformity as a function of different reinforcement schedules. *Journal of Personality and Social Psychology*, 1966, *4*, 175-180. (a)

Endler, N. S. Estimating variance components from mean squares for random and mixed effects analysis of variance models. *Perceptual and Motor Skills*, 1966, *22*, 559-570. (b)

Endler, N. S. The person versus the situation—a pseudo issue? A response to Alker. *Journal of Personality*, 1973, *41*, 287-303.

Endler, N. S. A person-situation interaction model for anxiety. In C. D. Spielberger and I. G. Sarason (Eds.) *Stress and anxiety* (Vol. 1). Washington: Hemisphere, 1975, 145-164. (a)

Endler, N. S. The case for person-situation interactions. *Canadian Psychological Review*, 1975, *16*, 12-21. (b)

Endler, N. S. & Hoy, E. Conformity as related to reinforcement and social pressure. *Journal of Personality and Social Psychology*, 1967, *7*, 197-202.

Endler, N. S., & Hunt, J. McV. Sources of behavioral variance as measured by the S-R Inventory of Anxiousness, *Psychological Bulletin*, 1966, *65*, 336-346.

Endler, N. S., & Hunt, J. McV. S-R Inventories of Hostility and comparisons of the proportions of variance from persons, responses, and situations for hostility and anxiousness. *Journal of Personality and Social Psychology*, 1968, *9*, 309-315.

Endler, N. S., & Hunt, J. McV. Generalizability of contributions from sources of variance in the S-R Inventories of Anxiousness. *Journal of Personality*, 1969, *37*, 1-24.

Endler, N. S., Hunt, J. McV., & Rosenstein, A. J. An S-R Inventory of Anxiousness. *Psychological Monographs*, 1962, *76*, No. 17 (whole No. 536), 1-33.

Endler, N. S., & Magnusson, D. Interactionism, trait psychology, psychodynamics and situationism. *Reports from the Psychological Laboratories*, the University of Stockholm, 1974, No. 418.

Endler, N. S., Wiesenthal, D. L., & Geller, S. H. The generalization of the effects of agreement and correctness on relative competence mediating conformity. *Canadian Journal of Behavioural Science*, 1972, *4*, 322-329.

Feather, N. T. The relationship of persistence at a task to expectation of success and achievement related motives. *Journal of Abnormal and Social Psychology*, 1961, *63*, 552-561.

Fiedler, F. E. Validation and extension of the contingency model of leadership effectiveness: A review of empirical findings. *Psychological Bulletin*, 1971, *76*, 128-148.

Fiske, D. W. *Measuring the concepts of personality*. Chicago: Aldine, 1971.

Frederiksen, N. Toward a taxonomy of situations. *American Psychologist*, 1972, *27*, 114-123.

Gibson, J. J. The concept of the stimulus in psychology. *American Psychologist*, 1960, *15*, 694-703.

Goldfried, M. R., & Kent, R. N. Traditional versus behavioral personality assessment: A comparison of methodological and theoretical assumptions. *Psychological Bulletin*, 1972, *77*, 409-420.

Guilford, J. P. *Personality*. New York: McGraw-Hill, 1959.

Hartshorne, H., & May, M. A. *Studies in the nature of character: Studies in deceit* (Vol. 1). New York: Macmillan, 1928.

Helson, H. Adaptation-level theory. In S. Koch (Ed.), *Psychology: A study of a science* (Vol. 1). New York: McGraw-Hill, 1959.

Helson, H. *Adaptation-level theory: An experimental and systematic approach to behavior*. New York: Harper & Row, 1964.

Hodges, W. F., & Felling, J. P. Types of stressful situations and their relation to trait anxiety and sex. *Journal of Consulting and Clinical Psychology*, 1970, *34*, 333-337.

Hunt, J. McV. Traditional personality theory in the light of recent evidence. *American Scientist*, 1965, *53*, 80–96.

Hunt, J. McV. The psychological basis for using preschool enrichment as an antidote for cultural deprivation. In O. J. Harvey (Ed.), *Experience, structure and adaptability*. New York: Springer Publishing Co., 1966.

Jones, E., & Nisbett, R. E. *The actor and the observer: Divergent perceptions of the causes of behavior*. New York: General Learning Press, 1971.

Jung, C. G. *Psychological types*. New York: Harcourt, Brace, 1923.

Kantor, J. R. *Principles of psychology* (Vol. 1). Bloomington: Principia Press, 1924.

Kantor, J. R. *Principles of psychology* (Vol. 2). Bloomington: Principia Press, 1926.

Kelly, G. A. *The psychology of personal constructs* (Vols. 1 and 2). New York: Norton, 1955.

Koffka, K. *Principles of gestalt psychology*. New York: Harcourt, 1935.

Krasner, L., & Ullmann, L. P. *Behavior influence and personality*. New York: Holt, Rinehart and Winston, 1973.

Krause, M. S. Use of social situations for research purposes. *American Psychologist*, 1970, *25*, 748–753.

Kretschmer, E. *Physique and character*. New York: Harcourt, Brace, 1926.

Lazarus, R. S. *Personality* (2nd Ed.). Englewood Cliffs, N.J.: Prentice-Hall, 1971.

Lewin, K. *A dynamic theory of personality. Selected papers*. New York: McGraw-Hill, 1935.

Lewin, K. *Principles of topological psychology*. New York: McGraw-Hill, 1936.

Lewin, K. *The conceptual representation and the measurement of psychological forces*. Durham, N.C.: Duke University Press, 1938.

Lewin, K. *Field theory in social science. Selected theoretical papers*. New York: Harper, 1951.

Magnusson, D. An analysis of situational dimensions. *Perceptual and Motor Skills*, 1971, *32*, 851–867.

Magnusson, D. The person and the situation in the traditional measurement model. *Reports from the Psychological Laboratories, the University of Stockholm*, 1974, No. 426. (b) 1973, No. 6.

Magnusson, D. The individual in the situation: Some studies on individuals' perception of situations. *Studia Psychologica*, 1974, *16*, 124–132.

Magnusson, D., Dunér, A., & Zetterblom, G. *Adjustment: A longitudinal study*. Stockholm: Almqvist & Wiksell. New York: Wiley, 1975 (in press).

Magnusson, D., & Ekehammar, B. An analysis of situational dimensions: A replication. *Multivariate Behavioral Research*, 1973, *8*, 331–339.

Magnusson, D., & Ekehammar, B. Anxiety profiles based on both situational and response factors. *Multivariate Behavioral Research*, 1975, *10*, 27–43. (a)

Magnusson, D., & Ekehammar, B. Perceptions of and reactions to stressful situations. *Journal of Personality and Social Psychology*, 1975, *31*, 1147–1154. (b)

Magnusson, D., Gerzén, M., & Nyman, B. The generality of behavioral data: I. Generalization from observation on one occasion. *Multivariate Behavioral Research*, 1968, *3*, 295–320.

Magnusson, D., & Heffler, B. The generality of behavioral data: III. Generalization potential as a function of the number of observation instances. *Multivariate Behavioral Research*, 1969, *4*, 29–42.

Magnusson, D., Heffler, B., & Nyman, B. The generality of behavioral data: II. Replication of an experiment on generalization from observation on one occasion. *Multivariate Behavioral Research*, 1968, *3*, 415–422.

Mårdberg, B. A model for selection and classification in industrial psychology. *Reports from the Psychological Laboratories*, the University of Stockholm, (Suppl. 19). 1973.

Mead, G. H. *Mind, self and society*. Chicago: University of Chicago Press, 1934.

Miller, D. R. The study of social relationships: Situation, identity, and social interaction. In S. Koch (Ed.), *Psychology: A study of a science*. New York: McGraw-Hill, 1963.

Mischel, W. *Personality and assessment.* New York: Wiley, 1968.

Mischel, W. Continuity and change in personality. *American Psychologist,* 1969, *24,* 1012–1018.

Mischel, W. *Introduction to personality.* New York: Holt, Rinehart and Winston, 1971.

Mischel, W. Toward a cognitive social learning reconceptualization of personality. *Psychological Review,* 1973, *80,* 252–283. (a)

Mischel, W. On the empirical dilemmas of psychodynamic approaches: Issues and alternatives. *Journal of Abnormal Psychology,* 1973, *82,* 335–344. (b)

Moos, R. H. Situational analysis of a therapeutic community milieu. *Journal of Abnormal Psychology,* 1968, *73,* 49–61.

Moos, R. H. Sources of variance in responses to questionnaires and in behavior. *Journal of Abnormal Psychology,* 1969, *74,* 405–412.

Moos, R. H. Differential effects of psychiatric ward settings on patient change. *Journal of Nervous and Mental Disease,* 1970, *5,* 316–321.

Moos, R. Assessment of the psychosocial environment of community-oriented psychiatric treatment programs. *Journal of Abnormal Psychology,* 1972, *79,* 9–18.

Moos, R. Conceptualizations of human environments. *American Psychologist,* 1973, *28,* 652–665.

Murphy, G. *Personality: A biosocial approach to origins and structure.* New York: Harper, 1947.

Murray, H. A. *Explorations in personality.* New York: Oxford University Press, 1938.

Nelsen, E. A., Grinder, R. F., & Mutterer, M. L. Sources of variance in behavioral measures of honesty in temptation situations: Methodological analyses. *Developmental Psychology,* 1969, *1,* 265–279.

Olweus, D. Personality and aggression. In J. K. Cole and D. D. Jensen (Eds.) *Nebraska symposium on motivation 1972.* Lincoln: University of Nebraska Press, 1973.

Overton, W. F., & Reese, H. W. Models of development: Methodological implications. In J. R. Nesselroade and H. W. Reese (Eds.), *Life span developmental psychology: Methodological issues.* New York: Academic Press, 1973.

Pervin, L. A. Performance and satisfaction as a function of individual–environment fit. *Psychological Bulletin,* 1968, *69,* 56–68.

Raush, H. L. Interaction sequences. *Journal of Personality and Social Psychology,* 1965, *2,* 487–499.

Raush, H. L. Process and change. *Family Process,* 1972, *11,* 275–298.

Raush, H. L., Dittmann, A. T., & Taylor, T. J. The interpersonal behavior of children in residential treatment. *Journal of Abnormal and Social Psychology,* 1959, *58,* 9–26. (a)

Raush, H. L., Dittmann, A. T., & Taylor, T. J. Person, setting and change in social interaction. *Human Relations,* 1959, *12,* 361–378. (b)

Raush, H. L., Farbman, I., & Llewellyn, L. G. Person, setting and change in social interaction: II. A normal control study. *Human Relations,* 1960, *13,* 305–333.

Rogers, C. R. *Client-centered therapy. Its current practice, implications and theory.* Boston: Houghton Mifflin, 1951.

Rogers, C. R. A theory of therapy, personality and interpersonal relationship, as developed in the client-centered framework. In S. Koch (Ed.) *Psychology: A study of a science* (Vol. 3). New York: McGraw-Hill, 1959.

Rotter, J. B. *Social learning and clinical psychology.* New York: Prentice-Hall, 1954.

Sakoda, J. M. Factor analysis of Oss situational tests. *Journal of Abnormal and Social Psychology,* 1952, *47,* 843–852.

Sandell, R. G. Effects of attitudinal and situational factors on reported choice behavior. *Journal of Marketing Research,* 1968, *5,* 405–408.

Schalling, D. Tolerance for experimentally induced pain as related to personality. *Scandinavian Journal of Psychology,* 1971, *12,* 271–281.

Schneider, D. J. Implicit personality theory: A review. *Psychological Bulletin*, 1973, *79*, 294–309.

Sells, S. B. Dimensions of stimulus situations which account for behavior variances. In S. B. Sells (Ed.), *Stimulus determinants of behavior*. New York: Ronald Press, 1963. (a)

Sells, S. B. An interactionist looks at the environment. *American Psychologist*, 1963, *18*, 696–702. (b)

Shapiro, D. *Neurotic styles*. New York: Basic Books, Inc., 1965.

Sheldon, W. H. *Varieties of delinquent youth*. New York: Harper, 1949.

Sherif, M., & Sherif, C. W. *An outline of social psychology*. New York: Harper & Brothers, 1956.

Sherif, M., & Sherif, C. W. Varieties of social stimulus situations. In S. B. Sells (Ed.), *Stimulus determinants of behavior*. New York: Ronald Press, 1963.

Sherif, M., & Sherif, C. W. *Social Psychology*. New York: Harper & Row, 1969.

Shute, C. Aristotle's interactionism and its transformations by some 20th century writers. *The Psychological Record*, 1973, *23*, 283–293.

Skinner, B. F. *Science and human behavior*. New York: Macmillan, 1953.

Skinner, B. F. Pigeons in a pelican. *American Psychologist*, 1960, *15*, 28–37.

Smith, N. W. Contextual interactionists: A symposium. *The Psychological Record*, 1973, *23*, 281–282.

Stagner, R. Traits are relevant: Theoretical analysis and empirical evidence. Paper read at the APA annual convention, Montreal, Quebec, August, 1973.

Stagner, R. *Psychology of personality* (4th ed.). New York: McGraw-Hill, 1974.

Sullivan, H. S. *The interpersonal theory of psychiatry*. New York: Norton, 1953.

Thurstone, L. L. *Multiple factor analysis*. Chicago: University of Chicago Press, 1947.

Tolman, E. C. *Purposive behavior in animals and men*. Berkeley: University of California Press, 1949.

Tolman, E. C. Psychology versus immediate experience. In E. C. Tolman, *Collected papers in Psychology*. Berkeley: University of California Press, 1951. (Reprinted from Philosophy of Science, 1935.)

Trickett, E. J., & Moos, R. H. Generality and specificity of student reactions in high school classrooms. *Adolescence*, 1970, *5*, 373–390.

Vale, J. R., & Vale, G. R. Individual differences and general laws in psychology: A reconciliation. *American Psychologist*, 1969, *24*, 1093–1108.

Vernon, P. E. *Personality assessment: A critical survey*. New York: Wiley, 1964.

Wachtel, P. Psychodynamics, behavior therapy and the implacable experimenter: An inquiry into the consistency of personality. *Journal of Abnormal Psychology*, 1973, *82*, 324–334. (a)

Wallace, J. What units shall we employ? Allport's question revisited. *Journal of Consulting Psychology*, 1967, *31*, 56–64.

Wallach, M. A., & Leggett, M. I. Testing the hypothesis that a person will be consistent: Stylistic consistency versus situational specificity in size of childrens' drawings. *Journal of Personality*, 1972, *40*, 309–330.

Weiss, P. A. The living system: Determinism stratified. In A. Koestler and J. R. Smythies (Eds.), *Beyond reductionism: New perspectives in the life sciences*. New York: Macmillan, 1969.

Wiesenthal, D. L., Endler, N. S., & Geller, S. H. Effects of prior group agreement and task correctness on relative competence mediating conformity. *European Journal of Social Psychology*, 1973, *3*, 193–203.

CHAPTER TWO

BASIC ISSUES

This chapter contains eight selections that focus on some basic issues in interactional psychology, in the area of personality. Some of these papers present empirical evidence relevant to the issues they discuss. Many of the selections in later chapters in this book are concerned with empirical investigations of the issues raised in this chapter. Modified versions of three of the papers in this chapter (those by Endler [2], Stagner [6], and Mischel [8]) formed the core of a symposium (at the American Psychological Association Annual Convention, Montreal, August 29, 1973) on "Traits, Persons and Situations: Some Theoretical Issues." The issues raised in this chapter include the conflict between trait psychologists and situationists, the need to specify and dimensionalize situations, and the nature of person–situation interactions.

In the first selection, Argyle and Little discuss four types of behavioral variability and relate these to five personality models: (a) personality as constant patterns of behavior, (b) personality as trait dispositions, (c) personality as a person's cognitive system, (d) personality as a series of unrelated S–R links, and (e) personality as the sum of role performance. On the basis of their own research on social behavior and social perception, they conclude that an interactional model is most appropriate for personality and point to the need for specifying situational factors. Argyle and Little suggest that for more adequately functioning groups, and with the passage of time in all groups, the situational factor is a more important source of behavioral variance than the person factor.

Endler discusses the complex personality issue of situational specificity (change) versus cross-situational consistency (stability) in the second selection. He suggests that there is little empirical evidence to support either the claim of the situationists that situations are the major source of variance, or that of the trait theorists (personologists) that personality traits are the major source of variance. The person-versus-situation issue has been phrased in such a way as to make it a pseudo-issue. Endler points to the need for examining and dimensionalizing situations psychologically and discusses various research strategies for the area of personality. He differentiates between a mechanistic model of interaction (interaction of two independent variables) and an organismic interaction model (mutual interaction between independent and dependent variables). Endler discusses the advantages of an interactionist approach, presents supporting empirical data, and proposes a person–situation interaction model for anxiety.

Pervin, in the third selection, discusses the research on the interaction between individual characteristics and situations (interpersonal and noninterpersonal environments) in effecting performance and satisfaction, and reviews the relevant theoretical viewpoints. He discusses various models for analyzing interactions between persons and environments. Finally, Pervin discusses three important issues that are relevant for interactional psychology: (a) whether to focus on the psychological (perceived) environment or the physical (actual) environment; (b) the units that should be used in describing situations and individuals; and (c) the nature of the processes involved in person–situation interactions.

In the fourth selection, Block states that there is an apparent inconsistency between the professed aim of personality theorists in seeking consistencies and regularities in behavior and the empirical evidence that fails to support the expected consistent relationship. Block suggests four conceptual reasons for the apparent inconsistency of personality, including conceptualizations of personality that do not attempt to account for environmental factors, the failure to specify the limits within which predicted consistent relationships should hold, the tendency to compare behavior of different levels of significance or importance for the individual, and the comparison of behaviors that may possibly be mediated by different underlying variables. He suggests that it is necessary to reconceptualize our notions about personality and to reformulate our research in line with these reconceptualizations.

Allport and Stagner (in the fifth and sixth selections) both attempt to defend the trait position. Allport believes that traits are an essential postulate for personality, and that they cannot be avoided by focusing on positivism or situationism or by examining statistical interaction effects. He proclaims his reservations without, however, indicating why he is reluctant to examine situations or interaction effects. He decries the preoccupation with methodology and suggests that we should accept the common sense assumption that individuals are real persons and that each has a neuropsychic (trait) organization. Allport points to the need to use theory as a guide in selecting trait dimensions and the need to empirically test the theories. He does not believe that traits can be defined in terms of interactions, but does accept the notion that behavior is variable and can be modified by ecological, social, and situational factors.

Wallace (1967), in discussing Allport's (1958) position, has suggested that instead of using the dispositional trait concept as the basic unit in personality, we substitute an ability or skill construct and treat response capability and response performance as the basic units for personality measurement. These units are modifiable by situations.

Stagner [6], however, states that traits are real entities, and that the concept of trait is a logical necessity and has some empirical support. He emphasizes that traits determine what will be reinforcing and which situations a person selects and approaches. Whereas Allport refers to traits as "neuropsychic dispositions," Stagner conceives of traits as *generalized expectancies*, which select situations we respond to and avoid. In conceiving of a trait as a cognitive structure, Stagner's position is not too far removed from Mischel's cognitive social learning reconceptualization of personality, which is presented in the last selection in this chapter. Mischel has moved from a situationist approach (Mischel, 1968, 1969, 1971) to an interactionist position, whereas Stagner, starting from a trait viewpoint, also seems to be moving towards an interactionist position. (While the present editors are not sympathetic to the trait viewpoint, the Allport and Stagner papers were included so that the reader may judge the trait position on its own merits, as presented by two of its leading proponents.)

Bowers, in the seventh selection, criticizes the recent overemphasis on situationism in personality research and theorizing. He suggests that situationism merely substitutes a behaviorist interpretation of personality for a trait position and neglects the importance of the person in personality research. Although he admits that behavior is situation specific, he points to the metaphysical, psychological, and methodological biases and assumptions of situationism which tend to ignore the person. Like Stagner and Mischel, Bowers believes that the person can influence the situation. Bowers reviews eleven empirical studies that support interactionism and proposes an interactionist viewpoint as an alternative to both the trait and situationist positions.

Mischel, in the final selection in this chapter, proposes a cognitive social learning reconceptualization of personality and emphasizes the interaction between person variables and psychological situations. This new theory (as indicated earlier) is a shift from Mischel's former (1968, 1969, 1971) overemphasis on the importance of situations. In the present selection Mischel provides data from various sources that tend to discredit the trait position of behavioral consistency across situations. He presents evidence in favor of situational specificity, but points to the necessity of concerning oneself with the learned meaning of stimuli. Mischel proposes five cognitive social learning variables as the basic units for studying persons (see chap. 1). He suggests a research strategy and program for testing these variables and analyzes the specific interactions between these person variables and psychological situation variables, within the context of a social learning orientation.

REFERENCES

Allport, G. W. What units shall we employ? In G. Lindzey (Ed.), *The assessment of human motives.* New York: Holt, Rinehart and Winston, 1958.

Mischel, W. *Personality and assessment.* New York: Wiley, 1968.

Mischel, W. Continuity and change in personality. *American Psychologist,* 1969, *24,* 1012–1018.

Mischel, W. *Introduction to personality.* New York: Holt, Rinehart and Winston, 1971.

Wallace, J. What units shall we employ? Allport's question revisited. *Journal of Consulting Psychology,* 1967, *31,* 56–64.

1

Do Personality Traits Apply to Social Behaviour?

MICHAEL ARGYLE and BRIAN R. LITTLE

I. INTRODUCTION

In recent years doubts have arisen as to whether personality can be usefully analysed in terms of traits. Vernon (1964), for example, has written that the trait-factor approach '. . . has not worked well enough and, despite the huge volume of research it has stimulated, it seems to lead to a dead end' (p. 239). More recently, Mischel (1968, 1969) has reviewed an extensive body of evidence and concluded that the orthodox trait-state paradigm has been misguided, and that traits are more usefully construed as products of the perceiver's categorizing behaviour than as substantive attributes of the perceived. If trait conceptions *are* basically misguided, as these recent critiques suggest, the implications for other areas of psychology where trait models have been used should receive serious attention. The purpose of the present paper is to look at these implications for the field of social psychology. Specifically, we will discuss the evidence and arguments about individual consistencies in social behaviour, consider those features of social behaviour which create difficulties for trait conceptions, and describe some of our empirical studies which suggest an alternative conceptual scheme for dealing with individual differences in social performance.

We believe that these questions are of fundamental importance for understanding personality. Social psychologists need to know how to conceptualize and measure personality in order to predict social behaviour like leadership, persuasibility, etc. The manner in which personality is conceived also affects the

From *Journal for the Theory of Social Behaviour*, 1972, 2, 1–35. Copyright 1972 by Basil Blackwell & Mott Ltd, and reproduced by permission of the authors and the publisher.

The authors wish to express appreciation to the S.S.R.C. for financial support, to Margaret McCallin for research assistance, and to Leo Meltzer and Robert Zajonc for helpful comments on an earlier version of this paper.

We also wish to acknowledge the use of M.R.C. Service for Analysing Repertory Grids under the direction of Dr. Patrick Slater.

ways in which clinical psychologists and other professional psychologists, social scientists and administrators approach their task. The question of individual consistencies in social behaviour also reflects the way people think about each other in everyday life, and the commonsense approach here may be seriously in error. For different practical purposes there may be traditional interest in only one side of the trait issue (e.g. clinical psychologists have a long-standing interest in personality-determined, rather than situation-determined aspects of social behaviour). We shall try to show, however, that awareness of the other side of the problem may have practical significance.

Theories of personality and social behaviour differ considerably in the extent to which they stress consistencies of individual behaviour. One of the important ways in which they differ is in the *amount* of variability in social behaviour which they hypothesize can be attributable to individuals, to situations, and to interactions between them. Figure 1 gives a diagrammatic representation of four types of variability which may characterize any social behaviour (e.g. assertiveness), in three individuals (P_1, P_2, P_3), observed in three different situations. The first type describes the most extreme trait position. Each person has a characteristic level of assertiveness, which is constant from situation to situation. Type B describes the most extreme alternative view, where each situation gives rise to a different level of assertiveness, and within each situation there is no variability. Type C shows person variability but without the condition that an individual's level of assertiveness remains constant. Here there are stable individual differences in social behaviour in a relative sense, with the rank order of persons remaining constant. We shall refer to this type below as a dispositional model. Type D variability describes an interaction between persons and situations, so that some people are highly assertive in some situations and the opposite in others. Specification of behaviour under this model must simultaneously consider aspects of the person and the situation.

Theories of social behaviour differ not only the amount of variability they attribute to persons versus situations, but also in the way in which such variability is interpreted. Several alternative perspectives will be briefly sketched.

1. *Personality as Constant Patterns of Behaviour*

Some aspects of persons are relatively constant, their eye colour or adult height, for example. Traits are sometimes viewed as patterns of behaviour which are similarly constant across different situations. An extravert would then be expected to be extraverted in a wide range of situations, and an honest person would be reliably honest. At its most extreme this view would stress Type A variability in Fig. 1.

2. *Personality as Trait Dispositions*

A rather different way of conceiving of traits is as dispositions to respond in certain ways, the actual response being a function of the situation as well as of

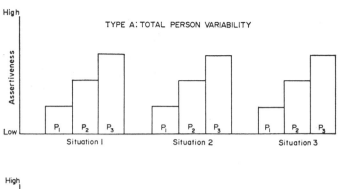

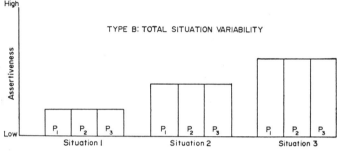

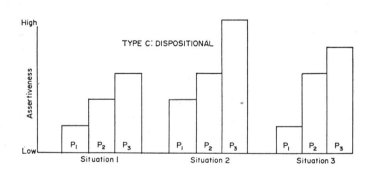

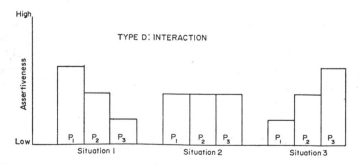

Fig. 1. Four types of variability in social behaviour.

the person. Lewin's formulation, $B = f(P, E)$, and Cattell's specification equation (Cattell, 1965) are explicit statements of this perspective. Thus whether or not a person is able to solve a particular intelligence test item is a joint product of his intelligence and the difficulty of the item. A person's level of anxiety is a joint product of his neuroticism and the stressfulness of the situation. To apply this equation there must be a measurable dimension of situations which is functionally related to performance. In each of these cases it is clear that in absolute terms the same person will respond quite differently on different occasions. However, the rank order of a number of persons should remain the same, unless the functional relationship is a complex, e.g. curvilinear, one. For most relationships the dispositional trait model assumes Type C variability as graphed in Fig. 1.

Under this model, then, the actual behaviour of people varies between situations, but there should be consistency in the sense that if A is, for example, more intelligent than B he should do better in a wide range of different items or tests, and the scores in the tests should correlate highly together. In the social realm, McGuire (1968) has proposed a model to account for individual differences in persuasibility in terms of two main traits, intelligence and anxiety. Each trait is postulated to interact with several aspects of the social situation in non-linear ways. This is an extremely interesting analysis, showing that apparent inconsistency can be related to stable dispositions of the individual and that individual performance can be predicted. In this case it would not be expected that a number of persons would keep the same rank order of persuasibility across different situations. Both Type C and Type D variability would seem to be stressed here.

Similar treatment might be given to popularity, proximity or other measures of social behaviour. However, we do not yet know the dimensions of social situations which need to be taken into account when making these predictions. (Two such dimensions in fact emerge from the study to be reported below.) There is also the problem that an individual's pattern of social performance appears to change *as a whole* between different situations and relationships, though it may be possible to reduce this to a number of dimensions, like dominance, poise, etc.

3. *Personality as a Person's Cognitive System*

Psychologists in the cognitive tradition (e.g. Levy, 1970, pp. 249–306), look at traits as not real attributes that reside in people but as concepts used by individuals to understand and predict the behaviour of themselves and others. If, as Kelly (1955) assumes, behaviour is determined by our personal construct systems, consistency of behaviour would occur when an individual has construed two or more situations as being similar. While there are some similarities to cognitive learning theories, the essential difference is that the constructs are not determined by stimulus features but are created by the person.

While cognitive personality research tends to underplay the role of situational variability in social behaviour it also undermines orthodox trait explanations. Bannister (1970) and Eysenck (1970) have recently debated the issues distinguishing trait psychology and personal construct psychology. The type of variability most consistent with the assumptions of cognitive personality research will be that which stresses the minimum influence of either stable aspects of the person or the situation—the interaction Type D. It should be noted, however, that a number of cognitive variables have been shown to be stable across domains and these tend to be treated as traits (e.g. field dependence, internal-external locus of control).

4. *Personality as a Series of Unrelated S-R Links*

This approach dispenses with trait concepts entirely. A person consists of a large number of response patterns attached to particular situations. This approach is favoured by some learning theorists and behaviour therapists. The latter will not ask whether a patient has a high score on the trait of 'neuroticism', but rather what are the particular situations which cause the patient anxiety or produce other undesirable responses. Mischel (1968) proposes a model of this kind, but allows for a certain amount of generalization of responses to related situations. Like the cognitive system approach, the S-R perspective would reject either of the extreme variability types and to the extent that it would subscribe to any general model of variability, would be most likely to opt for Type D. Because of the basic unrelatedness of the S-R links, however, no clear cut stabilities in social behaviour are expected. The S-R approach is far more concerned with the prediction of behaviour change (where situational factors become central) than with taxonomic-descriptive analysis and assessments of variability.

5. *Personality as the Sum of Role Performances*

Some sociologists dispense entirely with the concept of personality and proceed with the assumption that a person is simply the sum of a series of standard role performances. This approach differs from the previous one in that the role performances are assumed to be common to all occupants of the positions involved. Type B variability is given greatest stress in the approach. Individual differences *can* be handled in terms of combinations of roles (e.g. age, sex, class, etc.) and in terms of previous role experience. Situational variance, however, is the major focus here.

II. REVIEW OF THE EVIDENCE ON TRAITS
OF SOCIAL BEHAVIOUR

In the sections to follow we will review several lines of evidence that bear on the question of whether social behaviour can be usefully understood in terms of traits. The major assumptions of trait models is that there is scientific merit in using adjectives such as assertive, sociable, hostile, etc. as descriptions of individuals. To ascribe these characteristics to a person instead of to a sample of his behaviour is to beg the question of temporal and situational generality, however. Though this question is clearly a matter of empirical analysis, as we shall see there is considerable latitude for alternative interpretations of the same empirical data.

The evidence reviewed is based primarily on two types of statistical analysis. First, simple correlations are frequently cited, being used to check whether there is cross-situational generality in various types of behaviour. Correlational analysis will also appear when we consider whether predictions can be made about social behaviour from conventional personality tests. The second kind of statistic used will be analyses of the amount of variance in an area of behaviour that is attributable to situation and to persons. To the extent that most of the variance in a social behaviour is situational, the search for stable individual differences in that area will not prove very useful. A cautionary statement should be made at this point about the way in which these empirical data are interpreted. It is rather arbitrary what degree of correlation is needed in order to confirm or disconfirm trait models. In some non-social areas, such as intellectual behaviour, there seems to be good evidence that trait models work adequately, in that within most areas of intellectual functioning there are rather high correlations between different items, of the order of 0.6 to 0.8. Indeed there are also correlations between the different factors, though these are naturally lower. But when correlations are in the range 0.25–0.40, different investigators draw conflicting conclusions. Craik (1969) points out that '. . . the typically moderate correlations found among individual's behaviours in different "naturalistic" situations can serve to buttress the heuristic value of either dispositional or situational approaches' (p. 148). Similar ambiguity exists when situations, persons and interactions between them, each account for approximately the same amount of variation. Despite this degree of arbitrariness, however, some overall conclusions about the relative merits of trait and situational models of social behaviour can be attempted.

1. Behaviour Evidence for the Consistency of Social Behaviour

The most extensively studied aspect of social behaviour from this point of view is *informal leadership*. Although leadership was once looked at as a personality trait, it has been realized for some time that a person's leadership status in a group is a joint product of the group and the group task on the one hand, and various properties of the individual on the other. The same person is a leader in some groups and a follower in others.

The most relevant property of the individual is his ability at the group task (compared with the abilities of others) so that there are families of situations in which the same group members will tend to lead. There is a small amount of individual consistency here, in that some individuals are more strongly motivated to dominate, and some are more socially skilled, but these individual factors account for only a small amount of the variance (Gibb, 1969, Hollander & Willis, 1967).

Persuasibility was treated as a personality trait until recently, when it became clear that there are interactions between a number of properties of the individual and various properties of the message, the communication, etc. The properties of the person which are most relevant to whether he is persuaded are his intelligence, his anxiety, and his knowledge of the topic, but these interact with situational variables in quite complex ways so that it is not possible to ascribe persuasibility in general to individuals (McGuire, 1968).

An individual's *conformity* has also been found to vary greatly between different groups to which he belongs, so that some investigators have concluded that it is no more a trait than leadership is (Hollander & Willis, 1967). However, there is evidence for a rather small degree of consistency between different situations (Vaughan, 1964). There are presumably similar interactions between various personality and situational variables as in the case of persuasibility.

Popularity is also found to vary between situations. Stogdill (1953), for example, found that the popularity of members of an organization was more a function of their formal position than of their personalities. The correlations between popularity and familiar personality traits are extremely low (Mann, 1959), and are quite different depending on the group studied. If there is any common personality factor here it may be in 'rewardingness' (Jennings, 1950), which is not measured by the usual personality tests. But we do not know how far the same person is able to be rewarding in different groups or situations.

Mischel (1968) has reviewed a considerable body of evidence in this area, concluding that while cross-situational generality holds for variables such as intelligence, field dependence and reaction time, there does *not* appear to be generality for conditionability, dependence, attitudes to authority, rigidity or moral behaviour.

In our opinion the evidence for lack of generality of behaviour across situations is even more striking in the fields of social performance mentioned above.

2. *The Evidence for Social Traits from Questionnaire Studies*

Much of the presumed evidence for traits of social behaviour comes from the factor analysis of questionnaires. This evidence is rather confusing, however, since over 950 factors have now been extracted in different studies (French, 1953). The most familiar two factors are perhaps those of extraversion and neuroticism (Eysenck & Eysenck, 1969). Similar factors have been obtained in a number of studies by other investigators, though it is clear that the extraversion dimension really consists of two sub-factors—impulsiveness and social extraversion (Eysenck & Eysenck, 1963).

However, answering items like 'Do you generally take the lead in social occasions?' is quite unlike intelligence test items such as 'Complete the following series; 2, 5, 10, 17'. In the first place the subject is not limited by his abilities, as in the intelligence test case. Secondly, his answer is not in itself a sample of social behaviour (except perhaps as a minor instance of self-presentation) whereas the answer to the intelligence test item can be regarded as an examplar of intelligent behaviour. Wallace (1966) has recently argued that personality attributes *be assessed as abilities* rather than latent dispositions, though this alternative approach to personality assessment has not, to our knowledge, generated factor analytic studies. While the intelligence test item gives a very specific problem, the typical personality question is phrased in general terms. The question quoted above, for example, does not specify the particular social occasion or kind of group in which the subject might take the lead. When the situation is specified the correlation between items is very much smaller, and the presumed trait tends to disappear.

Mischel (1968) suggests that when correlations are found between different questionnaires or items this may be due not so much to the presence of traits, as to the operation of common response sets, such as acquiescence and social desirability, the common correlation of items with intelligence, or to the use of verbally similar items. The items of the authoritarianism F-scale, for example, are known to be affected by acquiescence and the level of education of respondents (e.g. Brown, 1965). The completion of a questionnaire can thus be seen not so much as a piece of social behaviour, nor as an accurate report on social behaviour, but as the resultant of cognitive sets which may or may not generate 'consistent' replies.

A similar line of argument is suggested by recent studies of political attitudes. Butler and Stokes (1969) found that only two per cent of a British sample gave ideologically consistent replies to questions about political policies; the correlation between attitudes to nationalization and to the social services was 0.55 for this two per cent but only 0.07 for the whole sample. Very similar results were obtained in the U.S.A. by Campbell, Converse, Miller and Stokes (1960). It appears, then, that consistency of answers to questionnaires depends upon the relevance of the questions to the individual (Campbell, 1963), upon his interest in the domain, and upon his past learning with respect to issues in that domain. To these criticisms proponents of trait models have a number of legitimate replies. To the charge that the factors extracted from questionnaire studies are mainly artefactual Rorer's (1965) review might be cited, which concludes that content plays a considerably more important role in test responses than 'response style' researchers have acknowledged. The above mentioned political studies might also be interpreted in a way that does not undermine trait models. They could be regarded as suggesting that we may have been too simplistic in the ways in which we have sought to assess consistencies of personality. The apparent unpredictability of much of behaviour might be reconciled with dispositional trait models, as long as attempts are made to tap domains that are salient to individuals.

3. *The Relation between Questionnaire and Overt Behaviour*

Campbell and Fiske (1959) have drawn attention to the fact that questionnaires often correlate with other questionnaires, but fail to correlate with different measures of behaviour. In other words considerable variance may be due to the measuring instrument rather than to the trait being measured. In the field of social behaviour questionnaires usually have very low correlations with overt behaviour. Mann (1959) reviewed all the studies of small group behaviour published between 1900 and 1957. The pattern of social behaviour which was most predictable was informal leadership. The median correlation with measures of intelligence was 0.15, with measures of dominance 0.20, extraversion 0.15, and adjustment 0.15; other measures had lower correlations. Correlations of personality questionnaries with popularity, conformity, total activity and socio-emotional activity were all lower and less consistent. Questionnaires also have very low and inconsistent correlations with more specific measures of social performance. Amount of gaze has a small correlation with extraversion (Kendon & Cook, 1970) though the size of this correlation has been found to vary greatly in different studies. Spatial proximity has not been found to correlate with personality questionnaires (Porter, Argyle & Saltern, 1970).

On the other hand a number of qualifications should be made before interpreting this evidence as challenging the assumption of behavioural consistency. First, there are some purely statistical reasons, such as unreliability of the overt behaviours assessed, that will obviously attenuate correlations between personality tests and other variables. (Block, 1963; see also Byrne & Holcomb, 1962). Second, while lack of correlation between personality trait measures and social behaviour is usually interpreted as undermining trait models, very few trait theorists argue that specific behaviour is predictable from measures of a single trait (Craik, 1969). Social behaviour will be determined by the interaction of *multiple* traits and the real task is one of finding the most reliable *combinations* of traits for the prediction of relevant social behaviours. Couch's (1960) work is noteworthy for following this strategy, as well as for showing how the inclusion of situational factors can lead to substantial increments in the prediction of overt social behaviour. Examples of this kind of research, however, are very rare.

Even with the use of single trait measures social behaviour can be predicted as long as it is analysed at a relatively molar level. Gough's work with some of the California Psychological Inventory Scales is a good example, indicating, for instance, that delinquency can be usefully predicted from the socialization scale (Gough, 1968).

The question was raised earlier whether people's responses to questionnaires may lack correspondence with their actual social behaviour. Again, there is evidence to favour both sides. Pinneau and Milton (1958) have reported an extensive analysis of what they call the 'ecology veracity' of test item responses, which they assessed by obtaining wives' ratings of their husbands' actual behaviours and correlating these with the husbands' test responses. They showed that the correlations between subjects and observers on a variety of tests were very high; as high approximately, as their reliabilities permitted. Thus, despite the fact that orthodox trait models make no assumption about a correspondence between the subjects' claims and his 'real behaviour', what small evidence there is suggest that this correspondence may be high. Perhaps the strategy of asking a person to provide an account of what he actually does in certain situations is as valid as it is obviously useful. On the other hand one can think of many situations in which distortion is likely to occur. The Pinneau and Milton study is best seen as a warning that the direct assessment of a person's self-reported social behaviour should not be rejected out of hand. Perhaps the most responsible course of research that might be taken by the personality oriented social psychologist would be to continue using self-report measures while frequently monitoring each new domain for evidence of convergence with overt behaviour.

As in the questionnaire studies reviewed above, the studies relating test responses to overt behaviour are equivocal in their support for trait models of social behaviour. What seems to be obvious is that there is very little in the way of useful prediction of circumscribed social behaviour from single trait measures. However, when global measures of overt behaviour are used and multiple trait predictors utilized the adequacy of the trait approach is improved.

4. Perceived Personality Traits

One of the reasons why people find trait conceptions intrinsically plausible is the experiences we have of other people in everyday interaction. We form impressions of one another as more or less consistent, stable, organisms that behave in predictable ways. However, this may not be because the perceived persons actually have general traits of social behaviour.

1. We usually see a particular individual in a very limited class of situations, e.g. at work, at parties, at home, etc. We do not have the opportunity to observe most people in a variety of situations. The exception to this is members of the family, and parents may explain that one of their children is for example 'shy with strangers', thus recognizing the lack of generality of the child's behaviour. Of course the most extreme exception to the generally impoverished view we have of people is perception of *ourselves*. More than any other person we see ourselves in a diversity of situations. The implications of this particular distinction between self-perception and perception of others does not seem to have been explored in the research literature.

2. A person (P) is usually directly observable by the O. The presence of the observer O is a constant factor which will tend to elicit a consistent style of

behaviour—the pattern of interaction that is elicited by and negotiated with O.

3. The consistent presence of O may lead P to engage in a similar self-presentation in order to avoid giving O an impression of inconsistency. If P has given O the impression that he is a certain kind of person he may be embarrassed if he gives a quite different performance on some occasion.

An important part of the scientific evidence on traits comes from the analysis of ratings by observers of the characteristics of subjects. Factor analysis of such ratings have consistently arrived at the two dimensions shown in Figure 2 (Leary, 1957; Lorr & McNair, 1965).

A number of recent studies have suggested that factors such as these may be better interpreted as being constructs of the observers rather than 'real' traits of those observed. Mulaik (1964) factor analyzed ratings by judges of real persons, stereotyped persons, and the meanings of trait words, and showed high factor similarity across these domains, suggesting that personality factors might well be the raters' conceptual factors.

Hallworth (1966) asked teachers to rate children on a number of 7-point scales, including scales from Osgood's semantic differential and scales assessing aspects of social behaviour. When the total set of scales was factor analysed, the social behaviour scales loaded on the same factors as the semantic differential:

1. Evaluation and 'good pupil' scales.
2. Activity and extraversion scales.
3. Potency and scales for self-assertion, etc.

Hallworth suggests that basic dimensions of personality have as their origin more general dimensions of meaning. He points out that this does not imply that the personality assessments are invalid, but it does suggest an alternative interpretation of their frequent appearance. D'Andrade (1965) asked students to

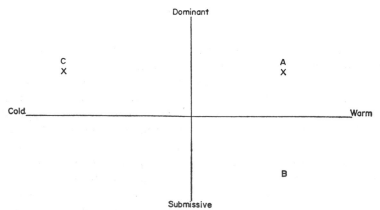

Fig. 2. Two basic dimensions of social behaviour.

rate the 16 categories of Leary's Interpersonal check list. Factor analysis of the ratings yielded the same two dimensions dominant-submissive and warm-cold that are commonly found in factor analyses of ratings of people.

It may, of course, be the case that the conceptual scheme used by raters have been built up because of their experience of the consistent behaviour of people. However, the Hallworth study suggests that the basic way of categorizing all objects and events may be the ultimate origin.

5. Studies on the Relative Contributions of Persons and Situations to Social Behaviour

One way of approaching the question of whether traits apply to social behaviour is to examine the amount of variance accounted for by personality and situational variables *vis-à-vis* a set of relevant behaviours. Though not concerned with interpersonal behaviour as such, Endler and Hunt and their colleagues have performed a series of studies that have analysed the effects of persons, situations and 'modes of responding' on behaviour such as anxiety and hostility (Endler, Hunt & Rosenstein, 1962; Endler & Hunt, 1966). The studies on anxiety have used the S–R Inventory of Anxiousness in which the subject is symbolically presented with a series of potentially anxiety-arousing situations such as a roller-coaster ride or a job-interview. He estimates on a scale from 'none' to 'very much' the likelihood that he would experience various indices of anxiety (e.g. sweating, heartbeat increase). Endler and Hunt then determine the relative contributions of main effects (persons, situations, modes of responding) and their various interactions.

The 'pure personologist' would expect Persons to constitute the main source of variance, while his sociological colleague might expect Situations to be the main source. But the data indicate that neither of these extreme viewpoints is supported. In a number of studies the average amount of variance attributable to persons is in the order of five per cent, and the amount of variance due to situations is similar (Endler & Hunt, 1966). *Interactions* between persons and situations, however, *did* account for comparatively large amounts of variance, and on the basis of their results in a number of different studies, Endler and Hunt conclude that the question of whether individual differences or situations are the major source of behavioural variance is 'a pseudo-issue', in that 'there is no simple major source of behavioural variance, at least so far as the trait of anxiousness is concerned' (p. 344).

A study more directly concerned with social behaviour has been reported by Ball (1969). Ball was interested in studying factors relating to the vertical dimension (sitting-standing) in social interaction, and explored the question of whether individual differences in etiquette-orientation versus one-upmanship orientation would be a better predictor of vertical behaviour than situational variables such as status differences. He reports that situational determinants were considerably better predictors, though his research design did not allow estimates of variance to be made.

While the previously mentioned studies used questionnaires rather than naturally occurring behaviour, two series of studies have been carried out in more naturalistic situations. Raush and his colleagues (Raush, Dittmann & Taylor, 1959; Raush, Farbman & Llewellyn, 1960) reported an extensive investigation of the behaviour of six hyperaggressive boys in a treatment home. They examined the relative contribution of different settings in the treatment centre (meal times, playtimes, etc.) and that of the individual boys. Their main finding was that the *interactive effects* between child and setting contributed far more information about behaviour than either Persons, Settings, or the sum of these two effects (Raush, Dittmann and Taylor, 1959). In this early study it was also reported that the contribution of settings (situations) to behaviour increased directly with the time the child had been under treatment. A subsequent study with a control group of normal boys in the same home (Rausch, Farbman & Llewellyn, 1960), found that this effect was not due merely to age but to treatment effects. Situations were found to account for more of normal boys' behaviour than Persons, suggesting that psychological disturbance may reflect itself in the inability to differentiate between different situations. Like the hyperaggressive boys, however, the behaviour of normal children was best predicted by the joint influence of Person and Setting rather than by either single effect alone of their sum.

Moos (1968, 1969) has extended and clarified some of these earlier studies, using both questionnaire and naturalistic observational data with psychiatric patients. In the first study (Moos, 1968) thirty psychiatric patients and ten staff members completed rating scales describing their feelings in different situations (e.g. small group therapy, getting up in the morning). Individual differences accounted for considerably more of the variance in ratings than situational differences, but only for the patient sample. Individual differences were *less* important in the staff ratings. For both groups the Person X Situation interaction was a significant source of variation. A second study (Moos, 1969) replicated the initial findings with a different sample, milieu and set of scales, and found that situational variance increased from an initial set of observations to one given several months later, lending support to the findings of Rausch *et al.* with boys.

The second study also included direct observation of S's behaviour in different situations. For behaviour such as smiling and general movement there is substantial Person variation and minimal Situation variation, while for behaviour such as talking, the reverse is true. Only two of eight reported behaviours had substantial Situation variance, the remaining six showing significant Person and Person X Situation effects. The most noteworthy finding of the behavioural analysis was that there is considerable variability in the contributions of different sources of behavioural variance.

Several conclusions can be drawn from these studies. First, the question of whether Persons or Situations contribute the most to social behaviour appears now to be posed in too simple a fashion. A more useful approach is to ask what are the relative effects of Persons, Situations, and their interactions, on different kinds of behaviour. The answers to this question, while still tentative, seem to be consistent from study to study. Person X Situation Interaction accounts for more variance than either Situations or Persons alone. With the passage of time and in more adequately functioning groups, Situations are relatively more important sources of variation than are Persons.

Second, the practical implications of these studies should not be overlooked. The amount of variance due to individual differences for any social behaviour sets an upper limit to the possible validity coefficients of individual difference measures (see Moos, 1969). If only twenty-five per cent of the variance is attributable to consistent individual differences the validity coefficient cannot exceed 0.5. The inclusion of situational variables would seem to be necessary if acceptable prediction levels are to be achieved.

III. INVESTIGATIONS OF REPORTED SOCIAL BEHAVIOUR IN DIFFERENT TYPES OF RELATIONSHIP

Another series of investigations has been carried out to determine the variability in social behaviour that is attributable to Persons and to Situations. These were started independently of those reported in II:5, but used a similar approach. Several features of this series differ from earlier studies. The variables under study included both verbal and non-verbal aspects of social behaviour, including some such as gaze and proximity that are of particular interest to students of social interaction. These studies differed from others also in that Ss were asked to report their behaviours in a number of different types of relationship (rather than situations). As in the Endler & Hunt, and Moos studies, estimates of Person, Situation and Interaction variances for each of the social behaviours were calculated. Additionally, however, a second stage of analysis was concerned with an examination of the principle components of social behaviour revealed by the ratings of both the total group and each individual.

The main study to be reported involved self-ratings by twenty-three poly-technic students on eighteen bipolar constructs which had been developed in our previous studies. In order to avoid eliciting stereotyped behaviour as much as possible, Ss were asked to provide the name of a real person they knew for each of twelve stimulus figures—(a) liked co-worker, (b) female friend, (c) liked member of family, (d) a professional person known in that capacity only, (e) liked neighbour or acquaintance, (f) less liked co-worker, (g) husband, wife, girlfriend, or boyfriend, (h) less liked member of family, (i) male friend, (j) less liked neighbour or acquaintance, (k) tradesman known in his trade capacity only, (l) boss or authority person.

The constructs, or dimensions, used are given in the Appendix.

Ss were tested in a single group. Each subject was given a questionnaire, a sheet with the list of stimulus figures and a sheet of instructions. Each sheet of the questionnaire had a construct written across the top and below this an 18 cm. line with the two poles of the construct on the left and right hand sides. Ss were asked to write in the letters A–L at appropriate points on the scale, depending on where each stimulus figure fell; for example, if, when talking to stimulus figure A, the conversation was mostly gossip or chat, S would write in 'A' towards the right-hand side of the scale for construct one, and so on for all twelve stimulus figures on each of the eighteen scales. The questionnaire was administered by one of the students' lecturers and took approximately twenty-five minutes to complete.

The completed sheets for each S were then transcribed into 12 X 18 grids, each cell of the grid consisting of the rating in cm. of a particular stimulus person on a particular construct. All measurements used the left-hand side of the scale as the zero point.

1. *Source of Variance, Analysis*

Total variation about each construct dimension was analysed into components attributable to Subjects, Stimulus Figures, and their Interaction. This analysis is formally identical to the previously mentioned studies looking at Person, Situation, and Interaction variance components. Table 1 reports the percentage of the total variance due to the different components for each of the eighteen social behaviour constructs. Results give clear evidence that on the average the stimulus figures (Situations) accounted for substantially more variance than did the Persons. As is found in other studies, however, constructs differ in the extent to which they are Situation dependent. Situation variance was approximately ten times higher than Person variance on constructs such as 'enjoyment', 'revealing ambitions', and 'formality', while Person variance was substantial on constructs such as 'care about personal appearance', 'concealing of affect', and 'gaze'. Interaction variance was uniformly high, though it should be noted that it is confounded with error variance and is therefore a slight over-estimate. Test-retest of subjects on the same scales would allow an estimate of 'true' interaction to be made.

2. *Principal Components of Combined Grids*

As there is a considerable amount of information contained in the grids it is helpful to reduce this information to more manageable form. One of the most useful techniques for data reduction is principal components analysis, and Slater (1964, 1969) has developed a programme, INGRID, which is specifically designed for the analysis of grid matrices.

INGRID analyses the total dispersion of the grid into its principal independent dimensions, and specifies separate loadings of stimulus figures and constructs on each dimension or component. These loadings can then be used to draw geometric representations. This programme was run on both the combined grids and on each indiviual's grid. For the combined grids analysis the first two

Table 1. Percentage of Total Variation about Interaction Construct Means Attributable to Persons, Situations, and their Interaction

	Person variance	Per cent Situation variance	Interaction
1. Gossip & chat . . . vs. little gossip and chat	9.5	23.5	67.1
2. Discuss personal problems . . . not at all	12.1	52.7	35.1
3. Behaviour is formal & rule governed . . . informal	4.0	61.7	34.3
4. Relaxes . . . tense	12.2	55.5	32.3
5. Swearing . . . never swear	15.9	33.5	50.5
6. Often refer to sex . . . never refer	6.6	56.7	36.7
7. Take great care with personal appearance, etc . . . less	37.8	19.2	43.0
8. Concerned about whether other thinks well . . . unconcerned	13.4	51.7	34.9
9. Openly show emotional states . . . conceal	16.7	35.6	47.7
10. Conceal anger, irritation . . . show freely	35.9	13.1	51.0
11. Freely express love, admiration, etc. . . . conceal	15.3	45.9	38.8
12. Openly reveal ambitions, financial sit . . . do not	5.9	62.2	31.8
13. Doing things depends on his doing things for me . . .	19.1	37.2	43.7
14. Look a lot in eye . . . avoid looking	30.2	26.6	43.2
15. Sit or stand very close . . . very distant	14.7	52.3	33.1
16. Relaxed posture . . . rather tense	19.0	37.7	43.3
17. Enjoy being with other . . . do not enjoy	6.5	67.8	25.7
18. Very much at ease . . . very ill at ease	15.2	51.8	33.1
Mean per cent var.	16.1	43.6	40.2

principal components accounted for eighty-five per cent of the total variance. On the first component the highest construct loadings were 'enjoy being with other', 'openly reveal ambitions, etc.', and 'discuss personal problems with'. This seems to be the familiar evaluative factor, and expressing it in interaction terms we'll label it the 'warm-cold' component. The second component loads the constructs 'concerned about whether other thinks well of me', 'care over personal appearance', and 'don't swear'. While closely related to dimensions of status and formality, this component seems to be one involving self-presentation, role-involvement, and ego-involvement. Expressing it, again, in interaction terms we can designate it 'constrained vs. casual'. In Figure 3 these two components are represented graphically as the principal axes. Upon these are placed the various role-figures as determined by their loadings on the two components. It can be seen that for the group as a whole various interaction clusters are discernible. Grid analysis thus seems to offer a useful way for grouping role relationships in terms of the interaction styles they elicit.

3. *Principal Components of Individual Grids*

Grid analysis also offers an interesting way of assessing a single individual. An example appears in Fig. 4.

The S, a nineteen-year old male, is a rather typical example in that he shows some degree of agreement with the combined analysis, while retaining some individuality in his ordering of relationships. The first dimension is similar to the first principal component on the combined grids. It is an evaluative component with high loadings for constructs like 'expressing love', 'eye contact', etc. The second component is also similar to the combined grid component, but the highest loading constructs are those concerned with swearing, care about appearance, references to sex, etc. and can be regarded as a polite-rough dimension. Of particular interest in this person's grid is his reported interaction with his boss. This figure is the mirror-image of the 'typical boss' appearing in the combined grid. Also, in contrast with most people this S does not seem to aggregate his relationships into clusters. While there is a small 'civil inattention'-like cluster in the cold-polite quadrant, and a 'friendship' cluster in the warm-polite quadrant, the other figures seem to occupy relatively isolated positions in his interaction space. The psychological meaning and personal importance of these kinds of discrepancies between combined grids and individual grids would seem to be a promising focus for clinical research.

4. *An Alternative Method of Analysing Individuals*

In another study, Ss were asked to describe their pattern of interaction with eighteen different target persons. The Ss were members of an American adult summer school in Oxford. For each of seventeen self-rating scales they were asked to write letters corresponding to the different target persons. Profiles were plotted showing how the group behaved towards each target person. Examples of two such profiles are shown below.

A detailed analysis was made of the responses of each subject using a distance analysis method. The similarity of interaction styles between every pair of target persons was calculated by subtracting the corresponding ranks on each of the seventeen scales. A McQuitty-type analysis was made of this set of relationships,

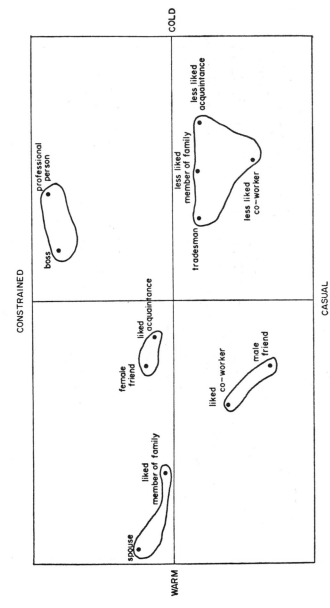

Fig. 3. Graphical representation of twelve stimulus figures upon the first two principal components for combined grids.

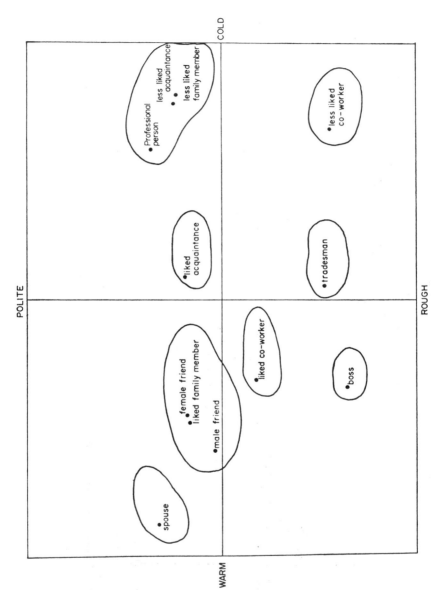

Fig. 4. Graphical representation of twelve stimulus figures upon the first two principal components for a single subject's grid.

and the pattern that emerged for one subject is shown in Fig. 6. The *S* was an unmarried female aged thirty, working in an academic job. The analysis shows clearly that she had four main styles of interaction. Her main style is the first one, and is typically represented by her behaviour towards her sister. There are a number of interesting features—for example, she behaves to her mother as to a subordinate.

The method is different in some respects from the one described above. It is not directly based on correlations, nor is it based on the individual's extracted dimensions, but rather goes directly to the assessment of similarity clusters. It has the additional advantage of making the designation of clusters less arbitrary than in the previous analysis. The method is extremely laborious when done by hand, but can be readily computerized.

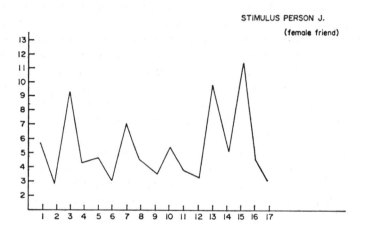

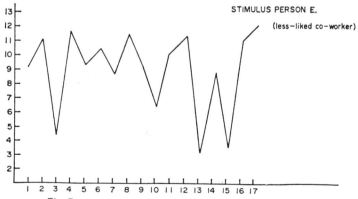

Fig. 5. Two profiles from preliminary study (n = 15).

IV. DISCUSSION AND CONCLUSIONS

1. *Conclusions about the Alternative Models of Personality*

The different models with which we began are not all testable directly. Nevertheless, the evidence which we have reviewed and the research we have reported are relevant to them, and some provisional conclusions can be made.

(a) **Personality as constant patterns of behaviour.** This model assumes substantial cross-situational generality to behaviour and a very high proportion of variance attributable to Persons. For most of the social behaviour reviewed no support for this assumption could be found. In our own main study Persons accounted for only sixteen per cent of the variance, and equally modest effects were found in the studies reviewed in section II.5. The amount of Person variance was different for different dimensions, however, and in physical adornment and concealing of negative affect there would seem to be some promise for finding stable individual differences.

The generally small amount of variance due to Persons may be partly an artefact of the method used in that Ss may have felt that they were being asked to show how their behaviour differed between target persons. However, the generally similar results in Moos' study with naturally occurring behaviour suggest that the findings are not artefactual.

It is also possible that the range of Ss used was small in relation to the range of the target persons and a possible way of solving this problem would be to use the same persons as Ss and target persons, so that the range is identical for both variables. But given the extensive evidence that the variance due to Persons is

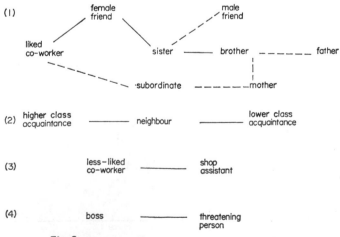

Fig. 6. Structure of target persons for one subject.

small, it is unlikely that more careful sampling will substantially help this basically discredited model.

(b) Personality as trait dispositions. On a simple version of this model, behaviour is a function of dimensions of the situation, and also a function of each individual's score on the trait. From this it would follow that all variance would be due either to Persons or to Situations. In our main study, however, we found that forty per cent of the variance was due to Person X Situation Interaction, which goes against such a model. However, in that both Persons and Situations did account for moderate amounts of variance, the dispositional model receives better support than the constant trait model. More complex models using several dimensions of situations and several underlying dispositions would be most likely to be consistent with the results.

(c) Personality as a person's cognitive system. While this model is probably untestable in terms of the kind of data we have considered, the strong evidence of Interaction (Type D) variability gives some support for the cognitive approach. It will be useful at this point to distinguish between our approach to assessment in this paper and that of personal construct theory (Kelly, 1955). A large number of studies have been carried out using Kelly's repertory grid technique to map out a person's personal construct system. Most often the constructs elicited are ones that are used by S in understanding other people. They represent, in other words, the concepts by which he decodes other people's personality. By using constructs pertaining to an individual's conception of his own social interaction we come closer to assessing an individual's *encoding of his own personality*—the ways in which he presents himself for decoding by others.

(d) Personality as unrelated S-R links, or the sum of role performances. Both of these approaches stress the lack of personal consistency across situations and in so far as Person variance was the lowest of the three major sources of variance they are given some support. The sum of role performances approach would place a heavy emphasis upon Situations as variance and so gains further support from the comparatively high (44%) amount of variance due to the relationship between S and the target figures. Two cautionary notes, however: There are some social behaviours which show very little in the way of Situational variation (e.g. concealing of negative emotion in our own study) and also a further kind of personal consistency appears when we consider that individuals interact along dimensions partly unique to them.

2. Why Social Behaviour does not follow a Trait Model

We have given detailed attention to the empirical data on traits of social behaviour. We turn now to some reasons why the more extreme trait positions are inapplicable to the field of social behaviour.

(a) **The rule governing particular situations.** Most social situations have rules and conventions prescribing how people should behave in them. Barker & Wright (1955) in their study of a small town in Kansas concluded that there were over 800 distinct public situations. As they put it: 'When we are in church we behave church, when we are in school, we behave school.' In some situations there is little scope for individual variation in behaviour—such as sitting in an audience. In many situations, traits such as leadership, dependence, etc. could not be easily manifested. In many situations the best way of predicting how a person will behave is to study the rules; Arabs, for example, stand considerably closer than the Americans or English (Watson & Graves, 1966). Goffman (1963) has drawn attention to the ways in which cultural conventions prescribe details of social performance, such as patterns of gaze, posture, etc. Most members of a culture would have difficulty in stating such conventions, but they become aware of them at once if someone breaks the rules.

(b) **Different role-relationships.** Within the *same* situation a person may perform in quite different ways because he may have to play different roles. He may be a teacher or pupil, committee chairman or committee member. He knows how to behave toward older and younger persons and towards males and females. These roles are parts of social structure in which superiors and subordinates, males and females are linked in a system of complementary roles. Breer (1960) has found that it is possible to make predictions of who would dominate whom from knowledge of the age, sex, and social class of two people: an older, more upper-class male usually dominates a younger, more lower-class female.

To use the analogy of playing games (which is also a form of social behaviour), the same person can follow the rules of football and cricket on different occasions—though he may have learnt different versions of the rules, as well as different styles of play in each of these games. And when he is playing cricket he can take turns at the roles of batting, bowling, and fielding. He may have a particular style of batting, or he may have exceptional skill at batting, but this will have little relation to the way he bowls.

(c) **The effects of the behaviour of others.** In the *same* situation, and when playing the *same* role, a person's performance will still vary with the behaviour of the other people present. Let us restrict the discussion to a dyadic encounter between A and B. A's behaviour depends on B, but B's behaviour also depends on A's. It is possible to make some prediction of what will happen from non-behavioural measures of A and B. For example, Carment, Miles & Cervin (1965) found that the *more* extraverted of two people spoke first in 28 out of 33 pairs, and spoke most in 23 out of 33 cases. Some combinations of people are more compatible than others. In Figure 2 two dimensions of preferred social performance are plotted. Here A and B would be compatible and it would be possible to predict how they would behave together. However A and C are not compatible and it is not possible to predict what would happen without further information. There would presumably be a struggle for dominance between A and C, the outcome depending on other variables. In general there is some kind of 'dyadic bargain' in which each person accommodates to some extent to the desires of the other.

(d) Arousal of motivation. An individual may become motivationally aroused in a variety of different ways, depending on the nature of the situation and the behaviour of the other person. Certain kinds of persons may induce sexual arousal, others may elicit anxiety, others aggressiveness and so on. Thus, not only will an individual be energized to a quite different degree on different occasions, but the nature of the motivation will also vary.

(e) Different personal attributes become relevant on different occasions. The prediction of patterns of social behaviour like leadership, popularity and conformity is complicated by the fact that all manner of attributes may become relevant on particular occasions. An individual is likely to become accepted as the leader of a particular group in a particular situation if he is the person with the greatest knowledge or ability relevant to the immediate group goal. He will be likely to be rejected by the group if he happens to hold attitudes or beliefs which are deviant in relation to topics which are important to the group at some point in time. His or her popularity will be affected by his or her physical appearance and how it fits current ideals of what people should look like.

3. Implications

(a) Implications for everyday person perception. Subjects in person perception experiments, and no doubt people in real-life as well, make judgments about the 'personalities' of other people. They decide how intelligent, honest, neurotic, dominant, etc. other persons are, these judgments being based on the evidence available, i.e. P's behaviour in the presence of O. As Secord and Backman say: 'One of the most widespread perceptual-cognitive processes operating in impression formation is temporal extension' (1964, p. 64). The data we have reviewed, however, show that this inference is basically invalid. Consider the judgments made of P by his wife, who considers that she knows him quite well. It is clear that the sample of P's behaviour which she sees is atypical. Similar considerations apply to judgments of P's personality by his boss or his neighbours, both of whom see quite different samples of P's social performance.

P usually supposes that Q always behaves as he does with P. This does not matter if P is only interested in his own interactions with Q. However if P wants to know how Q will get on with X, Y, and Z, he is liable to make serious errors of prediction. A boss may consider his subordinate, P, to be quiet and considerate; but he does not see P when with *his* subordinates.

The perceptual error of temporal extension is supported by the everyday use of words which appear to refer to roles as stable personality traits. It is a cultural assumption supported by dictionary definitions that individuals possess stable attributes. Allport and Odbert (1936) found between 4000 and 5000 dictionary words which indicated stable, permanent traits. It could be argued that these words need to be redefined either as patterns of behaviour (e.g. dominant), or as dispositional constructs (e.g. intelligent), or, as Mischel (1969) has suggested, as hyphen-words (e.g. aggressive-at-work, outgoing-parties, etc.).

(b) Applied implications. The problems discussed in this paper are most relevant to assessment for personnel selection and clinical assessment. Personnel selectors often try to form some impression of the personality and social skills of applicants for jobs, and for some jobs these are as important or more important than the abilities of the candidates. It follows from what we have said before that the candidate's performance during an interview or any other part of the selection procedure is likely to be a very poor guide to his style of social behaviour on the job. Further, in order to predict how a candidate will behave on the job it is necessary to specify the types of relationships and social situations in which he will be involved. This can be done by studying his social competence in situations similar to those in which he is going to be working—e.g. with female subordinates, at committee meetings, in conflict situations, etc. Such assessments can be made during an interview by exploring carefully the candidate's experience of such situations. They can also be made by asking referees to report in detail about the candidate's performance in specific situations.

REFERENCES

Allport, G. W. & Odbert, H. S. Trait-names: a psycho-lexical study. *Psychological Monographs*, 1936, 47, No. 211.

Ball, D. W. Biography, attitude or situation: Approaches to standing, sitting and definitions of the self. Unpublished doctoral dissertation, U.C.L.A., 1969.

Bannister, D. Comment, In R. Borger & F. Cioffi (eds.), *Explanation in the Behavioural Sciences*. Cambridge: Cambridge University Press, 1970, pp. 411–18.

Barker, R. G. & Wright, H. F. *Midwest and its Children*. Evanston, Ill.: Row, Peterson, 1955.

Block, J. The equivalence of measures and the correction for attenuation. *Psychological Bulletin*, 1963, 60, 152–56.

Block, J. Some reasons for the apparent inconsistency of personality. *Psychological Bulletin*, 1968, 70 210–212.

Breer, P. E. Predicting interpersonal behavior from personality and role. Unpublished doctoral dissertation, Harvard University, 1960.

Brown, R. *Social Psychology*. New York: Free Press, 1965.

Butler, D. & Stokes, D. E. *Political Change in Great Britain*. London: Macmillan, 1969.

Byrne, D. & Holcomb, Joan. The reliability of a response measure: Differential recognition-threshold scores. *Psychological Bulletin*, 1962, 59, 70–73.

Campbell, A., Converse, P. E., Miller, W. E. & Stokes, D. E. *The American Voter*. New York: Wiley, 1960.

Campbell, D. T. Social attitudes and other acquired behavioral dispositions. In S. Koch (ed.), *Psychology: A Study of a Science. VI.* New York: McGraw-Hill, 1963, pp. 94–172.

Campbell, D. T. & Fiske, D. W. Convergent and discriminant validation by the multitrait-multimethod matrix. *Psychological Bulletin*, 1959, 56, 81–105.

Carment, D. W., Miles, C. S. & Cervin, V. B. Persuasiveness and persuasibility as related to intelligence and extraversion. *British Journal of Social and Clinical Psychology*, 1965, 4, 1–7.

Cattell, R. B. *The scientific analysis of personality*. Baltimore, Md.: Penguin, 1965.

Couch, A. S. Psychological determinants of interpersonal behavior. Unpublished doctoral dissertation, Harvard University, 1960.

Craik, K. Personality unvanquished. *Contemporary Psychology*, 1969, 14, 147–8.

D'Andrade, R. G. Trait psychology and componential analysis. *American Anthropologist*, 1965, 67 (2), 215–28.

Endler, N. S., Hunt, J. McV., & Rosenstein, A. J. An S-R inventory of anxiousness, *Psychological Monographs*, 1962, 76 (17, Whole No. 536).

Endler, N. S. & Hunt, J. McV. Sources of behavioral variance as measured by the S-R Inventory of Anxiousness. *Psychological Bulletin*, 1966, 65, 336–46.

Eysenck, H. J. Explanation and the concept of personality. In R. Borger & F. Cioffi (eds.), *Explanation in the Behavioural Sciences.* Cambridge: Cambridge University Press, 1970, pp. 387–410.

Eysenck, S. B. G., & Eysenck, H. J. On the dual nature of extraversion. *British Journal of Social and Clinical Psychology*, 1963, 2, 46–55.

Eysenck, H. J., & Eysenck, S. B. G. *Personality Structure and Measurement*. London: Routledge & Kegan Paul, 1969.

Foa, U. G. Convergences in the analysis of the structure of interpersonal behavior. *Psychological Review*, 1961, 68, 341–53.

French, J. W. *The Description of Personality Measurements in Terms of Rotated Factors*. Princeton, N.J.: Educational Testing Service, 1953.

Gibb, C. A. Leadership. In G. Lindzey & E. Aronson (eds.), *The Handbook of Social Psychology*, Vol. 4, Reading, Mass.: Addison-Wesley, 1969, pp. 205–82.

Goffman, E. *Behavior in Public Places*. Glencoe, Ill.: Free Press, 1963.

Gough, H. G. An interpreter's syllabus for the *California Psychological Inventory*. In P. McReynolds (ed.), *Advances in Psychological Assessment*. Vol. I. Palo Alto, Calif.: Science and Behavior Books, Inc., 1968, pp. 55–79.

Hallworth, H. J. Perception of children's personalities by experienced teachers. *Educational Review*, 1966, 19, 3–12.

Hollander, E. P. & Willis, R. H. Some current issues in the psychology of conformity and non-conformity. *Psychological Bulletin*, 1967, 68, 62–76.

Jennings, H. H. *Leadership and Isolation*. New York: Longmans, 1950.

Kelly, G. A. *The Psychology of Personal Constructs*. New York: Norton, 1955.

Kendon, A. & Cook, M. The consistency of gaze patterns in social interaction. *British Journal of Psychology*, 1969, 60, 481–94.

Leary, T. *Interpersonal Diagnosis of Personality*. New York: Ronald, 1957.

Levy, L. *Conceptions of Personality*. New York: Random House, 1970.

Lorr, M. & McNair, D. M. Expansion of the interpersonal behavior circle. *Journal of Personality and Social Psychology*, 1965, 2, 813–30.

Mann, R. D. A review of the relationships between personality and performance in small groups. *Psychological Bulletin*, 1959, 56, 241–70.

McGuire, W. J. Personality and susceptibility to social influence. In E. F. Borgatta and W. W. Lambert (eds.), *Handbook of Personality Theory and Research*. Chicago: Rand McNally, 1968, Chapter 24, pp. 1130–87.

Mischel, W. *Personality and Assessment*. New York: Wiley, 1968.

Mischel, W. Continuity and change in personality. *American Psychologist*, 1969, 24, 1012–18.

Moos, R. Situational analysis of a therapeutic community milieu. *Journal of Abnormal Psychology*, 1968, 73, 49–61.

Moos, R. H. Sources of variance in responses to questionnaires and in behavior. *Journal of Abnormal Psychology*, 1969, 74, 405–12.

Mulaik, S. A. Are personality factors raters' conceptual factors? *Journal of Consulting Psychology*, 1964, 28, 506–11.

Pinneau, S. R. & Milton, A. The ecological veracity of the self-report. *Journal of Genetic Psychology*, 1958, 93, 249–76.

Porter, E. R., Argyle, M. & Saltern, V. What is signalled by proximity? *Perceptual and Motor Skills*, 1970, 30, 39–42.

Raush, H. L., Dittmann, A. T. & Taylor, T. J. Person, setting and change in social interaction. *Human Relations*, 1959, 12, 361–78.

Raush, H. L., Farbman, I. & Llewellyn, L. G. Person, setting and change in social interaction. II. A normal control study. *Human Relations*, 1960, 13, 305–32.

Rorer, L. G. The great response-style myth. *Psychological Bulletin*, 1965, 72, 48–59.

Secord, P. F. & Backman, C. W. *Social Psychology*. New York: McGraw-Hill, 1964.

Slater, P. *The Principal Components of a Repertory Grid*. London: Vincent Andrews & Company, 1964.

Slater, P. Notes on INGRID 67, unpublished Ms, 1969.

Stogdill, R. M. *The prediction of navy officer performance*. Personnel Research Board, Ohio State University, 1953.

Vaughan, G. M. The trans-situational aspect of conformity behavior. *Journal of Personality*, 1964, 32, 335–54.

Vernon, P. E. *The Structure of Human Abilities* (2nd ed.). London: Methuen, 1961.

Vernon, P. E. *Personality Assessment*. London: Methuen, 1964.

Wallace, J. An abilities conception of personality: Some implications for personality measurements. *American Psychologist*, 1966, 21, 132–8.

Watson, O. M. & Graves, T. D. Quantitative research in proxemic behavior. *American Anthropologist*, 1966, 68, 971–85.

APPENDIX

1. When you are talking to this person, how much of the conversation is gossip or chat (as opposed to conveying urgent information or solving pressing problems)?

very little   *mostly*
gossip or chat ⎯⎯⎯⎯⎯⎯⎯⎯⎯⎯⎯⎯⎯⎯⎯⎯⎯⎯ *gossip or chat*

2. How much do you discuss personal problems?

not at all ⎯⎯⎯⎯⎯⎯⎯⎯⎯⎯⎯⎯⎯⎯⎯⎯⎯⎯⎯ *a lot*

3. How far is behaviour formal and rule-governed?

very informal ⎯⎯⎯⎯⎯⎯⎯⎯⎯⎯⎯⎯⎯⎯⎯⎯⎯ *very formal*

4. How relaxed (as opposed to tense) are you when with this person?

very tense ⎯⎯⎯⎯⎯⎯⎯⎯⎯⎯⎯⎯⎯⎯⎯⎯⎯⎯ *very relaxed*

5. How often do you use swear words?

never ⎯⎯⎯⎯⎯⎯⎯⎯⎯⎯⎯⎯⎯⎯⎯⎯⎯⎯⎯⎯ *often*

6. How often do you refer to sex?

never ⎯⎯⎯⎯⎯⎯⎯⎯⎯⎯⎯⎯⎯⎯⎯⎯⎯⎯⎯⎯ *often*

7. How much care do you take about clothes, hair and personal appearance?

make no effort   *take great*
at all   _____   *care*

8. How concerned are you about whether the other person thinks well of you?

not at all   *very*
concerned   _____   *concerned*

9. How far do you reveal emotional states such as anxiety and depression?

try to   *show*
conceal   _____   *openly*

10. How far do you try to conceal anger, irritation or hostility towards the
    other?

try to   *show*
conceal   _____   *freely*

11. How far do you express feelings of love, approval or admiration for the
    other?

try to   *express*
conceal   _____   *freely*

12. How far do you reveal things about your financial situation, ambitions, etc.
    to this person?

do not   *reveal*
reveal   _____   *openly*

13. How far does your doing things for the other depend on his/her doing things
    for me?

                                                          depends on his/her
does not depend   *doing things for*
on this   _____   *me*

14. How much do you look the other person in the eye?

avoid looking   *look him/her in*
at him/her   _____   *the eye a lot*

15. How close do you normally sit or stand from the other?

very close   _____   *very distant*

16. How far do you adopt a relaxed, recumbent posture when with the other?

rather tense   *very relaxed*
posture   _____   *posture*

17. How much do you enjoy being with the other?

do not   *enjoy very*
enjoy   _____   *much*

18. How comfortable do you feel with this person?   very much

very ill   *very much*
at ease   _____   *at ease*

2

The Case for Person-Situation Interactions

NORMAN S. ENDLER

Cross-situational consistency (stability) versus situational specificity (change) is an important and complex issue in personality theorizing and research. Are there personality traits that are manifested in terms of response consistencies across a wide variety of situations, or is behaviour situation specific? As Mischel (1968), and Endler (1973) have indicated, personality research and theory have been primarily dominated by trait theories and by psychodynamic theories. These theories, which are response-response (R-R) theories, have assumed an underlying basic stability and continuity of personality, and have furthermore assumed the existence of trans-situational consistency.

Clinicians (Rapaport, Gill and Schafer, 1945), as well as personologists (Alker, 1972; Cattell, 1946, 1950; Cattell and Scheier, 1961; Guilford, 1959; McClelland, 1951; Murray, 1938) have proclaimed that *traits* are the prime or basic personality constructs or variables, and are the major determinants of behaviour. Traits are inferred from cross-situational response consistencies. Unfortunately different trait theorists derive different *kinds* of traits and different *numbers* of traits. If traits were really basic, then at the very least one would expect that different theorists derive the same kinds of traits, or at least the same number of traits. Furthermore, although the evidence for the reliability of traits is relatively good, *validity* coefficients for measures of personality traits are typically about .30, i.e., they account for about nine percent of the variance.

From the *Canadian Psychological Review*, 1975, *16*, 12–21. Copyright (1975) by the Canadian Psychological Association. Reprinted by permission.

This is a modified version of a paper presented at a symposium on "Traits, Persons and Situations: Some Theoretical Issues" at the American Psychological Association convention in Montreal, August 29, 1973. This symposium took place while I was on sabbatical at the University of Stockholm. I would like to thank Joe Hunt for reading this paper for me at the convention, and especially for stimulating many of the thoughts and ideas presented in the paper. The study was assisted under Grant No. 391 of the Ontario Mental Health Foundation, by Grant No. S73-1110 from the Canada Council and by a J. B. C. Watkins Leave Fellowship from the Canada Council (W 730350). The comments and suggestions of Marilyn Okada regarding this paper are appreciated.

Sociologists and social psychologists (Cooley, 1902; Cottrell, 1942a, 1942b; and George Herbert Mead, 1934) as well as social learning theorists (Bandura and Walters, 1963; Mischel, 1968, 1971; Rotter, 1954; Skinner, 1953, 1960) have proclaimed that *situations* are the prime determinants of behavioural variance. With respect to personality these theories are stimulus-response (S-R) theories, and many of these theorists have focused on the situations and the meanings these situations have for individuals in terms of cultural rules and roles. The assumption has been that S-R theories are more "scientific" than R-R theories of personality, because for the S-R theories it is possible to *control* the stimuli that evoke the responses, while no such control is possible for the R-R theories. However, as Bowers (1973) has pointed out, situationism has erroneously assumed that the S-R approach is identical to the experimental method and has taken a very myopic viewpoint regarding causality and explanation. Furthermore, the developmental aspect of the psychoanalytic position is basically an S-R approach to personality because it examines the relationships between childhood experiences and adult personality responses (Hilgard, Atkinson, and Atkinson, 1971), and yet it minimizes situational factors and maximizes response consistencies (traits).

Vernon (1964) and Mischel (1968, 1969, 1971) have both evaluated the data regarding personality traits and have found that there is little empirical evidence to support the trait theorists regarding trans-situational response consistencies. In emphasizing the importance of situational factors, Mischel (1971) has stated "that a person will behave consistently across situations only to the extent that similar behavior leads, or is expected to lead, to similar consequences across these conditions" (p. 74). That is, if situations have the same meaning for subjects, response consistency will occur, if situations have different meanings then inconsistency of responses should be expected.

Bowers (1973) has recently provided an extensive critique of situationism in terms of its metaphysical, psychological, and methodological assumptions, and Wachtel (1973) has suggested that some of the apparent discrepancies between psychodynamic trait theories and situation specific behaviour therapy theories may be due to differing perspectives of these two approaches in terms of the subjects studied, the content or phenomena of central interest, and research strategies. In a sense these two critiques of the situational approach serve as an antidote to the extensive critiques of trait theories provided by Farber (1964), Mischel, (1968, 1969, 1971, 1973), Peterson (1968), and Vernon (1964). Block (1968) has suggested some conceptual reasons for the apparent inconsistency of personality including "(a) the mixing of behaviors of different levels of salience, (b) the failure to recognize the effect of environmental factors, (c) the comparison of behaviors mediated by different underlying variables, and (d) the failure to specify or to recognize the bounds within which the posited relationship may be expected to exist" (p. 210).

Complexity of Personality

The trait (consistency) versus the situational (specificity) controversy is a complex and important issue for the area of personality. Although no one would deny the presence of personality stability and continuity (e.g. Block, 1971), there is persuasive evidence (e.g. Mischel, 1968, 1969, 1971) to suggest that there are both cross-situational personality differences at any given time for a particular individual, and substantial longitudinal personality changes over time.

There are differences with respect to consistency both *between* conceptual personality domains (e.g. cognitive versus social) and *within* a single domain (e.g. anxiety versus hostility). There is some evidence for trans-situational consistency and stability over time with respect to *intellectual* and *cognitive* factors (Mischel, 1969), but even here Hunt (1966) has provided evidence to indicate that the belief in fixed intelligence may well be a myth. With respect to *noncognitive personality dimensions* and *social behaviour* there is strong evidence for behavioural specificity. Argyle and Little (1972) have provided evidence in favor of situational factors with respect to social behaviour, social response questionnaires, and person perception; Endler (1966a), and Endler and Hoy (1967) have shown the importance of situational factors in social conformity; and Mischel (1968) has reviewed the evidence in favor of *situational specificity* for such character traits as aggression, attitudes to authority, conformity, dependency, rigidity and many other noncognitive personality variables. Mischel (1969) has suggested that on both an empirical and theoretical basis "the observed inconsistency so regularly found in studies of noncognitive personality dimensions often reflect the state of nature and not merely the noise of measurement" (p. 1014). The evidence then indicates that there is more consistency for the cognitive personality domain than for the noncognitive domain.

Within the *noncognitive personality* domain, Endler and Hunt (1968, 1969) found that individual differences account for 15-20 percent of the total variation for hostility but only 4-5 percent for the total variation for anxiety. Endler and Hunt suggest that the two traits may operate differently. Therefore, one cannot generalize from one trait to another with respect to consistency, and must pay attention not only to specific situations and various domains of personality but to the specific trait in question. We do not mean to deny the existence of traits, but merely to indicate the complexity of the human personality.

The complexity of the person versus the situation issue is also attested to by the phenomenon that *"there is a pervasive tendency for actors to attribute their actions to situational requirements, whereas observers tend to attribute the same actions to stable personal dispositions"* (Jones and Nisbett, 1971, p. 2). That is, when people explain their own behaviours they emphasize situational factors, but when they describe others they do so in terms of consistent dispositional personality constructs. Nisbett, Caputo, Legant and Marecek (1973), found that subjects describe *others* in terms of dispositional traits, but describe themselves in terms of "depends-on-the-situation" constructs. Lay, Ziegler, Hershfield and Miller (1973) using variations of the S-R inventories of Anxiousness (Endler, Hunt and Rosenstein, 1962) and Hostility (Endler and Hunt, 1968) found that predicted self-judgments produced less consistency over situations (i.e. less dispositional constructs) than judgments of others. Jones and Nisbett (1971) state that "the observer, even when he is a professional psychologist, is apt to conceive of the personalities of others as a collection of broad dispositions or traits, despite the scant empirical evidence for their existence" (p. 13). They suggest that this may be due to both biases of observer *information*, and biases of *information processing* on the part of the observer. Schneider (1973) has questioned "whether traits are the most appropriate units of person cognition and whether perceivers see traits as distributed across situations as well as stimulus persons" (p. 294).

Validity of Traits

Endler (1973, 1975), Endler and Hunt (1969), Hunt (1965), and Mischel (1968, 1969) have all indicated that validity coefficients for measures of personality traits typically range from .20 to .50 and are usually about .30. Stagner (1973) has provided evidence for the internal consistency reliability of trait measures. But it is not the *reliability* of traits that is being questioned, but rather their validity. It is true that validity coefficients are attenuated by errors of measurement, primarily reliability coefficients, and that self-report measures present methodological and statistical problems. However, it is equally evident that response indicators of presumed stable personality traits are specific and are dependent both on the modes of response used to assess the behaviours, and the evocative situations.

Situations

Although the S-R social learning theorists have emphasized the importance of the situation as a determinant of behaviour, very little has been done about defining and determining the nature of situations. While it is true that there have been attempts to classify situations (e.g. Sells, 1963, 1966) there has been little effort expended towards studying situations psychologically. Gibson (1960) has pointed to the difficulties inherent in defining a stimulus, let alone situations. Arsenian and Arsenian (1948) have proposed a psychosocial model for examining "tough" and "easy" cultures in terms of needs (persons) and paths of goals (situations) and the interaction between the two, and Chein (1954) has suggested a schema for investigating the objective behavioural environment. There is no indication that any investigators have attempted to empirically investigate either of these models. Endler, Hunt and Rosenstein (1962) have factor analyzed situations with respect to anxiousness and hostility, Magnusson (1971), and Ekehammar and Magnusson (1973) have analyzed individuals' perceptions of situations, Frederiksen (1972) has proposed a taxonomy of situations, and recently Moos (1973, 1974) has reviewed "six major methods by which characteristics of environments have been related to indexes of human functioning . . ." (Moos, 1973, p. 652). However, there has been no *systematic* attempt to study the situation *psychologically*. Situations do not exist in a vacuum but have psychological meaning and significance for people. Wachtel (1973) has pointed out that people select, create, and construct their own environments, and even Mischel (1973) has conceded this point. Stagner (1973) has suggested that traits determine what situations a person selects, and how he perceives situations. Furthermore, Wachtel has suggested that when stimuli are ambiguous, individual differences resulting from past experience are more discernable. All this points to the interaction between persons and situations, which is an issue we now wish to explore in greater detail.

PERSON–SITUATION INTERACTIONS

Endler and Hunt (1969) have presented self-report anxiety data, based on their S-R Inventories of Anxiousness (Endler *et al.*, 1962, Endler and Hunt, 1969) for 22 samples of males and 21 samples of female subjects. The samples of subjects varied in age, education level, geographical location, social class and mental health. They found that on the average, persons (individual differences) accounted for 4.44 percent of the variance for males, and 4.56 percent of the variance for females. Before the situationists gleefully proclaim that situations are more important than traits, let me point out that situational variance accounted for 3.95 percent of the variance for males and 7.78 percent of the variance for females. The interactions seem to be more important than either persons or situations. *Each* of the two-way interactions (Person by Situations, Persons by Modes of Response, and Situations by Modes of Response) account for, on the average, about 10 percent of the variance.

Bowers (1973) has summarized the results of 11 articles, published since 1959, that deal directly with the situation versus person controversy. These studies include data based on (a) self-report measures which most people have experienced personally or vicariously (e.g. S-R self-report inventories of anxiousness and hostility); (b) self-ratings of real situations (measuring feelings of trust, affiliation, affect, etc.); and (c) actual behaviour or observed behaviour in specific situations (e.g. honesty, hyperaggressive behaviour, smoking, talking). He found that the person by situation *interaction* accounts for more variance than either the person *or* the situation in 14 out of 18 possible comparisons, and the interaction accounts for more variance than the *sum* of the main effects in eight out of the 18 comparisons. Bowers (1973) found, that for these studies, the average variance due to persons was 12.71 percent, that due to situations was 10.17 percent, but that due to the person by situation interaction was 20.77 percent. Argyle and Little (1972) in reviewing the evidence with respect to person perception studies, social behaviour studies, and social response questionnaire studies have concluded that the "Person X Situation Interaction accounts for more variance than either situations or persons alone. With the passage of time and in more adequately functioning groups, Situations are relatively more important sources of variation than are Persons" (Argyle and Little, 1972, p. 16). While it is true that many of these results are based on self-reports and it would be desirable to have more behavioural measures, and in addition some physiological measures, one cannot dismiss these results as inconclusive.

Furthermore, studies in leadership, (Fiedler, 1971), aggressive behaviour (Berkowitz, 1973; Moyer, 1973; Feshbach, 1956) and on language performance (Moore, 1971) point to the importance of situational factors for these variables and to the relevance of a person by situation interaction in investigating personality. For example, Fiedler's (1971) contingency model of leadership indicates that the effectiveness of a leader is a function of the situation, the characteristics of the group and whether the leader is person oriented or task motivated. Berkowitz (1973) emphasizes the importance of cognitive and situational factors in aggression, and Moyer (1973) presents a physiological model of aggression which emphasizes the interaction of biological and learning factors in evoking violence. Moore (1971) reviews some literature that emphasizes "the interaction of characteristics of the speaker with characteristics of the situation in actual language performance" (pp. 18-19).

A Pseudo Issue

As Endler (1973) and Endler and Hunt (1966) have indicated "the question of whether individual differences or situations are the major source of behavioral variance, like many issues in the history of science, turns out to be a pseudo issue" (Endler and Hunt, 1966, p. 344). This does not mean to imply that persons and situations are unimportant sources of behavioural variance, nor does it deny that this is an important recurrent issue. "Rather it is the manner in which the question has been raised (e.g. which one, or how much is due to situations and how much to persons) that makes it a pseudo issue. Asking whether behavioral variance is due to either situations or to persons, or how much variation is contributed by persons and how much by situations (an additive approach) is analogous to asking whether air or blood is more essential to life or asking to define the area of a rectangle in terms of length or width" (Endler, 1973, p. 289). If we continue to ask inappropriate questions about this important personality issue, we will encounter the same difficulties as have been encountered with respect to intelligence and the nature-nurture issue. The appropriate and logical question is "*How* do individual differences and situations *interact* in evoking behavior?"

The notion of interaction is certainly nothing new. In the seventeenth century the physicist Robert Hooke proposed Hooke's law which stated that "within the elastic limit, strain is proportional to stress. For fluids and gases elasticity has a different meaning" (Bridgwater and Kurtz, 1963, p. 637). In other words, the elasticity of a substance is an interactive function of the nature of the material and the degree of situational stress. There is some evidence to suggest that there may be a Hooke's law for personality, in that anxiety reactions, for example, are an interactive function of personality traits (material) and situational stress (Endler and Shedletsky, 1973; Spielberger, 1972; Hodges, 1968).

However, as Mischel (1973) suggests it is insufficient to proclaim that interactions exist. One should be able to *predict* the nature of the interaction if the science of personality is to advance. Wallach and Leggett (1972) have made a similar point in their discussion of the failure to replicate interactions, and have also indicated their disenchantment with the moderator variable approach.

RESEARCH STRATEGIES FOR PERSONALITY RESEARCH

Let me briefly review some of the personality research strategies, and then suggest one approach to studying the nature of interactions. For a more extended presentation see Endler (1973).

Correlation Measures

The usual strategy has been to correlate measures (e.g. responses to question-naires) that are presumed indicators of a personality trait. This strategy has usually yielded correlations of .30, and the "failure to obtain construct validation using this strategy has been used as support for the situational-specificity model" (Endler, 1973, p. 295). However, while the correlational approach does not support the trait position, it also does not offer direct support for situational specificity. Low correlations may be due to a number of factors (e.g. reliability, methodological and statistical problems, interactions, etc.) in addition to the effect of situational specificity.

Moderator Variables

Situationists (e.g. Mischel, 1968, 1969; Bem, 1972) as well as trait theorists (Alker, 1972) have proclaimed that the "moderator" variable strategy (e.g. a variable affecting the relationship between two other variables) is very useful for seeking trans-situational consistency. Zedeck (1971) has suggested that there are inherent difficulties in identifying moderators, and that they present meth-odological and statistical problems. Wallach and Leggett (1972) do not believe that the moderator variable approach using selected sub-samples, is any different than the correlational approach using total samples. Both attempt to determine consistency by seeking evidence for dispositional traits. The interactions obtained in one study do not usually hold up in a replication of that study.

Behavioural Measures

Wallach and Leggett (1972) suggest that one should look for consistency in behav-ior and its products rather than looking for it in response indicators (test measures) of traits or constructs. The approach has merit since psychologists are ultimately interested in predicting actual behaviour. Wallach and Leggett (1972) compared childrens' drawing of a Santa Claus figure before, during, and after Christmas. Since they found no significant differences in size of drawings, as a function of the different occasions, but did find significant correlations (ranging from .47 to .68) of the size of the drawings across occasions, they suggest that this provides evidences for trans-situational consistency. However, it is our contention that their study neither proves nor disproves the consistency nor the situational specificity hypothesis. One cannot prove the null hypothesis, and the lack of difference across situations may point to the ineffectivensss of their technique, but does not imply consistency. Similarly, the correlations may represent test-retest reliabilities of their behavioural measure rather than consistency. The Wallach and Leggett (1972) paradigmatic approach is not appropriate in that it treats consistency and specificity as either situations *or* persons propositions. An interactionist approach would be more appropriate.

An Interactionist Approach

As indicated earlier human personality is very complex and therefore it is our contention that a useful paradigm (Kuhn, 1962) for the trait versus situation issue is an interactionist one, that examines *how* situations and persons *interact* in evoking behaviour. Methodology influences observations and results, and evidence from research on the nature-nurture intelligence controversy suggests that those favoring a heredity position use the correlational approach and those favoring environment use a mean-difference approach. We would therefore suggest that one should be openminded in one's approach to this problem. Note that low correlations of different measures of personality traits neither proves nor disproves consistency, and differences across situations do not conclusively demonstrate the primacy of situational factors.

We need a paradigm that can examine the interaction of situational and personal factors within the same experimental design (e.g. Bowers, 1973; McGuire, 1968). There are a number of different ways of approaching this problem. One method is to assess via variance components, derived from analysis of variance (Endler, 1966b), the relative variance contributed by situations and persons to behaviour and especially the contributions of person-situation interactions to behaviour. Endler and Hunt (1968, 1969) have done this with respect to the variables of anxiousness and hostility. Another approach exemplified by Raush (1965) in his research on the social behaviour of children, is to use multivariate information analysis to account for the relative contribution (in percent) of persons, situations and person by situation interactions in reducing the uncertainty of subsequent behavioural acts. In both these cases we are referring to the interaction of two independent variables (persons and situations) in effecting behaviour (the dependent variable) and *not* to the interaction between independent and dependent variables.

McGuire (1973) in discussing social psychology research, has recently criticized the simple linear sequential (cause and effect) model, including analysis of variance, and Fiske (1974) has been critical of current models in personality research. Overton (1973) in discussing the nature-nurture issue has stated that the interaction terms in analysis of variance are linear functions of independent elements and fall within, what he calls, the additive paradigm. He proposes an interactive paradigm where events are due to interactions that "are not decomposable into individual components" (p. 83). Vale and Vale (1969) have also proposed a paradigm that attempts to discover variables that underlie interactions.

Overton and Reese (1973) have made a useful distinction between the reactive organism (mechanistic) model of man and the active organism (organismic) model of man. For the mechanistic model, which uses analyses of variance procedures, the interaction term is concerned with an interdependency of determinants of behaviour. The "interaction is not between cause and effect, but between causes" (p. 78). For the organismic model, interaction refers to reciprocal causation or reciprocal action between environmental events and behaviour. In the present context, mechanistic interaction (which is unidirectional) would simply refer to the interactions of persons and situations in influencing behaviour, whereas organismic interaction (which is bidirectional) would refer to the mutual interdependence of persons-situations and behaviour so that the persons-situations influence behaviour and vice versa.

Mischel (1973), and Wachtel (1973) have recently focused on this dynamic view of interaction and Bowers (1973) has stated "that situations are as much a function of the person as the person's behavior is a function of the situation" (p. 327). Nevertheless, while it is important to study dynamic interaction and to develop appropriate techniques for doing this, we have still not fully explored the nature of mechanistic interaction. (It should be noted that Overton, 1973, would suggest that these two approaches imply differing, and possibly mutually exclusive, philosophies regarding the nature of man.) Concurrent with an investigation of dynamic interaction we must also examine how persons and situations interact (mechanistic interaction) in influencing behaviour. While Endler and Hunt (1968, 1969) have done this with respect to the variables of anxiousness and hostility (and Raush, 1965 with respect to social behaviour or children) their approach has been primarily descriptive. The next step is to experimentally examine the joint effects (on behaviour) of situations and of persons and to study behavioural measures as well as self-report measures, and subsequently to examine the effects of behaviour on persons and situations. To have any value such an approach must have predictive power rather than merely provide post hoc explanations.

A PERSON–SITUATION INTERACTION MODEL FOR ANXIETY

Let me briefly summarize a person-situation (mechanistic) interaction model for anxiety which is presented more extensively in Endler, (1974). Spielberger

(1966, 1972) has made an important distinction between *trait* anxiety (A-trait) (a personality variable) and *state* or acute anxiety (A-state) a transitory situational response. However, this theory has certain limitations in that it assesses trait anxiety unidimensionally. A multidimensional measure of trait anxiousness was developed (Endler and Okada, 1975) which provides independent measures of interpersonal A-trait, physical danger A-trait, and ambiguous A-trait. One can then examine the joint or interactive effects of A-trait (personality) and situational stress on state anxiety. However, in order for this person by situation interaction to be effective in inducing A-state anxiety, it is necessary for the A-trait measure to be congruent to the threatening situation. We are now conducting experiments in our laboratory in which we are predicting that *interpersonal* A-trait will interact with an *interpersonal* threat situation to elicit A-state changes, but will not interact with a physical danger threat situation. However, physical danger A-Trait will interact with a physical danger threat situation to elicit changes in A-state. This approach enables us to examine the interaction between personality and situational factors and examine their joint effects on behaviour. Ultimately we would have to extend this to determine how behaviour influences persons and situations (dynamic interaction).

The search for traits as prime determinants of behaviour has led to much misguided research. Similarly, an approach that focuses on situational factors can lead us astray. Human behaviour is complex and psychologists have to be willing to tolerate ambiguity and complex approaches rather than looking for simple solutions in terms of either traits or situations. A specific consideration of interactions would improve personality description "by emphasizing what kinds of responses individuals make with what intensity in various kinds of situations" (Endler and Hunt, 1966, p. 336).

REFERENCES

Alker, H. A. Is personality situationally specific or intrapsychically consistent? *Journal of Personality*, 1972, *40*, 1-16.

Argyle, M. and Little, B. R. Do personality traits apply to social behavior? *Journal for the Theory of Social Behaviour*, 1972, *2*, 1-35.

Arsenian, J. and Arsenian, J. M. Tough and easy cultures. *Psychiatry*, 1948, *11*, 377-385.

Bandura, A. and Walters, R. *Social Learning and personality development*. New York: Holt, Rinehart and Winston, 1963.

Bem, D. J. Constructing cross-situational consistencies in behavior: Some thoughts on Alker's critique of Mischel. *Journal of Personality*, 1972, *40*, 17-26.

Berkowitz, L. The case for bottling up rage. *Psychology Today*, 1973, *7*, 24-31.

Block, J. Some reasons for the apparent inconsistency of personality. *Psychological Bulletin*, 1968, *70*, 210-212.

Block, J. *Lives through time*. Berkeley, California: Bancroft, 1971.

Bowers, K. S. Situationism in psychology: An analysis and a critique. *Psychological Review*, 1973, *80*, 309-336.

Bridgwater, W. and Kurtz, S. *Columbia Encyclopedia (3rd Edition)*. New York: Columbia University Press, 1963.

Cattell, R. B. *The description and measurement of personality*. New York: World Book, 1946.

Cattell, R. B. *Personality: A systematic theoretical and factual study.* New York: McGraw-Hill, 1950.

Cattell, R. B. and Scheier, I. H. *The meaning and measurement of neuroticism and anxiety.* New York: Ronald, 1961.

Chein, I. The environment as a determinant of behavior. *The Journal of Social Psychology,* 1954, *39,* 115-127.

Cooley, C. H. *Human nature and the social order.* New York: Scribner's, 1902.

Cottrell, L. S., Jr. The analysis of situational fields. *American Sociological Review,* 1942, *7,* 370-382(a).

Cottrell, L. S., Jr. The adjustment of the individual to his age and sex roles. *American Sociological Review,* 1942, *7,* 618-625(b).

Ekehammar, B. and Magnusson, D. A method to study stressful situations. *Journal of Personality and Social Psychology,* 1973, *27,* 176-179.

Endler, N. S. Conformity as a function of different reinforcement schedules. *Journal of Personality and Social Psychology,* 1966, *4,* 175-180(a).

Endler, N. S. Estimating variance components from mean squares for random and mixed effects analysis of variance models. *Perceptual and Motor Skills,* 1966, *22,* 559-570(b).

Endler, N. S. The person versus the situation—a pseudo issue? A response to Alker. *Journal of Personality,* 1973, *41,* 287-303.

Endler, N. S. A person-situation interaction model for anxiety. In C. D. Spielberger and I. G. Sarason (Eds.), *Stress & Anxiety* Vol. 1. Washington: Hemisphere Publications (J. Wiley), 1975.

Endler, N. S. and Hoy, Elizabeth. Conformity as related to reinforcement and social pressure. *Journal of Personality and Social Psychology,* 1967, *7,* 197-202.

Endler, N. S. and Hunt, J. McV. Sources of behavioral variance as measured by the S-R Inventory of Anxiousness. *Psychological Bulletin,* 1966, *65,* 336-346.

Endler, N. S. and Hunt, J. McV. S-R Inventories of Hostility and comparisons of the proportions of variance from persons, responses, and situations for hostility and anxiousness. *Journal of Personality and Social Psychology,* 1968, *9,* 309-315.

Endler, N. S. and Hunt, J. McV. Generalizability of contributions from sources of variance in the S-R Inventories of Anxiousness. *Journal of Personality,* 1969, *37,* 1-24.

Endler, N. S., Hunt, J. McV. and Rosenstein, A. J. An S-R Inventory of Anxiousness. *Psychological Monographs,* 1962, *76,* No. 17 (Whole No. 536), 1-33.

Endler, N. S. and Okada, Marilyn. A multidimensional measure of Trait Anxiety: The S-R Inventory of General Trait Anxiousness. *Journal of Consulting and Clinical Psychology.* 1975, *43,* 319–329.

Endler, N. S. and Shedletsky, R. Trait versus state anxiety, authoritarianism and ego threat versus physical threat. *Canadian Journal of Behavioural Science,* 1973, *5,* 347-361.

Farber, I. E. A framework for the study of personality as a behavioral science. In P. Worchel and D. Byrne (Eds.), *Personality change.* New York: Wiley and Sons, 1964.

Feshbach, S. The catharsis hypothesis and some consequences of interaction with aggressive and neutral play objects. *Journal of Personality,* 1956, *24,* 449-462.

Fiedler, F. E. Validation and extension of the contingency model of leadership effectiveness: A review of empirical findings. *Psychological Bulletin,* 1971, *76,* 128-148.

Fiske, D. The limits for the conventional science of personality. *Journal of Personality,* 1974, *42,* 1-11.

Frederiksen, N. Toward a taxonomy of situations. *American Psychologist,* 1972, *27,* 114-123.

Gibson, J. J. The concept of the stimulus in psychology. *American Psychologist,* 1960, *15,* 694-703.

Guilford, J. P. *Personality.* New York: McGraw-Hill, 1959.

Hilgard, E. R., Atkinson, R. C. and Atkinson, R. L. *Introduction to Psychology* (5th Edition). New York: Harcourt Brace Jovanovich Inc., 1971.

Hodges, W. F. Effects of ego threat and threat of pain on state anxiety. *Journal of Personality and Social Psychology*, 1968, *8*, 364-372.

Hunt, J. McV. Traditional personality theory in the light of recent evidence. *American Scientist*, 1965, *53*, 80-96.

Hunt, J. McV. The psychological basis for using pre-school enrichment as an antidote for cultural deprivation. In O. J. Harvey (Ed.) *Experience, structure and adaptability*. New York: Springer Publishing Co., 1966, 235-276.

Jones, E. E. and Nisbett, R. E. *The actor and observer: Divergent perceptions of the causes of behavior*. New York: General Learning Press, 1971.

Kuhn, T. S. *The Structure of scientific revolutions*. Chicago: University of Chicago Press, 1962.

Lay, C., Ziegler, M., Hershfield, L., and Miller, D. The perception of situational consistency in behavior. Assessing the actor-observer bias. York University, Toronto, 1973 (Unpublished manuscript).

Magnusson, D. An analysis of situational dimensions. *Perceptual and Motor Skills*, 1971, *32*, 851-867.

McClelland, D. C. *Personality*. New York: Dryden, 1951.

McGuire, W. J. Personality and susceptibility to social influence. In E. F. Borgatta and W. W. Lambert (Eds.) *Handbook of personality theory and research*. Chicago: Rand McNally, 1968, 1130-1187.

McGuire, W. J. The yin and yang of progress in social psychology: Seven koan. *Journal of Personality and Social Psychology*, 1973, *26*, 446-456.

Mead, G. H. *Mind, self and society*. Chicago: University of Chicago Press, 1934.

Mischel, W. *Personality and assessment*. New York: Wiley, 1968.

Mischel, W. Continuity and change in personality: *American Psychologist*, 1969, *24*, 1012-1018.

Mischel, W. *Introduction to personality*. New York: Holt, Rinehart and Winston, 1971.

Mischel, W. Towards a cognitive social learning reconceptualization of personality. *Psychological Review*, 1973, *80*, 252-283.

Moore, D. R. Language research and pre-school language training. In C. Stendler Lavatelli (Ed.) *Language training in early childhood education*. Champaign-Urbana, Illinois: University of Illinois Press, 1971, 3-48.

Moos, R. Conceptualization of human environments. *American Psychologist*, 1973, *28*, 652-665.

Moos, R. Systems for the assessment and classification of human environments: An overview (Part 1, no. 1). In R. H. Moos and P. M. Insel (Eds.) *Issues in Social Ecology*. Palo Alto: National Press Books, 1974, 5-28.

Moyer, K. E. The physiology of violence. *Psychology Today*, 1973, *7*, 35-38.

Murray, H. A. *Explorations in personality*. New York: Oxford University Press, 1938.

Nisbett, R. E., Caputo, C., Legant, P. and Marecek, J. Behavior as seen by the actor and as seen by the observer. *Journal of Personality and Social Psychology*, 1973, *27*, 154–164.

Overton, W. F. On the assumptive base of the nature-nurture controversy: Additive versus interactive conceptions. *Human Development*, 1973, *16*, 74-89.

Overton, W. F. and Reese, H. W. Models of development: Methodological implications. (Chapter 4.) In J. R. Nesselroade and H. W. Reese (Eds.), *Life-span developmental psychology: Methodological issues*. New York: Academic Press, 1973, 65-86.

Peterson, D. R. *The clinical study of social behavior*. New York: Appleton-Century-Crofts, 1968.

Rapaport, D., Gill, M. and Schafer, R. *Diagnostic psychological testing*. Chicago: Year Book, 1945, 2 Volumes.

Raush, H. L. Interaction sequences. *Journal of Personality and Social Psychology*, 1965, *2*, 487-499.

Rotter, J. B. *Social learning and clinical psychology*. Englewood Cliffs, New Jersey: Prentice-Hall, 1954.

Schneider, D. J. Implicit personality theory: A review. *Psychological Bulletin,* 1973, *79,* 294-309.

Sells, S. B. (Ed.) *Stimulus determinants of behavior.* New York: The Ronald Press Co., 1963.

Sells, S. B. Ecology and the science of psychology. *Multivariate Behavioral Research,* 1966, *1,* 131-144.

Skinner, B. F. *Science and human behavior.* New York: Macmillan, 1953.

Skinner, B. F. Pigeons in a pelican. *American Psychologist,* 1960, *15,* 28-37.

Spielberger, C. D. The effects of anxiety on complex learning and academic achievement. In C. D. Spielberger (Ed.) *Anxiety and behavior.* New York: Academic Press, 1966.

Spielberger, C. D. Anxiety as an emotional state (Ch. 2). In C. D. Spielberger (Ed.) *Anxiety: Current trends in theory and research.* Volume I., New York: Academic Press, 1972, 23-49.

Stagner, R. Traits are relevant: logical and empirical analysis. Paper presented at a symposium on "Traits, Persons and Situations: Some Theoretical Issues" at the American Psychological Association annual convention in Montreal, August 29, 1973.

Vale, J. R. and Vale, C. A. Individual differences and general laws in psychology. *American Psychologist,* 1969, *24,* 1093-1108.

Vernon, P. E. *Personality assessment.* London: Methuen, 1964.

Wachtel, P. Psychodynamics, behavior therapy and the implacable experimenter: An inquiry into the consistency of personality. *Journal of Abnormal Psychology,* 1973, *82,* 324-334.

Wallach, M. A. and Leggett, M. I. Testing the hypothesis that a person will be consistent: Stylistic consistency versus situational specificity in size of children's drawings. *Journal of Personality,* 1972, *40,* 309-330.

Zedeck, S. Problems with the use of "moderator" variables. *Psychological Bulletin,* 1971, *76,* 295-310.

3

Performance and Satisfaction as a Function of Individual-Environment Fit

LAWRENCE A. PERVIN

This paper is concerned with the question of individual-environment fit. It assumes that for each individual there are environments (interpersonal and noninterpersonal) which more or less match the characteristics of his personality. A "match" or "best-fit" (Jahoda, 1961) of individual to environment is viewed as expressing itself in high performance, satisfaction, and little stress in the system whereas a "lack of fit" is viewed as resulting in decreased performance, dissatisfaction, and stress in the system. This paper presents selected studies in the experimental literature which exemplify and support the individual-environment fit approach, and discusses the theoretical models that have been suggested in relation to this view and the issues remaining to be considered.

It is beyond the scope of this paper to deal with the concept of the stimulus in psychology (Gibson, 1960) or with related theories of perception (Allport, 1955). For the purposes of this paper, environmental (situational) variables are defined as representing those stimuli external to the organism which affect its behavior. Within the framework of this paper, it is assumed that individuals vary in their sensitivity to different stimuli and in the nature of their responses to these stimuli. Behavior is represented as a function of the interaction or transaction between the individual and his environment. The issue of whether to define the environment independently of the individual or in relation to the individual is relevant to the research reviewed and is discussed later.

PERFORMANCE

The research reviewed in this section treats performance as a function of the interaction between the characteristics of the individual and those of the

From the *Psychological Bulletin*, 1968, *69*, 56–68. Copyright 1968 by the American Psychological Association. Reprinted by permission.

This review was conducted in conjunction with research supported by the National Institute of Mental Health (MH-08321) and the United States Office of Education. I am grateful to Stephen Klineberg, Bertram Koslin, and David Rosenhan for their critical readings of the manuscript.

environment. While it is often difficult to make a distinction between the interpersonal environment and the noninterpersonal environment, the studies are
defined and discussed in relation to these two categories.

Noninterpersonal Environment

The early work of drive theorists contributed little to the question of
individual-environment interaction. Differences between individuals were presumed to be reflected in the "constant" numerical values (Hull, 1943) but were
not systematically explored. Considerable research on anxiety as a drive state and
as a personality variable indicates that the effects of drive depend upon
situational and task variables. Concerning situational variables, for example,
Smith and Rockett (1958) found that when instructions were not intended to
reduce anxiety, low-anxiety subjects performed better than high-anxiety subjects
whereas when instructions were intended to reduce anxiety, high-anxiety subjects
out-performed low-anxiety subjects. Similar findings were reported by Sarason
(1961). Concerning task variables, Taylor (1956) reported that research on the
Manifest Anxiety Scale supported the conclusion that there is an interaction
between anxiety level and task complexity. As noted by Sarason (1960),
high-anxiety subjects may perform better than low-anxiety subjects on simple
tasks, but the low-anxiety subjects increasingly perform better than the high-
anxiety subjects as task complexity increases. Sarason (1960) has found that the
learning of verbal material is influenced by an interaction among task difficulty,
orienting instructions, and personality (test-anxiety) factors.

Other areas of research show similar findings. Feather (1961) reported an
interaction between personality and situational variables on persistence in a
laboratory setting, and Nakamura and Ellis (1964) reported an interaction between
the effect of reinforcement and the child's personality. In the latter study, high
rewards facilitated performance for children low in persistence but did not for
those high in persistence. Under conditions of low reward, children high in
persistence performed better than those low in persistence. In relation to task
variables, Claunch (1964) found that conceptually abstract subjects were superior
to concrete subjects on an examination task involving a complex criterion (essay)
but not on a quiz task. Forehand and Gilmer (1964) discussed the interactions
between personalities and job qualities leading to high organizational efficiency.
They also discussed the fear that too much of a match will prevent change.

Conclusions drawn from the literature on anxiety as a drive state correspond to
those Lazarus, Deese, and Osler (1952) concerning general stress behavior; that is,
to understand and predict responses to stress one must understand the individual's
motivations, his responses to stress, and the characteristics of the situation in which
he must perform. In a recent study based upon the interactionist point of view,
Hunt (Endler, Hunt, & Rosenstein, 1962) studied the trait of anxiousness.
Interactions among modes of response, situations, and persons were more
important in producing variations in behavior than any of the individual sources of
variance alone.

Interpersonal Environment

A number of studies show that a fit between the personality characteristics of one individual and those of another, or between an individual and the social climate created by a group of individuals, leads to high performance. For example, Smelser (1961) tried a variety of interpersonal combinations in operating two model railroad trains and found that the most productive group was composed of pairs in which the dominant subject was assigned a dominant role and the submissive partner a submissive role. He concluded that congruence of role and habitual pattern within subjects and complementarity of patterns between subjects were important variables.

Many studies of learning environment and learning performance fit into the interactionist framework. A number of these studies focus on the relationship between personality characteristics and the degree of structure in the environment. For example, Amidon and Flanders (1961) found that while independent children were unaffected by teaching method, dependent children performed better under indirect than direct teaching. Grimes and Allinsmith (1961) studied the relationship among compulsivity, anxiety, and performance in structured and unstructured settings. They found that anxiety and compulsivity interacted with one another and with teaching method. In a structured setting, compulsive children did better than noncompulsive children and anxiety made no difference. In the unstructured setting, compulsivity made no difference but anxiety impeded performance.

In a study of more general aspects of the learning environment, Beach (1960) found that students low on sociability perform better in lecture sections whereas more sociable students perform better in leaderless discussion groups. Finally, McKeachie (1961) found a significant interaction between student motives and classroom environment in determining grades.

Outside the learning environment, and related to a non-goal-directed behavior, the research of Raush, Dittmann, and Taylor (1959) represents a fine example of the interactions between personality characteristics and environmental conditions. They studied the social interactions of six hyperaggressive boys in different social settings. Their conclusion was as follows:

In general, there is individual consistency in social behavior across different settings and there is setting consistency across different individuals. But the interactive effects between child and setting contributed far more information about behavior than did the sum of the independent components [p. 375].

SATISFACTION

Noninterpersonal Environment

The studies previously discussed have suggested that performance may best be viewed as a function of the interaction among individual, task, and situational variables. This was found to be true regardless of whether the environmental variables were basically interpersonal or noninterpersonal. Similarly, a number of studies suggest that satisfaction may be most profitably understood within such a framework; that is, the satisfaction reported by an individual with his experiences reflects processes relating to the interactional or transactional model.

An example of this approach in the realm of noninterpersonal satisfaction has been the work on occupational choice and satisfaction. Englander (1960) found that the congruency of self-concept and the concept of the role of elementary school teacher was greater in students preparing to work in this field than in other students. Relating more specifically to satisfaction, Blocher and Schutz (1961) found that the similarity between self and liked occupation was greater than that between self and disliked occupation, and Brophy (1959) found that the similarity between self-concept and perceived occupational role requirements (occupational concept) was correlated with job satisfaction. The conclusion in the latter study was that occupational satisfaction is a function of the interaction between a personal concept and a related environmentally focused concept. These studies, and the theoretical viewpoint reflected in them, generally follow from Super's (Super, Starishevsky, Matlin, & Jordaan, 1963) theory of occupational choice and satisfaction: "Agreement between the self concept and one's own occupational concept is related to occupational preferences and to both internal and external criteria of success and satisfaction [p. 11]."

These studies involved the perceived occupational characteristics as opposed to some consensually validated description of the job. Furthermore, they limited themselves to the self-concept and to characteristics (adjectives) provided by the experimenter. An interesting departure from this is the work of Oppenheimer (1966). Using a modified Kelly Role Construct Repertory (REP) Test and a semantic differential, he had subjects rate themselves, their ideal selves, and a variety of occupational perceptions along dimensions provided by them from the REP test. He found that a small discrepancy between self and occupational perceptions was generally related to expressed occupational preference. However, this was most true for individuals with high self-esteem (a low self-ideal-self discrepancy). Individuals with low self-esteem were found to prefer occupations perceived as congruent with their ideal-self concepts rather than occupations perceived as congruent with their self-concepts.

In sum, the studies reviewed suggest that occupational satisfaction may be profitably studied as resulting from the interaction between personality and environment variables rather than the result of personality variables or environmental variables alone.

Interpersonal Environment

As stated by Miller (1963), the interactionist looks at satisfaction in interpersonal relationships as a function of the relationship between the characteristics of individuals rather than as a result of the characteristics of individuals in isolation. Much of the interactionist literature suggests a relationship between similarity and friendship choice or interpersonal satisfaction (Fiedler, Warrington, & Blaisdell, 1952; Kipnis, 1961; Morton, 1959; Newcomb, 1953, 1956, 1958; Rosenfeld & Jackson, 1959). This holds for both perceived similarity and actual similarity (Izard, 1960a, 1960b; Lindzey & Urdan, 1954; Triandis, 1959). However, other studies have found no relationship (Hoffman & Maier, 1966; Katz, Glucksberg, & Krauss, 1960) or relationships other than similarity (Miller, Campbell, Twedt, & O'Connell, 1966; Winch, Ktsanes, & Ktsanes, 1955). One study of particular interest is that of Lundy, Katkovsky, Cromwell, and Shoemaker (1955), which found that while self-descriptions were generally more similar to descriptions made of chosen persons than rejected persons, the description of a best-liked person was significantly more similar to a person's acceptable self while the reverse was true for the description of the least-liked person. The suggestion that people with high self-ideal-self discrepancies would dislike people similar to themselves is similar to the finding of Oppenheimer (1966) concerning occupational choice.

In a review of much of this literature, Lott and Lott (1965) concluded that

when we put all the evidence together, there can be little doubt that individuals tend to prefer friendly associations with others who are compatible to themselves in interests, values or personality. The major problem in this area is specification of what constitutes compatibility in situations of varying characteristics [p. 277].

Four issues are relevant to this area of research and to all transactional research:

1. *Do the relationships found relate to perceived or actual (consensually validated) characteristics?* In the Fiedler et al. (1952) study, similarity referred to assumed or perceived similarity whereas real similarity was not found to be significantly related to friendship choice. On the other hand, Izard (1960a) found such a relationship for actual similarity. It may be that a choice between perceived and actual similarity is inappropriate and that instead we should look at the conditions under which one or the other accounts for more of the variance. In any case, such studies point to the issue involved, to be discussed in the section on general theoretical viewpoints.

2. *What are the units that should be employed?* This issue was discussed by Allport (1958). Some studies look at needs, others at traits, and still others at attitudes and values. In many studies, attention is not given to the nature of the units employed and the possibility that different relationships may hold for different units.

3. *What is the nature of the processes involved in the relationships found?* One aspect of this issue is whether a relationship, such as that between friendship and similarity, indicates that similar individuals become friends or that friends become more similar. More generally, however, there is the issue of the reasons for similarity, complementarity or or compatibility being related to attraction and interpersonal satisfaction. Models of need satisfaction, cognitive consistency, and cognitive validation (Pepitone, 1964) are among those which have been suggested, but often research is either without a model or fails to make the model explicit.

4. *Do environmental conditions affect the nature of the relationships to be found?* It may be that different relationships hold for friendship choices than for marital partners, for friendship groups than for work groups, etc.; that is, that interpersonal attraction, already an interactive process, may vary further according to the conditions under which the individuals are interacting. This is likely the case, and it means that we need systematic exploration of this area, including the development of a classificatory scheme for environmental conditions.

The above issues relate to one another. In sum, the relationships found and our appreciation of the processes involved may vary according to the units employed, whether we look at perceived or actual characteristics, and the nature of the conditions under which the relevant individuals interact.

ACADEMIC PERFORMANCE AND SATISFACTION

The issues discussed in relation to performance and satisfaction have come to have particular relevance for the academic situation. We have increasingly ceased to speak of bright or dull students and good or bad colleges, and have instead focused on the relationships between students, curricula, and schools. Cronbach (1966) has emphasized the need for studying the interaction between student abilities and treatments of subject matter, and Sanford (1962) has emphasized the interaction between student personality and college characteristics: "An environment must be suited to the species; if it isn't, the organisms die or go elsewhere [p. 727]."

Three areas of research are representative of gains being made in understanding of the educational process through an emphasis upon individual-environment interaction: the college dropout, curriculum presentation, and faculty characteristics.

In one of the early works in this fast-growing field, Pace and Stern (1958) suggested the study of congruence between needs and press in determining successful performance and/or satisfaction in the college environment: "The total pattern of congruence between personal needs and environmental press will be more predictive of achievement, growth and change than any single aspect of either the person or the environment [p. 277]." Along these lines, Stern (1962) noted a study by Patton which found that authoritarians, a distinct minority at the University of Chicago, tended to have the highest dropout rate. They complained of looseness in the pedagogical approach that tolerated smoking in classrooms, did not require attendance, and expected students to answer their own questions. Similarly, Funkenstein (1962) reported results which suggest that many dropouts from medical schools result from an incongruity between the basic attributes of the individual and those of the college. Douvan and Kaye (1962) have suggested that the college dropout rate reflects serious errors in the choice process, Sanford (1962) has emphasized the strain created by lack of peer group support, and Snyder (1963) has noted the interplay between the adaptive patterns of the individual and those rewarded or penalized by the educational institution. Summerskill (1962), in reviewing the dropout literature, raised the following question: "Does the student have sufficient and appropriate motivation for a specified college with specified characteristics and objectives? [p. 640]."

Astin (1963) attempted to define the college environment in terms of attributes of the student body obtained from published sources (the Environmental Assessment Technique). More recently, he has developed the Inventory of College Activities, which attempts to define the college environment through observable events (Astin, 1965). He described the work of Pace and Stern as based on student perceptions of the environment and contrasted this "image" approach with that of the Environmental Assessment Technique, based on objective characteristics of students, and that of the Inventory of College Activities, based on observable events. Astin is working toward a definition of the college environment which is independent of subjective impressions given by students and independent of personal characteristics of students. His emphasis upon observable events is in keeping with his definition of the college environment as

a set of potential *stimuli*. The term "stimuli" refers here to those events or other observable characteristics of the college that are capable of changing the sensory input to the student attending the college. . . . Thus, while the student's subjective impression of his college may influence his behavior toward other students, his perception *per se* does not constitute a stimulus [Astin, 1965, p. 1].

This approach has given relatively little consideration to the interactions between students and colleges, and whether this definition of the college environment is empirically most useful remains an open question.

At the other extreme of attempts to measure the college environment is the research by Pervin (1967) which focuses on the way students as individuals and as groups perceive the environment. This research investigates the issue of student-college fit through the use of a semantic differential.[1] Students rate themselves and such concepts as My College, Faculty, Administration, and Students on the same scales. Discrepancies between ratings on pairs of concepts are then related to reported probability of dropping out and various types of satisfaction or dissatisfaction with the college environment. So far the results are quite promising. Students who perceived themselves as different from the college and other students on the semantic differential generally reported a higher probability of dropping out of college for nonacademic reasons, reported they felt more out of place, and were more dissatisfied with nonacademic aspects of life at their college. Furthermore, Self-Student discrepancies correlated best with dissatisfaction with students, Self-Faculty discrepancies best with dissatisfaction with faculty, and Self-Administration discrepancies best with dissatisfaction with the administration. Discrepancy scores appear to relate better to the criterion

----

[1] The form of the semantic differential that was used is called TAPE (Transactional Analysis of Personality and Environment) and was jointly developed by the author and D. B. Rubin as described in Pervin and Rubin (1967).

variables than simple perceptions of self, students, faculty, administration, or college. Further research will investigate the student and college environment variables that most influence these relationships, but the data to date give clear support to the theoretical rationale of student-college fit and the methodological approach employed.

The above sources relate to general campus atmospheres, but the issue of student-college fit can focus more specifically on the predominant nature of the curriculum. Malleson (1959) described the findings of Furneaux that certain types of students have difficulty in one area, while others have difficulty in another area, suggesting a relationship between type of work and type of student. Snyder (1966) reported similar findings at the Massachusetts Institute of Technology. McConnell and Heist (1962) emphasized that students who possess certain interests are more suited for some curricula than for others, and Katz and Sanford (1962) concluded:

Within the same institution, at the same time, there are undoubtedly students who would benefit most from one type of curriculum and other students who would benefit most from a different type, and yet that institution offers and defends as universally good a single curriculum [p. 431].

In spite of these calls to a transactional approach, most current research in this field investigates students or curricula rather than the interaction between the two.

Finally, we come to the faculty and mode of presentation of subject matter. The work of McKeachie (1961) pointed to an interaction between student and faculty motives in affecting academic performance. A later study of student need affiliation motives, instructor cues, and grade achievement concluded that

the interactions between situational and individual difference variables can be revealed in studies in natural settings, and that even with relatively unprecise measures such interactions are powerful enough and stable enough to emerge in replicated studies [McKeachie, Lin, Milholland, & Isaacson, 1966, p. 461].

Patton (1955) has found that students who reject traditional sources of authority and are highly motivated toward personal achievement are most favorably disposed toward experimental classes run by students themselves and most able to handle the responsibilities involved in such classes. Bay (1962) discussed the interaction between professors who reward independent intellectual efforts as opposed to those who reward efficiency in memorization and students who seek intellectual challenge as opposed to those who are more narrowly grade-oriented.

Related to style of presentation is the question of criteria of performance. Claunch (1964) found that abstract students were significantly superior to concrete students in performance on an examination involving a complex criterion (essay), but not in a multiple-choice task. On essay examinations abstract students were better able than the others to integrate comparisons of different theoretical points of view. Thus examination performance and grades reflect personality style or mode of cognitive functioning. More generally, grades reflect the interaction between the individual's mode of operation and the tasks set for him by his environment.

In sum, research in the area of academic performance and satisfaction clearly indicates that future investigators should consider the interaction between personality characteristics and qualities of the college environment (Lavin, 1965) and that college administrators should consider the possibility of reaching the same educational objectives in different ways for different students (Stern, 1962).

THEORETICAL POSITIONS

A number of psychologists have called attention to the importance of the environment in influencing behavior. Sherif and Cantril (1947) emphasized the importance of the social environment and criticized psychoanalysis for missing the continuous relationship between the individual and his social environment. Barker (1960) has worked on the importance of behavior settings as places containing opportunities for achieving multiple satisfaction of motives. In a similar way, Chein (1954) emphasized the environment as a limiting and determining factor in the way an individual satisfies his motives. The work of Bloom (1964) and Sells (1963) is also worthy of note, particularly the Sells view that situational or environmental measures must be obtained independently of the individual's perceptions of them.

While these psychologists have called attention to the environment, others have more clearly emphasized the need for an interaction approach to research (Meltzer, 1961; Miller, 1963; Shibutani, 1961; Wallace, 1965). Hunt (1961) has traced the history of a number of areas of research, such as that of intelligence, in terms of the relative emphasis upon the individual (heredity) or the environment. His conclusion from research in this area, and more recent research on anxiety (Hunt, 1965), is that the interactions between differences in individuals and variations among situations are the determinants of variations in behavior. Helson (1964) similarly analyzed alternative approaches to personality (instinct, typology, trait, S-R, eclectic) from an interactionist point of view. He defined personality as "the product of external and internal forces, acting at specific times, in specific situations, and having specific outcomes characteristic of the individual [p. 582]" and concluded that what is needed is an operational method for assessing the interactions between organism and environment. For some time, Brunswik (1955) emphasized the need for a "representative design" in experiments, including a range of stimuli along with a range of subjects, and more recently Cronbach (1957) has emphasized the need for joint use of experimental (situational) and correlational (individual) methods of research. Cronbach's conclusion was that future research must attempt to predict the behavior of an "organism-in-situation."

These psychologists have emphasized the need for an interaction approach to research, but have neither developed a theory of personality around this view nor, with the exception of Helson, a theory of the processes affecting the interactions or transactions between individuals and their environments. Angyal (1941) used the word "biosphere" to refer to the interaction between organism and environment, and Murphy (1947) used the term "organism-situation field." The two theories of personality which give greatest attention to the issue of individual-environment interaction are those of Lewin (1951) and Murray (1938). Lewin's "behavior is a function of personality and environment [B = F (P, E)]" has often served as a model for later Lewinian research. Murray's theory is particularly noteworthy in that it provides for a classificatory scheme, has a model for the relationship between the individual and his environment, and distinguishes between the environment as it is (alpha press) and as it is perceived by the individual (beta press). Essentially, Murray proposed that individuals and environments be classified along the same dimensions. As French (1963) noted, Lewin similarly emphasized the methodological utility of having the same conceptual dimension for individuals and environments. Murray's process model is one of need frustration or gratification, and thus the environment (press) is defined in terms of the benefits (facilitations, satisfactions) or harms (obstructions, dissatisfactions) it provides for the organism. Finally, Murray (1951) has emphasized that Lewin tried to avoid the alpha-beta press problem by affirming that the nature of the beta situation can be inferred from the subject's behavior and that the nature of the alpha situation can be neglected. Murray disagreed with this view, noting that there is not an invariable correlation between the beta situation and behavior, and that discrepancies between the alpha and beta press, as in delusions, are important for the researcher to be aware of.

Jahoda (1961) has emphasized the need for a best-fit concept between individuals and environments:

Culture patterns and the values and beliefs of an individual can, but need not, coincide. Where they do not coincide, an individual will experience a strain between his own inclinations and what the culture of his group requires. Where they do coincide, people will feel at ease in their environment without the experience of situational strains [p. 25].

A related emphasis has been on similarity. Thus Pepitone (1964) noted that the association between similarity and liking is seemingly ubiquitous in all human relationships. The problem with such analyses is that they fail to give an understanding of the process involved in individual-environment interaction. The criteria to be used for concluding that there is fit or similarity are often absent, as are discussions of why lack of fit or dissimilarity should lead to strain and avoidance. Finally, generally there is a lack of statement of the limiting conditions, if any, under which the relationships should hold.

Basically, two kinds of models have been proposed. The first tends to be based on reinforcement theory. For example, Murray (1938) saw the individual as interacting with various environments (press) according to the degree to which they gratify or frustrate his needs. An environment may have a positive or negative cathexis for the individual, or the individual may have a positive or negative sentiment toward the environment. Newcomb's (1956) model for interpersonal attraction emphasizes reciprocal rewards in the interactions between people and thus is also an example of a model based on reinforcement theory. Similarity is generally related to attraction because it is generally related to rewarding rather than punishing experiences in the interactional process. Advantages of this model are that it does specify the units to be employed (attitudes) and the limiting conditions under which the model applies (similarity in regard to objects of importance and common relevance), and notes the possibility that the model may not hold in the same way for all interpersonal relationships. However, the model also makes a number of questionable assumptions, such as that complementarity is but a special case of similarity and that one's self is a valued object to oneself. This assumption is brought into question by the findings of Lundy et al. (1955) and Oppenheimer (1966) that similarity is not desirable where the individual does not have a positive evaluation of himself.

In emphasizing cognitive as well as cathectic similarity, Newcomb's model at times borders on that of the second kind frequently found in the literature—a cognitive model. Models of balance (Heider, 1958), congruity (Osgood, Suci, & Tannenbaum, 1957), and dissonance (Festinger, 1957) all use cognitions as units and assume that imbalance, incongruity, and dissonance are painful states. As Brown (1962) noted, the models vary in the degree to which they define the situational properties of one or another state, in the degree of quantification of the processes involved, and in their provision for alternative means of achieving states of cognitive balance, congruity, and consonance. Furthermore, the models have a clear relationship with conflict theory in that states of imbalance express a call for mutually incompatible actions.

Pervin's (1967) research on student-college interaction used as its model the efforts of individuals to reduce discrepancies between their selves and their ideal selves. Several reports have suggested that individuals find large discrepancies between their selves and ideal selves to be painful and unpleasant (Block & Thomas, 1955; Kagan & Moss, 1962, p. 271; Wessman & Ricks, 1966, p. 243). The model assumes then that individuals are positively attracted toward objects in the environment that hold promise for taking them toward their ideal selves and are negatively disposed toward objects that hold promise for taking them away from their ideal selves. The findings of Lundy et al. (1955) and Oppenheimer (1966) that similarity is desirable where the individual has a low self–ideal-self discrepancy and undesirable where the individual has a high self–ideal-self discrepancy would fit with this model. Current research involves subjects rating themselves, their ideal selves, and the college environment on semantic differential scales. The *direction and distance* between self and environment in relation to the ideal self are being related to reports of satisfaction and dissatisfaction (Pervin, 1967).

It is important to note the relationship between the interactionist point of view as expressed by the psychologist and the similar issues emphasized by anthropologists and sociologists. Various anthropologists have emphasized the relationship between the personality characteristics of the individual and the system of rewards in the culture (Kluckhohn, 1954), the "fit" between the individual values and social norms (Benedict, 1934; Mead, 1952). These views point to an understanding of the socialization process as involving *continuous* interactions or transactions between individual and environment. Sociologists have focused on the interaction between personality mode or character structure and social structure (Gerth & Mills, 1953; Inkeles & Levinson, 1954). One important study in this area assessed the noncongruence between the modal personality patterns of Russian refugees and the Soviet socio-political system:

Most of the popular grievances were clearly based on real deprivations and frustrations, but the dissatisfactions appear to be even more intensified and given a more emotional tone because they were based also on the poor 'fit' between the personality patterns of many Soviet citizens and the 'personality' of the leaders as it expressed itself in the institutions they created . . . and in the resultant social climate in the U.S.S.R. [Inkeles, Hanfmann, & Beier, 1958, p. 16].

The thinking of Inkeles (1963) about the relationship between psychology and sociology, and his emphasis upon social action (R) as a result of social conditions (S) and personality needs (P), SP = R, represents an important contribution.

Anthropologists and sociologists who have been interested in the question of individual-environment interaction have also used reinforcement or conflict models, that is, the cultural or social system is seen as dependent upon environment gratification of the needs of individuals or upon shared expectations concerning patterns of behavior (Parsons & Shils, 1951). These developments hold promise for closer integration among the social sciences.

TRANSACTIONALISM

According to Dewey and Bentley (1949), there are three levels in the development of knowledge and the history of science. The first level is that of *self-action* and involves regarding objects as behaving under their own power. The second level is that of *interaction* and involves objects in a causal interconnection of one object acting upon the other. Finally, there is the level of *process transaction* which involves objects relating to one another within a system. In this third level, organism and environment influence one another as part of a total transactional field. Essentially, then, transactionalism has three properties: (*a*) Each part of the system has no independence outside of the other parts of the system or the system as a whole. (*b*) One part of the system is not acted upon by another part, but instead there is a constant reciprocal relationship. There are not cause-effect relationships but transactions. (*c*) Action in any part of the system has consequences for other parts of the system.

Much psychological research has been at the self-action level. As this review suggests, some recent research has emphasized interactional processes. Currently, there are some efforts to view human behavior within the transactional framework. While some time ago Ittelson and Cantril (1954) studied perception from a transactional point of view, recent use of this framework has come from those involved in the mental health fields. Thus Grinker (1956) spoke of the therapeutic process in terms of transactions and Kelly (1966) used this framework to redefine psychopathology:

Behavior is not viewed as sick or well but defined as transactional—an outcome of the reciprocal interactions between specific social situations and the individual. . . . The research task is to clarify the precise relationships between individual behavior and social structure that differentially affect various forms of adaptive behavior [p. 538].

Spiegel (1956) used the transactional model for the study of relationships within a family. He used role behaviors as units for analysis and saw processes as revolving around attempts to reduce conflict and incompatibility and increase integration. Integrative processes take into account disparities between motivation for role behavior and assigned role. His analysis of role conflict in the family (Spiegel, 1957) involved processes leading to equilibrium, disequilibrium, or re-equilibration. Strain was usefully defined as a discrepancy in expectations of ego and alter.

Spiegel's analysis is significant in terms of the specification of units of analysis and nature of the processes ongoing in the system. It may be that some parts of psychology are not ready for research in terms of the transactional framework, perhaps some not even for the interactional level. What is clear, however, is that human behavior is that complex and future analyses will be of a transactional kind.

SUMMARY AND CONCLUSION

In one way or another, the history of psychology reflects systems based upon an exaggerated emphasis on the individual or the environment—McDougall (1908) and Ross (1908), psychoanalysis and S-R theory, introspection and behaviorism, need theory and role theory, the nature versus nurture controversy. There is now sufficient literature to indicate that these are useless controversies since there is either truth in both points of view or in neither.

Lorenz (1966) described how the threshold for eliciting a particular instinct movement can be high, in which case only a particular stimulus will serve to elicit the behavior, or the threshold can be low, in which case almost any environmental stimulus will serve to elicit the behavior; that is, depending upon the threshold level, a more or less specific environmental stimulus may elicit the instinct movement. In a similar way, research on set and expectancy, and the work of Hernández-Peón, Scherrer, and Jouvet (1956), serves to illustrate how the individual and the environment may be at different levels of readiness to influence one another. These relationships indicate, on a relatively primitive level, what certainly must be true on a more complex level—individual and environment (interpersonal and noninterpersonal) are in a constant state of mutually influencing one another.

Within the framework of the "organism-in-situation" (Cronbach, 1957), a number of issues remain:

Should one consider the perceived or "actual" environment? Heider (1939) noted Titchener's error of describing psychological elements in terms of the physical environment and Kohler's error of describing stimuli in terms of the experiential object. Koffka (1935) distinguished between the geographical environment (the objective physical and social environment) and the behavioral environment (the environment as perceived and reacted to by the subject). His conclusion was that behavior could be more meaningfully understood if it was related to the behavioral environment. In general, this position was also held by Heider, Murray, Lewin, and Hunt, though Sells (1963) is a noteworthy exception in his emphasis upon obtaining situational measures independently of the individual's perceptions of them. The final answer to this question will likely involve an understanding of the circumstances under which one or the other kind of data would be most useful. Until then, of course, both kinds of data should be obtained wherever possible.

What units shall we employ and should they be the same units of analysis for individuals and environments? The literature on interpersonal attraction is significant in involving a number of investigators who explore similar phenomena but use different units. Needs, values, roles, attitudes, and cognitions have been used by various investigators. Such diversity makes comparison of results difficult. Murray's answer to the second part of this question is clearly that the same units should be used to describe and measure the individual and the environment. Rotter (1955) held a similar view and French (1963) noted that Lewin felt that "we can best maximize this sort of relevance of personality to environment by conceptualizing and measuring these two terms in commensurate dimensions . . . only those entities which have the same conceptual dimension can be compared as to their magnitude [p. 42]." It seems clear that study of the relationship between individuals and environments will be greatly facilitated by the development of such commensurate dimensions. The recently developed technique of three-mode factor analysis for the semantic differential (Levin, 1965) appears to hold some promise in this direction.

What is the nature of the processes involved in individual-environment relationships? A number of models have been discussed. Each seems to have promise in accounting for some relationships but to have limitations in accounting for other data. We must consider the possibility that individual-environment relationships vary according to the units employed, the conditions under which the individual and environment are relating, and the criteria for examining the behavioral phenomena of interest. Findings will not be truly comparable until all three properties of the research have been specified and studied in a systematic way.

REFERENCES

Allport, F. *Theories of perception and the concept of structure.* New York: Wiley, 1955.

Allport, G. What units shall we employ? In G. Lindzey (Ed.), *Assessment of human motives.* New York: Rinehart, 1958. Pp. 239-260.

Amidon, E., & Flanders, N. A. The effects of direct and indirect teacher influence on dependent-prone students learning geometry. *Journal of Educational Psychology,* 1961, **52,** 286-291.

Angyal, A. *Foundations for a science of personality.* New York: Commonwealth Fund, 1941.

Astin, A. W. Further validation of the Environmental Assessment Technique. *Journal of Educational Psychology,* 1963, **54,** 217-226.

Astin, A. W. The Inventory of College Activities (ICA): Assessing the college environment through observable events. Paper presented at the meeting of the American Psychological Association, Chicago, September 1965.

Barker, R. G. Ecology and motivation. In M. R. Jones (Ed.), *Nebraska symposium on motivation: 1960.* Lincoln: University of Nebraska Press, 1960. Pp. 1-49.

Bay, C. A social theory of higher education. In N. Sanford (Ed.), *The American college.* New York: Wiley, 1962. Pp. 972-1005.

Beach, L. R. Sociability and academic achievement in various types of learning situations. *Journal of Educational Psychology,* 1960, **51,** 208-212.

Benedict, R. *Patterns of culture.* New York: Mentor, 1934.

Block, J., & Thomas, H. Is satisfaction with self a measure of adjustment? *Journal of Abnormal and Social Psychology,* 1955, **51,** 254-259.

Blocher, D. H., & Schutz, R. A. Relationships among self-descriptions, occupational stereotypes, and vocational preferences. *Journal of Counseling Psychology,* 1961, **8,** 314-317.

Bloom, B. S. *Stability and change in human characteristics.* New York: Wiley, 1964.

Brophy, A. L. Self, role and satisfaction. *Genetic Psychology Monographs,* 1959, **59,** 263-308.

Brown, R. Models of attitude change. In T. M. Newcomb (Ed.), *New directions in psychology.* New York: Holt, Rinehart & Winston, 1962. Pp. 2-85.

Brunswik, E. Representative design and probabilistic theory in a functional psychology. *Psychological Review,* 1955, **62,** 193-218.

Chein, I. The environment as a determinant of behavior. *Journal of Social Psychology,* 1954, **39,** 115-127.

Claunch, N. C. Cognitive and motivational characteristics associated with concrete and abstract levels of conceptual complexity. Unpublished doctoral dissertation, Princeton University, 1964.

Cronbach, L. J. The two disciplines of scientific psychology. *American Psychologist,* 1957, **12,** 671-684.

Cronbach, L. J. The new definition of aptitude. Paper presented at the meeting of the Educational Testing Service, Princeton, N. J., June 1966.

Dewey, J., & Bentley, A. F. *Knowing and the known.* Boston: Beacon, 1949.

Douvan, E., & Kaye, C. Motivational factors in college entrance. In N. Sanford (Ed.), *The American college.* New York: Wiley, 1962. Pp. 193-224.

Endler, N. S., Hunt, J. McV., & Rosenstein, A. J. An S-R inventory of anxiousness. *Psychological Monographs,* 1962, **76**(17, Whole No. 536).

Englander, M. A. A. psychological analysis of vocational choice: Teaching. *Journal of Counseling Psychology,* 1960, **7,** 257-264.

Feather, N. T. The relationship of persistence at a task to the expectation of success and achievement related motives. *Journal of Abnormal and Social Psychology,* 1961, **63,** 552-561.

Festinger, L. *A theory of cognitive dissonance.* Stanford: Stanford University Press, 1957.

Fiedler, F. E., Warrington, W. G., & Blaisdell, F. J. Unconscious attitudes as correlates of sociometric choice in a social group. *Journal of Abnormal and Social Psychology,* 1952, **47**, 790–796.

Forehand, G. A., & Gilmer, B. von H. Environmental variables in studies of organizational behavior. *Psychological Bulletin,* 1964, **62**, 361–382.

French, J. R. P. The social environment and mental health. *Journal of Social Issues,* 1963, **19**, 39–56.

Funkenstein, D. H. Failure to graduate from medical school. *Journal of Medical Education,* 1962, **37**, 585–603.

Gerth, H., & Mills, C. W. *Character and social structure.* New York: Harcourt, Brace & World, 1953.

Gibson, J. J. The concept of the stimulus in psychology. *American Psychologist,* 1960, **15**, 694–703.

Grimes, J. W., & Allinsmith, W. Compulsivity, anxiety, and school achievement. *Merrill-Palmer Quarterly,* 1961, **7**, 247–271.

Grinker, R. (Ed.) *Toward a unified theory of human behavior.* New York: Basic Books, 1956.

Heider, F. Environmental determinants in psychological theories. *Psychological Review,* 1939, **46**, 383–410.

Heider, F. *The psychology of interpersonal relations.* New York: Wiley, 1958.

Helson, H. *Adaptation-level theory: An experimental and systematic approach to behavior.* New York: Harper & Row, 1964.

Hernández-Peón, R., Scherrer, H., & Jouvet, M. Modification of electrical activity in cochlear nucleus during "attention" in unanesthetized cats. *Science,* 1956, **123**, 331–332.

Hoffman, L. R., & Maier, N. R. F. An experimental reexamination of the similarity-attraction hypothesis. *Journal of Personality and Social Psychology,* 1966, **3**, 145–152.

Hull, C. L. *Principles of behavior.* New York: Appleton-Century-Crofts, 1943.

Hunt, J. McV. *Intelligence and experience.* New York: Ronald Press, 1961.

Hunt, J. McV. Traditional personality theory in the light of recent evidence. *American Scientist,* 1965, **53**, 80–96.

Inkeles, A. Sociology and psychology. In S. Koch (Ed.), *Psychology: A study of a science.* New York: McGraw-Hill, 1963. Pp. 317–387.

Inkeles, A., Hanfmann, E., & Beier, H. Modal personality and adjustment to the Soviet sociopolitical system. *Human Relations,* 1958, **11**, 3–22.

Inkeles, A., & Levinson, D. National character. In G. Lindzey (Ed.), *Handbook of social psychology.* New York: Addison-Wesley, 1954. Pp. 977–1020.

Ittelson, W. H., & Cantril, H. *Perception: A transactional approach.* New York: Doubleday, 1954.

Izard, C. E. Personality similarity and friendship. *Journal of Abnormal and Social Psychology,* 1960, **61**, 47–51. (a)

Izard, C. E. Personality similarity, positive affect, and interpersonal attraction. *Journal of Abnormal and Social Psychology,* 1960, **61**, 484–485. (b)

Jahoda, M. A social-psychological approach to the study of culture. *Human Relations,* 1961, **14**, 23–30.

Kagan, J., & Moss, H. A. *Birth to maturity: A study of psychological development.* New York: Wiley, 1962.

Katz, I., Glucksberg, S., & Krauss, R. Need satisfaction and Edwards PPS scores in married couples. *Journal of Consulting Psychology,* 1960, **24**, 205–208.

Katz, J., & Sanford, N. The curriculum in the perspective of the theory of personality development. In N. Sanford (Ed.), *The American college.* New York: Wiley, 1962. Pp. 418–444.

Kelly, J. G. Ecological constraints on mental health services. *American Psychologist,* 1966, **21**, 535-539.

Kipnis, D. M. Changes in self-concepts in relation to perception of others. *Journal of Personality,* 1961, **29**, 449-465.

Kluckhohn, C. Culture and behavior. In G. Lindzey (Ed.), *Handbook of social psychology.* New York: Addison-Wesley, 1954. Pp. 921-976.

Koffka, K. *Principles of Gestalt psychology.* New York: Harcourt, Brace, 1935.

Lavin, D. E. *The prediction of academic performance.* New York: Russell Sage Foundation, 1965.

Lazarus, R. S., Deese, J., & Osler, S. F. The effects of psychological stress upon performance. *Psychological Bulletin,* 1952, **49**, 293-317.

Levin, J. Three-mode factor analysis. *Psychological Bulletin,* 1965, **64**, 442-452.

Lewin, K. *Field theory in social science.* New York: Harper & Row, 1951.

Lindzey, G., & Urdan, J. A Personality and social choice. *Sociometry,* 1954, **17**, 47-63.

Lorenz, K. *On aggression.* New York: Harcourt, Brace & World, 1966.

Lott, A. J., & Lott, B. E. Group cohesiveness as interpersonal attraction: A review of relationships with antecedent and consequent variables. *Psychological Bulletin,* 1965, **64**, 259-309.

Lundy, R. M., Katkovsky, W., Cromwell, R. L., & Shoemaker, D. J. Self acceptability and descriptions of sociometric choices. *Journal of Abnormal and Social Psychology,* 1955, **51**, 260-262.

Malleson, N. Operational research in the university. *British Medical Journal,* 1959, **1**, 1031-1035.

McConnell, T. R., & Heist, P. The diverse college student population. In N. Sanford (Ed.), *The American college.* New York: Wiley, 1962. Pp. 225-252.

McDougall, W. *Introduction to social psychology.* London: Methuen, 1908.

McKeachie, W. J. Motivation, teaching methods, and college learning. In M. R. Jones (Ed.), *Nebraska symposium on motivation: 1961.* Lincoln: University of Nebraska Press, 1961. Pp. 111-142.

McKeachie, W. J., Lin, Y. G., Milholland, J., & Isaacson, R. Student affiliation motives, teacher warmth and academic achievement. *Journal of Personality and Social Psychology,* 1966, **4**, 457-461.

Mead, M. Some relationships between social anthropology and psychiatry. In F. Alexander & H. Ross (Eds.), *Dynamic psychiatry.* Chicago: University of Chicago Press, 1952. Pp. 401-448.

Meltzer, L. The need for a dual orientation in social psychology. *Journal of Social Psychology,* 1961, **55**, 43-47.

Miller, D. R. The study of social relationships: Situation, identity, and social interaction. In S. Koch (Ed.), *Psychology: The study of a science.* New York: McGraw-Hill, 1963. Pp. 639-737.

Miller, N., Campbell, D. T., Twedt, H., & O'Connell, E. J. Similarity, contrast and complimentarity in friendship choice. *Journal of Personality and Social Psychology,* 1966, **3**, 3-12.

Morton, A. S. Similarity as a determinant of friendship: A multidimensional study. Technical report, 1959, Princeton University, Contract Nonr 1858-15, Office of Naval Research.

Murphy, G. *Personality: A biosocial interpretation.* New York: Harper, 1947.

Murray, H. A. *Explorations in personality.* New York: Oxford University Press, 1938.

Murray, H. A. Toward a classification of interaction. In T. Parsons & E. A. Shils (Eds.), *Toward a general theory of action.* Cambridge: Harvard University Press, 1951. Pp. 434-464.

Nakamura, C. Y., & Ellis, F. F. Methodological study of the effects of relative reward magnitude on performance. *Child Development,* 1964, **35**, 595-610.

Newcomb, T. M. An approach to the study of communicative acts. *Psychological Review,* 1953, **60**, 393-404.

Newcomb, T. M. The prediction of interpersonal attraction. *American Psychologist,* 1956, **11**, 575-586.

Newcomb, T. M. The cognition of persons as cognizers. In R. Tagiuri & L. Petrullo (Eds.), *Person perception and interpersonal behavior.* Stanford: Stanford University Press, 1958. Pp. 179-190.

Oppenheimer, E. A. The relationship between certain self constructs and occupational preferences. *Journal of Counseling Psychology,* 1966, **13**, 191-197.

Osgood, C. E. Suci, G. J., & Tannenbaum, P. H. *The measurement of meaning.* Urbana: University of Illinois Press, 1957.

Pace, C. R., & Stern, G. G. An approach to the measurement of psychological characteristics of college environments. *Journal of Educational Psychology,* 1958, **49**, 269-277.

Parsons, T., & Shils, E. A. (Eds.) *Toward a general theory of action.* Cambridge: Harvard University Press, 1951.

Patton, J. A. A study of the effects of student acceptance of responsibility and motivation on course behavior. Unpublished doctoral dissertation, University of Michigan, 1955.

Pepitone, A. *Attraction and hostility.* New York: Prentice-Hall, 1964.

Pervin, L. A. A twenty-college study of Student X College interaction using TAPE (Transactional Analysis of Personality and Environment): Rationale, reliability, and validity. *Journal of Educational Psychology,* 1967, **58**, 290-302.

Pervin, L. A. Satisfaction and perceived self-environment similarity: A semantic differential study of student-college interaction. *Journal of Personality,* 1967, **35**, 623-634.

Pervin, L. A., & Rubin, D. B. Student dissatisfaction with college and the college dropout: A transactional approach. *Journal of Social Psychology,* 1967, **72**, 285-295.

Raush, H. L., Dittmann, A. T., & Taylor, T. J. Person, setting, and change in social interaction. *Human Relations,* 1959, **12**, 361-378.

Ross, E. A. *Social psychology.* New York: Macmillan, 1908.

Rotter, J. B. The role of the psychological situation in determining the direction of human behavior. In M. R. Jones (Ed.), *Nebraska symposium on motivation: 1955.* Lincoln Nebraska University Press, 1955. Pp. 245-268.

Rosenfeld, H., & Jackson, J. Effect of similarity of personalities on interpersonal attraction. *American Psychologist,* 1959, **14**, 366-367. (Abstract)

Sanford, N. (Ed.) *The American college.* New York: Wiley, 1962.

Sarason, I. G. Empirical findings and theoretical problems in the use of anxiety scales. *Psychological Bulletin,* 1960, **57**, 403-415.

Sarason, I. G. The effects of anxiety and threat on the solution of a difficult task. *Journal of Abnormal and Social Psychology,* 1961, **62**, 165-168.

Sells, S. B. Dimensions of stimulus situations which account for behavior variances. In S. B. Sells (Ed.), *Stimulus determinants of behavior.* New York: Ronald Press, 1963. Pp. 3-15.

Sherif, M., & Cantril, H. *The psychology of ego involvements.* New York: Wiley, 1947.

Shibutani, T. *Society and personality: An interactional approach to social psychology.* Englewood, N. J.: Prentice-Hall, 1961.

Smelser, W. T. Dominance as a factor in achievement and perception in cooperative problem solving interactions. *Journal of Abnormal and Social Psychology,* 1961, **62**, 535-542.

Smith, W. F., & Rockett, F. C. Test performance as a function of anxiety, instructor and instructions. *Journal of Educational Research,* 1958, **52**, 138-141.

Snyder, B. R. Student stress, In T. F. Lunsford (Ed.), *Campus cultures.* Boulder: Western Interstate Commission for Higher Education, 1963. Pp. 27-38.

Snyder, B. R. Adaptation, education, and emotional growth. In L. A. Pervin, L. E. Reik, & W. Dalrymple (Eds.), *The college dropout and the utilization of talent.* Princeton: Princeton University Press, 1966.

Spiegel, J. P. A model for relationships among systems. In R. Grinker (Ed.), *Toward a unified theory of human behavior.* New York: Basic Books, 1956. Pp. 16–26.

Spiegel, J. P. The resolution of role conflict within the family. *Psychiatry,* 1957, **20**, 1–16.

Stern, G. G. Environments for learning. In N. Sanford (Ed.), *The American college.* New York: Wiley, 1962. Pp. 690–730.

Summerskill, J. Dropouts from college. In N. Sanford (Ed.), *The American college.* New York: Wiley, 1962. Pp. 627–657.

Super, D. E., Starishevsky, R., Matlin, N., & Jordaan, J. P. *Career development: Self-concept theory.* New York: College Entrance Examination Board. 1963.

Taylor, J. A. Drive theory and manifest anxiety. *Psychological Bulletin,* 1956, **53**, 303–320.

Triandis, H. C. Cognitive similarity and interpersonal communication. *Journal of Applied Psychology,* 1959, **43**, 321–326.

Wallace, S. R. Criteria for what? *American Psychologist,* 1965, **20**, 411–417.

Wessman, A. E., & Ricks, D. F. *Mood and personality.* New York: Holt, Rinehart & Winston, 1966.

Winch, R. F., Ktsanes, T., & Ktsanes, V. Empirical elaboration of the theory of complimentary needs in mate selection. *Journal of Abnormal and Social Psychology,* 1955, **51**, 508–513.

4

Some Reasons for the Apparent Inconsistency of Personality

JACK BLOCK

The study of personality seeks regularities in behavior and this search is usually made operational by evaluations of the correlations among different, theoretically related behaviors. To date, the empirical evidence for personality consistency has not been inspiring. As a principle or aspiration of a science aimed at human understanding, the idea of continuity and coherence in personality functioning must be affirmed. Whereupon the question becomes: Why have psychologists, in their many research efforts, been unable to display the presumed harmonies in individual behavior?

The present note collects and lists some of the reasons for this state of affairs. The problem is viewed as arising both from deficiencies in the way psychologists operationalize their concepts and from deficiencies in the way they conceptualize their operations; and it is in these terms that our discussion will proceed. There are some psychometric reasons, as well, for the apparent inconsistency observed in behaviors, having to do with such matters as attenuation effects and the vexing influence of "method variance," but these statistical concerns have been dealt with elsewhere (Block, 1963, 1964; Humphreys, 1960); so the present argument can be entirely psychological.

To exemplify the several points to be made, the personality dimension of ego control will be used, although, of course, other personality constructs instead might have been employed. By ego control is meant something akin to excessive behavioral constraint or rigidity ("the overcontroller") at one end of the dimension and something like excessive behavioral reactivity or spontaneity ("the undercontroller") at the other end of the continuum. For further articulation of the ego-control concept, the reader may wish to consult other sources (e.g., Block, 1965; Block & Turula, 1963).

There is evidence for a common thread through a large variety of behaviors that can be accounted for by the concept of ego control. Undercontrollers in

From the *Psychological Bulletin*, 1968, 70, 210–212. Copyright 1968 by the American Psychological Association. Reprinted by permission.

one situation are often undercontrollers in another context as well and the same is true of overcontrollers. But also, and often, an individual who is impulsive in one situation will appear constrained in another circumstance; such behavior apparently denies the usefulness of a generalizing personality variable. This last kind of datum, of apparent inconsistency, can not be questioned or explained away by psychometric manipulation; it is there and further instances can be multiplied at will. What can be questioned, however, is the implication immediately, frequently, and strongly drawn from such observations to the effect that a personality dimension—in the present instance, ego control—necessarily loses its cogency as a basis for conceptualizing behavior because of the inconsistencies observed. We can question this implication if, and only if, a higher form of lawfulness can be found in the behaviors pointed to as evidence for temperamental inconsistency. The apparent discordancies must be resolved within a framework provided by a theory, or, at least, a theory must have the promise of integrating these otherwise upsetting data.

There are at least four ways in which these superficially embarrassing behavioral inconsistencies may come about:

1. *The behaviors being contrasted and correlated may not all be significant or salient for the individual.* Thus, it is psychologically uneconomical and as a rule not necessary to deliberate excessively before deciding whether to walk down the right aisle or the left aisle of a theatre. The decision problem confronting the individual in this particular situation is essentially unimportant. Consequently, an individual may make his theatre-lobby decision in a rather cavalier or "impulsive" way. Or he may give reign to a slight position preference which, because it is consistent, may suggest a "rigidity" or highly controlled patterning in his behavior. It is specious to contrast such peripheral behaviors of an individual with the way in which he copes with centrally involving situations such as friendship formation or aggression imposition, and yet, unwittingly, the comparison is often made. When correlation is sought between behaviors formulated in salient situations on the one hand and behaviors formulated in uninvolving situations on the other, then behavior will appear more whimsical than congruent. If we are to seek consistency, it must be sought among behaviors that are at comparable levels in the hierarchy of behaviors.

2. *Formulations of personality which are context blind or do not attempt to take environmental factors into account will encounter many behaviors that will appear inconsistent.* Thus, a generally spontaneous child may in certain circumstances behave in a highly constricted way. This vacillation and apparent inconsistency readily becomes understandable when it is realized that these certain circumstances are always *unfamiliar* ones for the child. Behavior often appears capricious because the nature of the stimulus situation in which the individual finds himself is not comprehended or attended to by the observer and his theory. Explicit theoretical conceptualization of

environmental factors is a fruitful way of integrating and assimilating behaviors which from a context-blind viewpoint appear inconsistent. It is still a
way that is almost untried.

3. *The behaviors being related may not be mediated by the same underlying
   variables.* Thus, in a basketball game two players may each demonstrate a
   wide variety of shots and sequencing of shots at the basket. The one player
   may have spent solitary, obsessive years before a hoop, planfully developing
   precisely the repertoire and combinations he is now manifesting. The second
   player, in the heat of athletic endeavor, may in spontaneous and impromptu
   fashion manifest a fully equivalent variety of basket-making attempts (and with
   no less accuracy if he is a good athlete). These phenotypically equivalent
   behaviors are in the first player mediated by controlled, deliberate development of a differentiated behavioral repertoire; in the second player,
   behavioral variety is mediated by his kinesthetic spontaneity. In a rather
   different situation, where prior cultivation of ability is not available as a
   resource, the first player may now appear rigid and behaviorally impoverished;
   the second player can continue to be spontaneous. These two individuals,
   behaviorally equivalent in the first situation, are quite different in the second
   situation; and this difference suggests an inconsistency of behavior. If the
   mediating variables underlying a given action are not analyzed or considered,
   behavior can appear paradoxical when closer assessment will reveal a lawful
   basis for the discrepancy.

4. *When an individual has reached certain personal limits, previous behavioral
   consistencies may break down.* Thus, an acutely paranoid individual will
   manifest both extremely overcontrolled behaviors and extremely under-
   controlled behaviors more or less conjointly. Etiologically, this contrary
   behavioral state appears to come about when the preparanoid individual finds
   his former ability to consistently contain his excessive impulses is becoming
   exceeded in certain directions of expression, with a resultant absence of
   control in these special areas. The former, often quite striking coherence the
   preparanoid personality manifests has been disrupted because the *bounds* or
   limits within which the coherence can be maintained have been transcended.
   Such extremist behaviors are especially likely to be judged psychopathological.
   Indeed, one of the explanations why psychiatrists and clinical psychologists
   often argue against the existence of an internally consistent ego apparatus is
   that they in their practice so often encounter those relatively few individuals
   in whom personal limits have been reached and therefore personal consonance
   shattered. More generally, psychologists have not given the notion of bounds
   or limits sufficient attention and application. Relationships tend to be posited
   unequivocally, without recognizing the bounds within which the relationship
   can be expected to hold and beyond which the relationship fails and is
   replaced by other relationships.

The foregoing remarks and recognitions are not new but their implications are
often neglected by the busy psychologist concerned more with the action of

research than with contemplative conceptualization. But both are required. If we are to respond to our empirical disappointments in the pursuit of personality consistency, that response should comprehend the reasons for former failure rather than perpetuate and proliferate a fundamentally unpsychological approach to the understanding of personality.

REFERENCES

Block, J. The equivalence of measures and the correction for attenuation. *Psychological Bulletin,* 1963, **60,** 152–156.

Block, J. Recognizing attenuation effects in the strategy of research. *Psychological Bulletin,* 1964, **62,** 214–216.

Block, J. *The challenge of response sets.* New York: Appleton-Century-Crofts, 1965.

Block, J., & Turula, E. Identification, ego control, and adjustment. *Child Development,* 1963, **34,** 945–953.

Humphreys, L. G. Note on the multitrait-multimethod matrix. *Psychological Bulletin,* 1960, **57,** 86–88.

5

Traits Revisited

GORDON W. ALLPORT

Years ago I ventured to present a paper before the Ninth International Congress at New Haven (G. W. Allport, 1931). It was entitled "What Is a Trait of Personality?" For me to return to the same topic on this honorific occasion is partly a sentimental indulgence, but partly too it is a self-imposed task to discover whether during the past 36 years I have learned anything new about this central problem in personality theory.

In my earlier paper I made eight bold assertions. A trait, I said,

1. Has more than nominal existence.
2. Is more generalized than a habit.
3. Is dynamic, or at least determinative, in behavior.
4. May be established empirically.
5. Is only relatively independent of other traits.
6. Is not synonymous with moral or social judgment.
7. May be viewed either in the light of the personality which contains it, or in the light of its distribution in the population at large.

To these criteria I added one more:

8. Acts, and even habits, that are inconsistent with a trait are not proof of the nonexistence of the trait.

While these propositions still seem to me defensible they were originally framed in an age of psychological innocence. They now need reexamination in the light of subsequent criticism and research.

CRITICISM OF THE CONCEPT OF TRAIT

Some critics have challenged the whole concept of trait. Carr and Kingsbury (1938) point out the danger of reification. Our initial observation of behavior is only in terms of adverbs of action: John behaves aggressively. Then an adjective creeps in: John has an aggressive disposition. Soon a heavy substantive arrives,

From the *American Psychologist*, 1966, *21*, 1-10. Copyright 1966 by the American Psychological Association. Reprinted by permission.

like William James' cow on the doormat: John has a trait of aggression. The result is the fallacy of misplaced concreteness.

The general positivist cleanup starting in the 1930s went even further. It swept out (or tried to sweep out) all entities, regarding them as question-begging redundancies. Thus Skinner (1953) writes:

When we say that a man eats *because* he is hungry, smokes a great deal *because* he has the tobacco habit, fights *because* of the instinct of pugnacity, behaves brilliantly *because* of his intelligence, or plays the piano well *because* of his musical ability, we seem to be referring to causes. But on analysis these phrases prove to be merely redundant descriptions [p. 31].

It is clear that this line of attack is an assault not only upon the concept of trait, but upon all intervening variables whether they be conceived in terms of expectancies, attitudes, motives, capacities, sentiments, or traits. The resulting postulate of the "empty organism" is by now familiar to us all, and is the scientific credo of some. Carried to its logical extreme this reasoning would scrap the concept of personality itself—an eventuality that seems merely absurd to me.

More serious, to my mind, is the argument against what Block and Bennett (1955) called "traitology" arising from many studies of the variability of a person's behavior as it changes from situation to situation. Every parent knows that an offspring may be a hellion at home and an angel when he goes visiting. A businessman may be hardheaded in the office and a mere marshmallow in the hands of his pretty daughter.

Years ago the famous experiment by La Piere (1934) demonstrated than an innkeeper's prejudice seems to come and go according to the situation confronting him.

In recent months Hunt (1965) has listed various theories of personality that to his mind require revision in the light of recent evidence. Among them he questions the belief that personality traits are the major sources of behavior variance. He, like Miller (1963), advocates that we shift attention from traits to interactions among people, and look for consistency in behavior chiefly in situationally defined roles. Helson (1964) regards trait as the residual effect of previous stimulation, and thus subordinates it to the organism's present adaptation level.

Scepticism is likewise reflected in many investigations of "person perception." To try to discover the traits residing within a personality is regarded as either naive or impossible. Studies, therefore, concentrate only on the *process* of perceiving or judging, and reject the problem of validating the perception and judgment. (Cf. Tagiuri & Petrullo, 1958).

Studies too numerous to list have ascribed chief variance in behavior to situational factors, leaving only a mild residue to be accounted for in terms of idiosyncratic attitudes and traits. A prime example is Stouffer's study of *The American Soldier* (Stouffer et al., 1949). Differing opinions and preferences are ascribed so far as possible to the GI's age, martial status, educational level, location of residence, length of service, and the like. What remains is ascribed to "attitude." By this procedure personality becomes an appendage to demography (see G. W. Allport, 1950). It is not the integrated structure within the skin that determines behavior, but membership in a group, the person's assigned roles—in short, the prevailing situation. It is especially the sociologists and anthropologists who have this preference for explanations in terms of the "outside structure" rather than the "inside structure" (cf. F. H. Allport, 1955, Ch. 21).

I have mentioned only a few of the many varieties of situationism that flourish today. While not denying any of the evidence adduced I would point to their common error of interpretation. If a child is a hellion at home, an angel outside, he obviously has two contradictory tendencies in his nature, or perhaps a deeper genotype that would explain the opposing phenotypes. If in studies of person perception the process turns out to be complex and subtle, still there would be no perception at all unless there were something out there to perceive and to judge. If, as in Stouffer's studies, soldiers' opinions vary with their marital status or length of service, these opinions are still their own. The fact that my age, sex, social status help form my outlook on life does not change the fact that the outlook is a functioning part of me. Demography deals with distal forces— personality study with proximal forces. The fact that the innkeeper's behavior varies according to whether he is, or is not, physically confronted with Chinese applicants for hospitality tells nothing about his attitude structure, except that it is complex, and that several attitudes may converge into a given act of behavior.

Nor does it solve the problem to explain the variance in terms of statistical interaction effects. Whatever tendencies exist reside in a person, for a person is the sole possessor of the energy that leads to action. Admittedly different situations elicit differing tendencies from my repertoire. I do not perspire except in the heat, nor shiver except in the cold; but the outside temperature is not the mechanism of perspiring or shivering. My capacities and my tendencies lie within.

To the situationist I concede that our theory of traits cannot be so simpleminded as it once was. We are now challenged to untangle the complex web of tendencies that constitute a person, however contradictory they may seem to be when activated differentially in various situations.

ON THE OTHER HAND

In spite of gunfire from positivism and situationism, traits are still very much alive. Gibson (1941) has pointed out that the "concept of set or attitude is nearly universal in psychological thinking." And in an important but neglected paper—perhaps the last he ever wrote—McDougall (1937) argued that *tendencies* are the "indispensable postulates of all psychology." The concept of *trait* falls into this genre. As Walker (1964) says trait, however else defined, always connotes an enduring tendency of some sort. It is the structural counterpart of such functional concepts as "expectancy," and "goal-directedness."

After facing all the difficulties of situational and mood variations, also many of the methodological hazards such as response set, halo, and social desirability, Vernon (1964) concludes, "We could go a long way towards predicting behavior if we could assess these stable features in which people differ from one another [p. 181]." The powerful contributions of Thurstone, Guilford, Cattell, and Eysenck, based on factor analysis, agree that the search for traits should provide eventually a satisfactory taxonomy of personality and of its hierarchical structure. The witness of these and other thoughtful writers helps us withstand the pessimistic attacks of positivism and situationism.

It is clear that I am using "trait" as a generic term, to cover all the "permanent possibilities for action" of a generalized order. Traits are cortical, subcortical, or postural dispositions having the capacity to gate or guide specific phasic reactions. It is only the phasic aspect that is visible; the tonic is carried somehow in the still mysterious realm of neurodynamic structure. Traits, as I am here using the term, include long-range sets and attitudes, as well as such variables as "perceptual response dispositions," "personal constructs," and "cognitive styles."

Unlike McClelland (1951) I myself would regard traits (i.e., some traits) as motivational (others being merely stylistic). I would also insist that traits may be studied at two levels: (a) dimensionally, that is as an aspect of the psychology of individual differences, and (b) individually, in terms of *personal dispositions*. (Cf. G. W. Allport, 1961, Ch. 15.) It is the latter approach that brings us closest to the person we are studying.

As for factors, I regard them as a mixed blessing. In the investigations I shall soon report, factorial analysis, I find, has proved both helpful and unhelpful. My principal question is whether the factorial unit is idiomatic enough to reflect the structure of personality as the clinician, the counselor, or the man in the street apprehends it. Or are factorial dimensions screened so extensively and so widely attenuated—through item selection, correlation, axis manipulation, homogenization, and alphabetical labeling—that they impose an artifact of method upon the personal neural network as it exists in nature?

A HEURISTIC REALISM

This question leads me to propose an epistemological position for research in personality. Most of us, I suspect, hold this position although we seldom formulate it even to ourselves. It can be called a *heuristic realism*.

Heuristic realism, as applied to our problem, holds that the person who confronts us possesses inside his skin generalized action tencencies (or traits) and that it is our job scientifically to discover what they are. Any form of realism assumes the existence of an external structure ("out there") regardless of our shortcomings in comprehending it. Since traits, like all intervening variables, are never directly observed but only inferred, we must expect difficulties and errors in the process of discovering their nature.

The incredible complexity of the structure we seek to understand is enough to discourage the realist, and to tempt him to play some form of positivistic gamesmanship. He is tempted to settle for such elusive formulations as: "If we

knew enough about the situation we wouldn't need the concept of personality";
or "One's personality is merely the way other people see one"; or "There is no structure in personality but only varying degrees of consistency in the environment."

Yet the truly persistent realist prefers not to abandon his commitment to find
out what the other fellow is really like. He knows that his attempt will not
wholly succeed, owing partly to the complexity of the object studied, and partly
to the inadequacy of present methods. But unlike Kant who held that the *Ding
an Sich* is doomed to remain unknowable, he prefers to believe that it is at least
partly or approximately knowable.

I have chosen to speak of *heuristic* realism, because to me special emphasis
should be placed on empirical methods of discovery. In this respect heuristic
realism goes beyond naive realism.

Taking this epistemological point of view, the psychologist first focuses his
attention on some limited slice of personality that he wishes to study. He then
selects or creates methods appropriate to the empirical testing of his hypothesis
that the cleavage he has in mind is a trait (either a dimensional trait or a
personal disposition). He knows that his present purposes and the methods
chosen will set limitations upon his discovery. If, however, the investigation
achieves acceptable standards of validation he will have progressed far toward his
identification of traits. Please note, as with any heuristic procedure the process of
discovery may lead to important corrections of the hypothesis as originally stated.

Empirical testing is thus an important aspect of heuristic realism, but it is an
empiricism restrained throughout by rational considerations. Galloping empiricism, which is our present occupational disease, dashes forth like a headless
horseman. It has no rational objective; uses no rational method other than
mathematical; reaches no rational conclusion. It lets the discordant data sing for
themselves. By contrast heuristic realism says, "While we are willing to rest our
case for traits on empirical evidence, the area we carve out for study should be
rationally conceived, tested by rational methods; and the findings should be
rationally interpreted."

THREE ILLUSTRATIVE STUDIES

It is now time for me to illustrate my argument with sample studies. I have
chosen three in which I myself have been involved. They differ in the areas of
personality carved out for study, in the methods employed, and in the type of
traits established. They are alike, however, in proceeding from the standpoint of
heuristic realism. The presentation of each study must of necessity be woefully
brief. The first illustrates what might be called *meaningful dimensionalism;* the
second *meaningful covariation;* the third *meaningful morphogenesis.*

Dimensions of Values

The first illustration is drawn from a familiar instrument, dating almost from
the stone age, *The Study of Values* (Allport & Vernon, 1931). While some of

you have approved it over the years, and some disapproved, I use it to illustrate two important points of my argument.

First the instrument rests on an a priori analysis of one large region of human personality, namely, the region of generic evaluative tendencies. It seemed to me 40 years ago, and seems to me now, that Eduard Spranger (1922) made a persuasive case for the existence of six fundamental types of subjective evaluation or *Lebensformen*. Adopting this rational starting point we ourselves took the second step, to put the hypothesis to empirical test. We asked: Are the six dimensions proposed—the *theoretic,* the *economic,* the *esthetic, social, political,* and *religious*—measurable on a multidimensional scale? Are they reliable and valid? Spranger defined the six ways of looking at life in terms of separate and distinct ideal types, although he did not imply that a given person belongs exclusively to one and only one type.

It did not take long to discover that when confronted with a forced-choice technique people do in fact subscribe to all six values, but in widely varying degrees. Within any pair of values, or any quartet of values, their forced choices indicate a reliable pattern. Viewed then as empirical continua, rather than as types, the six value directions prove to be measurable, reproducible, and consistent. But are they valid? Can we obtain external validation for this particular a priori conception of traits? The test's *Manual* (Allport & Vernon, 1931) contains much such evidence. Here I would add a bit more, drawn from occupational studies with women subjects. (The evidence for men is equally good.) The data in Table 1 are derived partly from the *Manual*, partly from Guthrie and McKendry (1963) and partly from an unpublished study by Elizabeth Moses.

For present purposes it is sufficient to glance at the last three columns. For the *theoretic* value we note that the two groups of teachers or teachers in preparation select this value significantly more often than do graduate students of business administration. Conversely the young ladies of business are relatively more *economic* in their choices. The results for the *esthetic* value probably reflect the higher level of liberal arts background for the last two groups. The

Table 1. Mean Scores for Occuaptional Groups of Women: Study of Values

	Female collegiate norms N = 2,475	Graduate nurses training for teaching N = 328	Graduate students of business administration N = 77	Peace Corps teachers N = 131
Theoretical	36.5	40.2	37.3	40.6
Economic	36.8	32.9	40.4	29.9
Esthetic	43.7	43.1	46.8	49.3
Social	41.6	40.9	35.0	41.2
Political	38.0	37.2	41.8	39.7
Religious	43.1	45.7	38.7	39.2

social (philanthropic) value is relatively low for the business group, whereas the *political* (power) value is relatively high. Just why nurses should more often endorse the *religious* value is not immediately clear.

Another study of external validation, showing the long-range predictive power of the test is an unpublished investigation by Betty Mawardi. It is based on a follow-up of Wellesley graduates 15 years after taking the Study of Values.

Table 2 reports the significant deviations (at the 5% level or better) of various occupational groups from the mean scores of Wellesley students. In virtually every case we find the deviation meaningful (even necessary) for the occupation in question. Thus women in business are significantly high in *economic* interests; medical, government, and scientific workers in *theoretical;* literary and artistic workers in *esthetic;* social workers in *social;* and religious workers in *religious* values.

One must remember that to achieve a relatively high score on one value, one must deliberately slight others. For this reason it is interesting to note in the table the values that are systematically slighted in order to achieve a higher score on the occupationally relevant value. (In the case of social workers it appears that they "take away" more or less uniformly from other values in order to achieve a high social value.)

Thus, even at the college age it is possible to forecast in a general way modal vocational activity 15 years hence. As Newcomb, Turner, and Converse (1965) say, this test clearly deals with "inclusive values" or with "basic value postures" whose generality is strikingly broad. An evaluative posture toward life saturates, or guides, or gates (choose your own metaphor) specific daily choices over a long expanse of years.

One reason I have used this illustration of trait research is to raise an important methodological issue. The six values are not wholly independent. There is a slight tendency for theoretic and esthetic values to covary; likewise for economic and political values; and so too with social and religious. Immediately the thought arises, "Let's factor the whole matrix and see what orthogonal dimensions emerge." This step has been taken several times (see *Manual*); but

Table 2. Significant Deviations of Scores on the Study of Values for Occupational Groups of Wellesley Alumni from Wellesley Mean Scores

Occupational groups	N	Theoretical	Economic	Esthetic	Social	Political	Religious
Business workers	64	Lower	Higher				
Medical workers	42	Higher	Lower			Lower	
Literary workers	40	Higher	Lower	Higher			
Artistic workers	37			Higher	Lower		
Scientific workers	28	Higher		Lower			
Government workers	24	Higher			Lower		Lower
Social workers	26				Higher		
Religious workers	11					Lower	Higher

always with confusing results. Some investigators discover that fewer than six factors are needed—some that we need more. And in all cases the clusters that emerge seem strange and unnamable. Here is a case, I believe, where our empiricism should submit to rational restraint. The traits as defined are meaningful, reliably measured, and validated. Why sacrifice them to galloping gamesmanship?

Covariation: Religion and Prejudice

Speaking of covariation I do not mean to imply that in restraining our empirical excesses we should fail to explore the patterns that underlie covariation when it seems reasonable to do so.

Take, for example, the following problem. Many investigations show conclusively that on the broad average church attenders harbor more ethnic prejudice than nonattenders. (Some of the relevant studies are listed by Argyle, 1959, and by Wilson, 1960.) At the same time many ardent workers for civil rights are religiously motivated. From Christ to Gandhi and to Martin Luther King we note that equimindedness has been associated with religious devoutness. Here then is a paradox: Religion makes prejudice; it also unmakes prejudice.

First we tackle the problem rationally and form a hypothesis to account for what seems to be a curvilinear relation. A hint for the needed hypothesis comes from *The Authoritarian Personality* (Adorno, Frenkel-Brunswik, Levinson, & Sanford, 1950) which suggests that acceptance of institutional religion is not as important as the *way* in which it is accepted. Argyle (1959) sharpens the hypothesis. He says, "It is not the genuinely devout who are prejudiced but the conventionally religious [p. 84]."

In our own studies we have tentatively assumed that two contrasting but measurable forms of religious orientation exist. The first form we call the *extrinsic* orientation, meaning that for the churchgoer religious devotion is not a value in its own right, but is an instrumental value serving the motives of personal comfort, security, or social status. (One man said he went to church because it was the best place to sell insurance.) Elsewhere I have defined this utilitarian orientation toward religion more fully (G. W. Allport, 1960, 1963). Here I shall simply mention two items from our scale, agreement with which we assume indicates the extrinsic attitude:

What religion offers me most is comfort when sorrows and misfortune strike.

One reason for my being a church member is that such membership helps to establish a person in the community.

By contrast the *intrinsic* orientation regards faith as a supreme value in its own right. Such faith strives to transcend self-centered needs, takes seriously the commandment of brotherhood that is found in all religions, and seeks a unification of being. Agreement with the following items indicates an intrinsic orientation:

My religious beliefs are what really lie behind my whole approach to life.

If not prevented by unavoidable circumstances, I attend church, on the average (more than once a week) (once a week) (two or three times a month) (less than once a month).

This second item is of considerable interest, for many studies have found that it is the irregular attenders who are by far the most prejudiced (e.g., Holtzmann, 1956; Williams, 1964). They take their religion in convenient doses and do not let it regulate their lives.

Now for a few illustrative results in Table 3. If we correlate the extrinsicness of orientation with various prejudice scales we find the hypothesis confirmed. Likewise, as predicted, intrinsicness of orientation is negatively correlated with prejudice.

In view of the difficulty of tapping the two complex traits in question, it is clear that from these studies that our rationally derived hypothesis gains strong support. We note that the trend is the same when different denominations are studied in relation to differing targets for prejudice.

Previously I have said that empirical testing has the ability to correct or extend our rational analysis of patterns. In this particular research the following unexpected fact emerges. While those who approach the intrinsic pole of our continuum are on the average less prejudiced than those who approach the extrinsic pole, a number of subjects show themselves to be disconcertingly illogical. They accept both intrinsically worded items and extrinsically worded items, even when these are contradictory, such as:

My religious beliefs are what really lie behind my whole approach to life.

Though I believe in my religion, I feel there are many more important things in my life.

Table 3. Correlation between Measures of Religious Orientation among Churchgoers and Various Prejudice Scales

Denominational sample	N	r
Unitarian	50	
Extrinsic—anti-Catholicism		.56
Intrinsic—anti-Catholicism		−.36
Extrinsic—anti-Mexican		.54
Intrinsic—anti-Mexican		−.42
Catholic	66	
Extrinsic—anti-Negro		.36
Intrinsic—anti-Negro		−.49
Nazarene	39	
Extrinsic—anti-Negro		.41
Intrinsic—anti-Negro		−.44
Mixed[a]	207	
Extrinsic—anti-Semitic		.65

[a]From Wilson (1960).

Table 4. Types of Religious Orientation and Mean Prejudice Scores

	Mean prejudice scores			
	Consistently intrinsic	Consistently extrinsic	Moderately inconsistent (proreligion)	Extremely inconsistent (proreligion)
Anti-Negro	28.7	33.0	35.4	37.9
Anti-Semitic	22.6	24.6	28.0	30.1

Note.—N = 309, mixed denominations. All differences significant at .01 level.

It is necessary, therefore, to inspect this sizable group of muddleheads who refuse to conform to our neat religious logic. We call them "inconsistently proreligious." They simply like religion; for them it has "social desirability" (cf. Edwards, 1957).

The importance of recognizing this third mode of religious orientation is seen by comparing the prejudice scores for the groups presented in Table 4. In the instruments employed the lowest possible prejudice score is 12, the highest possible, 48. We note that the mean prejudice score rises steadily and significantly from the intrinsically consistent to the inconsistently proreligious. Thus subjects with an undiscriminated proreligious response set are on the average most prejudiced of all.

Having discovered the covariation of prejudice with both the extrinsic orientation and the "pro" response set, we are faced with the task of rational explanation. One may, I think, properly argue that these particular religious attitudes are instrumental in nature; they provide safety, security, and status—all within a self-serving frame. Prejudice, we know, performs much the same function within some personalities. The needs for status, security, comfort, and a feeling of self-rightness are served by both ethnic hostility and by tailoring one's religious orientation to one's convenience. The economy of other lives is precisely the reverse: It is their religion that centers their existence, and the only ethnic attitude compatible with this intrinsic orientation is one of brotherhood, not of bigotry.

This work, along with the related investigations of Lenski (1961), Williams (1964), and others, signifies that we gain important insights when we refine our conception of the nature of the religious sentiment and its functions. Its patterning properties in the economy of a life are diverse. It can fuse with bigotry or with brotherhood according to its nature.

As unfinished business I must leave the problem of nonattenders. From data available it seems that the unchurched are less prejudiced on the average than either the extrinsic or the inconsistent churchgoers, although apparently more prejudiced on the average than those whose religious orientation is intrinsic. Why this should be so must form the topic of future research.

Personal Dispositions: An Idiomorphic Approach

The final illustration of heuristic realism has to do with the search for the natural cleavages that mark an individual life. In this procedure there is no reference to common dimensions, no comparison with other people, except as is implied by the use of the English language. If, as Allport and Odbert (1936) have found, there are over 17,000 available trait names, and if these may be used in combinations, there is no real point in arguing that the use of the available lexicon of a language necessarily makes all trait studies purely nomothetic (dimensional).

A series of 172 published *Letters from Jenny* (G. W. Allport, 1965) contains enough material for a rather close clinical characterization of Jenny's personality, as well as for careful quantitative and computational analysis. While there is no possibility in this case of obtaining external validation for the diagnosis reached by either method, still by employing both procedures an internal agreement is found which constitutes a type of empirical validation for the traits that emerge.

The *clinical* method in this case is close to common sense. Thirty-nine judges listed the essential characteristics of Jenny as they saw them. The result was a series of descriptive adjectives, 198 in number. Many of the selected trait names were obviously synonymous; and nearly all fell readily into eight clusters.

The *quantitative* analysis consisted of coding the letters in terms of 99 tag words provided by the lexicon of the General Inquirer (Stone, Bales, Namenwirth, & Ogilvie, 1962). The frequency with which these basic tag words are associated with one another in each letter forms the basis for a factor analysis (see G. W. Allport, 1965, p. 200).

Table 5 lists in parallel fashion the clusters obtained by clinical judgment based on a careful reading of the series, along with the factors obtained by Jeffrey Paige in his unpublished factorial study.

Table 5. Central Traits in Jenny's Personality as Determined by Two Methods

Common-sense traits	Factorial traits
Quarrelsome-suspicious ⎰	
Aggressive ⎱	Aggression
Self-centered (possessive)	Possessiveness
Sentimental	⎰ Need for affiliation ⎱ Need for family acceptance
Independent-autonomous	Need for autonomy
Esthetic-artistic	Sentience
Self-centered (self-pitying)	Martyrdom
(No parallel)	Sexuality
Cynical-morbid	(No parallel)
Dramatic-intense	("Overstate")

In spite of the differences in terminology the general paralleling of the two lists establishes some degree of empirical check on both of them. We can say that the direct common-sense perception of Jenny's nature is validated by quantification, coding, and factoring. (Please note that in this case factor analysis does not stand alone, but is tied to a parallel rational analysis.)

While this meaningful validation is clearly present, we gain (as almost always) additional insights from our attempts at empirical validation of the traits we initially hypothesize. I shall point to one instance of such serendipity. The tag words (i.e., the particular coding system employed) are chiefly substantives. For this reason, I suspect, *sexuality* can be identified by coding as a minor factor; but it is not perceived as an independent quality by the clinical judges. On the other hand, the judges, it seems, gain much from the running style of the letters. Since the style is constant it would not appear in a factorial analysis which deals only with variance within the whole. Thus the common-sense traits *cynical-morbid* and *dramatic-intense* are judgments of a pervading expressive style in Jenny's personality and seem to be missed by factoring procedure.

Here, however, the computer partially redeems itself. Its program assigns the tag "overstate" to strong words such as *always, never, impossible,* etc., while words tagged by "understate" indicate reserve, caution, qualification. Jenny's letters score exceedingly high on overstate and exceedingly low on understate, and so in a skeletonized way the method does in part detect the trait of dramatic intensity.

One final observation concerning this essentially idiomorphic trait study. Elsewhere I have reported a small investigation (G. W. Allport, 1958) showing that when asked to list the "essential characteristics" of some friend, 90% of the judges employ between 3 and 10 trait names, the average number being 7.2. An "essential characteristic" is defined as "any trait, quality, tendency, interest, that you regard as of major importance to a description of the person you select." There is, I submit, food for thought in the fact that in these two separate studies of Jenny, the common-sense and the factorial, only 8 or 9 central traits appear. May it not be that the essential traits of a person are few in number if only we can identify them?

The case of Jenny has another important bearing on theory. In general our besetting sin in personality is irrelevance, by which I mean that we frequently impose dimensions upon persons when the dimensions fail to apply. (I am reminded of the student who was told to interview women patients concerning their mothers. One patient said that her mother had no part in her problem and no influence on her life; but that her aunt was very important. The student answered, "I'm sorry, but our method requires that you tell me about your mother." The *method* required it, but the *life* did not.)

In ascribing a list of traits to Jenny we may seem to have used a dimensional method, but such is not the case. Jenny's traits emerge from her own personal structure. They are not imposed by predetermined but largely irrelevant schedules.

CONCLUSION

What then have I learned about traits in the last 4 decades? Well, I have learned that the problem cannot be avoided—neither by escape through positivism or situationism, nor through statistical interaction effects. Tendencies, as McDougall (1937) insisted, remain the "indispensable postulates of all psychology."

Further, I have learned that much of our research on traits is overweighted with methodological preoccupation; and that we have too few restraints holding us to the structure of a life as it is lived. We find ourselves confused by our intemperate empiricism which often yields unnamable factors, arbitrary codes, unintelligible interaction effects, and sheer flatulence from our computers.

As a safeguard I propose the restraints of "heuristic realism" which accepts the common-sense assumption that persons are real beings, that each has a real neuropsychic organization, and that our job is to comprehend this organization as well as we can. At the same time our profession uniquely demands that we go beyond common-sense data and either establish their validity or else—more frequently—correct their errors. To do so requires that we be guided by theory in selecting our trait slices for study, that we employ rationally relevant methods, and be strictly bound by empirical verification. In the end we return to fit our findings to an improved view of the person. Along the way we regard him as an objectively real being whose tendencies we can succeed in knowing—at least in part—beyond the level of unaided common sense. In some respects this recommended procedure resembles what Cronbach and Meehl (1955) call "construct validation," with perhaps a dash more stress on external validation.

I have also learned that while the major foci of organization in a life may be few in number, the network of organization, which includes both minor and contradictory tendencies, is still elusively complex.

One reason for the complexity, of course, is the need for the "inside" system to mesh with the "outside" system—in other words, with the situation. While I do not believe that traits can be defined in terms of interaction effects (since all tendencies draw their energy from within the person), still the vast variability of behavior cannot be overlooked. In this respect I have learned that my earlier views seemed to neglect the variability induced by ecological, social, and situational factors. This oversight needs to be repaired through an adequate theory that will relate the inside and outside systems more accurately.

The fact that my three illustrative studies are so diverse in type leads me to a second concession: that trait studies depend in part upon the investigator's own purposes. He himself constitutes a situation for his respondents, and what he obtains from them will be limited by his purpose and his method. But this fact need not destroy our belief that, so far as our method and purpose allow, we can elicit real tendencies.

Finally, there are several problems connected with traits that I have not here attempted to revisit. There are, for example, refinements of difference between trait, attitude, habit, sentiment, need, etc. Since these are all inside tendencies of some sort, they are for the present occasion all "traits" to me. Nor am I here exploring the question to what extent traits are motivational, cognitive, affective, or expressive. Last of all, and with special restraint, I avoid hammering on the distinction between common (dimensional, nomothetic) traits such as we find in any standard profile, and individual traits (personal dispositions) such as we find in single lives, e.g., Jenny's. (Cf. G. W. Allport, 1961, Ch. 15, also 1962.) Nevitt Sanford (1963) has written that by and large psychologists are "unimpressed" by my insisting on this distinction. Well, if this is so in spite of 4 decades of labor on my part, and in spite of my efforts in the present paper—I suppose I should in all decency cry "uncle" and retire to my corner.

REFERENCES

Adorno, T. W., Frenkel-Brunswik, Else, Levinson, D. J., & Sanford, R. N. *The authoritarian personality.* New York: Harpers, 1950.

Allport, F. H. *Theories of perception and the concept of structure.* New York: Wiley, 1955.

Allport, G. W. What is a trait of personality? *Journal of Abnormal and Social Psychology,* 1931, 25, 368–372.

Allport, G. W. Review of S. A. Stouffer et al., *The American soldier. Journal of Abnormal and Social Psychology,* 1950, 45, 168–172.

Allport, G. W. What units shall we employ? In G. Lindzey (Ed.), *Assessment of human motives.* New York: Rinehart, 1958.

Allport, G. W. Religion and prejudice. In, *Personality and social encounter.* Boston: Beacon Press, 1960. Ch. 16.

Allport, G. W. *Pattern and growth in personality.* New York: Holt, Rinehart & Winston, 1961.

Allport, G. W. The general and the unique in psychological science. *Journal of Personality,* 1962, 30, 405–422.

Allport, G. W. Behavioral science, religion and mental health. *Journal of Religion and Health,* 1963, 2, 187–197.

Allport, G. W. (Ed.) *Letters from Jenny.* New York: Harcourt, Brace & World, 1965.

Allport, G. W., & Odbert, H. S. Trait-names: A psycholexical study. *Psychological Monographs,* 1936, 47(1, Whole No. 211).

Allport, G. W., & Vernon, P. E. *A study of values.* Boston: Houghton-Mifflin, 1931. (Reprinted: With G. Lindzey, 3rd ed., 1960.)

Argyle, M. *Religious behavior.* Glencoe, Ill.: Free Press, 1959.

Block, J., & Bennett, Lillian. The assessment of communication. *Human Relations,* 1955, 8, 317–325.

Carr, H. A., & Kingsbury, F. A. The concept of trait. *Psychological Review,* 1938, 45, 497–524.

Cronbach, L. J., & Meehl, P. E. Construct validity in psychological tests. *Psychological Bulletin,* 1955, 52, 281–302.

Edwards, A. L. *The social desirability variable in personality assessment and research.* New York: Dryden Press, 1957.

Gibson, J. J. A critical review of the concept of set in contemporary experimental psychology. *Psychological Bulletin,* 1941, 38, 781–817.

Guthrie, G. M., & McKendry, Margaret S. Interest patterns of Peace Corps volunteers in a teaching project. *Journal of Educational Psychology,* 1963, 54, 261–267.

Helson, H. *Adaptation-level theory.* New York: Harper & Row, 1964.

Holtzmann, W. H. Attitudes of college men toward nonsegregation in Texas schools. Public *Opinion Quarterly,* 1956, 20, 559–569.

Hunt, J. McV. Traditional personality theory in the light of recent evidence. *American Scientist,* 1965, 53, 80–96.

La Piere, R. Attitudes *vs.* actions. *Social Forces,* 1934, 230–237.

Lenski, G. *The religious factor.* Garden City, N. Y.: Doubleday, 1961.

McClelland, D. C. *Personality.* New York: Dryden Press, 1951.

McDougall, W. Tendencies as indispensable postulates of all psychology. In, *Proceedings of the XI International Congress on Psychology: 1937.* Paris: Alcan, 1938. Pp. 157–170.

Miller, D. R. The study of social relationships: Situation, identity, and social interaction. In S. Koch (Ed.), *Psychology: A study of a science.* Vol. 5. *The process areas, the person, and some applied fields: Their place in psychology and the social sciences.* New York: McGraw-Hill, 1963. Pp. 639–737.

Newcomb, T. M., Turner, H. H., & Converse, P. E. *Social psychology: The study of human interaction.* New York: Holt, Rinehart & Winston, 1965.

Sanford, N. Personality: Its place in psychology. In S. Koch (Ed.), *Psychology: A study of a science.* Vol. 5. *The process areas, the person, and some applied fields: Their place in psychology and in science.* New York: McGraw-Hill, 1963. Pp. 488–592.

Skinner, B. F. *Science and human behavior.* New York: Macmillan, 1953.

Spranger, E. *Lebensformen.* (3d ed.) Halle: Niemeyer, 1922. (Translated: P. Pigors. *Types of men.* Halle: Niemeyer, 1928.)

Stone, P. J., Bales, R. F., Namenwirth, J. Z., & Ogilvie, D. M. The general inquirer: A computer system for content analysis and retrieval based on the sentence as a unit of information. *Behavioral Science,* 1962, 7(4), 484–498.

Stouffer, S. A., et al. *The American soldier.* Princeton: Princeton Univer. Press, 1949, 2 vols.

Tagiuri, R., & Petrullo, L. *Person perception and interpersonal behavior.* Stanford: Stanford Univer. Press, 1958.

Vernon, P. E. *Personality assessment: A critical survey.* London: Methuen, 1964.

Walker, E. L. Psychological complexity as a basis for a theory of motivation and choice. In D. Levine (Ed.), *Nebraska symposium on motivation: 1964.* Lincoln: Univer. Nebraska Press, 1964.

Williams, R. M., Jr. *Strangers next door.* Englewood Cliffs, N. J.: Prentice-Hall, 1964.

Wilson, W. C. Extrinsic religious values and prejudice. *Journal of Abnormal and Social Psychology,* 1960, 60, 286–288.

6

Traits Are Relevant: Theoretical Analysis and Empirical Evidence

ROSS STAGNER

The concept of a personality trait is widely used in popular discussions of human behavior; further, it is deeply embedded in the scientific literature. Gordon Allport (1961) stated that traits constitute "those aspects of personality in respect to which most people within a given culture can be profitably compared" (p. 340). And Guilford (1959) gives a more precise formulation: "A trait is any relatively enduring way in which one person differs from others. On a scalable trait, which can be represented by a straight line, each person has a characteristic position. If individuals have different positions on a common scale, the scale represents some quality or property that each person possesses to some degree, in common with other persons" (p. 6). In such conceptions, a *trait* is an abstraction from overt behavior, an intervening variable used to improve our understanding or our predictive accuracy with regard to some person.

In recent years a movement has developed in psychology that is critical of the trait concept and proposes that it be discarded. Hunt (1965) criticized the trait idea, commenting that trait studies "have all too often found even the reliability and validity coefficients of their measures falling within a range of 0.2 and 0.5" (p. 81). Mischel (1971) observed that ". . . the utility of describing people in broad trait terms (e.g., 'impulsive,' 'dependent') is . . . being questioned deeply" (p. 149). And Bandura (1969) says that

In the assessment process behavioral data, however obtained, are typically converted into trait or psychodynamic constructs that are far removed from the actual feelings and actions of the person being evaluated. . . . The evidence indicates that these hypothetical constructions are better predictors of diagnosticians' semantic and conceptual stereotypes than of clients' actual attributes and psychological reality. . . .

Printed by permission of the author.

This is a revised and expanded version of a paper presented at the 1973 APA Convention in Montreal, under the title, "Traits are relevant: Logical and empirical analysis." This was part of a symposium called "Traits, Persons, and Situations: Some Theoretical Issues." I wish to acknowledge the valuable comments of the other participants in the symposium: Norman S. Endler, J. McV. Hunt, Walter Mischel, and Kenneth S. Bowers, none of whom necessarily agree with anything said herein.

The tenacious belief in generalized response dispositions is attributed by Mischel (1968) to the tendency to construe behavioral consistencies even from variable performances. Hence, generality may emerge in the inferential construct domain, whereas a high degree of specificity may obtain at the behavioral level. (p. 15)

We cannot, of course, argue with Bandura's position that much of the so-called dynamic logic is circular. For example, a person with delusions, hallucination, and inappropriate emotional responses is labeled schizophrenic, and then the symptoms are explained by a hypothetical "schizophrenia." In this kind of usage the hypothetical construct is inexcusable. But Bandura should not throw out the baby along with the dirty bath water. There are many important examples of prediction of future human behavior from hypothetical inner states that are more precise than those based on knowledge of the external situation.

Mischel seems to have softened his attack on the trait concept in recent years (Mischel, 1973): "While some situations may be powerful determinants of behavior, others are likely to be exceedingly trivial" (p. 255). And he denies the widely held view that "social behavior theory, especially in its emphasis on the discriminativeness ('specificity') of behavior, implies a 'personalityless' view of man" (p. 254). This must, of course, be contrasted with his view (Mischel, 1971) that personality is so vague a term that he cannot define it!

It must be noted, however, that the general tenor even of the 1973 article is that traits are not defensible concepts. After a look at evidence indicating the role of the person in the determination of behavior outcomes, he writes, "While it would be bizarre to ignore the person in the psychology of personality, behavior often may be predicted and controlled efficaciously from knowledge about relevant stimulus conditions, especially when those conditions are powerful" (p. 277). We should not, I believe, confine our attention to the behavior of a person with a gun to his head. (Even under threats of pain and death, some individuals cling to their inner convictions, but most of us are more flexible.)

There is an impressive body of literature, most of which is ignored by the social-behavior theorists, to the effect that: traits are valuable constructs for explaining behavior; traits often outweigh situational determinants, even the "powerful" pressures of the experimental laboratory for prediction of behavior; a trait concept is compatible with extensive evidence from the laboratory and especially from neurophysiology; and trait theory fits closely with important new trends in cognitive theory.

With regard to the specific question of how traits relate to situations, I shall present arguments and evidence (a) that traits determine which situations a person will approach and which he will avoid; (b) that traits determine which "rewards" he will treat as reinforcers; (c) that traits will determine what he learns or what he rejects in a laboratory task; and (d) that traits predict behavioral outcomes over a long timespan or in markedly new situations, in a manner impossible if predictors are limited to behavior in specific situations.

I do not wish to try to argue out of existence the very substantive body of data indicating that a person, if persuaded to enter a laboratory experiment, may behave in accordance with the requirements of that situation *as he perceives these requirements*; nor do I deny that, even in nonlaboratory situations, a substantial portion of the variance in behavior may be related to person–situation interaction. However, I do propose that the limits of human cognitive capacity make a trait concept indispensable both for the observer of other personalities and for the individual himself; that the term *trait* or some synonym is essential in systematizing many observations of personality; that longitudinal studies indicate that consistency in personality development can be comprehended in terms of traits, but not in terms of specific situational responses; and that the trait concept is closely compatible with our expanding knowledge of cognitive psychology as exemplified by the works of Piaget, Bruner, and Chomsky. Finally, I shall cite some studies that indicate that measures of personality traits predict behavior in laboratory situations and behavior in long-term studies of careers.

TRAIT AS A DESCRIPTIVE UNIT

It is not surprising that when subjects were required to predict a person's behavior, and given a choice of how to categorize the available behavioral information, subjects overwhelmingly preferred to organize the data in terms of traits rather than in terms of situational settings (Jeffery & Mischel, 1972). A summarizing concept such as *trait* is indispensable because neither human cognitive capacity nor our communication channels are adequate to the task of encompassing all the complications of human behavior.

Suppose I ask Prof. Mischel to recommend to me a young Stanford Ph.D. for a faculty position. He will not respond by describing the behavior of this person in a seminar at 3:00 p.m. on Monday, May 8, 1973. Rather, he will ascribe to the individual such generalized traits as responsibility, fluency of expression, general vigor, acuity of intellectual analysis, and so on. He will undoubtedly support such attributions of traits by citing specific examples as evidence, but he knows, just as I know, that the specific situations facing a graduate student at Stanford will differ significantly from the situations facing a faculty member at another university. Thus, what he must communicate to me are the generalized patterns of perceptions and actions that statistically have characterized this person, and by extrapolation, *may be expected* to characterize his future performance.

TRAIT AS A SYSTEMATIZING CONCEPT

The crucial question seems to be: how much cross-situational consistency is observed? Can we describe personality in terms of situation-response consistencies, or do we need a higher-order concept that will provide a theoretical base for understanding these consistencies? I want to make two points about this issue: one is that situation-response consistency is grossly exaggerated by many psychologists; the other is that the kinds of uniformities observed lend themselves more readily to a trait formulation than to any other.

How consistent is a response to a situation? Animals are credited with forming a conditioned response when they reach a criterion of about eight out of ten correct responses. Even a highly overtrained rat will often make an error in a T-maze or choice box. Yet we do not discard the concept of conditioned response. Why demand complete consistency as regards a personality trait?

Situational consistency is related to meanings, not to overt acts. Liddell, James, and Anderson (1934, p. 57) performed an ingenious experiment as follows: they put a sheep in a harness and placed her foot on a metal plate, rang a bell, and delivered an electric shock. After a few trials she raised her hoof off the plate at the sound of the bell—a stimulus–response connection, some would say. Then Liddell turned the sheep upside down in the harness, with her head on the metal plate. When he rang the bell, did the sheep lift her hoof? No, she lifted here head off of the plate. Is this an absence of consistency in response? Or is it an indication that consistency depends on the perception of situations and consequences, and the selection of a response appropriate to that percept?

The cross-situational uniformities in behavior that we observe in human beings resemble the uniformity demonstrated by Liddell's sheep, that is, uniformity in dealing with *perceived* similarities. If a young man refuses an invitation to a party, drops a course that requires group discussion, and takes his vacation hiking alone in the mountains, we begin to get the idea that there is an inner consistency that involves the avoidance of situations that require close contact with other human beings. It is, however, rather difficult to treat these acts as examples of transfer of response, unless we postulate an underlying percept that ascribes threatening attributes to other persons. The concept of a trait of seclusiveness, it seems to me, makes better sense as a unifying concept here than any situation-specific kind of interpretation.

RESPONSE SPECIFICITY:
NEUROPHYSIOLOGICAL EVIDENCE

Current research in neurophysiological laboratories undermines the concept of a specific response to a specific stimulus in favor of a variable response to an abstracted or generalized stimulus. Aside from receptor processes, the first organismic response to a stimulus input is the cortical evoked response (CER). Far from being specific to a highly invariant input such as a flash of monochromatic light, the CER varies wildly. Generally speaking, it is overwhelmed by the greater magnitude of the ongoing electrical rhythms that make up the EEG. Only by averaging CERs over 25 to 100 repetitions of a stimulus do we achieve an identifiable wave-form. The very least we can make of this is that the "same" physical stimulus may evoke a variety of responses in the CNS. Variations may be induced by collateral inhibition (effects of simultaneous stimuli in the same or other modalities; context), by changes in tonic facilitative or inhibitory inputs from other sections of the CNS, and so on. John and Morgades (1969) trained cats to press one lever when a light flickered at 2 cps and another lever when the flicker was at 8 cps. They report that single unit responses were highly variable, but by the time a large population of neurons was involved, marked stability appeared. Their conclusion:

... Neural ensembles which reported the presence of the discriminated signals were broadly distributed throughout extensive regions and consistently displayed two different patterns of response to the two different stimuli ... Multiple unit ensemble responses displayed impressive stability suggesting an invariant mode of discharge to a particular stimulus. In contrast, *single unit activity was extremely variable* with many different response patterns displayed to the same stimuli. These findings suggested that the firing pattern of extensive neural ensembles constituted a far more reliable source of information on which to base differential response than did the firing patterns of single cells (pp. 205–206, italics added).

Neurophysiological data also give us clues as to how a new, different situation may come to elicit an already established response. Spinelli (1970) has described a generalization experiment as follows:

The records from the visual cortex of a cat trained to press a bar whenever a flicker of 4 cps was presented show 4 cps activity. If a flicker of 10 per second is now presented after learning, the animal still performs the avoidance response, but the records from visual cortex now show what look like a mixture of 10 per second and 4 cps activity ... it would seem that when the animal is generalizing to the 10 cps, two kinds of activities are generated in the cat's visual cortex: The 10 per second is produced by the stimulus; the other one, the 4 per second, could conceivably be a playback of what the animal had previously learned (p. 294).

This kind of observation throws still further doubt on the specificity interpretation and indicates, rather, that the organism constructs neural representations of external events that are composites of a variety of situations, not of a single situation. To quote Pribram (1969): "Somewhere between the retina and the visual cortex the inflowing signals are modified to provide information that is already linked to a learned response, for example, the monkey's intention to press one panel or another. Evidently what reaches the visual cortex is evoked by the external world but is hardly a direct or simple replica of it" (p. 76).

The foregoing conclusion was based on data reported by Pribram, Spinelli, and Kamback (1967), which showed that the CER takes different forms for visual inputs such as circles and vertical bars, for response intentions such as pressing the right or left panel, and for different consequences such as reinforcement or nonreinforcement. There is also a suggestion (though the data were not analyzed in this way) that would confirm Spinelli's remarks above: The CER wave-form for a circle incorrectly perceived as bars, hence leading to an incorrect response, seems to be intermediate between the "circle" pattern when correct and the "bar" pattern when correct. If this can be verified, it would give support to the notion that much response variation can be attributed to misperception of the stimulus; and this misperception in turn could be attributed to summated residuals of prior experiences with stimuli in the same category (cf. Helson, 1964).

Simultaneous presentation of a differential cue brings out this tendency even more sharply. Begleiter, Projesz, Yerra, and Kissin (1973) presented light flashes, bright or dim, and required the subject to press one button for bright, another for dim. A distinctive auditory stimulus accompanied each level of flash. After a training series, the experimenter began inserting flashes halfway between the original bright or dim stimuli. Half were accompanied by the auditory cue for bright, half by the cue for dim. In over 90 percent of trials, the switch pressed by the subject corresponded to the auditory cue, *and the CER corresponded to the subjectively reported brightness associated with that cue.* Thus, if contextual cues are present, an ambiguous stimulus can be converted into a member of a familiar schema and responded to (neurally and manually) as such; further, it is *consciously misperceived* as having the properties of the original stimulus.

The neurophysiological data, then, suggest the following conclusions: (a) successive presentations of physically identical stimuli lead to varying cortical responses; (b) the ongoing cortical rhythms overwhelm the CER, suggesting that established patterns are more potent than specific inputs; (c) only as CERs are summed across many repetitions does an identifiable pattern emerge; (d) the averaged CER apparently corresponds to a generalized model of the stimulus, since it does not correspond to any of the specific evoked responses; (e) ambiguous stimuli tend to be assimilated (Piaget) to an existing neural model or schema; and (f) stimuli so modified tend to evoke the conscious and manual responses appropriate to the original stimulus, not to the stimulus physically present. All of these, it seems to me, lead us away from a specifistic interpretation toward an emphasis on generalized patterns of perceiving and responding.

TRAIT AS CROSS–SITUATIONAL CONSISTENCY

The procedure used by Guilford and Zimmerman (1956), Comrey (1970), and other investigators guarantees that inventory measures of traits have significant cross-situational consistency. This is indicated by factor loadings of individual items on vectors obtained by purely objective statistical operations.[1]

Concurrent validity studies also support the consistency of trait measures. Raskin, Rondestvedt, and Johnson (1972) asked patients entering psychotherapy

---

[1] It is not, in a sense, essential that the inferred trait be identified by the content of the specific items on the inventory. The items may function as indicators solely in a statistical sense. Sarason (1969, p. 7) for example, seems to take such a stance in his comment that "interpretation of scores on particular scales should be based on statistical expectancies rather than on inferred meanings of particular items." A view of trait scores as a summation of probabilities was proposed by Stagner (1937, pp. 134–135). However, this approach evades the question of the underlying nature of traits. The main argument of the present paper asserts that we can define a trait as a generalized pattern of expectancies cutting across specific events. Prediction of a trait from specific indicators is still a matter of adding probabilities (Stagner, 1974, p. 219).

to fill out inventories describing themselves on states of anxiousness and depression. Later the therapist filled out a similar inventory for the same patient. The correlations were +.77 for anxiousness, +.68 for depression. Thus the traits measured seem to be consistent across instruments and across observers.

TRAIT AS LONGITUDINAL CONSISTENCY

Human beings also show consistency over time, but this is not always linked to specific responses. Indeed, regardless of the caveat issued by Bandura (1969), *consistency* in terms of traits may be manifested by *reversal* of a specific response. The research of Lewis (1967) dealt with crying in response to frustration in babies age 1 month and 12 months. Frustration at 1 month consisted of removing a nipple from the mouth for 30 seconds. At age 12 months it took the form of placing a barrier between the child and his mother with some attractive toys. Some babies cried in response to frustration at 1 month, and some cried at 12 months; *but the babies who cried on the first test were not those who cried on the second.* The correlation was negative; crying at time one predicted noncrying at time two. Bandura might conclude from this that human infants are very inconsistent, since their responses were reversed on the second test. But we may conclude—as Lewis did—that the group crying at age one month took an *active* attitude; at 12 months they crawled to the barrier or otherwise tried to modify the situation. The group not crying at one month were *passive*—they "froze" rather than acting—and at 12 months they sat and cried rather than taking any action. The interpretation by Lewis (which seems to me to be correct) is far closer to a trait theory than it is to a situation theory.

Long-term consistency in traits is indicated by a variety of studies. Block (1971) demonstrated that traits identified in childhood had predictive value for these individuals ten and twenty years later. Kagan (1971) gives impressive examples of consistency over time in personality traits. These studies automatically confirm the hypothesis of cross-situational consistency, since the situation facing a 10-year-old is axiomatically quite different from that facing a person at age 20 or 30.

Efforts to predict trait scores from specific situational items have been somewhat less successful. Stagner (1938) obtained self-reports of incidents in the biographies of college students and computed trait scores for those affirming and those denying a given situation. While the differences were far greater than chance, they were not of much practical importance. The same can be said of a similar study by Hearn, Charles, and Wolins (1965).

TRAIT AS COGNITIVE PATTERN

The trait concept may be viewed as a cognitive pattern, either within the person observed or within the observer. Situationists favor the view that inconsistencies are ignored by the observer in favor of a hypothesis of generalized trait consistencies.

Expanding on the hypothesis that the alleged consistency of personality is projected by the observer, Jones, Kanouse, Kelley, Nisbett, Valins, and Weiner (1971) point to the well-known tendency of human beings to achieve cognitive balance or consistency. Thus, they argue, the observer may misperceive the evidence so that it becomes more consistent. "It is not surprising that personal consistency is exaggerated in the eye of the beholder" (p. 90).

It is curious indeed that Jones et al. do not reverse this argument and say that the well-known tendency of human beings to achieve consistency supports the trait hypothesis. Not only does a child feel a need to be consistent in his evaluation of situations; he also feels a need to be consistent in his evaluation of himself. This tendency is not without its external supports. Parents will scold him for being inconsistent, and his peers will ridicule him if he changes his mind too often. Each of us needs a predictable environment (Stagner, 1951), and we are disturbed by unpredictable behavior of others. The negative reinforcements we deal out push the child toward consistency of the variety required by trait theory. Adults push themselves toward consistency; experienced inconsistencies give rise to tensions of dissonance, and reduction of these tensions is generally accomplished by bringing deviant specificities into line with the generalized pattern. Thus, a suspicious adult may observe that he has behaved in a trusting fashion in relation to some person; he may then conclude that he should not do this, because people in general are not trustworthy.

Since the time of Chomsky's (1959) critique of Skinner, it has become a commonplace that children do not acquire language by a succession of S–R classical, operant, or discriminative conditioned responses. George Miller, Roger Brown, and others have demonstrated the necessity of assuming that the child constructs an implicit grammar, a set of cognitive rules, and that he generates sentences in accordance with these rules, not by conditioning. Piaget has convinced most of us that the child progresses at a very early age from a specific and unchanging percept to an abstract concept, or *schema*. His behavior is guided by the schema, not by a specific percept.

I suggest that a trait be conceived as a schema, or a cognitive rule, that guides behavior in a variety of situations perceived as belonging to this schema or subject to this rule. Bem (1972) speaks of behavior as being similar in objectively dissimilar situations because these are perceived by the subject as belonging in an "equivalence class." This is what I mean by a trait. It is a cognitive process that equates otherwise different situations in terms of their attributes or consequences.

This notion of traits as cognitive structures is also compatible with a portion of Mischel's analysis. He says (1971, p. 46) "the essence of self-regulatory systems is the subject's adoption of *contingency rules* that guide his behavior in the absence of, and sometimes in spite of, immediate external situational pressures." As I see it, a contingency rule may take the form of a generalized expectancy that "revealing my inner emotions to others always leads to bad luck" or "bossing others is more likely to lead to reward than being bossed by others." These are the hidden structures that guide both perception of reward probabilities and action in ambiguous situations. The part of the Mischel quotation I especially like is the phrase "in spite of immediate situational pressures." The critical incident that verifies for me the presence of a trait is the situation in which the person refuses to accept an immediate reward, or tolerates immediate discomfort, in order to act according to a consistent pattern. Thus he may refuse to go to a dance with a pretty girl because he hates crowds, or he may accept ridicule rather than experiment with drugs, etc.

In my conception of this process, there is a series of thresholds (cf. Campbell, 1963) that can be considered measures of the strength of a trait. For example, a person may overcome his dislike of social situations if there is a large enough financial reward, or if he is threatened with physical violence if he refuses, or if he will suffer public humiliation for his uncooperative behavior. We can arrange these pressures on a Guttman scale and show that the generalized pattern may be held with sufficient intensity to pass one hurdle but not two, or three but not four. In other words, positions on the dimension (scores on a scale) correspond to the magnitudes of situational pressures the person will resist in order to hold to his preferred mode of behavior.

We can use Chomsky's hypothesis about language as a way of clarifying the trait concept. I suggest that a trait begins as a "deep structure." This might be an affective conviction in a child that "people are bad, dangerous." This deep structure, however, may be expressed overtly in many different ways, which may correspond to Chomsky's "syntactic transformations." Thus, the child may establish for himself a guiding rule of behavior, that adults are to be avoided as much as possible; or, people cannot be trusted, so you should never reveal your feelings; or, people will take advantage of you, so you should exploit them first; or, people will try to boss you, so you should try to dominate them first. A surface trait, an observable consistency of behavior, represents only one of several possible transformations of the deep structure.

While most children learn to conform to the grammar of the culture in which they live, the individual tends to retain some elements of his unique, idiosyncratic grammar; his personal style, as literary critics have long emphasized, endures for years and may never completely disappear. Similarly, I argue, the child conforms to situational demands with regard to social rules and institutional patterns; but his personality will continue to reveal underlying uniformities which correspond to these deep cognitive-affective structures that I call traits.

TRAIT AS A CORRECTION-RESISTANT HYPOTHESIS

The use of Chomsky's notions about deep structure and syntactic transformation depends on the assumption that these cognitive rules, once evolved by the child, are resistant to change. This is necessary because the individual is constantly being faced with situations in which he would get reinforcement for behaving in a way contrary to his hypothesis. Can an inner expectancy, once established, hold up in the face of contradictory reinforcement contingencies? A relevant animal study is that of Seligman and Maier (1967). They administered shocks to dogs held in a Pavlov sling (thus, no escape was possible). Later, they placed these animals in an open box with a grid floor. Even though severe shocks were administered, the animals did not learn to jump out, although normal controls learned this in one trial. The authors postulate an "expectancy of helplessness" as the intervening variable of residue of the prior experience which prevented learning the simple escape response. The animal behaved on the basis of expectancies.[2]

A human study supports this interpretation. Levine (1971) induced an expectancy that a problem could be solved by a sequence rule, e.g., AABAAABB, etc. After this expectancy was established, he switched to a simple problem involving size. Although control subjects solved this almost at once, those with the sequence hypothesis never succeeded. They emitted an unending variety of sequence possibilities and never tried other contingencies although reinforcements were being given when, by chance, they hit the correct item. This study suggests that when a person adopts a hypothesis (e.g., that people are untrustworthy), he may cling to it indefinitely. He does not explore or even consider others.

Psychotherapists have often deplored the difficulties of modifying personality in adults. The reasons may be found in the foregoing studies. Traits, once established, determine what situations the person will approach, what inputs he will perceive as reinforcing (and which ones he will ignore or reject), and what responses will be emitted in response to experimental instructions or situational pressures. He often ignores reinforcing events completely. The theorist who places all of his trust in reinforcement contingencies does so at his own risk.

TRAIT AS A PREDICTOR OF LABORATORY BEHAVIOR

In supporting the logical analysis of trait I have interpolated a few empirical investigations that seemed appropriate. Let me now turn to a brief survey of studies that confirm the foregoing analysis. If I am correct, then measured personality traits should predict behavior in a laboratory situation, and persons with traits incompatible with the response reinforced by the experimenter will fail to show the behavior predicted by the reinforcement contingencies. The following is a very limited sampling from a large number of studies confirming

---

[2] Ethical considerations prevent experimental attempts to establish specified traits in human subjects. Whimbey and Denenberg (1966), however, have demonstrated with rats that generalized patterns can be established and that predictions of new tasks not included in the experimental training sequence can be made with considerable accuracy.

the theoretical prediction that, despite the alleged high potency of situational pressures in the laboratory, subjects often behave in accordance with their enduring traits, not in accordance with this temporary situation. The following list is by no means an inclusive sampling of all the relevant studies; rather, it is chosen to indicate the wide variety of experiments in which trait measures prove to be as effective as, or more effective than, the specific situational pressure as a determinant of behavior.

1. Shemberg, Leventhal, and Allman (1968) had subjects rated on aggressiveness and later tested them in the Buss "aggression machine" situation, where they were pressed to administer shocks to a presumed victim. There was a statistically significant tendency for those rated above the median on aggressiveness to administer more, and also more severe, shocks than those below the median on these ratings.

2. Timmons and Noblin (1963) administered Blum's Blacky Test, a projective measure of Freudian trait tendencies, to college students and selected 15 fairly consistent orals, 15 consistent anals. These served as subjects in a verbal conditioning experiment. The orals showed significant yielding to the experimental pressure; 12 of 15 performed as predicted. The anals showed *significant counterconditioning*; only 4 of 15 behaved as predicted in the experiment. In fact, the remaining 11 subjects actually *reduced* their production of the reinforced word.

3. Getter (1966) used persons measured for internal control or external control on the Rotter scale. The externals formed conditioned verbal responses rapidly; the internals did not show significant conditioning. Similarly, Biondo and MacDonald (1971) exposed subjects to high and low influence pressures. Externals (as predicted) responded by yielding to influence at both levels. Internals showed no change to low influence, and reacted in the direction *opposite* to the influence in the high-influence condition.

4. Lester and Crowne (1970) showed that F-score (authoritarian trend) predicted a substantial portion of the variance in the behavior of girls who reported an insect phobia and were then pressed to pick up a giant cockroach.

5. Stricker, Messick, and Jackson (1970) obtained dramatic differences between a group of subjects characterized on a self-report inventory as "suspicious" and a nonsuspicious group when they were tried on the Asch conformity experiment. (Most of us have had the experience of having subjects deliberately "give the experimenter what he wants," or, negativistically, doing the opposite of what he believes is expected.)

6. Studies of persons treated by "behavior modification" methods indicate that the success or failure depends on personality traits. Andrews (1966) is especially emphatic on this point, but the same conclusion is suggested by Lang and Lazovik (1963).

Behavior modification by observing a model acting and being reinforced (Bandura, 1965) is unquestionably effective. But reinforcement is not an essential component of this kind of design, and behavior modeling is found in situations suggestive of trait influence. Consider the study by Hetherington and Frankie (1967). These investigators, operating on a trait approach, observed mother and father in the home and rated them in various situations. From these data they classified some fathers as the dominant parent, and some mothers as dominant. Later the child was offered an opportunity to model his behavior on the mother or the father. A significantly large percentage chose to model on the dominant parent, irrespective of sex. Thus the child must have believed in trait theory, since he chose the parent who was dominant in a variety of situations, and his behavior was not affected by reinforcement, since none was offered, but his acts were influenced by the perceived attributes of the model. Thus, a generalized trait in the parent can be identified by the child and can guide his behavior without regard to reinforcement.

TRAIT AS LONG-TERM PREDICTOR

Finally, let me turn to a class of investigations that indicate that trait measures have validity over a long period of time as predictors of academic behavior, occupational success, criminal behavior, etc.

Stagner (1933) showed that measured personality traits function as moderator variables affecting the individual's use of academic aptitude. For students in the upper third of the distribution on Bernreuter's self-sufficiency scale, the aptitude–grade-point correlation was +.59; for the lowest third on self-sufficiency, the correlation was +.37. Similarly, for the top third on dominance, the aptitude–grade correlation was +.71; for the bottom third, +.44. It should be noted that partial correlation will never reveal these effects; the correlations of the personality measures with both aptitude and GPA were of the order of .10. The trait operates to affect the person's effective use of his aptitude, but does not itself correlate well with either aptitude or achievement.

The same kind of moderator effect has been demonstrated by Hoyt and Norman (1954), using MMPI, and by Kipnis (1971), using his own measure of impulsiveness. Kipnis showed that impulsiveness had no relation to academic performance for persons of below average intelligence, but had a significant correlation (negative) with grades in the half of his group above median in ability.

At the neurophysiological level, Becker-Carus (1971) demonstrated a moderator effect of "neurotic tendency" (Eysenck) on brain process. When faced with a vigilance task, normal subjects showed a decrease of EEG rhythms in the 10–11 cps range, but those high on the neurotic scale showed an *increase*. (While a speculative interpretation is obvious, I simply cite the study to show that these moderator effects are ubiquitous.)

In the prediction of juvenile deliquency, Hathaway and Monachesi (1952) were able to show that a combination of MMPI scores on the Pd and Ma scales predicted delinquent behavior two years later at well above the chance level.

Robins (1966) showed that a combination of aggressive symptoms in childhood gave a better prediction of adult criminality than could be obtained from any single aggressive or delinquent act. This was not a personality trait measure, but the adding of symptoms corresponds rather closely to what is done in trait measurement.

In the prediction of occupational success, numerous investigators have reported that measured personality traits influence (or can be used to predict) future occupational status or income. The best studies in this area come from Harrell (1972) who tested several hundred young men receiving the MBA degree from Stanford University. Following up these men after ten years, he found that income status was effectively predicted by the ascendance scale on the Guilford-Zimmerman inventory and by the Ma scale on MMPI. Similarly, rapid rise into a general management status was predicted by these two scales, as well as by the general activity measure on the Guilford-Zimmerman.[3] It appears from the data that the predictive value of the personality measures will be even higher if intelligence level is held constant; however, these calculations have not yet been made.

CONCLUSIONS

While no one will deny that situational pressures may and often do determine behavior irrespective of dispositional traits, the evidence is equally clear in indicating that behavior often is predicted more accurately by a knowledge of established trait patterns than by a knowledge of the specific situation facing the person. This conclusion is particularly emphatic when the trait induces action contradictory to the situational pressure.

The evidence also indicates that long-range prediction, notably where the outcome behavior is nonspecific, taking such forms as high academic or occupational achievement, is significantly better when based on trait scores than when based on a knowledge of the situation. The relevance of trait measures increases as the span of time increases or as the generalized character of the outcome increases.

Theoretical analysis suggests that specific situations rarely if ever induce specific responses; rather, the situation is assimilated to a cognitive model of a category of similar situations, and the organism emits a response that is appropriate to the consequences to be expected in that class of situations. These researches on fine-grain analysis of organismic response seem to fit more comfortably with trait theory than with specifistic theory. Traits are conceived as

---

[3] Note should also be made of the excellent studies by Bray (1973) of management trainees in AT&T. These young men were assessed and assigned quantitative scores on various personality traits at time of employment, and inventory trait scores were also obtained. In a follow-up eight years later, both assessment evaluations and objective scores were found to have substantial value as predictors of success in management.

generalized expectancies that certain consequences can be expected from contact with certain categories of stimuli: with other persons, with authority figures, with submissive roles, etc. These expectancies, once established, function like source traits (Cattell) and give rise to surface traits by a process resembling Chomsky's "syntactic transformations." Since behavior in a specific situation depends on categorizing the situation, anticipating consequences in that situation, and choosing among alternative responses to such a situation, it would appear that analysis of day-to-day behavior is furthered by trait theory as opposed to situation-specific theory. Traits determine how the person will perceive the situation, whether he will enter the situation, whether he will perceive a proffered "reward" as reinforcing, and whether he will execute the response perceived by an experimenter as the one appropriate to the situational pressure.

REFERENCES

Allport, G. W. *Pattern and growth in personality.* New York: Holt, 1961.

Andrews, J. D. W. Psychotherapy of phobias. *Psychological Buleltin,* 1966, *66,* 455–480.

Bandura, A. Influence of models' reinforcement contingencies on the acquisition of imitative responses. *Journal of Personality and Social Psychology,* 1965, *1,* 589–595.

Bandura, A. *Principles of behavior modification.* New York: Holt, Rinehart & Winston, 1969.

Becker-Carus, D. Relationships between EEG, personality and vigilance. *Electroencephalogram and Clinical Neurophysiology,* 1971, *30,* 519–526.

Begleiter, H., Porjesz, B., Yerre, C., & Kissin, B. Evoked potential correlates of expected stimulus intensity. *Science,* 1973, *179,* 814–816.

Bem, D. Constructing cross-situational consistencies in behavior: Some thoughts on Alker's critique of Mischel. *Journal of Personality,* 1972, *40,* 17–26.

Biondo, J., & MacDonald, A. P. Jr. Internal–external locus of control and response to influence attempts. *Journal of Personality,* 1971, *39,* (3), 408–19.

Block, J. *Lives through time.* Berkeley, Calif.: Bancroft, 1971.

Bray, D. W. *The management recruit: Formative years in business.* New York: Wiley, 1973.

Campbell, D. T. Social attitudes and other acquired behavioral dispositions. In S. Koch (Ed.), *Psychology: A study of a science.* New York: McGraw-Hill, 1963.

Chomsky, N. Review of Skinner's *Verbal behavior. Language,* 1959, *35,* 25–28.

Comrey, A. L. *Manual for the Comrey Personality Scales.* San Diego, Calif.: Educational and Industrial Testing Service, 1970.

Getter, H. A. A personality determinant of verbal conditioning. *Journal of Personality,* 1966, *34,* 397–405.

Guilford, J. P. *Personality.* New York: McGraw-Hill, 1959.

Guilford, J. P., & Zimmerman, W. S. Fourteen dimensions of temperament. *Psychological Monographs,* 1956, *70* (10), Whole No. 417.

Harrell, T. W. High earning MBAs. *Personnel Psychology,* 1972, *25,* 523–530.

Hathaway, S. R., & Monachesi, E. D. The Minnesota Multiphasic Personality Inventory in the study of juvenile delinquents. *American Sociological Review,* 1952, *17,* 704–710.

Hearn, J. L., Charles, D. C., & Wolins, L. Life history antecedents of measured personality variables. *Journal of Genetic Psychology,* 1965, *197,* 99–110.

Helson, H. *Adaptation-level theory: An experimental and systematic approach to behavior.* New York: Harper, 1964.

Hetherington, E. M., & Frankie, G. Effects of parental dominance, warmth, and conflict on imitation in children. *Journal of Personality and Social Psychology*, 1967, *6*, 119–25.

Hoyt, D. T., & Norman, W. T. Adjustment and academic predictability. *Journal of Counselling Psychology*, 1954, *1*, 96–99.

Hunt, J. McV. Traditional personality theory in the light of recent evidence. *American Scientist*, 1965, *53*, 80–96.

Jeffery, K., & Mischel, W. *The layman's use of traits to predict and remember behavior.* Unpublished manuscript, Stanford University, 1973.

John, E. R., & Morgades, P. P. The pattern and anatomical distribution of evoked potentials and multiple unit activity elicited by conditioned stimuli in trained cats. *Communications in Behavioral Biology*, Part A. Vol. 3, No. 4. New York: Academic Press, 1969.

Jones, E. E., Kanouse, D. E., Kelley, H. H., Nisbett, R. E., Valins, S., and Weiner, B. *Attribution: Perceiving the causes of behavior.* Morristown, N. J.: General Learning Press, 1971.

Kagan, J., et al. *Change and continuity in infancy.* New York: Wiley, 1971.

Kipnis, D. *Character structure and impulsiveness.* New York: Academic Press, 1971.

Lang, P. J., & Lazovik, A. D. Experimental desensitization of a phobia. *Journal of Abnormal and Social Psychology*, 1963, *66*, 519–25.

Lester, L. F., & Crowne, D. P. A strict behavioral test of obedience and some childrearing correlates. *Personality: An international journal*, 1970, *1* (1), 85–93.

Levine, M. Hypothesis theory and nonlearning despite ideal S–R reinforcement contingencies. *Psychological Review*, 1971, *78* (2), 130–40.

Lewis, M. The meaning of a response, or why researchers in infant behavior should be oriental metaphysicians. *Merrill-Palmer Quarterly*, 1967, *13* (1), 7–18.

Liddell, H. S., James, W. T., & Anderson, O. D. The comparative physiology of the conditioned motor reflex, based on experiments with the pig, dog, sheep, goat, and rabbit. *Comparative Psychology Monographs*, 1934, *11* (1), 1–89.

Mischel, W. *Assessment of personality.* New York: Wiley, 1968.

Mischel, W. *Introduction to personality.* New York: Holt, Rinehart & Winston, 1971.

Mischel, W. Towards a cognitive social learning reconceptualization of personality. *Psychological Review*, 1973, *80* (4), 252–283.

Pribram, K. H. The neurophysiology of remembering. *Scientific American*, January 1969, pp. 73–86.

Pribam, K. H., Spinelli, D. N., & Kamback, M. C. Electrocortical correlates of stimulus, response, and reinforcement. *Science*, 1967, *157*, 94–96.

Raskin, M., Rondestvedt, J. W., & Johnson, G. Anxiety in young adults: A prognostic study. *Journal of Nervous and Mental Disease*, 1972, *154*, 229–237.

Robins, L. N. *Deviant children grown up; A sociological and psychiatric study of sociopathic personality.* Baltimore: Williams & Wilkins, 1966.

Sarason, I. G. *Contemporary research in personality* (2nd ed.). Princeton, N. J.: Van Nostrand, 1969.

Seligman, M. E. P., & Maier, S. F. Failure to escape traumatic shock. *Journal of Experimental Psychology*, 1967, *74*, 1–9.

Shemberg, K. M., Leventhal, D. B., & Allman, L. Aggression machine performance and rated aggression. *Journal of Experimental Research in Personality*, 1968, *3*, 117–119.

Spinelli, D. N. OCCAM: A content addressable memory model for the brain. In Pribram Karl H., and D. E. Broadbent, (Eds.) *The biology of memory.* New York: Academic Press, 1970.

Stagner, R. Relation of personality to academic aptitude and achievement. *Journal of Educational Research*, 1933, *26*, 648–660.

Stagner, R. *Psychology of personality.* New York: McGraw-Hill, 1937.

Stagner, R. Role of parents in development of emotional instability. *American Journal of Orthopsychiatry*, 1938, *8*, 122–129.

Stagner, R. Homeostasis as a unifying concept in personality theory. *Psychological Review,* 1951, *58,* 5–17.

Stagner, R. *Psychology of personality* (4th ed.) New York: McGraw-Hill, 1974.

Stricker, L. J., Messick, S., & Jackson, D. N. Conformity, anti-conformity, and dependence: Their dimensionality and generality. *Journal of Personality and Social Psychology,* 1970, *16,* (3), 494–507.

Timmons, E. O., & Noblin, C. D. The differential performance of orals and anals in a verbal conditioning paradigm. *Journal of Consulting Psychology,* 1963, *27,* 383–386.

Whimbey, A. E., & Denenberg, V. H. Programming life histories: Creating individual differences by the experimental control of early experiences. *Multivariate Behavioral Research,* 1966, *1,* 279–286.

7

Situationism in Psychology: An Analysis and a Critique

KENNETH S. BOWERS

Some recent and influential accounts of personality have emphasized the importance of the situational determinants of behavior while minimizing the importance of dispositional or intrapsychic determinants (Farber, 1964; Mischel, 1968). Ascendancy of this *situationism* (Allport, 1966) has been fostered in part by the positivistic approach to science, a Skinnerian model of man (as leavened by social behavior theories; W. Mischel, 1971), and the apparent success of various behavior therapies.

At the same time, the influence of trait theory as a viable model of man has dwindled (Mischel, 1968; Peterson, 1968). Indeed, the present article argues that situationism has served as a necessary and warranted corrective to a trait psychology. In the process, however, situationism has gone too far in the direction of rejecting the role of organismic or intrapsychic determinants of behavior (e.g., Bem, 1972). It is my argument that both the trait and the situationist positions are inaccurate and misleading and that a position stressing the interaction of the person and the situation is both conceptually satisfying and empirically warranted. Despite my disagreement with both the situationist and trait views, a great deal more effort is spent criticizing the former position than the latter one. This critical bias exists because the situationist assault on traits has by and large been quite successful. Since these criticisms are generally

From the *Psychological Review*, 1973, *80*, 307–336. Copyright 1973 by the American Psychological Association. Reprinted by permission.

Work on this article was begun when I was on sabbatical at Stanford University. Grateful appreciation is extended to Ernest R. Hilgard for his generous moral and financial support throughout the year, the latter under his Grant NIH MH 03859-10 from the National Institute of Mental Health. I would like to extend my thanks to Robert Alexander, Ernest Hilgard, Herbert Lefcourt, Donald Meichenbaum, Edward Renner, Michael Ross, Gregory White, and Paul Wachtel for their helpful criticism of an earlier draft of this paper. William Corning, Gary Griffen, and Edward Ware made helpful comments on a later draft. There are two other people who have been particularly helpful to me in arriving at the final version of this paper. One is my wife, Patricia, who likes ideas as much as I do. The other is an anonymous referee whose careful review and trenchant criticism of an earlier draft of this paper (Bowers, 1972) saved me from the public embarrassment of my worst excesses.

available (e.g., Bandura & Walters, 1963; Mischel, 1968), they are not reiterated here.

Although some recent work is beginning to take aim on the situationist point of view (Adinolfi, 1971; Alker, 1972; Carlson, 1971; Harré & Secord, 1972; Wachtel, 1973), there is still a great deal that remains to be said, and the hope is that the present article will help to serve this critical function. And even though the criticism emphasizes the work of relatively few authors, the present article is directed toward a current Zeitgeist, not just two or three embodiments of it. Hopefully, the broad base of the situationist viewpoint is revealed in the works of the relatively few investigators who have been selected to represent it.

Perhaps it is not yet altogether clear what is meant by the term "situationism." Hopefully, the full meaning of this term will emerge during the course of the article, but it is perhaps important to clarify in a preliminary way the domain under consideration. The word "situationism" has been employed instead of the more usual term "behaviorism," largely because the former term immediately calls attention to the explanatory bias espoused by a variety of otherwise heterogenous investigators. Simply stated, situationism's

analysis of the mode of connection of cause and effect is limited by the tendency either to ignore organismic factors, or to regard them as . . . subsidiary to the primary impact of the external stimulus [Harré & Secord, 1972, p. 27].

Indeed, situationism holds that the preservation of objectivity in psychology depends upon the observability of truly causal variables.

Although situationists agree that causal or controlling variables are generally external to the behaving organism, they do differ among themselves regarding the importance of intraorganismic or mediating variables in analysis of behavior. Skinner (1963), for example, objected to central events because "they offer no real explanation [of behavior] and stand in the way of a more effective analysis [p. 951]." Although Mischel has often espoused what seems to be similar sentiments, he has also maintained that "Assessing the acquired meaning of stimuli is the core of social behavior assessment [Mischel, 1968, p. 190]." And Osgood's development of the semantic differential certainly testifies to the important role that meaning, as a mediating variable, can have for the situationist point of view.

Situationists differ among themselves in other ways as well. Indeed, some investigators of situationist persuasion have effectively criticized others of an even more radically behavioristic bent. Bandura, for example, has made it perfectly clear that subjects can learn simply by observation, and that Skinner's insistence upon reinforcement as the sine qua non of learning is unwarranted (Bandura, 1969). Even within the ranks of social behaviorists, there are differences, at least in emphasis. Bandura (1969) and Kanfer (1970) both recognize that intraorganismic factors sometimes prevail over external circumstances in the determination of behavior. Kanfer has gone so far as to state that

the critical antecedent conditions and even the behavioral components in a self-controlled sequence may lie *entirely* in the domain of private experience [p. 179; italics added].

Mischel, on the other hand, though recognizing the importance of meaning in mediating behavior, consistently emphasizes the situational determinants of behavior:

This *utter dependence* of behavior on the details of the specific conditions reflects the great subtlety of the discriminations that people continuously make [Mischel[1]; italics added].

Given the variety of positions represented within the situationist point of view, it might be argued that it is presumptuous and misleading to classify them under one summarizing rubric. It must be acknowledged at the outset that there is indeed some danger in doing so, and that some of the criticisms that will be developed are perhaps less appropriate for certain representatives of situationism than others. Despite these dangers, it seems reasonable to proceed on the basis of what is more or less common to different situationists rather than dwelling any further on their distinctions. Hopefully, whatever distortions are introduced by proceeding in this fashion will not obfuscate the important differences between the situationist model of man and that of the interactionist position developed later in this paper.

One final caveat: The situationist position has generated a great deal of needed change in therapeutic practices. It is *not* the practical utility of situationism that is here being criticized. It is situationism as a model of man that is under attack. As Kanfer (1970) has astutely put it, "The clinical utility of behavioristic models may be limited to pragmatics [p. 212]."

This article is divided into five main sections. The first three sections discuss metaphysical, psychological, and methodological assumptions of situationism; the fourth section deals with an interactionist alternative to situationism, and in a fifth section, situationism and interactionism are compared regarding their interpretation of knowledge and objectivity in science.

METAPHYSICAL ASSUMPTIONS OF SITUATIONISM

The psychologist's view of human behavior is often quite at variance with the layman's. The latter, for example, is often disposed to see human behavior as somehow engendered and explained by qualities of the person—honesty, aggressiveness, stubbornness, and so on. By contrast, the situationist view of personality states that "the study of personality is essentially coterminous with the study of behavior [Farber, 1964, p. 5]," that

behavior is a function of its antecedents . . . and the laws relating behavior to its antecedents can be discovered in the manner of other natural sciences, by the observation and analysis of empirical events [Farber, 1964, p. 6].

Thus, while the layman may view a person as "honest," a situationist is apt to retort that telling the truth is under the control of the circumstances in which it

---

[1] W. Mischel. Specificity theory and the construction of personality. Speech delivered to the Faculty Seminar in Law and Psychology, Stanford University, October 24, 1972.

occurs. Consequently, the situationist is more apt to be interested in conditions that characteristically engender truth telling than in persons who ordinarily tell the truth.

This situationist or stimulus–response (S–R) analysis of behavior appeals to many psychologists because it seems to be an explicitly *causal* analysis. Thus, situationists are fond of contrasting R–R relationships which are "merely correlational" to experimentally determined S–R relationships which are deemed properly causal in nature. As one prominent situationist—Mischel (1968)—has put it,

the causal or controlling factors that determine . . . correlations of course remain uncertain. Correlations among response patterns do not reveal their controlling conditions; the latter can be clarified through experimental investigations [p. 95].

The above comments implicity reveal two metaphysical foibles of situationism that require clarification. Situationism (*a*) misidentifies an S–R *point of view* with the experimental *method* and (*b*) has adopted a limited and limiting understanding of scientific explanation and causality.

Stimulus–Response and Independent–Dependent Variables

Situationism tends to identify S–R relationships with the independent-dependent variable relationships yielded by the experimental paradigm. As it happens, the experimental method as generally employed is differentially sensitive to the impact of situational variables, and correspondingly insensitive to organismic variables. (The reverse is of course true of the correlational model; Cronbach, 1957.) However, the experimental method does not, so to speak, comment on this differential sensitivity; it is simply a procedure for acquiring a controlled observation. Thus, independent–dependent variable relationships are metaphysically neutral. This is not the case for their S–R counterparts, which do carry a great load of metaphysical freight. For example, S–R psychology typically suggests, however implicitly, that individual differences are reducible (at least in principle) to the cumulative impact of empirical differences in the situation. Individual differences constitute the sine qua non of personality theory, and their conceptual reduction to an accumulation of situational differences has led one enthusiastic situationist—Farber (1964)—to remark that, "I, for one, look forward to the day . . . when personality theories are regarded as historical curiosities [p. 37]."

Thus, with the subtly coopted prestige of the experimental method safely ensconced in its corner, the situationist metaphysic has gained ascendancy in the study of personality. As Rychlak (1968) elegantly put it,

the scientifically conscientious personality theorist . . . is unknowingly asked to equate S–R and IV–DV [independent–dependent variables], so that, having proven his proposition through the latter, he protects the integrity of the image of man implicit in the former [p. 217].

The relative insensitivity of the experimental paradigm to organismic factors thus becomes almost a virtue to the situationist; for if independent–dependent variable relationships cannot readily "see" the impact of persons on their behavior, perhaps it is because they are of relatively little importance.

Stimulus–Response and Causality

The whole notion of causality in psychological inquiry is very problematic (Harré & Secord, 1972; Locke, 1972). For many psychologists, the concept of causality seems to presuppose some ultimately reduced level of reality at which causality occurs (for a critique of reductionism, see Jessor, 1958; Koestler & Smythies, 1969). The rule of thumb for knowing when one has reached this level is simply to continue the reduction process until the sequence of observed events is so singularly reliable that the antecedent presence of "A" virtually guarantees the consequent presence of "B." At this point, one has presumably arrived at the level of reality in which input–output relations are revealed in all their pristine causal connectedness.

Some psychologists would rather abandon the notion of causality altogether, preferring instead the term "functional relation" (Skinner, 1953) to describe the connection between independent and dependent variables. In either case, it is a behavioral event that is accounted for or controlled by an environmental event.

The presumed functional or causal relationships that are established between environment and behavior are of undoubted practical importance. But an analysis of input–output events can also be misleadingly superficial. For example, it is true in a very practical sense that letting go of an object (e.g., an apple) "causes" it to fall. There is scarcely a psychological event that occurs with more regularity or predictability. But even if our control over behavior approached the level of control we can have over an apple, we might still have a very primitive understanding of the regularity that confronts us. As far as falling objects are concerned, the whole concept of gravitation is simply left out of the picture if we remain satisfied with the explanation that "letting go" of apples (the independent variable) "causes" them to fall (the dependent variable). If science had been satisfied with an input–output level of analysis, it is doubtful that man would ever have arrived in outer space, where letting go of objects does not "cause" them to fall. It is certainly true that understanding the laws of motion and gravitation does not, for the most part, increase the level of control we have over falling objects on earth. Yet appreciation of these laws behind familiar regularities both deepens our understanding of them and extends the range of observed regularity to less familiar instances of it.

Perhaps this example illustrates how causal explanations cannot simply be reduced to the isolation of observed regularities in nature. Scientific explanation derives from some kind of theoretical perspective appropriate to the regularities at hand. Yet a situationist psychology often seems to suggest that finding a reliable (S–R, response–reinforcement) relationship is tantamount to explaining it; the very words "stimulus" and "response" insinuate that the response *is* a response to the stimulus conditions that generated (caused) it. By contrast, R–R relationships do not seem to imply a causal connection. However, as Dulany (1968) has stated:

we must recongize that R–R relations and S–R relations have the same logical status and equal weight in supporting *theoretical* statements about the *causal influences of unobservables*. The usual objection [to R–R relations] rests on a simple confusion between what we can say about R–R relations and what we can say about the theoretical propositions they support [p. 369].

In other words, causation derives from a theoretical understanding of empirical relationships, whether these relationships be S–R or R–R in nature. This is a much different understanding of causality than the widespread view which simply assumes that antecedents cause consequences. If causality depends upon a theoretical understanding of observable relationships of either the S–R or R–R variety, then the experimental method loses some of its mystique; one cannot simply conclude that antecedent conditions (stimuli) cause the consequent responses.

To be sure, the experimental method does have distinct advantages in some circumstances and for some purposes. Nevertheless, as we shall later see, if the investigator is insensitive to the substantive issues involved in a particular area of inquiry, he may overapply the experimental method and obscure the very phenomena he is trying to clarify.

PSYCHOLOGICAL ASSUMPTIONS OF SITUATIONISM

The metaphysical foibles of situationism outlined above are supplemented by psychological assumptions regarding the nature of behavior and cognition. We will examine these assumptions in turn.

Situationism and Behavior

Behavior which is reinforced is acquired and maintained. The foregoing statement is necessarily true in a Skinnerian analysis of behavior, since a reinforcer is defined as a stimulus that increases the probability of response. There is, however, a distinct tendency for behaviorists to glide noiselessly from this initial assertion to a more problematic one that is *not* true by definition, nor does it follow logically from the definition of reinforcement, namely, behavior which is acquired and maintained is reinforced. Skinner's faith in the psychological validity of this second proposition is revealed by comments such as: "the musician plays or composes what he is reinforced by hearing . . . the artist paints what reinforces him visually [Skinner, 1957, p. 439]," and so on. As Chomsky (1959) was quick to point out, statements like these have entered Skinner into a vicious circle, since the reinforcing character of what is composed or painted is simply inferred from the fact that music was composed and a painting was painted; no longer is reinforcement an observable stimulus independent of the behavior it presumably reinforces. Moreover, it is unclear how inferring reinforcement from behavior in this fashion renders any more objective account of behavior than the mentalistic explanations that Skinner so deplores.

However deficient it may be in some respects, there is no doubt that a Skinnerian functional analysis has been forwarded as a crucially important basis for an objective account of human behavior and misbehavior (e.g., Bandura & Walters, 1963). As Peterson (1968) has noted,

a quasi-Skinnerian behavioral view seems at present to be the foremost candidate to replace the dynamic views which dominated thought about behavior disorders for the first half of the twentieth century [pp. 61–62].

Implicit in such formulations is the notion that ultimately it is the environment that accounts for behavior (Skinner, 1953, 1971). The question to be asked is whether this is a defensible claim.

The challenge of psycholinguistics. Research in psycholinguistics has provided empirical evidence that an organism's history of reinforcement cannot account for the acquisiton of language. For example, as Slobin (1971, p. 49) and others have pointed out, children learn early the correct forms of irregular verbs, such as came, broke, went, and so on. Presumably, this early acquisition of irregular verbs is due to the frequency with which they are used. Since these words are both early-appearing and correct, they are highly reinforced by parents. Nevertheless, these words drop out of the child's vocabulary as he learns the rule for regular verbs. At this point, the child

immediately replaces the correct irregular past tense forms with their incorrect overgeneralizations from the regular forms. Thus children actually say it came off, it broke, and he did it before they say it comed off, it breaked, and he doed it [Slobin, 1971, p. 49].

It is not clear how this sequence of events is consistent with a straightforward reinforcement account. Moreover, it might be noted that the children for whom these observations were made were the oldest siblings in middle-class families. Thus, the children are not likely to have simply modeled the bad grammar of older siblings or uneducated parents.

Lenneberg (1969) has observed children raised by deaf parents to determine whether the unusual nature of their verbal environment had any effect upon their language development. Among other things, Lenneberg found that babies of normal and of deaf parents tend to "fuss" equally often even though hearing parents are much more responsive to the fussing of their children than deaf parents are. "Thus the earliest development of human sounds appears to be relatively independent of the amount, nature, or timing of the sounds made by parents [Lenneberg, 1969, p. 637]."

Brown (1973; Brown & Hanlon, 1970) has reported two additional findings which cast doubt on the assumption that language acquisition can be understood solely in terms of environmental contingencies and constraints. As with Lenneberg, Brown and his colleagues utilized naturalistic observations and found that parents contingently approved not the syntactic structure of their children's utterance but its truth value. For example, the child might say "Mama isn't a boy, he a girl," and be contingently approved for saying so. However, the parents would disapprove correctly stated but inaccurate utterances such as "There's the animal farmhouse," when in fact the object was a lighthouse (Brown & Hanlon, 1970, pp. 45-48).

These same authors also observed that parents made comprehending (sequitor) responses equally often to their children's well-formed utterances as they did to badly formed utterances; similarly, children's well-formed and badly formed utterances received noncomprehending (nonsequitor) responses from their parents about equally often (Brown & Hanlon, 1970, pp. 42 f.). To summarize, children's syntax is neither selectively approved nor is it systematically reinforced by comprehending responses of the parent. Nevertheless, children's syntax improves with age.

While it is evidently true that language acquisition does not depend upon selective reinforcement of the child's early utterances, it is equally true that a child will not learn any language unless he has some contact with a verbal environment. For some retardates growing up in understaffed state institutions and for children of deaf parents, a great deal of language seems to be picked up from television and radio broadcasting (Lenneberg, 1969), which sources cannot, of course, be differentially responsive to the child's own verbal efforts. Evidently, the child's

engagement in language activity can be limited by his environmental circumstances, but the underlying capacity is not easily arrested. Impoverished environments are not conducive to good language development, but good language development is not contingent on specific training measures . . .; a wide variety of rather haphazard factors seems to be sufficient [Lenneberg, 1969, p. 637].

In commenting on these and related findings, Miller and McNeill (1969) have argued that

theories limited to observable stimuli, observable responses, and patterns that can be derived inductively from observable stimuli and responses, cannot explain how we understand the meaning of sentences, because many of the features on which the meaning depends do not exist in the surface structure [i.e., in actual utterances] and have no phonological representation [p. 675].

Slobin (1971) has agreed and has gone on to suggest that

what the child acquires in the course of language development is not a collection of S-R . . . connections, but a complex internal rule system . . . . [The child] is never exposed to the rule system itself, however: he is only exposed to individual sentences in individual situations. How, then, does he acquire the underlying linguistic system on the basis of such evidence [p. 56]?

Slobin continued by saying that apparently

the child has innate means of processing information and forming internal structures, and . . . when these capacities are applied to speech he hears, he succeeds in constructing a grammar of his native language [p. 56].

The importance of psycholinguistics for an understanding of personality may seem remote. Yet Skinner himself has long recognized the challenge that language acquisition proposed to his general theory of behavior (Skinner, 1957). And in emphasizing the biological basis of language, psycholinguists (e.g., Lenneberg, 1967) have raised serious doubts about whether language acquisition can ever be adequately reduced to a functional analysis of stimulus antecedents and response consequences. Since language seems to be the basis for a number of other important human activities (e.g., rule formulating and following), it is possible that a straightforward functional analysis will be inadequate at other levels of behavior as well (cf. Dulany, 1968; Kanfer, 1970, p. 212).

Two ways that environments influence behavior. Before leaving psycholinguistics entirely, it should be noted that it is with regard to this domain that Lenneberg (1960) has made the intriguing distinction between "training" variables and "environmental" variables. The latter simply provide the conditions necessary for the expression of behaviors such as nest building or courting rituals in animals and language acquisition in humans. Training variables refer to the more or less programmatic kinds of environment necessary for the acquisiton of special skills, such as ballet or carpentry. Now it is true that Lenneberg invoked "environmental variables" in connection with more or less innate as opposed to more or less learned behaviors. And it is unquestionably true that humans have fewer "preprogrammed" patterns of behavior than lower animals. Nevertheless, regardless of how a stable pattern of behavior has been acquired, it begins to take on qualities of autonomy and self-regulation that needs an environment more *permitting* than controlling its expression. Thus, in Breland and Breland's (1961) classic paper, "The Misbehavior of Organisms," should pigs or their environment be credited with the "instinctive drift" toward rooting behavior and away from well-practiced, systematically reinforced behavior? Should the varieties of unplanned, arbitrary, and oftentimes stultifying environments be credited with the near-universal acquisiton of language in children, or should we credit children's biocognitive readiness for language?

To extend this reasoning a bit further, consider the implications of a recent review which reported that operantly shaped patient behaviors typically revert to base-line or near-base-line levels after the termination of treatment (Kazdin & Bootzin, 1972). Should this characteristic relapse be attributed to the patient's posttreatment environment (as is typically done by behaviorists), or to some problematic condition of the subject that impairs his ability to function in an environment that does not programmatically reinforce his behavior? Finally, for a person who goes hiking or plays chess wherever and whenever he can, it seems curiously irrelevant to attribute this behavior to evoking and maintaining conditions as Walter Mischel (1968, 1969, 1971) consistently does. Instead, it seems more reasonable to attribute this behavior to a relatively stable pattern of skill, interest, and enjoyment of the activity for its own sake. If it is argued that this account of the matter is simply an explanatory fiction, the very least we can say is that skills, interests, and enjoyment are no more fictional explanations of behavior than is the reinforcement inferred from the occurrence of behavior.

Other evidence. Although psycholinguists have been most vociferous in their attacks upon a behavioristic model, other investigators have presented different kinds of evidence raising doubts about its adequacy. Schaffer and Emerson (1964), for example, interviewed a sample of mothers and adduced evidence for two kinds of infants, cuddlers and noncuddlers. The former sought (or at least accepted) and the latter rejected restriction of their movement such as occurred during feeding, changing, dressing, and so on. On examination of their evidence, the authors concluded that noncuddlers' avoidance of physical contact "is not peculiar to the relationship with the mother or indeed to social relationships in general [Schaffer & Emerson, 1964, p. 11]." See also Escalona (1968, 1972). The authors suggest that there may be a congenital basis for the difference in the two types of children. To be sure, differences of this kind may well have a profound effect on the quality of child-parent interactions and, consequently, upon subsequent infant development (cf. Bell, 1968, 1971; Rheingold, 1969).

A study by Rothbart and Maccoby (1966) also makes it doubtful that statements about persons can be entirely reduced to statements about their past and present circumstances. These investigators took tape-recorded utterances of a four-year-old child whose voice was not identifiably male or female. Some parents (of both sexes) were told that the voice belonged to a girl; others were told it was a boy's voice. The parents were asked to record their immediate reactions to each utterance. Parents' responses were then coded for each item, and items were grouped in seven different scales. Scores on all scales varied from permissiveness for a child's actions to nonpermissiveness.

A pattern of results emerged with fathers showing generally greater permissiveness toward girls than boys for both dependency and aggression, and with mothers showing greater permissiveness toward boys than girls [Rothbart & Maccoby, 1966, p. 237].

The authors pointed out that their results provide some difficulty for a social learning interpretation of sex differences in behavior. According to that view,

Dependent behaviors are less rewarded for males, and physically aggressive behaviors are less rewarded for females, in our culture; consequently there are mean differences between the sexes in the frequency of such behaviors after the first few years of life [Mischel, 1966, p. 75].

According to Rothbart and Maccoby (1966), it may well be that children are in fact not provided with a consistent reinforcement history for sex-typed behaviors. Parents evidently differ regarding what behaviors they reinforce, and a particular parent may be inconsistent by reinforcing some sex-type behaviors but not others. Moreover, sex differences in aggression have been observed before nonparental reinforcers become important in the child's environment. Generally, the findings of the Rothbart and Maccoby investigation fail to support the interpretation that differential reinforcement from both parents is of a kind to promote these differences at this early age level. Perhaps there is a biological component in these sex differences which is of importance either in its own right or in interaction with socialization practices [p. 243].

Interestingly, sex role identity is one area in which the social learning view and a more cognitive view have come into sharp focus. In a particularly illuminating passage, Kohlberg (1966) stated:

The social-learning syllogism is: "I want rewards, I am rewarded for doing boy things, therefore I want to be a boy." In contrast, a cognitive theory assumes this sequence: "I am a boy, therefore I want to do boy things, therefore the opportunity to do boy things (and to gain approval for doing them) is rewarding" [p. 89].

For a cognitive position, then, gender identity establishes what kind of events and stimuli are apt to be reinforcing, whereas reinforcement is the basis for sex role identity in social learning theory. *Neither* position totally ignores or dismisses either cognition or reinforcement as a basis for behavior. But a "biocognitive"[2] or interactionist position tends to emphasize that both behavior and reinforcement are subject to the selection and guidance of biocognitive structures. In the social behaviorist view, on the other hand, cognition is subject to and mediates the impact of external conditions and contingencies. It is to this latter view of cognition that we now turn.

Situationism and Cognition

As previously noted, situationism is methodologically biased toward enviromental explanations of behavior. It is not surprising, therefore, that psychologists of a situationist persuasion are ambivalent regarding the role of cognitive determinants of behavior. For example, Farber (1964) stated that

mental events exist, and in a commonsense way we know what we mean when we refer to them, but it is unnecessary to appeal to them in a thorough-going account of behavior [p. 8].

On the other hand, he does not want to "preclude the possibility that some kinds of systematic analyses of mental contents . . . may serve a useful purpose in the discovery of behavioral laws [p. 8]."

Similarly, Bandura and Walters (1963) argued that:

our social learning theory, instead of regarding internal processes as primary links in causal sequences that generate deviant patterns of response, treats such processes as mediating events . . . which must be inferred from the conjunction of certain manipulable stimulus conditions and observable response sequences [pp. 30–31].

---

[2] The term biocognitive is used here and on a few other occasions for several interrelated reasons: (a) It reminds the reader that cognition is rooted in the biological development of the organism (Flavell, 1963); (b) it emphasizes the extent to which our understanding and knowledge of external reality is inextricably a function of our biocognitive organization and development; and (c) it serves to distinguish the cognitive psychologist's concept of cognition from the situationist's view as the latter is outlined in the next section.

Although Mischel is now clearly coming to a position that emphasizes the role of cognition in behavior (e.g., Mischel, 1973a),[3] he has consistently viewed cognition primarily as a mediator of external causes. For example, in distinguishing a social learning view from a cognitive approach, Mischel (1966) stated:

In the present formulation, discriminable antecedent events, rather than inferred intrapsychic activities, are used to predict and analyze behavior. Thus, although the existence of mediating processes is acknowledged, they are not attributed the causal powers usually assigned to them in "cognitive" and "dynamic" theories. Instead, behavior is predicted on the basis of an analysis of the relevant social-learning history and the specific stimulus situations and contingencies in which the predicted behavior occurs [p. 62].

In another passage, Mischel (1968) argued that

Sometimes mental traits and states are invoked as if they were the causes of behavior while their own antecedents are ignored or forgotten. Unfinished causal sequences are found whenever mental states (cognitions, affects, motives, etc.) are employed as explanations of behavior while the determinants of the mental states themselves are omitted from the analysis [p. 95].

On yet another occasion, Mischel (1971) began a section with the question: "Are cognitions the causes of behavior?" He answered his own question as follows: "In spite of the obvious importance of personal constructs and other cognitions, one cannot assume that they are the main causes of the person's behavior . . . [p. 104]." Later, in the next paragraph, subtitled "Incomplete explanations," Mischel stated:

Perhaps the most fundamental criticism of cognitive and phenomenological explanations is that they are incomplete and do not provide a sufficiently detailed and comprehensive analysis of the causes controlling behavior. In [George] Kelly's theory, for example, personal constructs are viewed as key determinants of behavior, but what determines the constructs that a person has? Offering the construct as a cause of the observed behavior may be an example of an unfinished causal explanation. Such unfinished analyses are found whenever mental states, perceptions, cognitions, feelings, motives, or similar constructs are offered as explanations of behavior while the determinants of the mental states themselves are ignored [p. 104].

At this point, Mischel favorably invoked Skinner's term "mental way stations" as a means of characterizing the role of cognitions in behavior. Needless to say, the role of these "way stations" in an explanation of behavior is problematic.

---

[3] Just before finishing the final draft of this paper, I received Mischel's (1973) latest paper entitled, "Toward a Cognitive Social Learning Reconceptualization of Personality." Mischel's clarification of the importance of cognition for social learning theory is most welcome. It should be pointed out, however, that his latest formulation represents a fairly substantial shift in emphasis from earlier accounts. As if to underscore this shift, Mischel has largely abandoned references to "social learning theory" or "social behavior theory" as the phrase summarizing his position, and is instead calling it "cognitive social learning." It will not be possible for me to consider Mischel's reformulation in any detail, and my comments will necessarily focus on his earlier and very influential accounts (e.g., Mischel, 1968, 1969, 1971).

According to Skinner (1953)

> The objection to inner states is not that they do not exist, but that they are not relevant in a functional analysis. We cannot account for the behavior of any system while staying wholly inside it; eventually we must turn to forces operating upon the organism from without. Unless there is a weak spot in our causal chain so that the second link is not lawfully determined by the first, or the third by the second, then the first and third links must be lawfully related. If we must always go back beyond the second link for prediction and control, we may avoid many tiresome and exhausting digressions by examining the third link as a function of the first. Valid information about the second link may throw light on this relationship but can in no way alter it [p. 35].

The above passage clearly suggests that cognitions are superfluous to an objective understanding of behavior, even if they are not simply epiphenomenal, as Immergluck (1964) suggested. And in the following comment, we begin to understand why cognitions are so regarded even by very sophisticated neo-behaviorists:

> It is one thing to use notions like "competence," "knowledge" and "rules" as heuristic devices, as sources of hypotheses about performance; it is quite another thing to use them as *explanations* of performance—unless, of course, one is ready to give up his behavioristic moorings entirely in exchange for a frankly dualistic mentalism [Osgood, 1968, p. 505].

The mere mention of the word "mentalism" offends the sensibilities of a behaviorist in much the same way the word "masturbation" offends polite company. Consequently, ambivalence regarding cognition has sometimes led situationism into a hesitant and conflictful compromise between equivocating acceptance and outright rejection of mental events as explanations of behavior. The compromise position seems to regard reliance upon perceptual-cognitive explanations of behavior as a temporary expedient, and to consider the extent of their use to be a measure of our ignorance about the real determinants of behavior, which of course are presumed to be properly observable, at least in principle. This delaying tactic permits one to proceed as if perceptions and cognitions are temporarily useful, but ultimately specious. Thus, cognitions are scientific slaves, useful until the pyramids of science are complete, and then surreptitiously entombed in the monuments they helped construct. In this way, situationists can proclaim their philosophical purity (when the occasion arises) while promiscuously exploiting philosophically problematic notions of cognitions and constructs in their research. This "compromise" perhaps explains how cognitions can be both important and impotent at the same time. It also conveys one sense in which cognitive and phenomenological explanations are incomplete: They are incomplete until their situational determinants are uncovered; then they are obsolete.

Cognitions may also be considered incomplete in the sense that they have to be considered in conjunction with the environment in explaining behavior. Yet this sense of incompleteness suggests that behavior is also incompletely accounted for by its antecedent conditions. Indeed, the "test" question for the situationist is this: Would a thorough knowledge of antecedent inputs producing a particular behavioral effect also be considered an incomplete explanation? Or would such antecedents simply be accepted as *the* causal explanation, without further reference to such "mental way stations" as constructs, cognitions, perceptions, and so on.

Implicit in the above remarks is situationism's understanding that cognition is primarily a *response* to external events. It is precisely this assumption that has given cognitions the status of mediators of truly causal variables located outside the organism. To be sure, cognitive responses to external stimuli can themselves have stimulus properties, which can in turn engender overt responses. Nevertheless, so long as cognition is viewed primarily as a response mediating the causal impact of external stimuli, it cannot easily be viewed as initiating, maintaining, or explaining behavior (cf. Slobin, 1971, pp. 89 f.).

METHODOLOGICAL BIASES OF SITUATIONISM

Situationism presupposes the distinction between stimulus and response, and explains the latter in terms of the former. If a response is not accounted for in terms of a stimulus (either evoking or reinforcing), then (according to situationism) we have implicitly abandoned any claim to an objective account of behavior. The methodological guarantor of objectivity thus resides in the systematic application of the experimental method on one hand, and a functional (operant) analysis of behavior on the other. In the former method, the eliciting role of antecedent conditions is emphasized; in the latter, the reinforcing character of stimuli is central. Although both methods have their foibles, we shall at this point concentrate most of our critical remarks upon situationism's devotion to the experimental method.

Problematic Aspects of the Experimental Method

In the first place, the nearly exclusive use of the experimental method can fasten our attention on behavior *change* in a way that makes us inattentive to whatever behavioral stability exists. Recent research in hypnosis presents a particularly good example of this tendency. Barber (1969) has extensively advocated a positivistic application of the experimental paradigm to hypnosis, by which he found that variations in stimulus antecedents lead to variations in response consequences. In his conceptualization of hypnosis, he has systematically emphasized these treatment effects, virtually to the exclusion of striking and stable individual differences in hypnotic susceptibility (Hilgard, 1965, which even Barber, 1969, himself found and reported).

The point is that it is easier to notice behavior change with the experimental method, and behavioral stability with correlational techniques. Thus doth method move our minds to differing perceptions of reality: What a preferred method does not readily see can become less and less important to our conceptualization of the phenomena; what a method sees easily sometimes becomes the sole basis of our understanding. Since situationist users of the experimental method often seem to be less tolerant of correlational techniques than correlationists are of experimental techniques, psychology tends to be biased in the direction of a situationist view of human behavior (Cronbach, 1957).

There are several problems with this method-bound outlook. Instances in which *apparently* changed environments do not lead to corresponding changes in the behavior are oftentimes considered nonevents. It is as if a "truly" changed environment (like "true" insight of yore) will almost by definition produce changed behavior. The fact that a great deal of environmental tinkering is often necessary before clear treatment effects emerge is often shrouded from public view by the nonpublication of negative results. More important, such tinkering, when it is unsuccessful in rejecting the null hypothesis, is seldom taken as evidence regarding the relative stability of behavior across situations. Now, if one wants to argue that behavior is situation specific, then it must be possible to conclude that it is *not* situation specific; otherwise, the assertion that behavior is situation specific is nonfalsifiable. In other words, if (truly) changed environments can only be inferred from changed behavior, then the potential circularity of the situationist model becomes actual and vicious.

In light of these comments, consider the following proposition:

> When the eliciting and evoking conditions that maintain behavior change—as they generally do across settings—then behavior will surely change also [Mischel, 1969, p. 1016].

It is possible to view this comment as completely circular: When does behavior change? When the situation does. How do you know when the eliciting and evoking conditions change? When the behavior does. Viewed in this way, behavior becomes situation specific because it is impossible for it not to be situation specific.

Presumably, Mischel does not wish to endorse such a circular argument, and has offered the proposition quoted above as a sort of metahypothesis that is capable of disconfirmation. In principle, one could argue that this meta-hypothesis is in fact disconfirmed every time negative results are obtained from an experimental study of personality. In effect, such negative outcomes suggest that the dependent variable in question is stable across various treatment conditions. In order to interpret negative results in this fashion, however, one has to regard the various treatment conditions as truly different. In other words, we must be willing at some point to decide that negative results mean that the experimental hypothesis is not true, instead of questioning the adequacy of the procedures used to test the hypothesis.

How then are decisions made about the adequacy of one's experimental procedures? They can be legitimately made on theoretical, intuitive, or com-monsense grounds. But all too often, the adequacy of the manipulation is (implicitly) inferred from the outcome of the experiment, in a manner quite analogous to the circular way in which a reinforcing stimulus is often inferred from changed behavior.

Of course no one actually propounds such a circular argument, but psychologists sometimes proceed as if the situational specificity of behavior were irrefutably true instead of a disconfirmable (meta-) hypothesis. This tendency is both revealed and fostered by the habit of not taking negative results seriously, that is, as evidence for the falsity of the experimental hypothesis.

If negative results *are* taken seriously, an experiment can in fact be veiwed as *successful*, insofar as it suggests that meaningful behavioral stabilities are asserting themselves in the face of treatment differences. To be sure, it is helpful to demonstrate that the variance preventing treatment differences does not reflect mere random error, but is instead attributable to some correlated characteristic of the experimental subjects. However, in the face of a negative outcome, the usual strategy is to devise yet another treatment manipulation, not to investigate those characteristics of individuals which prevented treatment effects from occurring in the first place.

This situationist strategy is tempered somewhat by the occasional use of stratified samples, matched-subjects design, and/or pretesting subjects on a task pertinent to the dependent variable in question. Even when these methods are employed, however, it is often to enhance the likelihood of achieving treatment effects, not out of intrinsic interest in the subject variance. Treatment effects are valued by situationism; subject effects typically are not (e.g., Barber, 1969). It is thus curiously ironic that it is precisely the presence of subject effects in an experimental outcome which helps us to use the experimental method in a noncircular fashion. Instead of inferring that null results simply reflect the inadequacies of our treatment manipulation, we have the option of asserting that the two conditions may have indeed been different, but that they simply did not make a difference in the face of overriding behavioral stabilities.

A clear implication of the above remarks is that behavior has greater stability than situationism commonly recognizes, and that this stability does not necessarily depend upon the continuing presence of situational factors that may have helped to engender behavior change in the first place. The claim of behavioral stability across situations has ordinarily been identified with a trait psychology, and it is time to investigate the trait–situationism debate more thoroughly.

Trait versus Situational Sources of Behavioral Variance

The "classical" trait view (a) employs correlational techniques, (b) suggests that an individual's behavior should be relatively constant from one situation to the next, and (c) suggests that in the same situation, individual differences should emerge. Thus, the trait model provides for transsituational similarity of behavior within persons, and for subject differences in behavior within situations.

Situationism, on the other hand, (a) tends to employ experimental (or operant) techniques, (b) suggests that an individual's behavior should change from one situation to the other, and (c) regards individual differences in behavior within the same situation as something of an embarrassment—to be conceptualized as the result of past experience or simply as error variance. Thus, the situationist model provides for transsituational differences in behavior within subjects and for minimal subject variation within situations.

The situationist assault on the trait model has been more or less limited to demonstrating that within subjects, transsituational differences in behavior are more pervasive than the trait model suggests they should be. Almost invariably, the Hartshorne and May (1928) studies on deceit are invoked to press this point home. In this classic investigation, the honesty of children was quite variable from one temptation situation to another. Overall, the data seemed to suggest that children's behavior was less a function of an internal disposition to be honest and more a function of the particular temptation circumstances.

Actually, it is never clear just how much behavioral variation of this kind is consistent with a trait approach. Does trait theory become unraveled because the usually honest man lies to a rapist concerning the whereabouts of his wife? Transsituational variation is clearly an embarrassment to trait theory, just as subject differences within situations are awkward for situationism. Exactly when such embarrassment turns to disenchantment is an individual matter, but the judgment of one disillusioned trait theorist—Peterson (1968)—is certainly worth serious consideration. He stated:

the generality of these [personality] measures over method and situation was still not high enough to justify perpetuating the traditional conceptions of personality. . . . The findings required abandonment of a line of research to which I had devoted ten years of my life as a psychologist. The results also required a change in beliefs about the nature of personality. This research, per se, did not say which way the conceptual shift should go, but it suggested very strongly that traditional conceptions of personality as internal behavior dispositions were inadequate and insufficient [p. 23].

What must be emphasized is that rejection of traits is not synonomous with acceptance of situationism. For example, Wallach and Leggett (1972) have recently argued *for* behavioral consistency but *against* traits as an explanation of it. The situationist, for his part, is apt to disagree with the proposition that behavior is consistent across changing circumstances. For evidence, he is apt to invoke the successes of operant conditioning and social learning theory. It is inarguable that these developments have contributed a great deal to our understanding of how the environment influences behavior. Nevertheless, whether situationism is correct in advocating the situational specificity of behavior is subject to empirical test.

Some empirical evidence. This author has been able to locate 11 articles published since 1959 that evaluate the relative magnitude of person and situational influences on behavior. These studies have employed the analysis of variance model in an unusual manner. Instead of simply testing for a significant F, these studies have partitioned the sources of variance into various components in a way that allow one to determine the percentage of variance due to situations, to persons, and to Situation X Person interactions. Moreover, if broad factor categories like anxiety are employed, the percentage of variance due to specific modes of anxiety response can also be determined. For example, one person may tend to express anxiety more with muscular tension than with speech disturbances, whereas the reverse may be true of another individual. Such modes of response can of course enter into interactions with situations and with persons. In this brief review, however, I have concentrated on the Person X Setting interactions. Table 1 summarizes the findings of these studies.

It is helpful to anticipate what the trait theorist and the situationist might expect from such an analysis. Trait theory would suggest that the percentage of variance due to persons would be of overwhelming importance, since behavior is presumably determined primarily by a person's trait structures. Situationism, on the other hand, would suggest that most of the variance would be due to circumstances and little if any to the individual. In any event, situationism would certainly assert that the percentage of variance due to situations would exceed the percentage of variance due to persons (Argyle & Little, 1972).

At first, it looked as if this state of affairs might indeed be true. In an early (untabled) study by Endler, Hunt, and Rosenstein (1962), the authors found that the mean square for situations was up to 11 times the size of the mean square for persons. From this finding, Endler et al. were led to conclude that

the fact that a sampling of situations can contribute over 11 times the amount of variance contributed by individual differences among a sampling of Ss should give pause to clinicians, personologists, and psychometricians in general [p. 12].

In later publications, however, Endler and Hunt (1966, 1969) gracefully conceded that they had erred in drawing this conclusion. They acknowledged that the mean square due to settings and persons does not directly reflect the percentage of variance due to these sources. Included in Table 1 are the data for the Endler and Hunt (1966, 1969) studies on the S–R Inventory of Anxiousness which indicate that person variance is slightly in excess of setting variance.

More generally, the data in Table 1 clearly indicate that neither trait nor the situationist predictions are borne out. Far too little of the total variance ($\overline{X} = 12.71\%$) is due to the person to justify a thoroughgoing trait position. On the other hand, the percentage of variance due to situations is also meager ($\overline{X} = 10.17\%$). In fact, in 11 out of 19 comparisons, the percentage of variance due to situations is *less* than the variance attributable to persons. Furthermore, the interaction of persons and settings accounts for a higher percentage of variance than either main effect in 14 of 18 possible comparisons, and in 8 out of 18 comparisons the interaction term accounts for more variance than the sum of the main effects. The mean percentage of variance attributable to the Person X Situation interaction is 20.77%. Not represented in Table 1 is the fact that in some of the studies, modes of response (singly and in interaction with situations and persons) account for even more percentage variance than the tabled sources do. It also seems to be true that main effects due to persons are less evident in normal than in disturbed people.

The data in Table 1 can conveniently be subdivided into three major categories:

Table 1. Summary of Studies that Utilized the Analysis of Variance to Determine the Percentage of Variance Accounted for by the Situation, Persons, and the Situation X Person Interaction

Study	Setting (S)	Person (P)	S X P
Raush, Dittman, & Taylor (1959) Subjects = six hyperaggressive boys across six settings (averaged across two sets of observations).	2.50	2.22	11.30
Raush, Farbman, & Llewellyn (1960) Subjects = six normal control subjects matched with above subjects at age of first observation.	7.31	2.42	21.22
Subjects = six normal control subjects matched with above subjects at age of second observation.	7.30	3.29	22.41
Moos (1968) Subjects = 30 psychiatric patients across nine settings (data averaged across five different factors).	1.70	29.96	16.95
Subjects = 10 professional staff across nine settings (data averaged across five different factors).	12.56	6.78	25.41
Moos (1969) Subjects = 16 psychiatric patients across six different settings using self-report ratings on two different occasions (a and b) three months apart. Data are averaged across nine rating scales.	(a) 3.64 (b) 7.63	17.63 17.34	23.33 22.31
Subjects = same 16 patients, six settings, and two occasions (a and b) employing observer enumerations of subject behavior. Data are averaged across eight behavior categories.	(a) 19.79 (b) 23.31	23.01 21.98	29.21 28.01
Moos (1970) Subjects = 12 psychiatric patients across six settings, employing change scores from early to later assessment on subject rating scales. Data are averaged across eight dimensions.	.25	8.48	30.51
Subjects = same 12 psychiatric patients and six settings employing change scores from early to later assessment on observer ratings of subject behavior. Data are averaged across seven behavior categories.	3.08	9.93	32.27
Endler & Hunt (1966) Subjects = 289 students on S–R Inventory of Anxiousness. Data are averaged across three university samples.	6.20	7.68	9.97
Endler & Hunt (1968) Subjects = 264 men averaged across alternate forms of the S–R Hostility Inventory and across four university samples.	5.23	19.12	13.02

Table 1 (*continued*)

	Percentage of variance due to:		
Study	Setting (S)	Person (P)	S × P
Subjects = 235 women averaged across alternate forms of the S–R Hostility Inventory and across four university samples.	7.18	16.20	11.16
Endler & Hunt (1969) Median percentage variance across 22 *samples* of males on S–R Inventory of Anxiousness.	3.95	4.44	9.14
Median percentage variance across 21 *samples* of females on S–R Inventory of Anxiousness.	7.78	4.56	9.31
Nelsen, Grinder, & Mutterer (1969) Subjects = 47 boys and 59 girls averaging about 11.8 years old across six temptation situations.	14.15	20.70[a]	No solution[b]
Argyle & Little (1972) Subjects = 23 polytechnical students rating their own behavior vis-à-vis 12 specific target persons. Data are averaged over 18 bipolar constructs.	43.6	16.1	40.2
Endler (1973) Subjects = 308 normal and abnormal persons responding to an S–R Inventory of General Trait Anxiousness.	16.11	9.66	18.14

[a]The scores of this study actually represent an average of four different ways of treating the data. The authors applied both a random and fixed effects analysis of variance to findings that were scored as both interval and dichotomous data. For person effects, the four different results were 14.7%, 18.1%, 26.4%, and 23.6%. For setting effects, the results were 14.3%, 15.5%, 12.9%, and 13.9%.

[b]Since each subject was observed only once in each situation, there was no error term for the interaction variance.

1. The first category employs S–R inventories in which the subject is asked to respond to various (10–14) stimulus situations on a 5-point rating scale in each of several (10–14) response categories. (For example, one of the stimulus items reads: "Someone pushes ahead of you in a theatre line" and one of the rating categories reads: "Feel irritated; not at all . . . very much.") The Endler and Hunt (1966, 1968, 1969) studies are all of this type. A slight variation of this format is utilized by Endler (1973) and by Argyle and Little (1972). Notice that these data are derived from introspective reports by subjects whose past experience with similar situations is the basis for their ratings. The data from these studies are relatively easy to collect, and consequently, the *N*s are generally large. For example, in their 1969 article, Endler and Hunt

reported the median percentage variance due to persons and situations across 22 *samples* of males and 21 *samples* of females.

2. The second kind of data are also based upon self-observation. However, in this case, the stimulus is a real situation, not a hypothetical one. In other words, the subjects are actually exposed to one of several (up to 11) situations. Immediately after their participation in such settings, subjects are given a questionnaire on which they rate their experiences on several (9-33) scales tapping affect, feelings of trust, affiliativeness, etc. Some of Moos' (1968, 1969, 1970) data is of this kind. The logistics of using actual situations as the stimulus for subjects' self-observation are much more onerous than Endler and Hunt's procedure, and hence the Ns are much smaller (Ns range from the 12-40). Moreover, Moos' subjects were either psychiatric patients or professional staff in psychiatric settings, whereas Endler and Hunt usually employed college students as subjects.

3. The third kind of data is based on actual behavior or on observation of behavior in specific situations. This procedure requires an on the spot observer, and hence the Ns are relatively small. Some of Moos' (1969, 1970) studies are of this kind. The Raush et al. (1959, 1960) studies and the Nelsen, Grinder, and Mutterer (1969) study are all of this kind.

When these three different kinds of studies are classified in terms of whether the setting or person effects are larger, Table 2 is the result. Although the N is too small for satisfactory statistical computation, it is apparent that self-report measures are more often subject to weightier person effects than observed behaviors are. In no category was there a clear advantage of setting over person effects. Thus, irrespective of whether the dependent variable consists of behavior or self-ratings, both the trait and the situationist hypotheses seem seriously compromised by the data presented in Tables 1 and 2. Clearly, some kind of reformulation of the situationist-trait issue is in order. In this regard, the relatively large percentage of variance accounted for by the interactions is helpful. Obviously, and to some considerable extent, the person and the situation are codeterminers of behavior, and they need to be specified simultaneously if predictive accuracy is desired.

Table 2. Classification of Comparisons in which Setting Effects Exceed those of Persons (and vice versa) across Three Types of Dependent Measures

Variance	Behavior observation	Self-rating	Stimulus–response type inventories
Person variance greater than setting variance	3	3	5
Setting variance greater than person variance	4	1	3

Some ecological implications of Table 1. It would, of course, be quite possible to "prove" either the trait or the situationist point of view by employing the same methods that have here "disproved" both approaches. The trait view could be vindicated by selecting subject extremes (e.g., on hypnotic susceptibility) and monitoring the one (i.e., hypnotic) type of situation in which the subject differences will be most apparent. Alternatively, one could select a reasonably homogeneous group of subjects (e.g., college sophomores) and monitor their behavior in two entirely different situations (e.g., church versus a football game), thereby "proving" the situationist point of view. Of course, part of the value of the tabled studies is that they do not attempt to prove either point of view; they simply sample persons' behaviors over a sample of life circumstances. Consequently, the tabled data have a certain claim upon our credibility regarding the usual percentage of variance accounted for by persons and situations (allowing for the fact that many of the studies utilized psychiatrically disturbed subjects).

Incidentally, the comments in the preceding paragraph imply a generally unrecognized limitation of the experimental method as it is usually employed in psychology. Ordinarily, a distribution of subjects is randomly assigned to treatment conditions that are *not* randomly selected. Indeed, the latter are selected precisely because it is presumed they will make a difference to the behavioral outcome; few investigators try to prove the null hypothesis. It should not be surprising, therefore, that in planned experiments, the treatment variance is ordinarily expected to exceed the subject variance. (If it is anticipated that subject variance may be problematic, it can be eliminated by design—so to speak—never to reappear in a significance test, for lack of a proper error term.) Moreover, the population of environments from which the treatment and control conditions are "sampled" almost inevitably remains unknown. Ignorance on this score implicitly sanctions disregard for the representativeness of the treatment conditions, and encourages efforts to discover lawful S–R connections without respect to the ecological validity of the findings. Indeed, the more variance accounted for by antecedent conditions, the more indubitably lawful an S–R connection seems to be. Thus, we virtually never speak of "inflated" amounts of variance due to (sometimes extreme) treatment differences, whereas apologies are definitely in order if one reports an r^2 based on extreme groups of subjects. This asymmetry in our attitude toward the size of treatment and subject variance is a natural consequence of the fact that we generally know much less about the population of environments sampled than we do about the subject population. In other words, the issue of validity has been raised almost exclusively with regard to measurement of subjects and only occasionally with respect to environments (e.g., Brunswik, 1955).

The fact that treatment conditions are generally imposed without regard to their representativeness is a serious problem for psychology, for even under the unlikely event that a treatment manipulation accounted for 100% of the variance in subjects' behavior, it still remains to be asked whether the variance so accounted for is psychologically important. To answer *that* question, we must often rely upon naturalistic and clinical studies, and upon correlational and interactional analyses of data. This is a direction that research in psycholinguistics has taken, with some very interesting results summarized previously. It is not surprising, therefore, that noted psycholinguists—(Brown & Hanlon, 1970)—have recently commented as follows:

> The history of psychology generally and of psycholinguistics in particular shows that careful experimental work provides no sure path to the truth. Neither does naturalism. There are rich opportunities for error in either method. But on the whole, the opportunities arise at different points, and when the methods are used in combination, the truth has a chance to appear [p. 52].

The wisdom of such an eclectic approach contrasts sharply with situationism's attempt to chase "lawful" S-R, antecedent-consequent relationships across thousands of journal pages, while minimizing the importance of unconstrained behavior and individual differences. It is the latter, of course, which reveals and reflects just those dispositional, characterological, and stylistic qualities of behavior that are not clearly under stimulus control, and which are therefore viewed with suspicion by psychologists who prefer behavior to have objective (i.e., visible) antecedents and/or consequences that evoke and maintain it. Thus, in his highly influential book, *Personality and Assessment*, Michel (1968) derogated the

> small [about .30] albeit statistically significant relations between individual difference measures and behavior. . . . These weak associations, accounting for a *trivial* portion of the variance, become understandable when the *enormous* variance due to situationally specific variables that determine the consequences for behavior in any particular context is recognized [pp. 82–83; italics added].[4]

Situationists will sometimes object to their position being characterized as one that neglects or minimizes individual differences. Mischel (1968), for example, stated that "It would be a complete misinterpretation [of his position] to conclude that individual differences are unimportant [p. 38]." It is fair to state, however, that Mischel's own research has by no means emphasized individual differences; a sample of his investigations published since 1963[5] reveals that 7 out of 12 articles are virtually mute in this regard. In only 2 of the studies could

---

[4] In all fairness, Mischel himself has begun to realize that this position is untenable. In his most recent book (Mischel, 1971), he stated that

we may predict best if we know what each situation means to the individual, and consider the interaction of the person and the setting, rather than concentrating either on the situation itself or on the individual in an environmental and social vacuum [p. 149].

[5] Articles included in this sample were selected from the reference lists of Mischel's two books (1968, 1971) and from the *Journal of Personality and Social Psychology* from 1970 through May 1973. Only journal articles reporting original research were included, and then only if Mischel was senior author. The survey was begun in 1963 for symbolic reasons: it was exactly a decade ago that Bandura and Walters (1963) published their highly influential book *Social Learning and Personality Development*, which articulated the basic rationale behind the social learning position.

individual differences properly be said to constitute a focus of real concern. Barber, for his part, virtually never runs an experiment in which subjects are selected for their hypnotic susceptibility, despite overwhelming evidence concerning its importance (Hilgard, 1965). More generally, a recent review of the personality literature found that 128 out of 226 journal articles (57%) ignored subject variables altogether (Carlson, 1971). In this same review, only 51 studies (22%) compared sexes despite the fact that in 74% of these latter studies, sex was a significant factor. Evidently, subject variables are of relatively minor interest to current investigators in personality research. The lack of interest in subject variables reflects a lack of interest in persons, because in the series of studies reviewed by Carlson (1971), *"not a single published study attempted even minimal inquiry into the organization of personality variables within the individual* [p. 209]." So distressed was the author by this tendency to ignore subject variables in personality research that she entitled her article with a question: "Where is the person in personality research?"

Persons are still around of course, but their central importance for a psychology of personality has been obscured by the metaphysical and methodological biases of situationism. Indeed, a great deal of current research in personality exemplifies the methodological bigotry that Kaplan (1964) had in mind when he stated that occasionally

a conspicuously successful technique in some area of behavioral science is not only identified with "scientific method," but comes to be so mechanically applied that it undermines the very spirit of scientific inquiry [p. 29].

Further implications of Table 1. There are several other implications of the studies listed in Table 1 which require our attention. As Raush et al. (1959) pointed out in their study of hyperaggressive boys, the effects due to individual differences were "considerably enhanced" when the situation effects were held constant. And conversely, setting effects were much higher when examined for each child individually. This is a rather novel way of demonstrating that subject variation tends to obscure treatment effects, and that the role of individual differences can be rendered invisible by looking at one person's behavior over different situations.

The Skinnerian legacy of studying one organism at a time clearly has its virtues. However, employing this strategy makes it virtually impossible to see how different situations affect different individuals differently; the very possibility for an interaction term disappears. Yet it is precisely these interaction effects which help remind us that the environment is not monolithically responsible for behavior. This point totally escaped Farber (1964) when he stated that,

When we know the objective conditions under which a given behavior or behavioral characteristic occurs, we can explain any relevant behavior in terms of those conditions [pp. 28–29].

In an operant approach to behavior, it is of course quite legitimate to keep altering the reinforcement contingencies until an effective treatment regimen for a particular person is discovered. However, it cannot simply be concluded from successful conditioning of this sort that the situation accounts for behavior. For if instead of such an individualized program of conditioning we kept the situation constant and sought the person who operated most effectively within it (the standard procedure in personnel selection), we would be obliged, by some principle of symmetry, to conclude that intrapsychic determinants accounted for the behavior in question. The argument being advanced here is that neither conclusion is entirely warranted. Nevertheless, the many case studies reported in the behavior modification literature (e.g., Ullmann & Krasner, 1965) seem to suggest an omnipotence of the environment that it simply does not possess, except of course in the sense that it can be so hostile as to make life itself impossible.

The studies listed in Table 1 also remind us that behaviors differ in their vulnerability to situational influences. Moos (1969), for example, found that as far as patient smoking behavior was concerned, 41.9% of the variance was due to persons, whereas only 7.1% was due to the setting. For talking, the situation was pretty much reversed, with 68.3% of the variance due to settings and only 10.5% due to persons. Clearly, "The percentage of variance accounted for by different sources of variance varied greatly depending upon the particular behavior being considered [Moos, 1969, p. 409]." In other words, some behaviors are much more susceptible to environmental influences than others. Consequently, it cannot simply be assumed that success in changing one kind of behavior will mean similar success in changing another kind of behavior. Indeed, certain behaviors such as smoking, homosexuality, and infantile autism are often remarkably resistant to treatment efforts, and require massive and sometimes futile expenditures of resources to modify them permanently. Again, failure in achieving a "cure" for these behaviors is seldom taken by situationists as evidence of the role of organismic or intrapsychic factors in perpetuating the behavior; instead it simply suggests to them that the corrective situation remains undiscovered. In a sense, this attitude has a grain of truth to it. Nevertheless, one could almost wish for a metric that would indicate just how much expenditure of effort and resources is necessary to change a given problematic behavior. The size of this index could then be employed as a rough measure of the degree to which the behavior in question was originally attributable to characteristics of the person instead of to evoking and maintaining conditions.

Traits and Situationism; An Overview

It is time to bring the threads of my argument together. I have argued that situationism has thrived in part because of a misidentification of method and metaphysics, and in part because it has managed to minimize the role of individual differences in psychology. As a consequence, we have been left with an almost religious allegiance to a main effects psychology that emphasizes the situational impact on behavior almost to the exclusion of person or interaction effects (Vale & Vale, 1969). There is, perhaps a good reason for this state of affairs.

The psychology of personality was dominated for a long time by reifying intrapsychic traits as the explanations of behavior. The tendency for a trait psychology to emphasize these internal structures led to a corresponding neglect of situational factors affecting behavior. At the same time, the trait approach has been identified with a concern for the individual. Upon reflection, there is a curious anomaly in the fact that a leading exponent of the *individual* in psychology ends up defending a *typology* of individuals against the onslaught of situationism (Allport, 1966). Because a concern for traits and individuals has been the dual concern of trait psychologists, it has been easy simply to accept traits and situations as adversaries in accounting for variance, whereas it is more appropriate to juxtapose the individual and the situation. Traits are inventions, and there is no reason for believing that they should account for all of the available person variance. The data in Table 1 are helpful in this regard. The subjects employed therein were not preselected on the basis of some presumably important trait; instead, a sample of subjects was examined across a sample of situations. Under these circumstances, subject variance was as important as situational variance. For example, in the Nelsen et al. (1969) study, up to 26.4% of behavioral honesty was a function of persons, whereas the correspondingly high figure for settings was 15.5%. This finding places an important limitation on the widely cited conclusions of the original Hartshorne and May (1928) studies on deceit. These studies are most often invoked to support the claim that honesty is situation specific; apparently, it is also person specific (cf. Burton, 1963). It seems to be inordinately easy to overlook or underemphasize the latter conclusion while stressing the situation-specific character of behavioral honesty.[6]

It may not be the case that a particular trait (e.g., honesty) as measured on a paper-and-pencil inventory would correlate with and account for a great deal of this sort of subject variance. But there is no reason why this possibility should not be explored *after* the total amount of subject variance has been determined. This tactic allows a fairer determination of the relative amount of variance due

---

[6] By far the most persuasive case made for honesty as a consistent characteristic of persons has been made by Kohlberg (1969). His views on this issue are far too complex to present here. Suffice it to say that in one study, "The correlation between moral maturity scores at age 16 and in the mid-twenties was .78 (n = 24) [p. 389]." In another study,

Principled subjects appear much less likely to cheat then conventional subjects. Only one of nine principled subjects cheated while about one-half of the conventional subjects did so [Kohlberg, 1971, p. 229].

Evidently, the substitution of "honesty engendering circumstances" for honest people is somewhat premature.

to persons and to situations. What Table 1 makes quite clear, of course, is that the contribution of either of these main effects is relatively small compared to the amounts of variance due to their interaction.

What then is the psychological meaning of the statistical interaction in Table 1? Situationists, of course, acknowledge that persons interact with their environments, and that qualities of the person cannot simply be ignored in an understanding of behavior. Farber (1964, p. 27), for example, has conceded that an S–R analysis of behavior cannot proceed very far if the organism under study is replaced by a sack of potatoes.

Nevertheless, it is important to distinguish what situationism concedes from what it emphasizes. And if a behavioristic or situationist account emphasizes anything, it emphasizes that behavior is (ultimately) a function of the environment. By this account, it can be argued that the relatively high proportion of variance due to a Person X Situation interaction simply reflects the different conditioning histories of different individuals. As a result of the idiosyncratic circumstances of people's lives, similar behavior of different persons is evoked and maintained by different environments, and similar environments come to evoke and maintain different behavior in different people. In this manner, "Social behavior theory recognizes the individuality of each person and of each situation [Mischel, 1968, p. 190]." Suddenly it is situationism that is idiographic!

According to this interpretation, there is evidently nothing about the relative size of the Person X Situation interactions presented in Table 1 that forces us to abandon situationism, and this would be true even if the interaction term accounted for 100% of the variance. Indeed, there is a tendency for situationists to regard main effects due to the situation, and effects due to Person X Situation interactions as more or less interchangeable in demonstrating the power of the circumstances to control behavior. Thus, Goldfried and Kent (1972) have argued that

Endler and Hunt (1966, 1969) have ... demonstrated the importance of *situational effects* in their S–R Inventory of Anxiousness, where they found that the *interactions* between situations and subjects contributed more to the total variance than did the variance associated with individual differences alone [pp. 410–411; italics added].

Thus does a stout interaction term become grist for the situationist mill.[7]

There is of course, no a priori reason why the same interactions cannot be invoked as evidence for traits. Thus, it could be argued that stable characteristics of people are situation specific—that high hypnotic susceptibility, for example, will not reveal itself in all situations, but just hypnotic ones. The large interaction term which would likely result from exposing high- and low-susceptible subjects to hypnotic and nonhypnotic treatment conditions would

---

[7] It should be pointed out that such adaptability to almost any set of data is by no means flattering to situationism; indeed, a similar "flexibility" of the psychoanalytic point of view has been frequently and justly criticized by behaviorists.

support the trait concept of hypnotic susceptibility, while acknowledging the potentiating effect of circumstances favorable to hypnosis.

It thus seems true that the relatively large variance due to the interaction of subjects and settings (see Table 1) can be fashioned into post hoc consistency with either a trait or situationist point of view. But it is not necessary to do so. Instead, we can invoke an interactionist *interpretation* of the data in Table 1.

AN INTERACTIONIST (OR BIOCOGNITIVE) VIEW: AN ALTERNATIVE TO TRAITS AND SITUATIONISM

An interactionist or biocognitive view denies the primacy of either traits or situations in the determination of behavior; instead, it fully recognizes that whatever main effects do emerge will depend entirely upon the particular sample of settings and individuals under consideration. Thus interactionism views main effects as a sort of behavioral precipitate that does not readily dissolve in the fluid interaction of organism and environment. More specifically, interactionism argues that *situations are as much a function of the person as the person's behavior is a function of the situation.*

The fact that a person's behavior can be a function of the situation needs no explanation. Moreover, there is an obvious sense in which man creates the circumstances that sustain him; after all, most of us live in houses, not in caves. Nevertheless, there are other, somewhat more subtle ways in which situations are a function of persons. It is to these that we now turn.

Interactionism and Cognition

As indicated earlier, situationism suggests that current differences in persons' behavior to the same environment are attributable to earlier objective differences in the individuals' histories. However, this situationist recourse to earlier "objective conditions" is not entirely satisfactory, since at any point in an individual's development yet another appeal to still earlier "objective conditions" is necessary to account for differences he manifests vis-à-vis his peers. The invocation of ever-earlier objective conditions to explain individual differences finally runs headlong into a biological or genetic point of view which suggests that "*the effects of experience are always modified by the organism to which they occur* [Wiggins, Renner, Clore, & Rose, 1971, p. 40]." The point is, of course, that organismic differences exist at the very beginning, before "objective" differences in the situation can have any part in creating them. Thus, right from the outset, the situation must be specified in terms of the particular organism experiencing it (Escalona, 1968, 1972).

In this context, consider Piaget's genetic epistemology, which suggests that "the cognizing organism . . . actually *constructs* his world by assimilating it to schemas while accommodating these schemas to its constraints [Flavell, 1963, p. 71]." According to this view (see also Holt, 1972; Kelly, 1955; Neisser, 1967) reality virtually exists for a person as a function of his means and methods of knowing it. Even for scientists, "no observation is purely empirical—that is, free of any ideational element—as no theory . . . is purely ideational [Kaplan, 1964, p. 58]." Thus, the spectacle seen depends upon the methodological and conceptual spectacles worn; what is known depends as much upon schemas inside the knower as it does upon the world outside him (cf. Emmerich, 1966).

The above comments have immediate ramifications for the trait–situationism controversy. There is a fair bit of evidence (e.g., Dornbusch, Hastorf, Richardson, Muzzy, & Vreeland, 1965; Mulaik, 1964; Passini & Norman, 1966; Schneider, 1973) suggesting that traits, to some considerable extent, reflect the *perceiver's* cognitive organization and not the enduring characteristics of the person perceived (Mischel, 1968, p. 48). Cronbach (1955, 1958), for example, has argued that a rater's "implicit personality theory" is extraordinarily important in determining what he "sees" in the target person. This evidence implies that if traits do not exist in the person perceived, then they cannot account for his behavior. *Something* must account for a person's behavior, however, and for the situationist, more often than not, this explanatory "something" turns out to be environmental contingencies and constraints.

On the other hand, the fact that the observer's cognitive organization (or implicit personality theory) is inseparable from what he perceives is precisely what the interactionist position argues. Does it follow that the perceiver is cut off by his own cognitive organization from the reality of other persons? Do our conceptual spectacles serve as perceptual blinders?

If our adaptation to the environment were limited, in Piaget's terms, to assimilation, then this would indeed be the case. It is the accommodative aspects of adaptation that put us in touch with the "out-thereness" of things. And it is accommodation that makes us sensitive to the various particularities of individuals and situations. Thus, the correlation between observer ratings and self-ratings of persons observed increases as a function of the raters' familiarity with the target person (Norman, 1969; see also Lay & Jackson, 1969). Moreover, ingenious but neglected studies by Fancher (1966, 1967) have demonstrated that for some judges at least, accuracy in predicting patient behavior is progressively enhanced by correct feedback among the person being judged. These findings suggest that accommodation to the properties of the observed is more likely, the more contact the observer has with the observed—an unsurprising but important conclusion.

The delicate and vulnerable equilibrium between the perceiver's conceptual schemas and the characteristics of the phenomena or person perceived is revealed by further evidence showing that accuracy in predicting behavior is sometimes correlated *negatively* with judges' conceptual sophistication about personality (Fancher, 1967; see also Crow, 1957). In other words, the person perceived can be "overassimilated" to the organizing schemas of the perceiver. When this happens, the perceiver has, in effect, not accommodated to the characteristics of the person perceived, and judgment accuracy suffers.

Overassimilation of this kind is not unknown among professional mental health workers, who oftentimes became more engaged by abstract conceptualizations about personality than by the particular persons in their care (Adinolfi, 1971). Indeed, one sometimes gets the impression that clinicians and scientists alike occasionally don their preferred (conceptual and methodological) spectacles less to enhance their perceptiveness than to avoid being struck by reality. Keeping reality at bay in this fashion instead of in focus sometimes has ludicrous and even tragic consequences. For example, it is evidently very difficult for professional mental health workers to "see" normal behavior in persons they (mistakenly) believe to be schizophrenic. On the other hand, genuine psychiatric patients are often quite capable of recognizing normal behavior in hospitalized pseudopatients (Rosenhan, 1973). The superiority of genuine patients in identifying "normals" may be due to their nosological "innocence" and to their constant contact with the pseudopatients in question.

In sum, the situation is a function of the observer in the sense that the observer's cognitive schemas filter and organize the environment in a fashion that makes it impossible ever to completely separate the environment from the person observing it. This interactionist or biocognitive account is quite different from an S–R point of view (or its social learning derivative), which presupposes the separateness of stimulus and response, and views cognition as an implicit response mediating the impact of situational antecedents on behavioral outcomes. Thus, the fact that both points of view can emphasize cognition does not mean that there are no differences between an interactionist point of view on one hand and a cognitive social learning account (Mischel, 1973a) on the other.

Interactionism and Behavior

The second sense in which situations are a function of persons has recently been articulated in an extremely important article by Wachtel (1973; see also Bandura, 1969, pp. 45–48). Wachtel pointed out that a great deal of a person's social environment is engendered by his own behavior. Moreover, he argued that there is a fair amount of consistency in the kinds of environments people create for themselves. Thus, although it may be true as Mischel (1968) argued that behavior is situation specific,

we must ask why for some people the situation is so rarely different. How do we understand the man who is constantly in the presence of overbearing women, or constantly immersed in his work, or constantly with weaker men who are cowed by him and offer little honest feedback? Further, how do we understand the man who seems to bring out the bitchy side of *whatever* women he encounters, or ends up turning almost all social encounters into work sessions, or intimidates even men who usually are honest and direct [Wachtel, 1973]?

There is some evidence bearing directly on the assumption that people do indeed foster consistent social environments, which then reciprocate by fostering behavioral consistency.

Raush (1965) applied a sophisticated interactional analysis to naturally occurring interchanges among various samples of children and found that friendly acts were maintained at a high level among normal children throughout the course of their interaction with each other. Disturbed, hyperaggressive children, however, showed a steady and rather precipitous decline in friendly acts. The data corroborate the clinical observation that aggressive children have an "aptitude . . . for moving rapidly from an atmosphere of friendliness to one of wildly chaotic aggression [Raush, 1965, p. 497]." Normal children, by contrast, seem to be better able to sense the incipient deterioration of a friendly sequence, and behave in ways that save it from running a downhill course. Thus, aggressive, as distinct from normal children can be characterized by the fact that they foster aggression-engendering situations to which they in turn respond aggressively.

Somewhat similar conclusions were drawn by Kelley and Stahelski (1970) regarding the tendency for competitors to engender competitive behavior in persons who might otherwise have behaved cooperatively (in a prisoner's dilemma paradigm). The authors pointed out that cooperators are phenotypically heterogenous in their behavior, since they make cooperative moves when their partner does, but will adopt a competitive strategy to keep from being thoroughly exploited by a competitive partner. Competitors, however, are phenotypically homogenous in their behavior, since they consistently pursue a competitive strategy with every partner. In effect, a competitive player dominates the game, forcing an ordinarily cooperative person to adopt a competitive strategy in order to "survive." What is curiously ironic is that competitors tend to view their strategy as the only realistic one, since they have never seen cooperative behavior in their partners; how could they, since they have systematically engendered competitive behavior in any potentially cooperative person with whom they have played!

Moreover, competitors provoke this ubiquitously competitive environment while remaining innocent of their role in producing it. They are thus veridical in their perception of competitive behavior in others, but explaining their own competitive behavior in terms of a competitive environment is less than a complete account of the matter. The situation is somewhat reminiscent of the unwittingly provocative woman who feels self-righteously angry at men because they are always propositioning her.

This tendency for persons to engender typical environments (see also Bell, 1968, 1971; Rheingold, 1969) perhaps reveals an unexplored implication of the well-received proposition that

Actors tend to attribute the causes of their behavior to stimuli inherent to the situation, while observers tend to attribute behavior to stable dispositions of the actor [Jones & Nisbett, 1971, p. 15].

These authors implied that the observer's tendency to be a "trait theorist" about the actor's behavior is in error, and that the actor renders a truer account of his own behavior by pointing to the circumstances that evoke and maintain it.

Hence, Jones and Nisbett "suggest that the actor's view of his own personality is close to the [situation-specific] conception preferred by Mischel [p. 13]," and by themselves as well.

Although Jones and Nisbett's account is ingeniously argued, it remains incomplete insofar as it overlooks the actor's tendency to engender just those evoking and maintaining conditions which he then invokes to account for his behavior. As Wachtel (1973) has noted,

one can in many cases view consistency as a result of being in particular situations frequently, but *situations largely of one's own making and themselves describable as a characteristic of one's personality* [italics added].

Thus, the observer may render a more objective account of the actor's behavior after all. He may be taking into consideration the actor's tendency to generate situations that are typical for him, a tendency that the actor himself may not fully appreciate (cf. Berne, 1964).

A further implication of this line of thinking is that psychologists employing an experimental paradigm to study personality may, like the actor-subjects they observe, overlook the important role of the actor's own behavior in generating typical situations. By administering standard procedures to everyone in a treatment group, it is impossible to see, let alone investigate, those kinds of situations that a person ordinarily generates for himself. Wachtel (1973) has fittingly dubbed this tendency in current personality research to rely upon standard procedures and the experimental method as the model of the "implacable experimenter."[8]

In sum, emphasis upon the situation-specific character of behavior reveals an important truth, but a partial one that overlooks the person-specific character of situations. This oversight is due at least in part to situationism's reliance upon the experimental method, which has in turn produced enormous constraints on the kinds of observations that psychologists are likely to incorporate into their thinking[9] (cf. Harré & Secord, 1972; especially chap. 3). After all, an

experiment merely chooses between two hypotheses, it does not prove the correctness of either or exclude many of the other possible hypotheses that it was not specifically designed to test. Nor does an experiment determine whether the tested effects play an important role in the occurrence of the phenomenon during real life [Blurton-Jones, 1972, p. 11].

---

[8]Mischel (1973b) has dismissed Wachtel's "implacable experimenter" as a caricature. Koestler (1967) has engagingly dismissed the entire behavioristic movement on similar grounds. Evidently one man's caricature is another man's truth (cf. Gordon, 1972).

[9]Psychology is not the only discipline to be led astray by a limited observation base. A book by anatomist Sir Solly Zuckerman was published in 1932 reporting on the primacy of sexual instincts in baboons lodged at the London Zoo. Only somewhat later was the animals' captivity recognized as an important constraint on their behavior. "Neither the drives of hunger nor the fear of the predator stir the idleness of [their] hours [Ardrey, 1961, p. 37]." When baboons are observed in their natural habitat, much different behaviors are seen and conclusions drawn.

KNOWLEDGE AND OBJECTIVITY

This article has, among other things, drawn attention to various limitations of the experimental method—a preferred modus operandi of situationism. It should be pointed out that this "optimism of method" (Kessen, 1971, p. 291) emerges naturally out of an ontological preconception about the nature of reality. Situationism assumes that there is a discoverable and bedrock objectivity in the physicalistic realm of stimulus antecedents and response consequences (Kessen, 1971), and that

The main task of science is to specify quantitively how variations in one or a combination of antecedent variables affect the dependent variables—the behaviors that are to be explained [Barber, 1969, p. 14].

It is precisely this "bedrock" view of reality that interactionism challenges. It does so by fully acknowledging the "thought-impregnated character of observation [T. Mischel, 1971, p. 326]," and by suggesting that the objective state of affairs is less discovered than achieved. Interactionism argues that "reality" is constructed, that it emerges out of a continuously renewed equilibrium or balance between the knower and the known—between assimilation and accommodation. Thus, for interactionism, objectivity emerges out of a balanced *relationship* between the observer and the observed, and not out of some divination of an indubitable, rock-bottom reality (cf. Aune, 1967). More specifically,

Objectification of reality—the population of the external milieu with things recognized as independent of a self which cognizes them—can come about only when objects come to be inserted into a whole network of intercoordinated schemas [Flavell, 1963, p. 63].

Thus, a peculiar looking rock becomes a bone, becomes a fossil, becomes the jaw fragment of an ancient protoman, becomes evidence for the existence and the structure of Australopithecus Africanus—depending upon one's cognitive complexity and anthropological sophistication. And though the importance of thought and inference becomes more and more important as we go from "rock" to "A. Africanus," the subtle matrix of evidence and inference establishes the character of our ancient forebears with ever-increasing objectivity. In this fashion the most transcending abstractions can sometimes put us in closest touch with the structure of reality—as witness Einstein's theory of relativity.

Interactionism's reliance upon thought and inference to establish the objective state of affairs stands in stark contrast to situationism's preference for naive physicalism, which regards inference and abstraction as a retreat from the objectivity of "hard" facts. Situationism largely ignores the conceptual invasion of all percepts, and proceeds in a very pragmatic fashion to see how experimental manipulation of physicalistic stimuli affects physicalistic responses.

This wedding of method and metaphysics can conspire against the very reality of phenomena that might otherwise have some claim to scientific objectivity. To illustrate, Barber (1969) has repeatedly questioned the existence of a hypnotic trance, precisely because its reality is presently more inferred than observed. However, Barber's positivistic application of the experimental method can only "see" observable outcomes that are due to observable antecedents; an altered state of consciousness is simply invisible to an input–output analysis. Since the positivistic method and metaphysic are so inextricably interwoven, this invisibility of trance is tantamount to its nonexistence. Notice, however, that the existence of trance has actually been precluded on methodological, *not* on empirical grounds (Bowers, 1973). For Barber to deny the existence of trance on the basis of his own experiments is like denying the existence of four-inch fish after fishing with a net having five-inch holes.

If situationism often errs in the direction of naive physicalism, it frequently saves us from the tyranny of unaccommodating, Procrustean concepts. In clinical and applied fields, a behavioristic phychology has forced us to look more closely at, and accommodate to, the particularities of patient behavior and behavioral contexts (e.g., Neuringer & Michael, 1970). This kind of contact with patients' circumstances and behavior cannot help but be an improvement over the present state of affairs in psychiatric wards, where life-altering decisions about patients are often made by mental health professionals based on stereotyped judgments and grossly inadequate sampling of patient behavior (Gardner, Pearson, Bercovici, & Bricker, 1968; Rosenhan, 1973).

Despite this acknowledged advantage at a practical level, the situationist model, taken to its extreme, ultimately discredits man as an autonomous active agent. Situationism's foremost philosopher—Skinner (1955-56)—put it this way:

> Every discovery of an event which has a part in shaping a man's behavior seems to leave so much the less to be credited to the man himself; and as such explanations become more and more comprehensive, the contribution which may be claimed by the individual himself appears to approach zero [p. 52].

This model of man, which so emphasizes "objective" conditions and conditioning as the basis for thought and behavior is ultimately trapped in a paradox of its own making. Inherent in this emphasis is the absence of any clear distinction between conditioning on one hand and knowing on the other (cf. Kohlberg, 1971, pp. 151-152).[10]

There can be no doubt that conditioning is extraordinarily important in the affairs of mice and men, but this very assertion constitutes a *knowledge* claim based on systematic inquiry that cannot itself be entirely reduced to a history of

---

[10] To study cognition, one must have some sort of concept of knowledge in terms of which children's development is observed. Piaget's fundamental contribution to developmental psychology has been to observe children's development in terms of the categories (space, time, causality, etc.) which philosophers have deemed central to knowing. The fact that the cognitive categories of the philosopher are central for understanding the behavior development of the child is so apparent, once pointed out, that one recognizes that it is only the peculiar epistemology of the positivistic behaviorist which could have obscured it [Kohlberg, 1971, p. 152].

conditioning. If it could, then truths would be synonomous with what we are conditioned to believe. Surely, however, *knowing* that (and why) two plus two is four is different from simply saying so because the response has a consistent history of being reinforced. Surely Skinner and his followers wish to argue that they are *correct* in their claim that past and present reinforcement accounts for behavior; yet how can their argument be right *or* wrong if it is itself merely the product of conditioning. Clearly there is something missing in this ultra-situationist view. What is missing is man as *knower*, for whom the ongoing possibility of error continuously delivers him from the bondage of conditioning and "objective" conditions.

Although situationism does not have any explicit theory of knowledge, it implicitly suggests

that the uprooting of all voluntary components of belief will leave behind unassailed a residue of knowledge that is completely determined by the objective evidence [Polanyi, 1964, p. 269].

Polanyi has written eloquently about the problems that result from pursuing this kind of impersonal knowledge. Thus, he stated that the

great movement for independent thought instilled in the modern mind a desperate refusal of all knowledge that is not absolutely impersonal, and this implied in its turn a mechanical conception of man which was bound to deny man's capacity for independent thought [p. 214].

Polanyi (1964) objected to such a "universal mechanical interpretation of things, on the ground that it impairs man's moral consciousness [p. 153]." For in pursuing absolutely impersonal knowledge, man himself may become less morally accountable as his conduct and thought become ever more subject to and governed by supposedly "objective" conditions which prevail with increasing disregard for the men who know about them. According to Polanyi (1964), the ultimate consequences of such a trend are inauspicious: "In such a universe there is no one capable of creating and upholding scientific values; hence there is no science [p. 142]." To counter this trend, Polanyi (1964) educed and celebrated the subjective and personal character of all knowledge (see also Rogers, 1955).

SUMMARY AND CONCLUSION

This article has tried to show that the methodological and metaphysical biases of situationism have seriously constrained psychology's observation base and its model of man. Thus, overreliance upon the experimental method and operant techniques has fastened our attention upon behavior change, so that we tend to overlook behavioral stability, or reinterpret it as more apparent than real (e.g., Mischel, 1968, pp. 56 f.). However, if such perdurable differences in personality and style possessed by a John F. Kennedy and a Richard M. Nixon cannot be illuminated by the systematic application of experimental or operant techniques, so much the worse for these techniques. Enduring characterological and stylistic differences surely exist, and to investigate them we must fit our methods to the problems at hand, not vice versa.

Accordingly, it has been suggested that behavioral stabilities are more apt to emerge when correlational or interactional analyses are applied to naturalistic and clinical data. For it is under these relatively nonexperimental, unconstrained circumstances that a person is able to engender interpersonal circumstances characteristic for him—circumstances which can in turn sustain and lend consistency and stability to his behavior (Wachtel, 1973). By this analysis, we have behavioral consistency without a trait explanation of it (Wallach & Leggett, 1972).

It has been further argued that a situationist psychology has overrelied upon experimental and operant techniques because of certain preconceptions about reality. One such preconception more or less identifies objectivity with observability; another preconception holds that causality involves an invariant action of one observable upon another. Both of these preconceptions were challenged. It was argued that objectivity and causality are not simply impersonal givens to be divined, but part and parcel of man's deepening comprehension of nature (Polanyi, 1969). Not only observables but theories about them are necessary to an objective account of nature; not only the invariant contiguity of two events but some way of understanding the invariance is requisite to a causal account of the empirical connection. The extent to which reality and our knowledge of it are inextricably interwoven is the extent to which knowledge is personal as well as objective (Polanyi, 1964).

The importance of thought in the achievement of objectivity was placed in the broader context of Piaget's genetic epistemology. According to this view, reality emerges out of a balanced relationship between the knower and the known, between assimilation and accommodation. What we observe and perceive is invariably infiltrated by our thoughts and conceptions. Admittedly, this view involves the ever-present danger of overassimilating the "out-thereness" of things to unaccommodating concepts of it. This ongoing possibility for error suggests that men are not simply conditioned creatures of habit. Habits cannot be mistaken; they can only be (un)adaptive. The emphasis upon cognition as an organizing structure that determines our perception and knowledge of reality distinguishes it from a situationist account. The latter position views cognition as an implicit response that mediates the impact of an "objective" environment on "objective" behavior.

Finally, it is man's capacity for highly personalized, creative thought in combination with careful, disciplined observation that puts him in ever-closer touch with the structure of reality. The experimental method is simply one very good means of placing control upon observation. Its application does not, however, automatically provide a causal account of phenomena; nor does it necessarily deliver objective truth. Indeed, truth is both fragile and subtle; it can easily be crushed by a heavy-handed use of methodology. Alternatively, it can slip through fingers untrained in the methods of disciplined inquiry. Science at its best is thus like a firm but gentle hand that holds a butterfly without crushing it.

REFERENCES

Adinolfi, A. A. Relevance of person perception to clinical psychology. *Journal of Consulting and Clinical Psychology,* 1971, **37**, 167–176.

Alker, H. A. Is personality situationally specific or intrapsychically consistent? *Journal of Personality,* 1972, **40**, 1–16.

Allport, G. W. Traits revisited. *American Psychologist,* 1966, **21**, 1–10.

Ardrey, R. *African genesis.* New York: Dell, 1961.

Argyle, M., & Little, B. R. Do personality traits apply to social behavior? *Journal for the Theory of Social Behavior,* 1972, **2**, 1–35.

Aune, B. *Knowledge, mind, and nature.* New York: Random House, 1967.

Bandura, A. *Principles of behavior modification.* New York: Holt, Rinehart & Winston, 1969.

Bandura, A., & Walters, R. W. *Social learning and personality development.* New York: Holt, Rinehart & Winston, 1963.

Barber, T. X. *Hypnosis: A scientific approach.* New York: Van Nostrand-Reinhold, 1969.

Bell, R. Q. A reinterpretation of the direction of effects in studies of socialization. *Psychological Review,* 1968, **75**, 81–95.

Bell, R. Q. Stimulus control of parent or caretaker behavior by offspring. *Developmental Psychology,* 1971, **4**, 63–72.

Bem, D. J. Constructing cross-situational consistencies in behavior: Some thoughts on Alker's critique of Mischel. *Journal of Personality,* 1972, **40**, 17–26.

Berne, E. *Games people play.* New York: Grove Press, 1964.

Blurton-Jones, N. Characteristics of ethological studies of human behavior. In N. Blurton-Jones (Ed.), *Ethological studies of child behavior.* Cambridge: Cambridge University Press, 1972.

Bowers, K. Situationism in psychology: On making reality disappear. *Research Reports in Psychology,* University of Waterloo, 1972, No. 37.

Bowers, K. S. Hypnosis, attribution, and demand characteristics. *International Journal of Clinical and Experimental Hypnosis,* 1973, **21**, 226–238.

Breland, K., & Breland, M. The misbehavior of organisms. *American Psychologist,* 1961, **16**, 681–684.

Brown, R. Development of the first language in the human species. *American Psychologist,* 1973, **28**, 97–106.

Brown, R., & Hanlon, C. Derivational complexity and order of acquisition in child speech. In J. R. Hayes (Ed.), *Cognition and the development of language.* New York: Wiley, 1970.

Brunswik, E. Representative design and probabilistic theory in a functional psychology. *Psychological Review,* 1955, **62**, 193–217.

Burton, R. V. Generality of honesty reconsidered. *Psychological Review,* 1963, **70**, 481–499.

Carlson, R. Where is the person in personality research? *Psychological Bulletin,* 1971, **75**, 203–219.

Chomsky, N. Review of "Verbal Behavior," by B. F. Skinner. *Language,* 1959, **35**, 26–58.

Cronbach, L. J. Processes affecting scores on "understanding of others" and "assumed similarity." *Psychological Bulletin,* 1955, **52**, 177–193.

Cronbach, L. J. The two disciplines of scientific psychology. *American Psychologist,* 1957, **12**, 671–684.

Cronbach, L. J. Proposals leading to analytic treatment of social perception scores. In R. Tagiuri & L. Petrullo (Eds.), *Person perception and interpersonal behavior.* Stanford: Stanford University Press, 1958.

Crow, W. J. The effect of training upon accuracy and variability in interpersonal perception. *Journal of Abnormal and Social Psychology,* 1957, **55**, 355–359.

Dornbusch, S. M., Hastorf, A. H., Richardson, S. A., Muzzy, R. E., & Vreeland, R. S. The perceiver and the perceived: Their relative influence on the categories of interpersonal cognition. *Journal of Personality and Social Psychology,* 1965, **1**, 434–440.

Dulany, D. E. Awareness, rules, and propositional control: A confrontation with S-R behavior theory. In T. R. Dixon & D. L. Horton (Eds.), *Verbal behavior and general behavior theory.* Englewood Cliffs, N. J.: Prentice-Hall, 1968.

Emmerich, W. Personality assessments conceptualized as perspectives. *Journal of Projective Techniques and Personality Assessment,* 1966, **30**, 307–318.

Endler, N. S. The person versus the situation—A pseudo issue? A response to Alker. *Journal of Personality,* 1973, **41**, 287–303.

Endler, N. S., & Hunt, J. McV. Sources of behavioral variance as measured by the S-R Inventory of Anxiousness. *Psychological Bulletin,* 1966, **65**, 336–346.

Endler, N. S., & Hunt, J. McV. S-R inventories of hostility and comparisons of the proportions of variance from persons, responses, and situations for hostility and anxiousness. *Journal of Personality and Social Psychology,* 1968, **9**, 309–315.

Endler, N. S., & Hunt, J. McV. Generalizability of contributions from sources of variance in the S-R inventories of anxiousness. *Journal of Personality,* 1969, **37**, 1–24.

Endler, N. S., Hunt, J. McV., & Rosenstein, A. J. An S-R Inventory of Anxiousness. *Psychological Monographs,* 1962, **76** (17, Whole No. 536).

Escalona, S. *The roots of individuality.* Chicago: Aldine, 1968.

Escalona, S. K. The differential impact of environmental conditions as a function of different reaction patterns in infancy. In J. Westman (Ed.), *Individual differences in children.* New York: Wiley, 1972.

Fancher, R. E. Explicit personality theories and accuracy in person perception. *Journal of Personality,* 1966, **34**, 252–261.

Fancher, R. E., Jr. Accuracy versus validity in person perception. *Journal of Consulting Psychology,* 1967, **31**, 264–269.

Farber, I. E. A framework for the study of personality as a behavioral science. In P. Worchel & D. Byrne (Eds.), *Personality change.* New York: Wiley, 1964.

Flavell, J. H. *The developmental psychology of Jean Piaget: With a foreword by Jean Piaget.* Princeton, N. J.: Van Nostrand, 1963.

Gardner, J. E., Pearson, D. T., Bercovici, A. N., & Bricker, D. E. Measurement, evaluation, and modification of selected social interactions between a schizophrenic child, his parents, and his therapist. *Journal of Consulting and Clinical Psychology,* 1968, **32**, 537–542.

Goldfried, M. R., & Kent, R. N. Traditional behavioral personality assessment: A comparison of methodological and theoretical assumptions. *Psychological Bulletin,* 1972, **77**, 409–420.

Gordon, R. A very private world. In P. W. Sheehan (Ed.), *The function and nature of imagery.* New York: Academic Press, 1972.

Harré, R., & Secord, P. F. *The explanation of social behaviour.* Oxford: Basil Blackwell & Mott, 1972.

Hartshorne, H., & May, M. A. Studies in the *nature of character.* Vol. 1. *Studies in deceit.* New York: Macmillan, 1928.

Hilgard, E. R. *Hypnotic susceptibility.* New York: Harcourt, Brace & World, 1965.

Holt, R. R. On the nature and generality of mental imagery. In P. W. Sheehan (Ed.), *The function and nature of imagery.* New York: Academic Press, 1972.

Immergluck, L. Determinism-freedom in contemporary psychology: An ancient problem revisited. *American Psychologist,* 1964, **19**, 270–281.

Jessor, R. The problem of reductionism in psychology. *Psychological Review,* 1958, **65**, 170–178.

Jones, E. E., & Nisbett, R. E. *The actor and observer: Divergent perceptions of the causes of behavior.* New York: General Learning Press, 1971.

Kanfer, F. H. Self-regulation: Research, issues, and speculations. In C. Neuringer & J. L. Michael (Eds.), *Behavior modification in clinical psychology.* New York: Appleton-Century-Crofts, 1970.

Kaplan, A. *The conduct of inquiry.* San Francisco: Chandler, 1964.

Kazdin, A. E., & Bootzin, R. R. The token economy: An evaluative review. *Journal of Applied Behavior Analysis,* 1972, **5**, 343–372.

Kelley, H. H., & Stahelski, A. J. Social interaction basis of cooperators' and competitors' beliefs about others. *Journal of Personality and Social Psychology,* 1970, **16**, 66–91.

Kelly, G. A. *The psychology of personal constructs.* Vol. 1. New York: Norton, 1955.

Kessen, W. Early cognitive development: Hot or cold? In T. Mischel (Ed.), *Cognitive development and epistemology.* New York: Academic Press, 1971.

Koestler, A. *The ghost in the machine.* New York: Macmillan, 1967.

Koestler, A., & Smythies, J. R. *Beyond reductionism: New perspectives in the life sciences.* New York: Macmillan, 1969.

Kohlberg, L. A cognitive-developmental analysis of children's sex-role concepts and attitudes. In E. E. Maccoby (Ed.), *The development of sex differences.* Stanford: Stanford University Press, 1966.

Kohlberg, L. Stage and sequence: The cognitive-developmental approach to socialization. In D. A. Goslin (Ed.), *Handbook of socialization theory and research.* Chicago: Rand McNally, 1969.

Kohlberg, L. From is to ought: How to commit the naturalistic fallacy and get away with it in the study of moral development. In T. Mischel (Ed.), *Cognitive development and epistemology.* New York: Academic Press, 1971.

Lay, C. H., & Jackson, D. N. Analysis of the generality of trait-inferential relationships. *Journal of Personality and Social Psychology,* 1969, **12**, 12–21.

Lenneberg, E. H. Language, evolution, and purposive behavior. In S. Diamond (Ed.), *Culture in history: Essays in honor of Paul Radin.* New York: Columbia University Press, 1960.

Lenneberg, E. H. *Biological foundations of language.* New York: Wiley, 1967.

Lenneberg, E. H. On explaining language. *Science,* 1969, **164**, 635–643.

Locke, E. A. Critical analysis of the concept of causality in behavioristic psychology. *Psychological Reports,* 1972, **31**, 175–197.

Miller, G. A., & McNeill, D. Psycholinguistics. In G. Lindzey & E. Aronson (Eds.), *The handbook of social psychology.* Vol. 3. (2nd ed.), Reading, Mass: Addison-Wesley, 1969.

Mischel, T. Piaget: Cognitive conflict and the motivation of thought. In T. Mischel (Ed.), *Cognitive development and epistemology.* New York: Academic Press, 1971.

Mischel, W. A social-learning view of sex differences in behavior. In E. E. Maccoby (Ed.), *The development of sex differences.* Stanford: Stanford University Press, 1966.

Mischel, W. *Personality and assessment.* New York: Wiley, 1968.

Mischel, W. Continuity and change in personality. *American Psychologist,* 1969, **24**, 1012–1018.

Mischel, W. *Introduction to personality.* New York: Holt, Rinehart & Winston, 1971.

Mischel, W. Toward a cognitive social learning reconceptualization of personality. *Psychological Review,* 1973, **80**, 252–283. (a)

Mischel, W. On the empirical dilemmas of psychodynamic approaches: Issues and alternatives. *Journal of Abnormal Psychology,* 1973, in press. (b)

Moos, R. H. Situational analysis of a therapeutic community milieu. *Journal of Abnormal Psychology,* 1968, **73**, 49–61.

Moos, R. H. Sources of variance in responses to questionnaires and in behavior. *Journal of Abnormal Psychology.* 1969, **74**, 405–412.

Moos, R. H. Differential effects of psychiatric ward settings on patient change. *Journal of Nervous and Mental Disease,* 1970, **5**, 316–321.

Mulaik, S. A. Are personality factors raters' conceptual factors? *Journal of Consulting Psychology,* 1964, **28,** 506–5 11.

Neisser, U. *Cognitive psychology.* New York: Appleton-Century-Crofts, 1967.

Nelsen, E. A., Grinder, R. F., & Mutterer, M. L. Sources of variance in behavioral measures of honesty in temptation situations: Methodological analyses. *Developmental Psychology,* 1969, **1,** 265–279.

Neuringer, C., & Michael, J. L. *Behavior modification in clinical psychology.* New York: Appleton-Century-Crofts, 1970.

Norman, W. T. To see ourselves as others see us!: Relations among self-perceptions, peer-perceptions, and excepted peer-perceptions of personality attributes. *Multivariate Behavioral Research,* 1969, **4,** 417–443.

Osgood, C. E. Toward a wedding of insufficiencies. In T. R. Dixon & D. L. Horton (Eds.), *Verbal behavior and general behavior theory.* Englewood Cliffs, N. J.: Prentice-Hall, 1968.

Passini, F. T., & Norman, W. T. A universal conception of personality structure? *Journal of Personality and Social Psychology,* 1966, **4,** 44–49.

Peterson, D. R. *The clinical study of social behavior.* New York: Appleton-Century-Crofts, 1968.

Polanyi, M. *Personal knowledge: Towards a post-critical philosophy.* New York: Harper Torchbook, 1964.

Polanyi, M. The creative imagination. In M. Grene (Ed.), Toward a unity of knowledge. *Psychological Issues,* 1969, **6,** 53–70.

Raush, H. L. Interaction sequences. *Journal of Personality and Social Psychology,* 1965, **2,** 487–499.

Raush, H. L., Dittmann, A. T., & Taylor, T. J. Person, setting, and change in social interaction. *Human Relations,* 1959, **12,** 361–378.

Raush, H. L., Farbman, I., & Llewellyn, L. G. Person, setting, and change in social interaction: II. A normal control study. *Human Relations,* 1960, **13,** 305–332.

Rheingold, H. L. The social and socializing infant. In D. A. Goslin (Ed.), *Handbook of socialization theory and research.* Chicago: Rand McNally, 1969.

Rogers, C. R. Persons or science? A philosophical question. *American Psychologist,* 1955, **10,** 267–278.

Rosenhan, D. L. On being sane in insane places. *Science,* 1973, **179,** 250–258.

Rothbart, M. K., & Maccoby, E. E. Parents' differential reactions to sons and daughters. *Journal of Personality and Social Psychology,* 1966, **4,** 237–243.

Rychlak, J. F. *A philosophy of science for personality theory.* Boston: Houghton Mifflin, 1968.

Schaffer, H. R., & Emerson, P. E. Patterns of response to physical contact in early human development. *Journal of Child Psychology and Psychiatry,* 1964, **5,** 1–13.

Schneider, D. J. Implicit personality theory: A review. *Psychological Bulletin,* 1973, **79,** 294–309.

Skinner, B. F. *Science and human behavior.* New York: Free Press, 1953.

Skinner, B. F. Freedom and the control of men. *American Scholar,* 1955–56, **25,** 47–65.

Skinner, B. F. *Verbal behavior.* New York: Appleton-Century-Crofts, 1957.

Skinner, B. F. Behaviorism at fifty. *Science,* 1963, **140,** 951–958.

Skinner, B. F. *Beyond freedom and dignity.* New York: Knopf, 1971.

Slobin, D. I. *Psycholinguistics.* Glenview, Ill.: Scott, Foresman, 1971.

Ullmann, L. P., & Krasner, L. *Case studies in behavior modification.* New York: Holt. Rinehart & Winston, 1965.

Vale, J. R., & Vale, G. R. Individual difference and general laws in psychology: A reconciliation. *American Psychologist,* 1969, **24,** 1093–1108.

Wachtel, P. Psychodynamics, behavior therapy, and the implacable experimenter: An inquiry into the consistency of personality. *Journal of Abnormal Psychology,* 1973, **82,** 324–334.

Wallach, M. A., & Leggett, M. I. Testing the hypothesis that a person will be consistent: Stylistic consistency versus situational specificity in size of children's drawings. *Journal of Personality,* 1972, **40,** 309–330.

Wiggins, J. A., Renner, K. E., Clore, G. L., & Rose, R. J. *The psychology of personality.* Reading, Mass.: Addison-Wesley, 1971.

Zuckerman, S. *Social life of monkeys and apes.* New York: Harcourt, Brace & World, 1932.

8

Toward a Cognitive Social Learning Reconceptualization of Personality

WALTER MISCHEL

There has been a curious—indeed alarming—bifurcation between progress in theories regarding complex social behavior and cognition on the one hand, and in conceptualizations regarding the basic nature of personality on the other. Many of the therapeutic implications of social learning (social behavior) theories have become evident in the last few years. There have been notable advances in treatment techniques as well as significant reconceptualizations of the treatment process itself (e.g., Bandura, 1969). These developments are just starting to be accompanied by comparable parallel developments in personality theory. In the second direction, there has been vigorous progress in cognitive psychology (e.g., Neisser, 1967). But while cognitive and symbolic processes have received increasing attention both in the laboratory and in therapeutic applications, their implications for personality psychology have not yet been thoroughly explored and their impact on the basic traditional assumptions of personality psychology until recently has been limited.

During the last 50 years, when basic concepts were changing rapidly in most fields of psychology, the most fundamental assumptions about the nature of personality seem to have been retained with few substantial modifications. Of course there have been many changes in the names and particular characteristics of the trait dispositions advocated by different theoreticians and personality researchers in the last few decades. But in spite of the heterogeneity of hypothesized dimensions or structures, perhaps the most fundamental

From the *Psychological Review*, 1973, *80*, 252–283. Copyright 1973 by the American Psychological Association. Reprinted by permission.

Parts of this manuscript are based on the Address of the Chairman, Section III, Division 12, American Psychological Association, Washington, D. C., September 3, 1971. Preparation of this paper was facilitated by National Institute of Mental Health Grant M-6830 and National Science Foundation Grant GS-32582. Constructive comments have been received from more colleagues and students than can be listed here; the author is grateful for their help.

assumptions about them have remained almost monolithic until very recently. This paper briefly reviews the central assumptions of global dispositional approaches to personality, considers some of the main misconceptions, issues, and implications arising from recent challenges to those assumptions, and finally attempts a reconceptualization of person variables in the light of concepts from the study of cognition and social learning.

GLOBAL DISPOSITIONAL APPROACHES TO PERSONALITY

Assumptions of Traditional Trait Approaches

It has generally been assumed that personality dispositions or traits—the basic units of personality study—are relatively stable, highly consistent attributes that exert widely *generalized* causal effects on behavior. Whether one uses the language of factors, or of habits, or of basic attitudes, or of dynamics and character structure, this fundamental assumption has been shared: personality comprises broad underlying dispositions which pervasively influence the individual's behavior across many situations and lead to consistency in his behavior (e.g., Allport, 1937).[1] These dispositions are not directly observed but are inferred from behavioral signs (trait indicators), either directly or indirectly (Mischel, 1968). Guided by this assumption, personality research has been a quest for such underlying broad dimensions, for basic factors, or for pervasive motives, or for characteristic life styles. In personality assessment the trait assumptions regarding structure are seen in the existence of hundreds of tests designed to infer dispositions and almost none to measure situations. The same belief in global traits that manifest themselves pervasively is perhaps best seen in the projective test assumption that responses to vague or minimal stimuli will reveal individual differences in fundamental generalized dispositions (MacFarlane & Tuddenham, 1951).

Empirical Status of Assumptions

Given the pervasiveness of the consistency assumption of dispositional personality theory, its empirical status becomes especially important. There have been several recent reviews of that evidence (e.g., Mischel, 1968, 1969, 1971; Peterson, 1968; Vernon, 1964). The data cannot be summarized adequately here, but several themes emerge. To recapitulate briefly, impressive consistencies often have been found for intellective features of personality and for behavior patterns such as cognitive styles and problem-solving strategies that are strongly correlated

---

[1] In social psychology, the "attitude" has been the unit endowed with properties parallel to those assigned to the trait in the field of personality, and it appears to be subject to very similar criticisms and problems (e.g., Abelson, 1972).

with intelligence (e.g., Witkin, 1965). Consistency also is often high when people rate their own traits, as in questionnaires and other self-reports (e.g., E. L. Kelly, 1955). Temporal continuity also has been demonstrated often when the individual's behavior is sampled at different time periods but in similar situations. When one goes beyond cognitive variables to personality dimensions and when one samples personality by diverse methods and not just by self-report questionnaires, the data change and undermine the utility of inferring global personality dispositions from behavioral signs, as has been documented in detail (Mischel, 1968):

Response patterns even in highly similar situations often fail to be strongly related. Individuals show far less cross-situational consistency in their behavior than has been assumed by trait-state theories. The more dissimilar the evoking situations, the less likely they are to produce similar or consistent responses from the same individual. Even seemingly trivial situational differences may reduce correlations to zero. Response consistency tends to be greatest within the same response medium, within self-reports to paper-and-pencil tests, for example, or within directly observed non-verbal behavior. Intra-individual consistency is reduced drastically when dissimilar response modes are employed. Activities that are substantially associated with aspects of intelligence and with problem solving behavior—like achievement behaviors, cognitive styles, response speed—tend to be most consistent [p. 177].

Psychodynamic Approach to Consistency

Recognizing both the specificity and complexity of behavior, psychodynamic theorists long ago rejected the idea of broad overt behavioral consistencies across situations. Instead, psychodynamic theories emphasize that behavior varies, but diverse behavioral patterns serve the same enduring and generalized *underlying* dynamic or motivational dispositions. The search for dispositions thus rests on a distinction between surface behaviors ("signs" or "symptoms") and the motives that they serve. This involves the familiar distinction between the "phenotypic" and the "genotypic" and entails an indirect, rather than a direct measurement model (Mischel, 1968). Indeed, the most common argument for personality consistency in the face of seeming behavioral specificity is the distinction between the phenotypic and the genotypic. Granted that overt behavior is not highly consistent, might it not be useful to posit genotypic personality dispositions that endure, although their overt response forms may change? This genotypic–phenotypic model has been at the crux of dynamic dispositional theories of personality (Mischel, 1969). The psychodynamic model construes behaviors as highly *indirect* signs of the dispositions that underlie them, because defenses are hypothesized to distort and disguise the true meaning of the observed behaviors. If basic motives express themselves only indirectly after being distorted by defensive maneuvers, then their overt behavioral manifestations have to be interpreted symbolically as indirect signs. Thus, for example, using the white space of an inkblot in a percept may be taken as a sign of negativistic tendencies, or saying the inkblot looks like blood may be interpreted as a sign of a psychopathic personality. The psychodynamic approach thus shares with the trait approach a disinterest in behaviors except as they serve as signs—albeit more indirect signs—of generalized dispositions.

While inherently logical, the utility of the indirect sign approach to dispositions depends on the value of the inferences provided by the clinical judge. Consequently, the reliability and validity of clinicians' judgments become crucial. The extensive empirical studies on this issue have investigated in detail the value of clinicians' efforts to infer broad dispositions indirectly from specific symptomatic signs and to unravel disguises in order to uncover the motivational dispositions that might be their roots. As is now generally recognized, the accumulated findings give little support for the utility of clinical judgments, even when the judges are expert psychodynamicists working in clinical contexts and using their favorite techniques. Reviews of the relevant research generally show that clinicans guided by concepts about underlying genotypic dispositions have not been able to predict behavior better than have the person's own direct self-report, simple indices of directly relevant past behavior, or demographic variables (e.g., Mischel, 1968, 1971, 1972).

MISCONCEPTIONS AND ISSUES

The findings on the specificity–consistency of personality traits and the implications of social behavior theory for the psychology of personality may be leading to a paradigm crisis in the field (e.g., Fiske, 1973), and hence it is not surprising that they are easily misunderstood. These misunderstandings are evident in repeated critiques (e.g., Adelson, 1969; Adinolfi, 1971; Alker, 1972; Craik, 1969; Dahlstrom, 1970; Wachtel, 1973) aimed at applications of social behavior theory to the domain of personality (e.g., Mischel, 1968, 1969) and particularly to the issue of the specificity–generality of behavior. The thrust of these reactions is that social behavior theory, especially in its emphasis on the discriminativeness ("specificity") of behavior, implies a "personalityless" view of man.

Common Misconceptions

The position developed in Mischel's (1968) *Personality and Assessment* has been widely misunderstood to imply that people show no consistencies, that individual differences are unimportant, and that "situations" are the main determinants of behavior (e.g., Bowers, 1972). For example, Alker (1972) has thoroughly distorted the basic issues (as Bem, 1972, has shown), guarding the traditional personality paradigm against evidence that "behavior varies from situation to situation." But the fact that behavior varies across different situations is not questioned by anyone, including classical trait theorists. More serious issues, instead, are the consistency–specificity with which the same person reacts to situations that ostensibly are relatively *similar* (i.e., that are selected to evoke the same trait), and most important, the utility of predictions based on global trait inferences (Mischel, 1968). In the same vein, Wachtel (1973) defended psychodynamic theory against being forever consigned to a "scientific Valhalla" by emphasizing that psychodynamic theories in fact recognize people's responsiveness to variations in stimulus conditions. Unfortunately, he ignored the data and challenges that are relevant, most notably the failure of the psychodynamically oriented clinician to demonstrate the utility of the indirect sign approach when compared to more parsimonious alternatives (Mischel, 1968, 1972, 1973b).

Evidence for the lack of utility of inferring hypothesized global trait dispositions from behavioral signs should not be misread as an argument for the greater importance of situations than persons (Bowers, 1972). Is information about individuals more important than information about situations? The author has persistently refrained from posing this question because phrased that way it is unanswerable and can serve only to stimulate futile polemics. Moreover, in current debates on this topic, "situations" are often erroneously invoked as entities that supposedly exert either major or only minor control over behavior, without specifying what, psychologically, they are or how they function (Alker, 1972; Bowers, 1972; Wallach & Leggett, 1972). But while some situations may be powerful determinants of behavior, others are likely to be exceedingly trivial. The relative importance of individual differences will depend on the situation selected, the type of behavior assessed, the particular individual differences sampled, and the purpose of the assessment. In later sections, an attempt will be made to consider in detail how cognitive social learning person variables interact with conditions and how "situations" function psychologically. But first it is necessary to review further, and hopefully to clarify, some of the main issues and misconceptions regarding the status of global traits.

Moderator Variables and Person–Situation Interactions

Several recent trait studies have investigated the relative separate quantitative contributions of persons and situations as well as the variance accounted for by the interaction of the individual and the environment (e.g., Argyle & Little, 1972; Endler & Hunt, 1966, 1968, 1969; Endler, Hunt, & Rosenstein, 1962; Moos, 1968, 1969). The essential method consists of sampling the behavior of individuals (by questionnaire and/or by observation) across a series of situations and through various response modes. On the whole, these studies have indicated that the sampled individual differences, situations, and response modes when considered separately tend to account for less variance than does their interaction.

The overall results suggest, as Endler and Hunt (1969, p. 20) noted with regard to their own findings for anxiety, that behavior "is idiosyncratically organized in each individual. . . ." A similar conclusion emerges from Moos' (1968) studies of self-report reactions by staff and patients to various settings. Consider, for example, his obtained interactions between persons and nine settings with regard to "sociable, friendly, peaceful" versus "unsociable, hostile, angry" behavior. The results revealed that although different individuals reacted differently to the settings, a given person might be high on the dimension in the morning but not at lunch, high with another patient but not when with a nurse, low in small group therapy, moderate in industrial therapy, but high in individual therapy, etc. An entirely different pattern might characterize the next person. These results and interpretations are totally congruent with the conclusions emerging from earlier reviews that emphasize the idiosyncratic organization of behavior within individuals (Mischel, 1968, p. 190).

It would be wasteful to create pseudocontroversies that pit person against situation in order to see which is more important. The answer must always depend on the particular situations and persons sampled; presumably, studies could be designed to demonstrate almost any outcome. The interaction studies correctly demonstrated that the question of whether individual differences or persons are more important is a fruitless one that has no general answer. The views of Moos (1972, personal communication) regarding the limits of the kinds of interaction studies that he and Endler and Hunt pioneered seem extremely sensible. Moos recognized that these studies can be designed so that:

any result is possible. I think that all one can say is that given relatively real life situations (e.g., patients on wards or in outpatient psychotherapy, or your delay of gratification studies) that the major proportion of the variance simply does not appear to be accounted for by individual difference variables. One could certainly, however, easily design studies in which the major portion of the variance would be accounted for by individual difference variables. Frankly this is why I have stopped doing studies of this sort. It seems to me that the point has now been amply demonstrated, and it is time to get on with other matters.

It is encouraging that recent research on dispositions has started to recognize seriously the extraordinary complexity of the interactions found between subject variables and conditions. The concept of "moderator variables" was introduced to trait theory to refer to the fact that the effects of any particular disposition generally are moderated by such other variables as the subject's age, his sex, his IQ, the experimenter's sex, and the characteristics of the situation (Wallach, 1962). When one examines closely the interactions obtained in research on the effects of dispositions and conditions, the number of moderator variables required to predict behavior and the complexity of their interrelationships (e.g., McGuire, 1968) tend to become most formidable. For example, to predict a subject's voluntary delay of gratification, one may have to know how old he is, his sex, the experimenter's sex, the particular objects for which he is waiting, the consequences of not waiting, the models to whom he was just exposed, his immediately prior experience—the list gets almost endless (Mischel, 1973a). This seems to be another way of saying in the language of moderator variables and interaction terms that what a person does tends to be relatively specific to a host of variables, and that behavior is multiply determined by all of them rather than being the product of widely generalized dispositions. Some psychologists may find these interpretations more palatable if they are not phrased as reflecting the specificity of the acquired meanings of stimuli and the resulting specificity of behavior patterns (Mischel, 1968). Instead, they may prefer to construe the data as highlighting the uniqueness and complexity of personality. To say that what a person thinks, and does, and feels—and hence what he is at any moment—depends on many subject and condition variables is also to underline the complexity and uniqueness of his behavior.

The foregoing discussion does not imply that predictions cannot be made from subject variables to relevant behaviors, but it does suggest severe limits on the range and level of relationships that can be expected. Consider, as a representative example, a recent effort to relate individual differences in young children's expectancies about locus of control to their behavior in theoretically relevant situations (Mischel, Zeiss, & Zeiss, 1974). To explore these interactions, the Stanford Preschool Internal–External Scale was developed as a measure of expectancies about whether events occur as a consequence of the child's own action ("internal control") or as a consequence of external forces ("external control"). Expectancies about locus of control were measured separately for positive and negative events so that scores reflect expectancies for degree of internal control of positive events (I+), of negative events (I−), and a sum of these two (total I). Individual differences in I+, I−, and total I then were correlated with the children's ability to delay gratification under diverse working and waiting conditions. The results provided highly specific but theoretically meaningful patterns of relationships. To illustrate, relationships between total I and overall delay behavior were negligible, and I+ was unrelated to I−. As expected, I+ (but not I−) was found to be related to persistence in three separate situations where instrumental activity would result in a *positive* outcome; I− (but not I+) was related to persistence when instrumental activity could prevent the occurrence of a *negative* outcome.

The overall findings showed that individual differences in children's beliefs about their ability to control outcomes are partial determinants of their goal-directed behavior, but the relationships hinge on extremely specific moderating conditions, both with regard to the type of behavior and the type of belief. If such moderating conditions had not been considered and all indices of "delay behavior" had been combined regardless of their positive or negative valence, the actual role of the relevant individual differences would have been totally obscured. While the results were of considerable theoretical interest, the number and mean level of the achieved correlations were not appreciably higher than those typically found in correlational personality research. Moreover, the ability of these correlations to survive cross-validation remains to be demonstrated.

The more moderators required to qualify a trait, the more the "trait" becomes a relatively specific description of a behavior-situation unit. That is, the more highly circumscribed, "moderated," and situation specific the trait, the more it becomes indistinguishable from a specific behavior-situation description. At its extreme, when many strings of hyphenated moderator variables are required, the behavioral "signs" from which the disposition is inferred may become equivalent to the inferred disposition and make the inference gratuitous. As we increasingly qualify the description of a person to specify the exact response modes and conditions in which a particular behavior will occur, we move from characterizing him with generalized traits to describing his behavior in particular forms and under particular conditions.

The language of "interactions" and "moderator variables" provides simply another way of talking about the idiosyncratic organization of behavior and its dependence upon specific conditions unless (as Bem, 1972, p. 21, has noted) one can "*predict* on a priori grounds which moderators are likely to divide up the world into useful classes. . . ." Demonstrations that both subject and situational moderators can be used predictively, not merely to partial out the variance from each source post hoc, are especially important in light of the negative conclusions reached by Wallach, one of the main formulators of the moderator variable strategy in personality research. Commenting on the extensive results from his decade of work on the problem:

> Further analyses and additional data collection by us and others suggest that not only are findings ungeneralizable from one sex to the other, but even when, within sex, one simply tries to duplicate the results of a given study, such attempts do not pan out. . . . we cannot say that use of moderators has successfully pinpointed subgroups for whom consistency among diverse tests will be predictable. . . . The empirical basis for recommending moderators as the answer to the search for consistency thus seems more apparent than real [Wallach & Leggett, 1972, p. 313].

In regard to this last issue, the interaction studies of the sort conducted by Endler and Hunt and Moos, unfortunately, leave perhaps the most important question unanswered: once an individual's idiosyncratic pattern has been identified, can it be used accurately to *predict* consistencies in his subsequent behavior later in the same or (even more interestingly) in similar settings? While the interaction studies have demonstrated the existence of extensive Person X Situation interactions, they have not yet addressed themselves to the challenge of demonstrating that useful predictions can be made a priori about individual consistencies across a set of specified conditions. Such demonstrations are particularly necessary in light of the frequent failures to achieve replications in this domain (e.g., Averill, Olbrich, & Lazarus, 1972; Wallach & Leggett, 1972, pp. 313-314). Moreover, the interaction studies have not in any sense explained the nature of the obtained interactions. Later sections of this paper attempt to analyze the psychological bases for "interaction"; in the absence of such an analysis, an emphasis on interaction is in danger of being little more than the proclamation of a truism.

In sum, when interpreting the meaning of the data on Person X Situation interactions and moderator variables, it has been tempting to treat the obtained interactions as if they had demonstrated that people behave consistently in predictable ways across a wide variety of situations. But demonstrations of the predictive utility of the moderator variable–interaction strategy still lie in the future (e.g., Bem, 1972). The available data on this topic now merely highlight the idiosyncratic organization of behavior within individuals, and hence the uniqueness of stimulus equivalences and response equivalences for each person. Such data provide encouragement for idiographic study (Allport, 1937) but not for the predictive utility of "common" (nomothetic) personality traits.

"Specificity" or Discriminative Facility?

Viewed from the perspective of the traditional personality paradigm, the "specificity" and "inconsistency" found in behavior constitute an embarrassment that is generally attributed to methodological flaws and faulty measurements. Thus empirical evidence concerning the specificity of the relations between social behavior and conditions usually has been interpreted as due to the inadequacies of the tests and measures, faulty sampling, and the limitations of the particular raters or clinical judges. These and many other similar methodological problems undoubtedly are sources of error and seriously limit the degree of consistency that can be observed (e.g., Block, 1968; Emmerich, 1969).

An alternative interpretation, however, and one favored by a specific inter-action theory of social behavior, is that the "specificity" so regularly found in studies of noncognitive personality dimensions accurately reflects man's impressive discriminative facility and the inadequacy of the assumption of global dispositions, and not merely the distortions of measurement (Mischel, 1968). The term "discriminative facility" seems to fit the data better than "specificity" and avoids the unfortunate negative semantic connotations of specificity when applied to persons (e.g., the implications of inconsistency, insincerity, fickleness, unreliability; see also Gergen, 1968).

Whereas discriminative facility is highly functional (Gibson, 1969) diminished sensitivity to changing consequences (i.e., indiscriminate responding) may be a hallmark of an organism coping ineffectively. In fact, indiscriminate responding (i.e., "consistent" behavior across situations) tends to be displayed more by maladaptive, severely disturbed, or less mature persons than by well-functioning ones (Moos, 1968). For example, on the basis of their studies of hyperaggressive children undergoing therapeutic treatment, Raush, Dittmann, and Taylor (1959) reported: "there appears to be a trend for social behavior to become more related to situational influences with ego development . . . the children seem to have gained in the ability to discriminate between different situations [p. 368]." Yet although relatively more "indiscriminate behavior" tends to be found in more immature and/or severely abnormal persons, its extent should not be exaggerated. Even extremely autistic behavior, for example, is highly discriminative when closely analyzed (e.g., Lovaas, Freitag, Gold, & Kassorla, 1965).

Discrimination, Generalization, and Idiosyncratic Stimulus Meanings

The discriminativeness found in behavior is *not* so great that we cannot recognize continuity in people. It is also not so great that we have to treat each new behavior from a person as if we never saw anything like it from him before. But the findings remind us that what people do in any situation may be changed dramatically even by relatively trivial alterations in their prior experiences or by slight modifications in the particular features of the immediate situation. Rather than argue about the existence of "consistency," it would be more constructive to analyze and study the cognitive and social learning conditions that seem to foster—and to undermine—its occurrence.

If expected consequences for the performance of responses across situations are largely uncorrelated, the responses themselves should not be expected to covary strongly, as they indeed do not in most empirical studies. When the probable reinforcing consequences to the person for cheating, waiting, or working differ widely across situations depending on the particular task or circumstances, the behavior of others, the likelihood of detection, the probable consequences of being caught, the frustration induced, the value of success, etc., impressive generality will not be found. Conversely, when similar behaviors are expected and supported in numerous situations, consistency will be obtained.

Because most social behaviors produce positive consequences in some situations but negative ones in other contexts, the relatively low associations found among an individual's response patterns even in seemingly similar situations should not be surprising. Consider, for example, the intercorrelations among measures intended to sample dependent behaviors, such as "touching, holding, and being near." If a child has been rewarded regularly at nursery school for "touching, holding, and being near" with his teacher but not with his father at home, a high correlation between dependency measured in the two situations will not be found and should not be expected.

The consequences for similar content expressed in different response modes also tend to be drastically different. If on a projective test a person tells stories full of aggressive themes, he would be judged to have a healthy fantasy life, but he would be jailed if he enacted those themes in his relations with other people. It therefore should not be surprising that when different response modes are used to sample the individual's behavior (e.g., data from questionnaires, from behavior observation), consistency is even harder to demonstrate (Mischel, 1968).

To the degree that idiosyncratic social learning histories characterize each person's life, idiosyncratic (rather than culturally shared) stimulus equivalences and hence idiosyncratic behavior patterns may be expected. As was noted earlier (Mischel, 1968, p. 190, italics added):

> The phenomena of discrimination and generalization lead to the view that behavior patterns are remarkably situation–specific on the one hand, while also evokable by diverse and often seemingly heterogeneous stimuli on the basis of generalization effects. *The person's prior experiences with related conditions and the exact details of the particular evoking situation determine the meaning of the stimuli,* i.e., their effects on all aspects of his life. Usually generalization effects involve relatively *idiosyncratic* contextual and semantic generalization dimensions and are based on more than gradients of physical stimulus similarity . . . *one must know the properties or meaning that the stimulus has acquired for the subject.* If the history is unknown, the response has to be assessed directly.

Idiosyncratic histories produce idiosyncratic stimulus meanings. In clinical assessment of the individual, it is apparent, for example, that seemingly heterogeneous stimuli may come to elicit similar intense approach or avoidance patterns accompanied by strong arousal (Mischel, 1968). Because the conditions under which stimuli acquire their meaning and power are often both adventitious and unique, and because the dimensions of stimulus and response generalization tend to be idiosyncratic, it may be futile to seek common underlying dimensions of similarity on the basis of which diverse events come to evoke a similar response pattern for all persons. Especially when the individual's prior learning history is unknown, and when he is exposed to multiple and exceedingly complex stimuli as in virtually all life situations, it becomes important to assess the effective stimuli, or "stimuli as coded," which regulate his responses in particular contexts. These stimuli as coded should not be confused with the totality of objective physical events to which he is exposed. It is hardly novel now to assert that the objective distal stimulus impinging on sense organs does not necessarily correspond to the "effective" stimulus; organisms respond selectively to particular aspects of the objective stimulus event (Lawrence, 1959).

The meaning and impact of a stimulus can be modified dramatically by *cognitive transformations.* Such transformations are illustrated in research on the determinants of how long preschool children will actually sit still alone in a chair waiting for a preferred but delayed outcome before they signal with a bell to terminate the waiting period and settle for a less preferred but immediately available gratification (e.g., Mischel, Ebbesen, & Zeiss, 1972). We have been finding that the same child who on one occasion may terminate his waiting in less than half a minute may be capable of waiting by himself for long times on another occasion a few weeks earlier or later, if cognitive and attentional conditions are appropriate (Mischel, 1973a).

For example, if the child is left during the waiting period with the actual reward objects (e.g., pretzels or marshmallows) in front of him, it becomes extremely difficult for him to wait for more than a few moments. But through instructions he can cognitively transform the reward objects in ways that permit him to wait for long time periods (e.g., Mischel & Baker, 1973). If he cognitively transforms the stimulus, for example, by thinking about the pretzel sticks as little brown logs or by thinking about the marshmallows as round white clouds or as cotton balls, he may wait much longer than our graduate student experimenters. Conversely, if the child has been instructed to focus cognitively on the consummatory qualities of the reward objects, such as the pretzel's crunchy, salty taste or the chewy, sweet, soft taste of the marshmallows, he tends to be able to wait only a short time. Similarly, through instruction the children can easily transform the real objects (present in front of them) into a "color picture in your head," or they can transform the picture of the objects (presented on a slide projected on a screen in front of them) into the "real" objects by pretending in imagination that they are actually there on a plate in front of them (Mischel & Moore, 1973b).

The results clearly show that what is in the children's heads—not what is physically in front of them—determines their ability to delay. Regardless of the stimulus in their visual field, if they imagine the real objects as present, they cannot wait long for them. But if they imagine pictures (abstract representations) of the objects, they can wait for long time periods (and even longer than when they are distracting themselves with abstract representations of objects that are comparable but not relevant to the rewards for which they are waiting). Through instructions (administered before the child begins to wait) about what to imagine during the delay period, it is possible to completely alter (indeed, to reverse) the effects of the physically present reward stimuli in the situation and to cognitively control delay behavior with considerable precision. But while in experiments the experimenter provides instructions (which our subjects obligingly followed) about how to construe the stimulus situation, in life the "subject" supplies his own instructions and may transform the situation in many alternative (unpredictable) ways. The ability of individuals to cognitively transform the meaning and impact of stimuli in any given situation (e.g., by self-instructions) makes it even more unlikely that the assessor will discover a priori broad equivalence classes of stimulus meanings for many individuals across many situations, unless they all transform the stimuli in the same way.

Recognition of the idiosyncratic organization of behavior in each person suggests that individually oriented assessments are bound to have very limited success if they try to label a person with generalized trait terms, sort him into diagnostic or type categories, or estimate his average position on average or modal dimensions (Mischel, 1968).[2] Instead, it may be more useful for the clinician to assess the exact conditions that regularly covary with increments or decrements in the problem-producing behaviors for the particular person. For this purpose in a behavioral analysis, one attempts to sample directly the individual's relevant cognitions and behaviors in relation to the conditions of particular current concern:

In this sense, behavioral assessment involves an exploration of the unique or idiographic aspects of the single case, perhaps to a greater extent than any other approach. Social behavior theory recognizes the individuality of each person and of each unique situation. This is a curious feature when one considers the "mechanistic S-R" stereotypes not infrequently attached by critics to behavioral analyses. *Assessing the acquired meaning of stimuli is the core of social behavior assessment* . . . [Mischel, 1968, p. 190, italics added].

The above point is often misunderstood. For example, Adinolfi (1971, p. 174) asked: "How then does the social-behavioral critic of current clinical and personality theory propose to determine the stimulus conditions to which the observed is responding?" The answer to this question comes from actively

---

[2] It is possible that for each individual there are unique but broad classes of subjective stimulus equivalences, but these cannot be assessed by comparing individuals in situations that are construed as equivalent by the assessor. Such subjective equivalences certainly merit attention, but so far the clinician has not demonstrated his ability to find them reliably (Mischel, 1968).

enrolling the "observed" person in the assessment process (Mischel, 1968). In collaboration with the assessor the individual provides hypotheses about the conditions that lead to increases and decreases in his own problematic behaviors. To elaborate, verify, or modify these hypotheses, the stimulus conditions are introduced and systematically varied, and their impact on the person is assessed from his self-report and from other changes in his behavior. In this manner, one can analyze how changes in the particular stimulus conditions are correlated with changes in the behavior of interest. The acquired meanings of a stimulus can only be known by determining what the person does with it verbally and behaviorally, when it is introduced and varied in sampled situations. To reveal the acquired meanings of stimuli, one must assess what the individual says and does when they occur in symbolic form (e.g., when discussed in interviews) and more realistically when presented in hypothetical, role-playing or life situations, as has been discussed in detail (Mischel, 1968). Considerable evidence suggests that in this assessment enterprise, direct information from the person is the best source of data (Mischel, 1972).

Some of the clearest examples of the analysis of stimulus conditions influencing behavior are found in efforts to construct subjective anxiety hierarchies (e.g., Wolpe, 1961). In collaboration with the assessor, the individual can identify the specific conditions that generate fear in him and arranges them on a gradient of severity from least to most intense. For one client, items such as "thinks I only did an hour's work today," "sitting at the movies," "going on a casual stroll" and "staying in bed during the day (even though ill)" were some of the events arranged on a subjective continuum of "guilt"-producing stimuli. Such individually oriented assessments lead naturally to the design of individually oriented treatments intended to provide the best possible conditions for achieving each individual's objectives (Bandura, 1969). In the case of the client suffering from guilt, for example, after the subjective hierarchy of guilt-inducing stimuli had been identified, conditions could be arranged to help him make new responses incompatible with anxiety when the problem-producing stimuli are presented cognitively through thought-inducing instructions.

Uses and Misuses of Traits

In sum, obviously behavior is not entirely situation specific; we do not have to relearn everything in every new situation, we have memories, and our past predisposes our present behavior in critically important and complex ways. Obviously people have characteristics and overall "average" differences in behavior between individuals can be abstracted on many dimensions and used to discriminate among persons for many purposes. Obviously knowing how a person behaved before can help predict how he will behave again in similar contexts. Obviously the impact of any stimulus depends on the organism that experiences it. No one suggests that the organism approaches every new situation with an empty head, nor is it questioned by anyone that different individuals differ markedly in how they deal with most stimulus conditions. What has been questioned (Hunt, 1965; Mischel, 1968) is the utility of inferring broad dispositions from behavioral signs as *the* bases for trying to explain the phenomena of personality and for making useful statements about individual behavior. The available data do *not* imply that different people will not act differently with some consistency in different classes of situations; they *do* imply that the particular classes of conditions must be taken into account far more carefully than in the past, tend to be much narrower than traditional trait theories have assumed, and for purposes of important individual decision making, require highly individualized assessments of stimulus meanings (Mischel, 1968, pp. 235–280). The data also suggest that inferences about global underlying traits and dispositions tend to have less utility for most assessment efforts to predict or therapeutically modify individual behavior than do more economical, alternative analyses based on more direct data such as the person's past behavior in similar situations or his direct self-report.

A critique of traits as inadequate causal explanations and an indictment of the utility of indirect trait inferences for many individually oriented assessment and clinical purposes (Mischel, 1968) does not imply a rejection of their other possible uses. The layman as well as the trait psychologist generates and employs trait constructs. The question becomes not "do traits really exist?" but when are trait constructs invoked and "what are their uses and misuses?"

Research on the layman's attribution of causation to dispositional versus situational factors helps to clarify when person variables and individual differences are used in the everyday formation of impressions. Person (trait) explanations are invoked when the individual's behavior is "distinctive" (Kelley, 1967), that is, when it deviates from others' behavior in the same situation. Thus, behaviors that are at variance with relevant group norms (e.g., success when others fail, failure when others succeed) are attributed to the person or to "internal causes" (e.g., Frieze & Weiner, 1971; Weiner & Kukla, 1970). Conversely, when a person's behavior is consistent with the norms in the situation (when the person succeeds when others succeed, or fails when others fail), his performance is attributed to situational factors such as task difficulty (Weiner et al., 1971).

Traits are constructs which are inferred or abstracted from behavior. When the relations between the observed behavior and the attributed trait are relatively direct, the trait serves essentially as the summary term for the behaviors that have been integrated by the observer. People emit behaviors and these are perceived, integrated, and categorized by those who observe them, including those who emit them. The process of integrating the observed information is receiving much study but is still not completely understood (e.g., Anderson, 1971, 1972). Regardless of the exact genesis of trait impressions, trait labels may serve as summaries (essentially arithmetic averages) for categories of observed behavior (e.g., "dependent on peers," "physically aggressive with siblings"). For purposes of global characterizations of salient personal qualities, broad, highly abstract categories may be useful with minimal moderators or specific situational qualifiers. But for purposes of more specific communication and for prediction of specific behavior in relation to specific conditions, careful discriminative limits must be included.

Estimates of mean past behavior often are the best predictors of future behavior in similar situations, especially when there are no other bases for prediction (Mischel, 1968, 1972). The predictive limitations of traits become evident, however, when one attempts to predict from past behavior to behavior in different new situations. Moreover, when observers categorize an individual's behavior in trait terms, the "salient" (central, mean, primary) features of the behavior may become *the* basis for the categorization, so that the person becomes labeled as "anxious," for example, even if that term accurately characterizes only a small portion of his total social behavior. Then the "moderators" become omitted and the situation-free trait abbreviations that remain may serve more as global stereotypes and broad character sketches than as accurate bases for the prediction of specific behaviors.

When the consistency issue is viewed in terms of the *utility* of inferring broad response tendencies and not in terms of the more metaphysical question of the existence or validity of personality dispositions, it becomes evident that the answer must depend on the particular objective or purpose for which the inference is made. For example, while global trait inferences may have little utility for the prediction of the subject's specific future behavior in specific situations or for the design of specific treatment programs, they may have value for the person himself—for instance, when he must abstract attributes to answer such everyday questions as: Is your assistant reliable? or What kind of person is my psychotherapist? or Might this stranger lurking on the next corner be a murderer? or What are *you* like? Similarly, an indictment of the relative lack of utility of inferring broad dispositions for purposes of predicting and/or thera-peutically modifying the individual's behavior does not deny the utility of using such inferences for many other purposes—such as for gross initial screening decisions or for studying average differences between groups of individuals in personality research (Mischel, 1968).

The limitations of traditional personality theories which invoke trait con-structs as the psychologist's explanations for behavior should not deflect attention from the importance of the layman's everyday use of trait categories. How do trait categorizations function for the layman? Do they serve him well? For what purposes might they be used? In our research my students and I are asking such questions now. For example, we find that when required to predict a person's behavior and given a choice of how to categorize the available behavioral information, subjects overwhelmingly preferred to organize data in terms of traits rather than settings (Jeffrey & Mischel, 1973). But when the perceiver's purpose was structured as memorizing as much information as possible, setting categories were used. Clearly the functions of trait constructs for the layman deserve serious attention and hopefully will inform us further about the psychological uses and abuses of trait categorization.

From Behavior to the Construction of Personality

As Heider (1958) has noted, in the psychology of common sense the subject goes quickly from act to global internalized disposition. While behavior often may be highly situation specific, it seems equally true that in daily life people tend to construe each other as if they were highly consistent, constructing consistent personalities even on the basis of relatively inconsistent behavioral fragments.

This discrepancy may reflect in part that people go rapidly beyond the observation of *some* consistency which does exist in behavior to the attribution of greater perceived consistencies which they construct (e.g., Mischel, 1969; Schneider, 1973). After these construction systems have been generated, they may be adhered to tenaciously even in the face of seemingly disconfirmatory data (Mischel, 1968, 1969).

Many processes contribute to the construction and maintenance of consistent impressions of others. Tversky and Kahnemon (1971), for example, contended that both sophisticated scientists and naive subjects intuitively but often erroneously interpret small samples of observations as if they were highly representative. Moreover, after an initial impression of a person has been formed, observations of his subsequent behavior are biased toward consistency with the initial impression (Hayden & Mischel, 1973). Like the clinician (e.g., Chapman & Chapman, 1969), the layman's impressions may perpetuate consistent but invalid "illusory correlations." There even seems to be a substantial bias of memory for the attributes of behavior in the direction of preexisting cognitive structures or implicit personality theories (D'Andrade, 1970, 1973). Consequently, recall-based trait ratings may yield data that are systematic but unrelated to results based on direct observation of ongoing behavior as it occurs (Shweder, 1972).

The overattribution of consistency may be something people do unto others more than to themselves. Jones and Nisbett (1971) noted that when explaining *other* people's behavior we invoke their consistent personality dispositions: Steve is the sort of person who puts bumper stickers on his car; Jill tripped because she's clumsy. But when asked to explain our *own* behavior we consider specific conditions: "AAA sent me this catchy bumper sticker in the mail" or "I tripped because it was dark." Thus Jones and Nisbett (1971, p. 58) on the basis of some promising preliminary data theorized that "actors tend to attribute the causes of their behavior to stimuli inherent in the situation while observers tend to attribute behavior to stable dispositions of the actor." Jones and Nisbett analyzed many possible reasons for this seemingly paradoxical state of affairs, including the tendency to treat every sample of behavior we observe from another person is if it were modal or typical for him. It thus seems as if traits may be the consistent attributes that *other* people have. When describing other people, we seem to act more like trait theorists, but when we attempt to understand ourselves we function more like social behaviorists. Might there be a warning here for clinicians? Do we pin our clients with consistent dispositional labels and trait explanations more than we do ourselves? If that is true it may be because we have more information about ourselves and the multiplicity, variety, and complexity of the situations we encounter in our own lives, whereas we know others in only limited contexts and therefore tend to overgeneralize from their behavior in those instances.

Traits as Causes versus Traits as Summary Labels

According to the traditional trait paradigm, traits are the generalized dispositions in the person that render many stimuli functionally equivalent and that cause the individual to behave consistently across many situations (Allport, 1937). The present view, in contrast, construes the individual as generating diverse behaviors in response to diverse conditions; the emitted behaviors are observed and subsequently integrated cognitively by the performer, as well as by others who perceive him, and are encoded on semantic dimensions in trait terms. Thus while the traditional personality paradigm views traits as the intrapsychic *causes* of behavioral consistency, the present position sees them as the *summary terms* (labels, codes, organizing constructs) applied to observed behavior. In the present view, the study of global traits may ultimately reveal more about the cognitive activity of the trait theorist than about the causes of behavior, but such findings would be of great value in their own right.

COGNITIVE SOCIAL LEARNING PERSON VARIABLES

The previous sections have considered the limitations of the basic assumptions of traditional global dispositional theories of personality and some of the main misconceptions and issues arising from recent challenges to those assumptions. Progress in the area of personality will require more than criticism of existing positions and hinges on the development of an alternative conceptualization. In this section therefore a set of person variables is proposed, based on theoretical developments in the fields of social learning and cognition.

Given the overall findings on the discriminativeness of behavior and on the complexity of the interactions between the individual and the situation, it seems reasonable in the search for person variables to look more specifically at what the person *constructs* in particular conditions, rather than trying to infer what broad traits he generally *has*, and to incorporate in descriptions of what he does the specific psychological conditions in which the behavior will and will not be expected to occur. What people do, of course, includes much more than motor acts and requires us to consider what they do cognitively and affectively as well as motorically.

The proposed cognitive social learning approach to personality shifts the unit of study from global traits inferred from behavioral signs to the individual's cognitive activities and behavior patterns, studied in relation to the specific conditions that evoke, maintain, and modify them and which they, in turn, change (Mischel, 1968). The focus shifts from attempting to compare and generalize about what different individuals "are like" to an assessment of what they *do*—behaviorally and cognitively—in relation to the psychological conditions in which they do it. The focus shifts from describing situation-free people with broad trait adjectives to analyzing the specific interactions between conditions and the cognitions and behaviors of interest.

Personality research on social behavior and cognition in recent years has focused mainly on the processes through which behaviors are acquired, evoked, maintained, and modified (e.g., Bandura, 1969; Mischel, 1968). Much less attention has been given to the psychological products within the individual of cognitive development and social learning experiences. Yet a viable psychology of personality demands attention to person variables that are the products of the individual's total history and that in turn mediate the manner in which new experiences affect him.

The proposed person variables are a synthesis of seemingly promising constructs in the areas of cognition and social learning. The selections should be seen as suggestive and open to progressive revision rather than as final. These tentative person variables are not expected to provide ways to accurately predict broadly cross-situational behavioral differences between persons: the discriminativeness and idiosyncratic organization of behavior are facts of nature, not limitations unique to trait theories. But these variables should serve to demonstrate that a social behavior approach to persons does not imply an empty organism. They should suggest useful ways of conceptualizing and studying specifically how persons mediate the impact of stimuli and generate distinctive complex molar behavior patterns. And they should help to conceptualize person–situation interactions in a theoretical framework based on contributions from both cognitive and behavioral psychology.

The proposed cognitive social learning person variables deal first with the individual's *competencies* to construct (generate) diverse behaviors under appropriate conditions. Next, one must consider the individual's *encoding* and *categorization* of events. Furthermore, a comprehensive analysis of the behaviors a person performs in particular situations requires attention to his *expectancies* about outcomes, the *subjective values* of such outcomes, and his *self-regulatory systems and plans*. The following five sections discuss each of these proposed person variables. While these variables obviously overlap and interact, each may provide distinctive information about the individual and each may be measured objectively and varied systematically.

Cognitive and Behavioral Construction Competencies

Through direct and observational learning the individual acquires information about the world and his relationship to it. As a result of observing events and attending to the behavior of live and symbolic models (through direct and film-mediated observation, reading, and instruction) in the course of cognitive development the perceiver acquires the potential to generate vast repertoires of organized behavior. While the pervasive occurrence and important consequences of such observational learning have been convincingly demonstrated (e.g., Bandura, 1969; Campbell, 1961), it is less clear how to conceptualize just what gets learned. The phenomena to be encompassed must include such diverse learnings as the nature of sexual gender identity (e.g., Kohlberg, 1966), the structure (or construction) of the physical world (e.g., Piaget, 1954), the social rules and conventions that guide conduct (e.g., Aronfreed, 1968), the personal constructs generated about self and others (e.g., G. Kelly, 1955), the rehearsal strategies of the observer (Bandura, 1971a). Some theorists have discussed these acquisitions in terms of the products of information processing and of information integration (e.g., Anderson, 1972; Bandura, 1971a; Rummelhart, Lindsey, & Norman, 1971), others in terms of schemata and cognitive templates (e.g., Aronfreed, 1968).

The concept of *cognitive and behavioral construction competencies* seems sufficiently broad to include the vast array of psychological acquisitions of organized information that must be encompassed. The term "constructions" also emphasizes the constructive manner in which information seems to be retrieved (e.g., Neisser, 1967) and the active organization through which it is categorized and transformed (Bower, 1970; Mandler, 1967, 1968). It has become plain that rather than mimicking observed responses or returning memory traces from undisturbed storage vaults, the observer selectively *constructs* (generates) his renditions of "reality." Indeed, research on modeling effects has long recognized that the products of observational learning involve a novel, highly organized synthesis of information rather than a photocopy of specific observed responses (e.g., Bandura, 1971b; Mischel & Grusec, 1966). The present concept of construction competencies should call attention to the person's cognitive activities—the operations and transformations that he performs on information—rather than to a store of finite cognitions and responses that he "has."

Although the exact cognitive processes are far from clear, it is apparent that each individual acquires the capacity to construct a great range of potential behaviors, and different individuals acquire different behavior construction capabilities. The enormous differences between persons in the range and quality of the cognitive and behavioral patterns that they can generate is evident from even casual comparison of the construction potentials of any given individual with those, for example, of an Olympic athlete, a Nobel Prize winner, a retardate, an experienced forger, or a successful actor.

The person's behavior construction potential can be assessed readily by introducing incentives for the most complete constructions that he can render on particular performance tasks. In a sense, the assessment conditions here are identical to those in achievement testing (Wallace, 1966). The same strategy can be used to assess what subjects "know" (i.e., the cognitive constructions they can generate, for example, about abstract and physical properties and relationships as in mathematics and geography) and what they are capable of doing (enacting) in the form of social behaviors. For example, to assess what children had acquired from observing a model, attractive rewards later were offered to them contingent upon their reproducing the model's behaviors (e.g., Bandura, 1965; Grusec & Mischel, 1966). The results showed that the children had acquired a great deal of information from observation of the model which they could reconstruct elaborately but only when given appropriate incentives.

For many purposes, it is valuable to assess the quality and range of the cognitive constructions and behavioral enactments of which the individual is capable. In this vein, rather than assess "typical" behavior, one assesses *potential* behaviors or achievements. One tests what the person *can* do (e.g., Wallace, 1966) rather than what he "usually" does. Indeed one of the most recurrent and promising dimensions of individual differences in research seems to involve the person's *cognitive and behavioral (social) competencies* (e.g., White, 1959; Zigler & Phillips, 1961, 1962). These competencies presumably reflect the degree to which the person can generate adaptive, skillful behaviors that will have beneficial consequences for him. Personality psychology can profit from much greater attention to cognitive and intellectual competencies since these "mental abilities" seem to have much better temporal and cross-situational stability and influence than most of the social traits and motivations traditionally favored in personality research (e.g., Mischel, 1968, 1969).

The relevance of cognitive-intellective competencies for personality seems evident in light of the important, persistent contributions of indices of intelligence to the obtained networks of personality correlations (Campbell & Fiske, 1959; Mischel, 1968). In spite of extensive efforts to minimize or "partial out" the role of intelligence in personality studies, for example, cognitive competencies (as tested by "mental age" and IQ tests) tend to be among the very best predictors of later social and interpersonal adjustment (e.g., Anderson, 1960). Presumably, brighter, more competent people experience more interpersonal success and better work achievements and hence become more positively assessed by themselves and by others on the evaluative "good–bad" dimension which is so ubiquitous in trait ratings (e.g., Vernon, 1964). Cognitive achievements and intellective potential, as measured by mental age or IQ tests, also are receiving a central place in current cognitive-developmental theories (e.g., Kohlberg, 1969) and presumably are an important ingredient of such concepts as "ego strength" and "ego development." Indeed, it is tempting to speculate that the pervasive and substantial "first factor" found on tests like the MMPI (Block, 1965), often labeled with terms connoting "adjustment" at the positive end and maladaptive character structure at the negative end, reflects to a considerable degree the individual's level of cognitive-social competence and achievement. To the degree that certain demographic variables (e.g., socioeconomic class, high school graduation) reflect the individual's construction capacities and achievements, they also may be expected to predict "adjustment" and interpersonal competencies, as they often do (e.g., Robbins, 1972). The assessment of competence in response to specific problematic situations in the direct manner developed by Goldfried and D'Zurilla (1969) seems especially promising.

The relative stability of the person's construction capacities may be one of the important contributors to the impression of consistency in personality. The fact that cognitive skills and behavior-generating capacities tend to be relatively enduring is reflected in the relatively high stability found in performances closely related to cognitive and intellectual variables, as has been stressed before (Mischel, 1968, 1969). The individual who knows how to be assertive with waiters, for example, or who knows how to solve certain kinds of interpersonal problems competently, or who excels in singing, is *capable* of such performances enduringly.

Encoding Strategies and Personal Constructs

From the perspective of personality psychology, an especially important component of information processing concerns the perceiver's ways of encoding and grouping information from stimulus inputs. As discussed in earlier sections, people can readily perform *cognitive transformations* on stimuli (Mischel & Moore, 1973), focusing on selected aspects of the objective stimulus (e.g., the taste versus the shape of a food object): such selective attention, interpretation, and categorization substantially alter the impact the stimulus exerts on behavior (see also Geer, Davison, & Gatchel, 1970; Schachter, 1964). Likewise, the manner in which perceivers encode and selectively attend to observed behavioral sequences greatly influences what they learn and subsequently can do (Bandura, 1971a, 1971b). Clearly, different persons may group and encode the same events and behaviors in different ways. At a molar level, such individual differences are especially evident in the personal constructs individuals employ (e.g., Argyle & Little, 1972; G. Kelly, 1955) and in the kinds of information to which they selectively attend (Mischel, Ebbesen, & Zeiss, 1973).

The behaviorally oriented psychologist eschews inferences about global dispositions and focuses instead on the particular stimuli and behaviors of interest. But what are "the stimuli and behaviors of interest?" Early versions of behaviorism attempted to circumvent this question by simplistic definitions in terms of clearly delineated motor "acts" (such as bar press) in response to clicks and lights. As long as the behaviors studied were those of lower animals in experimenter-arranged laboratory situations, the units of "behavior" and "stimuli" remained manageable with fairly simple operational definitions. More recent versions of behavior theory, moving from cat, rat, and pigeon confined in the experimenter's apparatus to people in exceedingly complex social situations, have extended the domain of studied behavior much beyond motor acts and muscle twitches; they seek to encompass what people do cognitively, emotionally, and interpersonally, not merely their arm, leg, and mouth movements. Now the term "behavior" has been expanded to include virtually anything that an organism does, overtly or covertly, in relation to extremely complex social and interpersonal events. Consider, for example, "aggression," "anxiety," "defense," "dependency," "self-concepts," "self-control," "self-reinforcement." Such categories go considerably beyond self-evident behavior descriptions. A category like aggression involves inferences about the subject's intentions (e.g., harming another versus accidental injury) and abstractions about behavior, rather than mere physical description of actions and utterances.

A focus on behavior must not obscure the fact that even the definition and selection of a behavior unit for study requires grouping and categorizing. In personality research, the psychologist does the construing, and he includes and excludes events in the units he studies, depending on his interests and objectives. He selects a category—such as "delay of gratification," for example—and studies its behavioral referents. In personality assessment, however, it becomes quickly evident that the subject (like the psychologist) also groups events into categories and organizes them actively into meaningful units. The layman usually does not describe his experience with operational definitions: he categorizes events in terms of his *personal constructs* (G. Kelly, 1955), and these may or may not overlap either with those of the psychologist or of other individuals. As previously noted (Jeffery & Mischel, 1973), observers tend to group information about persons with dispositional categories (such as "honest," "intolerant," "freaky," "do gooder"). Skepticism about the utility of traditional trait constructs regarding the subject's broad dispositions in no way requires one to ignore the subject's constructs about his own and other's characteristics. People invoke traits and other dispositions as ways of describing and explaining their experience and themselves, just as professional psychologists do, and it would be strange if we tried to define out of existence the personal constructs and other concepts, perceptions, and experiences of the individuals whom we are studying. The study of personal construct systems (e.g., Little & Stephens, 1973), of implicit, personality theories (e.g., Hamilton, 1971; Schneider, 1973), and of self-concepts (e.g., Gergen, 1968) promises to illuminate an important set of still poorly understood person variables.

Cognitive consistency tends to be enhanced by selective attention and coding processes that filter new information in a manner that permits it to be integrated with existing cognitive structures (e.g., Norman, 1969). Cognitive processes that facilitate the construction and maintenance of perceived consistency (e.g., D'Andrade, 1970; Hayden & Mischel, 1973) have been mentioned earlier and are elaborated elsewhere (Mischel, 1968, 1969). After information has been integrated with existing cognitive structures and becomes part of long-term memory, it remains available enduringly and exerts further stabilizing effects. For example, the individual's subjective conception of his own identity and continuity presumably rests heavily on his ability to remember (construct) subjectively similar behaviors on his part over long time periods and across many situations. That is, the individual can abstract the common elements of his behavior over time and across settings, thereby focusing on his more enduring qualities.

There is considerable evidence that people categorize their own personal qualities in relatively stable trait terms (e.g., on self-ratings and self-report questionnaires). These self-categorizations, while often only complexly and tenuously related to nonverbal behavior, may be relatively durable and generalized (Mischel, 1968, 1969). Such stable styles of self-presentation and self-description may be reflected in personality test "response sets" like social desirability (Edwards, 1957), and in tendencies to depict oneself in relatively positive or negative terms found in the behavior of so-called "repressers" versus "sensitizers" on the Byrne (1961) Repression–Sensitization Scale (Mischel, Ebbesen, & Zeiss, 1973). While traditional personality research has focused primarily on exploring the correlates of such self-categorizations, in the present view they comprise merely one kind of person variable.

Behavior-Outcome and Stimulus-Outcome Expectancies

So far the person variables considered deal with what the individual is capable of doing and how he categorizes events. To move from potential behaviors to actual performance, from construction capacity and constructs to the construction of behavior in specific situations, requires attention to the determinants of performance. For this purpose, the person variables of greatest interest are the subject's expectancies. While it is often informative to know what an individual *can* do and how he construes events and himself, for purposes of specific prediction of behavior in a particular situation it is essential to consider his specific expectancies about the consequences of different behavioral possibilities in that situation. For many years personality research has searched for individual differences on the psychologist's hypothesized dimensions while neglecting the subject's own expectancies (hypotheses). More recently, it seems increasingly clear that the expectancies of the subject are central units for psychology (e.g., Bolles, 1972; Estes, 1972; Irwin, 1971; Rotter, 1954). These hypotheses guide the person's selection (choice) of behaviors from among the enormous number which he is capable of constructing within any situation.

On the basis of direct experience, instructions, and observational learning, people develop expectancies about environmental contingencies (e.g., Bandura, 1969). Since the expectancies that are learned within a given situation presumably reflect the objective contingencies in that situation, an expectancy construct may seem superfluous. The need for the expectancy construct as a person variable becomes evident, however, when one considers individual differences in response to the same situational contingencies due to the different expectancies that each person brings to the situation. An expectancy construct is justified by the fact that the person's expectancies (inferred from statements) may not be in agreement with the objective contingencies in the situation. Yet behavior may be generated in light of such expectancies, as seen, for example, in any verbal conditioning study when a subject says plural nouns on the erroneous hypothesis that the experimenter is reinforcing them.

In theories based on lower animal behavior, the expectancy construct has served as a limited heuristic (e.g., Bolles, 1972), since rats and pigeons cannot tell us their expectancies. Fortunately, humans are not so handicapped and under appropriate assessment conditions are willing and able to externalize their expectancies. Hence the expectancy construct applied to human rather than animal learning leads readily to measurement operations and to research strategies that can take account directly of the subject's hypotheses. Empirically, since direct self-reports seem to be one of the best data sources about the individual (Mischel, 1968, 1972), it should be possible to fruitfully assess behavior-outcome expectancies by asking the subject.

One type of expectancy concerns *behavior-outcome relations* under particular conditions. These *behavior-outcome expectancies* (hypotheses, contingency rules) represent the "if____; then____" relations between behavioral alternatives and probable outcomes anticipated with regard to particular behavioral possibilities in particular situations. In any given situation, the person will generate the response pattern which he expects is most likely to lead to the most subjectively valuable outcomes (consequences) in that situation (e.g., Mischel, 1966; Rotter, 1954). In the absence of new information about the behavior-outcome expectancies in any situation the individual's performance will depend on his previous behavior-outcome expectancies in similar situations. This point is illustrated in a study (Mischel & Staub, 1965) which showed that presituational expectancies significantly affect choice behavior in the absence of situational information concerning probable performance-outcome relationships. But the Mischel and Staub study also showed that new information about behavior-outcome relations in the particular situation may quickly overcome the effects of presituational expectancies, so that highly specific situational expectancies become the dominant influences on performance.

When the expected consequences for performance change, so does behavior, as seen in the discriminative nature of responding which was elaborated in earlier sections and documented elsewhere (Mischel, 1968). But in order for changes in behavior-outcome relations to affect behavior substantially, the person must recognize them. In the context of operant conditioning, it has become evident that the subject's awareness of the behavior-outcome relationship crucially affects the ability of response consequences (reinforcements) to modify his complex performances (e.g., Spielberger & DeNike, 1966). As previously stressed, the essence of adaptive performance is the recognition and appreciation of new contingencies. To cope with the environment effectively, the individual must recognize new contingencies as quickly as possible and reorganize his behavior in the light of the new expectancies. Strongly established behavior-outcome expectancies with respect to a response pattern may constrain an individual's ability to adapt to changes in contingencies. Indeed, "defensive reactions" may be seen in part as a failure to adapt to new contingencies because the individual is still behaving in response to old contingencies that are no longer valid. The "maladaptive" individual is behaving in accord with expectancies that do not adequately represent the actual behavior-outcome rules in his current life situation.

In the present view, the effectiveness of response-contingent reinforcements (i.e., operant conditioning) rests on their ability to modify behavior-outcome expectancies. When information about the response pattern required for re-inforcement is conveyed to the subject by instructions, "conditioning" tends to occur much more readily than when the subject must experience directly the reinforcing contingencies actually present in the operant training situation. For example, accurate instructions about the required response and the reinforcement schedule to which subjects would be exposed exerted far more powerful effects on performance than did the reinforcing contingencies (Kaufman, Baron, & Kopp, 1966). Presumably, such instructions exert their effects by altering response-outcome expectancies. To the extent that information about new response-reinforcement contingencies can be conveyed to motivated human beings more parsimoniously through instructions or observational experiences than through operant conditioning procedures (e.g., Kaufman et al., 1966), an insistence upon direct "shaping" may reflect an unfortunate (and wasteful) failure to discriminate between the animal laboratory and the human con-dition.

A closely related second type of expectancy concerns *stimulus-outcome relations*. As noted previously in the discussion of generalization and dis-crimination, the outcomes expected for any behavior hinge on a multitude of stimulus conditions that moderate the probable consequences of any pattern of behavior. These stimuli ("signs") essentially "predict" for the person other events that are likely to occur. More precisely, the individual learns (through direct and observational experiences) that certain events (cues, stimuli) predict certain other events. This concept of *stimulus-outcome expectancy* is similar to the S–S* expectancy representing stimulus-outcome contingencies proposed by Bolles (1972) in the context of animal learning.

Stimulus-outcome expectancies seem especially important person variables for understanding the phenomena of classical conditioning. For example, through the contiguous association of a light and painful electric shock in aversive classical conditioning the subject learns that the light predicts shock. If the product of classical conditioning is construed as a stimulus-outcome expectancy, it follows that any information which negates that expectancy will eliminate the con-ditioned response. In fact, when subjects are informed that the "conditioned stimuli" will no longer be followed by pain-producing events, their conditioned emotional reactions are quickly eliminated (e.g., Grings & Lockhart, 1963). Conversely, when subjects were told that a particular word would be followed by shock, they promptly developed conditioned heart-rate responses (Chatterjee & Eriksen, 1962). In the same vein, but beyond the conditioning paradigm, if subjects learn to generate "happy thoughts" when faced by stimuli that otherwise would frustrate them beyond endurance, they can manage to tolerate the "aversive" situation with equanimity (Mischel, Ebbesen, & Zeiss, 1972). Outside the artificial confines of the laboratory in the human interactions of life, the "stimuli" that predict outcomes often are the social behaviors of others in particular contexts. The meanings attributed to those stimuli hinge on a multitude of learned correlations between behavioral signs and outcomes.

Just as correlational personality research yields a host of validity associations between behavioral "signs" from persons in one context and their behavior in other situations, so does the perceiver's learning history provide him with a vast repertoire of meaningful signs. For example, as research on person perception suggests, "shifty eyes," "tight lips," "lean and hungry looks," obese body build, age, sex, and an enormous number of even subtler behavioral cues (e.g., regarding the status and power of others) come to predict for observers other correlated behaviors. If it were possible to compute them, many of these correlations probably would not average more than the .30 "personality coefficient" (Mischel, 1968) typically found in correlational personality research, but that may be sufficiently accurate (especially on an intermittent schedule) to assure their persistent use. Some of these stimulus-outcome associations presumably reflect the perceiver's idiosyncratic learning history and his own evolving personal rules about stimulus meanings. Many of these associations, however, are likely to be widely shared by members of a common culture and probably depend importantly on the transcultural semantic associations discussed by D'Andrade (1970) and Shweder (1971, 1972). An adequate study of stimulus-outcome expectancies therefore would require attention to the rule system of the individual as well as to the shared "sign" grammar of the culture and of the transcultural lexicon structure.

Both behavior-outcome and stimulus-outcome expectancies depend on inferences about the *intentions* motivating behavior (i.e., its perceived causes). For example, a person's reactions to a physical blow from another will crucially depend on whether it was perceived as accidental or deliberate. Similarly, whether praise and attention produces in the recipient a warm glow (and "conditioning" of his preceding behaviors) or suspicion (and a rebuff) depends on whether the behaviors are perceived as sincere or as ingratiating (Jones, 1964). Extremely subtle social and interpersonal cues affect the interpretation of the motivation (and hence the impact) of these complex human behaviors.

Although expectancy constructs often have been proposed, some of the main formulations have been based entirely on animal research (e.g., Bolles, 1972) which makes their relevance for human personality remote. Rotter's (1954) "subjective expectancy" construct was an important and theoretically influential exception. However, it deals only with one type of expectancy (similar to the present "behavior-outcome expectancies"); it does not consider stimulus-outcome expectancies. Moreover, Rotter's formulation focuses on "generalized expectancies" which are functionally similar to generalized traits and are not posited in the present approach.

In the present view, the person's expectancies mediate the degree to which his behavior shows cross-situational consistency or discriminativeness. When the expected consequences for the performance of responses across situations are not highly correlated, the responses themselves should not covary strongly (Mischel, 1968). As previously noted, since most social behaviors lead to positive consequences in some situations but not in other contexts, highly discriminative specific expectancies tend to be developed and the relatively low correlations typically found among a person's response patterns across situations become understandable (Mischel, 1968). Expectancies also will not become generalized across response modes when the consequences for similar content expressed in different response modes are sharply different, as they are in most life circumstances (Mischel, 1968). Hence expectancies tend to become relatively specific, rather than broadly generalized. Although a person's expectancies (and hence performances) tend to be highly discriminative, there certainly is some generalization of expectancies, but their patterning in the individual tends to be idiosyncratically organized to the extent that the individual's history is unique. (See the earlier section in this paper on generalization, discrimination, and idiosyncratic stimulus meanings.)

While behavior-outcome and stimulus-outcome expectancies seem viable person variables, it would be both tempting and hazardous to transform them into generalized trait-like dispositions by endowing them with broad cross-situational consistency or removing them from the context of the specific stimulus conditions on which they depend. At the empirical level, "generalized expectancies" tend to be generalized only within relatively narrow, restricted limits (e.g., Mischel & Staub, 1965; Mischel, Ebbesen, & Zeiss, 1973). As was noted before in this paper, for example, the generality of "locus of control" is in fact limited, with distinct, unrelated expectancies found for positive and negative outcomes and with highly specific behavioral correlates for each (Mischel, Zeiss, & Zeiss, 1973). If expectancies are converted into global trait-like dispositions and extracted from their close interaction with situational conditions, they are likely to become just as useless as their many theoretical predecessors. On the other hand, if they are construed as relatively specific (and modifiable) "if _____, then _____" hypotheses about contingencies, it becomes evident that they exert important effects on behavior (e.g., Mischel & Staub, 1965).

Subjective Stimulus Values

Even if individuals have similar expectancies, they may select to perform different behaviors because of differences in the *subjective values* of the outcomes which they expect. For example, given that all persons expect that approval from a therapist depends on verbalizing particular kinds of self-references, there may be differences in the frequency of such verbalizations due to differences in the perceived value of obtaining the therapist's approval. Such differences reflect the degree to which different individuals value the response-contingent outcome. Therefore it is necessary to consider still another person variable: the subjective (perceived value for the individual of particular classes of events, that is, his stimulus preferences and aversions. This unit refers to stimuli that have acquired the power to induce positive or negative emotional states in the person and to function as incentives or reinforcers for his behavior. The subjective value of any stimulus pattern may be acquired and modified through instructions and observational experiences as well as through direct experiences (Bandura, 1969).

Stimulus values can be assessed by measuring the individual's actual choices in life-like situations as well as his verbal preferences or ratings (e.g., Mischel, 1966; Mischel & Grusec, 1966). Verbal reports (e.g., on questionnaires) about values and interests also may supply valuable information about the individual's preferences and aversions, and appear to provide some of the more temporally stable data in the domain of personality (E. L. Kelly, 1955; Strong, 1955). Alternatively, subjects may be asked to rank-order actual rewards (Rotter, 1954), or the reinforcement value of particular stimuli may be assessed directly by observing their effects on the individual's performance (e.g., Gerwitz & Baer, 1958).

Reinforcement (incentive) preferences may also be assessed by providing individuals opportunities to select the outcomes they want from a large array of alternatives, as when patients earn tokens which they may exchange for objects or activities: the "price" they are willing to pay for particular outcomes provides an index of their subjective value (e.g., Ayllon & Azrin, 1965). The concept that any behavior which has a high natural frequency of occurrence can serve as a reinforcer for other less likely behaviors (Premack, 1965) also suggests that subjective reinforcers may be discovered by assessing the individual's naturally occurring high frequency behaviors in particular situations (Mischel, 1968).

A comprehensive assessment of stimulus values must include attention to stimuli that have acquired strong emotion-eliciting powers, as in the conditioned autonomic reactions seen in intense fears. For this purpose, specific self-report inventories, physiological measures, and direct behavior sampling of approach and avoidance behavior in response to the real or symbolically presented emotional stimulus may all be useful (Mischel, 1968).

The measurement operations for assessing stimulus values require considerable specificity. Just as the probable consequences of any behavior pattern hinge on a host of specific moderating considerations, so does the affective value (valence) of any stimulus depend on the exact conditions—in the person and in the situation—in which it occurs. The many variables known to affect the emotional meaning and valence of a stimulus include its context, sequencing, and patterning (e.g., Helson, 1964); social comparison processes (e.g., Festinger, 1945); and the cognitive labels the person assigns to his own emotional arousal state (Schachter & Singer, 1962). Thus, like instrumental responses, emotional reactions also tend to become far more discriminative than dispositional theories have assumed. Lazarus (1963), for example, has noted the specificity of sexual fears in frigid women. For instance, one woman could calmly imagine herself engaged in certain sexual caresses, but only if they occurred in the dark. Or consider the pilot who became debilitatingly anxious when flying, but only when his plane was higher than 9,000 feet (White, 1964), or the young woman who had asthmatic attacks mostly after she had contacts with her mother (Metcalf, 1956). Good illustrations of the analysis of stimulus conditions influencing emotional responses come from attempts to create subjective anxiety hierarchies (e.g., Wolpe, 1961).

Self-Regulatory Systems and Plans

While behavior is controlled to a considerable extent by externally administered consequences for actions, the individual also regulates his own behavior by self-imposed goals (standards) and self-produced consequences. Even in the absence of external constraints and social monitors, persons set performance goals for themselves and react with self-criticism or self-satisfaction to their behavior depending on how well it matches their expectations and criteria. The concept of self-imposed achievement standards is seen in Rotter's (1954) "minimal goal" construct and in more recent formulations of self-reinforcing functions (e.g., Bandura, 1971c; Kanfer, 1971; Kanfer & Marston, 1963; Mischel, 1968, 1973a).

The essence of self-regulatory systems is the subject's adoption of *contingency rules* that guide his behavior in the absence of, and sometimes in spite of, immediate external situational pressures. Such rules specify the kinds of behavior appropriate (expected) under particular conditions, the performance levels (standards, goals) which the behavior must achieve, and the consequences (positive and negative) of attaining or failing to reach those standards. Each of these components of self-regulation may be different for different individuals, depending on their unique earlier histories or on more recently varied instructions or other situational information.

Some of the components in self-regulation have been demonstrated in studies of goal setting and self-reinforcement (e.g., Bandura & Whalen, 1966; Bandura & Perloff, 1967; Mischel & Liebert, 1966). Perhaps the most dramatic finding from these studies is that even young children will not indulge themselves with freely available immediate gratifications but, instead, follow rules that regulate conditions under which they may reinforce themselves. Thus, children, like adults, far from being simply hedonistic, make substantial demands of themselves and impose complex contingencies upon their own behavior. The stringency or severity of self-imposed criteria is rooted in the observed standards displayed by salient models as well as in the individual's direct socialization history (e.g., Mischel & Liebert, 1966), although after they have been adopted, the standards may be retained with considerable persistence.

After the standards (terminal goals) for conduct in a particular situation have been selected, the often long and difficult route to self-reinforcement and external reinforcement with material rewards is probably mediated extensively by covert symbolic activities, such as praise and self-instructions, as the individual reaches subgoals. When individuals imagine reinforcing and noxious stimuli, their behavior appears to be influenced in the same manner as when such stimuli are externally presented (e.g., Cautela, 1971). These covert activities serve to maintain goal-directed work until the performance matches or exceeds the person's terminal standards (e.g., Meichenbaum, 1971). Progress along the route to a goal is also mediated by self-generated distractions and cognitive operations through which the person can transform the aversive "self-control" situation into one which he can master effectively (e.g., Mischel et al., 1972; Mischel & Moore, 1973a, 1973b). While achievement of important goals leads to positive self-appraisal and self-reinforcement, failure to reach significant self-imposed standards may lead the individual to indulge in psychological self-lacerations (e.g., self-condemnation). The anticipation of such failure probably leads to extensive anxiety, while the anticipation of success may help to sustain performance, although the exact mechanisms of self-regulation still require much empirical study.

Self-reactions and self-regulation also are influenced by the person's affective state. Following positive experiences, individuals become much more benign both toward themselves and others than after negative experiences. For example, after success experiences or positive mood inductions, there is greater selective attention to positive information about the self (Mischel et al, 1973), greater noncontingent self-gratification (e.g., Mischel, Coates, & Raskoff, 1968; Moore, Underwood, & Rosenhan, 1973), and greater generosity (e.g., Isen, Horn, & Rosenhan, 1973).

In conceptualizing the organization of complex self-regulatory behavior, it will be necessary to consider the individual's "priority rules" for determining the *sequencing* of behavior and "stop rules" for the *termination* of a particular sequence of behavior. The ideas concerning "plans" as hierarchical processes which control the order in which an organism performs a sequence of operations, proposed by Miller, Galanter, and Pribram (1960), seem relevant. Subjectively, we do seem to generate plans, and once a plan is formed (to go on a trip, to marry, to move to a new job, or write a paper) a whole series of subroutines follows. While intuitively plausible, the concept of plans has not yet stimulated the necessary personality-oriented cognitive research. Promising steps toward the study of plans are the concepts of behavioral intentions (Dulany, 1962), intention statements, and contracts (e.g., Kanfer, Cox, Greiner, & Karoly, 1973). Although self-instructions and intention statements are likely to be essential components of the individual's plans and the hierarchical organization of his self-regulatory behavior, at present these topics provide perhaps the largest void and the greatest challenge in personality psychology.

To summarize, a comprehensive approach to person variables must take account of the individual's self-regulatory systems. These systems include: the rules that specify goals or performance standards in particular situations; the consequences of achieving or failing to achieve those criteria; self-instructions and cognitive stimulus transformations to achieve the self-control necessary for goal attainment; and organizing rules (plans) for the sequencing and termination of complex behavioral patterns in the absence of external supports and, indeed, in the face of external hindrances.

Overview of Person Variables

In sum, individual differences in behavior may reflect differences in each of the foregoing person variables and in their interactions, summarized in Table 1.

First, people differ in their *construction competencies*. Even if people have similar expectancies about the most appropriate response pattern in a particular situation and are uniformly motivated to make it, they may differ in whether or not (and how well) they *can* do it, that is, in their ability to construct the preferred response. For example, due to differences in skill and prior learning, individual differences may arise in interpersonal problem solving, empathy and role taking, or cognitive-intellective achievements. Response differences also may reflect differences in how individuals *categorize* a particular situation (i.e., in how they encode, group, and label the events that comprise it) and in how they construe themselves and others. Differences between persons in their performance in any situation depend on their behavior-outcome and stimulus-outcome *expectancies*, that is, differences in the expected outcomes associated with particular responses or stimuli in particular situations. Performance differences also may be due to differences in the subjective *values* of the outcomes expected in the situation. Finally, individual differences may be due to differences in the *self-regulatory systems* and plans that each person brings to the situation.

COGNITIVE SOCIAL LEARNING VIEW OF INTERACTION

In this final section, some issues in current theorizing about personality will be reconsidered and interpreted in light of the proposed cognitive social learning person variables. These issues concern the role of individual differences and the specific interaction of person variables and situations.

Table 1. Summary of Cognitive Social Learning Person Variables

---

1. Construction competencies: ability to construct (generate) particular cognitions and behaviors. Related to measures of IQ, social and cognitive (mental) maturity and competence, ego development, social-intellectual achievements and skills. Refers to what the subject knows and *can* do.
2. Encoding strategies and personal constructs: units for categorizing events and for self-descriptions.
3. Behavior-outcome and stimulus-outcome expectancies in particular situations.
4. Subjective stimulus values: motivating and arousing stimuli, incentives, and aversions.
5. Self-regulatory systems and plans: rules and self-reactions for performance and for the organization of complex behavior sequences.

When Do Individual Differences Make a Difference?

From the present viewpoint, the conditions or "situational variables" of the psychological environment provide the individual with information which influences the previously discussed person variables, thereby affecting cognitive and behavioral activities under those conditions. "Situations" thus affect behavior insofar as they influence such person variables as the individual's encoding, his expectancies, the subjective value of stimuli, or the ability to generate response patterns. In light of the proposed set of person variables, it is now possible to return to the question of when situations are most likely to exert powerful effects and, conversely, when person variables are likely to be most influential.

Psychological "situations" and "treatments" are powerful to the degree that they lead all persons to construe the particular events the same way, induce *uniform* expectancies regarding the most appropriate response pattern, provide adequate incentives for the performance of that response pattern, and instill the skills necessary for its satisfactory construction and execution. Conversely, situations and treatments are weak to the degree that they are not uniformly encoded, do not generate uniform expectancies concerning the desired behavior, do not offer sufficient incentives for its performance, or fail to provide the learning conditions required for successful construction of the behavior.

Individual differences can determine behavior in a given situation most strongly when the situation is ambiguously structured (as in projective testing) so that subjects are uncertain about how to categorize it and have no clear expectations about the behaviors most likely to be appropriate (normative, reinforced) in that situation. To the degree that the situation is "unstructured," the subject will expect that virtually *any* response from him is equally likely to be equally appropriate (i.e., will lead to similar consequences), and variance from individual differences will be greatest. Conversely, when subjects expect that only *one* response will be reinforced (e.g., only one "right" answer on an achievement test, only one correct response for the driver when the traffic light turns red) and that no other responses are equally good, and all subjects are motivated and capable of making the appropriate response, then individual differences will be minimal and situational effects prepotent. To the degree that subjects are exposed to powerful treatments, the role of individual differences will be minimized. Conversely, when treatments are weak, ambiguous, or trivial, individual differences in person variables should exert significant effects.

There have been several empirical demonstrations of these points. Mischel and Staub (1965) examined some of the conditions determining the interaction and relative importance of individual differences and situations. Adolescent subjects were assessed on a measure of their expectancies for success in ability areas. Three weeks later, they worked on a series of problems and in one treatment obtained success, in a second, failure, and in a third, no information. Next, they had to make many choices, including one between a noncontingent but less preferred reward and a more preferred reward whose attainment was contingent upon their successful performance on a task similar to the one on which they had previously either succeeded, failed, or received no information. On this choice, situational success and failure had the expected effects: subjects who had succeeded chose much more often to work for the contingent preferred reward than did those who had failed. The effects of situational success and failure were so strong that they wiped out the role of individual differences in pre-experimental expectancy for success. But in the "no-information" condition (in which subjects obtained no feedback about their performance quality in the situation) preexperimental expectancy was a highly significant determinant of their choice to work for contingent rewards. Thus situational manipulations which provided new expectancies minimized the effects of relevant preexisting individual differences, but when situational variables were weak or ambiguous (the no-information about-performance condition) the expectancies that persons brought to the situation affected their behavior. Similar conclusions come from a recent study investigating the influence of success and failure experiences on subsequent selective attention to information about the self (Mischel et al., 1973).

The complex social settings of life also may be construed as varying in the degree to which they prescribe and limit the range of expected and acceptable behavior for persons in particular roles and settings and hence permit the expression of individual differences (e.g., Barker, 1966). In some settings the rules and prescriptions for enacting specific role behaviors impose narrow limits on the range of possible behaviors (e.g., in church, at school, in a theatre, at a conference), while in others the range of possible behaviors is broad and often the individual can select, structure, and reorganize situations with minimal external constraints. Because in particular settings certain response patterns are reinforced while others are not, different settings become the occasion for particular behaviors in different degrees. Raush (1965), for example, found that in a sample of normal American boys, friendly acts led to unfriendly responses in 31% of the instances in game situations but in only 4% of the time at mealtimes.

Person–condition interactions are never static, but environmental stabilities can be identified which help to account for continuities in behavior and permit useful predictions (e.g., Mischel, 1968). While it would be bizarre to ignore the person in the psychology of personality, behavior often may be predicted and controlled efficaciously from knowledge about relevant stimulus conditions, especially when those conditions are powerful (Mischel, 1968). The potency of predictions based on knowledge of stimulus conditions is seen, for example, in predictive studies regarding posthospital prognosis for mental patients. Of special interest are studies which revealed that the type, as well as the severity, of psychiatric symptoms depended strikingly on whether the person was in the hospital or in the community, with little consistency in behavior across changing situations (Ellsworth, Foster, Childers, Gilberg, & Kroeker, 1968). Moreover, accurate predictions of posthospital adjustment hinged on knowledge of the environment in which the ex-patient will be living in the community, such as the availability of jobs and family support, rather than on any measured person variables or in-hospital behavior (e.g., Fairweather, 1967). In another context, predictions of intellectual achievement are greatly improved if they take account of the degree to which the child's environment supports (models and reinforces) intellectual development (Wolf, 1966). Finally, when powerful treatments are developed, such as modeling and desensitization therapies for phobias, predictions about outcomes are best when based on knowing the treatment to which the individual is assigned (e.g., Bandura, Blanchard, & Ritter, 1969). On the other hand, when relevant situational information is absent or minimal, or when predictions are needed about individual differences in response to the same conditions, or when treatment variables are weak, information about person variables becomes essential.

Specific Interactions between Behavior and Conditions

Traditionally, trait research has studied individual differences in response to the "same" situation. But some of the most striking differences between persons may be found not by studying their responses to the same situation but by analyzing their selection and construction of stimulus conditions. In the conditions of life outside the laboratory the psychological "stimuli" that people encounter are neither questionnaire items, nor experimental instructions, nor inanimate events, but they involve people and reciprocal relationships (e.g., with spouse, with boss, and with children). The person continuously influences the "situations" of his life as well as being affected by them in a mutual, organic two-way interaction. These interactions reflect not only the person's reactions to conditions but also his active selection and modification of conditions through his own cognitions and actions.

As the analysis of complex social interactions illustrates (e.g., Patterson & Cobb, 1971), the person continuously selects, changes, and generates conditions just as much as he is affected by them. The mutual interaction between person and conditions (so easily forgotten when one searches for generalized traits on paper-and-pencil tests) cannot be overlooked when behavior is studied in the interpersonal contexts in which it is evoked, maintained, and modified.

Generally, changes in behavior toward others tend to be followed by reciprocal changes in the behavior of those others (Raush et al., 1959). In Raush's (1965) studies of naturalistic interactions, for example, "the major determinant of an act was the immediately preceding act. Thus if you want to know what child B will do, the best single predictor is what child A did to B the moment before [p. 492]." Construed from the viewpoint of Child A, this means that A's own behavior determines B's reactions to him. In that sense, the person is generating his own conditions. Such subject variables as the person's expectancies, self-regulatory rules, plans, and constructs presumably guide the situations which he selects, generates, and structures for himself.

The proposed cognitive social learning approach to person variables emphasizes most strongly the need to study the individual's behavior in specific interaction with particular conditions. Indeed, the conceptualization of behavior whether psychologist defined (as in research) or subject defined (as in clinical, individually oriented assessment) must be embedded in relation to the specific conditions in which the behavior occurs. Rather than talk about "behavior," it may be more useful to conceptualize *behavior-contingency units* that link specific patterns of behavior to the conditions in which they may be expected. Accurate descriptions require specifying as precisely as possible the response mode of the behavior as well as the contingencies in which it is expected to be of high or low frequency, as was discussed in earlier sections on situational moderator variables. Thus rather than describe a person as "aggressive," it would be necessary to qualify the mode of aggressive behavior (e.g., verbal insults but not physical attacks) and the specific contingencies (e.g., when criticized for poor athletic performance on playground but not in class). Such cumbersome, hyphenated descriptions (e.g., Mischel, 1969) would lack the "thumbnail sketch" appeal of global trait portraits. But they would remind us of the discriminativeness and complexity of the individual's behavior, its idiosyncratic organization, its dependence on conditions, and the hazards of attempting to abbreviate it grossly.

The previously discussed person variables should make it plain that a cognitive social learning approach does not construe the individual as an empty organism buffeted entirely by situational forces. Yet it should be equally apparent that the nature and effects of these person variables depend on specific interactions between the individual and the psychological conditions of his life. Construction capacities cannot be adequately understood without linking them to the cognitive social learning conditions through which they develop and are maintained and to the behaviors which they yield. Similarly, the study of expectancies must not lose sight of their roots in the individual's direct and vicarious experiences and of their ready modifiability in the light of changes in behavior-outcome and stimulus-outcome relationships. While subjective stimulus values and the individual's preferences and aversions may have a greater degree of stability, their meaning and impact also hinge on the specifics of the conditions in which they occur. Self-regulatory rules, standards, and plans serve to impose additional continuity and consistency upon behavior and guide the individual in the absence of immediate situational forces. Yet such standards, rules, and plans also are not situation free, and their flexibility in response to changing conditions provides further testimony to human adaptiveness.

Perhaps substantial immunity to situational changes is shown by some of the individual's personal constructs. The "theories" formed about behavior (as in the subject's implicit personality theories about self and others) may be some of the most stable and situation-free constructions. That has double-edged consequences; the person's constructs provide a measure of perceived stability in an otherwise excessively complex, disorganized, and unstable world, but they also may become hard to disconfirm. Yet even in the realm of constructs, consistency is far from pervasive. For example, Gergen's (1968) findings reveal that contrary to the popular belief, when it comes to their self-perceptions people do not have a consistent, unitary self-concept. Indeed, he concludes with regard to the phenomena of self-concepts that "inconsistency" rather than "consistency" seems to be the natural state of affairs.[3]

The proposed approach to personality psychology emphasizes the interdependence of behavior and conditions, mediated by the constructions and cognitive activities of the person who generates them, and recognizes the human tendency to invent constructs and to adhere to them as well as to generate subtly discriminative behaviors across settings and over time. It emphasizes the crucial role of situations (conditions) but views them as informational inputs whose behavioral impact depends on how they are processed by the person. It focuses on how such information processing hinges, in turn, on the prior conditions which the individual has experienced. And it recognizes that the person's behavior changes the situations of his life as well as being changed by them. The term "personality psychology" need not be preempted for the study of differences between individuals in their consistent attributes: it fits equally well the study of the individual's cognitive and behavioral activities as he interacts with the conditions of his life.

Three Perspectives in Personality Study

The study of persons may be construed alternatively from three complementary perspectives. Construed from the viewpoint of the psychologist seeking procedures or operations necessary to produce changes in performance, it may be most useful to focus on the environmental *conditions* necessary to modify the subject's behavior and therefore to speak of "stimulus control," "operant conditioning," "classical conditioning," "reinforcement control," "modeling" and so on. Construed from the viewpoint of the theorist concerned with how these operations produce their effects in the subject who undergoes them, it may be more useful to speak of alterations in processed information and specifically in constructs, expectancies, subjective values, rules, and other theoretical *person variables* that mediate the effects of conditions upon behavior. Construed from the viewpoint of the experiencing subject, it may be more useful to speak of the same events in terms of their *phenomenological impact* as thoughts, feelings, wishes, and other subjective (but communicable) internal states of experience. Confusion arises when one fails to recognize that the same events (e.g., the "operant conditioning" of a child's behavior at nursery school) may be alternatively construed from each of these perspectives and that the choice of constructions (or their combinations) depends on the construer's purpose. Ultimately, conceptualizations of the field of personality will have to be large enough to encompass the phenomena seen from all three perspectives. The

---

[3] In the same vein, in their analysis of sources of variance in personal constructs, Argyle and Little (1972) found that the average variation attributable to persons was only 16.1%, whereas the percentages for situations and interaction were 43.6 and 40.2, respectively.

present cognitive social learning approach to persons hopefully is a step in that direction.

REFERENCES

Abelson, R. Are attitudes necessary? In B. T. King & E. McGinnies (Eds.), *Attitudes, conflict, and social change.* New York: Academic Press, 1972.

Adelson, J. Personality. *Annual Review of Psychology,* 1969 **20,** 217–252.

Adinolfi, A. A. Relevance of person perception research to clinical psychology. *Journal of Consulting and Clinical Psychology,* 1971, **37,** 167–176.

Alker, H. A. Is personality situationally specific or intrapsychically consistent? *Journal of Personality,* 1972, **40,** 1–16.

Allport, G. *Personality: A psychological interpretation.* New York: Holt, 1937.

Anderson, J. The prediction of adjustment over time. In I. Iscoe & H. Stevenson (Eds.), *Persoanlity development in children.* Austin: University of Texas Press, 1960.

Anderson, N. H. Integration theory and attitude change. *Psychological Review,* 1971, **78,** 171–206.

Anderson, N. H. Information integration theory: A brief survey. (Tech. Rep. No. 24) La Jolla: University of California at San Diego, Center for Human Information Processing, 1972.

Argyle, M., & Little, B. R. Do personality traits apply to social behavior? *Journal of Theory of Social Behavior,* 1972, **2,** 1–35.

Aronfreed, J. *Conduct and conscience: The socialization of internalized control over behavior.* New York: Academic Press, 1968.

Averill, J. R., Olbrich, E., & Lazarus, R. S. Personality correlates of differential responsiveness to direct and vicarious threat: A failure to replicate previous findings. *Journal of Personality and Social Psychology,* 1972, **21,** 25–29.

Ayllon, T., & Azrin, N. H. The measurement and reinforcement of behavior of psychotics. *Journal of the Experimental Analysis of Behavior,* 1965, **8,** 357–383.

Bandura, A. Influence of model's reinforcement contingencies on the acquisition of imitative responses. *Journal of Personality and Social Psychology,* 1965, **1,** 589–595.

Bandura, A. *Principles of behavior modification.* New York: Holt, Rinehart & Winston, 1969.

Bandura, A. Analysis of modeling processes. In A. Bandura (Ed.), *Psychological modeling: Conflicting theories.* Chicago: Aldine-Atherton, 1971. (a)

Bandura, A. *Social learning theory.* New York: General Learning Press, 1971. (b)

Bandura, A. Vicarious and self-reinforcement processes. In R. Glaser (Ed.), *The nature of reinforcement.* New York: Academic Press, 1971. (c)

Bandura, A., Blanchard, E. B., & Ritter, B. Relative efficacy of desensitization and modeling approaches for inducing behavioral, affective, and attitudinal changes. *Journal of Personality and Social Psychology,* 1969, **13,** 173–199.

Bandura, A., & Perloff, B. Relative efficacy of self-monitored and externally imposed reinforcement systems. *Journal of Personality and Social Psychology,* 1967, **7,** 111–116.

Bandura, A., & Whalen, C. K. The influence of antecedent reinforcement and divergent modeling cues on patterns of self-reward. *Journal of Personality and Social Psychology,* 1966, **3,** 373–382.

Barker, R. *The stream of behavior.* New York: Appleton-Century-Crofts, 1966.

Bem, D. J. Constructing cross-situationsl consistencies in behavior: Some thoughts on Alker's critique of Mischel. *Journal of Personality,* 1972, **40,** 17–26.

Block, J. *The challenge of response sets.* New York: Appleton-Century-Crofts, 1965.

Block, J. Some reasons for the apparent inconsistency of personality. *Psychological Bulletin,* 1968, **70,** 210–212.

Bolles, R. C. Reinforcement, expectancy, and learning. *Psychological Review,* 1972, **79,** 394–409.

Bower, G. H. Organizational factors in memory. *Cognitive Psychology,* 1970, **1,** 18–46.

Bowers, K. Situationism in psychology: On making reality disappear. *Research Reports in Psychology, No. 37,* University of Waterloo, 1972.

Byrne, D. The repression–sensitization scale: rationale, reliability, and validity. *Journal of Personality,* 1961, **29,** 334–349.

Campbell, D. T. Conformity in psychology's theories of acquired behavioral dispositions. In I. A. Berg, & B. M. Bass (Eds.), *Conformity and deviation.* New York: Harper, 1961.

Campbell, D., & Fiske, D. W. Convergent and discriminant validation. *Psychological Bulletin,* 1959, **56,** 81–105.

Cautela, J. R. Covert conditioning. In A. Jacobs & L. B. Sachs (Eds.), *The psychology of private events.* New York: Academic Press, 1971.

Chapman, L. J., & Chapman, J. P. Illusory correlations as an obstacle to the use of valid psychodiagnostic signs. *Journal of Abnormal Psychology,* 1969, **74,** 271–280.

Chatterjee, B. B., & Eriksen, C. W. Cognitive factors in heart rate conditioning. *Journal of Experimental Psychology,* 1962, **64,** 272–279.

Craik, K. C. Personality unvanquished. *Contemporary Psychology,* 1969, **14,** 147–148.

Dahlstrom, W. C. Personality. *Annual Review of Psychology,* 1970, **21,** 1–48.

D'Andrade, R. G. Cognitive structures and judgment. Paper prepared for T.O.B.R.E. Research Workshop on Cognitive Organization and Psychological Processes, Huntington Beach, California, August 16–21, 1970. La Jolla: University of California at San Diego, Department of Anthropology, 1970.

D'Andrade, R. G. Memory and the assessment of behavior. Unpublished manuscript, University of California at San Diego, Department of Anthropology, 1973.

Dulany, D. H. The place of hypotheses and intentions: An analysis of verbal control in verbal conditioning. *Journal of Personality,* 1962, **30,** 102–129.

Edwards, A. L. *The social desirability variable in personality assessment and research.* New York: Dryden, 1957.

Ellsworth, R. B., Foster, L., Childers, B. Gilberg, A., & Kroeker, D. Hospital and community adjustment as perceived by psychiatric patients, their families, and staff. *Journal of Consulting and Clinical Psychology,* 1968, **32** (5, Pt. 2).

Emmerich, W. Models of continuity and change. Paper presented at the meeting of the Society for Research in Child Development, March 27, 1969, Santa Monica, California.

Endler, N. S., & Hunt, J. McV. Sources of behavioral variance as measured by the S–R inventory of anxiousness. *Psychological Bulletin,* 1966, **65,** 336–346.

Endler, N. S., & Hunt, J. McV. S–R inventories of hostility and comparisons of the proportions of variance from persons, responses, and situations for hostility and anxiousness. *Journal of Personality and Social Psychology,* 1968, **9,** 309–315.

Endler, N. S., & Hunt, J. McV. Generalizability of contributions from sources of variance in the S–R inventories of anxiousness. *Journal of Personality,* 1969, **37,** 1–24.

Endler, N. S., Hunt, J. McV., & Rosenstein, A. J. An S–R inventory of anxiousness. *Psychological Monographs,* 1962, **76** (17, Whole No. 536).

Estes, W. K. Reinforcement in human behavior. *American Scientist,* 1972, **60,** 723–729.

Fairweather, G. W. *Methods in experimental social innovation.* New York: Wiley, 1967.

Festinger, L. A theory of social comparison processes. *Human Relations,* 1945, **7,** 117–140.

Fiske, D. W. The limits of the conventional science of personality. Unpublished manuscript, University of Chicago, 1973.

Frieze, I., & Weiner, B. Cue utilization and attributional judgments for success and failure. *Journal of Personality,* 1971, **39,** 591–605.

Geer, J. H., Davison, G. C., & Gatchel, R. K. Reduction of stress in humans through nonveridical perceived control of aversive stimulation. *Journal of Personality and Social Psychology,* 1970, **16,** 731–738.

Gergen, K. J. Personal consistency and the presentation of self. In C. Gordon & K. J. Gergen (Eds.), *The self in social interaction.* New York: Wiley, 1968.

Gewirtz, J. L., & Baer, D. M. Deprivation and satiation of social reinforcers as drive conditions. *Journal of Abnormal and Social Psychology.* 1958, **57**, 165–172.

Gibson, E. J. *Principles of perceptual learning and development.* New York: Appleton-Century-Crofts, 1969.

Goldfried, M. R., & D'Zurilla, T. J. A behavioral-analytic model for assessing competence. In C. D. Spielberger (Ed.), *Current topics in clinical and community psychology.* Vol. 1. New York: Academic Press, 1969.

Grings, W. W., & Lockhart, R. A. Effects of anxiety-lessening instructions and differential set development on the extinction of GSR. *Journal of Experimental Psychology.* 1963, **66**, 292–299.

Grusec, J., & Mischel, W. Model's characteristics as determinants of social learning. *Journal of Personality and Social Psychology,* 1966, **4**, 211–215.

Hamilton, D. L. Implicit personality theories: Dimensions of interpersonal cognition. Paper presented at the meeting of the American Psychological Association, Washington, D.C., September 1971.

Hayden, T., & Mischel, W. Maintaining trait consistency in the resolution of behavioral inconsistency: The wolf in sheep's clothing. Unpublished manuscript, Stanford University, 1973.

Heider, F. *The pscyhology of interpersonal relations.* New York: Wiley, 1958.

Helson, H. *Adaptation-level theory.* New York: Harper & Row, 1964.

Hunt, J. McV. Traditional personality theory in the light of recent evidence. *American Scientist,* 1965, **53**, 80–96.

Irwin, F. W. *Intentional behavior and motivation.* New York: Lippincott, 1971.

Isen, A., Horn, N., & Rosenhan, D. Effects of success and failure on children's generosity. *Journal of Personality and Social Psychology,* 1973, **27**, 239–247.

Jeffery, K., & Mischel, W. The layman's use of traits to predict and remember behavior. Unpublished manuscript, Stanford University, 1973.

Jones, E. E. *Ingratiation: A social psychological analysis.* New York: Appleton-Century-Crofts, 1964.

Jones, E. E., & Nisbett, R. E. The actor and the observer: Divergent perceptions of the causes of behavior. In E. E. Jones et al. (Eds.), *Attribution: Perceiving the causes of behavior.* McCaleb-Seiler, 1971.

Kanfer, F. H. The maintenance of behavior by self-generated stimuli and reinforcement. In A. Jacobs & L. B. Sachs (Eds.), *The psychology of private events.* New York: Academic Press, 1971.

Kanfer, F. H., Cox, L. E., Greiner, J. M., & Karoly, P. Contracts, demand characteristics and self-control. Unpublished manuscript, University of Cincinnati, 1973.

Kanfer, F. H., & Marston, A. R. Determinants of self-reinforcement in human learning. *Journal of Experimental Psychology,* 1963, **66**, 245–254.

Kaufman, A., Baron, A., & Kopp, R. E. Some effects of instructions on human operant behavior. *Psychonomic Monograph Supplements,* 1966, **1**, 243–250.

Kelley, H. H. Attribution theory in social psychology. In D. Levine (Ed.), *Nebraska Symposium on Motivation:* 1967. Lincoln: University of Nebraska Press, 1967.

Kelly, E. L. Consistency of the adult personality. *American Psychologist,* 1955, **10**, 659–681.

Kelly, G. *The psychology of personal constructs.* New York: Basic Books, 1955.

Kohlberg, A. A cognitive-developmental analysis of children's sex-role concepts and attitudes. In E. E. Maccoby (Ed.), *The development of sex differences.* Stanford: Stanford University Press, 1966.

Kohlberg, L. Stage and sequence: The cognitive-developmental approach to socialization. In D. A. Goslin (Ed.), *Handbook of socialization theory and research.* Chicago: Rand McNally, 1969.

Lawrence, D. H. The nature of a stimulus: Some relationships between learning and perception. In S. Koch (Ed.), *Psychology: A study of a science*. New York: McGraw-Hill, 1959.

Lazarus, A. A. The treatment of chronic frigidity by systematic desensitization. *Journal of Nervous and Mental Disease*, 1963, **136**, 272–278.

Little, B. R., & Stephens, E. D. Psychological construing and selective focusing on content versus expressive aspects of speech. *Journal of Consulting and Clinical Psychology*, 1973, in press.

Lovaas, O. I., Freitag, G., Gold, V. J., & Kassorla, I. C. Experimental studies in childhood schizophrenia: I. Analysis of self-destructive behavior. *Journal of Experimental Child Psychology*, 1965, **2**, 67–84.

MacFarlane, J. W., & Tuddenham, R. D. Problems in the validation of projective techniques. In H. H. Anderson & G. L. Anderson (Eds.), *Projective techniques*. New York: Prentice-Hall, 1951.

Mandler, G. Organization and memory. In K. W. Spence & J. T. Spence (Eds.), *The psychology of learning and motivation: Advances in research and theory*. New York: Academic Press, 1967.

Mandler, G. Association and organization: Facts, fancies and theories. In T. R. Dixon & D. L. Horton (Eds.), *Verbal behavior and general behavior theory*. Englewood Cliffs, N.J.: Prentice-Hall, 1968.

McGuire, W. J. Personality and susceptibility to social influence. In E. F. Borgatta & W. W. Lambert (Eds.), *Handbook of personality theory and research*. Chicago: Rand McNally, 1968.

Meichenbaum, D. H. *Cognitive factors in behavior modification: Modifying what clients say to themselves*. (Research Report No. 25) Waterloo: University of Waterloo, 1971.

Metcalf, M. Demonstration of a psychosomatic relationship. *British Journal of Medical Psychology*, 1956, **29**, 63–66.

Miller, G. A., Galanter, E., & Pribram, K. H. *Plans and the structure of behavior*. New York: Holt, Rinehart & Winston, 1960.

Mischel, W. Theory and research on the antecedents of self-imposed delay of reward. In B. A. Maher (Ed.), *Progress in experimental personality research*. Vol. 3. New York: Academic Press, 1966.

Mischel, W. *Personality and assessment*. New York: Wiley, 1968.

Mischel, W. Continuity and change in personality. *American Psychologist*, 1969, **24**, 1012–1018.

Mischel, W. *Introduction to personality*. New York: Holt, Rinehart & Winston, 1971.

Mischel, W. Direct versus indirect personality assessment: Evidence and implications. *Journal of Consulting and Clinical Psychology*, 1972, **38**, 319–324.

Mischel, W. Processes in delay of gratification. In L. Berkowitz (Ed.), *Advances in social psychology*. Vol. 7. New York: Academic Press, 1973, in press. (a)

Mischel, W. On the empirical dilemmas of psychodynamic theory: Issues and alternatives. *Journal of Abnormal Psychology*, 1973, **82**, 335–344.

Mischel, W., & Baker, N. Cognitive appraisals and transformations in delay behavior. Unpublished manuscript, Stanford University, 1973.

Mischel, W., Coates, B., & Raskoff, A. Effects of success and failure on self-gratification. *Journal of Personality and Social Psychology*, 1968, **10**, 381–390.

Mischel, W., Ebbesen, E. B., & Zeiss, A. R. Cognitive and attentional mechanisms in delay of gratification. *Journal of Personality and Social Psychology*, 1972, **21**, 204–218.

Mischel, W., Ebbesen, E. B., & Zeiss, A. R. Selective attention to the self: Situational and dispositional determinants. *Journal of Personality and Social Psychology*, 1973, **27**, 129–142.

Mischel, W., & Grusec, J. Determinants of the rehearsal and transmission of neutral and aversive behaviors. *Journal of Personality and Social Psychology*, 1966, **3**, 197–205.

Mischel, W. Grusec, J., & Masters, J. C. Effects of expected delay time on the subjective value of rewards and punishments. *Journal of Personality and Social Psychology,* 1969, **11,** 363-373.

Mischel, W., & Liebert, R. M. Effects of discrepancies between observed and imposed reward criteria on their acquisition and transmission. *Journal of Personality and Social Psychology,* 1966, 3, 45-53.

Mischel, W., & Moore, B. Effects of attention to symbolically presented rewards upon self-control. *Journal of Personality and Social Psychology,* 1973, **28,** 172-179. (a)

Mischel, W., & Moore, B. Cognitive transformations of the stimulus in delay of gratification. Unpublished manuscript, Stanford University, 1973. (b)

Mischel, W., & Staub, E. Effects of expectancy on working and waiting for larger rewards. *Journal of Personality and Social Psychology,* 1965, 2, 625-633.

Mischel, W., Zeiss, R., & Zeiss, A. R. Internal-external control and persistence: Validation and implications of the Stanford Preschool I-E Scale. *Journal of Personality and Social Psychology,* 1974, 29, 265-278.

Moore, B. S., Underwood, B., & Rosenhan, D. L. Affect and altruism. *Developmental Psychology,* 1973, **8,** 99-104.

Moos, R. H. Situational analysis of a therapeutic community milieu. *Journal of Abnormal Psychology,* 1968, **73,** 49-61.

Moos, R. H. Sources of variance in response to questionnaires and in behavior. *Journal of Abnormal Psychology,* 1969, 74, 405-412.

Neisser, U. *Cognitive psychology.* New York: Appleton-Century-Crofts, 1967.

Norman, D. A. *Memory and attention.* New York: Wiley, 1969.

Patterson, G. R., & Cobb, J. A. Stimulus control for classes of noxious behaviors. In J. F. Knutson (Ed.), *The control of aggression: Implications from basic research.* Chicago: Aldine, 1971.

Peterson, D. R. *The clinical study of social behavior.* New York: Appleton-Century-Crofts, 1968.

Piaget, J. *The construction of reality in the child.* New York: Basic Books, 1954.

Premack, D. Reinforcement theory. In D. Levine (Ed.), *Nebraska Symposium on Motivation: 1965.* Lincoln: University of Nebraska Press, 1965.

Raush, H. L. Interaction sequences. *Journal of Personality and Social Psychology,* 1965, 2, 487-499.

Raush, H. L., Dittmann, A. T., & Taylor, T. J. The interpersonal behavior of children in residential treatment. *Journal of Abnormal and Social Psychology,* 1959, **58,** 9-26.

Robbins, L. N. Dissecting the "broken home" as a predictor of deviance. Paper presented at the NIMH Conference on Developmental Aspects of Self-Regulation, La Jolla, California, February 19, 1972.

Rotter, J. B. *Social learning and clinical psychology.* Englewood Cliffs, N.J.: Prentice-Hall, 1954.

Rummelhart, D. E., Lindsey, P. H., & Norman, D. A. A process model for long-term memory. (Tech. Rep. No. 17). La Jolla: University of California at San Diego, Center for Human Information Processing, 1971.

Schachter, S. The interaction of cognitive and physiological determinants of emotional state. In L. Berkowitz (Ed.), *Advances in experimental social psychology.* Vol. 1. New York: Academic Press, 1964.

Schachter, S., & Singer, J. E. Cognitive, social, and physiological determinants of emotional state. *Psychological Review,* 1962, **69,** 379-399.

Schneider, D. J. Implicit personality theory: A review. *Psychological Bulletin,* 1973, **79,** 294-309.

Shweder, R. A. Is a culture a situation? Unpublished manuscript, Harvard University, Department of Social Relations, 1971.

Shweder, R. A. Semantic structures and personality assessment. Unpublished doctoral dissertation, Harvard University, Department of Social Relations, March 1972.

Spielberger, C. D. & DeNike, L. D. Descriptive behaviorism versus cognitive theory in verbal operant conditioning. *Psychological Review*, 1966, 73, 306–326.

Strong, E. K., Jr. *Vocational interests 18 years after college*. Minneapolis: University of Minnesota Press, 1955.

Tversky, A., & Kahneman, D. Belief in the law of small numbers. *Psychological Bulletin*, 1971, 76, 105–110.

Vernon, P. E. *Personality assessment: A critical survey*. New York: Wiley, 1964.

Wachtel, P. L. Psychodynamics, behavior therapy, and the implacable experimenter: An inquiry into the consistency of personality. *Journal of Abnormal Psychology*, 1973, 82, 324–334.

Wallace, J. An abilities conception of personality: Some implications for personality measurement. *American Psychologist*, 1966, 21, 132–138.

Wallach, M. A. Commentary: Active-analytical versus passive-global cognitive functioning. In S. Messick & J. Ross (Eds.), *Measurement in personality and cognition*. New York: Wiley, 1962.

Wallach, M. A., & Leggett, M. I. Testing the hypothesis that a person will be consistent: Stylistic consistency versus situational specificity in size of children's drawings. *Journal of Personality*, 1972, 40, 309–330.

Weiner, B., Frieze, I., Kukla, A., Reed, L., Rest, S., & Rosenbaum, R. M. *Perceiving the causes of success and failure*. New York: General Learning Press, 1971.

Weiner, B., & Kukla, A. An attributional analysis of achievement motivation. *Journal of Personality and Social Psychology*, 1970, 15, 1–20.

White, R. W. Motivation reconsidered: The concept of competence. *Psychological Review*, 1959, 66, 297–333.

White, R. W. *The abnormal personality*. New York: Ronald Press, 1964.

Witkin, H. A. Psychological differentiation and forms of pathology. *Journal of Abnormal Psychology*, 1965, 70, 317–336.

Wolf, R. The measurement of environments. In A. Anastasi (Ed.), *Testing problems in perspective*. Washington, D.C.: American Council on Education, 1966.

Wolpe, J. The systematic desensitization treatment of neuroses. *Journal of Nervous and Mental Disease*, 1961, 132, 189–203.

Zigler, E., & Phillips, L. Social competence and outcome in psychiatric disorder. *Journal of Abnormal and Social Psychology*, 1961, 63, 264–271.

Zigler, E., & Phillips, L. Social competence and the process-reactive distinction in psychopathology. *Journal of Abnormal and Social Psychology*, 1962, 65, 215–222.

CHAPTER THREE

EMPIRICAL STUDIES

Although the theoretical basis for person–situation interactions in personality was postulated as early as the 1920s (e.g., Kantor, 1924, 1926) there was no substantial research in this area until the 1960s. The empirical support for person–situation interactions in personality developed almost independently of the theoretical basis for such interactions.

Raush, Dittmann, and Taylor (1959 [9]) and Raush, Farbman, and Llewellyn (1960) studied the behavior of hyperaggressive boys, in various situations, at two phases of treatment. Using a multivariate information transmission analysis, Raush and his colleagues found that person–situation interactions accounted for more behavior variance than either persons or situations per se. At about the same time Endler, Hunt, and Rosenstein (1962) developed their self-report S–R Inventory of Anxiousness that measured anxiety in various situations. Using this inventory and modifications of it, Endler and Hunt [10, 11], employing a variance components technique (Endler, [21], found that person–situation interactions accounted for more variance than either persons or situations per se. The Raush et al. studies and the Endler and Hunt studies were the first ones to directly assess person–situation interactions and compare them to persons and to situations in terms of variance contributions. Since then there have been a number of other studies that have assessed interactions for such variables as hostility, honesty, leisure time, choice behavior with respect to drinking, smoking, talking, social behavior, etc.

The twelve papers in this chapter provide empirical support for the importance of person–situation interactions for various personality variables. In the first selection, Raush, Dittmann, and Taylor [9] examine the social interactions of six hyperaggressive adolescent boys in six specific behavior settings over two phases of treatment, one and a half years apart. Using a multivariate transmission analysis procedure they find that different settings (situations) evoke different kinds of behavior, and that the interaction between the child (person) and the setting (situation) contributes more to behavioral variance than the sum of persons plus situations. Furthermore, with treatment and maturation the importance of the situation as a source of variance is increased. The authors conclude that in investigating the effects of psychotherapeutic changes in social behavior it is important to obtain a representative sample of situations and to examine person–situation interactions.

In the second selection in this chapter, Endler and Hunt [10] reanalyze the data from the Endler, Hunt, and Rosenstein (1962) S–R Inventory of Anxiousness by partitioning, via a variance components technique, the proportions of variance due to various main sources and their interactions. They suggest that the debate over the relative importance of situations and of individuals is a pseudo-issue and show that for self-report measures of anxiety person–situation interactions contribute more (10 percent) to behavioral variance than either persons (5 percent) or situations (5 percent). The next selection, also by Endler and Hunt [11], extends the work of the previous research and reports anxiety data for 22 samples of males and 21 samples of females, representing subjects varying in age, educational level, geographical location, social class, and mental health. The results show that on the average individual differences account for about 4 to 5 percent of the variance, situations about 4 percent for males, and about 8 percent for females, but person–situation interactions account for about 10 percent of the total variance. The importance of interactions reported by Endler and Hunt confirms the proposal that personality description and prediction would be improved by focusing on what responses (and their intensity) persons exhibit in various kinds of situations.

The fourth selection, by Nelsen, Grinder, and Mutterer [12], examines the issue of specificity versus generality with respect to the variable of honesty and compares and contrasts various methodologies with respect to this issue. Correlations among measures of reactions to six temptation situations are low to moderate, but a factor analysis indicates that the first factor accounts for 35 to 40 percent of the total variance. However, a variance components technique indicates that 15–26 percent of the variance is due to persons, 13–14 percent due to tasks (situations), and 60–71 percent was confounded between interaction and error sources. In general the results point to the importance of persons, situations, and especially person–situation interactions for the variable of honesty.

The fifth selection, by Endler and Hunt [13], examines person–situation interactions for hostility and compares the proportions of sources of variance for hostility and anxiousness. Using an S–R Inventory of Hostility and an S–R Inventory of Anxiousness, the authors show that individual differences contribute more to the total variance for hostility (15–20 percent) than for anxiousness (4–5 percent). For both "traits," the situations contribute about 7–8 percent for women and about 4 percent for men, and person–situation interactions contribute about 10 percent. Nearly 30 percent of the variance (for both "traits") is due to the three simple interactions. The importance of specifying the situation and the importance of person–situation interactions is emphasized for both hostility and anxiousness.

The Berkowitz and Geen paper [14], the sixth selection, while not specifically focusing on person–situation interactions, emphasizes the importance of situational factors in aggression, and thus indirectly has relevance for interaction. The authors suggest that for a comprehensive analysis of aggression, it is necessary to examine the stimulus (situational) characteristics of targets of aggression. That is, the target's *cue* value for aggression is one important component of aggressive behavior.

Fiedler [15], in the seventh selection, presents an extension of his contingency model of leadership and indicates the relevance of person–situation interactions for leadership. Presenting data from both field and laboratory studies, Fiedler shows how the situational dimension influences the relationship between leadership style (person variable) and group performance. His model predicts leadership performance better in field situations than in laboratory situations. In general, his paper emphasizes the importance of examining situational variables when studying leadership phenomena, and the importance of differentiating groups that exist to benefit an organization (task groups) from groups that exist for the benefit of the individual.

The eighth selection, by Magnusson, Gerzén, and Nyman [16], discusses the joint effect of task variation and group composition on ratings of behavior and on measures of talking time in group situations. Using data from two experiments, one with military conscripts and one with seven year old children, the authors show that when the situational variation simultaneously encompasses both the task and group composition, rating made independently by two teams of judges produce a random relationship. Correlations between the two teams of judges are maximal when judges rate the behavior of the subjects on the same type of situations or when there is a variation only with respect to the task *or* to group composition. The authors suggest that these results provide evidence for an interactional view of behavior.

The Moos [17] paper, the ninth selection, provides a situational analysis of a therapeutic community, by studying both patients and staff in various situations in a psychiatric setting. Studying a number of dependent variables (e.g., friendly–unfriendly, outgoing–shy, relaxed–tense, sure–unsure, attentive–inattentive, etc.) in eleven different situational settings, Moos finds that for patients individual differences account for more variance than setting (situational) differences, while for staff the reverse is true. However, the most important finding is that interaction of persons by settings (situations) accounts for about 20 percent of the total variance. Moos suggests that it is important to sample and measure situations, persons, modes of responses, and especially their interactions, when attempting to predict individual behavior.

Bishop and Witt [18], in the tenth selection, discuss the importance of interactions with respect to leisure time. Using a situation by leisure time response Inventory (modeled after the S–R Inventory of Anxiousness) and using a variance components technique for analyzing their data, the authors find that the various interactions account for substantially more variance than the main effects of persons or situations. The authors also compare their results on leisure time with the findings of Endler and Hunt on anxiety and hostility. The person by situation interaction variance, the modes of response variance and the situation variance are higher for both anxiousness and hostility than for leisure time. However, the person by modes of response variance is higher for leisure time than for the other two variables. Individual differences variance is higher for hostility than for the other two variables. The Bishop and Witt study differs from those of Endler and Hunt in at least three ways: Bishop and Witt (a) study leisure time activities instead of anxiety or hostility, (b) ask subjects for the probability of a response rather than the degree of a response, and (c) study situations that are events that *preceded* the response in question, while Endler and Hunt have subjects make responses to situations while they are *in* them (hypothetically). Bishop and Witt find strong person by mode of response interactions and strong situation by mode of response interactions, but rather weak person by situation interactions. This indicates the hazard of attempting to generalize from one behavior domain to another.

Sandell [19] in the eleventh selection studies choice behavior (i.e., the type of drink preferred) in various situations. He finds that individual differences and situations per se have very little effect on what type of drink is preferred. However situations are important in that they evoke certain preferred responses. For example, the situations by response interaction accounts for almost 40 percent of the variance. The person by situation interactions are rather weak. These results, like those of Bishop and Witt, indicate that the magnitude and nature of the interactions vary for the type of behavior under consideration.

The twelfth and final selection in this section, by Trickett and Moos [20], is concerned with person–situation interactions in highschool classrooms. They examine to what extent students' feelings and initiatives in the classroom are a function of individuals, classroom setting (situations), and their interactions, and compare these sources across several response dimensions (e.g., satisfaction, participation, etc.). Trickett and Moos find that the person by situation interaction accounts for as much or more of the variance than either individual differences or settings (situations). They also find that the percentage of variance due to different sources varies for different behavioral variables. For example, individual differences in satisfaction accounts for 27 percent of the variance, while individual differences in paying attention accounts for about 3 percent of the variance.

An examination of the Endler and Hunt selections, the Bishop and Witt selection, the Sandell selection, and the Trickett and Moos selection points to the complexity of personality and the fact that the nature and magnitude of interactions, persons, and situations vary from one personality domain to the next.

REFERENCES

Endler, N. S., Hunt, J. McV., & Rosenstein, A. J. An S-R Inventory of Anxiousness. *Psychological Monographs*, 1962, 76, No. 17 (whole no. 536), 1–33.

Kantor, J. R. *Principles of psychology* (Vol. 1). Bloomington: Principia Press, 1924.

Kantor, J. R. *Principles of psychology* (Vol. 2). Bloomington: Principia Press, 1926.

Raush, H. L., Dittmann, A. T., & Taylor, T. J. The interpersonal behavior of children in residential treatment. *Journal of Abnormal and Social Psychology,* 1959, *58,* 9–26.

Raush, H. L., Farbman, I., & Llewellyn, L. G. Person, setting and change in social interaction: II. A normal control study. *Human Relations,* 1960, *13,* 305–333.

9

Person, Setting, and Change in Social Interaction

H. L. RAUSH, A. T. DITTMANN, and T. J. TAYLOR

The present paper continues our report on the social interactions of a small group of hyperaggressive children in residential treatment (Raush, Dittmann, and Taylor, 32). In the earlier investigation we studied the social behavior that each of six such children directed toward others, both peers and adults, and the behavior that each child received from others, peers and adults. Interpersonal behaviors were described for two periods, a year and a half apart, and changes over the periods were examined. These changes were more pronounced in the interactions between the children and the adults of the child-care staff, but were consistent also in relations of the children to their peers. The direction of the change followed from the therapeutic aims of the program, e.g. decrease in hostility, increase in dependence on adults, decrease in inappropriately intense interactions.

The study presented here, although it deals with the same data, has a rather different focus. Its purpose is to explore the influence of the social setting on interpersonal behavior, to explore the interactions between individual and social factors for such behavior, and to explore these components in relation to behavioral change. These explorations may be put as a series of questions to be asked of the data:

1. Does knowledge about the social setting increase information about interactive behavior, that is, do disturbed children behave differently in different social settings? To this question an affirmative answer can be expected. Given such an answer, some consistencies in social-setting effects can be described.

From *Human Relations*, 1959, *12*, 361–378. Copyright (1959) by the Plenum Publishing Co. Ltd. Reprinted by permission of the authors and the publisher.

This report is one of a series of studies at the Child Research Branch, which is under the direction of Fritz Redl, at the National Institute of Mental Health. Donald S. Boomer and D. Wells Goodrich, particularly, contributed to the design and to the gathering and coding of much of the data. Elaine Irving and Irwin Farbman played a considerable role in the analyses of the data. William L. Hays of the University of Michigan, Richard A. Littman of the University of Oregon, and J. E. Keith Smith of the Massachusetts Institute of Technology were helpful in various aspects of the study.

2. To what extent are the effects of social situations generalized for all children, and to what extent do settings have specific effects for specific children? A related question asks to what extent individual reactions are consistent across situations and to what extent the specific setting is a component of individual consistency.[1] These questions concern the interaction between child and setting. While we can expect interaction, that is, that settings will have individual psychological 'meanings' as reflected in the behavior of individual children, we cannot forecast the magnitude of these effects.

3. With treatment and maturation, is there a shift in the relative contribution to information about behavior from situational and individual-difference sources? In other words, does the child come to be less influenced in his behavior by the social situation, or are his responses more differentiated from one setting to another as a function of increasing maturity? We expect that, as psychological maturity increases and pathology decreases, situational factors come to play a more potent role while individual-difference factors become less important as determinants of immediate overt social behavior.

4. Are changes in social behavior equal over all settings or do they appear greater in some situations than in others over a period of time? Our previous report (Raush, Dittmann, and Taylor, 32) indicated that not all children changed equally over the year and a half. Here, a similar question is raised with respect to social settings. Although we can expect change to be situation-specific to some degree, we cannot forecast the extent of such specificity or its nature.

Some Practical Aspects

Questions such as these have obvious practical implications (Redl and Wineman, 35; Redl, 33; Raush, 31). It is important to know, as part of any treatment or educative process, how we can gear situations toward maximizing certain behavioral potentials. Much work in learning and in social-psychological experiments is devoted to this problem, and a few studies (Barker and Wright, 2; Gump and Sutton-Smith, 18; Gump, Schoggen, and Redl, 17; Maier and Campbell, 23) have investigated the macroscopic settings of daily life and their influence on behavior. Most knowledge about macroscopic situational influences, however, tends to develop anecdotally from practical field experience, and it is difficult to distinguish between evidence, lore, and opinion. Practitioners plan, for example, different games or different degrees of structure for boys and for girls, for five-year-olds and for seven-year-olds, for withdrawn and for active children, for bright and for dull children, but there has been little empirical investigation of the relevant features, nor even of the efficacy of such planning.

Furthermore, how the individual and situational factors intermesh is for the most part a matter of theoretical persuasion, rather than specific empirical study. For example, to what extent are the effects of treatment of a child or of a

---

[1] General individual differences were noted in Raush, Dittmann, and Taylor (32).

schizophrenic patient dependent on the nature of personality modifications and to what extent are effects dependent on environmental supports for maintaining modifications in patterns of behavior? Discussion of such issues occupies considerable clinical thought: to take or not to take certain cases; to insist or not to insist on treatment of relevant family members; to remove or not to remove the patient to another environment; to send or not to send the hospital patient home.

Some Theoretical Considerations

The usual mode of studying personality is to examine the effect of variation in a trait or in a syndrome of traits on behavior in a single situation. The usual mode for investigating social effects is to vary several environmental situations and to examine the influence of such variations on behavior, irrespective of persons. Such investigations are demonstrations that result in binary statements: variable A is or is not relevant to variable B. Their success or failure as demonstrations depends to a considerable extent on the ingenuity of the investigator—in eliminating critical factors as much as selecting them, in choosing the 'right' situations for demonstrating personality variables, or the 'right' subjects for demonstrating situational variables. Egon Brunswik (6, 7) for many years criticized such psychological studies for their lack of sampling of situations, which he argued must be a requirement coordinate to the sampling of persons. Though one need not accept Brunswik's programmatic solutions to this problem, or his aim of arriving at probabilistic statements in an achievement-oriented psychology, the criticism is, nevertheless, a legitimate one. Hammond (19), in recognizing its legitimacy, quotes Fisher: 'The exact standardization of experimental conditions, which is often thoughtlessly advocated as a panacea, always carries with it the real disadvantage that a highly standardized experiment supplies direct information only in respect of the narrow range of conditions achieved by standardization. Standardization, therefore, weakens rather than strengthens our ground for inferring a like result, when, as is invariably the case in practice, these conditions are somewhat varied' (13, p. 97). The effects of the failure to consider situational aspects in clinical studies has been demonstrated by Hammond (20) and by Miller (27), among others. Peak comments on the issue in connection with problems of observational studies: 'As a rule, attention has been given to checking or controlling only limited aspects of the immediate situation, such as the instructions to be given, time limits to be used, and the questions to be asked. Perhaps the failure to cope more adequately with other aspects of this problem stems from the implicit assumption that the processes being measured are independent of most variables and therefore relatively static and stable, an assumption which is clearly false for such processes as attitudes, needs, adjustment mechanisms, interaction, and other group phenomena' (28, pp. 246–47). Cottrell (9) similarly emphasizes the need for defining situational contexts in the study of social interactions.

THE SOCIAL SETTINGS

In residential-treatment programs the opportunity is available for studying the interaction between social situations and individuals, in that the same subjects appear together in many situations. Here, indeed, the case is the reverse of the usual study: the persons are limited in number and may be studied as an entire population, whereas the situations are many and must be sampled. The characteristics of the persons are determined by the intake policy of the treatment program, which may or may not yield a group sufficiently homogeneous for the findings of any study to be generalized to a specific larger population. The characteristics of the situations, too, are limited by the treatment program in just as real a way.[2] But the situations available are still far too numerous for any research to encompass, and there is a very broad range for selection of samples.

Description of the Residence

The present study was carried out in the Child Research Branch of the National Institute of Mental Health. The residential treatment program of the Branch was located in the Clinical Center of the National Institutes of Health, a large building which housed, along with laboratories for both clinical and basic research in many medical and related disciplines, a 500-bed research hospital. The Children's Unit was one of many nursing units, modified to include the many activities required by long-term inpatient care of medically healthy boys. In one area were the bedrooms, dining facilities, and large living-room and play area, along with the offices of the child-care staff. In another area were the school rooms, the crafts room, play-therapy rooms, and offices of the research staff. The outer doors to the Unit were locked. Adjacent to the building was a large enclosed area with lawn, trees, and bushes, with swings, jungle gym, and other play equipment for nearby outdoor activities. This enclosure, along with a gymnasium, game courts, occupational therapy and physical therapy facilities, were shared with other patients in the hospital by scheduling with the various departments, so that when these children were using them other patients were not present. Activities such as swimming and trips for picnics and other recreational and educational purposes were frequently arranged.

The Specific Settings

From the many possible settings or recurring situations within the residential life, six were chosen for observations. All six were confined to the area of the Clinical Center and its immediate vicinity, since observers could be less obtrusive there than, for example, on trips. The six settings were:

---

[2] In most treatment residences that have been reported recently in the literature, for example, one could never study the situation of group punishment for infractions of rules.

1. **Breakfasts.** The period of getting up in the morning and of getting into the day's activities is said to be a critical one. Bettelheim (3) points to the ambivalent nature of the awakening process in the disturbed children at the Orthogenic School. On the one hand, the fears, fantasies, and asocial impulses of what is often a violent and terrifying night-life are still with the child, and ego controls are not yet established. On the other hand, the period is in some respects propitious for the establishment of communication, since distractions, demands, tensions, and frustrations from the outside world have not yet built up. It proved feasible to observe at breakfast, when one would still have a period prior to the induction of other activities and prior to cumulation of the conflicts that seemed to mount so readily for these children.

2. **Other meals.** These included lunch and supper. There seemed to be no theoretical reason for distinguishing between these two meal-times, and observations were distributed between them. Bossard (5, pp. 161–76) notes the special contribution of the meal-time period in the communication of familial values. The critical relevance of situations built around food has also been noted and utilized in the residential treatment of disturbed children. Bettelheim (3) comments on the role of food in the socialization process with disturbed children, and it seems likely that the eating situation is an important social setting for all children prior to adolescence. For most of the children in this study, some of whom had in earlier years suffered actual deprivation, food and eating were closely tied with issues of security.

3. **Structured game activities.** Social life for the preadolescent depends to a considerable extent on learning to play with other children. Group play provides opportunity for learing to get along with peers, for achieving a balance between a group and an individual identity, for the learning of multiple roles, for mastering problems around issues of competition and cooperation and around issues of success and failure, and for exploration of skills, physical ability, and external reality (Erikson, 12; Redl and Wineman, 35; Sullivan, 38). At the same time, group play tests such control capacities and learnings.

Structured, as used here, refers to those games in which there was a within-game body of rules, and in which there were scoring schemes and possibilities for winning or losing. The line was sometimes a narrow one, but such activities as fantasy play, skating in a gym or outdoors, throwing a ball back and forth, where specific within-game rules or scoring procedures were lacking, were not included. In the analyses only non-game behavior was studied. For example, body contacts and comments, such as claiming one's turn or calling 'you're out' or 'throw the ball', were not coded. That is, we were interested in behavior induced by, rather than intrinsic to, the game, though the distinction is somewhat tenuous. No distinction was made among the various structured games, which ranged from cards to basketball. This is unfortunate in that games have different potentialities for inducing different modes of behavior. They differ considerably in their use of dimensions of space, time, and objects; in the opportunities they provide for motoric expression and physical contact; and in the demands they make on capacities for tolerating frustration and delay in gratification (Redl, 34). Experimenters have intuitively used game features for the creation of social effects in order to study problems of group organization (cf. Thibaut, 39), and there have been a few studies on the psychological effects of different activity and game structures (Gump, Schoggen, and Redl, 17).

4. Unstructured group activities. Unstructured group activities encompassed informal social events that occurred outside the context of the other five settings. Discussions, social conversations, non-game interactions while skating or throwing a ball around or during a fantasy play about cowboys, comments during a group singing session or while watching a movie or a television show, were eligible for coding. The category was a confounded one, but, in general, the interactive role of the participants was more open, less defined, and less bound by formal rules than was the case with structured game activities.

5. Arts and crafts. Prior to coming to the Institution, all of these children had shown behavioral difficulties in school. With one exception they had been either excluded from schools or placed in special classes because of their behavioral problems. A useful area for observation would have been the special school situation at the Institution for these children. Observations in school were, however, limited by the fact that the early series of observations occurred during the summer when formal school sessions had ended. The arts-and-crafts situation served as an instructional setting substituting for school. As in the school setting, there were one to three adults instructing and guiding three to six children.

The setting is the most obviously task-oriented of the six. It should be noted that the tasks set for the children were most often individual ones. That is, each child generally worked on his own project—for example, each making his own map, or his own sailboat model—and only occasionally were the projects group-oriented, although some cooperation was necessary in the use of tools and materials.

6. Snacks at bedtime. The snacks period corresponds to breakfast. It was at the end of the day for the children, and, like the time of awakening, it probably had an ambivalent character. The structural features of the situation would seem to favor peaceful relaxation, but fatigue, night-time concerns, and residues of the day's conflicts might counter these features. The period was less formal than other mealtimes. The children were in pajamas, and milk and sandwiches were available. Generally, the children went to bed immediately after snacks, and observations often included the few minutes of transition from table to bedroom.

Relevant settings omitted from the study were psychotherapy sessions—four hours a week for each child; other two-person situations where the presence of an observer would be intrusive (cf. Goodrich, 16), and school situations other than periods devoted to arts and crafts. Thus, the sampling was not wholly representative, although it did cover a good portion of the kinds of activity engaged in by the children. No attempt was made at time-sampling. The nature of the settings selected did, however, ensure that various times of the day were included.

SUBJECTS, OBSERVATIONAL AND CODING SCHEME, AND PHASES OF OBSERVATION

The Subjects

The children under study here and problems in the treatment of such children have been described elsewhere (Raush, Dittmann, and Taylor, 32; Redl and Wineman, 35). Briefly, they were six hyperaggressive preadolescent boys, whose aggressiveness seemed born of insufficient ego controls rather than of the group mores of the delinquent gang. Although there was an age-spread of about two years in the group, all the boys were developmentally preadolescent and of very similar psychopathological history.

The Observations

The method of observing the children was described in some detail in Raush, Dittmann, and Taylor (32). Observations were about ten minutes in length, and concentrated on one child per observation plus all others with whom he interacted. Observers dictated their reports immediately, reporting as fully as possible all they had seen. The protocols were typescripts of the dictated reports, and these were coded in the 16 categories of the Circle of Interpersonal Mechanisms (Freedman *et al.*, 14). A series of studies of the reliability of this total procedure, both observing and coding, is reported by Dittmann (10) and in an additional note by Raush, Dittmann, and Taylor (32, p. 13). The coded interactions of each focal subject were treated separately for behavior toward peers and behavior toward adults. Since the frequencies under each category become markedly attenuated when they are partitioned into six children in each of six settings, bimodal classifications of behavior were made in order to ensure reasonably large frequencies for each cell. Codings were categorized into affectional and status dimensions on the 'Circle', i.e. friendly *versus* hostile, and dominant *versus* submissive.[3] Separate analyses were made of these two dimensions in relation to the other variables.

---

[3] Interactions coded at midpoints of the dimensions were distributed equally between the two categories, any odd entry being assigned randomly. It should be noted that the recodification of behavior into two categories was at the expense of whatever refinement and discrimination the original 16-category scheme allows. We may note parenthetically that there is evidence that the multiple categories yield greater discrimination than does the two-category classification.

The Phases of Observation

The children were observed at two phases. In the first phase, the median age was ten years. The second series of observations was approximately eighteen months later. In each phase, each of the six children was observed twice in each of the six settings. There were, thus, a total of 144 observations, 72 in each phase.

RESULTS

Mode of Analysis

The major scheme of analysis used here for describing the general phenomena of the study has been called *multivariate information transmission* (McGill, 1954) or *multivariate attribute analysis* (Smith, 37). The method was developed independently by McGill and by Smith as an extension of Shannon's (see Shanon and Weaver, 36) concepts. The scheme is related both to informaiton theory and to likelihood ratio techniques, and it is closely analogous to the analysis of variance (cf. McGill, 25, pp. 56-62; Quastler, 30, pp. 143-71; Garner, 15). Unlike analysis of variance, the method is appropriate to nominal data and for frequencies in discrete categories. No assumptions about linearity are required, and the tests are distribution-free. Furthermore, the analysis is exact and additive. The component measures of association plus the measure of error sum to the response information (McGill, 24, p. 107).

Two types of question may be answered by the scheme of analysis: (a) is there significant association among the variables and (b) what is the extent of the association among the variables? Question (b) asks, for example, how much information variable A furnishes about variable C, or how much information A and B jointly furnish about variable C. Question (a) is concerned with statistical significance in terms of sampling theory. It rests upon the fact that rate of information transmission may be converted to a chi-square value. Furthermore, both types of question may be answered with one variable or more held statistically constant.

The issues treated in this report are concerned with the influence of individual and situational variations on the behavior of the children in two phases, which, the reader will recall, were 18 months apart. Since one of the questions involved comparing the two phases for situational and individual effects, each phase was studied independently at first. There were four analyses in each phase, since behavior toward children and behavior toward adults were examined separately, and since, in each of these areas, affectional and status behaviors were analyzed independently. Thus, since there were six children, six settings, and two categories of behavior (friendly *vs.* hostile or dominant *vs.* submissive) in each analysis within a phase, each phase yielded four tri-dimensional (six by six by two) contingency tables—*affectional relations with children, affectional relations with adults, status relations with children,* and *status relations with adults.*

When the two phases were considered together, so as to evaluate the interaction of the treatment (or maturation) component with the other variables, there resulted four additional six-by-six-by-two-by-two matrices. One table, for example, included children by setting, by phase, by affectional behavior toward peers.

General Setting and Individual Effects

Table 1 summarizes the first-order analysis, the general effects of setting and individual differences for the four early-phase and the four later-phase analyses. A glance at the table indicates that both differences in settings and differences in children generally affected the type of behavior which occurred. Information based on different settings reduced predictive uncertainty by a mean of 2·50 per cent, and information from differences among children reduced predictive uncertainty by a mean of 2·22 per cent. The mean total predictive contribution of settings and children as independent sources is, then, 4·72 per cent (the sum of the two sources), which corresponds to the proportion of variance predictable from a Pearson r of about ·22.

A further look at the general setting-effects in light of the areas of exploration initially defined seems warranted. It was suggested that a sign of progress in ego integration for these children would be an increase in the influence of situational variance on behavior. In general, the setting becomes more relevant to behavior in the later phase; the mean contribution to reduction of uncertainty rises from 1·57 per cent to 3·43 per cent. The contribution of the individual-difference component remains about the same in the early and later phases, 2·34 and 2·10 per cent, respectively. Thus there appears to be a trend for social behavior to become more related to situational influences with ego development, although

Table 1. General Effects of Individual (I) and Setting (S) Variables on Behavior (B)

				Early Phase								
		To Peers ($N=580$)						To Adults ($N=557$)				
	Affectional Behavior			*Status Behavior*			*Affectional Behavior*			*Status Behavior*		
	χ^{2*} (df=5)	p	%sH(B)**	χ^2 (df=5)	p	%sH(B)	χ^2 (df=5)	p	%sH(B)	χ^2 (df=5)	p	%sH(B)
I;B	11·83	·050	1·47	34·49	·001	4·58	15·17	·010	1·99	10·06	·100	1·31
S;B	2·40	·900	0·30	15·63	·010	2·08	22·47	·001	2·94	7·25	·250	·95
				Later Phase								
		($N=430$)						($N=438$)				
I;B	12·92	·025	2·20	8·24	·200	1·41	13·02	·025	2·94	9·54	·100	1·83
S;B	38·30	·001	6·52	16·45	·010	2·82	11·79	·050	2·66	8·84	·200	1·70

* Since R (rate of information transmission) is defined as $\dfrac{-\log_e \lambda}{n}$, where λ is the likelihood ratio and n is the sample size, 2nR ($-2 \log_e \lambda$) is distributed as chi square, with degrees of freedom depending on the specific sources.
** The notation is to be read as follows: I;B is the effect of individual variations on behavior; S;B is the effect of setting variations on behavior. %sH(B) is the reduction in the uncertainty of the behavior classification through information from the individual-difference or setting sources. It is defined as the rate of information transmission from a source divided by the uncertainty of the behavioral classification (cf. McGill & Quastler, 26); the ratio is multiplied by 100.

the question of the specific relation of treatment to that development remains an open one. Put in another way, the children seem to have gained in the ability to discriminate between different situations.

Specific Setting Effects

Since settings, in general, were a source of variation in behavior, it is interesting to examine how the specific settings operate. Five intersetting comparisons were made. Each comparison involved an examination of differences between two settings or groups of settings in distributions of behavior over the four quadrants of the circle schema: hostile-dominant, hostile-passive, friendly-passive, and friendly-dominant.

(a) **Food vs. non-food.** The postulated relevance of the food situation for the disturbed child has been commented on. The comparison between all food-involved settings (breakfasts, other meals, and snacks) and with non-food settings (structured game, unstructured group, and arts-and-crafts activities) indicated that food situations tended to yield modes of interpersonal behavior differing from those of non-food situations. The major difference was in the relatively low frequency of passively hostile behaviors where food was present. It appears that the presence of food resulted in a more comfortable situation for these children characterized by fewer complaints, accusations, hostile demands, sulks, and whinings—both in relation to adults and in relation to other children.

(b) **Breakfast vs. other meals.** It was suggested previously that breakfast and snacks might occupy special positions in relation to other eating-situations. While it is true that most situations have potentialities for both relaxation and arousal of conflict, the balances in the early-morning situation and in the late-evening situation seemed particularly ambivalent, and special examination of these two settings might, it was felt, prove instructive. In the early phase, social behavior at breakfast did not differ from behavior at other meals. In the later phase, however, the children showed more friendly behavior toward each other at breakfast than they did at other meals. Breakfasts produced fewer attempts at aggressive domination of peers and there were more instances of friendly compliant behavior.

(c) **Snacks vs. other meals.** The snacks setting, although the differences are less firmly established, seemed to work in rather the opposite direction. It was in the early phase that snacks seemed to differ from other meals in the character of peer-oriented behavior produced. In that early period, snacks yielded a higher incidence of passive-hostile actions and a lower incidence of friendly-dominant actions than did other meals.

(d) **Structured game vs. unstructured group activities.** The structured game activity setting consisted of scored game situations with defined rules and with potentialities for winning and losing. The competitive features might be expected to produce a relatively high proportion of aggressive behavior toward other children. Care was taken, however, to avoid coding those actions which might be considered ordinary components of the particular game. Nonetheless, structured games tended to produce a relatively high proportion of hostile actions as compared with other settings. Comparison between the structured game setting and the unstructured activity setting indicated that social interactions with peers in the freer situation were in the later phase less apt to be hostile, and particularly less passively hostile, in orientation. The same trend appeared in social interactions with adults in the early phase.

(e) Structured game activities vs. arts and crafts. The arts-and-crafts setting also had a high degree of structure. But in the arts-and-crafts session the organization was of an instructional rather than a game situation. The role of the adult was that of teacher, and there was specific planning toward the reduction of potentially competitive features and of demands for group cooperation. Projects were, for example, most often individual ones, designed with careful consideration of the potentialities for frustration and for gratification. In the early phase the arts-and-crafts situation evoked less aggressive behavior toward adults than did the structured game activity setting, and in the later phase the instructional setting evoked less aggression, particularly passive aggression, in relations with peers as compared to the game situation. Thus, the data point to a difference between two types of high-structure setting, although the differences are not as consistent as one might hope throughout both phases.

Joint Effects of Settings and Individual Differences

So far we have been presenting the main effects of individual and setting differences on social behavior. *Table 2* presents a summary of the analyses of the interactive effects of differences among settings and among children in relation to the behavioral variable.[4] The major fact to be noted is that the effects of setting and individual differences were not summative. The interactive term between these two variables reduced uncertainty in the behavioral classification more than did the independent effects of the variables together. Thus, when the average contribution of the individual-difference component and that of the setting component from *Table 1* are summed, there is a mean reduction in behavioral classification uncertainty of 4·72 per cent; in contrast, when we look at the joint effect, which includes the interaction of the two components, the mean reduction in uncertainty is 11·37 per cent. The difference between these values

---

[4] The exact values in the table are to be interpreted with caution because of a generally significant interactive effect between children and settings in relation to the number of responses. In no case, however, in these and following analyses, were amplification terms negative (cf. McGill, 25, pp. 56–62).

Table 2. Joint Individual (I) and Setting (S) Effects on Behavior (B)

| | | To Peers (N=580) | | | | | To Adults (N=557) | | | | |
| | | Affectional Behavior | | | Status Behavior | | Affectional Behavior | | | Status Behavior | |
	df	χ^2	p	%sH(B)*	χ^2	p	%sH(B)	χ^2	p	%sH(B)	χ^2	p	%sH(B)
							Early Phase						
I,S;B	35	69·97	·001	8·70	75·90	·001	10·09	87·78	·001	11·49	77·16	·001	10·07
$I_S;B$	30	67·57	·001	8·40	60·27	·001	8·01	65·31	·001	8·55	69·90	·001	9·13
$S_I;B$	30	58·14	·005	7·23	41·41	·100	5·50	72·61	·001	9·50	67·10	·001	8·76
							Later Phase						
		(N=430)						(N=438)					
I,S;B	35	103·98	·001	17·69	58·05	·010	9·96	65·84	·005	14·87	42·14	·250	8·10
$I_S;B$	30	65·69	·001	11·18	41·60	·100	7·14	54·05	·005	12·21	33·31	·500	6·40
$S_I;B$	30	91·07	·001	15·49	49·81	·025	8·55	52·82	·010	11·93	32·60	·500	6·27

* The notation is to be read as follows: I,S;B is the joint effect of individual and setting variables on behavior; $I_S;B$ is the effect of individual variations on behavior within settings (or with settings held constant, statistically; $S_I;B$ is the effect of setting variations on behavior within individuals (or with individual children held constant, statistically); %sH(B) is the reduction in the uncertainty of the behavioral classification through information from the variables under consideration.

represents the gain in information from joint as opposed to single classification. By the same token, we may hold one of the independent variables statistically constant while examining the effects of the other. That is, we may study the effects of individual differences on behavior *within* each of the settings, and we may also study the effects of settings within individual children. Such an analysis markedly increased the information retrieved from both variables. For example, even where settings seemed to yield almost no information about behavior, as in the case of affectional behavior toward peers in the early phase (*Table 1*), the effect of settings was highly significant when each child was considered individually ($S_I;B$ in *Table 2*).

As was discussed above, different situations did, in general, affect behavioral trends; here we see that the general effects masked much of the potency of situational influences. The greater part of the yield of information about behavior from knowledge of the setting was recovered by considering setting influences for each child individually. The converse also held: there were, in general, consistent individual differences in behavior, but their effects were considerably enhanced when each setting was examined individually. It is clear, then, that situations had different meanings for different children and that individual differences among children were related to the nature of the situation. A clinical illustration, comparing the data for two children, has been presented (Raush, 31), but a brief example here may clarify the point. On the whole, 34 per cent of all responses produced by children toward adults were coded as hostile. One of the children, Frank, exhibited 60 hostile out of a total of 161 interactions with adults, an average of 37 per cent hostile responses. However, in the arts-and-crafts setting, a teaching situation, only 9 per cent of his behavior toward adults was hostile in orientation; this was in contrast with an average of 28 per cent hostile responses by all children toward adults in arts and crafts. At meal times, the case was reversed. There, 48 per cent of Frank's behavior toward adults was hostile in orientation in contrast to the lower group average of 29 per cent. The selection of an isolated example from the total matrix may, of course, capitalize on chance factors, but the analyses described above indicate the generality of similar phenomena in the data. Such findings are all the more striking since the children were selected as a homogeneous group and since they lived in a highly supervised and homogeneous environment.

Phase Relations with Settings and Individual Differences

An analysis of the behavioral changes in the children over a year and a half was presented previously (Raush, Dittmann, and Taylor, 32). Information transmission analysis of these same data incorporates some of the previous findings, but in addition it yields information about amounts by which un-certainties are reduced and the effects of interactions among the variables. Several conclusions may be drawn from the data (see *Table 3*). First, of the single components, time phase contributed little information about behavior toward peers; it was the major source of information about behavior toward adults. Second, interactions between phase and each of the other components contributed to information about behavior, but the contributions were far smaller than those from the previously discussed interaction between settings and individual differences. Third, there was a considerable multiple interaction among the three variables, settings, individual children, and time phase, such that, when settings and children were held constant statistically, there was marked gain in information from the contribution of phase effects.[5] Further analysis showed that the pattern of responsivity in different settings also changed. If we look at the number of responses, irrespective of their coding, over the six different

---

[5] Quastler (30, pp. 162-71) notes the increasing complexity of relations which result from the addition of a new part to the information system.

Table 3. Phase (T) Effects and their Interactions with Individual (I) and Setting (S) Effects on Behavior (B)

| | df | To Peers ($N=1010$) | | | | | | To Adults ($N=995$) | | | | | |
| | | Affectional Behavior | | | Status Behavior | | | Affectional Behavior | | | Status Behavior | | |
		χ^2	p	%sH(B)*	χ^2	p	%sH(B)	χ^2	p	%sH(B)	χ^2	p	%sH(B)
I;B	5	17·41	·005	1·01	35·47	·001	2·65	16·74	·010	1·32	12·94	·025	·97
S;B	5	25·27	·001	1·81	10·63	·100	·79	23·10	·001	1·82	16·08	·010	1·22
T;B	1	3·92	·050	·28	3·76	·100	·28	63·58	·001	5·01	29·33	·001	2·20
I,T;B	11	28·66	·005	2·05	46·48	·001	3·47	91·32	·001	7·19	48·91	·001	3·67
S,T;B	11	44·26	·001	3·20	35·83	·001	2·68	97·41	·001	7·81	45·41	·001	3·41
I,S,T;B	71	177·88	·001	12·75	137·70	·001	10·29	216·77	·001	17·07	148·63	·001	11·16
T_S;B	6	19·35	·005	1·39	25·21	·001	1·88	74·31	·001	5·85	29·33	·001	2·20
T_I;B	6	11·25	·100	·81	11·01	·100	·82	74·59	·001	5·87	35·98	·001	2·70
T_{IS};B	36	79·73	·001	5·71	62·72	·005	4·69	119·40	·001	9·40	81·89	·001	6·15

* Except for the introduction of phase (T) as an additional variable, the notation follows that of *Tables 1* and *2*.

settings, *total* distributions were the same for the two phases. When, however, separate analyses were made for interactions with peers and for interactions with adults, highly significant changes were noted in patterns for the two periods. Children showed an increase in interactions with peers and a decrease in interactions with adults in the breakfast setting, and a reverse decrease in interactions with peers and increase in interactions with adults in the arts-and-crafts setting. It would seem, then, that over the period breakfasts became a more social occasion and arts and crafts became a more task-oriented situation.[6]

Specific illustrations for the above phenomena may be found in the cell matrices, although again it should be noted that the selection of items for illustrative purposes may capitalize on chance factors, particularly as the cell entries become attenuated through multiple classification. Considering affectional behavior toward adults, the total proportion of hostile interactions dropped from 44 per cent in the early phase to 20 per cent a year and a half later. Not all settings, however, changed equally. For example, whereas the proportions of hostile responses went from 43 per cent to 9 per cent at breakfasts and from 61 per cent to 22 per cent in structured game activities, the arts-and-crafts situation showed little change in this respect, the proportions being 28 per cent and 27 per cent in early and late phases, respectively. Similarly, although each child showed a reduction in the proportion of hostile interactions with adults, some children changed more than others. Ed, for example, showed a reduction in hostile interactions from 49 per cent to 9 per cent whereas the reduction for Tony was from 37 per cent to 26 per cent. Finally, it would seem that the choice of setting where change appeared differed for different children. Between the two phases, Dave for example, showed a marked diminution in hostile responses toward adults in the structured group situation, whereas, for Frank, it was breakfasts and meal-times that changed most markedly.

DISCUSSION AND IMPLICATIONS

Person and Setting

People differ from one another across a variety of situations. We may characterize individual behavior as more or less aggressive, more or less dependent, more or less dominant, more or less friendly. Situations, too, evoke characteristic patterns of social action across a variety of persons. Situations are more or less competitive, more or less status-oriented, more or less friendly, more or less evocative of dependency. The present study delimited personality only to

---

[6] There appeared to be little relationship between the number of interactions and their friendly or unfriendly quality, either for different children or for different settings. This may be related to the fact that the context here is that of a closed, 'involuntary' group situation as compared to some of the open, 'voluntary' group situations described in the literature (Homans, 21).

the extent of considering individual children within a rather homogeneous group; it delimited situations in a rather 'rough, common-sense' way. Despite these limitations, both variables were shown to have relevance for interpersonal behavior. But there is, obviously, much more to be learned about the dimensions of personality and the dimensions of situations than these broad generalities.

Most recently, Campbell and Fiske (8) advocate that validational processes should utilize a matrix of intercorrelations among tests representing at least two traits, each measured by at least two methods. The approach they suggest for correlational studies resembles the methods used here, and the argument, for the most part, presents a cogent and explicit rationale for the approach in the present study. Campbell and Fiske, however, seem to imply that, for demonstration of validity, traits 'should' be fixed across variations in methods. Although such a requirement seems relevant for a 'psychology of traits', it should be noted that one could argue just as well from the point of view of a 'psychology of situations', that methods 'should' be fixed across variations in traits. Our own position is that neither one of these points of view is complete. We would view traits not as a once-and-for-all-time exclusive property of the organism irrespective of the environment but as directional potentialities under certain environmental circumstances; similarly, situations would be viewed as having arousal potential only for certain traits. The extent of contribution toward other variables, made by either trait or situational variations, will be, in part, a function of the level of conceptualization within a design. But we would suggest that it is most useful to consider neither situational nor trait variance as predictive error, but rather to move in the direction of explicit theoretical and empirical examination of sources of variance and their interactions. If such sources are defined, they add to, rather than detract from, predictive efficiency.

Which is more important for behavior, the individual personality or the situation? The question is a meaningless one. Neither component can be uncoupled from the other. The problem is similar to the heredity-environment one (cf. Anastasi, 1; Dobzhansky, 11). As Anastasi notes with respect to this latter issue, '. . . the nature and extent of the influence of each type of factor depend upon the contribution of the other. Thus the proportional contribution of heredity to the variance of a given trait, rather than being a constant, will vary under different environmental conditions. Similarly, under different hereditary conditions, the relative contribution of environment will differ' (1, p. 197). So, too, there are some situations where the potential range of individual variation is highly restricted and others where individual variations are maximized. Personality factors may be similarly differentiated—for example, cognitive functions are, it is likely, somewhat less subject to situational variations than are affective aspects of personality.

We found that setting variations influenced behavior more in the later than in the earlier phases of treatment. The gain in the ability to discriminate among situations was coordinate with other gains in the ability to make differentiations. Thus, despite the fact that the children were growing older, the differences between their behavior toward each other and their behavior toward adults increased with time. Even within the peer group itself the children responded more toward each child as an individual in the later phase. That is, in the later period each child was more apt to be treated differently by other children, although his own behavioral resemblance to others had not changed (cf. Raush, Dittmann, and Taylor, 32). It would seem, then, that there was an increasing trend for features associated with reality, and with increased capacity for reality-testing, to exercise more potent influence on social behavior.

Increased differentiation would seem to be an index of increased psychological maturity. Bjerstedt (4), for example, finds that sociometric choices of Swedish schoolchildren tend toward greater differentiation according to the situation with increasing age. To what extent the changes in our subjects were a function of age or of the treatment program is a tenuous question, and one that is not to be settled here. But again the heredity-environment analogy would appear to be appropriate. Growing up in the environment these boys came from, or growing up in a prison setting, is likely to differ from growing up in a milieu geared to therapy.

Person-in-Setting

Perhaps the most striking finding was the extent of interaction between child and setting. The unique confluence of child and setting contributed far more to behavior than did the summative effects of individual-difference and setting components. In fact, the potency of situational influences on behavior was somewhat obscured until setting variations were examined or each child individually; similarly, individual differences were more closely related to behavior when each setting was examined individually. It is not surprising to find interactive effects—that situations have different, though consistent, behavioral 'meanings' for different people. Thus, Maas (22), for example, found that the perception of group behavior by group leaders was a function neither of the type of group, *per se*, nor of the personality of the leader, *per se*, but rather of the interactive effect between type of leader and type of group. But the extent of such interaction poses both practical and theoretical problems.

Certainly, more adequate classification of both personality and setting dimensions should contribute to understanding such interactive effects. That is, there is no reason, at this point, to believe that the interaction represents individually unique and specific variance. We might speculate, however, on possibilities for classification and dimensionalization of person-situation configurations. A goal would be to refine and dimensionalize the interaction rather than concentrate on what we typically conceive of as the main variables. Consideration of such possibilities would demand revision in the boundaries we ordinarily, and perhaps arbitrarily, set in the matrix of events (cf. Peak, 29).

Setting and Change

Conclusions with respect to interactive effects between settings and change in interpersonal behavior can be only tentative from these data. Certainly, in an ongoing clinical operation, policies and procedures are modified in accordance with staff experience and with changes in clinical needs. Changes in policies, changes in experience, and changes in staff can all have effect on these results. Even so seemingly small a matter as the fact that during one period observations were made during the summer when children rose early, whereas during the other phase they were made in fall and winter, may affect the results. Still, it would seem that a conservative view, based on these results, would maintain that it is unlikely that change in social behavior is an all-or-none affair. If behavioral improvement varies according to the setting, and according to the constellation of the particular child and the meanings that particular settings have for him, then the study has obvious implications for investigations of therapeutic change. For one thing, it would seem likely that observers would differ somewhat in their estimates of improvement if their locales of observation differed. This problem is independent of, but is likely to be confounded with, problems in unreliability. Second, in lieu of accurate specification of variables—an untenable demand in most clinical situations, one would think—emphasis must be placed on respective sampling of situations where improvement in social behavior is being studied.

SUMMARY

The social interactions of six hyperaggressive boys were studied at two phases of residential treatment, a year and a half apart. In each phase each child was observed twice in six life settings and his behavior toward both peers and adults was described and coded.

The present report was concerned with several sources for the retrieval of information about social behavior. The following questions were raised, and the following answers were obtained by means of multivariate information transmission analyses:

1. Does knowledge about the social setting increase information about interactive behavior? The answer is, in general, yes. Some specific differences in the kinds of behavior evoked by specific settings were described.

2. To what extent are the effects of social settings generalized for all the children in the sample, and to what extent do settings have specific effects for specific children? To what extent are individual reactions consistent across situations and to what extent is individual consistency related to the specific settings? In general, there is individual consistency in social behavior across different settings and there is setting consistency across different individuals. But the interactive effects between child and setting contributed far more

information about behavior than did the sum of the independent components. Thus, it would seem that the kind of behavior a setting evokes would be to a considerable extent related to the personality of the particular child; the kind of behavior a child produces would be to a considerable extent related to the dimensions of the particular situation that are salient for him.

3. With treatment and maturation, is there a shift in the relative contribution to information about behavior from situational and individual-difference sources? The expectation was that, as psychological maturity increased, situational factors would come to play a more potent role for behavior. The trend of the data was toward confirmation of this expectation. The results were coordinate with other findings which indicated an increase in the ability of the children to make differentiations.

4. Are changes in social behavior equal over all settings or do they appear greater in some situations as compared to others? Tentatively, it would appear that, just as not all children show the same kind and degree of change over time and treatment, so not all settings show the same kind and degree of change. There may, however, be considerations that temper such conclusions.

The above phenomena were illustrated and some of their implications were noted.

REFERENCES

1. Anastasi, A. 'Heredity, Environment, and the Question "How?" ' *Psychol. Rev.,* Vol. 65, pp. 197–209, 1958.
2. Barker, R. G., and Wright, H. F. *Midwest and Its Children.* Evanston, Ill.: Row, Peterson, 1954.
3. Bettelheim, B. *Love Is Not Enough.* Glencoe, Ill.: Free Press. 1950.
4. Bjerstedt, Å. 'The Interpretation of Sociometric Status Scores in the Classroom.' *Acta psychol.,* Vol. 12, pp. 1–15, 1956.
5. Bossard, J. H. S. *The Sociology of Child Development* (Rev. ed.). New York: Harper, 1954.
6. Brunswik, E. *Systematic and Representative Design of Psychological Experiments.* Berkeley, Calif.: Univer. Calif. Press, 1947.
7. Brunswik, E. 'Representative Design and Probabilistic Theory in a Functional Psychology.' *Psychol. Rev.,* Vol. 62, pp. 193–218, 1955.
8. Campbell, D. T., and Fiske, D. W. 'Convergent and Discriminant Validation by the Multitrait-Multimethod Matrix.' *Psychol. Bull.,* Vol. 56, pp. 81–106, 1959.
9. Cottrell, L. S., Jr. 'The Analysis of Situational Fields in Social Psychology.' *Amer. sociol. Rev.,* Vol. 7, pp. 370–82, 1942.
10. Dittmann, A. T. 'Problems of Reliability in Observing and Coding Social Interactions.' *J. consult. Psychol.,* Vol. 22, p. 430, 1958.
11. Dobzhansky, T. 'On Methods of Evolutionary Biology and Anthropology. Part I. Biology.' *Amer. Scientist,* Vol. 45, pp. 381–93, 1957.
12. Erikson, E. H. *Childhood and Society.* New York: Norton, 1950.
13. Fisher, R. A. *The Design of Experiments.* (4th ed.) New York: Hafner, 1947.
14. Freedman, M. B., Leary, T. F., Ossorio, A. G., and Coffey, H. S. 'The Interpersonal Dimension of Personality.' *J. Personality,* Vol. 20, pp. 143–61, 1951.

15. Garner, W. R. 'Symmetric Uncertainty Analysis and its Implications for Psychology.' *Psychol. Rev.*, Vol. 65, pp. 183–96, 1958.
16. Goodrich, D. W. 'The Choice of Situation for Observational Studies of Children.' *Amer. J. Orthopsychiat.*, in press.
17. Gump, P., Schoggen, P., and Redl, F. 'The Camp Milieu and its Immediate Effects.' *J. soc. Issues*, Vol. 13, pp. 40–54, 1957.
18. Gump, P., and Sutton-Smith, B. 'Activity-Setting and Social Interaction: A Field Study.' *Amer. J. Orthopsychiat.*, Vol. 25, pp. 755–61, 1955.
19. Hammond, K. R. 'Representative vs. Systematic Design in Clinical Psychology.' *Pyschol. Bull.*, Vol. 51, pp. 150–60, 1954.
20. Hammond, K. R. 'Probabilistic Functioning and the Clinical Method.' *Psychol. Rev.*, Vol. 62, pp. 255–62, 1955.
21. Homans, G. C. *The Human Group.* New York: Harcourt, Brace, 1950.
22. Maas, H. S. 'Personal and Group Factors in Leaders' Social Perception.' *J. abnorm. soc. Psychol.*, Vol. 45, pp. 54–63, 1950.
23. Maier, H. W., and Campbell, S. G. 'Routines: A Pilot Study of Three Selected Routines and their Impact upon the Child in Residential Treatment.' *Amer. J. Orthopsychiat.*, Vol. 27, pp. 701–10, 1957.
24. McGill, W. J. 'Multivariate Information Transmission.' *Psychometrika*, Vol. 19, pp. 97–116, 1954.
25. McGill, W. J. 'Isomorphism in Statistical Analysis.' In Quastler, H. (Ed.) *Information Theory in Psychology.* Glencoe, Ill.: Free Press, 1955, pp. 56–62.
26. McGill, W., and Quastler, H. 'Standardized Nomenclature: An Attempt.' In Quastler, H. (Ed.), *Information Theory in Psychology.* Glencoe, Ill.: Free Press, 1955, pp. 83–92.
27. Miller, D. R. 'Prediction of Behavior by Means of the Rorschach Test.' *J. abnorm. soc. Psychol.*, Vol. 48, pp. 367–75, 1953.
28. Peak, H. 'Problems of Objective Observation.' In Katz, D., and Festinger, L. (Eds.), *Research Methods in the Behavioral Sciences.* New York: Dryden, 1953, pp. 243–300.
29. Peak, H. 'Psychological Structure and Psychological Activity.' *Psychol. Rev.*, Vol. 65, pp. 325–48, 1958.
30. Quastler, H. 'Information Theory Terms and their Psychological Correlates.' In Quastler, H. (Ed.) *Information Theory in Psychology.* Glencoe, Ill.: Free Press, 1955, pp. 143–71.
31. Raush, H. L. 'On the Locus of Behavior-Observations in Multiple Settings within Residential Treatment.' *Amer. J. Orthopsychiat.*, in press.
32. Raush, H. L., Dittmann, A. T., and Taylor, T. J. 'The Interpersonal Behavior of Children in Residential Treatment.' *J. abnorm. soc. Psychol.*, Vol. 58, pp. 9–27, 1959.
33. Redl, F. 'The Meaning of "Therapeutic Milieu".' In *Symposium on Preventive and Social Psychiatry.* Walter Reed Army Institute of Research. Washington, D.C.: U.S. Gov't Printing Office, 1957, pp. 503–17.
34. Redl, F. 'The Impact of Game Ingredients on Children's Play Behavior.' In Schaffner, B. (Ed.), *Group Processes, Trans. Fourth Conf.* New York: Josiah Macy, Jr. Foundation, 1959, pp. 33–82.
35. Redl, F., and Wineman, D. *The Aggressive Child.* Glencoe, Ill.: Free Press, 1957.
36. Shannon, C. E., and Weaver, W. *The Mathematical Theory of Communication.* Urbana: Univer. Illinois Press, 1949.
37. Smith, J. E. K. *Multivariate Attribute Analysis.* Engineering Research Institute, Univ. of Michigan, 1953.
38. Sullivan, H. S. *The Psychiatric Interview.* New York: Norton, 1954: London: Tavistock Publications, 1955.
39. Thibaut, J. 'An Experimental Study of the Cohesiveness of Underprivileged Groups.' *Hum. Relat.*, Vol. 3, pp. 251–78, 1950.

10

Sources of Behavioral Variance as Measured by the S-R Inventory of Anxiousness

NORMAN S. ENDLER and J. McV. HUNT

Whether the major source of variance in behavior derives from the situation or the person is an important recurrent issue between social psychologists and personologists. Social psychologists, especially those influenced by Cooley (1902) and George Herbert Mead (1934), have contended that the major source of behavioral variation resides in the situations in which individuals act (see Cottrell, 1942a, 1942b; Dewey & Humber, 1951; Lindesmith & Straus, 1949) and derives from the definitions or meanings these situations have for individuals in terms of cultural rules and the roles they call forth. Personologists (Cattell, 1946, 1950; Cattell & Scheier, 1961; McClelland, 1951; Murray, 1938; but excepting Allport, 1937, 1962) and clinicians (see Rapaport, Gill, & Schafer, 1945) have assumed that individual differences and their dynamic sources within individuals are essentially consistent across situations and thereby constitute the major source of behavioral variation.

Analyzing this issue, Hunt (1959, 1963) has pointed out that those emphasizing individual differences have found that interjudge coefficients of reliability and validity coefficients of tests assessing personality traits typically fall between .20 and .50. Using the square of these coefficients as an estimate of the proportion of variance contributed by person differences suggests that these proportions are limited to between 4% and 25% of the total. A range of proportions so small is hardly consonant with the notion of consistent across-situation differences among persons as the major source of behavioral variance.

From the *Psychological Bulletin*, 1966, 65, 336–346. Copyright 1966 by the American Psychological Association. Reprinted by permission.

This study was supported in part by United States Public Health Service grants (MH-K-6-18,567 and MH-08987) and in part by a grant from York University, Toronto. The authors wish to thank L. J. Cronbach, Goldine C. Gleser, D. W. Fiske, and John Gaito for their helpful comments and suggestions. The assistance of W. J. Jobst and Mrs. P. Offman with respect to some of the statistical analyses is also acknowledged.

What has been needed, however, is a direct comparison of the relative sizes of the contributions to the total variance in behavior, or reports of it, from persons (individual differences) and from situations for various indicator responses. Such comparison is needed for several such traits as proneness to anxiety, to haste, to hostility, etc., since the sizes of the variance from the various sources for one trait may not hold precisely for another. Anxiety is a widely investigated trait in which persons are commonly presumed to vary consistently across situations. Using the S-R Inventory of Anxiousness, Endler, Hunt, and Rosenstein (1962) have attempted such a test for this trait of anxiousness in terms of what their subjects reported they would do, feel, or show in various situations of various kinds.

The format of the S-R Inventory of Anxiousness had its origin in a logical analysis of the meaning of trait ratings, an analysis on which Hunt has lectured to his students for years (see Hunt, 1959). This format samples, separately, modes of response, situations, and persons. The form of the S-R Inventory employed by Endler, Hunt, and Rosenstein (1962) samples 14 reported modes of response in each of 11 situations with each person or subject. Each mode of response is reported for each of the situations; thus, the total number of items is 154. The form of the Inventory also employs a five-step scale for intensity of response ranging from "none" to "very much." The subject is asked to report the intensity of his response (physiological reaction, feeling, direction of response, or effect on action in progress) for each situation. All scales have the same direction, so that for each item, a high score (5) indicates a high level of anxiety and a low score (1) indicates a low level of anxiety. The format gives a page to each of the 11 situations, and the 14 modes of response are listed below the situation as follows:

"You are just starting off on a long automobile trip."

1. Heart beats faster   1 2 3 4 5

           Not at all   Much faster

2. Get an uneasy feeling   1 2 3 4 5

           None   Very strongly

3. Emotions disrupt action   1 2 3 4 5

           Not at all   Very disruptive

6. Perspire   1 2 3 4 5

           Not at all   Perspire much

7. . . 14. [See Endler, Hunt, & Rosenstein, 1962.]

Using a three-way analysis of variance of these reported intensities for the various modes of response, Endler, Hunt, and Rosenstein (1962) found that for a sample of 67 students at the University of Illinois selected for the extremes of anxiousness, the sampling of situations nevertheless yielded a mean square (158) which was 3.8 times the mean square from this sampling of subjects (40), and that for a random sample of 169 freshmen at Pennsylvania State University, the ratio of the mean square from situations (244) to the mean square from subjects (21) was 11.49. Although they also noted that the mean square for modes of response was considerably greater than the mean square for either situations or subjects and that the mean square for the interaction between modes of response and situations was nearly as large as that for persons (individual differences), they emphasized the comparison between the variance from situations and the variance from subjects (Endler et al., 1962, pp. 9–14). The fact that the variance from situations was substantially greater than that from individual differences clearly appeared to indicate that social psychologists have been more nearly correct than personologists.

Like many disputes in the history of science, however, this one between social psychologists and the personologists over whether the main source of variation in behavior is in situations or in persons turns out to be a pseudoissue, the discovery of which leads to new insight with import for behavioral prediction and for personal assessment. In the light of further analysis, the behavioral variance in reports of anxiety-indicating responses turns out to be due primarily neither to situations nor to persons. Although a comparison of mean squares for situations and for persons or subjects may have had a certain surprise value in the Endler, Hunt, and Rosenstein (1962) communication of their results, actually, the mean square for the situational source is a composite of variance from situations per se, from the interaction of situations with subjects, from the interaction of situations with modes of response, from the triple interaction, and from error. The mean square for subjects is a similar composite, as is also the mean square for modes of response. Because the mean square for each main contributor is a composite of a number of contributors to the variance, the logic of such comparing of mean squares is highly dubious.[1] The mean squares describe the variance among mean scores (i.e., over individual persons and over modes of response, for example, in the case of the mean square for situations) or among total scores (i.e., over situations and over modes of responses in the case of the mean square for individual differences). Actually, each component contributes something to the variance of each item score, and an analysis of the relative proportions of variance from each component should be based on an analysis of the total variation among the specific individual-item scores. It follows that, in order to discuss the relative proportion of variance contributed by each main component, it is necessary to determine the relative magnitude of variance

---

[1] Various investigators have compared mean squares in terms of their relative magnitude. That is, they compare the mean squares in terms of their relative magnitude and state, for example, that in a particular study the mean square for one source is greater than that for another source. These relative magnitudes do not, however, imply relative proportions of variance, since the sum of all the mean squares is greater than the total variance. This is because some components (residual, for example) may contribute to all the mean squares. For descriptive purposes (and limiting ourselves to the data at hand), a comparison of mean squares may be valid. For purposes of estimating the proportions of total variance from the various sources, it is invalid.

from each component. This is not to be derived directly from the mean squares but should rather come from specification equations. These specification equations are expectations of mean squares and are equated to sums of relevant components of variance, all properly weighted. We can then solve for each component source of variance.

Various statistical innovators have suggested procedures for partitioning the components of variance (see Bolles & Messick, 1958; Cornfield & Tukey, 1956; Endler, 1966; Endler & Jobst, 1964; Gaito, 1960; Lindquist, 1953; Scheffé, 1959).

This paper presents a reanalysis of the data reported by Endler, Hunt, and Rosenstein (1962). The reanalysis determines the relative contributions to the total variance from subjects, situations, and modes-of-response, and from all the various interactions. It consists of comparing estimated components of variance rather than either mean squares or sums of squares. In order to add information concerning the generality of the comparison across samples of subjects, moreover, a similar analysis of data from one new sample of subjects is included.

METHOD

Subjects and Procedure

The subjects in all three samples recieved the S-R Inventory of Anxiousness along with other measures not pertinent to the present report. The two samples of students described by Endler, Hunt, and Rosenstein (1962) were determined by considerations in other investigations. The Illinois sample included, in equal proportions, those who scored among the top 15% and among the lowest 15% of the students on the Mandler-Sarason (1952) Test Anxiety Questionnaire. These subjects were preselected by Rosenstein (1960) for another study. The Penn State students were not preselected, but some of them were used in another study (Grooms & Endler, 1960). While the Illinois sample was, for these reasons, highly selected, the sample from Penn State presumably approximated a random sample of freshmen in a large state-supported university. The third sample consisted of 53 male and female students in an elementary psychology course at York University and was presumably fairly representative of college students in a small liberal arts college in Canada.

Statistical Manipulation

The relative contributions of variance from situations, subjects, modes of response, two-way interactions, and residual (composed of the triple interaction and error or within-variance combined because the triple interaction cannot be separated from error with only one measure of each response of each subject in each situation) were assessed by means of a three-way analysis of variance, assuming a random-effects model.[2] The procedure used to partition variance from these various sources for the three samples is the one reported by Gleser, Cronbach, and Rajaratnam (1965), by Endler and Jobst (1964), and by Endler (1966).

For a three-way analysis of variance—situations (Sit), subjects (S), and modes of response (M-R)—using a random-effects model, the mean squares have the following expectations, in terms of the various component sources of variance (note that p = persons or subjects; i = situations; j = modes of response; r = residual and is equal to the triple interaction plus error or within variance; and n, k, and m = the numbers of subjects, situations, and modes of response, respectively):

$$E(MS_p) = \sigma_r^2 + km\sigma_p^2 + m\sigma_{pi}^2 + k\sigma_{pj}^2 \tag{1}$$

$$E(MS_i) = \sigma_r^2 + nm\sigma_i^2 + m\sigma_{pi}^2 + n\sigma_{ij}^2 \tag{2}$$

$$E(MS_j) = \sigma_r^2 + nk\sigma_j^2 + k\sigma_{pj}^2 + n\sigma_{ij}^2 \tag{3}$$

$$E(MS_{pi}) = \sigma_r^2 + m\sigma_{pi}^2 \tag{4}$$

$$E(MS_{pj}) = \sigma_r^2 + k\sigma_{pj}^2 \tag{5}$$

$$E(MS_{ij}) = \sigma_r^2 + n\sigma_{ij}^2 \tag{6}$$

$$E(MS_r) = \sigma_r^2 \tag{7}$$

The observed mean squares were substituted for their expectancies, and the equations above were solved for each of the component sources of variance.

---

[2] Some of our colleagues have questioned our use of a random-effects model rather than a mixed effects model. The latter may appear to be more appropriate since the situations and the modes of response in the S–R Inventory of Anxiousness are not random samples of all possible situations or of all possible modes of response. The S–R format for inventories, however, has one of its chief advantages in separate, and potentially random, sampling of situations and of modes of response, as well as of subjects. It may be noted that in the monograph (Endler, Hunt, & Rosenstein, 1962) no claim was made for statistical generality. Generality was to derive from the empirical reproducibility of the findings not only across samplings of situations, of modes of response, and of subjects, but also across traits. With a random-effects model, we could determine all the components of variance if each subject were asked to report each mode of response more than once in each situation. With the mixed-effects model, the only way we could solve for all the components would be by assuming the triple interaction to be zero. Since the triple interaction should be psychologically meaningful, we believe it is less hazardous to assume a random-effects model than a mixed-effects model. At any rate, the components of variance are comparable for random- and mixed-effects models (see Endler, 1966, for a more detailed discussion of the choice of model when solving for components of variance).

These component sources of variance were then summed to obtain a total or components sum for each sample, and the percentage contribution of each variance to the components sum was computed.

RESULTS

Table 1 presents degrees of freedom (*df*) and mean squares (*MS*) from three-way analyses of variance for the Illinois, Penn State, and York samples, respectively. The Illinois and Penn State columns of this table correspond to parts of Tables 3 and 4, respectively, in the S-R monograph of Endler, Hunt, and Rosenstein (1962), except that the order of the main sources of variance has been altered to present them according to increasing size, and the term residual has been substituted for the term triple interaction, that is, for $S \times Sit \times M\text{-}R$. The York columns are based on a three-way analysis of variance from data collected especially for this present study.

In Table 1, the mean squares for situations are much larger in all three cases than the mean squares for subjects. Similarly, the mean squares for modes of response are much larger than the mean squares for either situations or subjects. The results for the York sample correspond with those for the Illinois and Penn State samples in that the mean square for situations is inordinately larger than the mean square for subjects. Descriptively, this comparison of mean squares appears to be reproducible across samples of subjects and to indicate that the situations make more difference in the reported indices of anxiousness than do individual differences among the subjects.

Table 2 presents the reanalyzed data from the three samples. In this reanalysis, the variance has been partitioned among the main sources, and the various interactions according to the specification equations given above. The data from the Illinois sample are discussed separately because composing the sample of the top 15% and the bottom 15% of students preselected on another

Table 1. Analysis of Variance (Random-Effects Model) of Reported Responses to Situations in the S-R Inventory of Anxiousness from Illinois, Penn State, and York Samples

Source	Illinois[a] (N = 67)		Penn State[b] (N = 169)		York (N = 53)	
	df	MS	*df*	MS	*df*	MS
Subject (S) (*p*)	66	40.08	168	21.26	52	24.55
Situation (Sit) (*i*)	10	152.00	10	244.37	10	90.66
Mode of Response (M-R) (*j*)	13	307.46	13	836.51	13	257.12
S × Sit (*pi*)	660	3.43	1,680	3.16	520	3.18
S × M-R (*pj*)	858	4.44	2,184	2.86	676	2.85
Sit × M-R (*ij*)	130	9.38	130	20.62	130	7.14
Residual (*r*)	8,580	0.60	21,840	0.66	6.760	0.64

[a] From Endler, Hunt, and Rosenstein, 1962, Table 3, p. 10. This sample was composed of students scoring in either the top 15% or the bottom 15% on the TAQ (Mandler & Sarason, 1952).
[b] From Endler, Hunt, and Rosenstein, 1962, Table 4, p. 10.

Table 2. Estimated Variance Components and Percentages for each Component Derived from a Three-way Analysis of Variance (Random-Effects Model) of Reported Responses to Situations in the S-R Inventory of Anxiousness from Illinois, Penn State, and York Samples

Source	Illinois ($N = 67$)		Penn State ($N = 169$)		York ($N = 53$)	
	Variance component	Percent	Variance component	Percent	Variance component	Percent
Subject (S) (p)	.213	10.42	.103	5.75	.124	6.88
Situation (Sit) (i)	.149	7.29	.094	5.25	.109	6.05
Mode of Response (M-R) (j)	.399	19.53	.438	24.44	.425	23.57
S × Sit (pi)	.202	9.89	.179	9.99	.181	10.04
S × M-R (pj)	.349	17.08	.200	11.16	.201	11.15
Sit × M-R (ij)	.131	6.41	.118	6.58	.123	6.82
Residual (r)	.600	29.37	.660	36.83	.640	35.50
Total variation (Components sum)	2.043	99.99	1.792	100.00	1.803	100.01

measure of anxiety tends to exaggerate the variance from individual differences among subjects.

In spite of the exaggeration of the variance from subjects, the Illinois columns of Table 2 show the estimated proportion of the total variation from subjects to be only 10.42%. This exaggerated estimate of the proportion from subjects in this reanalysis is slightly larger than that from situations (i.e., 7.29%). Both, however, are relatively small proportions of the total variation (sum of the components of variances). The proportion deriving from modes of response for this Illinois sample is estimated at 19.53%, but, as pointed out by Endler et al., the large size of this proportion is a trivial finding inasmuch as one would expect subjects to "get an uneasy feeling" often, even though they might very seldom experience "having loose bowels." More important theoretically is the fact that the three simple interactions combined contribute an estimate of about one-third of the total variation. The interaction of subjects with modes of response (S × M-R = 17.08%) is probably exaggerated over the interaction of subjects with situations (S × Sit = 9.89%) and over the interaction of situations with modes of response (Sit × M-R = 6.41%) by the manner in which the Illinois sample was selected. In this sample, the estimated residual accounts for about 30% of the sum of variance components.

The last four columns of Table 2 present the reanalysis of the Penn State sample and a similar analysis for the new York sample. While one of these samples is representative of college students in a large state university and the other of students in a new, small Canadian college, it will be noted that the proportions of total variation from the main sources and from the various interactions are very similar indeed, and that the degree to which the various proportions differ from those for the highly selected Illinois sample in Table 2 is surprisingly small.

For the Penn State and York samples, the estimated proportions of the total variation are very similar, and those from subjects (5.75% and 6.88%, respectively) are about equal. These proportions from subjects are somewhat smaller, as would be expected, than that for the Illinois sample with the 70% of moderately anxious students removed. In the Penn State and York samples, the estimated proportions of total variation from the modes of response are increased to about one-fourth, and this increase over that for the Illinois sample would also be expected from the nature of the differences in the sampling of subjects. Again the simple interactions combined contribute nearly a third of the total variation in each sample. The interaction of Subjects with Situations accounts for an estimate of about 10%, that for Subjects with Modes of Response about 11%, and that for Situations with Modes of Response about 7%; and these proportions apply to both samples. Again the residual contributes just over a third of the total variation in each sample.

DISCUSSION

This reanalysis changes the answer to the question of whether behavioral variation is primarily a function of individual differences or of situations. It would appear that behavioral variation is attributable to neither of these factors per se. The fact that reliability and validity coefficients are low for the inventories purporting to measure various personality traits (behavioral characteristics presumed to be consistent across situations) would be expected from the fact that considerably less than a tenth of the variance derives from individual differences. While situations make a substantial difference in behavior and may be all-important when society demands conformity (see F. H. Allport, 1934), when the individual is free to respond according to his own inclinations, as in the case of answering the S-R Inventory, the situation per se makes no more contribution to the total variation than do individual differences. Moreover, the interaction of subjects with situations contributes more of the variance than does either by itself. While the modes of response continue to contribute nearly a quarter of the variance, they too show substantial interactions with both subjects and situations, and the triple interaction itself may be a substantial contributor (one may guess it to be of the order of 10%) even though it could not be assessed by the approach used here because no subject responded to any item more than once.

The fact that the proportions of total variability coming from the various sources are found to be similar in three samples of subjects indicates that these results tend to generalize across groups of subjects. On the other hand, the relatively small portion of the variance contributed by individual differences among subjects may reflect the fact that all the subjects are about the same age, all from the middle class, and all from the English-speaking North American culture. This relatively small portion of variance from individual differences may also reflect less of a genuine generalizability of actual response across subjects than it reflects the generalization of reports of response. A culture may more readily standardize what people are willing and able to report than it standardizes actual variation in heart rate, in palmar sweat, and in tendencies toward nausea or loose bowels. Only by measuring actual responses of individuals in such real situations as those here presented only verbally can one estimate how well reports reflect behavior.

The proportion of the total variability from the sampling of situations in this study may well be considerably smaller than that to be found in life in general. This sampling is loaded with situations which were chosen to evoke substantial amounts of anxiety. Had the sampling included also such situations as "sitting down to eat a holiday dinner," "sitting down to read the evening paper," "getting undressed for bed," etc., the proportion of variance from situations might be higher. Investigations now in progress will attempt to answer this question by administering and analyzing reports from inventories with other samplings of situations.

It is possible that the large proportion of variance coming from modes of response may be exaggerated here. Some of the responses called for are socially desirable and others are socially undesirable; this factor may have exaggerated the variance of reports more than acutal behavior would vary. Again, it would be necessary to measure these various modes of response from samplings of subjects in real situations before such a question could be answered.

The finding that nearly a third of the total variation comes from the simple interactions is important. The interaction of Subjects with Situations (about 10% in all three samples) indicates that while behavior is shaped by the situation, the shape it takes is not independent of the individual. Individuals respond more or less to various situations, independently of the mode of response called for.

The interaction of Subjects with Modes of Response (about 11% of the variance) would imply that individuals vary substantially in the patterns of autonomic response to which they are prone, as Lacey and Lacey (1958) have noted and emphasized.

The interaction of Situations with Modes of Response (of the order of 7% of the variance) indicates that at least some of the situations must tend to induce certain modes of response somewhat consistently in people. The fact that this interaction contributes so little of the variance reminds one of the inadequacy of that earliest hope for simple, consistent S-R laws. On the other hand, the fact that such a source of variance does exist is consonant with the finding that certain kinds of stimuli do evoke specific kinds of autonomic responses fairly consistently (see Darrow, 1929; Davis & Buchwald, 1957; Davis, Buchwald, & Frankmann, 1955; Lacey & Lacey, 1958).

The triple interaction is probably meaningful psychologically even though it was not possible to isolate it in this study. The triple interaction states that in a particular situation, a particular person has a particular mode of response. For example, a given individual may not need to urinate frequently, nor need he be generally anxious about automobiles or about riding in them, but when he is about to start off on a long automobile trip, he may find himself needing to urinate frequently. Such triple interactions may be quite real, and they may differ in important ways from main effects, from simple interactions, and from error.

Unfortunately, when each person reports each of his responses in each situation only once, it is not possible to differentiate estimates of the triple interaction from estimates of the error. It is not easy to obtain repeated realistic reports of specific responses in each of the situations because subjects may become irritated by the repetition or they may merely repeat their first report of response from memory. On the other hand, it should be quite feasible to record actual responses of individuals in several encounters with each of the various situations. Under such investigative circumstances, the triple interaction could readily be separated from the error or within-variance.

Choice of Mathematical Model

The approach in this paper has been to determine what components of variance are included in each mean square, to estimate the magnitude of each source from each sample of data, and to compare the magnitude of each source with the sum of all sources of variance in the analysis. An alternative approach to the partitioning of variance consists of computing "coefficients of utility" by forming ratios of the sum of squares for each source of variance to the total sum of squares for the analysis (Bolles & Messick, 1958). Although coefficients of utility are simple to compute and are often empirically similar to estimated components of variance, such an approach is not advocated because it suffers from at least two defects.

First, the ratios of the sum of squares for the various sources to the total sum of squares are the same irrespective of whether a fixed-effects, a mixed-effects, or a random-effects model is assumed. Thus, comparing ratios for the various sums of squares disregards what has been learned about statistical models during the past 25 years, while the approach by way of components of variance is sensitive to the various models. Empirical discrepancies between the two approaches may be small, but the results obtained with the two models do differ. Gaito (1958) presented a set of data where the results and conclusions from the two models differed radically.

Second, comparing the ratios of the various sums of squares with the total sum eliminates the possibility of removing the effects of insignificant sources of variance. In the approach by way of components of variance, one can pool the mean squares for nonsignificant sources. Thus, with the approach by way of comparing ratios for the sums of squares from the various sources, one throws away information by failing to make use of the tests of the null hypothesis. This can make a substantial difference in results. On these considerations, Gaito (1958) suggested in his critique of the Bolles-Messick coefficient of utility that for both ease of interpretation and definitiveness of results, the approach by way of components of variance is to be preferred to that by way of sums of squares.

Tucker's Three-Mode Factor Analysis

A highly appropriate alternative treatment of such data would be Tucker's (1964) three-mode factor analysis if the existing storage limitations of computers did not make computation so difficult. The highly significant interactions in the analysis of variance indicate that situations and modes of response are neither single factored nor independent of one another. In their simple factor analyses of the situations and of the modes of response, Endler, Hunt, and Rosenstein (1962) found three types of situations and three types of modes of response. Levin's (1965) three-mode factor analysis of the data from the Penn State sample included here confirms these findings, at least in general, and indicates significant interactions. His core matrix consists of three idealized subjects or types. Each type is an interaction matrix of Situation Factors X Response Factors; that is, for each type, we obtain the scores of response factors to the situation factors (see Levin, 1965, p. 451). Since Levin's results from a three-mode factor analysis are highly consistent with our own, they provide a confirmation of the method of estimating the size of components of variance used in this study.

Suggestions for Personality Assessment

The fact that very substantial portions of the total variance come from the interactions of subjects with situations, of subjects with modes of response, and of situations with modes of response, and from the triple interaction, has importance for personality description and for the design of inventories to predict either behavior or feelings. First, it implies that accuracy of personality description in general calls for statements about the modes of response that individuals manifest in various kinds of situations as well as statements about their general proneness to make certain responses rather than others, and about their proneness to be responsive rather than unresponsive. Such a direction in personality description would have its ultimate limit in the uniqueness of the individual emphasized by G. W. Allport (1937, 1962). Like many limits, uniqueness in generalized description of persons may be unfeasible, but considerable refinement might be achieved with appreciable profit by categorizing situations and by categorizing modes of response and, then, by describing individuals in terms of those categories of responses they are prone to make in various categories of situations. The format of the S-R Inventory permits separation of the situations to be symbolically encountered by the subjects from the responses they are asked to report. It also permits sampling of situations and of responses separately. Considerable improvement in the validity of trait assessment might well be obtained from the use of this format with the samples of situations and modes of response designed for the purpose of assessment.

Second, the fact that substantial portions of variance come from the interactions suggests that the validity of predictions of personal behavior should be substantially improved by asking the individuals concerned to report the trait-indicating responses of interest in the specific situations, or at least in the specific kinds of situations, concerned. Evidence that use of the format of the S-R Inventory in such a fashion does improve both the precision of description and the validity of prediction, at least so far as anxiety is concerned, has recently come from several sources.

On the side of precision of description, Endler and Bain (1966) have employed the original form of the S-R Inventory of Anxiousness to study social class differences and have found college students from the lower class more anxious than those from the middle class in situations loaded heavily on the interpersonal factor but not in situations offering inanimate, physical danger or in psychological situations. Concretely, the class differences in reported responses were limited to such situations as "You are going into an interview for an important job" or "You are entering a competitive contest before spectactors"; they did not appear for such situations as "You are crawling along a ledge high on a mountain side" or "You are going as a subject into a psychological experiment." Moreover, in a comparison of high school boys from lower and higher socioeconomic backgrounds on the various categories of responses in the S-R Inventory, Haywood and Dobbs (1964) found those of lower socioeconomic status scoring higher than those of higher socioeconomic status on those responses loading heavily on either the autonomic factor or the exhilaration factor. These studies suggest that the separation of categories of situations from categories of responses afforded by the S-R Inventory permits an improvement in the precision with which class differences in anxiousness can be described.

On the side of validity of prediction, two studies have yielded interesting evidence. In a study of the effects of three therapy-like approaches to the modification of frequency of recitation during quiz sections in a course in elementary psychology, D'Zurilla (1964) has related reported degrees of response in the various kinds of situations in the S-R Inventory to the number of times each student actually talked out in class before the treatments were instituted. The anxiety scores for the situation described as "You are getting up to give a speech before a large group" showed a correlation of $-.63$ with the numbers of pretreatment recitations. Significant but lower coefficients were found between anxiety scores for other interpersonal situations and this criterion, but the correlations became low and insignificant for anxiety scores for other kinds of situations and for global measures of anxiety. In a study comparing the efficacy of insight therapy and desensitization in reducing anxiety in public speaking situations, Paul (1966) found anxiety scores based on the 14 anxiety-indicating modes of response in the S-R Inventory to the public speaking situation to show validity coefficients of the order of .7 to .8 with subjects' reports of anxiety when actually speaking. Such anxiety scores also showed significant but lower correlations with rater observations of anxiety from subjects' speaking behavior. Anxiety scores based on subjects' responses to three other interpersonal situations in the Inventory showed significantly lower correlations with reported and observed anxiety of subjects in the speaking sutuation. These results suggest strongly that validity of prediction is a function of the similarity of the test situations to which subjects are asked to report their responses to the criterion situation. The format of the S-R Inventory permits specifying test situations that are much like any criterion situation in which one may wish to predict subjects' responses.

CONCLUSION

In the light of this reanalysis of the data from the study by Endler, Hunt, and Rosenstein (1962) and of the analysis from the additional sample from York University, the question of whether individual differences or situations are the major source of behavioral variance, like many issues in the history of science, turns out to be a pseudoissue. In effect, there is no single major source of behavioral variance, at least so far as the trait of anxiousness is concerned. Human behavior is complex. In order to describe it, one must take into account not only the main sources of variance (subjects, situations, and modes of response) but also the various simple interactions (Subjects with Situations, Subjects with Modes of Response, and Situations with Modes of Response) and, where feasible, the triple interaction (Subject with Situations with Modes of Response). Behavior is a function of all of these factors in combination.

The marked similarity for the proportions of total variation (sum of variance components from the various main sources and interactions) across the three samples of subjects in this study indicates considerable consistency, at least among college-age youth, for this sampling of situations and this sampling of modes of response. Work now in progress is attempting to ascertain whether this generality holds for other samples of situations and other samples of modes of response.

The fact that the interactions contribute approximately a third of the variance implies that personality description can be improved by describing people in terms of the kinds of response they manifest in various kinds of situations. Studies are cited in which this implication is empirically confirmed.

REFERENCES

Allport, F. H. The J-curve hypothesis of conforming behavior. *Journal of Social Psychology,* 1934, **5**, 141–183.

Allport, G. W. *Personality.* New York: Holt, 1937.

Allport, G. W. The general and unique in pscyhological science. *Journal of Personality,* 1962, **30**, 405–422.

Bolles, R., & Messick, S. Statistical utility in experimental inference. *Psychological Reports,* 1958, 4, 223–227.

Cattell, R. B. *The description and measurement of personality.* New York: World Book, 1946.

Cattell, R. B. *Personality: A systematic theoretical, and factual study.* New York: McGraw-Hill, 1950.

Cattell, R. B., & Scheier, I. H. *The meaning and measurement of neuroticism and anxiety.* New York: Ronald Press, 1961.

Cooley, C. H. *Human nature and the social order.* New York: Scribner's, 1902.

Cornfield, J., & Tukey, J. W. Average values of mean squares in factorials. *Annals of Mathematical Statistics,* 1956, **27**, 907–949.

Cottrell, L. S., Jr. The analysis of situational fields. *American Sociological Review,* 1942, 7, 370–382. (a)

Cottrell, L. S., Jr. The adjustment of the individual to his age and sex roles. *American Sociological Review,* 1942, 7, 618–625. (b).

Darrow, C. W. Differences in the physiological reactions to sensory and ideational stimuli. *Pscyhological Bulletin,* 1929, **26,** 185–201.

Davis, R. C., & Buchwald, A. M. An exploration of somatic response patterns: Stimulus and sex differences. *Journal of Comparative and Physiological Psychology,* 1957, **50,** 44–52.

Davis, R. C., Buchwald, A. M., & Frankmann, R. W. Autonomic and muscular responses, and their relation to simple stimuli. *Psychological Monographs,* 1955, 69(20, Whole No. 405).

Dewey, R., & Humber, W. J. *The development of human behavior.* New York: Macmillan, 1951.

D'Zurilla, T. J. Effects of behavioral influence techniques applied in group discussion on subsequent verbal participation. Unpublished doctoral dissertation, University of Illinois, 1964.

Endler, N. S. Estimating variance components from mean squares for random and mixed-effects analysis-of-variance models. *Perceptual and Motor Skills,* 1966, **22,** 559–570.

Endler, N. S., & Bain, J. M. Interpersonal anxiety as a function of social class. *Journal of Social Psychology,* 1966, **70,** 221–227.

Endler, N. S., Hunt, J. McV., & Rosenstein, A. J. An S-R inventory of anxiousness. *Psychological Monographs,* 1962, 76(17, Whole No. 536).

Endler, N. S., & Jobst, W. J. Components of variance derived from mean squares for random, mixed, and fixed effects analysis of variance models. Urbana, Ill.: University of Illinois, Psychological Development Laboratory, 1964. (Mimeo)

Gaito, J. The Bolles-Messick Coefficient of Utility. *Psychological Reports,* 1958, **4,** 595–598.

Gaito, J. Expected mean squares in analysis of variance techniques. *Psychological Reports,* 1960, **7,** 3–10.

Gleser, G. C., Cronbach, L. J., & Rajaratnam, N. Generalizability of scores influenced by multiple sources of variance. *Psychometrika,* 1965, **30,** 395–418.

Grooms, R. R., & Endler, N. S. The effect of anxiety on academic achievement. *Journal of Educational Psychology,* 1960, **51,** 299–304.

Haywood, H. C., & Dobbs, V. Motivation and anxiety in high school boys. *Journal of Personality,* 1964, **32,** 371–379.

Hunt, J. McV. On the judgment of social workers as a source of information in social work research. In A. W. Shyne (Ed.), *Use of judgments as data in social work research.* New York: National Association of Social Workers, 1959, Pp. 38–54.

Hunt, J. McV. Five instances where investigative observations are modifying personality theory. Paper read at a symposium on "Personality: Theories and Systems," XVII International Congress of Psychology, Washington, D.C., August 1963.

Lacey, J. I., & Lacey, B. C. Verification and extension of the principle of autonomic response stereotype. *American Journal of Psychology,* 1958, **71,** 50–73.

Levin, J. Three-mode factor analysis. *Psychological Bulletin,* 1965, **64,** 442–452.

Lindesmith, A. R., & Strauss, A. L. *Social psychology.* New York: Dryden Press, 1949.

Lindquist, E. F. *Design and analysis of experiments in psychology and education.* New York: Houghton-Mifflin, 1953.

Mandler, G., & Sarason, S. B. A study of anxiety and learning. *Journal of Abnormal and Social Psychology,* 1952, **47,** 166–173.

McClelland, D. C. *Personality.* New York: Wm. Sloane Assoc. (now Holt, Rinehart, & Winston), 1951.

Mead, G. H. *Mind, self, and society.* Chicago: University of Chicago Press, 1934.

Murray, H. A. *Explorations in personality.* New York: Oxford, 1938.

Paul, G. L. *Insight vs. desensitization in psychotherapy: An experiment in anxiety reduction.* Stanford: Stanford University Press, 1966.

Rapaport, D., Gill, M., & Schafer, R. *Diagnostic psychological testing.* Chicago: Year Book, 1945. 2 vols.

Rosenstein, A. J. Psychometric vs. physiological anxiety and serial learning. *Journal of Personality,* 1960, **28,** 279–292.

Scheffé, H. *The analysis of variance.* New York: Wiley, 1959.

Tucker, L. R. The extension of factor analysis to three-dimensional matrices. In N. Frederiksen (Ed.), *Contributions to mathematical psychology.* New York: Holt, Rinehart & Winston, 1964.

11

Generalizability of Contributions from Sources of Variance in the S-R Inventories of Anxiousness

NORMAN S. ENDLER and J. McV. HUNT

For nearly half a century, anxiety has been a focal matter in psychological theorizing. Anxiety began to take on focal status in the twenty-fifth of Freud's (1917) introductory lectures, even though in the fourth of his new introductory lectures (Freud, 1932) he relinquished his theory of its origin in frustration or "undischarged libidinal excitation" in favor of a theory in which he saw anxiety originating from punishment of the infant in the form of castration threats. Anxiety got full focal status in the theory of acquired drive (see Hull, 1943; Miller & Dollard, 1941). Nevertheless, the conceptual nature of anxiety has been confused. It has been viewed sometimes as a reaction to situations in which the person has encountered pain (Freud, 1932; Hull, 1943; Miller & Dollard, 1941). It has been viewed sometimes as a state of the organism which varies from occasion to occasion (Cattell & Scheier, 1961; Spielberger, 1966a). It has been viewed also as a chronic characteristic of persons which is relatively constant across both situations and occasions, and this view has been implicit for most of those who have constructed instruments for assessing individual differences in anxiousness as a trait (see Cattell, 1957; Hathaway & Meehl, 1951; Mandler & Sarason, 1952; Taylor, 1953). Moreover, the distinction between situationally evoked reactions or states of anxiety and a common trait of anxiousness has been a special case in the debate over whether variability in behavior is more a matter of situational

From *Journal of Personality*, 1969, *37*, 1–24. © 1969 by the Duke University Press. Reprinted by permission of the authors and publisher.

This study was supported in part by grants from the United States Public Health Service Nos. MH-08987 and MH-K6-18567, and in part by grants from York University, Toronto, from the Canada Council, and from the Research Board of the University of Illinois. The assistance of Kelly Hsia and Cheryl Schlafer with respect to some of the statistical analyses is gratefully acknowledged. We also wish to thank the many students who participated in this study, and the teachers, professors, and administrators of the participating institutions for their cooperation and assistance.

determinants, commonly held by those social psychological theorists (e.g., Cottrell, 1942a, 1942b; Dewey & Humber, 1951) who have taken their lead from George Herbert Mead (1934), or more a matter of personality traits, commonly held by both clinicians and personologists (e.g., Cattell, 1946, 1950; Cattell & Scheier, 1961).

It was this issue of the relative importance of individual differences and of situations which originally led to the idea of constructing S-R Inventories of Traits (see Endler, Hunt, & Rosenstein, 1962). These S-R Inventories are distinctive because they separate explicitly described *situations* from the *modes of response* which serve as indicators of the reaction, state, or trait in the format. They thereby permit investigators to sample separately the situations, the modes of response, and the subjects, and they also permit them to partition the total variance in the responses or reports of responses among these main sources and their interactions.

On the basis of the results from the original form of the S-R Inventory of Anxiousness, Endler and Hunt (1966) found that neither individual differences nor situations contributed substantially, as main sources, more than about 4 to 6 per cent of the total variance (components sum) in the reported modes of response indicating anxiety. The modes of response themselves contributed of the order of 25 per cent of the variance. Nearly a third of the variance came from the simple interactions (subjects with situations: about 10 per cent; subjects with modes of response: about 11 per cent; and situations with modes of response: about 7 or 8 per cent). These findings helped to explain the traditionally low (.20 to .25) validity coefficients for omnibus inventories of anxiety. They suggested that validity coefficients might well be raised substantially by specifying the particular situations in which the response indicators of anxiety are reported by subjects on inventories and in which the subjects are to be observed. They also suggested that personality diagnosis and description might generally be improved by specifying the kinds of responses that persons make in various kinds of situations.

The results from which these fairly radical suggestions derive were based upon but the original, single form of the S-R Inventory of Anxiousness (Form O). This form contains a sample of 11 situations and a sample of 14 modes of response. The results reported came from but three samples of college students. In view of these limitations in sampling, the generalizability of the results for even the single trait of anxiousness may be questioned.

The purpose of the investigation reported here has been to determine to what extent the proportion of variance for subjects holds for still other samples of subjects, to what extent the proportion of variance from situations holds for other samples of situations, and to what extent the proportion of variance from modes of response holds for other samples of modes of response indicating anxiousness. This investigation, in contrast to the previous ones, moreover, compares the results from men and women separately in order to determine if consistent sex differences exist with respect to the sizes of the proportions of variance contributed by the three main sources and their interactions.

METHOD

The strategy of this investigation has been to construct five new forms of the S-R Inventory of Anxiousness, and to administer the original form and each of these new forms to each of several groups of men and women, or of adolescent boys and girls. In certain forms of the Inventory, the range of threat in the situations was deliberately exaggerated from situations which are typically innocuous ("You are just sitting down to dinner," or "You are undressing for bed") to others highly threatening (e.g., "You are getting up to give a speech before a large group"; "You receive a summons from the police"; "You are driving down the road when you meet two racing cars approaching you abreast") in order to determine how much of this would increase the proportion of variance contributed by situations. Moreover, a list of 125 situations was constructed to constitute a finite population, and several approximations of random samples were selected from this list to test the generality of the original findings. A similar procedure has been employed in sampling modes of response, even though it is not as easy to vary any dimension of anxiousness by choice of response indicators. Individual differences have been extended by sampling subjects of differing age and mental health. For each form of the Inventory with each sample of subjects, we have partitioned the variance derived from a three-way analysis of variance from the various main sources and their inter-actions by means of the variance components method reported by Gleser, Cronbach, and Rajaratnam (1965), Endler and Jobst (1964), and by Endler (1966). The variances for each source from all of the 43 samples of subjects and for all forms across their respective samples of subjects are presented for comparison in summary fashion as medians, semi-intequartile ranges, and ranges.

The Forms of the S-R Inventory of Anxiousness

The original form of the S-R Inventory of Anxiousness (Form O, consisting of 11 situations and 14 modes of response, totaling 154 items) has been used along with five other quite different forms in the present study. The format for each form provided a page for each of the situations, with the situations described at the top (e.g., "You are about to take the final examination for a course in which your status is doubtful"), and with the modes of response listed below. The subjects reported their various responses on rating scales of five steps which ranged in likelihood or intensity from none to very much. A low score (of one) always indicated the absence of or a very low level of that particular response-indicator of anxiousness; a high score (of five) always indicated the presence of and an intense reaction for that particular response-indicator of anxiousness.

The five new forms were: Form 1-X-62 consisting of 18 situations and 10 modes of response (180 items), Form U-I-64-A, Form EY-L-64-A, and Form U-I-66-A, each containing 14 situations and 10 modes of response (140 items), and Form SA-66 containing 12 situations and 10 modes of response (120 items).

Selection of Situations

In the case of Form O, the choice of the 11 situations was based on an intuitive attempt to select a variety of situations that would be familiar, through either first-hand or vicarious experience, to most college students and which would include both social and nonsocial situations varying from ones regarded typically as innocuous ("You are starting on a long automobile trip") to others typically regarded as very threatening ("You are on a ledge high upon a mountain side") and with most of them regarded as potentially quite threatening.

Since the factor analysis of situations in Form O (Endler, Hunt, & Rosenstein, 1962) had uncovered three kinds of situations (interpersonal danger, inanimate danger, and ambiguous danger), the 18 situations selected for Form 1-X-62 were arbitrarily chosen from a master list of 125 composed from suggestions by ourselves and our colleagues with about equal representation of each kind. The 14 situations in Form U-I-64-A were deliberately selected from the master list, now extended to 200 in order to extend the range of danger. At the innocuous end, we added such situations as "sitting down to eat at your favorite restaurant" and "getting ready to go to bed." At the threatening end, we added such situations as "failing examinations," "being approached by cars racing abreast," and "receiving a police summons." This deliberate extension of the range of danger was done, as already noted, to determine the limits of proportion of variance that might come from situations as a single main-source. For the other three forms, the selection moved toward a random sampling of situations from the finite population of the master list of 200. In each case, however, the selection included representatives of each of the three kinds (interpersonal, inanimate, and ambiguous danger). Moreover, for Form EY-L-64-A and Form SA-66 the selection and descriptions of the situations were modified to be appropriate for use with young adolescents. All the others were used with samplings of adults and college students.

Selection of Modes of Response

For the original Form O, the 14 modes of response indicating anxiety or fear were chosen to represent both positive and negative reactions to situations because feelings of keen anticipatory excitement are commonly reported from the same situations that evoke excited withdrawal, because Hunt, Cole, and Reis (1958) had found some of their subjects reporting hope where others reported fear, and because both approach and withdrawal reactions incorporating various levels of excitement have been emphasized by Olds (1955) and by Schneirla (1959, 1964). We presumed that excited approach is the obverse of anxiousness. In this original Form O, moreover, the indicator responses were also chosen to sample the subjects' reported perceptions of their physiological reactions (the traditional expressive indicators of emotion) because these would be most amenable to validation via recording of the physiological reactions. Finally, the

Table 1. Synoptic Description of the Various Forms of the S-R Inventory of Anxiousness with Number of Situations, Modes of Response, and Number of Samples Analyzed.[a]

Form of the S-R Inventory	O	1-X-62	UI-64-A	EY-L-64-A	SA-66	UI-66-A
Number of situations	11	18	14	14	12	14
Number of modes of response	14	10	10	10	10	10
Number of male samples	7	3	3	6	2	1
Number of female samples	7	2	3	6	2	1

[a]See footnote 1 for ADI references for the availability of the situations and modes of response in each of the forms.

indicator responses were also chosen to include from the MMPI (Hathaway & Meehl, 1951) some of the items most useful diagnostically in the Taylor Anxiety Scale (Taylor, 1953).

Because the factor analyses of the 14 modes of response in Form O had discovered three kinds (distress, exhilaration, and autonomic reactions), the 10 modes of responses selected for Form 1-X-62, Form U-I-64-A, Form EY-L-64-A, and Form UI-66-A always included the three scales with the highest loadings on each of these factor-kinds. Form SA-66 used eight modes from Form O plus two new ones ("hands trembling" and "get fluttering feeling in stomach").

Thus far, we have not yet constructed a master list of modes of response indicating anxiousness or fear. Moreover, we have found ourselves hard put to think of many beyond those already included among the 14 in Form O. Thus, the samples of situations in the various forms have been greatly varied, while the samples of response-indicators have consisted primarily of subsamples of the 14 originally employed in Form O plus the two new ones in Form SA-66.

Table 1 presents a synoptic description of the several forms of the S-R Inventory of Anxiousness with the numbers of situations and the numbers of modes of response in each and with the numbers of samples of men and women who responded for each form.[1]

Subjects

A total of 43 samples of subjects (22 of males and 21 females) have served in the work reported here. More than one sample of subjects have responded to each form of the Inventory. Except for Form UI-66-A, more than one sample of

---

[1] A table (Table A) containing all of the situations and modes of response for each and all of the various forms of the S-R Inventory of Anxiousness has been deposited with the NAPS, Order NAPS Document No. NAPS-00027 from ASIS National Auxiliary Publications Service, c/o CCM Information Sciences, Inc., 22 West 34th Street, New York, N. Y. 10001; remitting $1.00 for microfilm or $3.00 for photocopies.

both males and females have responded to each form, with six samples of each having responded to Form EY-L-64-A and seven samples to the original form, Form O (see Table 1).

The various samples of subjects have been selected to represent not only a wide variation in collegiate populations, but also in ages from adolescence to middle age, and in social classes from upper middle to upper lower, and in mental health from typical samplings of high school and college students to adolescent patients of a mental health clinic. The college students have come from both private and public colleges and universities. They represent a geographical distribution ranging from institutions in the eastern, midwestern, and western portions of the United States and from one province (Ontario) in Canada. These samples also represent adults attending evening colleges in Toronto, adolescents attending both junior and senior high schools, and patients of the East York Mental Health Clinic. An attempt was made to give the original form of the S-R Inventory of Anxiousness (Form O) to a sample of 31 psychotic patients of the Toronto Psychiatric Hospital, but interviewers had to fill out the inventory, and the cooperation of the patients was highly uncertain. The results from this sample have not been included among the results reported here. Table 2 presents the name of the institution from which each sample of subjects came, the size of the various samples, and the form of the S-R Inventory administered to each.

Table 2. Name, Size of Sample, and Form of S-R Inventory of Anxiousness Administered

Name of sample	Form of S-R	Number of males	Number of females
Penn State University	O	93	76
Penn State University	O	206	99
Penn State University	O	—	98
Dartmouth College	O	125	—
York University (Toronto)	O	30	23
York University (Toronto)	O	103	46
Forest Hill Collegiate (High School)	O	41	34
University of Illinois	O	53	55
York University	1-X-62	62	49
Atkinson College (evening, adult)	1-X-62	74	77
Atkinson College (evening, adult)	1-X-62	74	—
University of Illinois	UI-64-A	31	37
University of Colorado	UI-64-A	29	41
York University	UI-64-A	81	68
East York Collegiate (High School)	EY-L-64-A	140	95
Westwood Junior High	EY-L-64-A	55	59
St. Clair Junior High	EY-L-64-A	45	51
Oak Park Junior High	EY-L-64-A	58	61
Cosburn Junior High	EY-L-64-A	57	59
East York Mental Health Clinic	EY-L-64-A	49	33
St. Andrews Junior High	SA-66	75	68
St. Andrews Junior High	SA-66	72	74
University of Illinois	UI-66-A	46	71

Table 3. Medians, Semi-interquartile Ranges (Q), and Ranges of Variance Components and Percentages of Total Variance for Each Component Source for Reported Response-indicators to Situations on the Various Forms of the S-R Inventory of Anxiousness

| | Part A—Males (N = 22 samples) | | | | | |
| | Median | | Q[a] | | Range | |
Source	Variance component	Pct.	Chi-square component	Pct.	Chi-square components	Pcts.
Subject (S)	.095	4.44	.024	1.66	.021- .231	0.74- 9.73
Situation (Sit)	.083	3.95	.015	0.77	.049- .369	2.24- 13.66
Mode of Response (M-R)	.594	24.76	.166	4.97	.344-1.084	14.62- 40.13
S x Sit	.193	9.14	.025	1.16	.101- .527	3.74- 22.19
S x M-R	.225	10.34	.039	1.87	.128- .381	4.92- 16.12
Sit x M-R	.157	7.51	.071	2.25	.067- .297	4.05- 12.77
Residual	.746	37.06	.108	3.61	.585-1.082	22.46- 45.92
Total variation (Components sum)	2.285	100.00	.338	0.01	1.607-2.972	99.99-100.00
	Part B—Females (N = 21 samples)					
Subject (S)	.096	4.56	.027	1.15	.047- .183	1.62- 7.58
Situation (Sit)	.182	7.78	.048	1.34	.082- .575	3.14- 19.86
Mode of Response (M-R)	.627	26.61	.348	4.32	.400-1.185	16.53- 45.45
S x Sit	.226	9.31	.033	1.88	.133- .289	4.61- 13.05
S x M-R	.245	11.06	.040	1.80	.172- .370	6.76- 15.20
Sit x M-R	.180	6.95	.071	2.04	.100- .333	4.68- 12.51
Residual	.731	34.33	.146	3.06	.622-1.106	22.93- 41.42
Total Variation (Components sum)	2.607	100.00	.336	0.00	1.898-3.012	99.99-100.01

[a]Q is the semi-interquartile range: $Q = (Q_3 - Q_1)/2$.

RESULTS

Consistency among Proportions of Variance from Each Source

Table 3 presents the medians, semi-interquartile ranges (Q),[2] and the ranges of the variance components and of the percentages of the total variance (components sum) from each component source for the reported response-indicators

---

[2] The semi-interquartile range, Q, is the measure of variation most often used in connection with the median, $Q = (Q_3 - Q_1)/2$, where Q_3 and Q_1 are the third and first quartiles (i.e, the 75th and 25th percentiles), respectively. The semi-interquartile range represents one-half of the range of the middle 50 per cent of the observations. In general the relationship between Q and the median is analogous to the relationship between the mean and the standard deviation. See Edwards (1967, pp. 13-14).

of anxiousness for all of the samples responding to each and all of the forms of the S-R Inventory.[3]

An inspection of Table 3 shows that, at least in general, the proportions of total variance reported by Endler and Hunt (1966) from three samples of college students on the original form of the S-R Inventory of Anxiousness are corroborated. Except in the case of modes of response, the interaction between situations and modes of response and the residual, the semi-interquartile ranges (Qs), are below 2 per cent. The median proportions from subjects and situations are both below 5 per cent for males,[4] but a sex difference appears wherein the median proportion of total variance from situations for females (7.78 per cent) is nearly twice that for males (3.95 per cent). The median proportion of the total variance contributed by the modes of response is about a quarter for both females and males. Again, the median proportions of variance from each of the three two-way interactions is larger than that from either subjects or situations, except in the case of females for whom the interaction between situations and modes of response (6.95 per cent) is slightly less than that for situations (7.78 per cent). Again, slightly more than a third of the total variance derives from the three-way interaction and error (Residual).

Yet an inspection of the ranges in the proportions of variance from the various sources shows some instability across the samples of subjects and the samples of situations and of modes of response in the several forms of the S-R Inventory of Anxiousness. This instability is the largest for modes of response, among the main sources, and for the residual.

Effects of Varying the Samples of Subjects

Although some variation among the proportions of total variance contributed by each of the main sources and their interactions does occur, what is important

---

[3] The estimated variance components and percentages of total variation contributed by each component source for each sample of subjects have been deposited as Tables B-I with the American Documentation Institute. Order Document No. NAPS-00027 (as per instructions in footnote 1). The original analysis of variance tables can readily be derived from the variance components' tables plus the data regarding number of situations, modes, and subjects presented in Tables 1 and 2 of this paper.

[4] An exception to this statement must be made for the sample of 31 male psychotic patients for which individual differences among subjects contributed 14.56 per cent. The other sources contributed as follows: situations, 2.63 per cent; modes of response, 12.14 per cent; subjects $\times$ situations, 12.14 per cent; subjects $\times$ modes of response, 14.94 per cent; situations $\times$ modes of response, 1.88 per cent; and the residual of 39.59 per cent of the total variance. In the case of the 26 psychotic women, the contributions to the total variance were subjects, 6.58 per cent; situations, 5.77 per cent; modes of response, 15.30 per cent; subjects $\times$ situations, 16.67 per cent; subjects $\times$ modes of response, 18.08 per cent; situations $\times$ modes of response, 2.55 per cent; and the residual, 35.05 per cent. Contact with these patients was so poor, however, that we have no assurance that their reports were discriminating with any consistency among either situations or modes of response.

is how small variations are. Despite variations in the ages of subjects in the various samples and in the social classes from whence they came, and despite efforts to extend the variation of threat in the samples of situations, the proportion of total variance contributed by individual differences among subjects across situations never reaches as much as 10 per cent. Despite efforts to extend the variation of threat in the samples of situations, the proportion of total variance contributed by situations never reaches 15 per cent for men and never reaches 20 per cent for women. Moreover, the proportions of variance contributed by each of the three two-way interactions are nearly always higher than either of these two main sources, and typically the proportion of total variance from one of these two-way interactions is of the order of the combined proportion from these two-main sources (not counting modes of response, the contribution of which is regularly large).

Sex differences. Nevertheless, some sex differences emerge which should be considered. The one most evident from Table 3 is that for the proportion of total variance contributed by situations. This is nearly twice as large for women (7.78 per cent) as for men (3.95 per cent). Other sex differences emerge when the range of threat or danger in the sample of situations is extended, but these can best be mentioned below.

Age differences. Some evidence of age trends in the proportions of variance contributed by the various sources can also be seen in Table 4. Especially marked is an increase in the proportion of total variance contributed by modes of response with age. This increase is especially marked between junior high school and high school, is absent between high school and college, but continues between college-aged students and adults attending night school. Another downward trend with age appears for the proportion contributed by the interaction between subjects and modes of response, and a very slight downward trend with age appears also for the proportion contributed by subjects. These trends may result from an increasing appreciation of the social desirability of the various modes of response and an increasing tendency to expect certain modes of response in certain kinds of situations. These trends appear to be somewhat steeper for females than for males, perhaps indicating that appreciation of social desirability plays a larger role for girls than for boys.

Social class. The factor of social class is considered in Table 5. This table considers only the findings from samples of students in high schools and junior high schools. The characteristics of the neighborhoods of the various schools provide a basis for assessing at least the modal social class of the individuals sampled. Forest Hill Collegiate (high school), for instance, is predominantly lower-upper class with a sprinkling of upper-middle class (for the criteria of social class, see Warner, Meeker, & Ells, 1949). St. Andrews Junior High School

Table 4. A Comparison of Samples of Subjects from Predominantly Adult, College, High School, and Junior High School Age Levels in Terms of Medians and Ranges of Percentages of Total Variation from Each Component Source

Part A—Males

Source	Adult (N = 2)		College (N = 11)	
	Median	Range	Median	Range
Subject (S)	3.53	3.4- 3.7	4.93	0.7- 7.6
Situation (Sit)	3.14	2.9- 3.4	4.45	2.2-13.7
Mode of Response (M-R)	32.72	30.9-34.6	25.46	21.7-40.1
S x Sit	8.05	7.0- 9.1	9.65	3.7-12.7
S x M-R	7.05	6.8- 7.4	10.79	4.9-12.1
Sit x M-R	12.30	11.8-12.8	8.08	4.1-12.5
Residual	33.21	32.0-34.4	36.40	22.5-42.1

Source	High school (N = 2)		Junior high school (N = 6)	
Subject (S)	4.18	2.8- 5.6	5.30	3.8- 9.7
Situation (Sit)	4.34	3.8- 4.9	3.76	2.7- 5.8
Mode of Response (M-R)	26.09	20.9-32.9	20.04	14.6-24.7
S x Sit	9.90	7.5-12.3	9.20	7.7-22.2
S x M-R	10.81	7.9-13.7	12.35	8.9-16.1
Sit x M-R	7.74	4.1-11.4	5.07	4.5- 7.7
Residual	36.14	32.7-39.6	36.68	35.8-38.8

Part B—Females

Source	Adult (N = 1)		College (N = 11)	
	Median	Range	Median	Range
Subject (S)	2.55	—	3.61	1.6- 6.9
Situation (Sit)	8.97	—	7.78	3.1-19.9
Mode of Response (M-R)	28.64	—	26.61	21.4-45.5
S x Sit	9.35	—	9.15	4.6-13.1
S x M-R	6.76	—	10.73	5.0-14.3
Sit x M-R	10.14	—	6.97	4.7-12.5
Residual	33.60	—	33.14	22.9-36.3

Source	High school (N = 2)		Junior high school (N = 6)	
Subject (S)	4.09	3.5- 4.7	5.03	2.4- 7.6
Situation (Sit)	8.34	7.5- 9.1	7.70	6.3- 9.7
Mode of Response (M-R)	27.36	23.4-31.3	24.96	16.5-32.7
S x Sit	9.66	7.7-11.7	9.15	6.3-12.0
S x M-R	11.57	7.9-15.3	9.52	7.0-11.9
Sit x M-R	8.34	5.9-10.8	6.79	6.1- 8.3
Residual	31.14	29.7-31.6	36.97	35.8-40.3

Note.—Median of total variation source is always 100 per cent. N refers to the number of samples in all cases. Where N = 1, the median is equal to the percentages for that praticular sample, and there obviously is no range.

Table 5. A Comparison of Samples of Subjects from Predominantly Lower-upper to Upper-middle; Upper-middle and Upper-lower Social Classes in Terms of Medians and Ranges of Percentages of Total Variation from Each Component Source

	Part A—Males					
	Lower-upper, etc. (N = 1)		Upper-Middle (N = 2)		Upper-Lower (N = 6)	
Source	Median	Range	Median	Range	Median	Range
Subject (S)	5.57	—	9.19	8.7- 9.7	3.84	2.8- 6.5
Situation (Sit)	3.81	—	4.76	3.7- 5.8	3.76	2.7- 4.9
Mode of Response (M-R)	20.87	—	15.53	14.6-16.4	24.70	16.9-32.9
S x Sit	12.34	—	17.24	12.3-22.2	9.09	7.5- 9.4
S x M-R	13.73	—	10.79	8.9-12.7	11.06	7.9-16.1
Sit x M-R	4.05	—	5.07	4.7- 5.4	7.51	4.5-11.4
Residual	39.62	—	37.43	36.1-38.7	40.95	32.7-45.9

	Part B—Females					
Source	(N = 1)		(N = 2)		(N = 6)	
Subject (S)	4.72	—	6.67	5.8- 7.6	3.99	2.4- 6.5
Situation (Sit)	7.53	—	8.19	8.1- 8.3	7.26	3.8- 9.7
Mode of Response (M-R)	23.43	—	16.70	16.5-16.9	28.70	23.1-32.7
S x Sit	11.66	—	11.76	11.5-12.0	8.16	6.3-10.6
S x M-R	15.26	—	11.51	11.1-11.9	7.99	7.0-11.1
Sit x M-R	5.86	—	6.09	6.0- 6.1	7.39	5.0-10.8
Residual	31.55	—	39.10	37.9-40.3	36.68	29.7-41.4

Note.—Median of total variation source is always 100 per cent. N refers to the number of samples in all cases. Where N = 1, the median is equal to the percentages for that particular sample and there is obviously no range.

represents predominantly the upper-middle class. The East York Mental Health Clinic, East York Collegiate (high school), and the other four junior high schools (Westwood, St. Clair, Oak Park, and Cosburn) represent chiefly the upper-lower class. Again no one form of the Inventory went to all these groups (see Table 2), so the apparent trends are confounded with differing samples of situations and slightly differing samples of modes of response.

If one considers only the differences in the percentages for the upper-middle and the upper-lower classes, omitting the Forest Hill sample which was given Form O only, the percentage of total variance from subjects is greater for the upper-middle than for the upper-lower class. A similar but much less marked difference appears for the percentages of variance from situations. On the other hand, the differences in percentages of variance from modes of response are opposite in direction, substantially larger for both upper-lower class boys and girls than for upper-middle class boys and girls. This difference appears to result from less reticence about needing to urinate and having loose bowels among adolescents of the upper-lower class than among those of the upper-middle class. This still tentative finding also calls for further investigation.

While consistency in the proportions of total variance contributed by the various main sources and their interactions is the major finding, samples of subjects differing in age and in social class yield some variations in these proportions, and further investigation of the effects of age and social class is indicated. Combining these various samples into a single large sample and partitioning the variance might well raise to some degree the proportion of variance contributed by individual differences among subjects across situations and modes of response. This remains to be done. Yet, inasmuch as the mean and standard deviation for the sample of clinic patients differs little from the means and standard deviations of the various samples of adolescents, any increase in the contribution from subjects brought about from combining samples can hardly be expected to be large.

Effects of Extending the Range of Threat in Samples of Situations

Extending the range of danger or threat in the sampling of situations increases somewhat the proportion of total variance contributed by this source and increases also the proportion contributed by the interaction between situations and modes of response. Table 6 presents the medians and ranges of percentages of total variation from each component source for the sampling of situations in each form of the S-R Inventory of Anxiousness, excepting UI-66-A which was administered to only single samples of men and of women.[5] The situations in the original Form O and all the others, except UI-64-A, contained at least a moderate degree of danger or threat and ranged considerably. The sampling of situations in UI-64-A was deliberately exaggerated in range of threat by including such innocuous items as "You are sitting down to read the evening paper," and "You are going to bed after a long day." At the other extreme, this sampling also included such extremes of threat as "You are driving down the road when you meet two racing cars approaching you abreast," and "You are reading about the situation in Cuba and a new threat of nuclear war." The sampling of situations in UI-64-A was bimodal. Such increasing of the range of threat had several effects upon the proportions of total variance. First of all, it served to increase the proportion from situations from a maximum of 5.1 per cent in males to a median of 10.71 per cent, and from a maximum of 9.7 per cent in females to a median of 13.1 per cent. Even so, the maximum proportion from situations never exceeds 13.7 per cent for males or 19.9 per cent for females. It

---

[5] Form UI-66-A was administered to only one male and one female sample. For these samples the percentages for the component sources in the case of males were 4.93 for subjects, 3.30 for situations, 35.05 for M-R, 7.23 for subjects × situations, 11.05 for subjects × M-R, 0.08 for situations × M-R, and 30.36 for residual; and in the case of females, 2.74 for subjects, 3.14 for situations, 45.45 for M-R, 8.06 for subjects × situations, 6.99 for subjects × M-R, 9.76 for situations × M-R, and 23.87 for residual.

Table 6. Medians and Ranges of Percentages of Total Variation for Each Component Source for Each Form of the S-R Inventory of Anxiousness

Part A—Males

Source	Form 0 (N=7) Median	Range	Form 1-X-62 (N=3) Median	Range	Form UI-64-A (N=3) Median	Range
Subjects (S)	6.45	4.7- 7.6	3.40	2.0- 3.7	1.74	0.7- 4.2
Situation (Sit)	4.24	3.5- 5.1	2.88	2.2- 3.4	10.71	10.1-13.7
Mode of Response (M-R)	23.83	20.9-25.5	31.84	30.9-34.6	37.10	35.0-40.1
S x Sit	10.21	9.7-12.7	9.01	7.0- 9.1	5.33	3.7- 5.7
S x M-R	11.59	8.0-13.7	7.35	6.8- 9.6	9.04	4.9-10.8
Sit x M-R	5.50	4.1- 8.5	12.49	11.8-12.8	10.00	8.6-11.0
Residual	38.31	36.4-42.1	32.85	32.0-34.4	24.21	22.5-30.8

Source	Form EY-L-64-A (N=6)		Form SA-66 (N=2)	
Subject (S)	3.84	2.8- 6.5	9.19	8.7- 9.7
Situation (Sit)	3.76	2.7- 4.9	4.76	3.7- 5.8
Mode of Response (M-R)	24.70	16.9-32.9	15.53	14.6-16.4
S x Sit	9.09	7.5- 9.4	17.24	12.3-22.2
S x M-R	11.06	7.9-16.1	10.79	8.9-12.7
Sit x M-R	7.51	4.5-11.4	5.07	4.7- 5.4
Residual	40.95	32.7-45.9	37.43	36.1-38.7

Part B—Females

Source	Form 0 (N=7) Median	Range	Form 1-X-62 (N=2) Median	Range	Form UI-64-A (N=3) Median	Range
Subject (S)	4.98	3.6- 6.9	3.02	2.6- 3.5	1.62	1.6- 1.8
Situation (Sit)	7.53	5.8- 8.3	7.34	5.7- 9.0	14.03	13.1-19.9
Mode of Response	23.43	21.4-26.6	30.22	28.6-31.8	38.45	34.5-38.9
S x Sit	11.41	9.0-13.1	9.25	9.2- 9.4	4.70	4.6- 5.6
S x M-R	11.51	10.7-15.3	6.70	6.7- 6.8	5.58	5.0- 7.4
Sit x M-R	5.86	4.7- 7.0	11.33	10.1-12.5	11.06	10.6-11.3
Residual	34.33	31.6-36.3	32.07	30.5-33.6	23.01	22.9-24.1

Source	Form EY-L-64-A (N=6)		Form SA-66 (N=2)	
Subject (S)	3.99	2.4- 6.5	6.67	5.8- 7.6
Situation (Sit)	7.26	3.8- 9.7	8.19	8.1- 8.3
Mode of Response (M-R)	28.70	23.1-32.7	16.70	16.5-16.9
S x Sit	8.16	6.3-10.6	11.76	11.5-12.0
S x M-R	7.99	7.0-11.1	11.51	11.1-11.9
Sit x M-R	7.39	5.0-10.8	6.09	6.0- 6.1
Residual	36.68	29.7-41.4	39.10	37.9-40.3

Note.—Median of total variation is always 100 per cent. N refers in all cases to the number of samples of subjects. Form UI-64-A is excluded from this table because there is only one sample for each sex.

served also to increase the proportion of total variance from modes of response for both males and females. The effects of increasing the range of threat on the two-way interactions are (a) to decrease the contribution from the interaction between subjects and situations, (b) to decrease the contribution from the interaction between subjects and modes of response (and to do it substantially more for females than for males), and (c) to increase the contribution from the interaction between situations and modes of response. Despite these alterations of the proportions deriving from increasing the range of threat, the proportion of the variance contributed by the three two-way interactions remains higher than that from the main sources of subjects and situations combined. Thus, even maximizing the range of threat fails to alter in any fundamental fashion the relationships among the proportions found with Form O for the three samples of college students.

DISCUSSION

These findings have a number of theoretical implications, which are relevant to the conceptual distinction between *state* and *trait* for anxiety. They are relevant to the issue of whether individual differences across situations are more or less important than situations in determining the reports of response-indicators of anxiousness. They are relevant to the measurement of anxiety. And, finally, if these findings hold true for such other common traits as hostility and honesty, they have something to say about personality description in general.

State Anxiety vs. Trait Anxiety

Cattell and Scheier (1958, 1961) distinguished chronic (trait) anxiety, defined as a relatively permanent characteristic of persons, from momentary (state) anxiety, defined as a state which varies from day to day and from moment to moment. The former they measured by means of a score-persons matrix (R-technique), the latter by means of a score-occasions matrix (P-technique). While they found evidence for this distinction between momentary states and individual differences in chronic anxiety levels, the instruments by means of which these factors were assessed failed to tie the anxiety indicators to specific situations.

Indicators of anxiety are required for responses or reactions to situations, for states, or for chronic levels. These indicators may be physiological or behavioral, and the behavioral may include the subject's report of feelings, actions, and physiological responses as is the case with the S-R Inventories of Anxiousness. Considerable ordinality exists among the indicators of anxiousness. Loose bowels and a compulsion to urinate, for instance, indicate more anxiety than sweaty palms and feelings of uneasiness. In the findings of this investigation, this ordinality provides the reason for the high proportion of variance (a quarter of the total or more) contributed regularly by modes of response. Highly threatening situations are more likely to evoke these response-indicators of high-level anxiety than less threatening ones, and this is shown by the fact that increasing the range of threat or danger in the sampling of situations (Table 6, Form UI-64-A) clearly increases the contribution to the total variance from the interaction between situations and modes of response.

Despite such evidence of relatively consistent S-R relationships, their contribution is limited (at least in the reports of our many subjects) to about 10 per cent of the total variance. On the other hand, our findings provide clear evidence of the idiosyncratic organization of anxiousness; they demonstrate again that individuality in personality which Allport (1937, 1962) so long stressed. The evidence derives form the fact that over a fifth of the total variance derives regularly from the two two-way interactions in which subjects participate (subjects by situations, and subjects by modes of response). In addition, there is the proportion of variance contributed by the three-way interaction among subject, situations, and modes of response which we have thus far failed to assess.[6] In the light of such findings and considerations, either occasion scores, without knowledge of the evocative situations, or trait scores can give but relatively little of the total information about the anxiousness of persons.

Trait anxiety does exist, however, and it may have at least three bases. It may be a chronic manifestation of the indicators of anxiety across situations evoked by conflicts or situations which people carry around in their minds. It may be a tendency to manifest the indicators of anxiety in a large proportion of situations. It may be manifest as a tendency to show especially strong response-indicators to a relatively few situations. Omnibus questionnaires about anxiousness do yield measures of trait anxiety. Unfortunately, from the fact that individual differences among subjects across situations contribute only about 5 per cent of the total variance, such measures of trait anxiety cannot be expected to predict anxious behavior very accurately. Among omnibus inventories, the S-R Inventory of Anxiousness is as good as any. In fact, total scores for subjects derived from it show higher correlations with the scores for the same subjects from the Cattell (1957) IPAT Anxiety Scale, the Mandler-Sarason (1952) Test Anxiety Questionnaire, and the Taylor (1953) Manifest Anxiety Scale than scores from any of these instruments show with each other (see Endler, Hunt, & Rosenstein, 1962, p. 17). Even so, from the statistical principle that the percentage of variance in common between two variables can be estimated by squaring the coefficient of correlation between measures of them, it is clear that the validity coefficients for

---

[6] Since the original (1962) studies, we have become aware of the need for and possibilities of administering several samplings of situations to each sampling of subjects. This avoids confounding the effect of a sampling of situations with a sampling of subjects and permits separation of the contribution of the triple interactions from the error. We have made one attempt to do this (see Endler & Hunt, 1968b). We have also compared the contributions from the various component sources for hostility with those for anxiety (see Endler & Hunt, 1968a).

such omnibus measures of anxiety can be expected to rise consistently no higher than those customarily found. They range between .2 and .25. Similarly, this finding that individual differences among subjects across situations contributes only about 5 per cent of the total variance in the response indicators of anxiety helps to explain why the effects of psychometrically assessed extremes of differences among individuals in anxiety typically yield small effects on conditioning (see Bitterman & Holtzman, 1952; Farber & Spence, 1953; Spence & Taylor, 1951; Taylor, 1951; Taylor & Spence, 1954) and on such relatively more complex learning as rote memorizing of a series of nonsense syllables (Farber & Spence, 1953; Montague, 1953; Spielberger, 1966b; Taylor & Spence, 1952). These studies have tended to show that anxiety facilitates conditioning of such simple responses as the eye blink and the galvanic skin response and that anxiety hampers the more complex memorizing of a series of nonsense syllables, but the differences between even extreme groups, based on their scores on omnibus measures of trait anxiety, have regularly been small and barely significant from a statistical standpoint. On the other hand, when Beam (1955) compared the conditioning of the galvanic skin response in a group of students under the situational stress of being about to appear in a play on opening night or about to have their doctoral orals with that of a presumably equivalent group well-removed in time from such situational stress, the differences in both the rate and the degree of conditioning were tremendous and very highly significant ($p <$ .001). Moreover, when, in the same study, Beam compared the number of repetitions required by a group of students to memorize a series of nonsense syllables while under these forms of situational stress with the number of repetitions required by the same students to memorize an equivalent list at another occasion well removed in time from these stressful situations, the group averaged 1.5 as many repetitions under the situational stress as they did in the relatively stressless situation. Some of these students required six times as many repetitions to achieve the criterion under the situational stress than they did without it. From such considerations, it would appear that the differences in anxiety indicators obtainable within given individuals in contrasting situations is clearly much larger and more dependable than that between extreme groups obtained psychometrically with omnibus measures of anxiety.

The Issue of Subjects vs. Situations

The finding that neither individual differences across situations or situations per se contribute heavily to the total variance lends confirmation to the conclusion drawn by Endler & Hunt (1966) that this issue of the relative importance of subjects and situations is but a pseudo-issue.[7] The fact that these

---

[7] In the original study, we missed this point and stressed the relative importance of situations over individual differences (Endler, Hunt, & Rosenstein, 1962). We missed this point because I (Hunt) erroneously overruled my ex-student collaborators, albeit on what we

two main sources combined typically contribute no more to the total variance in the response-indicators of anxiousness than does either of the two-way interactions in which subjects participate strongly suggests that anxiety is idiosyncratically organized in each individual and that the issue of the relative importance of subjects and situations disappears.

Toward More Valid Measurement of Anxiousness

The fact that the contributions of the two-way interactions to the total variance loom so large suggests that improving the validity of measures of anxiousness demands specifying the situations concerning which subjects are asked to report their response-indicators and limiting the validating observations of their behavior to those specified situations. When the situations are so specified, validity coefficients ranging between .6 and .8 appear (see D'Zurilla, 1964; Hoy, 1966; and Paul, 1966). Thus the suggested importance of specifying situations is corroborated. Doing it increases validity coefficients from the range of .2 to .25, typically found for omnibus measures of individual differences in anxiety, to a range from .6 to .8.

Implications for Personality Description

If such findings hold for such other common traits as hostility and honesty, they have implications for personality description in general. First, they imply that attempting to devise better instruments with which to measure individual differences in traits across situations is doomed to the failure epitomized by validity coefficients ranging from .2 to .25. Second, they imply that it may be possible to save some of the loss of validity for personality description in general, where specifying particular situations may be unfeasible. These findings, as did those of Endler, Hunt, and Rosenstein (1962), suggest that it should be feasible to move in a fruitful direction by categorizing both situations and the response-indicators of the traits in question. Tucker's (1964) three-mode factor analysis constitutes one promising approach once the storage limitations of computers are sufficiently overcome to permit handling of sufficiently large samples of situations and modes of response. Until such a time, situations can be

---

took for expert advice, on how appropriately to partition the variance among the sources. So long as one merely compares the main sources, situations do appear to contribute several times as much of the variance as individual differences. This appeared to support the contention of the social psychologists over that of the personologists. But once the components method of partitioning the total variance (Gleser, Cronbach, & Rajaratnam, 1965; Endler, 1966) was employed, it became clearly evident that the variance contributed by each of the interactions is substantially larger than that from either of the main sources: individual differences or situations.

categorized by factor-analyzing situation-scores across individuals and modes of response somewhat after the fashion of Cattell's (1950) P-technique. In turn, modes of response can be categorized by factor-analyzing mode scores across individuals and situations. Once the situations and the modes of response are each categorized, it should become feasible to describe individuals in terms of the kinds of responses they are likely to make in the various kinds of situations.

SUMMARY

Six different forms of the S-R Inventory of Anxiousness, with differing samples of situations and of modes of response, were administered to 22 samples of male and to 21 samples of female subjects who varied in age, in social class, and in mental health. This was done to test the generalizability of the proportions of total variance from the several main sources and their interactions found by Endler and Hunt (1966) with but one form of the inventory used with three samples of college students.

Of the main sources of total variance, individual differences contribute typically only 4-5 per cent of the total variance, situations only about 4 per cent for males and about 8 per cent for females, but, because a certain ordinality exists among the reported modes of response indicating anxiety, these modes of response contribute about a quarter of the total variance. Each of the two-way interactions contributes typically about 10 per cent, and the triple interaction coupled with error contributes about a third of the total variance.

Some indications of age trends and of social-class differences in the proportions of variance from the several sources exist. Even though these are relatively small, they deserve further study. Deliberately increasing the range of threat in the sampling of situations increases the proportion of variance from situations to a maximum of 13.7 per cent for males and of 19.9 per cent for females; it also increases somewhat the proportion from the interaction of situations with modes of response.

These findings have implications for the theory of anxiety. They imply that the issue of the relative importance of individual differences and of situations is but a pseudo-issue. The fact that individual differences across situations and across modes of response contribute only about 5 per cent of the total variance in the reported indicators of anxiousness dooms omnibus inventories of anxiety to validity coefficients of the customary order of .2 to .25. On the other hand, the validity of reported anxiety indicators can be raised to coefficients ranging from .6 to .8 by specifying the situation. These findings also suggest that personality description in general might be improved considerably by categorizing both situations and modes of response and then by describing individuals in terms of the kinds of responses they tend to manifest in the various kinds of situations.

REFERENCES

Allport, G. W. *Personality.* New York: Holt, 1937.

Allport, G. W. The general and unique in psychological science. *J. Pers.,* 1962, **30,** 405-422.

Beam, J. C. Serial learning and conditioning under real-life stress. *J. Abnorm. soc. Psychol.,* 1955, **51,** 543-551.

Bitterman, M. E., & Holtzman, W. H. Conditioning and extinction of the galvanic skin responses as a function of anxiety. *J. abnorm. soc. Psychol.,* 1952, **47,** 615-623.

Cattell, R. B. *The description and measurement of personality.* New York: World Book, 1946.

Cattell, R. B. *Personality: A Systematic theoretical and factual study.* New York: McGraw-Hill, 1950.

Cattell, R. B. *Handbook for the I.P.A.T. Anxiety Scale.* Champaign, Ill.: Institute for Personality and Ability Testing, 1957.

Cattell, R. B., & Scheier, I. H. The nature of anxiety: A review of 13 multivariate analyses comparing 814 variables. *Psychol. Rep.,* Monograph Supplement, 1958, **5,** 351-388.

Cattell, R. B., & Scheier, I. H. *The meaning and measurement of neuroticism and anxiety.* New York: Ronald Press, 1961.

Cottrell, L. S., Jr. The adjustment of the individual to his age and sex roles. *Amer. sociol. Rev.,* 1942, **7,** 618-625. (a)

Cottrell, L. S., Jr. The analysis of situational fields. *Amer. sociol. Rev.,* 1942, **7,** 370-382. (b)

Dewey, R., & Humber, W. J. *The development of human behavior.* New York: Macmillan, 1951.

D'Zurilla, T. J. Effects of behavioral influence techniques applied in group discussions on subsequent verbal participation. Unpublished doctoral dissertation, Univer. of Illinois, 1964.

Edwards, A. L. *Statistical methods.* (2nd ed.) New York: Holt, Rinehart & Winston, 1967.

Endler, N. S. Estimating variance components from mean squares for random and mixed effects analysis of variance models. *Percept. Mot. Skills,* 1966, **22,** 559-570.

Endler, N. S., & Hunt, J. McV. Sources of behavioral variance as measured by the S-R Inventory of Anxiousness. *Psychol. Bull.,* 1966, **65,** 6, 338-346.

Endler, N. S., & Hunt, J. McV. S-R Inventories of Hostility and comparisons of the proportions of variance from persons, responses, and situations for hostility and anxiousness. *J. Pers. soc. Psychol.* 1968, **9,** 309-315. (a)

Endler, N. S., & Hunt, J. McV. Triple-interaction variance in the S-R Inventory of Anxiousness. *Percept. mot. Skills,* 1968, **27,** (3). (b)

Endler, N. S., Hunt, J. McV., & Rosenstein, A. J. An S-R Inventory of Anxiousness. *Psychol. Monogr.,* 1962, **76,** No. 17 (Whole No. 536), 1-33.

Endler, N. S., & Jobst, W. J. Components of variance derived from mean squares for random, mixed, and fixed effects analysis of variance models. Technical Report: Project No. MH-08987-USPHS. Urbana, Ill.: Univer. of Illinois, Psychological Development Laboratory, Oct., 1964, mimeographed.

Farber, I. E., & Spence, K. W. Complex learning and conditioning as a function of anxiety. *J. exp. Psychol.,* 1953, **45,** 120-125.

Freud, S. *Introductory lectures of psychoanalysis* (1917). (2nd ed.; trans. by Joan Riviere.) London: Allen & Unwin, 1940.

Freud, S. *New introductory lectures on psychoanalysis* (1932). (Trans. by W. J. H. Sprott). New York: Norton, 1933.

Gleser, G. C., Cronbach, L. J., & Rajaratnam, N. Generalizability of sources influenced by multiple sources of variance. *Psychometrika,* 1965, **30,** 395-418.

Hathaway, S. R., & Meehl, P. E. *An atlas for the clinical use of the MMPI.* Minneapolis: Univer. of Minnesota Press, 1951.

Hoy, Elizabeth. The influence of incongruity on reported anxiety. Unpublished master's thesis, York University, 1966.

Hull, C. L. *Principles of behavior.* New York: Appleton-Century-Crofts, 1943.

Hunt, J. McV., Cole, Marie-Louise Wakeman, & Reis, Eva E. S. Situational cues distinguishing anger, fear, and sorrow. *Amer. J. Psychol.,* 1958, 71, 138-151.

Mandler, G., & Sarason, S. B. A study of anxiety and learning. *J. abnorm. soc. Psychol.,* 1952, 47, 166-173.

Mead, G. H. *Mind, self, and society.* Chicago: Univer. of Chicago Press, 1934.

Miller, N. E., & Dollard, J. *Social learning and imitation.* New Haven, Conn.: Yale Univer. Press, 1941.

Montague, E. K. The role of anxiety in serial rote learning. *J. exp. Psychol.,* 1953, 45, 91-96.

Olds, J. Physiological mechanisms of reward. In M. R. Jones (Ed.), *Nebraska symposium on motivation: 1955.* Lincoln: Univer. of Nebraska Press, 1955.

Paul, G. L. *Insight versus desensitization in psychotherapy: An experiment in anxiety reduction.* Stanford, Calif.: Stanford Univer. Press, 1966.

Schneirla, T. C. An evolutionary and developmental theory of biphasic processes underlying approach and withdrawal. In M. R. Jones (Ed.), *Nebraska symposium on motivation: 1959.* Lincoln: Univer. of Nebraska Press, 1959.

Schneirla, T. C. Aspects of stimulation and organization in approach/withdrawal processes underlying vertebrate behavioral development. In D. H. Lehrman, R. Hinde, & Evelyn Shaw (Eds.), *Advances in the study of behavior.* New York: Academic Press, 1964.

Spence, K. W., & Taylor, Janet A. Anxiety and strength of the UCS as determiners of the amount of eyelid conditioning. *J. exp. Psychol.,* 1951, 42, 183-188.

Spielberger, C. D. Theory and research on anxiety. In C. D. Spielberger (Ed.), *Anxiety and behavior.* New York: Academic Press, 1966, Pp. 3-20. (a)

Spielberger, C. D. The effects of anxiety on complex learning and academic achievement. In C. D. Spielberger (Ed.), *Anxiety and behavior.* New York: Academic Press, 1966. Pp. 361-398. (b)

Taylor, Janet A. The relationship of anxiety to the conditioned eyelid response. *J. exp. Psychol.,* 1951, 41, 81-92.

Taylor, Janet A. A personality scale of manifest anxiety. *J. abnorm. soc. Psychol.,* 1953, 48, 285-290.

Taylor, Janet A., & Spence, K. W. The relationship anxiety level to performance on serial learning. *J. exp. Psychol.,* 1952, 44, 61–64.

Taylor, Janet A., & Spence, K. W. Conditioning level in the behavior disorders. *J. abnorm. soc. Psychol.,* 1954, 49, 497-502.

Tucker, L. R. The extension of factor analysis to three-dimension matrices. In N. Frederiksen (Ed.), *Contributions to mathematical psychology.* New York: Holt, Rinehart & Winston, 1964.

Warner, W. L., Meeker, Marchia, & Ells, K. *Social class in America: A manual for the measurement of social status.* Chicago: Science Research Associates, 1949.

12

Sources of Variance in Behavioral Measures of Honesty in Temptation Situations Methodological Analyses

EDWARD A. NELSON, ROBERT E. GRINDER, and MARCIA L. MUTTERER

In nineteenth-century genetic psychology, conscientious behavior was said to issue from a unitary moral faculty. Unless its development was arrested during childhood, the moral faculty was assumed to assure stable and habitual honest behavior. It was also assumed that individual differences would be consistent across situations and that the "strength" of the moral faculty would constitute the primary source of behavioral variation. This early genetic viewpoint has been preserved most prominently in orthodox psychoanalytic theory which holds that an integrated superego emerges from successful resolution of the oedipal conflict (Blum, 1953; Sears, Rau, & Alpert, 1965).

The belief that honesty may be accounted for by a unitary moral faculty appears to have flourished until the turn of the century, when Morgan (1896), Thorndike (1903), Thorndike and Woodworth (1901), and McDougall (1910) collectively attacked its basic assumptions. None was more damning in his criticism than McDougall (1910), to wit:

because they treated the individual in artificial abstraction from the social relations through which his moral sentiments are formed, they [older moralists] were led to maintain the hypothesis of some special faculty, the conscience, . . . in seeking to account for moral conduct [p. 229].

In the early 1920s, Hartshorne and May (1928) and Hartshorne, May, and Shuttleworth (1930) set out "to test scientifically the truth or falsity of this theory . . . that honesty is a unified character trait [Hartshorne, 1932, p. 209]."

From *Developmental Psychology*, 1969, *1*, 265–279. Copyright 1969 by the American Psychological Association. Reprinted by permission.

The analyses presented in this paper are based upon data collected for a master's thesis submitted to the University of Wisconsin (Mutterer, 1965). A partial report of the results was presented at the Biennial Meetings of the Society for Research in Child Development, Minneapolis, Minnesota, March 25, 1965.

Over a period of 5 years, they studied the behavior of several thousand children in 29 temptation situations. On the basis of mean differences and low correlations among the temptation measures, Hartshorne and May (1928) concluded that moral behavior could not be conceptualized as emanating from "an inner entity operating independently of the situations in which the individuals are placed [p. 385.]" Apparent generality of moral behavior seemed to them a function of situational similarity; individuals who have learned certain responses in temptation situations will react similarly to other temptation conflicts to the degree that the conflicts share identical stimulus elements.

The Hartshorne and May (1928) emphasis on situational factors has been challenged recently by Burton (1963), who, on the basis of factor analyses, found that a first principal component accounted for at least 40% of the common variance of a matrix of intercorrelations selected from the Hartshorne and May study. Burton (1963) concluded that:

the strong emphasis on lack of relation between the tests is removed. Our analyses indicate that one may conclude there is an underlying trait of honesty which a person brings with him to a resistance to temptation situation. However, the results strongly agree with Hartshorne and May's rejection of an "all or none" formulation regarding a person's character [p. 492].

Although Burton's (1963) factor analyses did assess the extent of intra-individual consistency across the tasks more precisely, the study leaves certain issues unresolved. First, Hartshorne and May (1928), as well as Burton, noted several methodological problems with the data that might affect interpretation of factor-analytic results. The inter-r's, for example, were not obtained from the same cases throughout the study. Furthermore, Hartshorne and May failed to report the sample sizes in their correlations.

Second, additional replications of the study are needed because measures of the extent of generality are specific to given population and task parameters. For example, higher correlations, hence greater generality, will be obtained from a population that is relatively heterogeneous with respect to a given distribution of scores (McNemar, 1963). Likewise, the heterogeneity of tasks may affect the size of the correlations. Hence, replications and extensions of Hartshorne and May's and Burton's studies are necessary before drawing general conclusions concerning the extent of intraindividual consistency.

Third, the factor-analytic procedures employed by Burton (1963) did not allow for separate assessment and comparison of the influence of situations, persons, and Situation X Person interactions as sources of behavioral variance. For example, the contribution of situations to the total behavioral variance cannot be assessed since the correlational procedures, in effect, standardize the means and standard deviations of the measures. In a series of recent investigations, Hunt and his colleagues (Endler & Hunt, 1966; Endler, Hunt, & Rosenstein, 1962; Hunt, 1965) have argued that individual differences, situations, and interactions should be distinguished as sources of behavioral variance. Moreover, on the basis of measures of anxiousness derived from a self-report inventory, these researchers have demonstrated that personality description may be improved by comparing persons, situations, and modes of response, *and* the corresponding interactions among these sources of behavioral variance.

In view of these issues, the current study was designed (*a*) to replicate and extend the Hartshorne and May (1928) and Burton (1963) studies; (*b*) to apply the Endler and Hunt (1966) framework to assess the relative contributions of persons, situations, and interactions as sources of behavioral variance in temptation conflicts; and (*c*) to discuss the advantages and limitations of Burton's factor-analytic approach to the generality problem as compared with Endler and Hunt's ANOVA approach. In addition, the paper discusses several technical problems concerned with distribution and scaling of resistance to temptation measures; these problems pertain to underlying assumptions and interpretation of both the factor-analytic and ANOVA methods.

METHOD

Subjects

The subjects were 47 boys and 59 girls in five sixth-grade classes drawn from four public elementary schools of a rural community. For boys the mean age was 11.9 years ($SD = 7.5$), and for girls, 11.7 years ($SD = 5.7$). The sample was white, except for one American Indian. One hundred and twenty-seven children were initially available in all the classes; 21 subjects were absent for one or more temptation tests. Hence, the experimental sample was comprised of 106 children. Henmon-Nelson Intelligence Test scores were available from school records for all subjects. The mean score for boys was 108.8 and for girls, 114.5. Standard deviations were 13.4 and 13.7 for boys and girls, respectively.

Both the sequence for presentation of the temptation situations and the time interval between the sessions were randomized for the four participating schools. Two classes in one of the schools were regarded as unitary for purposes of randomization to minimize interclass communication. Details of the presentation sequence and intervals are presented in Mutterer (1965).

Each of the six tests of temptation was administered by the same female experimenter over a period of 2½ months. The experimenter was a stranger to all the children, and neither teachers nor pupils knew when the experimenter might appear or when she might again return. Nothing occurred during the experimental sessions to indicate that school personnel or pupils perceived that the tests concerned children's conscience development.

Measures

Every subject participated once in each of the following six temptation conflicts:

1. The ray-gun game: The subjects operated a shooting gallery individually according to a prescribed set of rules. The game was programmed to produce a fixed score when all rules were followed, and badges were offered to those yielding to temptation. The features of the apparatus and instructions for playing the game have been described in Grinder (1961, 1962).

2. The magic mirror task: A tangible incentive (M & Ms), to be delivered several days after the task, was offered in an individual setting. Instructions for playing the game were similar to those of the ray gun. The subjects were seated in front of a 16 X 15 X 4 inch wooden box, which held a 12 X 10 inch translucent glass plate in a horizontal position, and a bank of 30 score lights tilted upward at 45 degrees. The subjects were asked to illuminate the path of an imperceptible Porteus-type maze, mounted directly under the glass plate, by tracing its course with a pencil light. The path and score lights were divided into six segments. Each portion changed in color from white to red as it was completed, while, simultaneously, the score for the section was indicated on brightly illuminated red lights.

   The path was controlled and the score lights were prearranged with microminiature light-activated switches. The apparatus was designed in order that preceding segments of the path have to be completed before successive segments operate. Each subject was asked to record his scores separately for each of the six segments, and to keep a cumulative record of his progress. The game was programmed to yield 20 points. The subjects were told that if they earned more than 20 points they would be given 20 M & Ms plus an M & M for every point after their twentieth. Transgression scores were based upon the extent to which subjects falsified their points to exceed the programmed score.

3. The multiple-choice (copying) test: Contrived from the duplicating technique (Hartshorne & May, 1928, p. 51) whereby the subjects make illegitimate use of answers, a 25-item multiple-choice test was prepared in which the first 10 items were made extremely easy and the remaining 15 items, although worded simply, were made impossibly difficult. The subjects were told that the names and scores of those who got 18 or more points would be posted on a colored "top-of-the-class" sheet and that the names of those who got less than 18 points would be posted on a smaller white sheet. A few hours later, after the tests had been scored by the experimenter, they were returned to the subjects who were then asked to score their own papers. Transgression scores were based on discrepancies between obtained points and reported points.

4. The speed test: This measure was adapted directly from the double-testing technique of Hartshorne and May (1928, pp. 76, 82). The speed subtests comprised addition, number matching, cancellation of As, digit-symbol substitution, placing dots in small squares, and digit-cancellation tests. First subjects took each subtest twice. After these were collected, the subjects were informed that these were practice trials and were handed a third set. On this

trial, the subjects scored their own papers after being told that the fastest class in the community would win a "speed-king" trophy. Following Hartshorne and May procedures, transgression scores were based on the number of points on the third test that fell beyond 2.88 standard deviations above the mean of comparable third test scores for the control group, whose papers were scored for them.

5. The squares (peeping) test: This test was a replication of a peeping test adapted from the Improbable Achievement Technique (Hartshorne & May, 1928, p. 61). The subjects were presented with a single sheet of paper upon which five large squares were drawn, one inside the other, and were asked to shut their eyes and to follow the path between the lines of the squares with their pencils for five timed trials. The subjects scored their own papers on the basis of the number of corners turned without crossing a line. Those who turned at least 14 corners correctly were to be awarded 10 M & Ms and an extra M & M for each additional corner. Following Hartshorne and May (1928, p. 64), transgression scores were based upon the number of corners turned without a crossover beyond 13. The subjects' papers were graded independently by two judges, who agreed 97% of the time or on 102 out of 106 papers. A third judge graded the remaining papers and cast the deciding opinion.

6. The circles (peeping) test: This test was similar in most respects to the preceding test. The subjects were presented a drawing, apparently without design, of 10 circles of various sizes. They were asked to close their eyes and to "hit" each of the circles with the point of a pencil. After each of three timed trials, the subjects were asked to open their eyes and to record their hits. No prizes were offered the subjects, but they were told that "kids your size generally get 20 hits." The only temptation, therefore, was that of surpassing the performance of an ambiguous referent. In accordance with Hartshorne and May (1928, p. 254), transgression scores were based upon the number of hits beyond 13.

Scaling Procedures

Researchers have traditionally used two different types of scales for analyzing performance in temptation situations, dichotomous and interval. Dichotomous scales treat performance in terms of resist–yield categories indicating in either-or terms whether the subject has transgressed. Interval scales, on the other hand, are based upon the number of raw score units beyond a transgression criterion, thereby indicating the extent of transgression.

With dichotomous scales, the variance of each measure depends upon the resist-yield proportion. For example, the variance is maximal for a 50-50 split. With interval scales, the variance is affected more by the amount of transgression. Thus, variance would be maximal for a test that produced a large proportion of transgressors and that differentiated many degrees of transgression. Conversely, variance would be minimal in a task where a large proportion resisted temptation and, thus, necessarily scaled within a single interval unit.

To the extent that personality and task parameters affect extent of transgression in a nonlinear manner, interval and dichotomous scales yield noncomaprable measures. For example, the extent of transgression as measured by the interval techniques might be affected by the extent to which subjects perceive that high scores increase likelihood of detection. Moreover, high transgression might be motivated by the desire to excel, whereas low transgression might be motivated by fear of failure. These differences would be masked by dichotomous scales.

Since neither type of scaling is clearly advantageous on a priori bases, and since each type has a tradition in resistance to temptation research, both types of scales were employed in this investigation. Thus, the study allowed for comparison of the alternative scaling procedures as they might affect the results of the various statistical analyses.

Reliability of the Measures

Assessment of test-retest reliability for each of the six tasks was precluded by the exigencies of data collection. However, some relevant data were provided by previous research. A pilot study involved administration of the ray gun to 56 boys under two slightly different conditions. The correlation between the interval scores for the two administrations was .85; when scaled dichotomously the tetrachoric correlation (r_t) was .94. Hartshorne and May (1928) reported alternate form reliabilities, based upon interval scores, of .70, .44, and .46 for their versions of the copying, speed, and peeping tasks, respectively.

Unreliability of resistance to temptation measures is enhanced by the difficulty of determining whether the subjects have transgressed. In the present study, this is particularly problematical with tasks such as speed, squares, and circles, since the transgression criterion for each is arbitrarily determined as some very improbable score. Hence, some transgressors may be classed as having resisted temptation. Such discrepancies will contribute error variance to the computations, especially those that are based upon dichotomous scales.

If a measure is unreliable, intercorrelations involving that measure will be attenuated. As Burton (1963) noted in his study, the extent of generality is also underestimated to the extent that the measures are unreliable. Hence, estimates in his study, as well as this investigation, should be regarded as conservative.

RESULTS AND DISCUSSION

Initially, the data were analyzed for males and females separately to determine the extent of sex differences. These analyses did reveal significant but small sex differences in the extent of transgression and in certain correlations among the measures. However, subsequent statistical analyses with both the ANOVA and

Table 1. Frequency Distributions for Six Transgression Measures

Ray gun		Magic mirror		Multiple choice		Speed		Squares		Circles	
Score	N	Score	N	Score	N	Score	N	Score	N	Score	N
0	15	0	46	0	39	0	81	0	41	0	58
1–4	15	1	24	1	9	1	1	1	5	1–2	3
5–8	11	2	16	2	5	2	14	2	1	3–4	9
9–12	13	3	8	3	7	3	3	3	7	5–6	10
13–16	7	4	7	4	17	4	3	4	8	7–8	7
17–20	14	5	1	5	12	5	1	5	12	9–10	7
21–24	9	6	2	6	5	6	0	6	16	11–12	4
25–28	8	7	0	7	8	7	0	7	16	13–14	3
29–32	8	8	2	8	1	8	3			15–16	2
33–36	3			9	2					17–18	1
37–40	1			10	1					19–20	2
41–44	1										
45–48	1										
Totals											
Resisting	15		46		39		81		41		58
Transgressing	91		60		67		25		65		48

principal components techniques indicated that the extent of intraindividual consistency and related indexes were not materially different for males and females. Therefore, this study presented data for the sexes combined.[1]

Frequency Distributions

Table 1 presents the frequency distributions of the six resistance-to-temptation measures in terms of the dichotomized resist—yield scores and the interval score. To simplify interpretation, the raw score units on each scale were transformed so that 0 equals resist, and units 1 or greater indicate extent of transgression. Visual inspection of the distributions of the six measures in terms of the interval scales reveals marked differences in their shapes. On the other hand, categorization of the transgression scores in terms of the dichotomous groupings indicated that the resist-yield proportions range from about 15–85% to 80–20%.

The discrepancies among the distributions of both dichotomous and the interval scores indicate that the subjects' performances varied considerably from

[1] Table A (means, standard deviations, and analysis of variance of resistance to temptation according to classrooms, sex, and tasks). Table B (intercorrelations and principal components analyses of six resistance to temptation measures for males and females), and Table C (comparisons of persons, tasks, and interactions as sources of variance among six measures of resistance to temptation for males and females) may be obtained for a fee from the National Auxiliary Publications Service. Order Document No. 00300 from National Auxiliary Publications Service of the American Society for Information Science, c/o CCM Information Science, Inc., 22 West 34th Street, New York, New York, 10001; remitting $1.00 for microfiche or $3.00 for photocopies.

situation to situation. On the speed test, few subjects transgressed; on the magic-mirror test, most subjects transgressed only a few points beyond the criterion. Yet on the ray-gun and squares measures most subjects transgressed extensively. Such wide variations in performance may be taken as prima facie evidence that temptation behavior was affected by situational variables, that is, by variations of task parameters as were employed in this study.

Besides allowing for certain inferences about the role of situational factors, the frequency distributions also provided indirect evidence concerning the extent of intraindividual consistency. To the extent that the amount of transgression varied across situations, indexes of intraindividual consistency were restricted or limited. For example, one might expect that product-moment correlations based upon such discrepant distributions as the speed measure, in which most of the subjects resisted, and the ray-gun measure, in which most yielded, could hardly be high. Most of the variance on the ray-gun measure was not accounted for in the speed test because about 15% resisted temptation of the former, while about 80% resisted on the latter. Correlations based upon the dichotomous scores, of course, were also affected by such discrepancies, but presumably to a lesser degree because differences in the degree of transgression were not a source of variance. The noncomparability of the distributions lends additional support for using both dichotomous and interval techniques.

Correlations

Table 2 presents both the product-moment (r) and tetrachoric (r_t) correlation coefficients among the various temptation measures. The product-moment correlations were computed from the interval scores and the tetrachoric correlations from the dichotomized scores. These data permit comparisons between the measures of interrelationships based upon the two types of scales. Analyses in terms of the product-moment correlations reveal a range of values from .05 to .55, with a median r of .20. By comparison, analyses in terms of the dichotomized resist–yield scores with r_t reveal a range of values from $-.10$ to .77, with a median of .28. Although the difference between the median r and r_t

Table 2. Intercorrelations between Six Transgression Measures

Test	Ray gun	Magic mirror	Multiple choice	Speed	Squares	Circles
Ray gun	—	.21	.40	.18	.07	−.08
Magic mirror	.18	—	.33	.13	.43	.28
Multiple choice	.36	.10	—	.59	.34	.42
Speed	.09	.06	.26	—	−.10	.01
Squares	.32	.14	.23	.05	—	.77
Circles	.15	.23	.22	.20	.55	—

Note.—Tetrachoric correlations are above the diagonal, product-moment correlations are below; $N = 106$.

values is not great, the matrices show that sizable discrepancies do exist between the two measures of correlation. Three of the r_t values are lower (.01 to −.10) than the lowest r (.05), and four r_t values are higher (.40 to .59) than the highest r (.36).[2] The differences between corresponding pairs of correlation coefficients range in value from .03 to .33, with a median difference of .19. Furthermore, 11 of the 15 r_t values are greater than the corresponding r values. Thus, it appears that the product-moment correlations are in some instances attenuated.

These discrepancies may be explained in part because of greater sampling error intrinsic to r_t but, more importantly, on the basis of the large deviations from normality in some of the distributions of the interval scores. The r_t statistic assumes a normal distribution underlying the dichotomized data, and if the interval scores were normally distributed, the r and r_t values would be expected to correspond closely. Given the obtained frequency distributions, the assumption is violated; however, r_t is meaningful in that it estimates the product-moment correlations that might be obtained if the underlying trait of honesty-dishonesty were indeed normally distributed. McNemar (1963), for example, has said that it "can be argued that the use of the tetrachoric r automatically normalizes the distributions [p. 197]." If one makes this assumption, the results imply that differing trait structures might be reflected by the two types of scales. On the other hand, even if one does not wish to assume underlying normality, nor to regard r_t as an estimate of an r based upon hypothetical distributions, the r_t statistic does describe the relationships between the dichotomized scores.

It is noteworthy that the results based on the interval scores in this study are similar to those reported by Hartshorne and May (1928) for comparable measures. For example, the intercorrelations among Hartshorne and May's transgression measures ranged from −.02 to .45 with a median r of about .20, based upon summed scores for each type of test; and from −.01 to .31 with a median of .20, based upon the averaged scores for each type of test. Furthermore, the distributions of scores in the Hartshorne and May study, like those of the present investigation, appear in several instances to have been markedly skewed and multimodal (Hartshorne & May, 1928, pp. 118, 121, 315). It would seem, therefore, that as in this study, some of their r's may have been attenuated as a result of widely discrepant distributions of scores for the different tasks.

Principal Components Analyses

To determine the overall extent of relationships among the six transgression measures, the intercorrelation matrices of both interval and dichotomous scores were subjected to principal components analyses. According to these analyses, the degree of generality ("g") among the measures is reflected by the loadings

---

[2] Excluding the r of .55 between squares and circles, which Hartshorne and May (1928) treated as alternate forms of the peeping tests.

and percentage of variance extracted with the first principal component. Following Burton (1963), the criterion for a "g" characteristic on the first principal component was set at 30% of the total variance in the matrix.

The results, presented in Table 3, indicate that the first principal components account for 35% and 41% of the total variances within the product-moment and tetrachoric matrices, respectively. The loadings of all measures on the first components are above .35, and for each matrix, four of the six variables have loadings greater than .60.

The magic-mirror and speed tests, which have the lowest loadings on the first component for the product-moment matrix, were also the most highly skewed. Thus, the attenuated variance associated with this skewedness may underlie the low loadings for these measures. On the other hand, the weaker loadings of the speed and ray-gun tests on the first principal component of the tetrachoric matrix seem to result from the disproportionality of the resist–yield distributions: 80% of the subjects resisted on the speed tests and only about 15% did so on the ray-gun test; performance on all other measures was more evenly divided, with no more than 35–65% yielding or resisting on any given test. Thus the results are clearly consistent with the interpretation that lower intercorrelations and lower loadings result in those cases where a given test produces a distribution which deviates widely from the others. Presumably, exclusion of the tests with unusual distributions from the principal component analyses would increase the percentage of variance accounted for by the first component.

The findings from the principal components analyses are remarkably consistent with Burton's (1963) results, which indicated that about 35–43% of the total variance in the matrix was included in a first component. These results lend further support to the generality position as stated by Burton.

There is also evidence, however, that additional intraindividual consistency in performance is accounted for by another stable dimension reflected in the loadings on the second principal component. Employing the criterion of accepting all principal components with eigenvalues greater than one, the first two components were retained and, following Kaiser's (1958) varimax procedure, these components were subjected to orthogonal rotation. The results of the rotation are presented in Table 4.

The first factor (I') is most clearly defined by the two peeping tests (squares and circles), with intermediate loadings from the magic-mirror test. Factor II' is most clearly defined by the speed and multiple-choice tests, with slightly weaker loadings from the ray-gun game. The loadings of the remaining tests on the factors were either low or inconsistent according to both interval and dichotomous scoring procedures.

The best criteria for differentiating between the two factors may be the academic and achievement characteristics of some of the tests. The multiple-choice and speed tests are most similar to classroom situations, employing addition, subtraction, writing, and information tests. The incentives offered for excellent performance were individual recognition for the former and group

Table 3. Principal Components Analyses of Six Transgression Measures

Test	Based on product-moment correlations						Based on tetrachoric correlations					
	I[a]	II	III	IV	V	VI	I	II	III	IV	V	VI
Ray gun	.60	.16	-.63	-.10	.42	-.18	.36	-.54	-.65	.38	-.10	.20
Magic mirror	.41	-.24	-.16	.85	.08	.20	.64	.04	-.39	-.66	.05	.05
Multiple choice	.62	.50	-.22	-.13	-.55	.03	.79	-.43	.20	.14	.32	-.15
Speed	.38	.66	.53	.20	.30	.10	.38	-.72	.48	-.17	-.27	.04
Squares	.73	-.42	.09	-.33	.09	.41	.76	.54	-.07	.12	-.23	-.24
Circles	.72	-.34	.44	-.06	-.08	-.41	.74	.51	.26	.20	.03	.29
Percentage of variance	35.0	17.6	15.8	15.1	10.0	6.4	40.8	25.8	15.2	11.3	4.0	2.9

278

Table 4. Orthogonal Rotation of Factors

Test	Interval scales based on product-moment correlations		Dichotomous scales based on tetrachoric correlations	
	I'ᴀ	II'	I'	II'ᴀ
A. Ray gun	.40	.48	.01	.65
B. Magic mirror	.48	.05	.56	.33
C. Multiple choice	.21	.77	.44	.79
D. Speed	−.08	.76	−.07	.81
E. Squares	.83	.09	.93	−.04
F. Circles	.78	.14	.90	−.03

ᴀ These factors have been reflected.

recognition (class trophy) for the latter. The ray gun, although not of an academic nature, also seems to imply "real life" achievement, since the subjects were offered recognition in the form of marksman, sharpshooter, and expert badges as awards for outstanding achievement. By contrast, the peeping and the magic-mirror tests appear to possess more novel, gamelike qualities. Further, the nonacademic connotations of these tests may have been reinforced by the incentives offered, that is, M & Ms or simply encouragement to do well without public recognition. The ray gun possesses gamelike qualities as well, and, in the instance of the interval-scale analysis, such qualities may be reflected in the loadings on Factor I'.

Burton's (1963) factor-analytic study also differentiated between academic and nonacademic tests, although his evidence regarding the loadings of peeping tests on the academic factor was equivocal. According to one of the statistical procedures employed by Hartshorne and May (1928) (correlations among total scores), the peeping tests loaded on the factor.

In this study, as in Burton's (1963), several tests loaded differentially according to the different measurement and scaling procedures. Thus, in both studies it appears that differences between methods of scaling may account for inconsistencies in the factor structures.

Analyses of Variance

In order to compare persons, tasks, and other sources of variance, two-way analyses of variance were computed, using data based upon both interval and dichotomous scales. This procedure allowed for assessment of the percentage of total variance contributed by each source. First, variance attributable to persons reflected directly the extent of intraindividual consistency across the six tasks. Second, variance attributable to tasks reflected directly the extent to which the tasks consistently elicited greater or lesser degrees of transgression, that is, due to differences among situations (e.g., amount and type of incentive, group versus individual setting, etc.) as well as differences among the response modes from task to task (e.g., peeping versus adding points versus changing answers). Third, the remaining variance was attributable to interaction and/or error, depending on certain assumptions and choices of ANOVA models, to be discussed in the proceeding paragraphs.

Before considering the results of the ANOVA, it should be noted that one encounters a serious problem in attempting to apply ANOVA to data from a study such as this, because the different measures of transgression involve different metrics (e.g., number of points added beyond a programmed criterion versus number of dots produced in the peeping situation). In other words, the unit intervals are not equivalent and, hence, not readily comparable. Estimates of the relative contributions of situations, therefore, would probably be considerably inflated by the unit-metric differences between the various measures, over and above "true" effects of the situations upon degree of transgression.

One can make various adjustments in the metrics, in order to approximate equivalence among the measures, but the various criteria for making the adjustments all entail certain difficulties. For example, it would be meaningless to standardize the means and variances of the measures, because this would automatically equalize all means and variances, virtually eliminating any differences among the situations. Alternatively, one might adjust the measures such that the ranges of possible scores are equivalent. This procedure does not insure equivalence of the units, and ANOVA requires assumptions of normality and homogeneous error-of-measurement variance. Nevertheless, this procedure seems preferable since the variance is minimally affected by differences in the shapes of the distributions. The estimate based upon actual range entails the assumptions that the uppermost levels of transgression are the same in all situations and that the size of an arbitrary, fixed number of units within the range is approximately equivalent. One obvious disadvantage to this procedure is that the range of transgression is unstable across different samples.

The above arguments actually make questionable the applicability of repeated-measures ANOVA designs as a basis for comparing different situations, especially when interval scales are used. The problem of metric differences is perhaps less serious when the dichotomous scales are employed, since only two levels of performance are described, that is, resisting or yielding. Despite the difficulties with the interval scales, however, the analyses with both types of scales were continued because of the exploratory nature of the study and because of the robustness of ANOVAs.

The data based on both scaling procedures are presented in Table 5. The design allowed for identification of persons and tasks as sources of behavioral variance in the six temptation situations. (The contributions of interactions, unfortunately, cannot be directly assessed, since this source was confounded with error variance.) The F tests revealed that, for both dichotomous and interval scales, statistically significant proportions of the variance were accounted for by both persons and tasks.

Table 5. Analysis of Variance of Transgression Scores

Source	df	Interval scores		Dichotomous scores	
		MS	F	MS	F
Persons	105	1,506.12	2.61*	.407	2.26*
Tasks	5	13,544.20	23.48*	4.404	24.40*
Residual	525	576.91		.180	

* $p < .001$.

Although both persons and situations accounted for a statistically significant portion of the variance, the variance components had to be portioned in order to assess the relative contributions of the various sources. Table 6 presents the variance components for both random-effects and mixed-effects models. The mixed model may be more appropriate for use with these data since the temptation situations were not random samples of all possible situations; however, with this model one cannot separate the interaction effects from error effects. With the mixed-effects model one can solve for all the variance components only by assuming the two-way interaction to be zero, or alternatively, by assuming the error to be zero. Since the two-way interaction might be meaningful, following Endler and Hunt (1966), the variance components were also arranged in terms of a random-effects model, which combines error variance with the two-way interaction variance to form the residual variance.

Table 7 presents the estimated variance components and percentages for both models. For the random-effects model, using the interval scores, about 18% of the variance was accounted for by persons and 14% by tasks; the residual contributed 68% of the total variance. The corresponding figures for the dichotomous data were 15%, 16%, and 70%.

For the mixed-effects model, applied to the interval scores, persons accounted for about 26%, tasks for 13%, and the residual 61% when one assumes that the interaction was maximal and error was not contributing to the residual. The

Table 6. Analysis of Components of Variance with Random- and Mixed-effects Model

Random-effects model	Mixed-effects model
$E(MS_p) = \sigma_r^2 + m\sigma_p^2$	$E(MS_p) = \sigma_e^2 + m\sigma_p^2$
$E(MS_t) = \sigma_r^2 + n\sigma_t^2$	$E(MS_t) = \sigma_e^2 + \sigma_{pt}^2 + n\theta_t^2$
$E(MS_r) = \sigma_r^2$	$E(MS_r) = \sigma_e^2 + \sigma_{pt}^2$

Table 7. Estimated Variance Components and Percentages for Each Component According to Random-Effects and Mixed-Effects Models

Source	Interval scores		Dichotomous scores	
	Variance component	Percentage	Variance component	Percentage
Random effects model[a]				
Persons	154.9	18.1	.038	14.7
Tasks	122.3	14.3	.040	15.5
Residual	576.9	67.5	.180	69.8
Total variation (components sum)	854.1	99.9	.258	100.0
Mixed effects model[b]				
Persons	251.0	26.4	.068	23.6
Tasks	122.3	12.9	.040	13.9
Interaction	576.9	60.7	.180	62.5
Total variation (components sum)	950.3	100.0	.288	100.0

[a] Assumes $\sigma_r^2 = \sigma_e^2 + \sigma_{pt}^2$.
[b] Assumes $\sigma_{pt}^2 = $ maximum, $\sigma_e^2 = 0$. If one assumes $\sigma_{pt}^2 = 0$ and $\sigma_e^2 = $ maximum, then the results are identical with those from the random case.

corresponding figures with the dichotomous data were 24%, 14%, and 63%. If one assumes the error was maximal and the interaction was not contributing to the residual, the results for the mixed model correspond with the figures for the random-effects model.

Comparing the results for the two types of scales, one may note that for both models the findings correspond rather closely. There appears to be a tendency for the interval scales to attribute a slightly greater percentage (about 3%) to persons and slightly less (about 2%) to the residuals. The percentages attributable to tasks appeared virtually identical for both types of scales.

Comparing the results for the mixed versus random-ANOVA models, the results were also in substantial agreement, especially with regard to the relative contribution of tasks: About 13–15% of the variance appeared attributable to task differences, regardless of which model was assumed. On the other hand, with regard to the contribution of persons, the two models differed by 8–9%. The greater proportion of person variance was accounted for by the mixed model, if one assumes the interaction to be maximal, with zero error variance. On the other hand, if one assumes the interaction within the mixed model was zero, with maximal error, the results for the two models were identical, and persons accounted for only 15–18% of the variance.

One can likewise compare the relative contributions of persons and situations within the mixed model according to the alternative assumptions of zero interaction and maximal error, or maximal interaction and zero error. The figures for the random case described the solution for the former case of the mixed model. First, it was apparent that differential contributions of interactions versus errors did not materially affect the estimated contributions of tasks. In either case about 13–15% of the total variance was attributable to tasks. On the other hand, the differential contributions by interaction versus errors did modestly affect the percentages attributable to persons to the extent of 8–9% of the variance. A maximum of about 26% (for interval scores) was reached as the interaction approached a maximum.

Finally, one may conclude that between 60–70% of the variance was attributable to Person X Task interaction and/or error variance. It is unlikely that either term is zero, but no comparisons can be made, since the two factors were confounded. It would be highly desirable, of course, to separate the interaction effects from the error effects, but this would necessarily involve readministration of the same tasks to the same subjects under identical conditions. This does not appear feasible because the previous experience of the subjects, for example, transgression not followed by detection or punishment, would be very likely to have an effect upon the second performance.

One additional interpretation of the analysis of variance procedure is also related to the problem of generality across the temptation situations. Hoyt (1941) has developed an internal consistency reliability coefficient, based on a random-effects analysis of variance model. The Hoyt coefficient, based upon the formula,

$$r = 1 - \frac{MS \text{ error}}{MS \text{ persons}},$$

has been shown to be equivalent to the Kuder-Richardson (Formula 20) split-half reliability coefficient. Thus the coefficient offers a measure of behavioral consistency with the effect of situation variance removed. Taking the six temptation situations as separate "items" of a single measure of transgression, the Hoyt (1941) r's were computed for both dichotomous and interval measures. The dichotomized scores yielded an $r = .56$, and the interval scores, an $r = .62$. Comparable computations by Hartshorne and May (1928) based upon their obtained average correlations of .227 for nine types of tests, yielded a Spearman-Brown reliability coefficient of .73. In terms of conventional interpretations made of internal consistency reliability, considering that the figures were based on relatively few items, the data suggested that individuals were only moderately predictable across situations.

Comparison of Factor-Analytic and ANOVA Methods

The generality problem was originally approached informally by Hartshorne and May (1928). They based their conclusions regarding the specificity of moral behavior upon visual inspections of the mean differences and low correlations among the measures. In the current study, both principal components analyses and the ANOVA designs were chosen as alternative approaches to the generality problem. Both procedures offer relatively sophisticated statistical indexes for describing the degree of generality or unidimensionality in quantitative terms.

The results of the principal components analyses indicated that about 35–41% of the total variance of the intercorrelation matrices was attributable to a first principal component, depending upon how the transgression measures were scaled. On the other hand, partitioning variance according to the ANOVA models indicated that about 15–26% of the total variance among the measures was attributable to persons.

The apparent discrepancy between the figures from these two methods was due to the different bases for computing the total variance. The principal components identified the variance within an intercorrelation matrix, and the measures which composed the matrix were, in effect, standardized in the process of computing the correlations. By contrast, the ANOVA method included variance attributable to tasks in the computation of total variance. If one eliminates variance attributable to tasks, the proportion due to persons increases to about 17–30% according to the various models. Another index of uni-dimensionality that may be derived from the ANOVAs is the Hoyt (1941) reliability coefficient. Squaring the Hoyt r's, the unidimensional variances for the dichotomous and interval scales, respectively, amount to 31% and 38% of the total variances after the mean squares for tasks have been removed. Thus, in view of the different bases for computing the extent of generality, the results of the factor-analytic and ANOVA methods were in substantial agreement.

Besides this agreement, however, the two methods each yielded certain unique ancillary findings regarding *other* sources of variance over and above uni-dimensional person variance. The ANOVA method, as noted above, provides a specific assessment of the relative contributions of tasks. In addition, this method allows for analysis of the effects of differential error and interaction variance upon the contributions of persons and tasks.

On the other hand, factor-analytic methods also offer certain unique in-formation. By means of rotational procedures, secondary sources of person variance, not extracted with the first principal component, may be identified. In this study the second principal components accounted for about 18% and 26% of the total variances. When the first two components were rotated, parameters relating to academic versus nonacademic achievement-task cues appeared to differentiate two personality dimensions. Each dimension presumably reflected the disposition to resist or transgress on a certain subset of the total set of tasks. Thus, the factor-analytic methods lend themselves more readily than the ANOVA methods to the extraction and identification of certain sources of personality variance, over and above the unidimensional variance across a full set of tasks.

CONCLUSIONS AND IMPLICATIONS

Insofar as this study replicates certain facets of the Hartshorne and May (1928) investigation of the generality issue, the results of the two studies appear to be in substantial agreement. First, the correlation matrices from the two studies appear similar according to various criteria, and, second, in both this and the Burton (1963) study the first principal components account for about 35–40% of the variance of the intercorrelation matrices. These similarities appear in spite of a time differential of about 40 years between the data collection periods of the two studies, and in spite of differing populations, tasks, and other procedures.

In that the authors' results are in agreement with those from Burton's (1963) reanalysis of the Hartshorne and May (1928) data, they provide additional support for his conclusion that "there is an underlying trait of honesty." In other words, the results of this study provide evidence for conceptualization of a disposition toward honesty versus transgression across a variety of temptation situations.

In addition to the unidimensional person variance revealed by the above procedures, additional facets of the analyses revealed other sources of behavioral variance. Rotations of the first two principal components suggest that *two* personality dimensions may account for even greater proportions of the total variance than the unidimensional variance considered alone. One factor was interpreted as based upon the disposition to respond to cues pertaining to academic achievement; the other factor appeared to be based upon responses to achievement-related cues of a nonacademic nature.

Besides personality variance, situations appeared to account for a moderate proportion of the total variance. The calculations according to the various ANOVA models and scaling procedures all indicated that about 13–15% of the total variance was attributable to task differences. This figure describes the extent to which some situations characteristically elicited more transgression than others.

It is also significant that according to the ANOVA calculations between 60% and 70% of the total variance is confounded between error and Person X Task interaction. The analyses suggest that the error and unspecified interaction variance result in part from peculiar distributional properties of the measures, from lack of equivalence among the units of measurement, and from low reliabilities for some of the measures.

The above findings hold important methodological implications for those concerned with research on moral behavior. Previous research concerning child rearing, personality, and situational determinants of temptation behavior has frequently overlooked problems of measurement, perhaps because behavioral measures were assumed to be reliable and valid. The findings from this study, for example, the relatively low indexes of internal consistency of a summary measure based on all six tasks, suggest that any *single* behavioral measure holds little or no validity as a measure of a general trait of honesty. Indeed, the summary measure itself was only moderately generalizable. Hence, it is not surprising that literature surveys by Kohlberg (1963), for example, report very little replication or consistency of results across various investigations, each employing a different measure of resistance to temptation. The measurement problems also may explain why carefully conducted investigations rarely report high correlations among personality or child-rearing variables and resistance to temptation. It is clear that future research must pay more attention to measurement problems such as these.

The findings in this study also hold certain implications for both theory and experimental design of research concerning temptation behavior. Most importantly, the findings support the Endler and Hunt (1966) contention that neither persons nor situations alone account for major behavioral variance. Thus future theory and research aimed toward a comprehensive account of moral behavior must take into account interactions as well as main effects.

In order to accomplish this, however, there is need for sophisticated conceptualizations of the manner in which situational and personality factors interact to determine temptation behavior. On the basis of his analyses, Burton (1963) provided a learning model to account for both personality and situational determinants of moral behavior. His model involved both primary and secondary (mediated) generalization gradients which can explain both consistency and variability across different situations. While such a model represents a beginning in the effort to provide a comprehensive theoretical framework, its value for purposes of guiding future research remains limited. For example, the model provides only limited means for specifying the personality parameters for predicting secondary generalization, and virtually no basis for specifying the parameters of primary stimulus generalization. The model, in addition, fails to provide specific bases for predicting the nature of interactions between situational and personality variables.

As such conceptual problems are resolved, there will also be need for more complex experimental designs and more sophisticated statistical methods such as multivariate analysis of variance (Bock, 1966) and three-mode factor analysis (Tucker, 1964). Meanwhile, however, the procedures of principal components analysis and factor analysis, as applied in this study, remain useful for evaluating operations designed from existing conceptualizations of personality traits, and for exploring and identifying on a gross level some of the relevant situation and personality parameters which account for behavioral variance in temptation situations.

REFERENCES

Blum, G. S. *Psychoanalytic theories of personality.* New York: McGraw-Hill, 1953.

Bock, R. D. Contributions of multivariate experimental design to educational research. In R. B. Cattell (Ed.), *Handbook of multivariate experimental psychology.* Chicago: Rand McNally, 1966.

Burton, R. V. Generality of honesty reconsidered. *Psychological Review,* 1963, **70,** 481–499.

Endler, N. S., & Hunt, J. McV. Sources of behavioral variance as measured by the S-R Inventory of Anxiousness. *Psychologcial Bulletin,* 1966, **65,** 336–346.

Endler, N. S., Hunt, J. McV., & Rosenstein, A. J. An S-R Inventory of Anxiousness. *Psychological Monographs,* 1962, 76(17, Whole No. 536).

Grinder, R. E. New techniques for research in children's temptation behavior. *Child Development,* 1961, **32,** 679–688.

Grinder, R. E. Parental childrearing practices, conscience, and resistance to temptation of sixth-grade children. *Child Development,* 1962, **33**, 803–820.

Hartshorne, H. *Character in human relations.* New York: Scribner, 1932.

Hartshorne, H., & May, M. A. *Studies in the nature of character.* Vol. 1. *Studies in deceit.* New York: Macmillan, 1928.

Hartshorne, H., May, M. A., & Shuttleworth, F. K. *Studies in nature of character.* Vol. 3. *Studies in the organization of character.* New York: Macmillan, 1930.

Hoyt, C. J. Test reliability estimated by analysis of variance. *Psychometrika,* 1941, **6**, 153–160.

Hunt, J. McV. Traditonal personality theory in the light of recent evidence. *American Scientist,* 1965, **53**, 80–96.

Kaiser, H. F. Varimax criterion for analytic rotation in factor analysis. *Psychometrika,* 1958, **23**, 187–200.

Kohlberg, L. Moral development and identification. In H. W. Stevenson (Ed.), *The sixty-second yearbook of the National Society for the Study of Education.* Chicago: University of Chicago Press, 1963.

McDougall, W. *An introduction to social psychology.* (3rd ed.) Boston: Luce, 1910.

McNemar, Q. *Psychological statistics.* New York: Wiley, 1963.

Morgan, C. L. *Habit and instinct.* London: Arnold, 1896.

Mutterer, M. L. Factors affecting the specificity of preadolescents' behavior in a variety of temptation situations. Unpublished master's thesis, University of Wisconsin, 1965.

Sears, R. R., Rau, L., & Alpert R. *Identification and child rearing.* Stanford, Calif.: Stanford University Press, 1965.

Thorndike, E. L. *Educational psychology.* New York: Lemcke & Beuchner, 1903.

Thorndike, E. L., & Woodworth, R. S. The influence of improvement in one mental function upon efficiency of other functions. *Psychological Review,* 1901, **8**, 247–261.

Tucker, L. R. The extension of factor analysis to three-dimensional matrices. In N. Frederiksen & H. Gulliksen (Eds.), *Contributions to mathematical psychology.* New York: Holt, Rinehart & Winston, 1964.

13

S-R Inventories of Hostility and Comparisons of the Proportions of Variance from Persons, Responses, and Situations for Hostility and Anxiousness

NORMAN S. ENDLER and J. McV. HUNT

This paper describes two different forms of the S-R Inventory of Hostility. It also presents data from them for samples of both sexes, and compares the proportions of the total variation (components sum) from persons, responses, and situations on them with the proportions of variance from these respective sources on S-R Inventories of Anxiousness. The S-R Inventories of what have been considered to be general personal traits provide a format that separates persons, responses, and situations as sources of the total variation in reported behavior. Such inventories define any trait in terms of samples of the responses which have been considered to be behavioral indicators of that trait, and they obtain reports of these responses from samples of persons under samples of individually specified conditions. The purpose of the study reported here is to determine whether the proportions of variance found to be so consistent across samplings of each source for the trait of anxiousness by Endler, Hunt, and Rosenstein (1962) and by Endler and Hunt (1966, 1969) will also hold for S-R Inventories of another such trait as angriness or hostility.

In a series of studies, Endler et al. (1962, 1966, 1969) have given S-R Inventories of Anxiousness employing several samples of reports of response

From the *Journal of Personality and Social Psychology*, 1969, 37, 1–24. Copyright 1969 by the American Psychological Association. Reprinted by permission.

This study was supported in part by United States Public Health Service grants (MH-08987 and MH-K-618567 from the National Institute of Mental Health), in part by a grant from the Canada Council, and in part by a grant from the Research Board of the University of Illinois. The assistance of Kelly Hsia with respect to some of the statistical analyses is gratefully acknowledged. We also wish to thank the students of York and Illinois who participated in this study, and their professors, for their cooperation. We would especially like to thank Professor Donald Weatherley of the University of Colorado and his class for their participation in this study.

indicators of anxiousness with several samples of situations to several samples of persons or subjects. Despite the variations in the samplings from these separate contributors to the variance made feasible by the S-R Inventory format, the proportions of total variance from each of these sources and from the interactions among them is quite stable for the trait of anxiousness. Contrary to the traditional belief of personologists that such a trait as anxiousness is a major determinant of behavior, for the various samples of persons individual differences across situations contributed only about 4% or 5% of the total variance, in reported responses (see Endler & Hunt, 1966). Contrary also to the often-stated contention of the school of social psychologists stemming from the work of George Herbert Mead, the various samples of situations contribute only about the same small proportion of the total variance. On the other hand, the various samples of reported response indicators contribute approximately a quarter of the variance. Thus, the variation among responses considered to be the indicators of the trait of anxiousness carry more weight in judgments of anxiousness than either of the main sources in the controversy. Moreover, the contribution from the simple interactions is greater than that from any one of the main sources of variance, and each of the various simple interactions contributes more to the total variance than do either persons or situations. The interaction between subjects and situations contributes approximately 10% of the total variance; that between subjects and the response indicators contributes approximately another 10%; and that between situations and response indicators contributes about 8%. The residual, composed of the triple interaction and error, contributes about 35%. Inasmuch as the variations in the samplings of both modes of response and situations were deliberately exaggerated to test the limits, the consistency among these proportions of variance from various main sources and their interactions has appeared to be surprisingly great.

METHOD

The basic strategy of this investigation has been simple. First, we have constructed two forms of an S-R Inventory of Hostility. These have been based on two samplings of responses indicating hostility. Second, we have given each of these forms to two samplings of college students. Third, we have partitioned the variance in the reported responses from the four samplings of persons. Finally, the proportions of variance attributable to each of the main sources and each of the interactive sources have been compared with the corresponding proportions of variance obtained for the S-R Inventories of Anxiousness.

Anxiousness Instrument

The various forms of the S-R Inventory of Anxiousness, with the various samples of persons, of reported responses, and of situations, have already been described (Endler et al., 1962; Endler & Hunt, 1966, 1969). In each of the forms, the responses included in the sample have all been as indicators of a state of anxiety or anxiousness, and, with a very few exceptions chosen to minimize threat so as to maximize variability in the degree of threat, the situations in the samples have all been reported as sources of fear by someone.

Hostility Instrument

In this study, anger, aggression, and hostility are considered to be synonymous. The evocative situations for such responses are presumed to have in common something which interferes with the ongoing, goal-directed behavior of individuals. The forms of the S-R Inventory of Hostility used here, and reported for the first time, obtain reports of samples of 10 modes of response in each of the 14 situations which constitute the sample of situations. Each item in the inventories, consisting of a response to a specific situation, is measured by the report of the subject on a five-step scale ranging from "not at all" to "very much." All of the items in the inventories are arranged to scale in the same direction with a low score indicating a low level of anger or hostility and a high score indicating a high level of anger or hostility. The format provides a page for each of the situations, described at the top, and it lists the sample of responses with a scale following each one. The inventories of hostility used in this study employ samples of 14 situations with 10 modes of responses to each situation, a total of 140 reported responses. The number 140 was dictated by the capacity of the computer to process the data. The samples of situations are larger than the samples of responses simply because it was easier to find situations than responses.

Sampling of situations. Situations were selected from the gamut of those likely to be familiar, through either direct or vicarious experience, to most college students, the populations from which our samples of subjects were taken. Several of the situations were taken from the sample utilized by Hunt, Cole, and Reis (1958) to evoke anger. Some represent what Rosenzweig (1944) has considered to be personal frustrating circumstances and some represent impersonal frustrating agents. The sample of situations in the first form (H-YU-65-A) used in this study includes the following 14 situations:

1. You are talking to someone and he (she) does not answer you;
2. You accidently bang your shins against a park bench;
3. Your instructor unfairly accuses you of cheating on an examination;
4. Someone has lost an important book of yours;
5. You have just found out that someone has told lies about you;
6. You are driving to a party and suddenly your car has a flat tire;
7. You arrange to meet someone and he (she) doesn't show up;
8. You are trying to study and there is incessant noise;
9. You are waiting at the bus stop and the bus fails to stop for you;
10. You are in a restaurant and have been waiting a long time to be served;

11. Someone has opened your personal mail;
12. You wake up early to get to a special 8 A.M. class and the instructor doesn't show up;
13. You are carrying a cup of coffee to the table and someone bumps into you;
14. You are very tired and have just gone to sleep, when you are awakened by the arrival of some friends.

The sample of situations in the second form of the S-R Inventory of Hostility (Form H-UI-65-A) includes the following 14:

1. You are talking to someone and he (she) does not answer;
2. The grocery store closes just as you are about to enter;
3. Someone has splashed mud over your new clothing;
4. Someone persistently contradicts you when you know you are right;
5. You have just found out that someone has told lies about you;
6. Someone makes an error and blames it on you;
7. You are reading a mystery and find that the last page of the book is missing;
8. You miss your train because the clerk has given you faulty information;
9. You are typing a term paper and your typewriter breaks;
10. You use your last 10¢ to call a friend and the operator disconnects you;
11. Someone has opened your personal mail;
12. You wake up early to get to a special 8 A.M. class, and the instructor doesn't show up.
13. You are carrying a cup of coffee to the table and someone bumps into you;
14. Someone pushes ahead of you in a theater-ticket line.

Samplings of responses. The samples of responses include, first of all, certain physiological reactions typically found in anger because reports of these can most readily be validated by means of physiological recording. They include, second, various extrapunitive reactions to frustration, and third, various intropunative reactions to frustration, both of which have been described by Rosenzweig (1944). The 10 modes of response for the first form (H-YU-65-A) were:

1. Heart beats faster	not at all . . . much faster
2. Want to strike something or someone	not at all . . . very much
3. Lose patience	not at all . . . very much
4. Feel irritated	not at all . . . very much
5. Perspire	not at all . . . very much
6. Emotions disrupt actions	not at all . . . very much
7. Curse	not at all . . . very much
8. Become tense	not at all . . . very much
9. Want to shout	not at all . . . very much
10. Frown	not at all . . . very much

For the second form (H-UI-65-A) of the S-R Inventory of Hostility employed in this study, the 10 modes of response were:

1. Heart beats faster   not at all . . . much faster
2. Want to hit something or someone   not at all . . . very much
3. Hands tremble   not at all . . . very much
4. Swear   not at all . . . very much
5. Perspire   not at all . . . very much
6. Become enraged   not at all . . . very much
7. Splutter   not at all . . . very much
8. Grind teeth   not at all . . . very much
9. Want to yell   not at all . . . very much
10. Grimace   not at all . . . very much

Subjects and Procedure

All of the subjects in this study were college students. Two samples of subjects were administered Form H-YU-65-A (14 situations, 10 modes of response), and two samples were administered Form H-UI-65-A (14 situations, 10 modes of response) of the S-R Inventory of Hostility. The two samples receiving Form H-YU-65-A consisted of 45 men and 73 women from York University, and 38 men and 23 women from the University of Colorado. The two samples receiving Form H-UI-65-A consisted of 98 men and 91 women from York University, and 83 men and 48 women from the University of Illinois.

Statistical Manipulations

The reliabilities for the situation scales and the modes of response scales were assessed by means of Cronbach's (1951) coefficient alpha, which is the average of all possible split-half correlations for each scale.

The responses to situations in the S-R Inventories were analyzed via a three-way analysis of variance (subjects, situations, modes of response) random-effects model.[1] Separate analyses were conducted for each sample (with the sexes being analyzed separately). The observed mean-square equations were solved for each of the component sources of variance. The procedures used to partition variance from the various sources, subjects, situations, modes of response, Subjects × Situations, Subjects × Modes of Response, Situations × Modes of Response, and residual (composed of triple interaction and error or within variance combined) have been described by Endler (1966b) and by Gleser, Cronbach, and Rajaratnam (1965). The component sources of variance summed to obtain the total variation and the percentages of the total variation (components sum) from each of the component sources computed.

Median values for the various sources of hostility variance were compared with median values of anxiousness variance derived from data used in another study (Endler & Hunt, 1967).

---

[1] For the justification of the use of a random effects model, see Endler and Hunt (1966), Footnote 3, pages 338–339.

RESULTS

Reliability of the Subscales of the S-R Inventories of Hostility

Both the situation scales and the mode-of-response scales for both inventories are highly reliable.[2] For Form H-YU-65-A, the coefficient alphas for all the 14 situation scales and for all the 10 mode-of-response scales were all in the .80s and .90s except that for Situation 3 for York men; for this scale $\alpha = .72$. For Form H-UI-65-A, the alphas for all the situation scales and for all the mode-of-response scales were in the .80s and .90s for men and all but the scale for Situation 1 were above .75 for women. For Illinois women on Situation 1, $\alpha = .61$.[3]

Proportions of Variance from Sources

The proportions of the total variance contributed by the various main sources and interactions, as derived from the mean-squares of three-way analyses of variance, for the two forms of the S-R Inventory of Hostility for both men (top part of table) and for women appear in Table 1.[4] Considerable consistency is evident in the proportions of variance from the various sources across the two forms of the inventory and across the four samples of subjects. This consistency is not, however, as great as that found for the various forms of the S-R Inventory of Anxiousness (see Endler & Hunt, 1966, 1967) and considerable differences exist between the sexes.

---

[2] The means, standard deviations, and the coefficient alpha reliabilities (Cronbach, 1951) for the 14 situation scales and the 10 mode-of-response scales for men and women, for the samples that received Form H-YU-65-A (York and Colorado) of the S–R Inventory of Hostility have been deposited as Tables A and B with the American Documentation Institute (ADI). Similarly the analogous results for the samples that received Form H-UI-65-A (York and Illinois) of the hostility inventory have been deposited as Tables C and D with the ADI. Order Document No. 10020 from the ADI Auxiliary Publications Project, Photoduplication Service, Library of Congress, Washington, D.C., 20540. Remit in advance $1.25 for photocopies, or $1.25 for microfilm, and make checks payable to Chief, Photoduplication Service, Library of Congress.

[3] The reliabilities of the situation scales and the mode-of-response scales for the S-R Inventories of Anxiousness were of a similar order. For those and for the means and the standard deviations, see Endler, Hunt, and Rosenstein (1962, Tables 5 and 6, pages 14–15).

[4] In order to conserve space, the analysis of variance tables are not presented here. However, they can easily be derived from the information presented in Table 1. The mean-squares can be derived by substituting the variance components into the specification equations of the expected mean-squares (see Endler, 1966a). The df can be determined from the information provided in this paper concerning the numbers of subjects, situations, and modes of response. Sums of squares can be derived from the MS and df.

Table 1. Estimated Variance Components and Percentages for Each Component of Reported Responses to Situations on the S-R Inventory of Hostility

A. Men

| Source | Form H-YU-65-A | | | | Form H-UI-65-A | | | |
| | York (n=45) | | Colorado (n=38) | | York (n=98) | | Illinois (n=83) | |
	σ^2 component	%	σ^2 component	%	σ^2 component	%	σ^2 component	%
Subjects (S)	.314	19.62	.389	22.01	.251	18.54	.254	16.33
Situations (A)	.079	4.95	.148	8.37	.045	3.29	.067	4.32
Mode of response (B)	.258	16.14	.205	11.60	.194	14.33	.210	13.48
S × A	.185	11.58	.296	16.75	.125	9.21	.226	14.53
S × B	.180	11.26	.185	10.46	.255	18.79	.218	13.99
A × B	.083	5.19	.074	4.21	.038	2.80	.034	2.21
Residual	.500	31.26	.470	26.59	.448	33.04	.547	35.15
Total variation (components sum)	1.598	100.00	1.767	99.99	1.356	100.00	1.556	100.00

B. Women

| Source | Form H-YU-65-A | | | | Form H-UI-65-A | | | |
| | York (n=73) | | Colorado (n=23) | | York (n=91) | | Illinois (n=48) | |
	σ^2 component	%	σ^2 component	%	σ^2 component	%	σ^2 component	%
Subject (S)	.256	14.04	.367	15.60	.178	13.45	.361	21.69
Situation (A)	.156	8.55	.267	11.35	.042	3.20	.094	5.63
Mode of Response (B)	.318	17.42	.376	15.99	.195	14.76	.184	11.00
S × A	.237	12.98	.284	12.07	.115	8.72	.181	10.88
S × B	.197	10.78	.277	11.78	.304	23.05	.345	10.71
A × B	.124	6.78	.096	4.08	.050	3.76	.042	2.51
Residual	.537	29.45	.685	29.12	.437	33.08	.459	27.53
Total variation (components sum)	1.824	100.00	2.352	99.99	1.322	100.00	1.667	100.00

Males versus Females for Hostility Variance

The proportion of variance contributed by persons tends to be greater for men than for women except in the case of the Illinois sample, and, conversely, the variance contributed by situations tends to be a little less for men than for women. The proportions of variance contributed by the other sources are similar for the two sexes.

Hostility versus Anxiousness

Persons constitute a source of the total variance for hostility nearly four times what it is for anxiousness in the case of men and nearly three times what it is for anxiousness in the case of women (see Table 2). Situations contribute about the same portion of the total variance for hostility as for anxiousness. Modes of response contribute a higher portion of the total variance for anxiousness than for hostility. For the various interactions, the portions for hostility are about the same as for anxiousness except in the case of that between situations and modes of response, where the contribution for anxiousness is nearly twice that for hostility in the case of women.

DISCUSSION

In this S-R Inventory of Hostility the responses reported by the subjects represent what are sometimes called the emotional state of anger. Insofar as a

Table 2. Median Percentages of the Various Components from the Several Sources for Reported Anxiousness and Hostility for the S-R Inventories

Source	Median percentages			
	Anxiousness		Hostility	
	Men ($n=22$)	Women ($n=21$)	Men ($n=4$)	Women ($n=4$)
Subject (S)	4.44	4.56	19.08	14.82
Situation (A)	3.95	7.78	4.64	7.09
Mode of Response (B)	24.76	26.61	13.90	15.37
$S \times A$	9.14	9.31	10.40	11.48
$S \times B$	10.34	11.06	12.62	16.24
$A \times B$	7.51	6.95	3.01	3.92
Residual	37.06	34.33	32.15	29.28
Total variation (components sum)	100.00	100.00	100.00	100.00

Note.—n in all cases is the number of samples used in deriving the median.

trait of hostility exists, it must consist of a tendency to manifest these indicator responses consistently across a variety of situations. The stronger the indicator responses and the more consistently the various situations evoke them, the stronger would be the trait of hostility and the more hostile would be the individual manifesting these behavioral indicators of anger.

Although the consistency in the proportions of total variance contributed by the various sources across forms of the S-R Inventory of Hostility and across samples of subjects is somewhat lower than that across forms of the S-R Inventory of Anxiousness and across samples of subjects, it is still considerable. On the other hand, the proportions of variance found to be so consistent across samplings of each source for anxiousness do not hold for hostility, where subjects contributed consistently between approximately 15% (for women) and 20% (for men) of the variance for hostility.

An explanation of this greater contribution of subjects to the total variance for hostility than for anxiousness is not readily apparent. From the fact that the situations which are presumed to evoke the indicators of anger are somewhat more strictly defined by the containment of some element of frustration in the present, one might expect a smaller contribution from situations to the total variance of hostile responses than anxious responses to compensate for the greater contribution from subjects, but not so. It is the modes of response and their interaction with situations which show the compensatory reduction in the contribution to the total variance for hostility as compared with anxiousness. This suggests that the response indicators of hostility show less variation than those of anxiousness, and that this lesser variation leaves room for only a lower level of interaction with situations for hostility than for anxiousness.

These results indicate that individual differences in the intensity of a trait of hostility are genuinely more prominent than individual differences in the intensity of a trait of anxiousness. The two traits appear to operate differently. Hostility is relatively less desirable socially than anxiousness. Prohibitions against expressions of anger may be more effective with some subjects than with others, and this may lead to greater individual differences in hostility than in anxiousness. Most of the situations used in these hostility inventories have in common the notion of frustration operating in the present. Hunt, Cole, and Reis (1958) have indicated this is one of the situational cues distinguishing anger (the trait of hostility) from fear (the trait of anxiousness) where timing is in terms of anticipation or dread of future events. Possibly a more heterogeneous sampling of situational events would increase the proportion of the variance from situations for hostility to some degree even though it failed to increase much the variance from situations per se for anxiousness (see Endler & Hunt, 1969).

The proportions of the total variance from individual differences for hostility were greater for men than for women. For both anxiousness and hostility, the situations contribute more to the total variance for women than for men. This may mean that women are more influenced by situational factors than are men. Such an interpretation would be congruent with the findings that women are typically more field dependent than men (Rudin, 1955; Witkin, Lewis, Hertzman, Machover, Meissner and Wapner, 1954) and that women conform more than men (Endler, 1966a).

While it is important for high validity coefficients to specify the situations in which the indicators of hostility are to be manifest, it follows from the evidence obtained here that it is somewhat less important for hostility than for anxiousness. Validity correlations for omnibus measures of hostility can be expected to reach a level of .40 or .50, whereas validity correlations for such measures of anxiousness can be expected to be no higher than those of .20 or .25 traditionally found (see Beam, 1955; Endler et al., 1962; Grooms & Endler, 1960; Haywood & Spielberger, 1966). It follows also that one cannot expect to obtain such marked improvements to validity correlations by specifying the situations in the case of measures of hostility as in the case of measures of anxiousness. In the case of the latter, the improvements in the size of the validity and coefficients have been found to go from the traditional size of .20 to .25 for omnibus inventories to between .60 and .80 (cf. D'Zurilla, 1964; Endler & Bain, 1966; Haywood & Dobbs, 1964; Hoy, 1966; Paul, 1966).

Finally, it also follows that it would be profitable to investigate many of the common traits which have been considered to be of importance in the description of persons by the method of the S-R inventories in which the influence of the main sources of variance (individuals, situations, and modes of response) and their interactions are separated.

REFERENCES

Beam, J. C. Serial learning and conditioning under real life stress. *Journal of Abnormal and Social Psychology*, 1955, **51**, 543–551.

Cronbach, L. J. Coefficient alpha and the internal structure of tests. *Psychometrika*, 1951, **16**, 297–334.

D'Zurilla, T. J. Effects of behavioral influence techniques applied in group discussion on subsequent verbal participation. Unpublished doctoral dissertation, University of Illinois, 1964.

Endler, N. S. Conformity as a function of different reinforcement schedules. *Journal of Personality and Social Psychology*, 1966, **4**, 175–180. (a)

Endler, N. S. Estimating variance components from mean squares for random and mixed-effects analysis of variance models. *Perceptual and Motor Skills*, 1966, **22**, 559–570. (b)

Endler, N. S., & Bain, J. M. Interpersonal anxiety as a function of social class. *Journal of Social Psychology*, 1966, **70**, 221–227.

Endler, N. S., & Hunt, J. McV. Sources of behavioral variance as measured by the S-R Inventory of Anxiousness. *Psychological Bulletin*, 1966, **65**, 336–346.

Endler, N. S., & Hunt, J. McV. Generalizability of contributions from sources of variance in S-R Inventories of Anxiousness. *Journal of Personality*, 1969, **37**, 1–24.

Endler, N. S., Hunt, J. McV., & Rosenstein, A. J. An S-R Inventory of Anxiousness. *Psychological Monographs*, 1962, **76**(17, Whole No. 536).

Gleser, G. C., Cronbach, L. J., & Rajaratnam, W. Generalizability of scores influenced by multiple sources of variance. *Psychometrika*, 1965, **30**, 395–418.

Grooms, R. R., & Endler, N. S. The effect of anxiety on academic achievement. *Journal of Educational Psychology*, 1960, **51**, 299–304.

Haywood, H. C., & Dobbs, V. Motivation and anxiety in high school boys. *Journal of Personality,* 1964, **32**, 371–379.

Haywood, H. C., & Spielberger, C. D. Palmar sweating as a function of individual differences in manifest anxiety. *Journal of Personality and Social Psychology,* 1966, **3**, 103–105.

Hoy, E. Incongruity and reported anxiety. Unpublished master's thesis, York University, 1966.

Hunt, J. McV., Cole, M-L. W., & Reis, E. E. S. Situational cues distinguishing anger, fear, and sorrow. *American Journal of Psychology,* 1958, **71**, 138–151.

Paul, G. L. *Insight versus desensitization in psychotherapy: An experiment in anxiety reduction.* Stanford: Stanford University Press, 1966.

Rosenzweig, S. An outline of frustration theory. In J. McV. Hunt (Ed.), *Personality and the behavior disorders.* New York: Ronald Press, 1944.

Rudin, S. A. The influence of context on perception of complex stimuli. Unpublished doctoral dissertation, University of Illinois, 1955.

Silverman, R. E. The manifest anxiety scale as a measure of drive. *Journal of Abnormal and Social Psychology,* 1957, **55**, 94–97.

Spielberger, C. D. The effects of anxiety on complex learning and academic achievement. In C. D. Spielberger (Ed.), *Anxiety and behavior.* New York: Academic Press, 1966.

Witkin, H. A., Lewis, H. B., Hertzman, M., Machover, K., Meissner, P. B., & Wapner, S. *Personality through perception.* New York: Harper, 1954.

14

Stimulus Qualities of the Target of Aggression: A Further Study

LEONARD BERKOWITZ and RUSSELL G. GEEN

What determines the intensity of the aggression that is directed against a particular target? Most answers to such a question undoubtedly would attribute the strength of a given attack primarily to internal factors, such as drive or emotion arousal, previously acquired aggressiveness habits, and/or inhibitions against this form of behavior. External determinants must also be considered, however. Continuing an argument advanced in a number of papers (Berkowitz, 1962, 1964, 1965b), we will here attempt to show that the stimulus characteristics of the available target can also govern the magnitude of the attack.

In two recent experiments (Berkowitz & Geen, 1966; Geen & Berkowitz, 1966) male college students were first made angry with a peer and then were shown a brief film. Some of these people watched a fairly violent prize fight scene, while other subjects saw an exciting but nonaggressive track race. Then, immediately after the film, each subject was provided with a socially sanctioned opportunity to give electric shocks to the person who had provoked him. The main hypothesis underlying this research contends that a target will elicit aggressive responses from an individual who is ready to act aggressively to the extent that the target is associated with aggressive behavior generally. This association was established in some conditions by giving the anger instigator in the same name as the victim of the filmed violence, either the name of the actor portraying the victim (Berkowitz & Geen, 1966) or the fictitious name used in the story (Geen & Berkowitz, 1966). In both instances the greatest number of shocks was given to the anger instigator whose name connected him with the victim of the witnessed aggression, while such naming had no effect on the people seeing the nonaggressive movie.

Although highlighting the importance of the available target's stimulus characteristics, the findings in these two studies are open to a number of alternative

From the *Journal of Personality and Social Psychology,* 1967, 5, 364–368. Copyright 1967 by the American Psychological Association. Reprinted by permission.

This study was carried out by RGG under LB's supervision as part of a project sponsored by Grant G-23988 from the National Science Foundation to the senior author.

explanations. In this paper we will focus our attention on a possible explanation suggested by the Spence (1956) incentive conception. Adherents of this mode of thought would (or should) point to the experimental procedure followed in establishing the target person's name-mediated association with the film victim; in both experiments the confederate was introduced *before* the movie was shown. Seeing a film character with the same name as the anger instigator conceivably could have reminded the angered subjects of the provocation they had suffered, so that, in essence, they were kept aroused by the film, while the subjects in the other conditions were permitted to calm down. Other evidence indicates, however, that our findings are not due to a simple reminder of the anger instigator. In an unpublished experiment by the present writers, deliberately angered subjects were shown the exciting but nonaggressive track-race film employed in this research program after having been led to believe their tormentor had the same name as either the winner or the loser in the race. Even though the subjects, hearing this name, could have been reminded of the anger instigator the men in these conditions did not give their frustrater more shocks immediately afterwards than did the people in the control groups. The name evidently had to appear in an aggressive context if it was to have an effect upon subsequent aggression.

Spence's incentive formulation can readily account for these results, however. When the subject saw a person beaten who had the same name as his own frustrater he could have been stimulated to make anticipatory aggressive responses. The excitation produced by this anticipatory aggression then might have led to the great number of attacks upon the frustrater soon afterwards.

The present experiment was designed as a test of this alternative, "anticipation" explanation of the earlier results. Subjects were angered and then shown the prize-fight film, as in the Berkowitz-Geen and Geen-Berkowitz studies, but this time they were not told the frustrater's name until the movie had ended. If, in the earlier studies, the film victim's name had elicited anticipatory aggression as the subjects watched the prize-fight scene, this altered procedure should now eliminate or lessen the effects of the available target's name. On the other hand, greater aggression should be directed against the frustrater having the same name as the victim of the witnessed violence if this label increases the frustrater's cue value for aggression.

Subjects

The subjects were 90 male undergraduates at the University of Wisconsin who volunteered without knowing the purpose of the experiment in order to earn points counting toward their final grade in introductory psychology.

Method

When each subject, scheduled singly, came to the laboratory, he was met by the experimenter (RGG) and a confederate who was posing as another subject. The experimenter told the two men the study had to do with problem solving under stress. He said the stress would be induced by administering mild electric shocks and gave the subject an opportunity to withdraw from the experiment if he so desired. (None of the people did so, although one person left later after revealing he had heard about the investigation.) The two men then went to separate rooms where they were to hear further instructions over an intercom. Actually delivered by a tape recording, the oral instructions given to the subject informed him that he would have to work on a problem while his partner in the other room watched a brief film. In about 5 minutes, at the conclusion of the film, the partner would judge the quality of the subject's problem solution. These evaluations were to be administered in the form of electric shocks; one shock for an excellent solution, up to 10 shocks for a very poor solution.

The subject then was given the specific problem he was to solve: to devise a contest that would be part of an advertising campaign for a store. He was also told at this time that his partner's later task would be to formulate a promotion campaign for a new laundry detergent. At the end of the tape recording, the experimenter came into the subject's room and gave him a pad of paper onto which he was to write his solution to the assigned problem. Five minutes later the experimenter returned, strapped a shock bracelet onto the subject's forearm, and picked up the subject's work, supposedly to take it to the other person for an evaluation. In acutality, however, the experimenter went to a nearby room from which he gave the subject seven shocks in order to produce a moderate emotion arousal in him. He then went back into the subject's room and asked him to complete a brief questionnaire assessing his present mood.

When this was done the experimenter introduced the film the subject was to see as part of the next phase of the study. Three film conditions were established. Two-thirds of the cases (*aggressive film* groups) were to be shown the prize-fight scene used in all of the experiments in this research program, but the introduction to this film was varied. The experimenter played a tape recording supposedly summarizing the film story up to the witnessed scene, ostensibly so that the subject would have a better understanding of the scene. For one *aggressive film* condition this story synopsis portrayed the movie protagonist in a very unfavorable light so that the subject would regard the beating the protagonist was to receive in the film as relatively proper (*justified-film-aggression* condition). The other *aggressive film* groups were given a story depicting the protagonist in a more favorable manner. Being more sympathetic to the protagonist, the men in this condition presumably would regard the beating the hero took in the movie as *less-justified film aggression*. The remaining third of the cases saw the exciting but nonaggressive track-race film used in the earlier experiments (*track-race-film* condition). Previous investigations in this series (Berkowitz, 1965a; Berkowitz, Corwin, & Heironimus, 1963; Berkowitz & Rawlings, 1963) have demonstrated that the portrayal of the film protagonist as a scoundrel by means of the *justified aggression* introduction effectively lowered the subject's inhibitions against aggression on his part immediately after the film. The *less-justified film-aggression* introduction was added in order to determine whether the accomplice's name would govern the magnitude of the attacks made upon him even under relatively strong restraints against aggression.

At the conclusion of the film the subject filled out a second mood questionnaire. The confederate, who supposedly had been working on the problem assigned to him, then entered the room saying he had finished his task. The experimenter took this person's problem solution and then set the stage for the final experimental manipulation. Saying he wanted to make sure he did not get their records mixed up, he asked the two men for their names. After the subject had given his name, within each of the film conditions the confederate said his name was either *Kirk Anderson* or *Bob Anderson.* (If the subject had witnessed the prize-fight scene in which the actor, Kirk Douglas, played the role of the person taking the beating, and the confederate had just introduced himself as "Kirk," the experimenter made a remark about the coincidence in the names. When queried at the end of the session, 4 subjects indicated they had become suspicious at this point, and they are not included in the 90 subjects. None of the other men said they had doubted the coincidence after the deceptions were explained at the conclusion of the session.)

The two men were sent to separate rooms again, and about 30 seconds later the experimenter gave the subject what was supposedly his partner's solution to his problem. The subject was reminded that he was to give his partner from 1 to 10 shocks as his evaluation of his partner' solution, and also that this was the last time shocks were to be administered. After providing this information, the experimenter left the room so that the subject would be alone while giving the shocks. Although these shocks serve as the principal measure of aggression, a final questionnaire was also employed for secondary measures. The subject completed this questionnaire shortly after giving his "evaluation" of the other person's problem solution, indicating his attitude toward his partner on four 7-step scales. At the conclusion of the session the deceptions were explained, and each subject was asked not to talk about the experiment for the remainder of the semester.

RESULTS

Film-Induced Mood Changes

The first question to be considered has to do with the effects of the film treatments on the subjects' experimental mood. As was mentioned above, the men filled out a mood questionnaire first after they had been emotionally aroused by receiving seven shocks and then again immediately after seeing the film (and before shocking their partner). The conditions did not differ reliably on any of the mood scales completed on the first occasion. Change scores were then computed for each subject on each of the 10 mood scales, and the three film conditions were compared on the 10 change scores. Table 1 summarizes the findings on six of the scales. The first two scales were the only ones of the 10 yielding a significant among-groups effect in the preliminary analyses of variance. The men witnessing the prize-fight scene, surprisingly enough, reported a greater

Table 1. Mean Changes in Mood from Before to After Film

Mood scale	Justified film aggression	Less-justified film aggression	Track film	Among-groups F ratio
Sad-HAPPY	-0.33_a	-0.54_a	0.40_b	7.39**
Pleasant-unpleasant	0.64_{ab}	0.74_a	-0.27_b	4.65*
Angry-NOT angry	-0.54_a	-1.04_a	-0.40_a	1.16
Anxious-relaxed	-0.53_a	-0.40_a	0.30_a	2.47
Calm-TENSE	0.33_a	-0.07_a	-0.22_a	1.49
Not worried-worried	0.00_a	-0.10_a	0.03_a	1.63

Note.—Separate analyses of variance were conducted for each scale. In regard to any one scale, cells having a subscript in common are not significantly different, at the .05 level, by Duncan multiple-range test. The capitalized word indicates the direction of a high, positive-change score.

*$p < .05$.
**$p < .01$.

increase in feelings of sadness and unpleasantness than the men shown the nonaggressive track film. As is apparent in the third line, there was no significantly greater increase in experienced anger in the people seeing the fight. Finally, looking at the last three scales, we can note that the film conditions did not differ reliably in reported changes in felt anxiety, tension, and worry. All in all, rather than producing an increased anger or anxiety, the aggressive movie evidently made the men feel somewhat sadder.[1]

Aggression toward Target Person

Considering the moods existing in the three film conditions, the usual common-sense theory of aggression would undoubtedly not have predicted the results obtained with the shock measure. Over all 90 subjects, the men who had witnessed the aggressive movie subsequently gave somewhat more shocks to their tormenter than did the people seeing the nonaggressive film, even though the former were sadder rather than angrier. But more important than this, the greatest number of shocks were administered by the provoked subjects who had seen *justified film aggression* and whose target had a name (Kirk) associating him with the victim of this observed violence. Kirk generally received somewhat more shocks than did Bob, but only after the subjects had watched a man named "Kirk" being beaten on the movie screen. The only significant difference in this

---

[1] It is an interesting question as to why this increased sadness arose. But whatever the reason, this is irrelevant to our present theme. The point remains that the greatest overt aggression was displayed in one of the aggressive film conditions, even though the mood change produced by the film was not one of increased anger.

Table 2. Mean Number of Shocks to Confederate

Confederate's name	Justified film aggression	Less-justified film aggression	Track film
Total sample[a]			
Kirk	5.87_a	5.13_{ab}	4.13_b
Bob	5.00_{ab}	4.67_{ab}	4.60_{ab}
Omitting 5 most anxious men in each group[b]			
Kirk	6.4_a	5.0_b	4.4_b
Bob	4.8_b	4.3_b	4.7_b

Note.—Cells having a subscript in common are not significantly different, at the .05 level, by Duncan multiple-range test.

[a] $N = 15$ in each group.

[b] $N = 10$ in each group.

total sample, however, was between the *justified-film-aggression–Kirk* group and the *track-film–Kirk* group.

A secondary analysis of the data was carried out under the assumption that strong anxiety had led to an inhibition of aggressive responses in the most strongly instigated group. Scores on three intercorrelated mood scales, anxious-not anxious, calm-tense, not worried-worried (the three scales shown at the bottom of Table 1), were combined for each subject to yield an anxiety index, and the five most anxious men in each condition were then set aside. We then determined the mean number of shocks given by the less anxious people *after* the mood scales had been filled out. The results are shown in the bottom half of Table 2. A much clearer picture now emerges. The available target whose name associated him with the victim of justified violence received a significantly greater number of shocks than the target person in any other condition. As we had predicted, the available target's name had a significant effect even when this name-mediated association with the observed aggression was established after the aggression was witnessed.

Questionnaire Measures of Hostility

The four questionnaire measures of hostility toward the confederate gave rise to results essentially similar to those obtained with the electric-shock measure; on three of the four items the strongest disapproval of the confederate was expressed by the men who had witnessed the *justified film aggression* and then rated the confederate named Kirk. This group was tied with the *justified-film-aggression–Bob* condition on the fourth item. Significant condition differences were obtained with only two of the items, however. The results with these two measures are summarized in Tables 3 and 4.

Table 3. Mean Expressed Desire to Have Confederate as Personal Friend

Confederate's name	Justified film aggression	Less-justified film aggression	Track film
Total sample[a]			
Kirk	4.80_a	4.13_{bc}	3.67_c
Bob	4.40_{ab}	4.13_{bc}	3.80_{bc}
Omitting 5 most anxious men in each group[b]			
Kirk	4.70_a	4.40_{ab}	3.70_{bc}
Bob	4.40_{ab}	4.20_{abc}	3.60_c

Note.—Cells having a subscript in common are not significantly different, at the .05 level, by Duncan multiple-range test. A high score indicates an unfavorable attitude.
[a]$N = 15$ in each group.
[b]$N = 10$ in each group.

Looking at the findings for the total sample, as shown in the top halves of the tables, we can see that the men provoked by the confederate who was associated with the *justified film aggression* subsequently expressed a reliably lower desire to have him as a personal friend (Table 3) and as a roommate (Table 4) than the other subjects also angered by Kirk but who had watched the nonaggressive movie. Although the *justified-film-aggression–Kirk* group was not significantly more hostile to the confederate than was the *justified-film-aggression–Bob* condition, the men in the latter group did not differ reliably from their track-film controls. (This latter difference did become significant in the case of

Table 4. Mean Expressed Desire to Have Confederate as Roommate

Confederate's name	Justified film aggression	Less-justified film aggression	Track film
Total sample[a]			
Kirk	5.20_a	4.33_{ab}	4.20_b
Bob	4.80_{ab}	4.53_{ab}	4.27_{ab}
Omitting 5 most anxious men in each group			
Kirk	5.20_a	4.70_{ab}	4.30_{ab}
Bob	5.00_{ab}	4.80_{ab}	4.00_b

Note.—Cells having a subscript in common are not significantly different, at the .05 level, by Duncan multiple-range test. A high score indicates an unfavorable attitude.
[a]$N = 15$ in each group.

the "personal friend" item when the five most anxious subjects were omitted—bottom half, Table 3—because the *track-film-Bob* mean became somewhat lower.) In general, the questionnaire findings parallel those obtained in the earlier experiment (Geen & Berkowitz, 1966). Instead of there being a cathartic purge of aggressive tendencies in the men giving the greatest number of electric shocks, the strong instigation produced in them by giving them a target associated with the source of their aggressive predisposition evidently led to relatively persistent aggressive response chains; they continued to display the strongest aggression on the next occasion when the aggression was to be expressed verbally rather than physically.

DISCUSSION

Taken together, the findings in the writers' research program point to the importance of considering the available target's stimulus characteristics in any comprehensive analysis of aggression. Particular people are attacked, the senior author has contended, not only because they are safe and visible targets, but also because they have cue properties causing them to elicit aggressive responses from persons who are ready to act aggressively. Supporting this reasoning, available target persons who are associated with the victim of observed violence receive more attacks from angered individuals than do other possible targets lacking this association. This result is obtained, furthermore, even when the available target's connection with the observed victim is established after the aggressive event is witnessed.

Our results do not unequivocally demonstrate, however, just how aggressiveness cues function. While the previous papers in this series had suggested that target stimuli "pull out" aggressive responses, the possibility still remains that the actions were "pushed out" by a strong, although short-lived, internal arousal state produced by the stimuli. McClelland's (1953) affect conception of motivation takes this type of position. He had proposed that motives were aroused when some cue redintegrated a previously experienced affective state. Hearing a name connected with the just-witnessed aggressive film conceivably could have redintegrated the affect that had been aroused by the film, and this reawakened affect could then have "driven" the attacks upon the target person. The mood changes shown in Table 1 appear to argue against this formulation. The aggressive movie seems to have generated greater sadness than anger, and it is unlikely that this felt sadness had impelled the subsequent aggression. We prefer to suggest that the violent movie had elicited implicit aggressive responses within the men witnessing this film, rather than experienced anger. These implicit responses presumably increased the audience's readiness to act aggressively, enabling the subsequently encountered aggressive cue to evoke strong aggressive actions from the men.

REFERENCES

Berkowitz, L. *Aggression: A social psychological analysis*. New York: McGraw-Hill, 1962.

Berkowitz, L. Aggressive cues in aggressive behavior and hostility catharsis. *Psychological Review*, 1964, **71**, 104–122.

Berkowitz, L. The concept of aggressive drive: Some additional considerations. In L. Berkowitz (Ed.), *Advances in experimental social psychology*. Vol. 2. New York: Academic Press, 1965. Pp. 301–327. (a)

Berkowitz, L. Some aspects of observed aggression. *Journal of Personality and Social Psychology*, 1965, **2**, 359–369. (b)

Berkowitz, L., Corwin, R., & Heironimus, M. Film violence and subsequent aggressive tendencies. *Public Opinion Quarterly*, 1963, **27**, 217–229.

Berkowitz, L., & Geen, R. G. Film violence and the cue properties of available targets. *Journal of Personality and Social Psychology*, 1966, **3**, 525–530.

Berkowitz, L., & Rawlings, E. Effects of film violence on inhibitions against subsequent aggression. *Journal of Abnormal and Social Psychology*, 1963, **66**, 405–412.

Geen, R. G., & Berkowitz, L. Name-mediated aggressive cue properties. *Journal of Personality*, 1966, **34**, 456–465.

McClelland, D. C., Atkinson, J. W., Clark, R. W., & Lowell, E. L. *The achievement motive*. New York: Appleton-Century-Crofts, 1953.

Spence, K. W. *Behavior theory and conditioning*. New Haven: Yale University Press, 1956.

15

Validation and Extension of the Contingency Model of Leadership Effectiveness: A Review of Empirical Findings

FRED E. FIEDLER

A contingency model of leadership effectiveness, described in a theoretical paper 7 years ago (Fiedler, 1964), has stimulated numerous studies in the area testing the model as well as attacking it in a recent issue of this journal (Graen, Alvares, Orris, & Martella, 1970). The present paper reviews 25 investigations purporting to test or extend the model.

The contingency model postulates that the performance of interacting groups is contingent upon the interaction of leadership style and situational favorableness. It has been suspected for some time that group effectiveness depends on attributes of the leader as well as of the situation (e.g., Tannenbaum & Schmidt, 1958; Terman, 1904). The question in leadership theory has been, What kind of leadership style for what kind of situation? The contingency model specifies that the so-called "task-oriented" leaders perform more effectively in very favorable and very unfavorable situations, while "relationship-oriented" leaders perform more effectively in situations intermediate in favorableness. The theory operationalizes leadership style as well as situational favorableness and, therefore, lends itself to empirical testing.

This study first defines the main terms of the theory, and briefly reviews the findings on which the model is based. It then presents (*a*) validation evidence relevant to the model's prediction of group performance in real-life studies and

From the *Psychological Bulletin*, 1971, 76, 128–148. Copyright 1971 by the American Psychological Association. Reprinted by permission.

This review was prepared under Contract N00014-67-A-0103-0012 with the Office of Naval Research and the University of Washington, Seattle (Fred E. Fiedler, Principal Investigator). Research was supported in part by Contract N00014-67-A-0103-0013 with the Advanced Research Projects Agency of the Office of Naval Research.

I am indebted to my colleagues, Anthony Biglan, Uriel Foa, Terence R. Mitchell, and Gerald Oncken for their invaluable criticisms and suggestions for the successive manuscripts.

laboratory experiments; (b) extensions of the model to a more broadly defined hypothesis; and (c) an analysis of results bearing upon the reclassification and prediction of performance of coacting groups.

Definitions

The main terms of the theory—*leadership style, situational favorableness,* and *leadership* or *group effectiveness*—are briefly described below, as are the definitions of *interacting* and *coacting* groups.

Interacting groups. These are groups in which the members work cooperatively and interdependently on a common task. The contributions of individual members of these groups cannot, therefore, readily be isolated, and the members, for this reason, are typically rewarded or penalized as a group. In contrast, in *coacting* groups members perform their tasks in relative independence of one another, as for example, members of bowling teams, men in piecework production or in training situations in which each participant typically receives an individual score or evaluation at the end of training.

Leadership style. The predictor measure used in studies of the contingency model is the least preferred co-worker (LPC) score. This score is obtained by first asking an individual to think of all co-workers he has ever had. He is then asked to describe the one person with whom he has been least able to work well, that is, the person he least prefers as a co-worker. This need not be someone with whom he works at the time. The description is made on 8-point, bipolar adjective scales, for instance,

friendly $:\overline{\quad}_{8}:\overline{\quad}_{7}:\overline{\quad}_{6}:\overline{\quad}_{5}:\overline{\quad}_{4}:\overline{\quad}_{3}:\overline{\quad}_{2}:\overline{\quad}_{1}:$ unfriendly

cooperative $:\overline{\quad}_{8}:\overline{\quad}_{7}:\overline{\quad}_{6}:\overline{\quad}_{5}:\overline{\quad}_{4}:\overline{\quad}_{3}:\overline{\quad}_{2}:\overline{\quad}_{1}:$ uncooperative

As a rule, 16 to 24 items have been used in LPC scales. The LPC score is obtained by summing the item values, giving a value of 8 to the favorable pole of each scale. Thus, a high score indicates that the subject has described his least preferred co-worker in relatively favorable terms, that is, with an average item value in the neighborhood of 5 on the 8-point scale. A low score means that the least preferred co-worker is described in a very negative, rejecting manner, that is, an LPC score of about 2 (Fiedler, 1967a, p. 43). It should also be noted that the low LPC person describes his least preferred co-worker in a uniformly, hence undifferentiated or stereotyped manner as "all bad." The high LPC person's description has a considerably greater item variance (a standard deviation of 1.43 for the high versus .43 for the low LPC person).

The score has been difficult to interpret. While labels of relationship-oriented versus task-oriented have been given to high versus low LPC persons, the terms are somewhat misleading. First, only in situations which are unfavorable (that is, stressful, anxiety arousing, giving the leader little control) do we find leader behaviors which correspond to these terms (Fiedler, 1967a). Second, Mitchell (1970) has found evidence that high LPC leaders tend to be cognitively more complex in their thinking about groups, while low LPC leaders tend to give more stereotyped cognitively simple responses. Similar results (i.e., a correlation of .35) have been reported by Schroder and his co-workers (H. Schroder, personal communication, 1969).

Thus, the LPC score must be seen as a measure which at least in part reflects the cognitive complexity of the individual and which in part reflects the motivational system that evokes relationship-oriented and task-oriented behaviors from high versus low LPC persons in situations which are unfavorable for them as leaders.

Situational favorableness. The variable that moderates the relationship between LPC and group performance is the situational favorableness dimension. It is conceptually defined as the degree to which the situation itself provides the leader with potential power and influence over the group's behavior. Situational favorableness appears to be quite important in affecting a wide range of group phenomena, as well as interpersonal behaviors. It seems likely that this dimension may have far-reaching significance in other personality research, as well as in social psychological investigations.

Situational favorableness has been operationalized in a number of ways which are discussed later. The original work on the contingency model presented one method based on three component dimensions that affect the degree to which the situation provides the leader with potential power and influence. These are leader-member relations, task structure, and position power. The hypothesis was that (a) it is "easier" to be a leader of a group that respects and accepts its leader, or in which the leader feels accepted, than in a group that distrusts and rejects its leader. Likewise (b), it is considered easier to be a leader of a group that has a highly structured, clearly outlined task than of a group that has a vague, unstructured, nebulous task; (c) it is easier to be a leader when the position is vested with power (when the leader has the power to hire and fire, promote and transfer, give raises or lower salaries) than it is to be a leader who enjoys little or no power over his members: It is easier to be a general manager than the chairman of a volunteer group.

Leader-member relations were considered to be the most important of these situational factors, and subsequent studies have supported this supposition (Fishbein, Landy, & Hatch, 1969; Mitchell, 1969). Detailed instructions for obtaining measures of leader-member relations, task structure, and position power have been described. Leader-member relations can be measured by means of sociometric preference ratings or by a group atmosphere scale which is similar in form and content to LPC, but asks the subject to rate his group as a whole.

Scales for rating task structure and position power are described in Fiedler (1967a, pp. 24, 28, 269, 281–291).

We could then classify group situations by means of the three dimensions. For this purpose, all groups were classified as falling above or below the median on each dimension. This led to an eight-celled classification system which can be depicted as an eight-celled cube (Figure 1). Each of the eight cells or "octants" can be scaled in terms of how much power and influence a leader might have in such a situation. Obviously, a liked and accepted leader who has a clear-cut task as well as power over the fate of his members (Octant I) will have a very favorable situaton. Conversely, a distrusted chairman of a volunteer group with a vague problem-solving or policy-making task (Octant VII) will be in a very unfavorable situation to exert power. Other octants fall between these two extremes.

Leadership effectiveness. The performance of the leader is here defined in terms of the major assignment of the group; that is, the leader's effectiveness is measured on the basis of the group's performance of its major assigned task.

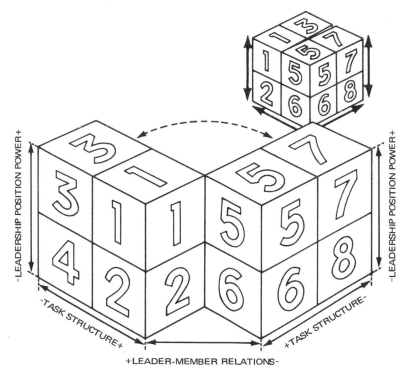

Fig. 1. A model for the classification of group task situations. (Reproduced with permission from *The Harvard Business Review*, September–October, 1965, p. 117).

While such other aspects of group behavior as morale, member satisfaction, or personal growth might be important concomitants of group effectiveness, they are here not considered to be the primary criterion, but rather contributors to performance. In other words, we evaluate the performance of an orchestra conductor not by his ability as a musicologist or the happiness of his musicians, but by how well his orchestra plays. Whether happy musicians play better than unhappy musicians, or whether the man who is a great musicologist is a better conductor is an important research question in its own right. The major question asked here is the relationship of leadership style (specifically LPC) and group or organizational effectiveness.

Previous Results

Interacting groups from 15 studies, antedating 1963, were classified according to their situational favorableness, and the correlation between leader LPC and performance was then computed for each set of groups. The correlations between the leader's LPC score and the group's effectiveness measures, when plotted against situational favorableness, generated a bow-shaped distribution indicating that the low LPC leaders performed more effectively than high LPC leaders in very favorable and very unfavorable situations; high LPC leaders performed more effectively in situations intermediate in favorableness (see Figure 2).

We here review the validation evidence that has accumulated since publication of the model in 1964. Before specifically reporting any of the studies, it should be stressed that the group classification system was viewed "as a very convenient starting point for presenting the empirical results which we have obtained in our research on interacting groups [Fiedler, 1967a, p. 34]." Improved methods for measuring situational favorableness were expected to be developed in time. The three component dimensions did, however, turn out to be a very convenient method for testing the model since operationalized measures were available.

VALIDATION EVIDENCE OF THE CONTINGENCY MODEL

Classification of Studies

A number of studies designed to test the model have been conducted by various independent investigators as well as by the writer and his associates. Some of these investigators, by design, and others, by oversight, have not followed the methodology originally described. Different operationalizations of situational favorableness were used in some studies, while others extended the model to coacting groups (e.g., Hill, 1969; Hunt, 1967), and some used leadership style measures unrelated to LPC (Shaw & Blum, 1966). These differences in methodology and divergencies from the model are, of course, quite

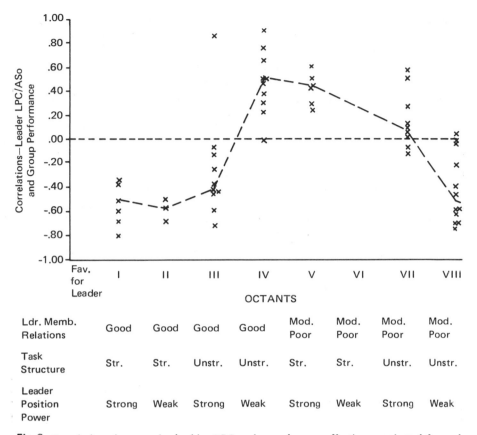

Fig. 2. Correlations between leadership, LPC scales, and group effectiveness plotted for each cell or octant of the situational favorableness dimension for studies of interacting groups conducted prior to 1963.

appropriate and desirable. However, studies that do not conform to the explicit methodology of the earlier work cannot be used as exact tests of the model.

This divergence in method presents difficulties only where the investigator and his reviewer disagree on the appropriateness of a study for testing the contingency model, or where the methodology is inadequate to test the model. This problem has here been handled as follows:

1. Four independent judges carefully read the definition of interacting and coacting groups, and the definitions of the various subdimensions of the situational favorableness dimension presented by Fiedler (1967a).
2. The judges were then given all studies that purported to test the contingency model. They were asked to read the entire methodology section in the case of shorter investigations, and relevant sections of very extensive studies. They

were not asked to read the results. Using the scales described by Fiedler (1967a), the judges classified each study in terms of the group situation into which it should be classified.

3. Groups were included among the validation studies of interacting groups if three of the four judges could agree that the groups were interacting, and if at least three of the judges agreed into which octant the groups should be classified.

Because of the nature of the pre-1963 research on which the original analysis was based, all groups in Octant I, II, and V were from field studies of natural groups and organizations, and all but one set of groups in Octants III, IV, VII, and VIII were from laboratory experiments using ad hoc groups. It is very difficult to reproduce certain effects commonly found in natural groups under experimental conditions. These include, for example, high leader position power, high stress, and very poor leader-member relations. For this reason, the model can be more meaningfully evaluated as a predictor if natural groups and ad hoc groups in laboratory experiments are considered separately, as well as together.

Field Studies

The Hunt studies. The first field study to test the contingency model was conducted by Hunt (1967) in three different organizations, namely, a large physical science research laboratory, a chain of supermarkets, and a heavy machinery plant. In each case Hunt obtained group atmosphere scores from managers and foremen, and ratings of position power and task structure from management personnel at higher levels in the hierarchy. Higher management of the research laboratory and in the manufacturing plant also provided performance ratings, while objective criteria based on an index of sales per employee manhour was derived for managers of meat markets.

The position power of all managers and foremen was judged to be high. Task structure was rated to be high for developmental research and for meat market managers, and low for managers of basic research groups and for general foremen of the heavy machinery plant. The correlations obtained for each of these groups, by octant, are presented in Table 1. (Hunt's results on coacting groups are presented in a later section.)

Electronics firm. A second set of real-life groups was investigated by Hill (1969). The research was conducted in a large electronics firm. The study dealt with supervisors of engineering teams and with instructors of assembly groups. Assembly-line instructors were rated by Hill's judges as having structured tasks and low position power, while supervisors of engineering groups were rated as having unstructured tasks and high position power. Leader-member relations were measured by supervisors' group atmosphere scores, trichotomized, with the upper third considered to have good leader-member relations, and the lower third considered to have poor leader-member relations.

Table 1. Test of the Contingency Model in Hunt's Studies

Sample	Octants			
	I	III	V	VII
Research chemists: basic research		.60 (6)		.30 (5)
Research chemists: development	−.67 (7)			
Meat markets	−.51 (10)		.21 (11)	
General foremen: heavy manufacturing		−.80 (5)		−.30 (5)

Note.—Numbers in parentheses indicate number of cases.

The correlation for nine assembly instructors' teams with high group atmosphere (Octant II) was −.10, and for the nine teams with low group atmosphere (Octant IV), −.24. The correlation between eight engineering supervisors' LPC and performance for high group atmosphere (Octant III) was −.29, and for eight supervisors with low group atmosphere groups (Octant VII), it was .62.

Public Health Teams: I. Fiedler, O'Brien, and Ilgen (1969) conducted a study of public health volunteers in Honduras during the summer of 1966. The sample consisted of 225 teenagers who were assigned to teams in Honduras to operate public health clinics and to perform community development work in outlying towns and villages. Formal leaders were not assigned. The teams' informal leaders were identified at the end of the volunteer period on the basis of sociometric questionnaire responses. The task of these groups, namely, to run a public health clinic and, time permitting, to perform some community development work, was fairly well-specified by the sponsoring organization. Problems arose when the villagers and the town officials failed to cooperate and when the population was unsupportive or hostile. Under these conditions the volunteers experienced considerable stress, often verbalized as "feeling at a loss about what to do." Under these stressful conditions, the team members were more or less on their own in trying to cope with the problems they encountered. All judges who evaluated the study agreed that the position power of the leader was low, and three of four judges considered the task to be relatively structured in the stress-free condition, but unstructured in the situation in which village support was absent.

The informal leader's group atmosphere scores were used to measure the leader-member relations. Groups operating in cooperative or favorable villages could then be classified as falling into Octants II or VI, depending on the leader's group atmosphere score; groups in uncooperative, unfavorable villages could be classified as falling into Octants IV or VIII, again depending on the leader's group atmosphere scores.

Table 2. Correlations between Leader LPC Scores and Rates: Team Performance in Two Studies (1966, 1968) of Public Health Volunteer Teams

Situation				1966		1968		
Group atmosphere	Task structure	Position power	Octant	Correlation	n	Correlation	n	Median
High	High	Low	II	−.21	13	−.46	7	−.33
High	Low	Low	IV	.00	15	.47	9	.23
Low	High	Low	VI	.67*	9	−.45	8	.11
Low	Low	Low	VIII	−.51	12	−.14	7	−.32

*$p < .05$.

Public Health Teams: II. A second study, practically identical in procedure, was conducted in the same organization (but with different volunteers) 2 years later by O'Brien, Fiedler, and Hewett.[1] One major difference in training was that most volunteers had received a culture training program developed for use of the project. This program made the situation somewhat more favorable since it provided some information that enabled the volunteers to understand and to communicate more effectively with their host nationals. A study of the effects of this program on adjustment and performance, conducted in 1967, provided evidence that individuals who had received "culture assimilator" training had adjusted and performed more effectively abroad than those who had not.

The correlations between leader LPC and performance ratings of the head-quarters staffs are presented in Table 2 for both studies. The median correlations for these groups support the model (correlations for Octant VI were not predicted).

The patterns of the 1966 and 1968 correlations both form a bow-shaped pattern, but the positive correlation was found in Octant VI in the 1966 group, but in Octant IV in the 1968 group.

Unclassifiable Field Studies

A number of other studies designed to test the contingency model cannot be included in the present analysis because the judges rating the published research could not agree on the classification of the groups. Thus, a major study by Butterfield (1968) attempted to compare five theories of leadership, namely, four theories developed at the University of Michigan and the contingency model. The study was conducted in an administrative unit of a federal agency. The sample of groups was not clearly described. References to groups indicated, however, that

---

[1] O'Brien, G. E., Fiedler, F. E., & Hewett, T. The effects of programmed culture training upon the performance of volunteer medical teams in Central America. Urbana, Illinois: Group Effectiveness Research Laboratory, University of Illinois, 1969.

"the various work units were engaged in rather different functions ranging from delivering mail to performing financial audits ... [p. 61]," and measures of effectiveness such as "typed papers, delivered mail, dispatched automobiles, coding systems ... [Appendix B]." These descriptions led all four judges to the conclusion that a number of groups must have been coacting (e.g., messenger services, typing pools, motor pool dispatchers, etc.). Equally important, however, Butterfield's measure of leader-member relations consisted of only two questionnaire items, one of which dealt with how much annoyance an employee feels with the manager. The important leader-member relations dimension was, therefore, not adequately represented in Butterfield's study.

A field study by Kretzschmar and Lueck (1969) dealt with 67 managers in business administrations of four industrial companies in Germany. In contrast to other studies, all measures of task structure, leader-member relations, and position power were based on supervisors' own ratings. In addition, supervisors also rated their own effectiveness. Our studies have shown that leaders' evaluations of their own performance typically do not correlate with objective measures, and these methodological differences made it impossible to compare this study with others in the group.

The field studies which can be used to test the contingency model are, then, those by Hunt (1967), by Hill (1969), by Fiedler et al. (1969), and by O'Brien et al. (see Footnote 3). These results are now discussed, along with those obtained in laboratory studies.

Laboratory and Field Experiments

The contingency model was based on field studies in Octants I, II, and V, and on controlled experiments in Octants III, IV, VII, and VIII. Since that time a number of field and laboratory experiments have attempted to test the predictions of the model in all octants.

The Belgian Navy Study. This was a large field experiment conducted in cooperation with the Belgian naval forces. The study involved 96 three-man teams which were experimentally assembled so that 48 teams would be culturally homogeneous (all French or all Dutch speaking) and 48 teams were heterogeneous (the leader from one language sector and the members from the other). In 48 teams the leader was a petty officer who had high position power, while the other 48 teams were headed by a recruit who had low position power. The groups were given four different tasks, one of which was coacting (teaching men to assemble an automatic pistol). The coacting task and one of the two structured tasks could not be reliably scored, and only one structured and one unstructured task were, therefore, suitable for more intensive analysis.[2] Leader-member relations were

---

[2] The Graen et al. review (1970) included all three interacting tasks in the analysis of evidential results of the contingency model. However, it was clearly pointed out by the

Table 3. Correlations between Leader LPC Scores and Group Performance Scores Obtained in Structured and Unstructured Tasks of the Belgian Navy Study

	Homogeneous groups					Heterocultural groups				
Octant	GA	TS	PP	Correlations[a]		Octant	GA	TS	PP	Correlations[a]
I	+	+	+	−.72	−.77	IX	+	+	+	.03	.77
II	+	+	−	.37	.50	X	+	+	−	.77	−.53
III	+	−	+	−.16	−.54	XI	+	−	+	.20	−.26
IV	+	−	−	.08	.13	XII	+	−	−	−.89	.70
V	−	+	+	.16	.03	XIII	−	+	+	.08	−.19
VI	−	+	−	.07	.14	XIV	−	+	−	.53	−.90
VII	−	−	+	.26	−.27	XV	−	−	−	−.37	.08
VIII	−	−	−	−.37	.60	XVI	−	−	−	−.36	−.60

Note.—GA = group atmosphere, TS = task structure, PP = position power.
[a]Two correlations were obtained per cell corresponding to the order of presentation ($n = 6$).

assessed on the basis of group climate scores obtained from leaders after each of the task sessions.

Since the contingency model, presented in 1964, was based on culturally homogeneous groups, that is, groups in which all members had the same mother tongue, only these will be used for validation purposes at this time. Table 3 presents the correlations between leader LPC scores and group performance scores. Two correlation coefficients, each with $n = 6$, were computed since the tasks were presented in counterbalanced order. As can be seen, the findings do not support the contingency model which postulates a curvilinear relationship.

A post facto analysis of the data suggested that the laboratory manipulations had not been adequate for the purpose of creating a sufficiently unfavorable situation for the leader. The homogeneous groups probably did not develop really poor leader-member relations, and there was also a question whether the supposedly structured task (requiring the group to find the shortest route for a ship which had to cover 12 ports) was sufficiently structured. The task, basically a topological puzzle, requires problem solving, and subsequent studies have shown this type task to be intermediate in structure. A bow-shaped relationship similar to that of the contingency model did emerge when heterocultural groups were included in the analysis to intensify the situational difficulty for the leader. Heterocultural groups are, of course, much more difficult to handle, and leaders reported significantly higher anxiety and greater tension in heterogeneous groups than in homogeneous groups. This effect was, however, not predicted.

---

present writer (1967a, p. 161) that the first structured task was methodologically inadequate: 9 groups obtained perfect scores and 62 groups made a total of 189 errors by not following instructions. The first task was, therefore, quite unsatisfactory and could not very well have yielded anything but random results.

The Japanese student study. Shima (1968) tested the contingency model in Japan, using two Guilford[3] tests, namely, the Unusual Uses Test considered to be moderately structured, and an "integration" task which required groups to invent a story using 10 unrelated words. All subjects were high school students, and these were assembled into 32 groups. The leaders were elected by the group members, and the group's relations with the leader were, therefore, assumed to be good. However, the judges rating this study disagreed with Shima's classification of position power. Since the leader was elected and, therefore, had obtained his position from his fellow students, and since the groups were ad hoc, the judges rated position power in this study as being low. Based on the assumption that leader position power was low, the groups would be classified as falling into Octants II and IV. The corresponding correlations were $-.26$ ($n = 16$) and .71 ($n = 16$, $p < .05$), thus supporting the model.

Church leadership groups. Mitchell (1969) conducted a small study of group performance as part of a leadership training workshop to determine the relationship between cognitive complexity and LPC. The participants were members of Unitarian churches who attended a leadership workshop. Each of the groups performed two of four tasks, one structured, and one unstructured. The tasks consisted of finding the shortest route for (a) a school bus and (b) a cross-country road race. The two unstructured tasks were to write a position paper on the church's stand on (c) legalizing abortion and (d) a "Black Caucus" within the Unitarian-Universalist church. Leader position power was low.

Mitchell (1969) originally computed correlations for groups with poor as well as with good leader-member relations, and these correlations were included in the Graen et al. (1970) critique. The Mitchell study was not, however, designed as a test of the model, and an analysis of the data showed that only 2 of the 64 group sessions in this study had group atmosphere scores below 55, a score which is roughly at the median of group atmosphere scores for similar studies. As pointed out before, a finding of this type is neither unusual nor unexpected in ad hoc groups. Most researchers, testing the model, have, therefore, tried to increase the difference between groups with high and low group atmosphere scores by using only the upper and lower thirds of the distribution, whenever this was possible. In light of the high group atmosphere scores in the Mitchell study, all groups were classified as falling into Octants II and IV depending upon task structure. The resulting rank-order correlations for Octant II were .24 and .17 ($n = 16$), and for Octant IV, .43 and .38 ($n = 16$).

Executive development workshop. An almost identical study was conducted by Fiedler as part of an executive development program. Here again, all but one of

---

[3] Guilford, J. P., Berger, R. M., & Christiansen, P. R. A factor analytic study of planning I: Hypothesis and description of tests. Los Angeles, California: Psychological Laboratory, University of Southern California, 1954.

the group atmosphere scores was above the usual cutting score, and all groups were classified as having high group atmosphere. The groups were given a relatively structured task and an unstructured task (i.e., routing a truck convoy and writing a recruiting statement inviting college students to become junior executives). All leaders were rated as having low position power, and thus all groups fell into Octants II and IV. The correlations were .34 and .51 for the structured and unstructured tasks, respectively ($ns = 11$). (See also the section reviewing results on groups in training which might apply to the church leadership and the executive development workshop studies.)

West Point Cadets. Skrzypek[4] recently completed a study of 32 four-man groups composed of cadets at West Point. Leaders were chosen from among a pool of 400 men whose LPC scores fell either one standard deviation above or below the mean. Members were assigned at random. Unlike other laboratory studies, which used postsession questionnaires, leader-member relations in this study were determined a priori on the basis of previously obtained sociometric ratings that identified well-accepted and not-accepted leaders among the cadets. Position power was varied by informing the group that the leader in the high position power would be evaluating each of his group members at the conclusion of the tasks and that these evaluations would become part of the individual's leadership score (a very important aspect of West Point's system). The leaders in the low position power were instructed to act as chairmen, and the group was told that the members as a group would be evaluated on their performance.

Each group performed one structured task and one unstructured task in counterbalanced order. The structured task consisted of drawing a plan for barracks and a military-post area to scale. The unstructured task required the groups to design a program which would educate enlisted men in overseas assignments on world politics and maintain their interest throughout their tour.

The results were as follows for each of the eight octants: Octant I, $-.43$; Octant II, $-.32$; Octant III, .10; Octant IV, .35; Octant V, .28; Octant VI, .13; Octant VII, .08; Octant VIII, $-.33$. Thus, while none of the correlations reached the .05 level of significance, all but the correlation for Octant III were in the predicted direction.

Nonclassifiable Studies

Student nurses. A study by Reilly[5] was excluded because the judges could not agree with one another or with the investigator on the position power of the leaders. Reilly studied groups composed of nurses who were given successively

---

[4] Skrzypek, G. J. The relationship of leadership style to task structure, position power, and leader-member relations. West Point, New York: United States Military Academy, 1969.

[5] Reilly, A. J. The effects of different leadership styles on group performance: A field experiment. Ames, Iowa: Industrial Relations Center, Iowa State University, 1968.

structured and unstructured discussion problems. Whether the leader actually had high position power was questioned because the leader was a fellow student, and her additional responsibilities were limited: They consisted of making certain arrangements for the groups as well as assigning 20% of the grade each student would obtain. This study is discussed in a later section, since it may also be classified as a training study.

Experimental change of position power. A second nonclassifiable study was conducted by Nealey and Shiflett (S. Nealey, personal communication, 1969) who attempted experimentally to induce a change of situational favorableness from Octant III to Octant IV and vice versa. The groups were assembled on the basis of LPC and intelligence scores. The experimental manipulation, changing the groups, did not succeed although the study prior to the experimental manipulation yielded relations between LPC and group performance.

Here again, the judges did not agree on whether the leader's position was, in fact, strong, since in the appropriate experimental condition the leader's position power was established basically by instructing the leader to role play a person with a powerful or weak position power.

Graen, Orris, and Alvares (1971) described two laboratory experiments which were specifically designed to test the contingency model. These studies also constituted the main basis for a recent article in this journal by Graen et al. (1970), which questioned the adequacy of the model.

Graen et al. (1971) used 78 and 96 male college students randomly assembled into 52 and 64 three-man groups, respectively. Each group worked on two tasks. The students were paid for their participation, and one person in each three-man group was chosen at random to serve as the leader during the first task. Another member of the same group served as leader during the second task.

Each of the groups was given one structured and one unstructured task in counterbalanced order. Using an 8-point scale for assessing task structure (Fiedler, 1967a, p. 25ff) Graen et al. (1971) chose two structured and two unstructured tasks. Position power was varied by giving the leaders of one set of groups

superior formal status relative to the members . . . special information about the task, and . . . the highest decision-making authority and responsibility. In the weak leader condition, the leader role was one of discussion leader without special information and with decision-making authority and responsibility close to that of the members. Each group worked on both tasks under only one of the two power conditions. The task sequence was randomized within power conditions [Graen et al., 1971, p. 198].

Group atmosphere scores were obtained after each task session, and the groups were divided into those whose group atmosphere scores had fallen above and below the median for the entire set. Groups were then assigned to the appropriate cell of the contingency model by dichotomizing the three situational variables of position power, task structure, and group atmosphere. The results of the two experiments are given in Table 4.

Table 4. Correlations between Leader LPC and Performance in the Graen et al. Studies

Experiment	Octant							
	I	II	III	IV	V	VI	VII	VIII
1	.47[a]	−.41	.46[a]	.33	.25	−.39	.43	−.33
2	−.13	.18[a]	.02[a]	−.08[a]	−.52[a]	−.43	.45	.44[a]

[a]Correlations in a direction counter to the hypothesis of the model.

Graen and his associates claim that their two studies followed as closely as possible the prescriptions of the contingency model and research methodology used in its development. Because their results were nonsignificant, the authors concluded that their studies, therefore, "cast doubt on the plausibility of the contingency model [Graen et al., 1971, p. 201]."

Nonsignificant results obviously can occur for any number of reasons, including inadequate experimental design. A study that attacks a theory, therefore, must not only be methodologically sound (especially if it does not support an alternative hypothesis), but it must also guard against the possibility of obtaining nonsignificant and randomly distributed data because of inappropriate or marginal experimental manipulations.

A methodological critique in the *Journal of Applied Psychology* (Fiedler, 1971) pointed to various weaknesses in the manipulation of three independent variables in the Graen et al. (1971) experimental design. The manipulations were inadequate and make the studies inappropriate for inclusion in the present analysis. A summary of the inadequacies is presented below. The discussion is based on data in the original Graen et al. (1971) paper as well as subsequent data included in a rejoinder to the methodological critique of their studies.

1. Task structure. Task structure was assessed by means of a rating scale with scores ranging from a maximum of 8.0 to a minimum of 1.0 (Fiedler, 1967a). The average task structure scores of the studies on which the original contingency model paper was based averaged 7.39 for the structured and 3.15 for the unstructured tasks. In contrast, the scores in the Graen et al. (1971) studies were 5.85 and 5.45 for the two structured tasks, and 3.69 and 3.60 for the two unstructured tasks. The scores for the structured task were, therefore, less than 1 scale point above the cutting score of 5.0 and the differences between structured and unstructured tasks were only 2.17 and 1.85 scale points. This clearly represents a very weak manipulation as compared with the differences of 4.24 in the original tasks.

While it may be argued that the task structure scores in some of the original studies were similar to those in the Graen et al. studies, an experiment which seeks to disconfirm a theory should not use marginal manipulations in testing the null hypothesis.

2. Position power. Graen et al. (1971) manipulated this variable by giving the randomly chosen leader "superior formal status" and "special information about the task," and delegating to him "the highest decision-making authority and responsibility." This was done here by talking directly to the leader in the presence of the members, presenting written task instructions to the leader only, "maintaining body orientation and eye contact with the leader," and giving an official timing device to the leader. In the weak position power condition, the formal status of the leader was not reinforced, verbal instructions were addressed to the group, written instructions were given to no one in particular, and the timing device was placed in the center of the table.

A number of reasons suggest that this power manipulation is inadequate. First of all, it is difficult to believe that the particular experimenter behaviors—like looking the leader in the eye, and giving the leader of an ad hoc group a timing device and written instructions—are sufficiently powerful manipulations to do all the things the authors expected to accomplish. Position power is conceptualized as providing the leader with some real power to give rewards and sanctions. In other words, the leader must have some fate control over his members. It is very difficult to give high position power to a leader in any laboratory situation. Where this was done successfully, it was usually accomplished by using individuals who had some formal position power outside the laboratory. Thus, the Belgian Navy study (Fiedler, 1966) compared petty officers with recruit leaders; a study of ROTC cadets by Meuwese and Fiedler (Fiedler, 1967a) and a study of West Point cadets by Skrzypek (see Footnote 5) used cadet officers who held higher rank than their members. Moreover, Graen et al. (1971) demoted the leader appointed for the first task session to member status in the second session and made another member of the same group the leader in the second session. This procedure is likely to dilute the formal leadership power.

Graen et al. (1971) subsequently reported data on perceived leader influence in support of their claim that the position power manipulation actually had been effective. Cell means of perceived influence ratings are reported in Table 5.

Thus, the difference in means over octants in Experiment 2 was only .16. A *t* test comparing the perceived influence ratings in the strong and weak position power conditions was 1.746, which is not significant. As can be seen, some of the weak position power octants had means which were higher than some of the supposedly high position power octants. Specifically, two of the "weak" octants had mean scores of 5.38, while two of the "strong" octants in the first experiment had mean scores of only 5.14. The position power manipulation in Experiment 2 appears, therefore, not to have been effective.

3. Distribution of LPC scores. Leaders were assigned at random and LPC scores were obtained after the three-man groups had been assembled. This procedure does not properly assure that leader LPC scores within each octant will have similar means and distributions. It is obvious that a meaningful test of the contingency model cannot be obtained if, for example, all groups within one

Table 5. Cell Means of Perceived Influence Ratings in
Graen et al. Study

Condition	Octant				$\overline{X}$
		Experiment 1			
Strong position power	5.83	6.17	5.14 5.14		5.57
Weak position power	4.33	4.83	3.24 4.86		4.32
M_{diff}					1.25
		Experiment 2			
Strong position power	5.75	5.63	6.13 3.50		5.29
Weak position power	5.38	5.00	5.38 4.75		5.13
M_{diff}					.16

octant have leaders with high LPC scores, while all groups in another octant have leaders with very low scores. An appropriate test is an analysis of variance to determine whether the means of various octants are reasonably similar; if so, the F test will be nonsignificant.

Data provided by Graen et al. (1971) show that the means of LPC scores within the various octants ranged from 84.7 to 42.7 in the first experiment and from 77.3 to 52.9 in the second experiment. A one-way analysis of variance was performed for each study with the eight octants as cells in the design. The F ratio for the second study was not significant (1.17), indicating that the various octants did not differ in mean LPC. The F ratio for the first study was, however, 3.10, which is significant at the .01 level and indicates that the distribution of leader LPC scores differed markedly from octant to octant. In other words, some octants (e.g., Octant IV) contained few, if any, low LPC leaders, while others (e.g., Octant V) contained few, if any, high LPC leaders.

Since the position power manipulation in addition to the weak task structure manipulations in Experiment 2 and the LPC score distributions in Experiment 1 were inadequate for testing the contingency model, neither experiment was included in the validation analysis.

Summary of Results

Table 6, which summarizes all correlations from acceptable studies, shows that the median correlations for six of the seven octants are in the predicted direction (Octant VI was not predicted). Of these, the joint probabilities of the correlations in Octants I, III, and IV are significant below the .05 level. Also, 34 of the 45 correlations are in the predicted direction, a finding significant at the .01 level by binomial test. It should be noted that the number of correlations in the predicted direction would be significant at the .01 level by binomial test even if we included the two Graen et al. (1970, 1971) experiments. These results permit the conclusion that we are not dealing with random effects: Group performance appears to be contingent upon leadership style and situational favorableness.

On the other hand, 5 of the 10 correlations obtained in Octant II are in the positive rather than in the negative direction. These counter-expectational positive correlations, although found only in this octant, throw considerable doubt on the overall generality of the relationship predicted in the Fiedler 1964 paper. It is, therefore, essential that we examine the relations in greater detail.

It will be recalled that in the 1964 study, data for Octants I, II, and V came from field studies, while the data for Octants III, IV, VII, and VIII came, with but one exception, from laboratory studies. Field and laboratory results should, therefore, be examined separately.

Field studies. The median correlations for field studies are quite similar to those predicted in the Fiedler 1964 paper. All of the medians are in the predicted

Table 6. Summary of Field and Laboratory Studies Testing the Contingency Model

Study	Octants							
	I	II	III	IV	V	VI	VII	VIII
Field studies								
Hunt (1967)	−.64		−.80		.21		.30	
	−.51		.60				−.30	
Hill (1969)[a]		−.10	−.29			−.24	.62	
Fiedler et al. (1969)		−.21		.00		.67*		−.51
O'Brien et al. (1969)		−.46		.47		−.45		.14
Laboratory experiments								
Belgian Navy	−.72	.37	−.16	.08	.16	.07	.26	−.37
	−.77	.50	−.54	.13	.03	.14	−.27	.60
Shima (1968)[a]		−.26		.71*				
Mitchell (1969)		.24		.43				
		.17		.38				
Fiedler exec.		.34		.51				
Skrzypek[a]	−.43	−.32	.10	.35	.28	.13	.08	−.33
Median								
All studies	−.64	.17	−.22	.38	.22	.10	.26	−.35
Field studies	−.57	−.21	−.29	.23	.21	−.24	.30	−.33
Laboratory experiments	−.72	.24	−.16	.38	.16	.13	.08	−.33
Median correlations of Fiedler's original studies (1964)	−.52	−.58	−.33	.47	.42		.05	−.43

Note.—Number of correlations in the expected direction (exclusive of Octant VI, for which no prediction had been made) = 34; number of correlations opposite to expected direction = 11; p by binomial test = .01.

[a]Studies not conducted by the writer or his associates.

*$p < .05$.

direction, and 13 of the 15 predicted correlations are in the expected direction, which is significant at the .05 level. The curve, based on relatively few studies, is not as regular as that obtained in 1964. Octant VI was not predicted. The predicted median correlation of .05 in Octant VII which we based on 12 correlations in the 1964 study, now is shown with a median correlation of .30, based on three correlation coefficients. Overall, considering the small number of studies and the small number of cases within each of these studies, the results seem rather remarkably consistent with the 1964 data, suggesting that the model is valid for the prediction of leadership performance under field conditions.

Experiments and laboratory studies. Only the Belgian Navy, the West Point, and Graen et al. (1971) studies provided data for all predicted octants. It is, therefore, hazardous to draw more than tentative conclusions for any octants but II and IV for which sufficient data are available. Data for Octants I and IV tended to support the prediction of the contingency model, while they did so only directionally in Octants III, V, VII, and VIII. The data clearly indicate that the model does not adequately predict leadership performance in Octant II of laboratory studies. On the other hand, 22 of the 29 predicted correlation coefficients were in the expected direction, which is significant at the .01 level for binomial tests.

A number of possible explanations for the nonpredicted results suggest themselves. The most parsimonious and obvious of these might simply be that it is difficult to manipulate leadership variables in laboratory experiments, and some important aspects of real-life situations do not permit themselves to be readily built into the laboratory.

EXTENSIONS OF THE CONTINGENCY MODEL

A number of studies have tested the more general hypothesis that the situational favorableness affects the relationship between leadership style and performance. Some of these studies tested groups in situations ranging from the very favorable to the very unfavorable; other studies considered groups falling on only two points on the situational favorableness continuum. The various group situations were categorized as being favorable, intermediate, or unfavorable situations by two or more judges. However, since the degree of situational favorableness in some of these investigations was not operationally specified in advance, the rejection of the null hypotheses becomes correspondingly more hazardous in these cases. This is especially so in studies in which the statistical relations do not reach the commonly accepted level of significance. On the other hand, it is difficult to obtain a large sample of groups or organizations in any one study; and it is essential, therefore, that we consider the cumulative evidence from different investigations.

Experimental variation in leadership behavior. Shaw and Blum (1966) instructed nine leaders to act in a highly controlling and directive manner, while a second set of 9 leaders was told to be permissive and passive. The groups were given three tasks in counterbalanced order, and the tasks varied in degree of structure. Permissive, passive leaders performed more effectively in the two relatively unstructured tasks (roughly Octant IV), the directive leaders, as predicted by the investigators, performed more effectively in the highly structured tasks (roughly Octant II). These results conform to the general expectations of the model.

Objectification of situational favorableness by structural role theory. O'Brien (1969) measured situational favorableness objectively by applying methods of structural role theory (Oeser & Harary, 1962, 1964). O'Brien assumed that a situation would be more favorable to the leader the greater the number of paths he had to the task structure. The more readily and directly the leader could influence task performance, the greater his influence and control of task-relevant group behavior.

The structural role theory deals with relations among three elements, namely, persons, positions, and tasks. Relations among the first indicate the interpersonal relationships, relations among the positions indicate authority relations, and relations among the tasks indicate allocations and task sequences. O'Brien assembled groups on the basis of personal compatibility depending upon the members' similarity or dissimilarity in scores on Schutz' FIRO scale (1958). The group task consisted of constructing models from spheres and sticks according to a given pattern. Position and task allocation were manipulated by determining the means by which the leader could interact in the task performance. A coefficient of situational favorableness could then be computed which, in oversimplified form, expressed the leader's paths to the task structure as a ratio of all possible paths. The higher the ratio, the more favorable the leader's position power.

The results of O'Brien's study, based on the correlation between leader LPC and the number of models produced, showed the predicted relationships. For 16 groups with high situational favorableness the correlation was −.08; for 16 groups with intermediate favorableness it was .77 (significant at .01); and for 32 groups with low situational favorableness the correlation was −.13.

Heterocultural American and Indian groups. Anderson (1966) conducted a laboratory experiment which used graduate students from India as well as from the United States. These groups consisted of one American leader, one American group member, and one Indian group member. The tasks required the groups to negotiate an agreement on hiring practices between an Indian village and an American company, and to compose two different stories based on the same TAT card. Half the leaders had high LPC, and half had low LPC scores. Of these, half were instructed to be as considerate as possible in their leadership behavior, while the other half were told to structure the situation as firmly as possible.

Anderson performed a post hoc analysis that scaled the situations on the basis of favorableness. This scaling suggested that the TAT tasks were more favorable than the hiring problem (which required negotiation) and that the considerate condition would be more favorable than the structuring condition. This ordering of situations was supported by leader responses to questions about their anxiety and tension in each of these conditions.

The correlations for the four tasks in order of favorableness (TAT-considerate, TAT-structuring, negotiation-considerate, negotiation-structuring) were $-.50$, .21, $-.22$, and $-.12$, thus suggesting a curvilinear relationship between LPC-performance correlations and situational favorableness ($ns = 8$).

Chemical processing companies. Lawrence and Lorsch (1967) compared the performance of six chemical processing companies, each of which had four subsystems: production, sales, applied research, and basic research. Each subsystem was under the direction of a senior management official, either at the vice-presidential level or immediately below. The structure of these subsystem tasks was rated by a number of judges. Fundamental research was rated as lowest in structure, while production was rated as highest. This reviewer correlated the manager's LPC and rated performance from the Lawrence and Lorsch data. The results follow the expectation that a low LPC manager would perform better on structured tasks, while a high LPC manager would perform better in unstructured situations. The correlations, in order of rated structure, were for production, $-.50$; sales, $-.31$; applied research, $-.10$; and fundamental research, .66. ($ns = 6$).

Since these results were obtained without reference to leader-member relations, they suggest that the leader-member relations dimension might be relatively less important at higher levels of the organization. This seems reasonable since the manager at the third and higher levels usually has very few direct contacts with production workers at the nonsupervisory levels, and relatively few contacts with first-line supervisors.

Psychiatric nursing organization. Nealey and Blood (1968) investigated the psychiatric nursing service of a large Veterans Administration hospital. LPC scores were obtained from supervisors at the first and second levels of the organization, namely, head nurses in charge of a ward, and "unit supervisors" in charge of one of the hospital's six large units, which are both quite comparable as to structure and function. Performance of wards and of units was judged by management personnel at the level above the head nurse and the unit supervisor, respectively.

The most important difference between the job of the head nurse and that of the unit supervisor for purposes of the present analysis appears to be the structure of her subordinates' tasks. The work of the psychiatric aide is relatively structured since there are fairly specific guidelines available on the management of psychiatric patients and ward personnel. The job of the unit supervisor, or more precisely, the work of the head nurses she supervises, requires considerably more policy and decision making, and it is correspondingly less structured. Nealey and Blood correlated the LPC scores of these nursing supervisors with rated performance. In a very similar study, Nealey and Owen (1970) about 18 months later recomputed these correlations on 25 head nurses, 15 of whom had participated in the first study. The correlations between head-nurse LPC and performance for the first and second studies were −.22 ($n = 21$) and −.50 ($n = 25$, $p < .05$), and for unit supervisors tested in the first study, .79 ($n = 8$, $p < .01$). Thus, as in the Lawrence and Lorsch study, the structure of the supervisory task strongly moderates the direction of the relationship between LPC and organizational performance.

Stress as an index of situational favorableness. A study by Fiedler and Barron (cited in Fiedler, 1967a) investigated the relationship between leader LPC and creative group performance under varying conditions of stress. Fifty-four three-man teams composed of ROTC cadets participated in this study under relatively stress-free conditions, intragroup conflict, and relatively severe external stress. Within each of these stress conditions the groups were divided into those with high, medium, and low leader group-atmosphere scores. The resulting LPC-performance relations were then plotted against stressfulness of the situation and resulted in a bow-shaped curve with low LPC leaders performing better than high LPC leaders in relatively stress-free and stressful conditons, and high LPC leaders performing better in situations of intermediate stress.

Summary of studies testing the contingency theory. The results presented in this section are, in one respect, quite weak, and in another, quite strong. The investigations do not permit an exact test of a theory since the methodology, the criteria, and the subject populations vary from study to study. At the same time,

Table 7. Summary of LPC-Group Performance Correlations of Studies Extending the Contingency Hypothesis

Study and date	Favorable			Intermediate			Unfavorable		
O'Brien (1969)	−.08			.77[a]				−.13	
Anderson (1966)	−.50	.21		−.22				.12	
Lawrence & Lorsch (1967)[a]	−.50	−.10	−.13	.66					
Nealey & Blood (1968)	−.22			.79[a]					
Nealey & Owen (1970)	−.50[a]								
Fiedler & Barron[b]									
Task I	−.42	−.56	−32	.67	−.08	−.01	−.53	−.72	.18
Task II	−.71	−.59	.69	.41	−.15	−.20	−.47	−.61	−.14
Median		−.37			.20			−.30	

Note.—The location of the correlation coefficient in the table indicates degree of judged favorableness of the leadership situation. The farther to the left, the more favorable the situation.

[a] Study not conducted by writer or his associates.

[b] In Fiedler (1967a).

these studies provide consistent cumulative evidence that the correlation between leadership style and group performance is moderated by the situational favorableness dimension even though this dimension is operationalized in a wide variety of ways. Thus, the Shaw and Blum experiment, the Lawrence and Lorsch investigation, as well as the Nealey and Blood and the Nealey and Owen studies show that the structure of the task is important in determining the direction of the correlation between LPC and group performance. The Fiedler and Barron (Fiedler, 1967a) study used stress as an index of situational favorableness. The O'Brien experiment presented an ingenious new metric of situational favorableness based on structural role theory, and the results of his study yielded relations in the expected direction with one of the correlations highly significant. Finally, the Anderson (1966) experiment, based on post hoc analysis of the data, also yielded data that tended to show an interaction of task and leadership style. Thus, notwithstanding the diversity of the studies, there is clear evidence that identified situational components determine, in part, the type of leadership style that a particular group requires for effective performance.

EXTENSION OF THE MODEL TO COACTING GROUPS

A number of field studies have attempted to investigate the relation of leader LPC scores to the performance of coacting groups and organizations (Fiedler, 1967b). The number of studies reported is now sufficient so that a review of the findings appears appropriate.

Task Groups and Organizations

Craft shops and grocery markets. Two organizations studied by Hunt (1967) were coacting. These were craft shops in the physical science laboratory and grocery departments of chain stores. Both of these types of organizations performed coacting tasks that were highly structured. In both organizations the leader's position power was high. Performance of craft shops was assessed by ratings, while grocery departments were evaluated on the basis of an objective measure of number of man-hours over total sales volume.

The correlations for six workshops with high, and five with low group atmosphere scores (comparable to Octants I and V), were, respectively, $-.48$ and $.90$ ($p < .05$), those for 13 supermarkets with high group atmosphere, $-.06$, and those with low group atmosphere, $.49$.

Hospital departments. Hill's (1969) study included various departments in a hospital, including the nursing service, the controller's department, dietetics, housekeeping, stores, central supply, and maintenance. All were rated to be coacting, and all supervisory personnel were rated as having high position power. The nursing service was rated by Hill as having an unstructured task, while other departments were rated as having structured tasks. Classifying the groups on the basis of the contingency model classification would make the nursing service fall into Octants III and VII and other departments into Octants I and V, depending on the leader's group atmosphere score. The correlations for the Octant I and V groups were $-.21$ ($n = 8$) and .52 ($n = 8$) and for the Octant III and VII groups (nursing) $-.32$ ($n = 7$) and .87 ($n = 7$, $p < .05$).

Telephone offices. Bates (1967) conducted a study of telephone supervisors in two offices of the Bell Telephone Company. The total sample consisted of 112 operators working in 13 groups. Of these employees, 21 were first-line supervisors who provided LPC and group atmosphere scores. The task was rated as highly structured, and the position power as high. These groups would then fall into Octants I and V.

Bates obtained two criterion scores, a "quality index" reflecting the accuracy and courtesy with which the operators handle calls as well as the accuracy in billing calls. A second index, called the "load factor," reflects the average number of calls handled by an office. Three telephone executives who were independently interviewed agreed that the quality index is the more important and that offices rarely performed below the minimum load factor. Since the quality and load indexes were negatively correlated ($-.43$), only the quality index was here considered. Bates divided his groups into six with relatively high group atmosphere and seven with low group atmosphere scores. The corresponding correlations between supervisors' LPC scores and quality indexes were $-.77$ and .75.

School principals. McNamara (1967) investigated the effectiveness of elementary school principals in 32 elementary schools of the Edmonton, Alberta, school system. The schools were relatively small in size, some containing as few as six teachers. Although McNamara spoke of his schools as interacting, all four judges classified the schools as coacting. Their reason was that there is relatively little interaction among teachers in the performance of their instructional duties, nor is it likely that the principal's job demands that he share his administrative duties with his staff or teachers. The principal's position power was rated as being high.

The effectiveness of schools was judged by five members of the school system's administrative staff. Leader-member relations were indexed by group atmosphere scores, with the upper third of the schools and the lower third of the schools used, and the middle third deleted from the sample.

The correlation between principal's LPC and performance in high group atmosphere schools (Octant I) was $-.48$ ($n = 11$), while that in low group atmosphere schools (Octant V) was .31 ($n = 12$).

Training Situations

Naval aviation cadets. Fiedler and Hutchins (Fiedler, 1967a) conducted a study of aviation cadets (including some commissioned officers in flight training) and their instructors. The student pilots were in the advanced course which concentrated on formation flying, a rather anxiety-arousing phase of training. The cadets were assigned to "flights" of eight men, and each flight was under the direction of an instructor team. The performance of the men in each flight was evaluated by instructors regularly assigned to another squadron of the training base.

Two samples of 16 instructors were tested, using their groups' performance scores as criterion of leadership (Octants I and V). The correlation of head instructors' LPC scores and performance of their flights was .45 and .17. Fiedler (1967a) also obtained correlations between the sociometrically chosen men, that is, informal leaders with very little position power. Since all were sociometrically chosen, all had good leader-member relations. The correlation between the LPC scores of 22 leaders and performance ratings was .55 ($p < .02$) and .28 for ns of 22 and 15. The lower correlations in the second set of teams may be due to the smaller range and standard deviation of performance scores in the second sample of teams.

Management trainees. A study by Seifert (1969) used 14 management training groups in Germany. These groups, each consisting of 25 to 30 participants, remained together for almost 1 year. Similar to the naval aviation cadet study, each group had a team of instructors and a head instructor. Each group also had an informal leader, designated as spokesman of the group, but having very little position power. Similar to the naval aviation cadets, Seifert reported that the men were under considerable pressure and anxiety lest they fail. (Although Seifert treated these groups as interacting, all four judges considered the Seifert study one of coacting groups.) Effectiveness was rated by instructors and was based on several scales of motivational and performance characteristics of the men.

Correlations between the LPC of head instructors and performance was .56 for those with high group atmosphere and −.20 for those with low group atmosphere scores. The correlation between spokesmen's LPC and performance scores was .45, regardless of group atmosphere.

Student nurses. A study by Reilly, mentioned above (see Footnote 6), was designed to test the contingency model. However, the judges rating Reilly's method were divided on the leader's position power. The study involved the assembly of 14 groups of student nurses with each group required to complete 10 sets of discussion problems and examination questions posed by the faculty of the school over the course of the year. Some of these problems were highly structured; that is, there was an answer or a solution available. Other problems were highly unstructured; that is, the group had to discuss a case or an ethical issue for which no definite answer was available. Reilly reported a correlation of .63 between leader LPC and group performance, irrespective of leader group atmosphere scores.

The leader had responsibility for arranging the sessions and seeing that the group's solutions were typed and handed in to the faculty. She also had the responsibility to assign 20% of each of her fellow students' grades. Leaving aside for the moment the question of position power on which our judges disagreed, or that these groups may well have been interacting in most tasks, the most important point might well be that the Reilly study, as well as the naval aviation cadet study by Fiedler and Hutchins (Fiedler, 1967a) and the Seifert study of German management trainees, is distinguished by having as its purpose the training of the group members rather than the performance of some task that results in an output beneficial to the organization.[6] In all of the studies, the exercise was designed to be beneficial to the individual group member. There might well be a psychological difference in leading a group for the purpose of benefiting the members and leading a group for the purpose of benefiting the organization. Our data suggest that this may be the case.[7]

Summary of results from coacting groups. As we suggested in the discussion of the Reilly (see Footnote 6) study, the results obtained from studies of coacting groups can best be discussed by separating results from task groups and results from training groups (Table 8).

The results from task groups are highly consistent in showing that groups or organizations with structured tasks and high leader position power perform more effectively under low LPC leaders when the group climate is rated as favorable, and more effectively under high LPC leaders when the group climate is unfavorable. Classifying coacting groups in the same manner as interacting groups indicates that the correlations are quite similar in the two octants for which data are available, namely, Octants I and V.

Hill, in his study of a hospital, classified the supervising nurses' job as unstructured. The correlation for Octant III is in the predicted direction, and the correlation for Octant VII, while much higher than would be expected for this octant, is not incompatible with data from interacting groups.

The data on coacting *task* groups suggest that the distinction between interacting and coacting task groups might be unnecessary, while the distinction between *task* groups and *training* groups might be essential. The latter appear to follow quite dissimilar rules.

The Seifert (1969), the Fiedler and Hutchins (Fiedler, 1967a), and Reilly (see Footnote 6) studies suggest that groups in training might constitute a valid subclassification for leadership studies, a classification that needs to be intensively examined further. The possibility should be considered that this set of

---

[6] An earlier unpublished study of classroom performance by Marse (1958) showed negative correlations of −.70 ($n = 6$) and −.36 ($n = 12$) for physics and rhetoric section instructors at the University of Illinois where rated student performance was the criterion. In that study, however, the class members never interacted in groups as part of their training. Whether this is an important determining factor remains to be seen.

[7] Note, however, that a school principal's group membership consists primarily of teachers and clerical staff, not of students.

Table 8. Correlational Summary of Studies Extending the Contingency Model to Coacting Task and Training Groups

Group	Octants							
	I	II	III	IV	V	VI	VII	VIII
Task groups								
Craft shops	−.48				.90[a]			
Groceries	−.06				.49			
Hospital departments[a]	−.21		−.32		.52		.87	
Telephone offices	−.77				.75			
School principals[a]	−.48				.31			
Median	−.48		−.32		.52		.87	
Training groups								
Naval aviation								
Chief instructors	.45							
	.17							
Informal leaders			.55					
			.28					
Management trainees[a]								
Head instructors	.56					−.20		
Informal leaders	.45		.45					
Student nurses[a]			.63					
Medians	.45		.50			−.20		

[a]Studies not conducted by writer or his associates.

studies might also include those by Mitchell (1969) and Fiedler which used participants in leadership workshops.

Recent empirical findings from research on leadership training. Despite intensive efforts, research has failed to show that leadership experience or leadership training systematically improve organizational performance (Campbell et al., 1970). These disappointing results can be deduced from the contingency model. Specifically, we can interpret leadership experience and training as improving situational favorableness (e.g., human relations training is supposed to improve leader-member relations; technical training would make the task appear more structured). Training and experience should then differentially affect the performance of high and low LPC leaders. The contingency model would then predict that training for intermediate situations will improve the performance of high LPC leaders—but *decrease* that of low LPC leaders. Likewise, training and experience for favorable and unfavorable situations will improve performance of low LPC leaders—but *decrease* performance of high LPC leaders. These results have now been obtained in several studies and further support the contingency model (Fiedler, in press).

SUMMARY

A review of studies testing and extending the contingency model evaluated the model's predictive power in field and laboratory situations and in coacting task and training groups.

The model seems to predict leadership performance in field situations, but not completely in laboratory situations. The major discrepancy between the model and the field studies on the one hand, and the laboratory studies on the other, was in Octant II, where the model predicted negative correlations, while the laboratory studies showed predominantly positive correlations between LPC and group performance. This discrepancy, if it is not due to chance, may well bring to light important aspects of leadership interactions that are not usually reproduced in laboratory situations.

A series of studies, extending the theory, was reviewed. Taken as a group, these studies provide strong evidence that the situational favorableness dimension does indeed moderate the relationship between leadership style and group performance, and that it therefore provides an important clue to our understanding of leadership phenomena.

Finally, studies of coacting groups and organizations suggested that we differentiate between groups that exist primarily for the benefit of the organization—that is, the typical task groups—and groups that exist for the benefit of the individual—groups of trainees. Coacting task groups appear to follow the predictions of the contingency model, at least for Octants I and V. Data from groups-in-training showed consistently positive relations between leader LPC and group performance measures in Octants I and III, and only one small negative correlation in Octant VI. These findings suggest a new approach to the classification of coacting groups and training groups which might lead to a better understanding of managerial performance in task and training organizations.

REFERENCES

Anderson, L. R. Leader behavior, member attitudes, and task performance of intercultural discussion groups. *Journal of Social Psychology,* 1966, **69**, 305–319.

Bates, P. A. Leadership performance at two managerial levels in the telephone company. Unpublished bachelor's thesis, University of Illinois, 1967.

Butterfield, D. A. An integrative approach to the study of leadership effectiveness in organizations. Unpublished doctoral dissertation, University of Michigan, 1968.

Campbell, J. P., Dunnette, M. D., Lawler, E. E., & Weick, K. E. *Managerial behavior, performance, and effectiveness.* New York: McGraw-Hill, 1970.

Fiedler, F. E. A contingency model of leadership effectiveness. In L. Berkowitz (Ed.), *Advances in experimental social psychology.* New York: Academic Press, 1964.

Fiedler, F. E. The effect of leadership and cultural heterogeneity on group performance: A test of the Contingency Model. *Journal of Experimental Social Psychology,* 1966, **2**, 237–264.

Fiedler, F. E. *A Theory of leadership effectiveness.* New York: McGraw-Hill, 1967. (a)

Fiedler, F. E. Führungsstil und Leistung koagierender Gruppen. *Zeitschrift für experimentelle und angewandte Psychologie,* 1967, **14**, 200–217. (b)

Fiedler, F. E. Note on the methodology of the Graen, Orris, and Alvares studies testing the contingency model. *Journal of Applied Psychology*, 1971, **55**, 202–204.

Fiedler, F. E. *Leadership*. A module for the General Learning Press, in press.

Fiedler, F. E., O'Brien, G. E., & Ilgen, D. R. The effect of leadership style upon the performance and adjustment of volunteer teams operating in a stressful foreign environment. *Human Relations*, 1969, **22**, 503–514.

Fishbein, M., Landy, E., & Hatch, G. Consideration of two assumptions underlying Fiedler's Contingency Model for the prediction of leadership effectiveness. *American Journal of Psychology*, 1969, **4**, 457–473.

Graen, G., Alvares, K., Orris, J. B., & Martella, J. A. Contingency model of leadership effectiveness: Antecedent and evidential results. *Psychological Bulletin*, 1970, **74**, 285–296.

Graen, G., Orris, J. B., & Alvares, V. M. Contingency model of leadership effectiveness: Some experimental results. *Journal of Applied Psychology*, 1971, **55**, 196–201.

Hill, W. The validation and extension of Fiedler's theory of leadership effectiveness. *Academy of Management Journal*, 1969, March, 33–47.

Hunt, J. G. Fiedler's leadership contingency model: An empirical test in three organizations. *Organizational Behavior and Human Performance*, 1967, **2**, 290–308.

Kretzschmar, V., & Luecke, H. E. Zum Fiedlerschen Kontingenzmodell Effektiver Führung, *Arbeit und Leistung*, 1969, **23**, 53–55.

Lawrence, P., & Lorsch, J. Differentiation and integration in complex organizations. *Administrative Science Quarterly*, June 1967, **12**, 1–47.

Marse, J. E. Assumed similarity between opposites and the performance of leadership functions. Unpublished master's thesis. University of Illinois, 1958.

McNamara, V. D. A descriptive-analytic study of directive-permissive variation in the leader behavior of elementary-school principals. Unpublished master's thesis, University of Alberta, 1967.

Mitchell, T. R. Leader complexity, leadership style, and group performance. Unpublished doctoral dissertation, University of Illinois, 1969.

Mitchell, T. R. Leader complexity and leadership style. *Journal of Personality and Social Psychology*, 1970, **16**, 166–174.

Nealey, S. M., & Blood, M. Leadership performance of nursing supervisors at two organizational levels. *Journal of Applied Psychology*, 1968, **52**, 414–422.

Nealey, S. M., & Owen, T. M. A multitrait-multimethod analysis of predictors and criteria of nursing performance. *Organizational Behavior and Human Performance*, 1970, **5**, 348–365.

O'Brien, G. E. Group structure and the measurement of potential leader influence. *Australian Journal of Psychology*, 1969, **21**, 277–289.

Oeser, O. A., & Harary, F. A mathematical model for structural role theory I. *Human Relations*, 1962, **15**, 89–109.

Oeser, O. A., & Harary, F. A mathematical model for structural role theory II. *Human Relations*, 1964, **17**, 3–17.

Schutz, W. C. *FIRO: A Three-dimensional theory of interpersonal behavior*. New York: Holt, Rinehart & Winston, 1958.

Seifert, K. H. Untersuchungen zur Frage der Führungseffektivität. *Psychologie und Praxis*, 1969, **13**, 49–64.

Shaw, M. E., & Blum, J. M. Effects of leadership style upon group performance as a function of task structure. *Journal of Personality and Social Psychology*, 1966, **3**, 238–242.

Shima, H. The relationship between the leader's modes of interpersonal cognition and the performance of the group. *Japanese Psychological Research*, 1968, **10**, 13–30.

Tannenbaum, R., & Schmidt, W. H. How to choose a leadership pattern, *Harvard Business Review*, 1958, **36**, 95–101.

Terman, L. M. A preliminary study of the psychology and pedagogy of leadership. *Pedagogical Seminary*, 1904, **11**, 413–451.

16

The Generality of Behavioral Data I: Generalization from Observations on One Occasion

DAVID MAGNUSSON, MARIANNE GERZEN and BÖRJE NYMAN

Behavioral data are used both in fundamental research and in applied psychology as a basis for generalizations about the individuals to whom the data refer. We usually are not interested in data if they are valid only for the particular occasion of observation and not for other situations. Data must be robust and lead to generalizations of broader interest. We draw general conclusions from data collected on one occasion or a number of occasions, and apply them to other occasions and other situations.

This generalization occurs above all in two common and well-known contexts. First, we use data to infer personality traits as determinants of behavior. We endeavor, for example, to determine what is characteristic of an individual in a certain respect, and this is assumed to be more or less valid in other situations. Second, in applied psychology, data collected in some situations are often used as a basis for prediction of behavior in situations with other conditions. The assumption underlying this practice is that there are valid behavioral dimensions with the help of which people's behavior can be explained. A question of importance for both fundamental research and application is then: "How far and under what conditions is it possible to make such generalizations on the basis of data collected in observations from a limited number of situations?"

Data are based on observation of behavior. Every individual can reveal a very large number of behavioral responses. The following are usually assumed to be valid for these responses:

From *Multivariate Behavioral Research*, 1968, *3*, 295–320. Copyright 1968. Publication authorized by Multivariate Behavioral Research.

We wish to thank J. McV. Hunt, Univ. of Illinois, and Erik Leander, Univ. of Stockholm, for discussions of the psychological and the statistical problems involved. The Military Psychological Institute has been very cooperative in the collection of data.

The experiments have been made possible by financial support from the Swedish Council for Social Science Research.

1. In a given situation, the probability of different responses varies for the individual in respect to both occurrence and strength; some responses occur, others do not, and those occurring vary in respect to intensity.
2. The probability that a certain response will occur for an individual changes from one situation to another.
3. The probability of a certain response is different for different individuals in the same situation.
4. Variations in probability over situations for a certain response by a person are less than the variations in the probability over persons for the same response in a certain situation. The probability of a certain response does not change so much for one individual between different situations as it would if a new individual, chosen randomly, were taken for each new situation.

Each separate observational situation provides a sample of the behavior of each individual observed. For practical reasons we are compelled to make our observations of an individual in one or a limited number of situations. Whether, and how far generalizations of behavior are then possible is a question of (a) the relative size of the sample of responses from him, (b) the representativeness of this sample. When the number of situations in which it is possible to make systematic observations is small, a certain insecurity arises concerning the possibilities for generalization. A more serious shortcoming may be when the situations in which we usually make systematic observations differ essentially in character and conditions from the situations to which we wish to generalize. When, therefore, we must reckon with observational situations which are not representative samples of the population of situations to which we wish to generalize regarding behavior, the answer to the following question will determine how far we can generalize: "How does the probability of behavioral responses and therefore the measurable behavior vary from one situation to another with changes in the situational conditions?"

In so much as it is shown that behavior varies greatly with variations in the situational conditions, the problem of sampling observational situations will be important for the possibilities of generalizing in respect to the presence of personality traits and in respect to prediction of behavior.

The problem now formulated is an old one: To what degree can we account for the total variation in data for individuals' behavior in a series of different situations in terms of

"a) individual differences (represented by measures of aptitude, interest, attitude and personality), b) situational or environmental variables, c) the interaction of individual and the situational (environmental) variables?" (Sells, 1964, p. 1)

It is not surprising that this question has been the object of much debate since its answer has important consequences. If the individual factors per se are dominant, the behavior of the individual will be stable and consistent from situation to situation with different characteristics. Data covering the behavior in different situations will then show high intercorrelations independent of the degree of change in the characteristics of the situations. Knowing the individual will make it possible to predict his behavior in any situation with some certainty. If the situational or the interactional factors are most important, the behavior will change from situation to situation, where the magnitude of the change is a function of the degree of change in the characteristics of the situations. Data covering behavior in different situations will show varying intercorrelations, the size of which will be some function of the similarity between the situations. For the most probable case, where the interaction between the individuals and the situations accounts for most of the total variation in behavior, we have to know both the individual and the situation in order to predict his behavior in a specific situation.

The emphasis on various factors has changed between fields of research and between researchers in these fields (see, e.g. Endler, Hunt & Rosenstein, 1962, or Miller, 1963, pp. 641–642). Although already Fechner while seeking for a systematic relationship between the properties of a stimulus and the occurrence and intensity of the response emphasized the importance of situational conditions for behavior, there is no doubt that most of the interest and work has been devoted to the study of individual factors.

Although psychologists in their practical work probably agree that individual, situational and interactional factors determine behavior, there is no doubt that situational and interactional factors are considered in practice only to a limited extent. Sometimes it seems as if it is implicitly assumed that the whole problem of a valid description and prediction is merely a question of reliable instruments to measure stable interindividual differences. In any case, this seems to be true outside the clinical field. If the interindividual variation in one situation or a certain type of situations is responsible for only a small part of the total variation over situations with varying conditions, it is hardly astonishing that the descriptions and predictions that make use of only this variation are restricted to validity.

During recent years, stress has been laid on the necessity of paying more attention to situational and interactional variables (see, e.g. Sells, 1963; Hunt, 1965; Bieri et al., 1966). In a summary of his views on the state of personality research, Abelson says (1962, p. 241): "In particular there has been a rather serious neglect of situational variables." The same interest in situational factors in a wider sense is reflected in the rapid development of ecological psychology (Barker, 1965).

In spite of the central role of the reply to the question of the significance of the situational and interactional factors, the problem has only to a small extent been the object of experimental studies leading to general conclusions.

"The literature abounds with research on individual variation where the situation is held constant; increasingly, there are studies in the effects of different situations where the individual differences are held constant. Few studies have involved interrelations between variations in behavior and different situations" (Miller, 1963, p. 643; see also Forehand & Gilmer, 1964).

One of the best planned and best performed studies in this field of research was published by Endler, Hunt & Rosenstein (1962). In this the problem discussed was elucidated by data from a questionnaire on anxiousness. The subjects indicated on a five-point scale the intensity of their reaction in each of fourteen different respects (e.g. "Feels exhilarated and thrilled," "Mouth gets dry," "Have loose bowels"), and for each of eleven different situations (e.g., "Going to meet a date," "Sailing a boat on a rough sea," "Getting up to give a speech in a large group"). The data first published were reanalyzed to partition the various sources of variance (Endler & Hunt, 1966). Modes-of-response contributed nearly 25 per cent of the total variance, situations and subjects contributed about 5 per cent each, simple interactions about one-third together (about 10 per cent each) and the residual comprised the remaining third of the total variance. Results in accordance with those of Endler, Hunt & Rosenstein recently have been reported for choice behavior (Sandell, 1966).

In a comment on the results reported together with Endler and Rosenstein, Hunt states:

"Rather, the generality of our findings would have to derive from their reproducibility with other samples of modes-of-response, with other samples of situations, with other samples of subjects, and with other personality traits. If these results should prove to be reproducible in general, as I have defined general, they imply that our brethren from social psychology have a conceptual slant which is more nearly congruent with reality than has been the slant of us personologists" (1965, p. 82).

THE PRESENT STUDY

Two experiments are reported here, which are relevant to the problem under consideration.

The data collected in the experiments are ratings of personality variables, based on direct observation of behavior in "natural" social situations, where the situational factors have been varied systematically. What is actually studied is the generalizability of such data obtained in one situation for each subject. An analysis of the results can give an immediate answer to the question of how far this sort of data for an individual's behavior in a certain situation is valid also for other situations. The results also can be used as a basis for a discussion concerning the more general question about the generality of behavior and personality traits.

Situational Factors of Importance
for Variation in Behavior

The planning of an empirical study about how far data can be generalized to situations other than the one in which they were collected presupposes an analysis of the situational factors which may be of importance in determining behavior. On the whole, psychologists have been remarkably indifferent to systematic analyses of this kind as bases for meaningful description of situations (see, e.g. Bieri, 1962; Miller, 1963). The following situational factors, similar to those suggested by Sherif and Sherif (1963), were judged to be of great importance for how a situation is expressed totally, and defined by a person:

1. Whether the individual is alone or a member of a group.
2. The other individuals of the group, with which he interacts; i.e. the composition of the group.
3. The task of the individual or group.

Variations in individual behavior between situations may be attributed largely to variations in one, some, or all of the factors mentioned. In the experiments reported here the effect of variation of the last two conditions has been studied.

Of the two main variables tested, the task and the composition of the group, the influence of the latter on individual's behavior in particular has been studied in various investigations (see, e.g. Haythorn, 1952; Gibb, 1959). Bieri (1962, p. 229) writes: "The behavior of the other person is a very powerful stimulus condition in social behavior and has been recognized theoretically."

Design for the Collection of Data

In order to test the extent to which ratings of an individual's behavior in one situation can be generalized to other situations the following factorial design was planned (Magnusson, 1965):

	Variation of task	
Variation of group	No	Yes
No	$A_1 - A_2$	$B_1 - B_2$
Yes	$C_1 - C_2$	$D_1 - D_2$

Ratings of personality variables were collected after the observation of behavior in group situations. A_1, A_2, B_1, B_2, C_1, C_2, D_1, and D_2 are situations in which the observations were made.

Cell A: Each subject is observed on two occasions. He is together with the same group members and they have the same task on both occasions.
The conditions of the situation are repeated.

Cell B: Each subject is observed on two occasions. He has the same companions on both occasions but the task for the group is different.
The task is varied, while group composition is repeated.

Cell C: Each subject is observed twice. He has the same task but different companions on the two occasions.
The composition of the group is varied, while the task is repeated.

Cell D: Each subject is observed on two occasions. Both the task and the companions are changed.

The task and the composition of the group are both varied.

A, B, C, and D are called treatments in the following discussion.

In each cell 12 subjects have been observed and rated. Thus data have been obtained for 48 subjects.

On each occasion the subject participated with two (Experiment I) or three (Experiment II) other individuals. The persons participating were not told which of them was the subject. This role was assigned randomly.

Two teams of raters worked in each of the experiments. The members of each team rated independently of each other.

The composition of the teams of raters remained unchanged during the experiments. The experimental design was made so that no rater saw the same subject more than once and each rater saw all 48 subjects.

EXPERIMENT I: COLLECTION OF DATA

Subjects

In this experiment, the experimental groups consisted of 192 military conscripts, of which 48 were rated as subjects.

Raters

Eight well trained psychologists, with long experience in this type of observation and rating, worked as observers and raters. The raters formed two teams of four judges in each, where one team always observed the first situation and the other team the second situation in each treatment. They had been trained for the special task in a pilot study.

Tasks

One factor studied in the experiment is variation of task. The magnitude of the variation expressed by data will naturally depend upon the characteristics of the tasks chosen. With very different tasks, the variation in data will probably be greater than when tasks are similar in character. A general expression of how great a part of the variation over situations can be attributed to variation in tasks requires a random sample of items, representative of the population of tasks which may confront an individual in a group. The experiment as planned, is a model experiment intended to test the methods and the prospects of more comprehensive investigations which may give more generalizable results. We have therefore chosen two tasks of a character commonly employed in observations and ratings of this kind.

The tasks cannot be regarded as very similar or very different in character. The fact that they were chosen in the way they were, however, means that the variation in tasks cannot be generalized to refer to the variation between any other tasks.

Task 1. The group was given a large-scale map of a district with main and secondary roads, a railway, a river, and lakes. The members were supplied with blocks representing houses, public buildings, factories, shops and the like. The task for the group members was to plan a town, such as they would like to live in.

In treatments A and B each subject was confronted with the same task twice. In order to minimize the effect of the confrontation with the task the first time on the behavior of the subject on the second confrontation, two parallel planning tasks were constructed differing in respect to the details of the map.

Task 2. Each member of a group was given a set of 10 photographs of male persons, a list of 12 professions, and a list of 12 nationalities. He was told that his task in the first stage was to couple the male in the photograph with one of the nationalities and one of the professions. When all group members had made the judgment they were to deliver the copy of the results to the research leader. Thereupon, all group participants were to come to a group decision with regard to the task given to each individual participant. The photographs in the parallel task were of women.

Motivation

One important factor in tests of this type is the level of the subject's motivation. The situation is probably experienced by the subjects as being unlike an ordinary workaday situation. It is therefore highly desirable to encourage the group members to do their best with the tasks.

The group members were motivated by a sum of money, which was given for the best result. In the planning task they were told that the group which obtained the result judged by a jury to be the best would get 50 dollars, the next best group would get 30 dollars, and the third best group would get 10 dollars.

In the combination task the subjects were told that the group which got the most correct solutions would be given 50 dollars and that the best subject in the group would be given 10 dollars extra. A second and third prize also were given. The purpose of the instructions was to motivate the subjects to do their best when working alone and then try to drive through their opinions when a decision was to be made by the group.

Ratings

With reference to the principal aim of the investigation three variables used for psychological selection of military leaders were chosen.

Variable I: Cooperative Ability
Variable II: Self-Confidence
Variable III: Leadership

The ratings were recorded on a scale of the following type. Each variable to be rated was also defined by a series of statements about the behavior, characterizing the extremes of the scale.

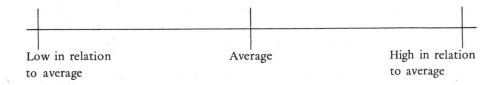

Low in relation   Average   High in relation
to average   to average

In the instructions to the raters, military conscripts were given as the frame of reference for the ratings. In order to establish, as far as possible, a common and stabilized frame of reference the raters were trained in a pilot study.

Talk Time

The main data used in the experiment were ratings of behavior. What can be studied directly is the effect of variations in the experimental conditions on these data. The extent to which variations in data as a result of variations in experimental conditions also reflect variations in the subjects' actual behavior will be a problem of interpretation and judgment. A direct objective measure of a behavioral variable also has been studied; namely, the amount of time each subject talked during each situation (talk time).

For each situation the total time taken for the discussion was noted and the time each subject spoke. In the latter case, even very brief talk was registered.

Because of a technical mishap, talk time was registered for only 93 of the 96 testing sessions.

Interview Ratings

An interview with each subject followed immediately after the last observational occasion. The interviewer had extensive experience with interviewing conscripts. Another interviewer, with the same experience and training, watched the interview through a one-way screen. The same two interviewers worked throughout the entire investigation.

The interviewers, who never participated in the observational section of the experiment, rated the same variables on the basis of the same instructions as those given to the judges in the observational sessions. The ratings were based only on the interview.

RESULTS

Agreement among Observers on the Same Occasion

The degree of agreement among the four judges, who observed and rated the subjects on the same occasion, was calculated by an intraclass coefficient of correlation for each team of judges in respect of each rated variable and treatment (Ebel, 1951). The results revealed no systematic or significant differences between the two teams of judges as far as level of coefficients was concerned. The means of the coefficients obtained are shown in Table 1.

The coefficients reported in Table 1 may be interpreted as estimates of the coefficients that would have been obtained for the correlation with ratings made by another team of four judges if they had observed the same subjects on the same occasion. This means that the coefficients in Table 1 are estimates of the maximum value that can be expected for the correlation between the teams of judges when the situational conditions varied. The coefficients which are obtained for the correlation between ratings made by two teams, when the judges made their observations on different occasions, must thus be interpreted in relation to the coefficients reported in Table 1. In this connection it is worth observing that the coefficients for agreement among judges show no systematic trend over treatments in respect of size.

Agreement among the judges within the teams was studied in respect to possible developmental tendencies which might be considered to be related to practice, etc. Intraclass coefficients were calculated for each team of judges, for the first and for the second halves of the observation sessions. No systematic trends or significant differences were found.

Variation in Ratings as an Effect of Variation in Situational Conditions

For each subject, the mean of the ratings of the four judges in each separate variable was calculated as the best available measure of the subject's behavior in each separate situation.

The coefficients for the correlation between the two series of ratings obtained for each variable in the two situations in each treatment are reported in Table 2.

Each single coefficient, irrespective of treatment, was tested for significance according to a series of hypotheses. The tests of significance were carried out by analysis of variance.

The following results were obtained:

1. When the two situations were identical (treatment A), the null-hypothesis for the correlation between ratings given on two different occasions can be rejected for all variables at the 1 per cent level of confidence. The result

Table 1. Mean Intraclass Coefficients for the Agreement Among Four Raters Observing the Same Situation

	Task varied	
Group varied	No	Yes
No	I. 0.822	0.872
	II. 0.897	0.941
	III. 0.912	0.960
Yes	I. 0.848	0.884
	II. 0.870	0.860
	III. 0.927	0.915

supports the alternative hypothesis that it is possible to predict with some certainty a person's behavior in one situation from his behavior in another, similar situation.

2a. When the task was varied (treatment B), the null-hypothesis for the correlation between the two series of ratings can be rejected, for one variable at the 1 per cent level of confidence, and for the other two variables at the 5 per cent level. The result supports the alternative hypothesis that it is possible to predict with some certainty a person's behavior in one situation from his behavior in another situation, which differs in regard to the purpose of the group's activities.

2b. The null-hypothesis cannot be rejected, that certainty in the prediction of behavior from one situation to the other is as great when task is varied as when the conditions are repeated. The differences between the coefficients

Table 2. Coefficients for the Correlation between Ratings Given in One Situation by Four Raters and Ratings Given by Four Other Raters in Another Situation[a]

	Task varied	
Group varied	No	Yes
No	I. 0.764	0.658
	II. 0.726	0.693
	III. 0.685	0.598
Yes	I. 0.494	−0.081
	II. 0.793	0.044
	III. 0.852	−0.018

[a] N = 16.

in treatments A and B are all in the expected direction, but they are not great enough to justify any conclusions.

3a. When the composition of the group was varied (treatment C), the null-hypothesis for the correlation between the two series of ratings can be rejected for two of the variables at the 1 per cent level, and for the third at the 10 per cent level. The result supports the alternative hypothesis that it is possible to predict with some degree of certainty a person's rated behavior in one situation on the basis of his behavior in another situation in which he interacts with persons other than those present in the observed situation.

3b. The null-hypothesis, that certainty in the prediction of a person's behavior is independent of whether the composition of the group is varied or not, cannot be rejected for any of the variables at the 5 per cent level. Two of the coefficients are in fact higher for treatment C than for treatment A.

4a. When both the task and the groups were varied at the same time (treatment D), the null-hypothesis for the correlation between the two series of ratings cannot be rejected for any of the variables. As a matter of fact, all three coefficients are well clustered around 0, and two of them are negative. The results provide no grounds for the alternative hypothesis that it is possible to predict a person's rated behavior in one situation on the basis of his behavior in another situation, differing from the first in respect to the task and the composition of the groups.

4b. The null-hypothesis that certainty in the prediction of a person's rated behavior is as great when both the task and the composition of the group are varied as when the situational conditions are the same can be rejected for all three variables. This supports the alternative hypothesis that simultaneous variation in both task and composition of group has a systematic and significant effect on the possibilities of predicting a person's rated behavior in one situation on the basis of observations made in another.

As mentioned earlier, the size of the correlations in Table 2 should be judged in relation to the coefficients obtained for agreement among the four judges in each treatment (Table 1). It should be observed that the latter are at the same level for all treatments. Thus differences between treatments in respect to the possibility of judging the behavior in separate situations or in respect to interindividual variance in the samples of individuals cannot be the cause of the results which are interpreted as effects of the treatments. The total picture is the same and the conclusions are not changed if the correlations given in Table 2 are placed in direct relation to the coefficients in Table 1.

The sets of coefficients in Table 1 and 2 are directly comparable as far as size is concerned, since both are estimates of the correlations of four judges with four other judges. A direct comparison between the tables shows that the coefficients of the correlation between ratings made on different occasions are lower for all variables in all treatments than the coefficients of the correlation between ratings made on the same occasion. This is also true of treatment A, where the situational conditions are repeated.

Table 3. Coefficients for the Correlation between Talk
Time Measures on the Two Occasions for each Treatment

	Cell A	Cell B	Cell C	Cell D
	N = 11	N = 12	N = 11	N = 11
r	0.636	0.613	0.895	0.418

Talk Time

Talk time is an objective measure of one aspect of behavior. The reliability of this measure expressed as the agreement between different timetakers was not established. In another experiment performed in the same series such a measure has been calculated. It shows that the registration of talk time can be made almost without any errors in respect to differences between timetakers.

The coefficients for the correlation between talk time in the two situations for each treatment are reported in Table 3.

The null-hypothesis that talk time on one occasion is not related to talk time on another can be rejected for treatment A and B at the 5 per cent level and for treatment C at the 1 per cent level. For treatment D the null-hypothesis cannot be rejected. The null-hypothesis that the correlation between occasions in respect to talk time is independent of treatment can be rejected for the difference between the coefficients for treatments C and D. The coefficient for treatment D is significantly lower at the 5 per cent level than the coefficient for treatment C.

The result supports that obtained for the rating data. When the situational conditions are varied simultaneously, in respect to task and group, only about 17 per cent of the variance for this objectively measured variable is predictable from one occasion to the other.

Interview Ratings

Agreement of ratings was calculated between the two psychologists who, on the basis of interviews, had rated the subjects in respect to the same variables as the judges in the observational situations.

The coefficients of agreement in ratings for the two judges are shown in Table 4.

Table 4. Coefficients for the Agreement between
Ratings Based on Interview[a]

		r
Variable I	Cooperative Ability	0.804
Variable II	Self-Confidence	0.783
Variable III	Leadership	0.854

[a] N = 48

Table 5. Coefficients for the Correlation between Mean Ratings Based on Interviews (2 Interviewers) and Mean Ratings Based on Observation (4 Observers)

	Team A—Interview ratings	Team B—Interview ratings
Variable I	0.161	0.148
Variable II	0.306	0.336
Variable III	0.438	0.345

The level of the coefficients is as expected. Agreement between two judges, who base their ratings on identical interviews, is greater than the coefficients obtained for the correlation between two judges who base their judgments on independent direct observation.

The coefficients of correlation were calculated between the means of interview ratings and the means of observation ratings. The coefficients are given in Table 5.

The coefficients of correlation deviate significantly from 0 for both teams of observers for two of the variables, namely Self-Confidence and Leadership.

The picture is as follows. When the situations change, as they do in treatment D, the correlation between the observation ratings is negligible. At the same time, the ratings made by the interviewers in a completely different situation have a systematic and positive correlation with the ratings from each of the situations. This fact will be discussed later.

EXPERIMENT II: COLLECTION OF DATA

Subjects

This study was based on ratings of children in play situations.

A total of 12 groups was observed in each of the four cells, each group consisting of four children (two boys and two girls) where one of the boys was rated as the subject. Forty-eight children, all belonging to normal classes of the first grade of the Swedish school system, were thus rated. The members of each group were chosen randomly for a class.

The average age of the subjects was approximately 7 years and 3 months.

Raters

Four female, well-trained child psychologists participated as observers and raters. They formed two teams. The combination of members in the teams was unchanged through the whole experiment. One of the teams always saw the first situation for observation of the subject and the other team always saw the second situation.

The raters were carefully prepared by special training for the experiment. A pilot study was performed in which each rater, for a period of 12 hours, observed and rated 48 children of the same age as in the experimental situations. The raters and the experiment leader discussed the problems connected with the rating procedure for totally 6 hours before the pilot study and 14 hours before the main study.

Tasks

Many psychologists have pointed to the potentiality in observations of children in game situations (Freud, 1963; Peller, 1952; Philips, 1960; Piaget, 1932). Redl (1959, p. 33) has summarized some important points of view:

"It seems to me that children's games are a sort of little 'universe in miniature', something like an experiment in nature with the creation of social systems, activity structures and many other potent ingredients. Most of the considerations that go into an experiment for a miniature social structure and activity design for a specific group of patients or normal people . . . seem to me also implied in the patterns of games, and there is the advantage, that they can be varied at will, can be inserted for ten minutes".

On the basis of preliminary studies of fifteen different child games, one dice game and one card game was found to be of suitable difficulty for children of age 7 and were chosen as Task 1 and Task 2 respectively.

Task 1. The dice game, called Chorea, was modified somewhat for the purpose of this experiment. The game is played on a square plate of wood. The task is to move from the nest and back along given paths in accordance with the rules and as fast as the verdict of the dice permits.

Task 2. A classical Swedish card game called Black Peter was used as the second task. The one who gets the card with Black Peter has lost the game.

Variables

Preliminary definitions of three rating variables were first formulated in a series of discussions with child psychologists and therapists. The definitions formulated in this way were tried out in the pilot study. Some modifications were made on the basis of the information obtained and on the opinions given by the raters in the pilot study. The variables used were the following:

Variable I: Ability to Follow the Rules of the Game
Variable II: Endurance and Concentration
Variable III: Reaction toward Frustration

Rating Procedures

Ratings were recorded on a graphic scale of a type originally constructed by Champney (1941 a, b) for use in interviews with parents ("The Fels Behavior

Rating Scale"). It has been revised by Richards and Simons (1941) for ratings of children of preschool age.

The scale consisting of a vertical line has verbal cues for different scale values. The rater has to mark anywhere on the scale the position judged to be correct for the subject. The positions on the scale for the verbal cues were empirically determined in a careful pre-experimental procedure carried out by six child psychologists who were not involved in the following experiment.

The games in the groups were led by one of the authors, who also organized and administered this experiment. While playing the children and she sat around a square table. Her role was to give the instructions and repeat them if necessary, and to lead in a flexible way the work of the children so as to give them the opportunity to show their behavior as freely as possible. The two observers also sat in the same room, visible to the children. The children were informed the day before the experiment that they were to play a game.

Each session took 40 minutes.

RESULTS

Agreement between Observers On the Same Occasion

As previously mentioned, two judges formed a rating team for each observational session. Agreement between the ratings made by the two judges was calculated as product-moment coefficients of correlation. The estimated coefficients obtained by the Spearman-Brown formula giving the expected values of the correlation between the mean ratings made by the two judges and mean ratings made by two other equivalent judges are reported in Table 6.

The fact that the coefficients in Table 6 refer to ratings made by two judges provides a natural explanation of the greater variation in these values than in the variation of the corresponding values for judges in Experiment I.

Table 6. Estimated Coefficients for the Reliability of Mean Ratings Given by Two Observers on the Same Occasion

	Task varied	
Group varied	No	Yes
No	I. 0.847	0.713
	II. 0.901	0.933
	III. 0.726	0.713
Yes	I. 0.895	0.693
	II. 0.961	0.658
	III. 0.870	0.773

Table 7. Coefficients for the Correlation between Mean Ratings Given by Two Observers on One Situation and Mean Ratings Given by Two Other Observers in Another Situation

Group varied	Task varied	
	No	Yes
No	I. 0.514	0.205
	II. 0.790	0.026
	III. 0.313	0.787
Yes	I. 0.767	0.103
	II. 0.595	−0.046
	III. 0.603	0.059

Variation in Ratings as an Effect of Variation in Situational Conditions

The mean of the two judges' ratings was used as the best available measure for each variable studied in each situation.

The coefficients of the correlation between the two series of ratings obtained for each variable were calculated for each treatment. They are given in Table 7.

The greater variation in these values than in the corresponding values for Experiment I must be seen in the light of the fact that they refer to the relation between means of two judges' ratings, while the coefficients in Experiment I are based on means of four judges' ratings.

As in Experiment I the coefficients for the correlation between ratings made on different occasions (Table 7) must be assessed in relation to the size of the correlation between ratings made on the same occasion (Table 6) for corresponding cells.

In these results the picture is not so unambiguous as in Experiment I. On one decisive point it shows complete agreement, however. This refers to the result for treatment D in comparsion with the coefficients for the other treatments. The coefficients in treatment D differ systematically from the coefficients in the other treatments, and in the same way as in Experiment I. Testing of significance with Fisher's z as a test variable gave the following results:

1. On the average, over all treatments there is positive correlation between ratings from the first observational session, and the ratings from the second observational session. The correlation differs significantly from 0 for each variable at the 1 per cent level.
2. Such a correlation is not present for any variable if, on the other observational occasion, both the task and the composition of the group are changed. For ratings in treatments A, B and C, the alternative hypothesis is

supported that it is possible to predict a person's behavior in one situation with some certainty on the basis of observations in another situation which is identical with or differing from the first one in respect to task or composition of group. When the variations in situational conditions are made for tasks and groups simultaneously, the null-hypothesis cannot be rejected that the data obtained in one situation are not valid for the other situation.

SUMMARY AND COMMENTS

The principal problem has been whether and to what extent data obtained in observations of behavior under given conditions are valid as expressions of the individual's behavior in other situations under other conditions. The results also may be discussed in connection with a closely related problem on another level: To what extent do situation factors, singly or in interaction with each other and the individual, determine behavior over and above the individual traits which may be valid over situations?

The problem has been investigated by studying the effects of variation of task and composition of group, separately and simultaneously, on ratings of behavior based on direct observations of individuals in group situations. Two experiments were carried out, one with ratings of conscripts in respect to the variables Cooperative Ability, Self-Confidence, and Leadership; and one with ratings of seven-year-old children on the variables Ability to Follow the Rules of the Game, Endurance and Concentration, and Reaction toward Frustration. The results obtained in these two experiments agree on the decisive points, which may be summarized as follows:

1. The correlation between ratings made by two independent teams of judges after observation on one occasion for each of the teams of judges, is significantly different from zero a) when the conditions are the same on the two occasions, b) when the variation in conditions refers to only the task, and c) when the variation in conditions refers to only the composition of the groups.
2. No systematic differences in relationships are present between these various treatments.
3. When the variation between the two observational sessions refers to the task and the composition of group simultaneously, the correlation is random between the ratings made by the two teams of judges who saw one situation each. For none of the three variables did the correlation exceed ± 0.10 in either of the experiments. The rating data obtained for treatment D thus show no generality at all.

The investigation was planned as a model experiment to test whether the main problem could be attacked in a meaningful way by varying the above-mentioned situation factors. The variation in the situational conditions was not made by a random selection of tasks or members of groups. Variation of task was thus studied for only two tasks in each of the experiments. In Experiment I, where both subjects and the other group members belonged to the same category of conscripts, the composition of groups was probably more homogeneous than it would otherwise have been, regardless of how a meaningful population is defined. This means that the interindividual variation in this experiment was reduced to an extent that cannot be estimated, which affects the possibilities of using the results as a basis for conclusions on the relative importance of the interindividual differences independent of situational conditions. On the other hand, the interindividual variation was large enough to produce very high agreement within the teams of judges, when the members rated the same behavior independently of each other. It should also be observed that the same random relationship between ratings from the two situations in treatment D was obtained in Experiment II, where school children, chosen randomly from unselected classes, were observed.

What may be regarded as the main result is summarized in point 3 above. Although the conditions reported earlier make care necessary in the generalization of the results, it must be pointed out that the results of two experiments with clearly different groups of individuals, different tasks, different rating variables and different situational conditions have otherwise given unambiguous results on this point. This circumstance may justify a discussion of the result in some of the contexts that may be of interest. Here the consequences of a completely random correlation between ratings made on different occasions, with variation of both task and composition of group will be touched upon (a) for the possibilities of using data from one observational session for diagnosis and prediction in applied psychology, (b) for a discussion of different definitions of reliability and measures of reliability, and (c) for discussions of individual, situational and interactional factors as determinants of behavior.

Diagnosis and Prediction

The results in treatment D, with variation of both task and composition of group, suggest that the rating data obtained by observations on one occasion are not valid for other situations when the conditions are changed considerably. Such a circumstance has important consequences for applied psychology, since the variables judged were chosen with, among other things, the intention that they were to be such as are used in applied psychology; in diagnosis, guidance, selection and classification. The result brings into focus the necessity of sampling observational situations in these contexts.

It must be stressed that the tentative conclusions on the possibilities of generalizing from data obtained at one observational session so far refer to ratings of observed behavior. Interview data also were collected on one occasion, but the results suggest that the data may possibly be generalized to refer to each of the observational situations lacking in mutual relationship. This result will be discussed later in another connection.

The Concept of Reliability

The results both from the ratings and the objectively measured variable, talk time, show drastically the deficiencies of the concept of reliability in its classic meaning. When data are to be evaluated, assessments of how reliably the instrument "measures what it measures" are based almost without exception on measures obtained by coefficients of internal consistency, coefficients of the correlation between scores from parallel tests, or test-retest coefficients. High coefficients are regarded as proof that the data have high reliability. In all these cases, the condition is that the calculations are made on data collected either on one occasion only, or in situations made as much alike as possible, which implies that the situational factors were invariant. In most situations, however, it is of little value to know how exactly an individual variable can be measured in a certain situation. The intention is rather to obtain a measure which holds for the individual independently of the situational conditions. The results reported in the present investigation suggest that traditional coefficients of reliability are of limited value in such cases. This holds especially when measures of inter-rater agreement are used as estimates of the reliability of ratings. There is reason to assume that discouraging results in different kinds of validation, where rating data have been used as predictors or criteria, often have as backgound an over-estimation of the value of high coefficients for inter-rater agreement. Instead, the results support such views and models as those advocated, among others, by Cronbach, Rajaratnam & Gleser (1963).

Interpretation of Specific Behavioral Responses

Ratings of behavior reveal a high degree of stability over occasions, when situational conditions are held constant or changed moderately, but vary randomly when situational conditions vary greatly. This supports the conclusion that situational conditions are of great importance for the behavior rated. Superficially the result may seem even to support the conclusion that no stable individual variation in behavior exists when the situational conditions are varied as in treatment D. But even when the shortcomings in the sampling of situations are ignored, such a conclusion cannot be drawn for another important reason. It is necessary to bear in mind that the main data are not direct expressions of behavior. Behavior has been interpreted, which presents an interpersonal perception problem. Let it be assumed that we take randomly two samples of responses by observing an individual in two different situations. It is quite possible that the individuals show, objectively, the same rank order in the two situations in respect to certain responses, e.g. in the time they talk, but that the correlation between ratings of variables of the type used in this investigation may still be negligible because each response occurs in (a) different contexts of behavior for the individual in the two situations, and (b) in the frames of reference of different situations which may give different total interpretations (cf. Asch's classic experiment, 1946).

An Interactional View of Behavior

In his conclusion about the problem of the relative importance of individual and situational factors Hunt states:

"Thus it is neither the individual differences among subjects, per se, nor the variations among situations, per se, that produce the variations in behavior. It is, rather, the interactions among these which are important". (1965, p. 83)

This view has earlier been advocated by psychological theorists, e.g. Brunswik (1956), Helson (1959), Lewin (1939), Mausner (1955), and Murphy (1947). The important interindividual variation is not in the stability of behavior in situations with different conditions, but in the change of type and degree of behavior in a consistent and specific way with changes in situational conditions. Then we must study the individual in more than one situation in order to obtain data which may be generally valid. The fact that interview ratings reveal some degree of generality, expressed in positive correlations with ratings from each of the observation situations, may be interpreted as support for such an interpretation of the zero coefficients for treatment D. An interview may be regarded as an observation of the respondent in a sample of situations in his previous life. Then the basis for judgments of the individual's behavior in these situations is given by the individual himself, together with the additional information that may be present in the way the respondent transmits the information.

Data also have been obtained for an objectively measured variable, talk time. When the situational conditions were changed as in treatment D, the predictable variance with respect to talk time was only about 17 per cent. Then it must be remembered that this variable can be measured directly almost without error, which means that the rest of the total variance can be attributed to situational and interactional factors. The results also indicate that for such behavior as can be regarded as an expression of the individual's general activity level, situational and interactional factors are of great importance.

Further Research

As already mentioned, the results emphasize the importance of paying more attention to situational and interactional factors in both predictions and clinical descriptions. This also implies, among other things, that the observation situations should be sampled in an adequate way for measurement in applied psychology. This brings important and partly new research tasks into the focus of interest; analyses of, for example, (a) which situational factors are of importance for variations in behavior, and (b) how these, in interaction with each other and with individual factors, contribute to the structuring of behavior in a given situation (see, e.g. Arnoult, 1963; Bellows, 1963; Forehand & Gilmer, 1964; Helson, 1964; Mausner, 1963; Sells, 1963). A systematic study of situational and interactional factors assumes sampling of situations as well as sampling of individuals.

The results reported here are of immediate interest for further research, both for the discussion of personality traits and situational variables, and for the discussion of interpersonal perception, in particular, how a valid perception of other people is built up. The results reported, however, say something only about the possibilities of generalizing from one observational situation. For both the application of the result in applied psychology and for the further enunciation of theories, (a) a replication of the experiments with another and more differentiated set of situations, and (b) a study of the generality of data as a function of the number of observational sessions are urgently needed.

REFERENCES

Abelson, R. P. Situational variables in personality research. In S. Messick and J. Ross (Eds.), *Measurement in Personality and Cognition*, New York: Wiley, 1962.

Arnoult, M. D. The specification of a "social" stimulus. In S. B. Sells (Ed.), *Stimulus Determinants of Behavior*. New York: Ronald Press, 1963, 16-30.

Asch, S. E. Forming impressions of personality. *Journal of Abnormal and Social Psychology*, 1946, *41*, 258-290.

Barker, R. G. Explorations in ecological psychology. *American Psychologist*, 1965, *20*, 1-14.

Bellows, R. Towards a taxonomy of social situations. In S. B. Sells (Ed.), *Stimulus Determinants of Behavior*. New York: Ronald Press, 1963, 197-212.

Bieri, J. Analyzing stimulus information in social judgments. In S. Messick and J. Ross (Eds.), *Measurement in Personality and Cognition*. New York: Wiley, 1962.

Bieri, J., Atkins, A. L., Briar, S., Leaman, R. L., Miller, H., and Tripodi, T. *Clinical and Social Judgment: The Discrimination of Behavioral Information*. New York: Wiley, 1966.

Brunswik, E. *Perception and the Representative Design of Psychological Experiments*. Berkeley: University of California Press, 1956.

Champney, H. The measurement of parent behavior. *Child Development*, 1941, *12*, 131-166.

Champney, H. The variables of parent behavior. *Journal of Abnormal and Social Psychology*, 1941, *36*, 525-542.

Cronbach, L. J., Rajaratnam, N., and Gleser, G. C. Theory of generalizability: A liberalization of reliability theory. *British Journal of Statistical Psychology*, 1963, *15*, 137-163.

Ebel, R. L. Estimation of the reliability of ratings. *Psychometrika*, 1951, *16*, 407-424.

Endler, N. S., Hunt, J. McV., and Rosenstein, A. J. An S-R inventory of anxiousness. *Psychological Monographs*, No. 17, Vol. 76, 1962.

Endler, N. S. and Hunt, J. McV. Sources of variance in reported anxiousness as measured by the S-R Inventory. *Psychological Bulletin*, 1966, *65*, 336-346.

Forehand, G. A. and Gilmer, B von H. Environmental variation in studies of organizational behavior. *Psychological Bulletin*, 1964, *62*, 361-382.

Freud, A. The concept of developmental lines. *The Psychoanalytic Study of the Child*. New York: International Universities Press, 1963.

Gibb, C. A. Leadership. In G. Lindzey, *Handbook of Social Psychology*. Vol. II. Reading, Mass.: Addison-Wesley, 1959.

Haythorn, W. The influence of individual members on the characteristics of small groups. *Journal of Abnormal and Social Psychology*, 1953, *48*, 276-284.

Helson, H. Current trends and issues in adaptation-level theory. *American Psychologist,* 1964, *19,* 26-38.

Helson, H. Adaptation-level theory. In S. Koch (Ed.), *Psychology: A Study of a Science.* Vol. 1. New York: McGraw-Hill, 1959, 565-621.

Hunt, J. McV. Traditional personality theory in the light of recent evidence. *American Scientist,* 1965, *53,* 80-96.

Lewin, K. Field theory and experiment in social psychology: Concepts and methods. *American Journal of Sociology,* 1939, *44,* 868-896.

Magnusson, D. The generality of behavioral data. Planning an investigation (Mimeographed prepublication.) Stockholm, 1965.

Mausner, B. Studies in social interaction: I. A conceptual scheme. *Journal of Social Psychology,* 1955, *41,* 259-270.

Mausner, B. The specification of the stimulus in a social interaction. In S. B. Sells (Ed.), *Stimulus Determinants of Behavior.* New York: Ronald Press, 1963, 107-116.

Miller, D. R. The study of social relationships: Situation, identity, and social interaction. In S. Koch (Ed.), *Psychology: A Study of a Science.* Vol. 5. New York: McGraw Hill, 1963, 639-737.

Murphy, G. *Personality: A Biosocial Approach to Origins and Structure.* New York: Harper & Row, 1947.

Peller, L. E. Models of children's play. *Mental Hygiene,* 1952, *36,* 66-83.

Philips, R. H. The nature and function of children's formal games. *Psychoanalytic Quarterly,* 1960, *29,* 200-207.

Piaget, J. *The Moral Judgment of the Child.* New York: Harcourt, 1932.

Redl, F. The impact of game ingredients on children's play behavior. In B. Schaggerer (Ed.), *Group Processes.* New York: Corlies, Macy & Comp., 1959.

Richards, T. W. and Simons, M. P. The Fels child behavior rating scales. *Genetic Psychology Monographs,* 1941, *24,* 259-309.

Sandell, R. G. The importance of attitudinal and situational factors in reported choice behavior. 1966. (Mimeographed prepublication.)

Sells, S. B. Dimensions of stimulus situations which account for behavior variance. In S. B. Sells (Ed.), *Stimulus Determinants of Behavior.* New York: Ronald Press, 1963, 3-15.

Sells, S. B. Dimensions of stimulus situations which account for behavior variance. Annual Progress Report, Institute of Behavioral Research, Texas Christian University, 1964.

Sherif, M. and Sherif, C. W. Varieties of social stimulus situations. In S. B. Sells (Ed.), *Stimulus Determinants of Behavior.* New York: Ronald Press, 1963, 82-106.

17

Situational Analysis of a Therapeutic Community Milieu

RUDOLF H. MOOS

The research reported here deals with one facet of the generality-specificity problem, that is, the problem of the consistency of different types of behavioral reactions across a variety of different settings. The attribution of a personality trait to an individual assumes some degree of consistency in that individual's trait across a variety of settings. For example, when an individual is described as dominant, the implicit assumption is that the individual will tend to be relatively consistently dominant in a variety of different settings. The results of several recent research investigations have been calling this general assumption into serious question.

One of the earliest and most widely cited series of studies bearing on this problem was that by Hartshorne and May (1928), which concluded that conflict between honest and deceitful behavior was quite specific to each situation, and that one could not generalize about a subject's (S's) honesty from a few samples of his behavior. Consistency of behavior from one situation to another, they concluded, was due to similarities in the situations and not to a consistent personality trait in people. The basis for their conclusions was that the correlations between the cheating tests they utilized were too low to provide evidence of a unified character trait of honesty or deceitfulness. These conclusions about honesty have been upheld by some (Allinsmith, 1960) and vigorously challenged by others (Allport, 1937; Burton, 1963; MacKinnon, 1938).

This general issue has been dealt with recently by several other investigators (Bolles, 1959; Endler & Hunt, 1966; Sells, 1963; Zinner, 1963). For example,

From the *Journal of Abnormal Psychology*, 1968, *73*, 49–61. Copyright 1968 by the American Psychological Association. Reprinted by permission.

The manuscript is based, in part, on a paper presented at the California State Psychological Association Convention, San Francisco, January 1966.

The author wishes to express his appreciation to the patients and staff who were kind enough to participate in this research, and to David Daniels, Katherine Baker, Martha Merk, and Bernice Moos for their help in various phases of the preparation of the manuscript.

Raush and his co-workers (Raush, Dittmann, & Taylor, 1959a, 1959b; Raush, Farbman, & Llewellyn, 1960) studied the social interactions of a group of preadolescent boys at two phases of residential treatment, a year and a half apart. They also studied the social interactions of a matched group of six normal boys. In each phase each child was observed twice in each of six life settings (breakfast, other meals, structured game activities, unstructured game activities, arts and crafts, and snacks at bedtime).

Results indicated that, on the one hand, the boys did differ from one another across a variety of situations; that is, individual behavior could be characterized as more or less aggressive, more or less dependent, more or less dominant, more or less friendly. On the other hand, however, the life settings also evoked characteristic patterns of social action, that is, settings were more or less competitive, more or less status-oriented, more or less friendly, more or less evocative of dependency. In general, then, there was individual consistency in social behavior across different settings and there was setting consistency across different individuals. Most importantly, the interactive effects between child and setting contributed far more information about behavior than did the sum of the independent components. The normal children tended to differentiate among the social settings more than did the disturbed children, and situational factors generally came to play a more potent role in behavior with treatment and maturation. These results argue very strongly for representative sampling of situations in studies of social behavior.

There have also been some questionnaire-oriented approaches to this problem. For example, Endler, Hunt, and Rosenstein (1962) presented a logical analysis of what different things might be meant by stating that one individual shows more of a given common trait than does another. This analysis suggested a new format for trait inventories which would sample separately responses, situations, and individual differences, and would thereby permit a formal investigation of their relative contributions to variance and of their interactions.

The authors attempted this for the trait of anxiety by asking their Ss to report, in a sample of 11 specific situations (e.g., "entering a final examination in an important course"), the degree to which they had manifested a sample of 14 modes of response commonly considered indicative of anxiety, for example, "heart beats faster," "get an uneasy feeling," "need to urinate frequently," and "mouth gets dry." When the authors did a three-way analysis of variance of these questionnaire reports, the largest mean square came from modes of response and the second largest mean square came from situations rather than from persons. In one sample the mean square for situations was somewhat more than 11 times that for persons.

When the authors estimated the percentage of variance accounted for by the different sources in three independent samples, they found that individual and setting differences each accounted for only between 5 and 10% of the total variance, whereas, the three first-order interactions (Individuals $\times$ Situations, Ss $\times$ Modes of Response, and Situations $\times$ Modes of Response) each accounted for approximately 5–15% of the total variance (Endler & Hunt, 1966). The modes of response contributed 20–25% of the variance and the second-order interaction contributed about 30–35%.

Thus, neither the individual differences among *S*s, per se, nor the variations among situations, per se, accounted for much of the variation in behavior; it was, rather, the interactions among *S*s, situations, and modes of response which were most important.

These results suggest that the assumption that most of the variation in behavior resides within the individual is very much open to question. In order to investigate this problem systematically, it is necessary to be able to study the reactions of each of a set of individuals in each of a variety of common everyday settings. How consistent are individual differences across various settings; that is, how much variance is accounted for by individual differences? On the other hand, how consistent is a particular group of settings in the reactions it "pulls" from a variety of individuals; that is, how much behavioral variance is accounted for by setting differences?

A psychiatric inpatient ward provides an excellent general milieu in which research relevant to these questions can be conducted, since it is relatively easy to study the reactions of each of a group of individuals in each of a variety of settings. A previous study conducted on a psychiatric inpatient ward, utilizing patient and staff diaries for data collection, indicated both that the patients and the staff had a tendency to react in a particular manner regardless of the setting (i.e., they possessed traits), and that the settings utilized tended to evoke a particular hierarchy of reactions regardless of whether patients or staff were responding in (Moos, Daniels, Zukowsky, Sassano, Hatton, Dueltgen, Beilin, & Moos, 1964). The study reported here is an extension of this previous work.

The major purpose of the present study was to investigate the reactions of patients and staff in a representative sample of daily settings in a psychiatric in-patient therapeutic community ward. The most important questions studied were:

1. What are the relative amounts of variance in behavior accounted for by settings, individual differences, modes of response, and their interactions? For example, to what extent do people react consistently across a representative sample of ward settings? To what extent do ward settings elicit consistent reactions regardless of the individual in the setting? To what extent is variance accounted for by an interaction between the individual and the setting?

2. How consistent are these relative amounts of variance for the patients and the staff? For example, are setting effects greater for the staff than for the patients? As mentioned above, some previous evidence has suggested that the relative amount of variance accounted for by settings may be greater for normals than for patients, thus implying that staff members may be expected to discriminate more among different ward settings than do patients.

3. How consistent are these relative amounts of variance for different categories of responses? For example, are setting effects greater for some categories of responses than for others?

METHOD

Settings and Subjects

The project was carried out on an open-door 30-patient research unit located in a large Verterans Administration hospital. The treatment was based in part upon patient responsibility, decision making, and self-regulation as a corrective experience within the framework of the ward community and the institution. In part it was based upon the exploration, understanding, and modification of behavior that interfered with productivity, self-maintainence, and satisfaction. Open communication in multidirectional pathways, qualified permissiveness, and active patient participation were encouraged.

At the time of the study, community meetings were held 5 days a week, whereas small group therapy was held 4 days a week. Individual therapy was formally arranged for most patients, but for some it centered around brief and informal contacts. The remainder of the treatment program consisted of recreational activities and various hospital workshop and industrial work assignments.

The patients were a representative sample of male veterans with diagnoses of neuropsychiatric disorder. The typical demographic characteristics of these men were as follows: they were in their 30s or early 40s, single, divorced, or in some way estranged from their families. They were of lower socioeconomic status and came from families with a large number of children. They usually had a high school education or less and had a low level of occupational skill or attainment. The men frequently had had rather long careers as mental patients, some having had several previous hospitalizations dating from World War II or the Korean War. Problems of high dependency, immaturity, limited ego strength, and social isolation were frequent.

The staff participating in the project included two nurses, two psychiatric technicians, three psychiatrists, two psychologists, and one social worker.

Procedure

Each of the 30 patients and each of the 10 staff members were asked to describe their reactions in a number of different everyday ward settings. These settings, which were chosen on the basis of the earlier diary study, which had been conducted on the same ward, are listed below.

1. Going to bed at night.
2. With a patient.
3. Staff rehash.
4. Community meeting.
5. Small group therapy.
6. Individual therapy.
7. Industrial therapy.
8. Alone.

9. With a nurse.
10. Getting up in the morning.
11. Lunch.

The settings were chosen in an attempt to sample systematically the different types of situations in which patients and staff participated. Not all the settings were equally relevant for both groups; for example, patients never participated in staff rehash, and thus were not asked to describe their reactions in that setting. In addition, some of the settings which occurred on the ward for the patients, for example, "Going to bed at night" and "Getting up in the morning," occurred off the ward for the staff. These differences between the two groups will be discussed more fully later.

The settings were each rated on 33 adjective pairs, for example, attentive-inattentive, friendly-hostile, outgoing-shy, sure-unsure, trusting-suspicious, relaxed-tense, etc. The adjective pairs had also been chosen on the basis of the earlier study in an attempt to cover systematically the different types of responses which patients and staff had described in their diaries.

Essentially then, each S was administered a semantic differential (entitled the Setting-Response Inventory–SRI) with 11 concepts (settings), and was asked to rate these settings on 33 adjective pairs, which comprised different reactions which that individual might have in the setting. The Ss were given the following directions:

On the following pages you are asked to describe your reactions or feelings in different kinds of situations. Below the name of each kind of situation you will find a list of 33 pairs of words to describe your reactions or feelings in that situation. This questionnaire is intended to get your feelings in a number of everyday ward and treatment program situations, therefore it is very important to record your feelings in the situations at the time you are in that situation. For example, one of the situations is getting up in the morning. You should check your feelings in the situation getting up in the morning right after getting up.

RESULTS

Both the patients and staff were generally able to complete the questionnaire adequately. In order to obtain sets of Ss in which each individual had checked his reactions in every setting, it was necessary to exclude some Ss and some settings from this phase of the data analysis. For patients it was necessary to exclude the settings of staff rehash (none of the patients participated in this setting) and community meeting (several of the patients had not participated in the community meeting during the particular 2-day period in which the questionnaire had been administered). These exclusions left 9 settings, and there were 22 patients who had described their reactions in each of these 9 settings. For staff, it was necessary to exclude the settings of small group therapy and individual therapy, since only about half of the staff members had participated in these settings. These exclusions left 9 settings, and all 10 of the staff meembers had described their reactions in each of these 9 settings.

Table 1. Adjective Factors on SRI with Sets of
Defining Adjective Pairs and Factor Loadings

Factor	Adjective pair	Factor loading
I	Trusting-Suspicious	.75
	Approving-Disapproving	.72
	Useful-Useless	.68
II	Outgoing-Shy	.61
	Extroverted-Introverted	.56
	Independent-Dependent	.50
III	Secure-Insecure	.48
	Sure-Unsure	.45
	Strong-Weak	.31
IV	Involved-Uninvolved	.61
	Attentive-Inattentive	.30
	Energetic-Tired	.24
V	Sociable-Unsociable	.26
	Friendly-Hostile	.25
	Peaceful-Angry	.25

The adjective intercorrelations based on the remaining data were calculated and then factor analyzed by the principal-components method, and five rotated factors were obtained by an orthogonal rotation of the factor matrix. The five rotated factors, which accounted for over 85% of the total variance, are shown in Table 1, together with the three adjective pairs which showed the highest loadings on each factor.

An analysis of variance was then conducted, separately for patients and for staff, for each set of adjective pairs. With this technique it was possible to specify, for each of the sets of adjective pairs (i.e., for each response factor), the amount of variance accounted for by individuals, by settings, by responses, and by their interactions.

Table 2 summarizes the analysis-of-variance results for the patients for each of the five factors considered.[1]

The results indicate that there is significant between-patient variance for all five of the sets of adjective pairs and significant between-settings variance for two

---

[1] The analysis of variance employed a model which assumed that each of the three sources of variance was sampled randomly, even though this was not strictly the case. However, as Endler, Hunt, and Rosenstein (1962) have pointed out, the setting-response format for personality inventories has, as one of its chief advantages, the potential for randomly sampling all three sources of variance. Furthermore, in these particular analyses, statistically significant results for individual-difference and setting-difference effects generally would be obtained using a model in which, for example, the sampling of settings and Ss was assumed to be random and the sampling of responses was assumed to be fixed. In any case, the statistical significance of these results is considered to be less important than either the results relevant to the proportions of variance accounted for by the different sources of variance or the reproducibility of the results on other samples. The analyses-of-variance calculations utilized for the F tests follow those discussed by Winer (1962). In a three-way random model, in which the interactions cannot be pooled, quasi F ratios with estimated degrees of freedom for both numerator and denominator must be calculated. The appropriate formulas may be found on pages 199–202 in Winer.

Table 2. Summary of Analyses of Variance for Patients

Source	df	Factors									
		I		II		III		IV		V	
		MS	F	MS	F	MS	F	MS	F	MS	F
Between patients	21	48.03	10.74**	36.15	7.69**	33.38	6.27**	32.30	3.75**	33.65	6.37**
Between settings	8	7.27	1.58	3.68	1.30	10.74	2.14*	11.00	1.83	10.86	2.73**
Between responses	2	4.52	1.53	6.67	1.34	7.88	2.91	86.06	9.96**	7.68	1.94
Patients × Settings	168	3.83	2.49**	2.45	1.06	4.59	2.94**	3.74	2.51**	3.24	2.75**
Patients × Responses	42	2.18	1.42	4.57	1.97**	2.29	1.47*	6.37	4.28**	3.22	2.73**
Settings × Responses	16	2.31	1.50	2.71	1.17	1.98	1.27	3.76	2.52**	1.92	1.63
Residual	336	1.54		2.32		1.56		1.49		1.18	
Total	593										

* $p < .05$.
** $p < .01$.

of the sets. There is also a significant Patients × Settings interaction for four of the response sets, a significant Patients × Responses interaction for four of the sets, and a significant Settings × Responses interaction for one set.

Table 3 summarizes the analysis-of-variance results for the staff for each of the five factors considered.

These results indicate that there is significant between-staff-members variance for three of the sets of adjective pairs and significant between-settings variance for four of the sets. In addition, there is significant Staff × Settings interaction for all five of the response sets, significant Staff × Responses interaction for three sets, and significant Settings × Responses interaction for four sets.

Table 4 summarizes the relative percentages of total variance accounted for by each source of variance for patients and staff for each of the response factors.[2]

---

[2] The percentages of variance accounted for by each source of variance were calculated for this random-effects analysis-of-variance model utilizing the rationale and equations given by Gleser, Cronbach, and Rajaratnam (1965) and Endler (1966). These authors have pointed out that the analysis-of-variance technique can be used to estimate the relative magnitude of each individual component of variance, expressed as a percentage of the sum of the different variance components. The general logic of this technique involves breaking the expected mean squares into their various variance components and solving separately for each component.

Table 3. Summary of Analyses of Variance for Staff

Source	df	Factors									
		I		II		III		IV		V	
		MS	F	MS	F	MS	F	MS	F	MS	F
Between staff	9	5.79	2.84**	9.43	2.53*	5.19	1.75	4.05	1.15	8.64	3.38**
Between settings	8	9.00	2.17*	9.65	3.15**	4.48	1.15	26.04	8.01**	12.79	3.43**
Between responses	2	3.08	.96	29.22	12.49**	8.95	3.01	31.14	18.99**	5.47	1.84
Staff × Settings	72	1.98	2.04**	2.56	3.76**	2.29	3.27**	2.98	3.55**	2.03	2.71**
Staff × Responses	18	1.03	1.06	1.84	2.71**	1.38	1.97*	1.37	1.63	1.28	1.71*
Settings × Responses	16	3.14	3.24**	1.18	1.74*	2.29	3.27**	1.11	1.32	2.45	3.27**
Residual	144	.97		.68		.70		.84		.75	
Total	269										

* $p < .05$.
** $p < .01$.

Table 4. Summary of Percentage of Total Variance
Accounted for by each Source of Variance

Source	Factors				
	I	II	III	IV	V
Patients					
Between individuals	39.56	30.45	27.15	20.80	31.82
Between settings	.98	.26	2.35	1.89	3.03
Between responses	.25	.26	.78	9.22	.61
Individuals × Settings	18.67	1.05	26.37	17.73	20.91
Individuals × Responses	1.72	6.56	2.09	12.77	6.97
Settings × Responses	.98	.52	.52	2.36	.91
Residual	37.84	60.89	40.73	35.22	35.76
Staff					
Between individuals	7.14	9.46	4.88	.73	11.68
Between settings	8.79	9.91	1.22	27.64	15.23
Between responses	.00	13.51	4.27	12.00	1.52
Individuals × Settings	18.68	28.38	32.32	25.82	21.83
Individuals × Responses	.00	5.86	4.88	2.18	3.05
Settings × Responses	12.09	2.25	2.36	1.09	8.63
Residual	53.30	30.63	35.22	30.55	38.07

There are several conclusions which may be drawn from these results: (*a*) Individual differences between patients account for considerably more of the variance (20–40%) than individual differences between staff members (1–12%). Individual differences between patients account for a higher percentage of variance than do individual differences between staff on each of the five response sets. (*b*) Individual differences between patients account for considerably more of the variance than setting differences for patients. Again, individual differences between patients account for a higher percentage of variance than setting differences for each of the five response sets. (*c*) Individual differences between staff, on the other hand, generally account for somewhat less of the variance than setting differences for staff. This is the case for four of the five response sets. (*d*) Setting differences for staff members generally account for more of the variance than setting differences for patients. Again, this is the case for four of the five response sets. (*e*) The Individuals × Settings interaction effect, with only one exception, accounts for a significant and important percentage of total variance in the patient and staff analyses. For patients, the Individuals × Settings interactions account for between 1 and 26% of the variance, and for staff they account for between 18 and 32% of the variance. (*f*) The Individuals × Responses and Settings × Responses interaction effects both consistently account for smaller, but mostly still statistically significant, proportions of the total variance. The percentage of variance associated with general differences between the different responses in any one response set is also rather small, although it was statistically significant in three instances. These results are probably due to the fact that the response pairs were chosen from responses which were highly intercorrelated. (*g*) The residual variation accounted for between 30 and 60% of the total variance, with the average variance accounted for being around 30–35%. The residual variation is composed of both second-order interaction variance (Individuals × Settings × Responses) and error variance. Since each *S* checked his response on each adjective pair in each setting only once, there is no independent measure of error variance, and therefore the error and second-order interaction

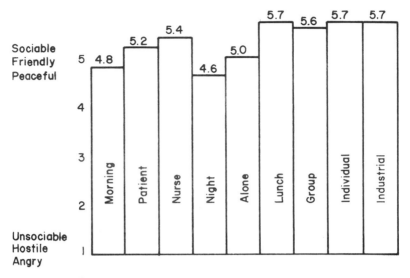

Fig. 1. Average setting scores for patients on Factor V.

variance are confounded. (*b*) The relative percentage of variance accounted for by any particular source of variance varies rather widely depending upon the particular individuals (patients or staff) and the particular set of responses analyzed.

The data for the set of adjective pairs on Factor V will be presented in detail in order to illustrate these results more fully. Figures 1 and 2, which show,

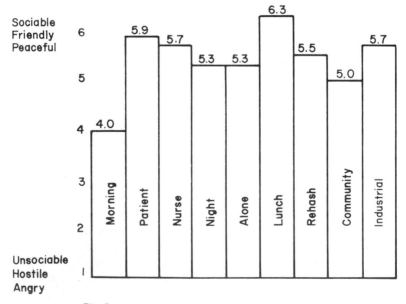

Fig. 2. Average setting scores for staff on Factor V.

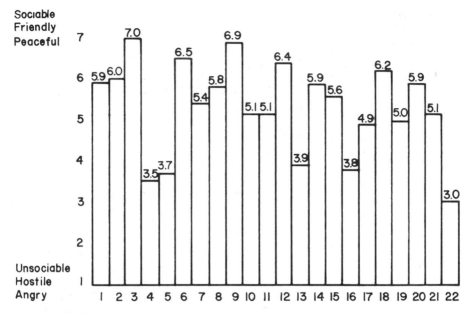

Fig. 3. Average individual scores for each of the 22 patients on Factor V.

respectively, the data for patients and staff, indicate that patients tend to make fewer distinctions between settings than do staff. The variation for the patients is from an average score of 4.6 in the setting going to bed at night to an average score of 5.7 in the settings lunch, individual therapy, and industrial therapy, whereas for the staff, the variation is from an average score of 4.0 in the setting getting up in the morning to an average score of 6.3 in the setting lunch. These figures illustrate that staff show greater differences between settings than do patients.

Figures 3 and 4, on the other hand, which show, respectively, the data for the patients and staff, indicate that individual differences between the patients are much greater than individual differences between the staff.

Figures 5 and 6 give examples of the Individuals X Settings interaction for the patients and staff. In Figure 5 curves are plotted for selected patients for the three settings of lunch, group therapy, and individual therapy. The interaction effect may be illustrated by observing that Patient 21 feels much more sociable in individual therapy than in group therapy, whereas Patient 13 reacts in exactly the reverse manner; that is, he feels much more sociable in group therapy than in individual therapy.

In Figure 6 curves are plotted for selected staff for the three settings of being with a nurse, being with a patient, and community meeting. The Individual X Setting interaction effect may be illustrated by observing that Staff Member 46 feels more sociable during community meeting than when with a nurse, whereas

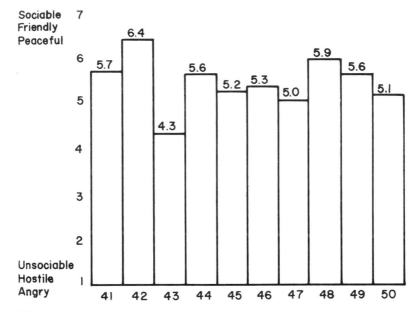

Fig. 4. Average individual scores for each of the 10 staff members (numbered 41–50) on Factor V.

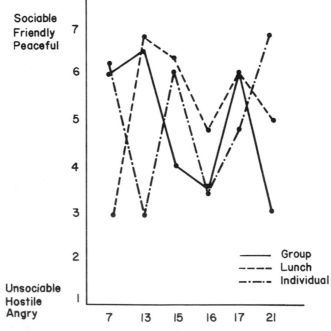

Fig. 5. Example of Patient X Setting interaction on Factor V for 6 selected patients.

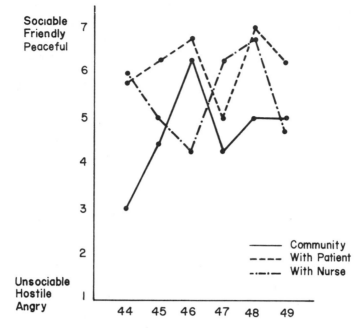

Fig. 6. Example of Staff X Setting interaction on Factor V for 6 selected staff members.

Staff Member 44 reacts the reverse, feeling more sociable when with a nurse than during community meeting.

More detailed examples of these and other specific interaction effects will be presented in a later paper.

DISCUSSION

The results clearly indicate that, in general, individuals, settings, and Individual X Setting interactions account for statistically significant and important proportions of variance.

For the patients, individual differences were significant for all five of the response sets, setting differences were significant for two sets, and Patient X Setting interactions were significant for four sets. Individual differences between patients accounted for considerably more variance on all five of the response sets than did setting differences; that is, settings did not elicit consistently different reactions from patients. This implies that there is very little that one can say about how patients will feel on these response dimensions from knowledge of the particular setting alone.

On the other hand, the interaction between patients and settings accounted for relatively large proportions of the total variance on four of the response sets. This result implies exactly what clinicians have always been emphasizing, that is, that different individuals react differentially to different settings. It also suggests that the setting is important not necessarily because it elicits the same reactions across all patients, but rather because it elicits different reactions in different patients, different reactions which cannot be accurately predicted from knowing only the general response tendencies of the patient.

For the staff, individual differences were statistically significant for three of the five response sets, setting differences were significant for four sets, and Patient X Setting interactions were significant for all five sets. Individual differences between staff generally accounted for less of the total variance than did consistent differences between settings. For the staff, then, setting differences were relatively more important in accounting for total variance than were individual differences. To some extent, settings did elicit consistently different reactions from all staff members. This implies that there are predictions about how staff will react which may be made solely on the basis of knowledge of the particular setting they are in.

As with the patients, the interaction between staff and settings accounted for relatively large proportions of the total variance. Again, this result implies what some personality theorists have long been emphasizing, that is, that different people react differentially to different settings. For staff, it suggests that the setting is important partly because it elicits the same reactions across all staff members, and, even more importantly, because it elicits different reactions in different staff members, different reactions which cannot be accurately predicted from knowing only the characteristic responses of the staff members. Settings may elicit consistent reactions from all the staff; however, individual staff members also react differently to different settings.

The patients showed significant Individual X Response interactions for four response sets and the staff for three sets, suggesting that individual patients and staff have consistent tendencies to react with one of the response modes rather than another. Even within one "trait," then, there are significant individual differences in the tendency to respond with different response indicators of that trait. For example, one patient may feel generally very shy but not very dependent, whereas another patient may feel generally very dependent but not very shy.

The patients showed significant Setting X Response interactions for only one response set, whereas the staff showed significant Setting X Response interactions for four of the sets. A Settings X Response interaction effect occurs when some settings tend to elicit one response indicator of a particular trait whereas other settings tend to elicit another response indicator of that same trait. For example, the staff in general felt much more "useful" than "trusting" or "approving" in the settings with a patient and with a nurse, whereas they felt much more "trusting" and "approving" than "useful" in the setting lunch.

Unfortunately, in these analyses, the Individual X Setting X Response variance cannot be separated from the error variance, since each individual only responded once to each item in the setting. The second-order interaction and error together accounted for quite large percentages of the variance in each analysis. These percentages ranged from 35 to 60% for the patients and from 30 to 50% for the staff. The second-order interaction effect appears to have both important psychological meaning and to be practically important for prediction purposes. For example, a patient may not usually be shy, nor need he even usually be dependent or introverted; when he is interacting with a nurse, however, he may feel particularly shy.

These results are generally consistent with both our own earlier results and those of other investigators. In our earlier diary study the results had shown that both patients and staff reacted consistently across settings and that settings tended to have consistent "pull" for particular reactions across both patients and staff.

Both Raush et al. (1959a, 1959b, 1960) and Endler et al. (1962, 1966) have found that both individuals and settings contribute significantly to overall behavioral variance. It is very important to note their conclusions about interaction effects. Raush et al. concluded that interactions between the child and the setting were far more important in accounting for individual reactions than either the child or the setting alone. Endler and Hunt (1966) found, in three different samples, that about 10% of their total variance was due to the S X Situation interaction, and that the three simple interactions combined (S X Situation, S X Response, and Situation X Response) contributed an estimated one-third of the total variation. In the present study, for patients, the three simple interactions accounted for between 8 and 33% of the total variance, and for staff, they accounted for between 30 and 40% of the total variance. Clearly, the simple interactions can be very important. For example, in four of the five staff analyses the Individual X Setting interaction accounted for a greater percentage of the variance than either consistent individual differences or consistent differences between settings.

Individual differences between patients accounted for a much greater proportion of variance than individual differences between staff members. This was true for all five response sets. Setting differences, on the other hand, accounted for a greater proportion of staff variance than of patient variance for four of the five response sets. Thus, consistent individual differences between patients contribute more information about patients than consistent individual differences between staff members do about staff. Conversely, the staff as a whole varies its reactions much more from setting to setting than do the patients as a whole. These results are consistent with those of Raush et al., who found that normal children showed greater differences between settings than disturbed children. They also found that when disturbed children improved clinically, they also showed greater setting effects; that is, more of their behavior was determined by the setting and they were more able to vary their behavior according to the setting.

Even though there is some consistency with Raush et al.'s results, the differences between patients and staff shown here must be interpreted with caution. This is because the sampling of settings represented a greater variety of settings for the staff than they did for the patients. For the patients, all of the settings actually took place on the ward, whereas for the staff some of the settings took place on the ward and others took place off the ward, for example, "Going to bed at night," "Lunch," "Getting up in the morning." Thus, staff might have shown greater setting variance because the sample of settings represented a greater variety for them than they did for the patients. The patients were always responding in one role, that is, the role of patient, whereas the staff was responding part of the time in other roles. Unfortunately, with the existing data, it is not possible to compare patient and staff variability in the same settings in order to obtain some empirical evidence on this question, because there are only three settings which both patients and staff responded to which are also role related for both patients and staff.

In any case, this consideration suggests the possibility that patients (and possibly staff) may show less variability in different settings related to the same role than in settings in which they play different roles. When an individual assumes a role, this may decrease the variability of response he shows in different settings related to that role. Even though this might be the case, it is also possible that, in addition, patients show less setting variability than staff, and sicker patients show less setting variability than healthier patients. Further work is needed in this area.

The results also indicate that there is a large amount of variation in the percentages of variance attributable to the different sources depending upon the particular response set analyzed. Part of this variation is probably due to sampling variations, and part to consistent differences between different response modes. For example, both the staff and the patients show a greater proportion of variance accounted for by individual differences on Response Set 1 than on Response Set 4. It is certainly conceivable that certain response modes ("traits") might consistently be more a function of the individual than the setting, or vice versa.

There is very little evidence which bears on this point. Endler and Hunt found the percentages of variance in anxiety attributable to different sources highly consistent across three different samples of college students. They are currently working on a hostility test and they will be able to compare the percentages of variance related to different sources of variance for anxiety and hostility.

Raush et al. analyzed both affectional behavior and status behavior in normal and disturbed boys. Their results suggest that joint individual and setting effects were greater for affectional behavior than for status behavior in both groups. This was also true for general effects of individual and setting variables on behavior; that is, the reduction in the uncertainty of the behavior classification through information from individual-difference or setting sources was greater for affectional than for status behavior for both groups of boys. These results taken together suggest that the hypothesis that different sources of variance account for different percentages of variance in different traits is worth further empirical investigation.

There are many important implications of these results. The relative amount of variance accounted for by individuals, settings, responses, and their interactions varies importantly depending upon the particular sample of individuals, settings, and responses which have been chosen for detailed study. This suggests that the old question of whether individual differences or social situations are more important in determining behavior reactions has no clear-cut answer. It depends upon the particular sample of settings and individuals under study. The question of whether one is more important than the other is meaningless in any absolute sense. If the investigator is interested in individual differences, then the variance related to individual differences is more important to him. If, on the other hand, the investigator is concerned with differentiating among settings, then the variance attributable to setting differences is more important for him.[3]

Raush et al. (1959) came to a similar conclusion and stated that "in general, there is individual consistency in social behavior across different settings and there is setting consistency across different individuals [p. 375]." Endler and Hunt similarly conclude that the issue of whether variance from settings is greater than variance from individuals is a pseudo-issue, primarily because, in their analyses, the simple interactions accounted for more of the variance than either individual or setting differences alone.

The consistently high percentage of variance accounted for by the Individual X Setting interactions also has great potential practical significance. One aspect of a process of treatment or education is to learn how situations can be geared toward maximizing particular behavioral potentials for particular individuals; there have been only a few systematic studies, however, which have investigated the macroscopic settings of daily life and their influence on behavior (Barker, 1963; Barker & Gump, 1964). As part of any milieu treatment process, it is important to investigate how different ward settings can be geared toward maximizing particular behavioral potentials in particular patients. Most of the knowledge about general environmental influences and their interactions with individual behavior potentials has developed anecdotally from practical clinical experience, but has not been subjected to systematic empirical evaluation. For example, the staff spends a great deal of time planning for individually tailored changes in a therapeutic community milieu for individual patients, and a large amount of staff time and discussion usually goes into debating whether or not the proposed changes are advisable; however, there has been little investigation of the efficacy of this type of planning. If individual reactions really do depend importantly on the interaction between the individual and the particular setting to which he is exposed, then the value of these types of studies is potentially very great.

The importance of this type of analysis for measurement and prediction is at least as great as its importance for therapy and therapeutic practices. If individual

---

[3] B. I. Engel and R. H. Moos, The generality of specificity. Unpublished manuscript, 1965.

differences really account for only an average of 20% of the variance in behavior, then it is not surprising that the validity coefficients of tests assessing personality traits fall in the range of .20–.50. Endler and Hunt have discussed this issue and have concluded, using the square of these validity coefficients as an estimate of the proportion of variance contributed by individual differences, that these proportions are generally between 4 and 25% of the total. The implications clearly call for measurement procedures which systematically sample not only individuals, but which also systematically sample settings and modes of response.

Endler et al. (1962) have suggested that it would be fruitful to be able to categorize settings and responses into types and to make predictions about individual behavior in terms of specific types of responses which might occur in specific types of settings. This suggests the possibility of attempting to categorize and type ward settings on important dimensions and to study the reactions of individual patients in these ward-setting types.

Discussion of further possible implications of these results should properly await replication both by questionnaire and by naturalistic observational methods. The extent to which results would be replicated if the data utilized were observations of actual behavior in different settings is exceedingly important. It is possible that patients are not as aware as staff members of the degree to which their responses vary from setting to setting. On the other hand, staff members might believe that their behavior varies more from setting to setting than it actually does. It is also possible that setting variations would be consistently greater or consistently less when actual behavior is observed, rather than when responses are obtained by questionnaire.

Other potentially fruitful areas suggest themselves. What are the types of settings which tend to elicit consistent reactions across certain types of individuals? What are the types of settings which tend especially to facilitate behavioral change? In any case it appears quite clear that the relatively neglected area of the contribution of everyday settings to behavioral reactions needs greater attention. Not only individuals, but also settings and particular indicator responses must be sampled in attempts to measure and predict individual behavior.

REFERENCES

Allinsmith, W. The learning of moral standards. In D. R. Miller & G. E. Swanson (Eds.), *Inner conflict and defense.* New York: Holt, 1960, Pp. 141-176.

Allport, G. *Personality, a psychological interpretation.* New York: Holt, 1937.

Barker, R. G. (Ed.) *The stream of behavior.* New York: Appleton-Century-Crofts, 1963.

Barker, R. G., & Gump, P. V. *Big school, small school.* Stanford: Stanford University Press, 1964.

Bolles, R. C. Group and individual performance as a function of intensity and kind of deprivation. *Journal of Comparative and Physiological Psychology,* 1959, **52**, 579-585.

Burton, R. V. Generality of honesty reconsidered. *Psychological Review,* 1963, **70**, 481–499.

Endler, N. S. Estimating variance components from mean squares for random and mixed effects analysis of variance models. *Perceptual and Motor Skills,* 1966, **22**, 559-570.

Endler, N. S., & Hunt, J. McV. Sources of behavioral variance as measured by the S-R Inventory of Anxiousness. *Psychological Bulletin,* 1966, **65,** 336–346.

Endler, N. S., Hunt, J. McV., & Rosenstein, A. J. An S-R Inventory of Anxiousness. *Psychological Monographs,* 1962, **76**(17, Whole No. 536).

Gleser, G. C., Cronbach, L. J., & Rajaratnam, N. Generalizability of scores influenced by multiple sources of variance. *Psychometrika,* 1965, **30,** 395–418.

Hartshorne, H., & May, M. A. *Studies in deceit.* Vol. 1. New York: Macmillan, 1928.

MacKinnon, D. W. Violation of prohibition. In H. A. Murray (Ed.), *Explorations in personality.* New York: Oxford University Press, 1938. Pp. 491–501.

Moos, R. H., Daniels, D. N., Zukowsky, E., Sassano, M., Hatton, J., Dueltgen, A., Beilin, L., & Moos, B. S. The ecological assessment of behavior in a therapeutic community. *International Journal of Social Psychiatry,* Special Congress Ed., No. 1, 1964, 87–96.

Raush, H. L., Dittmann, A. T., & Taylor, T. J. The interpersonal behavior of children in residential treatment. *Journal of Abnormal and Social Psychology,* 1959, **58,** 9–26. (a)

Raush, H. L., Dittmann, A. T., & Taylor, T. J. Person, setting and change in social interaction. *Human Relations,* 1959, **12,** 361–378. (b)

Raush, H. L., Farbman, I., & Llewellyn, L. G. Person, setting and change in social interaction: II. A normal control study. *Human Relations,* 1960, **13,** 305–332.

Sells, S. B. (Ed.) *Stimulus determinants of behavior.* New York: Ronald Press, 1963.

Winer, B. J. *Statistical principles in experimental design.* New York: McGraw-Hill, 1962.

Zinner, L. The consistency of human behavior in various situations: A methodological application of functional ecological psychology. Unpublished doctoral disseration, University of Houston, 1963.

18

Sources of Behavioral Variance during Leisure Time

DOYLE W. BISHOP and PETER A. WITT

Several recent studies by Endler and his colleagues (Endler & Hunt, 1966, 1968; Endler, Hunt, & Rosenstein, 1962) have dealt with the general problem of sources of behavioral variability due to the situation, personality, and type of response.

The two kinds of behavior that they dealt with were hostility and anxiety. Endler et al. (1962; Endler & Hunt, 1968) have shown that hostility and anxiety cannot be adequately characterized by emphasizing either the situation (as many sociologically oriented theorists are prone to do) or the personality (as many personologists do). Instead, the studies by Endler and others suggest that hostility and anxiety can be adequately understood only if we take into account the type of response that a type of individual makes to a type of situation. In other words, hostility and anxiety are complex functions of the three factors—situations, personalities, and responses.

Recent articles by Endler and Hunt (1968, 1969) have also indicated that the relative proportions of variance in reported behavior that are attributable to persons, situations, modes of response, and their interactions differ for the hostility and anxiety domains, and to a lesser degree for males and females. It appears, then, that statements about the relative contributions of sources of behavioral variance will have to be qualified to note the *kinds* of behavior, subjects, and (the investigators might guess) situations that one is investigating.

The present research used the Endler et al. (1962) methods to investigate a domain of behavior that the investigators believe to be quite different from anxiety or hostility. The main purpose was to compare the relative contributions of sources of variance in anxiety and hostility found by Endler et al. (1962;

From the *Journal of Personality and Social Psychology*, 1970, *16*, 352–360. Copyright 1970 by the American Psychological Association. Reprinted by permission.

This study was supported in part by a grant from the Title III Higher Education Act—Kentucky Project, Terry O'Banion, principal investigator, and in part by a grant from the University of Illinois Research Board, and from National Institute of Mental Health Grant MH 17913, D. W. Bishop, principal investigator.

Endler & Hunt, 1968) to those obtained when leisure-time responses were the focus of investigation. The emphasis, then, was on greater knowledge of how much we can generalize about sources of behavioral variance across different domains of behavior. Leisure was regarded as contrasting domain of behavior because it usually involves more pleasant emotions than hostility and anxiety. In addition, its various response forms are probably normally considered less socially undesirable or pathological than are many responses indicating hostility or anxiety.

A second reason for studying leisure behavior was to compare the variance due to the Persons X Modes of Leisure Response interaction with that due to the Situations X Modes of Response interaction. This comparison was stimulated by two classical viewpoints about leisure behavior which roughly categorize leisure theorists into "personologists" and "situationists." The first of these, which comes close to the classic Aristotelian view of leisure, tends to regard leisure as being free, unobligated behavior; leisure is activity engaged in for its own sake or as its own end, and is relatively unaffected by specific events or needs. Leisure responses are considered "free" for a number of reasons, the major ones being that (a) they are not required for biological survival (e.g., in contrast to eating, sleeping, etc.), (b) they are not culturally or socially necessary in order for an individual to function in a society (e.g., in contrast to work which often involves economic, social, and even religious sanctions), and (c) they are less controlled by specific normative and role requirements or expectations than are other kinds of behavior (e.g., family obligations, professional duties, etc.). (See DeGrazia, 1962, and Berlyne, 1969, for further discussions of this view of leisure.)

In short, this view has emphasized that many physical and social prescriptions or proscriptions (i.e., situational events or experiences) do not influence a person's leisure responses. Rather, the emphasis has been on leisure responses being "free choices" and being part of the individual's personality style, or at least determined by personality traits such a social extroversion. It is also assumed, however, that leisure behavior is not unitary, and that a given individual will include several specific activities in his repertoire and exclude others. But the set of activities preferred by one individual will be different from that preferred by another. For present data this implies a strong Persons X Modes of Leisure Response interaction.

The contrasting, "situational" views of leisure have often been proposed by some sociologists, professional recreationists, and occasionally medical doctors (cf. Hagedorn & Labovitz, 1968; Hahn, 1965; Sapora & Mitchell, 1961). There are various theories of play and leisure that represent this situational category; among the more prominent ones are the relaxation, surplus energy, catharsis, compensation, and task generalization theories. These theories differ on the antecedents to leisure responses which they propose; they are alike, however, in implying that some situational event or set of events induce a need state that can be satisfied by appropriate leisure responses (e.g., the relaxation theory proposes that a person will seek out relaxing, nonstrenuous activities after being in fatiguing situations). These theories are essentially S-R theories in a broad sense. None of them is very precise, however, about the stimuli or responses that it predicts. These theories obviously do not regard leisure behavior as unitary, since they predict that only certain kinds of leisure responses will follow as a consequence of the prior situation. Thus, given information about a variety of situations representing these theories and a variety of leisure responses that could be made to each, a strong Situation X Mode of Response interaction would be predicted.

This study sought further evidence on the above two major views of leisure behavior by comparing the proportions of variance for the Persons X Modes of Response and Situations X Modes of Response interactions. A strong Persons X Modes of Response interaction but weak Situations X Modes of Response interaction would be consistent with the "freedom" view of leisure, which implies personal idiosyncracies in leisure response patterns. The reverse outcome would favor the situational views of leisure, which tend to disregard individual differences. Obviously, it is possible for both views to be partly supported by large Persons X Modes of Response and Situations X Modes of Response variances. Also, a large Persons X Situations X Modes of Response variance might indicate a need to incorporate the two views to take account of personal idiosyncracies in specific situations. These possibilities were the focus of the second part of this investigation. The Method section describes in more detail the selection of situations and responses and elaborates on the situational views of leisure.

To summarize, this study (a) investigated the relative proportions of variance associated with persons, situations, modes of response, and their interactions for leisure as compared to anxiety and hostility behavior and (b) compared the Person X Modes of Leisure Response and the Situations X Modes of Leisure Response interaction variances. The authors investigated the responses that individuals said they would make during their leisure time as a consequence of having been in various imagined situations. The data obtained were in the form of a three-dimensional matrix, the three dimensions corresponding to persons, situations, and modes of response. The responses were choices of leisure activities. The form of the data, then, was exactly like that of Endler and Hunt (1968), whereas the content was substantially different. The comparisons of sources of variance for leisure, anxiety, and hostility behavior were done separately for males and females because of the sex differences reported by Endler and Hunt (1968).

METHOD

Subjects

Two different samples of subjects were used in order to gain some information about the generality of the present results and their relationship to those of Endler et al. (1962). The first sample consisted of a class of 49 students in an introductory recreation course at the University of Illinois. There were 16 males and 33 females. The second sample consisted of 91 students from a relatively new junior college in Kentucky. There were 33 males and 58 females.

In neither sample, as far as the investigators could tell from registration data, were many of the students similar in terms of declared or anticipated major or home background factors, such as socioeconomic status. The authors do not know whether there are differences between the samples on intellectual factors, such as aptitude for college. From the authors' general knowledge of the two samples, they doubt that there are any striking differences in this area.

Leisure Behavior Inventory

The Situation X Leisure Response inventory was a 10-page questionnaire. On the front of the questionnaire, following a general introduction, the subject was given the following instructions:

Imagine that you have been in or experienced each of the situations on the following pages. Then for each situation, indicate how much you would feel like doing *each* of the listed activities by marking the accompanying scale. You can assume that such factors as the weather, season, availability of facilities, etc., do not inhibit participation in any activity. In other words, indicate what you think you would do, assuming that you could do it.

These instructions were followed by an illustrative situation and an example of how a person might mark the scales. Each of the situations was described on a separate page, followed by the statement, "Having had this experience (or one like it)." This statement was followed by the list of 11 (Illinois) or 13 (Kentucky) activities beside each of which was a five-position scale. The five scale positions were labeled near the top of the list, such that the labels were beside the statement in quotation marks given above. The five scale positions were "Almost certainly; more than likely; there is a 50/50 chance that; more than likely, and almost certainly; I would not (or would) feel like."

The *number* of situations and responses included in the leisure behavior inventory was determined largely by considerations of the time and motivation that subjects would have to fill out a lengthy inventory and by data analysis capacities of available computer facilities. The types of leisure responses included on the leisure behavior inventory were chosen on the basis of the authors' experience with responses from six previous community surveys of what people do in their leisure time. Content and factor analyses and discriminant analyses of occupational groups using these data have suggested a number of dimensions underlying leisure responses. These analyses have suggested the following major types of leisure activities: active games and sports involving extensive use of arms and legs and frequently involving body contact; prestigeful-intellectual activities, such as attending plays and concerts and reading books; rugged outdoor activities and serene, relaxing contacts with the out-of-doors; sociable-partying activities; and nonintellectual, nonstrenuous activities such as watching TV or napping. A factor analysis of the responses used in the leisure behavior inventory of this study revealed five factors that appeared to cover the above types, although the small number of items made exact identification difficult. The investigators were satisfied, however, that a range of types of leisure activities had been included.

The situations chosen for the leisure behavior inventory were the authors' intuitive attempts to design specific situations that represent five major *types* of situations; these types have been suggested by classical theories of leisure behavior as the major antecedents or determinants of leisure activity. The classical theories and types of situations are (*a*) compensation theory—referring to situations in which the person has experienced specific frustrations (i.e., failed to achieve specific goals) and then compensates by substitute activities and goals during leisure; (*b*) catharsis theory—somewhat like the compensation theory, but referring to situations that produce generalized frustration or emotional arousal which the person then releases through "cathartic" leisure activity; (*c*) surplus-energy theory—referring to situations in which the person has an abundance of energy (and by implication situations of inactivity that induce a "need for activity"), which he releases through leisure pursuits; (*d*) relaxation theory—referring to situations in which the person is harried, tense, and needs to relax during leisure to "unwind," or in which he is fatigued and needs to relax in order to restore himself; this theory comes closest to describing the professional recreationist's view of "recreation" or leisure activity; (*e*) task generalization—not so much a theory about causal antecedents as a descriptive term used by sociologists (Hagedorn & Labovitz, 1968) to describe the tendency for one's "work" to be similar to his leisure, presumably because of certain positive reinforcements in one's work; the term is akin to the psychological concept of response generalization.

For further discussion of the above theories see Berlyne (1969) and Sapora and Mitchell (1961). None of the theories is specific enough to permit a straightforward derivation of particular situations. The authors used them as guides to develop the specific leisure behavior inventory situations; this gave the authors some assurance of variation among situations along dimensions that other investigators have considered important. The situations (with corresponding theories) and modes of response for the leisure behavior inventory are given in Table 1; Situation 10 was developed to have a general positive tone and has no specific corresponding theory.

Statistical Analysis

A three-way analysis of variance was computed on the Persons X Situations X Responses matrix, using a random-effects model. Endler and Hunt (1966) presented a rationale for the use of a completely random model with such data. Also, in the present study the choice of a random or mixed model did not greatly affect the outcome. The component of variance for each source of variation was derived from the equations for expected values of the mean

Table 1. Situations and Modes of Response Used in the Leisure Behavior Inventory

Situations (and corresponding theories)	Coefficient alpha reliability
1. You have just completed an afternoon's work in the library. Although you've spent a lot of time the work was worth it because you found many materials that gave shape to your ideas for an important term paper (task generalization).	.82
2. You have just gotten results from the biggest exam of the year and you have either failed or not done as well as you expected to do (compensation).	.90
3. It is Saturday morning. Just yesterday you caught up on your school work. You have had a good night's sleep and awake fully refreshed and full of energy (surplus energy).	.91
4. After months of trying to be appointed as a member of an important student committee, you find that you have been turned down. You get this information via a letter which is waiting for you when you return from your classes (compensation).	.89
5. You have just finished a strenuous day of running from class to class, doing a great number of errands and in general being under extreme tension and pressure. It is now midafternoon and your last errand has been taken care of (relaxation).	.91
6. Today you got up full of energy and never really wanted to go to class. As a result, the long hours of sitting in lectures has made you very restless. It is now afternoon and you have finished your last class (surplus energy).	.91
7. You get back from the library where you have had a great deal of trouble studying due to the incessant noice (catharsis).	.94
8. It is Friday afternoon and although not under any pressure or duress, the events of the past week have kept you extremely busy without much chance for recreation (relaxation).	.92
9. You have just lost all of your class notes for your hardest class. You return from searching for them feeling frustrated and under extreme tension (catharsis).	.94
10. You have had an average day of classes. It is midafternoon and a representative of an important student group, which you have wanted very much to join, calls you and asks you to meet him next day about joining the group (general positive situation—no specific underlying theory).	.93

Modes of response	
1. Watch television.	.91
2. Spend time on my favorite hobby such as playing a musical instrument, painting or drawing, or working on some form of arts and crafts.	.91
3. Take a nap.	.87
4. Go to where my friends gather or talk or socialize.	.91
5. Visit a friend.	.93
6. Play in a competitive game such as tennis, handball, squash, or badminton with another person.	.89
7. Spend time in the out-of-doors walking or hiking.	.93
8. Go partying.	.91
9. Spend time catching up on odd tasks such as letters or errands.	.90
10. Find a quiet place to sit and relax by myself.	.92
11. Spend time on academically related activities such as studying.	.87
12. Play in a contact game such as football, soccer, or basketball.	.96
13. Go shopping for clothes.	.95

Note.—Items 12 and 13 were not used in University of Illinois sample.

squares, and the percentage of variance accounted for by the component was calculated. With the present ANOVA model, the residual (or triple-interaction) mean square contains two variance components—that due to sampling error and that due to the triple-interaction effect. Since there is no independent estimate of variance due to sampling error, the two components together were treated as a residual variance.

RESULTS

Reliabilities of the Leisure Behavior Inventory

Table 1 gives the coefficient alpha reliability estimate (Cronbach, 1951) for each situation and mode of response. The coefficients in Table 1 are those for the Kentucky sample; those for the Illinois sample were virtually identical. All of the coefficients are in the .80s and .90s and are comparable to those reported by Endler and Hunt (1968) for the anxiousness and hostility inventories. Individuals' scores on the various situation and mode-of-response scales of the leisure behavior inventory are evidently highly reliable.

Proportions of Variance for Leisure Behavior

The proportions of the total variance contributed by the various sources for the two samples and for men and women are shown in Table 2.[1] The proportions of variance were similar for the two samples and the two sexes. There were a few notable differences, however, between the two samples, between the sexes, and between sex-sample combinations.

Overall sample differences. The only strong difference between the samples that was the same for both sexes was in the variance contributed by situations. This variance was relatively small in both samples, but was more than three times greater for the Kentucky than for the Illinois sample.

Overall sex differences. The most notable difference between males and females occurred in the proportion of variance contributed by the Situations X Modes of Response interaction. This source of variance was somewhat greater for women than for men, especially in the Kentucky sample, where the percentage for women was over two times greater than that for men.

Sex-sample combination differences. The Situation X Modes of Response interaction variance just discussed, while primarily revealing a difference between

---

[1] Mean squares for the leisure behavior sources can be obtained by substituting the variance components in Table 2 into the specification equations for expected mean squares. Sums of squares can then be derived from the mean squares and the appropriate degrees of freedom, which can be determined from the reported numbers of persons, situations, and modes of response.

Table 2. Estimated Variance Components and Percentages for each Component from the Leisure Behavior Inventory and Their Comparisons with Those from S-R Inventories of Anxiousness and Hostility

Source	Leisure activity (Illinois)		Leisure activity (Kentucky)		Anxiousness	Hostility
	Variance component	%	Variance component	%	Median percentage[a]	Median percentage[a]
			Men			
Persons (A)	.082	4.4	.117	6.4	4.4	19.1
Situations (B)	.008	.5	.061	3.3	4.0	4.6
Responses (C)	.124	6.7	.170	9.3	24.8	13.9
A × B	.053	2.9	.098	5.4	9.1	10.4
A × C	.452	24.3	.385	21.2	10.3	12.6
B × C	.228	12.3	.139	7.7	7.5	3.0
Residual	.910	48.9	.850	46.7	37.1	32.2
Total	1.857	100.0	1.820	100.0	100.0	100.0
			Women			
Persons (A)	.093	5.3	.034	1.9	4.6	14.8
Situations (B)	.014	.8	.058	3.3	7.8	7.1
Responses (C)	.190	10.8	.148	8.4	26.6	15.4
A × B	.054	3.1	.079	4.5	9.3	11.5
A × C	.361	20.6	.329	18.6	11.1	16.2
B × C	.303	17.3	.289	16.4	7.0	3.9
Residual	.740	42.1	.830	46.9	34.4	29.3
Total	1.755	100.0	1.767	100.0	100.0	100.0

Note.—For the Illinois men and women and Kentucky men and women samples, $n =$ 16, 33, 33, and 58, respectively.

[a]All percentages, including that for total, are medians of 22 samples (anxiousness) or of 4 samples (hostility) taken from Endler and Hunt (1968).

the sexes, also shows differences that are associated with both sex and sample—because the difference in variance between males and females was greater for Kentucky than for Illinois. Another more notable "interactive effect" of Sex X Sample occurred for the variance contributed by persons. Although this variance was relatively small (compared to other sources) in all four subgroups, it was even smaller for Kentucky women compared to Illinois women or men, or Kentucky men.

While the above differences are notable and probably deserve further investigation, the overall consistency of results for the two samples and the sexes is also apparent; this consistency is especially visible when one compares the subgroups on the relative levels and rank orders of the various sources of variance. Also, most of the above differences were not as notable as were the differences between the sources of variance for leisure behavior and those for anxiousness and hostility, to which the authors now turn.

Leisure Behavior versus Anxiousness and Hostility

Considering those sources of variance where anxiousness and hostility had higher percentages than leisure behavior, it can be seen that (a) anxiousness and hostility were substantially higher than leisure in the simple effects of modes of response, the percentage for anxiousness being about three times and that for hostility about twice as great. (b) The percentage of variance attributable to the Situations X Persons interaction was about two to three times greater for both anxiousness and hostility. (c) The simple effects of situations were somewhat higher for anxiousness and hostility, and this difference was especially pronounced for women, the situation variance being two or three times greater for anxiousness and hostility than for leisure. In fact there was almost an interactive effect of domain of behavior with sex of subject here: the situational variance in leisure was virtually identical for men and women, but women showed a larger situational variance than men for anxiousness and hostility.

Considering those sources of variance where leisure actvity had higher percentages than anxiousness and hostility, the authors found that (a) leisure behavior was substantially higher in the Persons X Modes of Response interactive effects, the percentage of variance being about twice as great as that for hostility and anxiousness; this difference was sharply reduced, however, in the case of the leisure-hostility comparison for women; here the Persons X Modes of Response variance was only slightly larger for leisure. (b) The percentage of variance attributable to the Situations X Modes of Response interactive effects on leisure behavior was about twice as great as it was for anxiousness, especially for women; for men the two domains were more similar in the Situations X Modes of Response variance, although that for leisure was still slightly higher. Situations X Modes of Response variance in leisure behavior was about three times (for men) or four times (for women) larger than that for hostility. (c) The residual variance for leisure was somewhat higher than that for anxiousness for hostility; it cannot be clearly determined how much of this difference was due to error and how much to a true Persons X Situations X Modes of Response triple interaction. The latter interpretation would be supported by the fact that estimated reliabilities for the leisure behavior inventory are comparable to those for anxiousness and hostility inventories.

Finally, anxiousness and leisure had about the same proportion of variance contributed by the persons source, but hostility showed about three to four times more variance due to persons than leisure behavior.

Persons X Modes of Response versus Situations X Modes of Response Interactions in Leisure Behavior

A strong Persons X Modes of Response interaction is suggested by the classic Aristotelian view of leisure, which implies personalized choice patterns that are free from the influence of specific situational events. A strong Situational X Modes of Response interaction is suggested by five situational theories which the authors attempted to represent by the selection of leisure behavior inventory situations. The results provided some support for both of these views, because both interactions were comparatively high (see Table 2). There were interesting differences between men and women on this comparison, however. For men the Persons X Modes of Response interaction variance was substantially higher than the Situations X Modes of Response interaction variance. For women, however, the two variances were about the same, with the Persons X Modes of Response variance being only slightly larger. This differential outcome for men and women is primarily accounted for by their differences on the Situations X Modes of Response variance, which is the largest difference between men and women for sources of leisure behavior variance.

DISCUSSION

With regard to the issue of whether the major source of variation in behavior derives from the situation or from simple individual differences (Endler & Hunt, 1966), this study forced the investigators to the same conclusion reached by Endler and Hunt about anxiousness and to a lesser extent about hostility: neither persons nor situations, in terms of their simple effects, have a great deal of influence on reported leisure behavior. The various interactions accounted for substantially more of the variance than did the main effects of persons, situations, or modes of response. The strong Persons X Modes of Response interaction suggests that the assessment of a person's leisure interests and habits, a frequent concern of leisure-time agencies, could be improved by attempting to characterize individuals by their *patterns* of leisure choices, instead of treating single choices separately or combining them into an omnibus score as is often done. In addition, the relatively strong Situations X Modes of Response interaction, which was the second highest source of variance (ignoring the residual), indicates that validity of leisure behavior descriptions could be improved by specifying the situations in which various response patterns might be observed; this appears to be less important for men, however, than for women. This difference in Situations X Modes of Response variance was the largest difference between men and women for the authors' data. The authors have no ready explanation for it except to note that it is consistent with a widespread belief that women are more emotionally responsive than men to situational events. Endler and Hunt (1968) found that simple situational variance was greater for women than men, and quoted evidence that women are more field dependent than men. Why this greater influence of situations on women should reveal itself as a main effect for hostility and anxiousness but as an interaction with modes of response for leisure is not entirely clear. Evidently, the domain of behavior (leisure, anxiousness, or hostility) or the form of response (degree of response for the Endler et al. (1962; Endler & Hunt, 1968) inventories, probability of response for the leisure behavior inventory) has something to do with these different outcomes.

That the domain of behavior or form of response can affect the magnitude of a source of variance is apparent from present comparisons of variances for leisure, anxiousness, and hostility. Endler and Hunt (1968) anticipated the effects of domain of behavior in their comparisons of anxiousness and hostility. This study has demonstrated even greater differences between leisure and either anxiousness or hostility. Anxiousness and hostility had higher percentages of variance than leisure for the simple effects of responses, of situations, and for the Persons X Situations interaction. Leisure had higher percentages of variance for the Persons X Modes of Response and Situations X Modes of Response interactions, and for the residual. The fact that the reliability coefficients for situations and modes of response on the leisure behavior inventory were about the same magnitude as those for the Endler et al. (1962; Endler & Hunt, 1968) inventories suggests that the greater residual variance for leisure might contain a larger triple-interaction effect. In studying leisure behavior, therefore, it might be especially important to sample persons, situations, and modes of response, and to attempt to characterize persons by their patterns of response to different situations. Tucker's (1964) work on three-mode factor analysis could be one useful means of doing this.

The above differences between domains of behavior plus those outlined by Endler and Hunt (1968) in their comparisons of anxiousness and hostility clearly indicate that generalizations about sources of behavioral variance are limited. The fact that domain of behavior sometimes interacts with sex in describing a source of variance (e.g., the Persons X Modes of Response and Situations X Modes of Response variances) further restricts the authors' ability to generalize. None of this is to say that generalizations are not possible. Evidently, the percentages of variance for various sources do not fluctuate randomly, as shown by the similarity of results for different samples of subjects of the same sex *within* a given domain of behavior. A more correct statement, then, would be that the relative magnitude of any source of variance is related to systematic factors. But at present we do not know enough about these factors to know the limits of our generalization attempts.

Knowing more about the sources of variance investigated here and the factors that affect them is important not only for methodology (as in constructing an inventory), but also for theorizing about various kinds of behavior. The importance for theory is illustrated by the comparison of Persons X Modes of Response and Situations X Modes of Response variances—a comparison suggested by two classical traditions of theorizing about leisure behavior. Neither of these classical views is very concrete, and neither specifically predicts the result that the authors associated with it. Rather, these views imply different sources of variance by their different philosophies about the meaning of leisure and its antecedents. Present data suggest that both views have some merit. In fact, the residual variances for the leisure behavior samples might include large triple-interaction components. If so, this might suggest the need to integrate both points of view in the development of theories that allow for individualized response patterns to different situations. Again, however, male-female differences might eventually alter such conclusions. For example, the present findings suggest that the various situational views of leisure are more applicable to the leisure activities of females than to those of males (as indicated by the greater Situations X Modes of Response variance for females). This conclusion is strengthened by the authors' attempts to select situations to represent the major situational views and by some evidence of our success in these attempts (Witt & Bishop, 1970).

Besides investigating a different domain of behavior, this study differed in two other ways from those of Endler et al. (1962; Endler & Hunt, 1968). First, the studies differ in the form of response elicited from the subject; their studies asked about the degree of response, whereas the present study asked about the probability of a response. Second, the situations used by Endler et al. (1962; Endler & Hunt, 1968) were immediate, and responses were made while the subject was *in* them (hypothetically); present situations were events that shortly *preceded* the response in question. Both types are stimulus situations, but differ in their (hypothetical) proximity to the reported responses. Additional research is needed to isolate the effects of these factors from those associated with the domain behavior.

It would also be profitable to investigate various samplings of persons, situations, and modes of response for the leisure behavior inventory, as Endler and Hunt (1969) did in their generalizability paper for anxiousness. Finally, there is need to investigate sources of variance under more realistic conditions where situations and responses can be objectively recorded.

REFERENCES

Berlyne, D. E. Laughter, humor, and play. In G. Lindzey & E. Aronson (Eds.), *The handbook of social psychology.* Vol. 3. Reading, Mass.: Addison-Wesley, 1969.

Cronbach, L. J. Coefficient alpha and the internal structure of tests. *Psychometrika*, 1951, 16, 297–334.

DeGrazia, S. *Of time, work and leisure.* New York: Twentieth Century Fund, 1962.

Endler, N. S., & Hunt, J. McV. Sources of behavioral variance as measured by the S-R inventory of anxiousness. *Psychological Bulletin*, 1966, 65, 336–346.

Endler, N. S., & Hunt, J. McV. S-R inventories of hostility and comparisons of the proportions of variance from persons, responses, and situations for hostility and anxiousness. *Journal of Personality and Social Psychology*, 1968, 9, 309–315.

Endler, N. S., & Hunt, J. McV. Generalizability of contributions from sources of variance in the S-R inventories of anxiousness. *Journal of Personality*, 1969, 37, 1–24.

Endler, N. S., Hunt, J. McV., & Rosenstein, A. J. An S-R inventory of anxiousness. *Psychological Monographs*, 1962, 76(17, Whole No. 536).

Hagedorn, R., & Labovitz, S. Participation in community associations by occupations: A test of three theories. *American Sociological Review*, 1968, 33, 272–283.

Hahn, P. *Recreation: A medical viewpoint.* New York: Columbia University Press, 1965.

Sapora, A. V., & Mitchell, E. D. *The theory of play and recreation.* New York: Ronald Press, 1961.

Tucker, L. R. The extension of factor analysis to three-dimensional matrices. In N. Fredericksen & H. Gulliksen (Eds.), *Contributions to mathematical psychology.* New York: Holt, Rinehart & Winston, 1964.

Witt, P. A., & Bishop, D. W. Situational antecedents to leisure behavior. *Journal of Leisure Research,* 1970, **2,** 64–77.

19

Effects of Attitudinal and Situational Factors on Reported Choice Behavior

ROLF GUNNAR SANDELL

Choice behavior is commonly explained, according to a dominant model for theories in personality and social psychology, by reference to some evaluation system in the individual's mind. This system is referred to as "preferences," "attitudes," "sentiments," "valences," "cathexes" or "distribution of libido," "ego-ideal," "utility," etc. Attitudes, to use this concept collectively, are generally defined as dispositions to react to objects on various occasions with signs of like or dislike. For example[1] Krech, Crutchfield and Ballachey define attitudes and their role as follows:

The social actions of the individual reflect his attitudes—enduring systems of positive or negative evaluations, emotional feelings, and pro or con action tendencies with respect to social objects [11, p. 139].

While stressing the correspondence between attitudes and overt actions, this definition implies that the attitude object itself is the stimulus for actions of either of two kinds: acceptance or rejection, approach or avoidance. Thus, the action is evidently conditional on the attitude object but not on the situation in which the individual encounters the object.

These assumptions are also implied in operational definitions of the attitude concept. The object is usually judged or rated independently of any specified conditions in a choice situation. Judgments are further reduced to a single scale value, indicating the individual's reaction to the object stimulus in terms of one-dimensional like or dislike.

From Sandell, R. G., Effects of attitudinal and situational factors on reported choice behavior, vol. 5, 1968. Reprinted from *Journal of Marketing Research* published by the American Marketing Association.

This study was supported by grants from Statens Konsumentråd och Statens Råd för Samhällsforskning. The computational work was done with the help of Sylvia Jansson. The author is greatly indebted to Professor J. Mc V Hunt for his valuable advice on this article.

[1] See also [1, p. 810; 3, p. 31; 9, p. 428, and 10, p. 152].

According to the concept of behavior implied in these definitions (for convenience referred to as the *attitude model*), the variation in choice behavior should be attributable to the variation between objects and the interactions between objects and individuals. Variation resulting from situations prevailing on choice occasions should be negligible—in most operational definitions of attitudes it is not even allowed.

An alternative concept regards a choice reaction as conditional on an object-independent situation. The object does not necessarily function as a choice instigator but rather as the consequence of a choice elicited by a more general situation.

Operationally, this idea requires situations to be specified in the measurement instructions. Stimulus for the verbal report should be a description of a situation; the verbal report should be a description of the reaction made to the specified situation, not a "like" or "not like" to the stimulus of an attitude object. In relation to choice behavior, the purpose of the operations is to find the situations that, at least at the verbal level, elicit the choice of the object in question. To reduce trial-and-error by the investigator the subject could be provided with a sample of short descriptions of alternative reactions, e.g., for choice objects, and asked to choose among, rate, or rank them for specified strategic situations. In the *situation-reaction model*, situational factors are responsible for most of the variation in choice behavior, in interaction with objects and with objects and persons.

In personality theory, similar views were suggested by Rotter [12] and Hunt [8]. Usually, in formulations about personality, traits—operationally defined as dimensions of interindividual differences—seem to be regarded as the dominant source of variation in behavior. The definitional correspondence between the concept of trait and that of attitudes is obvious and has, among others, been noted by Allport [2, p. 295] and Green [7, p. 335]. Traits, as well as attitudes, relate to differences between people's likes for different "things."

Hunt [8, p. 83] argues, "for either understanding variations of behavior or making clinical predictions, we should be looking toward instruments that will classify people in terms of the kinds of responses they make in various categories of situations." He refers to a study [4] with data from an instrument like the S–R Inventory of Anxiousness [5] to determine the proportions of variance within a certain behavioral class which could be attributed to reactions, situations, persons, and various interactions among these.

This experiment exploits the approach taken by Hunt and his collaborators to compare the assumptions implied in the attitude concept with those of a situation-oriented view, for reported choice behavior.

METHOD

Design and Procedure

The experiment was to have student subjects state how much they would like to have each of alternative items in each of a sample of specified situations. By having the same set of alternatives rated in all situations, situational variance can hardly be attributed to differences between situations for the set sampled for choice. The alternative items chosen were drinks. Reasons for using this kind of alternatives are based solely on the point that the alternative reactions are supposedly different enough to be clearly described and discriminated among, but at the same time, they are all related to the single drive stimulus complex, thirst. This should reduce the possibilities for variation from situations and eliminate explanations of situational variance in terms of need or drive variations.

Situations and drinks were sampled randomly from larger listed sets of thirst situations and drinks. The samples are presented in Table 1. The S–R inventory used here has an instruction page and seven rating pages. At the top of each of the seven pages, a situation is stated from the sample in Table 1. Under this description, the drinks are ordered randomly in a vertical column. To the right of each drink is a seven-step graphic rating scale, the extremes of which are defined as "extremely willingly" and "extremely unwillingly," respectively. The situations are also ordered randomly, common to all subjects.

The instruction page was an attempt to learn whether the drinks sampled actually were alternatives empirically. This was done by testing whether the subjects could place all alternatives on a one-dimensional preference scale from "like extremely" to "dislike extremely." The ability to do so is taken to define operationally the commensurability of the drinks, as being alternatives to each other. Conversely, if subjects refuse, protest, or otherwise indicate difficulties in ordering or rating all items on a single scale, the items are not alternatives. No difficulties in following instructions were observed. After this control, the subjects were instructed to mark on each scale on each of the following pages

Table 1. Situations and Alternatives in the S–R Inventory

Situations		Drinks
When really thirsty	I drink[a]	Corn or potato brandy[b]
Smoking after dinner	I drink	Coffee
When alone	I drink	Liqueur
Feeling sleepy in the afternoon	I drink	Mineral[c]
		Squash[d]
Reading the paper in the morning	I drink	Tea
		Water
Before sitting down at the table	I drink	Wine
		Whiskey
With a really delicious piece of meat	I drink	Beer

[a] "Extremely unwillingly"   "Extremely willingly"

|—|—|—|—|—|—|—|

[b] Swedish: brännvin.
[c] Swedish: läskedryck.
[d] Swedish: saft.

how willingly or unwillingly they would drink each scale's beverage in the situation specified at the top of the page.

Subjects

The subjects were 36 students at the Institute of Advertising, Stockholm. The experiment was part of the regular class work and participation was required. The data from five subjects were discarded because of incomplete records or failure to follow instructions. Thus, data were obtained from the 31 students' ten ratings in seven situations, i.e., 2,170 observations in all.

Statistical Analysis

A three-way analysis of variance, assuming a random effects model, was performed on the willingness ratings, with individuals, situations, and alternatives as factors. For reasons stated by Endler and Hunt [5] no meaningful comparisons can be made between mean squares. Comparisons should be made between the relative proportions of the total variance attributable to each factor. These relative proportions must be derived through specification equations suggested by Gleser, Cronbach, and Rajaratnam [6] and used by Endler and Hunt [4]. This procedure equates mean squares to sums of weighted variance components.

If i is persons, s is situtions, a is alternatives, and r is residual (which here equals the triple interaction plus error) and if n is the number of persons, k is the number of situations, and m is the number of alternatives, then the variance components can be solved by the following equations:

$$E(MS_i) = \sigma_r^2 + km\sigma_i^2 + m\sigma_{is}^2 + k\sigma_{ia}^2$$

$$E(MS_s) = \sigma_r^2 + nm\sigma_s^2 + m\sigma_{is}^2 + n\sigma_{sa}^2$$

$$E(MS_a) = \sigma_r^2 + nk\sigma_a^2 + k\sigma_{ia}^2 + n\sigma_{sa}^2$$

$$E(MS_{is}) = \sigma_r^2 + m\sigma_{is}^2$$

$$E(MS_{ia}) = \sigma_r^2 + k\sigma_{ia}^2$$

$$E(MS_{sa}) = \sigma_r^2 + n\sigma_{sa}^2$$

$$E(MS_r) = \sigma_r^2.$$

Observed mean squares were substituted for expected mean squares, $E(MS)$, and the equations were solved for the relevant component in each. These variance components were then summed, and the sum proportions attributable to each component were computed.

Table 2. Summary of Variance Analysis of Willingness Ratings in S-R Inventory

Source	d.f.	Mean squares	Variance com-ponents	Per-cent
Individuals (I)	30	8.289	0.025	0.5
Situations (S)	6	100.867	0.219	2.7
Alternatives (A)	9	213.509	0.690	14.6
I × S	180	2.596	0.129	2.7
I × A	270	5.232	0.560	11.8
S × A	54	59.714	1.884	39.8
I × S × A	1620	1.313	1.313	27.8

RESULTS

Results of the analysis of variance and specification equations are summarized in Table 2. From assumptions implied in general and operational definitions of the attitude concept, one would expect the dominant part of the variance to be attributable to factors independent of the situation factor. Attitudes shared by all subjects correspond to the variation between alternatives (14.59 percent), but the individual person's attitudes correspond to the interaction between alternatives and persons, i.e., differences between persons regarding differences between alternatives (11.84 percent). There is also the variation due to persons, i.e., differences between persons for some "general beverage attitude" (0.53 percent). These attitude factors thus account for about 27 percent of the variation.

According to a situation-oriented view, one would expect a substantial proportion of variance to result from interaction between situations and alternatives, corresponding to universally established dependencies between situations and reactions (39.83 percent), and from interaction between individuals, situations, and alternatives, which corresponds to individually established dependencies (27.76 percent). To this could be added the variance component from situations, i.e., differences between situations on the appropriateness of the beverages in general, (2.73 percent). Interaction between situations and persons refers to modifying individual differences (2.73 percent). Situational factors thus determine, alone and in interaction with others, about 73 percent of the total variation.

DISCUSSION

The meaning of the results is clear: a person's choice is highly dependent on the situation. An alternative with a high choice probability for a person in one situation does not necessarily have a high choice probability for the same person in another situation. Here high choice probability is defined in relative terms. The results could also be expressed in terms of individual differences. Thus, a person relatively high on the trait of choosing a certain alternative in one situation is not necessarily high on the same trait in another situation.

The triple interaction contains random factors that cannot be isolated from true interaction. However, since the large proportion of variance resulting from triple interaction was hypothesized, the randomness should not be over-emphasized.

Undoubtedly, another outcome is available from sampling situations from a homogeneous universe. It is also true that a more nearly homogeneous sample of alternatives, e.g., different brands of a single product, would probably yield a different outcome for the influence of situational factors. This would not, however, mean that choices reported would follow other laws or principles. It would merely constitute a restriction of the range effect of the homogeneous sampling and therefore make only special cases of the normal outcome. The principle, as such, still holds even if different samples allow the factors different chances to affect the dependent variable. In fact, the sampling of situations here was from a nearly homogeneous universe. A more nearly homogeneous sampling of alternatives would also result in the restriction of the range of functional stimuli, which would be difficult to match in sampling situations.

It should be recognized that a situation-reaction kind of theory would use stimulus generalization or another convergent mechanism to explain situation-independent effects. Since the results are partly either attitude or stimulus-response modelled, the critical issue for distinguishing the two models is the significance of the situation factor effects. Logically and statistically, a model that recognizes only two of three factors as important cannot accept any significant effects except the main effects of either and their interaction. A model that recognizes all three factors as important, however, can account for all effects involving one, two, or all three of the factors.

Therefore, the model implied in definitions of the attitude concept is obviously only valid in some special cases. For predictive purposes the concept should be redefined according to assumptions of conditional relations between reactions and situations. Or it could be substituted by existing concepts making these assumptions, e.g., learning theory. Redefining is most important at its operational level. Apparently, the conventional attitude measurement techniques do not allow an important factor to influence results, if not in an informal way, through subjects' uncontrolled initatives. We tested the validity of the conventional preference scale obtained as a control in the experiment, using the S–R inventory as the criterion. Over 100 randomly drawn pairs of observations were used in computing the correlation between the rated willingness of a subject for a certain drink in a certain situation and the same subject's rating of the same drink on the conventional preference scale. The validity coefficient was .51. The "explained" 25 percent conforms rather well to the estimated variance proportions. Methods of greater predictive power than offered by conventional preference and attitude measurement techniques should apparently be pursued, perhaps following the previously outlined directions. The technique used in this experiment seems to exemplify what Hunt [8] suggested as desirable: investigation of specific dependencies between choice reactions and situations is possible.

CONCLUSIONS

These results strongly support a situation-oriented view of choice behavior, but not the traditional view that explains choices among alternatives by reference to general and stable evaluations, attitudes, preferences, valences, etc. The situation-oriented view should reorient research toward studies on choice behavior as a function of situational variation and on mechanisms that establish and mediate these dependencies, and toward the development of reliable study methodology. This experiment exemplifies an indirect, verbal technique that is probably the most practical and economic form in terms of application. For the necessary basic research on the subject, however, observation of choice behavior under systematically manipulated conditions appears to be the most favorable approach.

REFERENCES

1. G. W. Allport, "Attitudes," in C. Murchison, ed., *A Handbook of Social Psychology,* Worcester: Clark University Press, 1935.
2. _____ *Personality: A Psychological Interpretation,* New York: Holt, Rinehart and Winston, 1937.
3. D. T. Campbell, "The Indirect Assessment of Social Attitudes," *Psychological Bulletin,* 47 (1950), 15–38.
4. N. S. Endler, and J. Mc V. Hunt, "Sources of Behavioral Variance as Measured by the S-R Inventory of Anxiousness," *Psychological Bulletin,* 65 (1966), 336–46.
5. _____ and A. P. Rosenstein, "An S-R Inventory of Anxiousness," *Psychological Monographs,* 76 (1962), 1–33.
6. Goldine C. Gleser, L. J. Cronbach, and N. Rajaratnam, "Generalizability of Scores Influenced by Multiple Sources of Variance," *Psychometrika,* 30 (1965), 395–418.
7. B. F. Green, "Attitude Measurement," in G. Lindzey, ed., *Handbook of Social Psychology,* Vol. 1. Reading, Pa.: Addison-Wesley, 1954.
8. J. Mc V. Hunt, "Traditional Personality Theory in the Light of Recent Evidence," *American Scientist,* 53 (1965), 80–96.
9. D. Katz and E. Stotland, "A Preliminary Statement to a Theory of Attitude Structure and Change," in S. Koch, ed., *Psychology: A Study of a Science,* Vol. 3. New York: McGraw-Hill Book Co., 1959.
10. D. Krech, and R. S. Crutchfield, *Theory and Problems of Social Psychology,* New York: McGraw-Hill Book Co., 1948.
11. _____ and E. L. Ballachey, *Individual in Society,* New York: McGraw-Hill, Book Co., 1962.
12. J. B. Rotter, "Some Implications of a Social Learning Theory for the Prediction of Goal Directed Behavior from Testing Procedures," *Psychological Review,* 67 (1960), 301–16.

20

Generality and Specificity of Student Reactions in High School Classrooms

EDISON J. TRICKETT and RUDOLF H. MOOS

The old Lewinian adage that behavior is a function of *both person and environment* has made increasing inroads into educational and psychological thinking in recent years. From the perspective of a mental health consultant, Sarason et al, (18) explicitly stress the importance of the situational context of behavior by reporting changes in children's behavior as a consequence of changing their environment (e.g., transferring a child to a different class) without changing the "personality" of the particular child. From the guidance field, Danskin, Kenneday and Friesen (2) present a conception of the emergent guidance counselor as a "human development engineer" who should broaden his frame of reference and invest "a much larger part of his total resources into observation of and systematic research into the learning climate of the school" (p. 135). A growing research literature in educational psychology demonstrates an increased concern with the interaction of pupil and classroom as a better way of predicting student learning. For example, Grimes and Allinsmith (7), studying the relationship among compulsivity, anxiety, and performance in structured and unstructured settings, found that anxiety and compulsivity interacted with one another and with teaching methods. In a structured setting, compulsive children performed better than non-compulsive children, with anxiety making no difference. In the unstructured setting, however, compulsivity made no difference and anxiety impeded performance.

Implicit in this shifting emphasis from various fields is a dissatisfaction with the predictive power of a "personality" model of behavior which attributes a high degree of generality or consistency to individual behavior across different settings. Within clinical psychology "the belief that people display stable

From *Adolescence*, 1970, 5, 373–390. Copyright 1970 by Libra Publishers, Inc. Reprinted by permission of the authors and the publisher.

The authors express their thanks to Marilyn Cohen and Martha Merk for their assistance in the preparation of the manuscript.

generalized behavior across diverse situations is reflected in the continuing practice of identifying, labeling and categorizing individuals on such broad dimensions as anxiety or ego strength" (12). Such phrases from the educational vocabulary as "behavior problem" also seemingly imply a consistency of personality or behavior patterns across settings. For example, an adolescent described as "rebellious" should logically be expected to exhibit some mode of rebellious behavior in a variety of settings. If he did not, then prediction of his behavior on the basis of only his personality trait of "rebelliousness" would be quite limited.

Though much current thinking is moving toward stressing the importance of situational and interactional determinants of behavior (1, 4, 14, 9, 10, 19), empirical research systematically investigating various aspects of the problem is still rare. The available literature, however, strongly suggests a re-examination of the assumption that much of the variation in behavior can be accounted for by "personality" or individual differences (12). With respect to the educational setting, perhaps the oldest and most pertinent example is the Character Education Inquiry of Hartshorne and May (8). In studying "honesty" these authors exposed large numbers of children to several different situations in which they could exhibit a number of dishonest behaviors (e.g., lie, cheat, steal). They found that the correlations among the cheating tests were too low to provide evidence for a unified personality trait of honesty. The correlations among the cheating tests were highest when highly similar situations were compared, and "as we progressively change the situation, we progressively lower the correlations between the tests" (8, p. 384 as reported in 12, p. 25). The findings that the correlations between settings decrease as the similarity between the settings decreases has been recently corroborated by Ellsworth et al (3), Magnusson et al (11), and Moos (13). These studies suggest that setting differences and the interaction of person and setting must be taken into account if prediction of behavior is to improve.

This issue of the generality and specificity of behavior has clear relevance to the classroom behavior of adolescents who, in most public schools, experience a variety of different classroom settings daily. While it is commonplace to hear adolescents describe classes as "good" or "bad," or "organized" or "disorganized," it is equally common to hear of a student who cannot cope effectively with a particular class, but who is seen as an exemplar in another. These everyday anecdotes, when put in the context of the previously mentioned research, suggest that an important empirical issue is the degree to which classroom behavior is a function of individual differences, setting or classroom differences, and the interaction of student and classroom. It is the purpose of the present study to present data on this issue by investigating the following two questions:

1) To what extent are students' feelings and initiatives in the classroom a function of individual differences, different classroom settings, and their

interaction? For instance, to what degree do students react consistently across a variety of classrooms? To what extent do different classrooms "pull" for different reactions (i.e., are students generally more satisfied in English or Math?)? And, finally, how much variance is accounted for by the interaction of student and classroom?

2) Are the relative amounts of variance accounted for by persons, settings, and their interaction consistent across several response "dimensions"? Is, for example, satisfaction more person-determined than participation?

METHOD

Subjects and Procedure

The subjects were 12 high school sophomores (7 boys and 5 girls) in a public high school with high academic standards and innovative educational programs. The students, all 15 to 16 years of age, were from upper middle class homes and were in Advance Placement courses. Several had shared classes in junior high school and knew each other very well. Thus, they were less representative of high school sophomores in general than of those with well above average intelligence coming from upper middle class families.

During the third month of school, each of these 12 students was given a questionniare on which they were asked to rate their feelings and the initiatives they took in each of four daily classes which they shared. The classes were:

1. English
2. Mathematics
3. Biology
4. Government

For each class, the students rated their reactions on 28 seven-point scales. Fifteen of these scales consisted of *feelings* or *mood* adjective pairs such as "satisfied—dissatisfied" and "tense—relaxed", while 13 of the scales were *initiatives* such as "I speak out in class" and "I 'goof off' in this class". The *feelings* and *initiatives* were chosen on the basis of relevance to classrooms as ascertained by student interviews and a review of prior literature.

The instructions asked the students to think about how they usually felt in each of the four classes. Included in the instructions was the following:

Let us say that you are in the situation *English Class* and the first word pair is "interested-disinterested". Ask yourself which of the two words best describes your feeling *in that particular situation*. Then circle the number on the scale which best describes the degree to which you feel *interested* or *disinterested* in that situation.

In sum, each of the 12 sophomore students was administered a questionnaire with four settings (classes) and was asked to rate each of these settings on 28 seven-point scales.

Results

All of the students adequately completed the questionnaire. First, item intercorrelations were calculated among the 28 items across the four classes and five dimensions were selected for further analysis. The average intercorrelations of these groups of items are shown in Table 1. The average intercorrelation of each item with the other items in its dimension was always higher than that item's average intercorrelation with the items in each of the other dimensions. "Seating" was included as an initiative because in each of the classes students could choose where to sit.

A three-way fixed effects analysis of variance was then conducted for each of the five dimensions (23). This analysis allows one to specify for each dimension the amount of variance accounted for by each of the three main effects (students, classes, response dimensions) and their interactions.

Table 2, which summarizes the analyses of variance results, indicates that there were significant individual differences in all five of the response dimensions, significant between-class differences for four of the dimensions, and significant between-responses differences for two dimensions. Further, the Subject $\times$ Class interaction was significant for all five dimensions, the Subject $\times$ Response interaction for two dimensions, and the Classes $\times$ Response interaction for one.

Next, the relative percentages of total variance accounted for by each source was calculated for each of the five response dimensions using the fixed-effects

Table 1. Response Items on Each of the Five Dimensions and Their Average Intercorrelations*

Dimension	Responses	Average intercorrelation
I. Paying attention	Excited about learning	
	Alert	
	Curious	
	In class I pay close attention to what the teacher is saying	.59
	**I goof off in this class	
II. Participation	Active	
	Involved	
	I speak out in class	.66
	I ask questions in class	
III. Anxious uncertainty	Tense	
	Lost	.61
	Confused	
IV. Satisfaction	Satisfied	
	Contented	.86
V. Seating	I usually sit at the front	
	**I usually sit at the back	−.73

*For convenience, only one pole of the feeling adjectives is presented in the Table.
**Item reversed in analysis.

Table 2. Summary of Analyses of Variance for Five Dimensions

	I			II			III			IV			V		
	df	Ms	F	df	MS	F	df	MS	F	df	MS	F	df	MS	F
Between students	11.	8.99	13.08**	11.	20.36	26.65**	11.	6.71	7.75**	11.	10.33	27.25**	11.	15.25	11.97**
Between classes	3.	14.33	20.86**	3.	6.90	9.02**	3.	31.01	35.84**	3.	26.34	69.49**	3.	0.74	0.58
Between responses	4.	0.75	1.09	3.	19.15	25.06**	2.	5.86	6.77**	1.	0.84	2.23	1.	2.04	1.60
Students × classes	33.	6.46	9.41**	33.	5.81	7.61**	33.	4.28	4.94**	33.	2.60	6.86**	33.	7.09	5.57**
Students × responses	44.	1.82	2.65**	33.	2.88	3.77**	22.	1.43	1.65	11.	0.71	1.87	11.	1.16	0.91
Classes × responses	12.	1.42	2.06*	9.	0.98	1.29	6.	0.62	0.72	3.	0.12	0.32	3.	2.40	1.89
Residual	132.	0.69	—	99.	0.76	—	66.	0.87	—	33.	0.38	—	33.	1.27	—
Total	239.	—	—	191.	—	—	143.	—	—	95.	—	—	95.	—	—

*p < .05.
**p < .01.

402

model described by Gleser, Cronbach and Rajaratnam (6). The results of this analysis are summarized in Table 3.

The most important result is that, for every dimension, the Student X Class (Person X Setting) interaction accounted for statistically significant and practically important proportions of the total variance (from 30 to 60%). The Person X Setting interaction actually accounted for the largest proportion of variance in all five of the dimensions. The results also indicated that: (a) consistent individual differences among students accounted for between 3% (paying attention) and 27% (satisfaction) of the total variance; (b) consistent differences among classes accounted for between zero (seating) and 30% (satisfaction) of the variance; (c) consistent differences among responses accounted for less than 10% of the total variance on each dimension; and, (d) the two first-order interactions involving responses (Students X Responses and Classes X Responses) always accounted for less than 15% of the total variance. Variance attributable to responses and the interaction between responses and students and classes is low because of the high item intercorrelations on each of the dimensions utilized.

The Person, Setting and Person X Settings effects for the satisfaction dimension will be presented diagrammatically for illustrative purposes. Figure 1 demonstrates the person main effect in that Subject #7 obtained a higher mean satisfaction score than Subject #10 in all four classes. Also, Subject #7 differentiated very little between classes, whereas Subject #10 viewed Government as far more satisfactory than his other three classes.

Figure 2 portrays the average satisfaction score across all students for each of the four classes. The class main effect is shown by the fact that the science-oriented classes were rated as less satisfying than the humanities-oriented ones.

Figure 3 illustrates the Person X Setting interaction. The interaction effect is most clearly observed in Biology and Government, where Subject #2 is more satisfied in Biology than in Government, whereas the reverse is true of Subject #3.

Table 3. Summary of Percentage of Variance Accounted for by Each Source for Each Dimension

Source	Dimensions				
	I	II	III	IV	V
Students	2.98	20.98	4.98	26.55	20.83
Classes	5.09	0.49	23.97	28.70	–
Responses	–	9.03	3.12	0.24	–
Students X Classes	49.42	34.08	36.38	31.89	58.60
Students X Responses	12.12	14.29	4.51	2.36	1.89
Classes X Responses	2.60	0.49	–	–	–
Residual	29.39	20.63	27.60	10.88	25.42

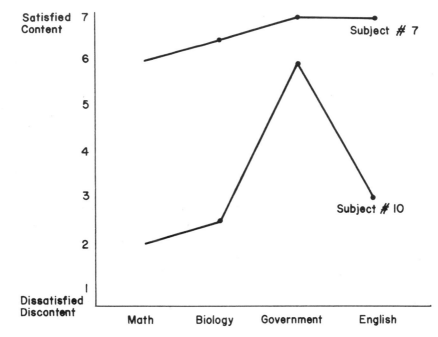

Fig. 1. Average Satisfaction scores across classes for Subjects #7 and #10.

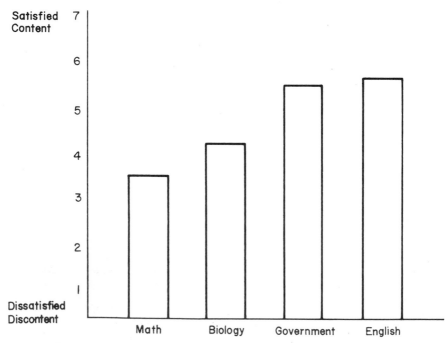

Fig. 2. Average Setting scores on the Satisfaction dimension across all Subjects.

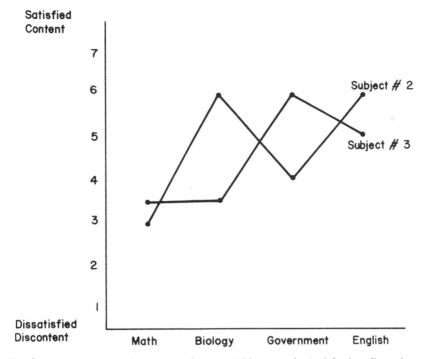

Fig. 3. Person X Setting interactions for two Subjects on the Satisfaction dimension.

Discussion

The results indicate that, in general, students, classes, and Student X Class interactions each account for important proportions of the total variance. Consistent differences among students were significant for four of five dimensions, and the Student X Class interactions were significant for all five of the dimensions.

The consistently large amounts of variance accounted for by the Student X Class interaction supports the rationale for shifting from a "personality-based" approach to predicting behavior, to one more explicitly concerned with the interaction of person and setting. While both students and classes generally accounted for statistically significant portions of variance, in every response dimension used in the present study, the interaction between the two accounted for more. This large interaction effect is even more striking when one considers the socioeconomic and intellectual homogeneity of the students, two criteria often used as differentiating variables in and of themselves. If a more random sample of students was selected, one may anticipate an even greater amount of variance related to the Person X Setting interaction. The relatively smaller amount of variance accounted for by the class main effect indicates that the classroom setting does not have a particularly strong tendency to elicit the same reactions in different students. Further, the variance accounted for by individual differences is small enough to suggest that predicting student reactions on the basis of student personality traits or response tendencies alone is of limited utility.

While caution should be exercised in generalizing the present results due to the restricted range of both students and classes involved, the results are consistent with earlier studies done in quite different environments. Previous studies have found that both individuals and settings contribute significantly to overall behavioral variance in the "traits" of anxiety and hostility among college students (4, 5), in the reactions of hyper-aggressive and normal boys in a residential setting (15, 16, 17), and in the reactions of patients and staff in a psychiatric ward (14).

It is important to note the conclusions of these investigators about interaction effects. Endler and Hunt, using data from several samples of college students, found that about 10% of the total variance was due to the Subject X Situation interaction and that "nearly 30% of the total variance for both 'traits' comes from the three simple interactions (Person X Situation, Person X Mode of Response, and Situation X Mode of Response) . . . ." (4). Raush et al, concluded that interactions between the child and the setting were far more important in accounting for individual reactions than either the child or the setting alone. Moos found that the three first-order interactions accounted for between 8 and 33% of the variance for psychiatric patients and for between 30 and 40% for staff. Thus, previous research has found that the Person X Setting interaction effect accounts for as much or more of the variance than either consistent individual differences or consistent differences among settings. This is exactly what was found in the present study.

A second finding of the present study, also consistent with previously mentioned research, is that the percentage of variance attributable to different sources varies in different response dimensions. For example, individual differences in Dimension I (paying attention) accounted for about 3% of the variance, whereas individual differences in Dimension IV (satisfaction) accounted for about 27%. While part of these differences may indeed be attributable to sampling variations, it may be that some response dimensions such as satisfaction are more person determined than others, e.g., paying attention. Consequently, an important research domain within educational settings lies in the assessment of various traits or coping styles such as aggressiveness, dominance, or withdrawal to determine to what extent and under what conditions such "personal styles" are determined by persons, settings and their interactions.

The importance of this type of analysis for the measurement and prediction of classroom behavior is also great. For example, the relatively small amount of variance accounted for by individual differences sets a limit on the predictive validity of personality tests used to predict classroom behavior. When individual differences account roughly for 20% of the variance, one would not expect validity coefficients to exceed a range of .40-.50. Endler and Hunt (5) have discussed this issue and have concluded, using the square of validity coefficients as an estimate of the amount of variance accounted for by individual differences, that these proportions are generally between 4% and 25% of the variance. This range is almost identical with the results of the present study. Following this same logic, the consistently large proportion of variance accounted for by the Student X Class interaction makes it mandatory to develop ways of conceptualizing person-environment interdependence if prediction of behavior is to improve. While much time has been spent assessing characteristics or "traits" of persons, far less effort has been directed toward assessing characteristics of environments. Recently, however, Walberg has created an assessment technique for the high school classroom (20, 21, 22). With assessment techniques for *both people and settings*, it is possible to test hypotheses related to the interaction of the two. Since our data indicates that this interaction effect is substantial, such *interactive* research holds great promise for future investigations.

To summarize, the results of the present study suggest that prediction of classroom behavior may be enhanced by measurement procedures which systematically sample individuals, settings, and modes of response for various behavioral dimensions. Further, the interactional aspect of student classroom behavior is an extremely important source of variance and as such deserves greater attention. Future work concerning this interactional variance necessitates a conceptual scheme and an empirical assessment technique which encompass both student and classroom environment. In addition, such work should go beyond questionnaires to the naturalistic observation of actual student behavior in diverse settings.

REFERENCES

1. Barker, R. G. *Ecological Psychology.* Stanford: Stanford Univ. Press, 1968.
2. Danskin, D. G., Kenneday, C. E., Jr. and Friesen, W. S. "Guidance: the Ecology of Students." *Personnel and Guidance Journal,* 1965, *44,* 130-135.
3. Ellsworth, R. B., Foster, L., Childers, B., Arthur, G. and Kroeker, D. "Hospital and Community Adjustment as Perceived by Psychiatric Patients, their Families and Staff." *Journal of Consulting and Clinical Psychology Monograph,* 1968, *32,* Part 2.
4. Endler, N. S. and Hunt, J. McV. "S-R Inventories of Hostility and Comparisons of the Proportions of Variance from Persons, Responses, and Situations for Hostility and Anxiousness. *Journal of Personality and Social Psychology,* 1968, *9,* 309-315.
5. Endler, N. S. and Hunt, J. McV. "Sources of Behavioral Variance as Measured by the S-R Inventory of Anxiousness." *Psychological Bulletin,* 1966, *65,* 336-346.
6. Gleser, G. C., Cronbach, L. G. and Rajaratnam, N. "Generalizability of Scores Influenced by Multiple Sources of Variance." *Psychometrica,* 1965, *30,* 395-418.
7. Grimes, J. W. and Allinsmith, W. "Compulsivity, Anxiety, and School Achievement." *Merrill-Palmer Quarterly,* 1961, *7,* 247-271.
8. Hartshorne, H. and May, M. A. *Studies in Deceit,* Vol. *1,* New York: Macmillan, 1928.
9. Kelly, J. G. "Ecological Constraints on Mental Health Services." *American Psychologist,* 1966, *21,* 535-539.
10. Kelly, J. G. "Naturalistic Observations and Theory Confirmation: An Example." *Human Development,* 1967, *10,* 212-222.
11. Magnusson, D. and Heffler, B. "The Generality of Behavioral Data, IV: Cross-situational Invariance in an Objectively Measured Behavior." Applied Psychology Unit, Psychological Laboratories, University of Stockholm, 1967 (mimeo).

12. Mischel, W. *Personality and Assessment.* New York: John Wiley and Sons, 1968.
13. Moos, R. H. "The Generality of Questionnaire Data: Ratings by Psychiatric Patients." *Journal of Clinical Psychology,* in press, 1969.
14. Moos, R. H. "Situational Analysis of a Therapeutic Community Milieu." *Journal of Abnormal Psychology,* 1968, *73,* 49-61.
15. Raush, H. L., Dittmann, A. T. and Taylor, T. J. "The Interpersonal Behavior of Children in Residential Treatment." *Journal of Abnormal and Social Psychology,* 1959, *58,* 9-26 (a).
16. Raush, H. L., Dittmann, A. T. and Taylor, T. J. "Person, Setting and Change in Social Interaction." *Human Relations,* 1959, *12,* 361-378 (b).
17. Raush, H. L., Farbman, I. and Llewellyn, L. G. "Person, Setting and Change in Social Interaction: II. A Normal Control Study." *Human Relations,* 1960, *13,* 305-332.
18. Sarason, S. B., Levine, M., Goldenberg, I. I., Cherlin, D. L. and Bennett, E. M. *Psychology in Community Settings: Clinical, Educational, Vocational, Social Aspects.* New York: John Wiley and Sons, 1966.
19. Trickett, E. J., Kelly, J. G. and Todd, D. M. "The Social Environment of the High School: Guidelines for Individual Change and Organizational Redevelopment." In Golan, S. E. and Eisendorfer, C. (eds.), *Community Psychology and Mental Health,* in press, 1970.
20. Walberg, H. J. Classroom Climate Questionnaire. Cambridge, Mass.: Harvard University, 1967, mimeograph.
21. Walberg, H. J. Structural and Affective Aspects of Classroom Climate. *Psychology in the Schools,* 1968, *5,* 247-252.
22. Walberg, H. J. and Anderson, G. J. Learning Environment Inventory. Cambridge, Mass.: Harvard University, 1967, mimeograph.
23. Winer, B. J. *Statistical Principles in Experimental Design.* New York: McGraw-Hill, 1962.

CHAPTER FOUR

METHODOLOGIES FOR ANALYZING PERSON BY SITUATION INTERACTIONS

The modern interactionistic theory of behavior, as summarized in chap. 1, has important consequences for the choice of models and for methods of data collection and data treatment. However, in the past, appropriate methods for the treatment of person by situation interaction data were lacking, and it is not until recently that such methods have been available. Probably, the empirical study of person by situation interactions was delayed by the lack of such methods. A good example of the influence of methodology on empirical developments in this area is the effect of the introduction of the S-R Inventory of Anxiousness by Endler, Hunt, and Rosenstein (1962). Although this inventory presented a theoretical advance by simultaneously sampling persons, situations, and responses, the authors erroneously concluded that situations were more important than persons (rather than concluding that interactions were more important than either persons or situations) because of inappropriate statistical methodologies.

This chapter contains three papers: by Endler [21], by Raush [22], and by Magnusson and Ekehammar [23]. The methods discussed in these papers are closely bound to what Overton and Reese (1973) have called a reactive model of behavior (see chap. 1). In order for interactional psychology to produce further developments and progress, it is essential that new methods are developed. These new methods should be appropriate for the treatment of data within an organismic model of behavior (see for example, Raush, 1972).

In investigations of the trait (inner-directed), situationism (outer-directed), and interaction personality models discussed in chap. 1, one main problem of interest is the relative contribution of different sources to the total behavioral variance (see Endler & Hunt, [10], Sells, 1963). This cannot be accomplished by directly comparing mean squares from different sources, since mean squares are not independent of one another. Bolles and Messick (1958) suggested a method for partitioning variance due to different sources by forming ratios of the sums of squares for each variance source divided by the total sum of squares. A preferable method is to use a variance components technique. Endler [21], in the first paper in this chapter, presents a variance components technique and compares this method for random and mixed effects analysis of various techniques. He suggests that the choice of model should be determined by the nature of the data under investigation. An example, using anxiety data from Endler, Hunt, and Rosenstein (1962), compares the relative contributions of different sources of variance, and shows that for this particular example person by situation interactions contribute more to variance than either persons or situations *per se*. The method proposed by Endler and presented in this paper has subsequently been widely used (see [10], [11], [12], [13], [17], [18], [19], [20], [33], for example).

In the second paper Raush [22] discusses two methods for data treatment: multivariate information analysis and transition probability analysis. He applies these methods to affectional behavior data in order to investigate interaction sequences among normal and disturbed children in different situations. Multivariate information analysis, which does not require linearity, or continuity, or a metric, or order relations among data, is used to study the main effects of situations, groups, and antecedent behavioral acts on subsequent behavior, as well as the relative contributions of different components. Using transition probability analysis, the probability of a certain behavior in a dyadic interaction can be predicted on the basis of data from the two antecedent events in this interaction. Raush compares such predictions with the actual outcome in his data, and finds that interactions are more important than main effects. He suggests that the methods can be used in future studies on temporal processes of behavior.

Magnusson [28], in his paper on stituational dimensions, summarizes the results of some recent studies on the generality of behavioral measures by stating "... that individuals differ not mainly with regard to certain stable aspects of behavior but particularly regarding their specific, characteristic ways of adjusting to the varying characteristics of different situations" (see Magnusson [28], chap. 5). Therefore, the behavioral pattern across situations should be a major source of interest in empirical studies conducted within a person–situation interaction model. There is, however, a lack of methodology for determining interactional patterns when studying individuals and groups. In the third paper in this chapter, Magnusson and Ekehammar [23] use Latent Profile Analysis (LPA) (see Mårdberg, 1973) as a basis for classifying individuals in homogeneous groups in terms of their reaction patterns across situations. The data are taken from an inventory of the Endler–Hunt S–R Inventory format. Magnusson and Ekehammar compare, contrast, and discuss the profiles for sexes and for different subgroups based on their reactions across different situations. For example, three categories of individuals were obtained for each sex, two of which differed in *level* of anxiety, with the third group being characterized by a high trans-situational inconsistency.

REFERENCES

Bolles, R., & Messick, S. Statistical ability in experimental inference. *Psychological Reports,* 1958, *4,* 223–227.

Endler, N. S., Hunt, J. McV., & Rosenstein, A. J. An S–R Inventory of Anxiousness, *Psychological Monographs*, 1962, *76*, No. 17 (whole No. 536), 1–33.

Mårdberg, B. A model for selection and classification in industrial psychology. *Reports from the Psychological Laboratories, University of Stockholm*, 1973, suppl. 19.

Overton, W. F., and Reese, H. W. Models of development: Methodological implications. In J. R. Nesselroade and W. H. Reese (Eds.), *Life-span developmental psychology: Methodological issues*. New York: Academic Press, 1973.

Raush, H. L. Process and change. *Family Process*, 1972, *11*, 275–298.

Sells, S. B. The interactionist looks at the environment. *American Psychologist*, 1963, *18*, 696–702.

21

Estimating Variance Components from Mean Squares for Random and Mixed Effects Analysis of Variance Models

NORMAN S. ENDLER

Analysis of variance procedures can be used for: (a) F tests of the null hypothesis (the traditional use); (b) investigating theoretical models as suggested by Grant (1962); and (c) estimating, from mean squares, the relative contributions of variance components.

Most psychologists have used F ratios. A neglected use of analysis of variance is to estimate, from mean squares, the relative magnitude of each component of variance. Many authors (Anderson & Bancroft, 1952; Lindquist, 1953; Schultz, 1955; Cornfield & Tukey, 1956; Scheffé, 1959; Gaito, 1958, 1960; Edwards, 1960; Winer, 1962; McNemar, 1963; etc.) have discussed expectations of mean squares $[E(MS)]$, but primarily in terms of the appropriate error terms for F ratios, rather than with respect to solving empirically for the different variance components. Gaito has estimated variance components for a two-way classification model; Medley and Mitzel (1963), and Gleser, Cronbach, and Rajaratnam (1965) for a three-way model. Medley and Mitzel (1963), comparing random and fixed effects models, have been primarily interested in reliability estimation,

Endler, N. S. Estimating variance components from mean squares for random and mixed effects analysis of variance models. *Perceptual and Motor Skills,* 1966, 22, 559-570. Reprinted by permission.

The investigation was partially supported by United States Public Health Service Grant MH−08987, from the NIMH (funded through the University of Illinois) and partially supported by a grant from York University, Toronto. The author is indebted to L. J. Cronbach and G. C. Gleser, whose ideas on components of variance and whose comments on our S-R monograph stimulated the writing of this paper. He also wishes to thank John Gaito, J. McV. Hunt, and D. W. Fiske for their helpful comments and suggestions, and W. J. Jobst for his assistance in reanalyzing the S-R data. Any errors and obscurities are the responsibility of the author. Parts of this paper are derived from an earlier unpublished paper by Endler and W. J. Jobst (1964), entitled "Components of variances derived from mean squares for random, mixed and fixed effects analysis of variance models."

while Gleser, *et al.* (1965) have compared the absolute values of the different variance components for a random effects model. This study elaborates and extends the Gleser, *et al.* paper to the mixed model.

The purposes of this expository paper are: (1) to indicate how the analysis of variance can be used to determine the relative magnitude of different variance components as a percentage of the sum of the different variance components (total variation); (2) to discuss the relative merits of random and mixed effects models[1] when using the procedure of variance components; and (3) to illustrate the above with an example from the field of personality assessment. A three-way classification analysis of variance with one observation per cell will be used.[2]

The rationale for the use of variance components is that one can determine the relative contribution to variance of different sources (factors). *F* ratios primarily determine whether or not a particular source of variance is significant, but do not indicate how much a particular source contributes to variance or the relative importance of different factors. Specifically, the variance components procedure may aid in resolving the controversy in personality theory as to the relative importance of individuals and situations as sources of behavioral variation. Furthermore, this procedure can be used in reliability estimation (Medley & Mitzel, 1963; Gleser, *et al.*, 1965) and for determining sources of unreliability. For example, disagreement among judges may be due to the effects of situational variance, or to Ss by situation variance. The variance components procedure therefore supplements information obtained by other procedures (e.g., *F* ratios, correlations) and may be used to answer questions not readily answered by other statistical procedures.

VARIANCE COMPONENTS

In the analysis of variance, each *MS* computed from a particular sample is a function of the sum of the relevant component sample variances, each component being multiplied by an appropriate coefficient. However, mean squares *cannot* be added since each may be a composite of variance due to independent variables, their interactions, and error. Nor can they be used to describe the

---

[1] For a discussion of variance components with respect to a fixed effects model see the unpublished Endler and Jobst (1964) paper. A three-way analysis of variance fixed effects model with one observation per cell presents certain problems. No error term for *F* is available and one cannot determine the variance components unless one assumes that σ_{pij}^2 (the triple interaction) is zero, an assumption that is often unwarranted. Therefore, most fixed effects designs will have more than one observation per cell. When one of the factors is persons (Ss) (e.g., in personality assessment; see illustrative example in this paper) the fixed effects model is unwarranted, because rarely, if ever, can one justify that persons represent a fixed effect. Therefore, this paper will limit itself to random and mixed effects models.

[2] This particular model presents certain difficulties because there is no independent estimate of σ_e^2 and certain assumptions have to be made about the triple interaction (e.g., the triple interaction is zero). However, this model was chosen because it is frequently reported in the literature and it is pertinent to the field of personality assessment.

relative contribution of different sources of variance. It is necessary to break down the mean squares into the variance components and to solve for each component separately.

In order to obtain a unique solution for each separate variance component in a three-way classification analysis of variance, it is necessary to have more than one observation per cell.[3] However, in the area of personality research, e.g., it is often unfeasible to have more than one observation per cell.[4]

Some Notation and Definitions

We will deal with a three-way analysis of variance with one observation per cell, where one of the factors is subjects or persons (p), and the other two factors or facets are i and j. This particular model assumes completely matched data or crossings. Each level of i is matched with each level of j, and this occurs for each person (p). That is, for each p there are all possible i and j crossings. The number of levels or observations for p is n; the number of levels for facet i is k; and the number of levels for facet j is m. Therefore, there are eight sources of variance for each score, namely: σ_p^2, σ_i^2, σ_j^2, σ_{pj}^2, σ_{pi}^2, σ_{ij}^2, σ_{pij}^2, and σ_e^2 (where e stands for within or error of measurement variance). We can also define a residual variance as σ_r^2 which is equal to $\sigma_e^2 + \sigma_{pij}^2$.

Therefore, a three-way analysis of variance would yield the following mean squares: $MS_p = SS_p/(n-1)$; $MS_i = SS_i/(k-1)$; $MS_j = SS_j/(m-1)$; $MS_{pi} = SS_{pi}/(n-1)(k-1)$; $MS_{pj} = SS_{pj}/(n-1)(m-1)$; $MS_{ij} = SS_{ij}/(k-1)(m-1)$; $MS_r = SS_r/(n-1)(k-1)(m-1)$.

---

[3] For the random effects model the error and triple interaction components of variance are confounded in each $E(MS)$. However, it is possible to use the residual variance (triple interaction) to determine a unique solution for each other variance component, for a three-way classification with one observation per cell. In the mixed model, a unique solution is only possible for some of the components unless certain assumptions are made. (See below.)

[4] For example, it is often unfeasible to administer the same *multidimensional* personality inventory to the same Ss more than once because Ss' boredom, resistance, etc. would increase the error of measurement. Repeated measurements of the same Ss also would lead to carryover effects with unequal covariances. This paper used a univariate procedure as an approximation to a multivariate problem. Danford, Hughes, and McNee (1960) state that as N becomes large, univariate and multivariate F tests approach identical results. Possibly the covariances stabilize as N increases and therefore approximately the same constants appear in the numerator and denominator of the F ratios. In the $E(MS)$ coefficients p or $1 - p$ which refer to variance may bias the results (see Box, 1954). However, Gaito and Wiley (1963) state that the $E(MS)$ for the general multivariate case with unequal variances and covariances "would be complex and difficult to derive and are not available in the literature at the present time" (p. 74). A univariate procedure (assuming equal variances and zero covariances, an assumption seldom met in practice) is suggested as a first approximation which can serve as a screening device and provide better than chance results. However, because of the possibility of correlated scores, the reader is cautioned that the variance components are biased. (See note of caution at the end of paper.)

Each mean square can be broken down into different components of variance; the components included in a mean square partially determined by the type of model. We will use σ^2 to represent a component due directly to a random effect; θ^2 a component due to a fixed effect [see Schultz (1955), Edwards (1960), and Gaito (1960), for methods for obtaining the $E(MS)$ or variance components[5]].

Case I: The Random Effects Model

In the random effects model, the assumption is made that the levels for each of the three factors have been randomly sampled from larger populations. The $E(MS)$ can be broken down into components of variance, in terms of seven equations. Since the terms $\sigma_e{}^2$ and $\sigma_{pij}{}^2$ occur in all equations, let $\sigma_e{}^2 + \sigma_{pij}{}^2 = \sigma_r{}^2$ (residual) and the equations take the following form:[6]

$$E(MS_p) = \sigma_r{}^2 + km\sigma_p{}^2 + m\sigma_{pi}{}^2 + k\sigma_{pj}{}^2 \qquad [1]$$

$$E(MS_i) = \sigma_r{}^2 + nm\sigma_i{}^2 + m\sigma_{pi}{}^2 + n\sigma_{ij}{}^2 \qquad [2]$$

$$E(MS_j) = \sigma_r{}^2 + nk\sigma_j{}^2 + k\sigma_{pj}{}^2 + n\sigma_{ij}{}^2 \qquad [3]$$

$$E(MS_{pi}) = \sigma_r{}^2 + m\sigma_{pi}{}^2 \qquad [4]$$

$$E(MS_{pj}) = \sigma_r{}^2 + k\sigma_{pj}{}^2 \qquad [5]$$

$$E(MS_{ij}) = \sigma_r{}^2 + n\sigma_{ij}{}^2 \qquad [6]$$

$$E(MS_r) = \sigma_r{}^2 . \qquad [7]$$

The above seven equations can be solved for the seven variance components by substituting the observed mean squares (from the analysis of variance) for their expectancies.

This provides the following estimates of the variance components in terms of mean squares:

$$\sigma_p{}^2 = (MS_p - MS_{pi} - MS_{pj} + MS_r)/km \qquad [8]$$

---

[5] The $E(MS)$ for a given source includes the error variance $\sigma_e{}^2$, a component of variance directly attributable to that source and all other components (σ^2 terms) which include the subscripts under consideration, providing the remaining subscripts refer to random effects. The coefficient of each component for any given source is the product of the number of levels of the variables not included in the subscript of the σ^2 being considered. These coefficients are multiplied by n the number of observations per cell, which in this particular paper is equal to 1. The coefficient of $\sigma_e{}^2$ is always 1.

[6] It is assumed that the covariances between ith and jth factors are zero. Therefore the covariance terms are not included in the $E(MS)$. See Footnote 5 and note of caution.

$$\sigma_i{}^2 = (MS_i - MS_{pi} - MS_{ij} + MS_r)/nm \tag{9}$$

$$\sigma_j{}^2 = (MS_j - MS_{pj} - MS_{ij} + MS_r)/nk \tag{10}$$

$$\sigma_{pi}{}^2 = (MS_{pi} - MS_r)/m \tag{11}$$

$$\sigma_{pj}{}^2 = (MS_{pj} - MS_r)/k \tag{12}$$

$$\sigma_{ij}{}^2 = (MS_{ij} - MS_r)/n \tag{13}$$

$$\sigma_r{}^2 = MS_r \ . \tag{14}$$

Since variances are additive, we can sum the seven components, obtain a component sum or total, and determine the proportion or percentage of the component sum contributed by each individual components. (Note that $\sigma_e{}^2$ cannot be estimated in this situation.) This enables us to compare the relative magnitude of the different components.

Note that for the random effects model the assumption is made that the levels for each factor are random samples from an indefinitely large population. This assumption is often unwarranted in psychological research, where mixed and fixed models are frequently more appropriate. Random and mixed effects models are quite dependent on the assumption of normality; the fixed model is robust despite failures in assumptions.

Case II: The Mixed Effects Model

In the mixed effects model, the assumption is made that for some of the factors, the levels have been randomly sampled, while for other factors, the levels have not been randomly sampled.

Suppose one of the factors, p, is randomly sampled, while the other two factors, i and j, have not been randomly sampled.[7] Therefore, p is a random effect and i and j are fixed effects.

In this case, the $E(MS)$ can be broken down into components of variance as follows (see Schultz, 1955). Note that σ^2 represents a component due to a random effect, and θ^2 represents a component due to a fixed effect.

$$E(MS_p) = \sigma_e{}^2 + km\sigma_p{}^2 \tag{15}$$

$$E(MS_i) = \sigma_e{}^2 + nm\theta_i{}^2 + m\sigma_{pi}{}^2 \tag{16}$$

$$E(MS_j) = \sigma_e{}^2 + nk\theta_j{}^2 + k\sigma_{pj}{}^2 \tag{17}$$

---

[7] The procedure for having two levels random and one fixed is analogous to the model described here where two are fixed and one is random.

$$E(MS_{pi}) = \sigma_e^2 + m\sigma_{pi}^2 \tag{18}$$

$$E(MS_{pj}) = \sigma_e^2 + k\sigma_{pj}^2 \tag{19}$$

$$E(MS_{ij}) = \sigma_e^2 + \sigma_{pij}^2 + n\theta_{ij}^2 \tag{20}$$

$$E(MS_r) = \sigma_e^2 + \sigma_{pij}^2 \tag{21}$$

This provides seven simultaneous equations and eight unknowns. However, here the terms σ_e^2 and σ_{pij}^2 do not occur in all equations. Therefore, the equations in the present form are insoluble in terms of unique solutions unless we make certain assumptions. In deriving F ratios, some investigators have assumed that σ_{pij}^2 is equal to zero.[8] If, therefore, the assumption is made that σ_{pij}^2 is equal to zero, Equations 15 to 19 are not altered and 20 and 21 become:

$$E(MS_{ij}) = \sigma_e^2 + n\theta_{ij}^2 \tag{20a}$$

$$E(MS_r) = \sigma_e^2 \tag{21a}$$

This provides seven equations and seven unknowns. Therefore, these equations can be solved for each variance component by substituting the observed mean squares for their expectancies.

The estimates of variance components in terms of mean square are then:

$$\sigma_p^2 = (MS_p - MS_r)/km \tag{22}$$

$$\theta_i^2 = (MS_i - MS_{pi})/nm \tag{23}$$

$$\theta_j^2 = (MS_j - MS_{pj})/nk \tag{24}$$

---

[8] Assuming that σ_{pij}^2 is equal to zero in effect assumes that the triple interaction is zero. In psychological research this is probably not warranted but is less unrealistic than assuming that the error variance is zero. This point is elaborated in the discussion section of this paper. In many cases in hypothesis testing the investigator is primarily interested in three F ratios: the main effect for factor i; the main effect for factor j; and the i by j interaction. In these cases it does not matter what the three-way interaction is. However, if in hypothesis testing the investigator is interested in the F ratio due to the main effect of p (persons) and its interactions with i and with j, it is necessary to make some assumptions about the triple interaction (e.g., $\sigma_{pij}^2 = 0$) or about σ_e^2. The discussion section of this paper *compares* variance components results under the assumptions of $\sigma_{pij}^2 = 0$ versus $\sigma_e^2 = 0$, i.e., the lower and upper limits of the triple interaction. One can also possibly use the error of measurement of item scores or single responses (derived from the reliability of the measuring instrument) as an estimate of σ_e^2. While this is feasible for estimating variance components, it is not justified for F testing where one must use the data provided by the experiment.

$$\sigma_{pi}^2 = (MS_{pi} - MS_r)/m \qquad [25]$$

$$\sigma_{pj}^2 = (MS_{pj} - MS_r)/k \qquad [26]$$

$$\theta_{ij}^2 = (MS_{ij} - MS_r)/n \qquad [27]$$

$$\sigma_e^2 = MS_r \ . \qquad [28]$$

The variance components can be summed and the proportion or percentage of this sum or total contributed by each component can be determined. (Equations 22 to 28 hold only for one factor random and two fixed, and not for two factors random.)

Note that for the mixed effects model, the assumption is that the triple interaction, σ_{pij}^2, is equal to zero. This assumption is not always warranted in psychological research where the triple interaction may have psychological meaning.

Illustrative Example

The S-R Inventory of Anxiousness (Endler, Hunt, & Rosenstein, 1962) is used as an example to illustrate how the percentage of variance due to each of several factors can be determined. The S-R Inventory employs a sample of 14 modes of response to a sample of 11 situations. Each response is matched with each situation, and the total number of items is 154. It is possible to use different numbers of situations and modes of response. Therefore, the three factors are p = persons or Ss, i = situations, and j = modes of response. There are n persons, k situations, and m modes of response.

Table 4 of the monograph (Endler, *et al.*, 1962, p. 10) reports an analysis of variance of the S-R Inventory (11 situations by 14 modes of response) for 169 Ss from Pennsylvania State. Mean squares for the various sources were as follows: Subjects (Ss) = 21.26; situations (Sit.) = 244.37; modes of response (M-R) = 836.51; Ss X Sits. = 3.16; Ss X M-R = 2.86; Sits. X M-R = 20.62; and residual (Ss X Sits. X M-R) = 0.66.

The variance components can be estimated from the specification equations previously discussed. Each component can be expressed as a percentage of the sum of all the components or total variation. For a random model (as assumed by the authors of the monograph) one solves Equations 8 to 14 for variance components; for a mixed model one solves Equations 22 to 28.

The first four numerical columns of Table 1 present the variance components and percentages of variance (of the components' sum) due to each component for random and mixed effects models, respectively. (The last two columns are not pertinent at this point but will be discussed later.)

For the mixed model $\sigma_{pij}^2 = 0$ is assumed. In general, the results from the two models are comparable and appear to indicate that individual differences *per*

Table 1. Estimated Variance Components and Percentages of Variance Components Derived from a Triple-classification Analysis of Variance of the S-R Inventory of Anxiousness for Random and Mixed Effects Models

Source	Random Model*		Mixed Model** $(\sigma_{pij}{}^2 = 0)$		Mixed Model*** $(\sigma_e{}^2 = 0)$	
	σ^2 Comp.	%	σ^2 Comp.	%	σ^2 Comp.	%
Subjects (p)	.103	5.75	.134	7.28	.138	7.06
Situations (i)	.094	5.25	.102	5.54	.102	5.21
Modes of Response (j)	.438	24.44	.448	24.33	.448	22.90
Ss × Sits. (pi)	.179	9.99	.179	9.72	.226	11.55
Ss × M-R (pj)	.200	11.16	.200	10.86	.260	13.29
Sits. × M-R (ij)	.118	6.58	.118	6.41	.122	6.24
Residual (r)	.660	36.83	.660	35.85	.660	33.74
Total Variation (Components Σ)	1.792	100.00	1.841	99.99	1.956	99.99

*Assuming $\sigma_r{}^2 = \sigma_{pij}{}^2 + \sigma_e{}^2$.
**Assuming $\sigma_{pij}{}^2 = 0$.
***Assuming $\sigma_{pij}{}^2 =$ maximum of .660 (i.e., $\sigma_e{}^2 = 0$).

se ($\sigma_p{}^2$) and situations ($\sigma_i{}^2$) do not contribute very much to the total variation (between 5% and 7% each), while individuals in interaction with situations or with modes of response contribute about 10% each. Modes of response ($\sigma_j{}^2$) contribute about 25% of the variance.

It is important to note, however, that in order to interpret adequately estimated variance components, it is necessary to determine their standard errors or confidence intervals (see Brownlee, 1960; Lindquist, 1953).

DISCUSSION

The Choice of a Model

What model should be used in estimating variance components? The mixed effects model is usually more appropriate than the random effects model for research in the behavioral sciences, where random samplings of all the dimensions (factors) are infrequent. However, on mathematical grounds, the mixed model has certain pitfalls in that we have had to assume that the triple interaction is zero,[9] in order to obtain unique solutions for each component of variance.

---

[9] It may be possible to test whether the triple interaction is zero by extending Tukey's (1949) test of non-additivity from a two-factor experiment to a three-factor experiment. However, if the non-additivity F ratio is significant, we have to assume a non-additivity model and cannot state that the triple interaction is zero. With large samples, the computation of the non-additivity sums of squares becomes a tedious and cumbersome task.

In using the random model, the following basic assumptions have been made: (a) the levels for each of the three factors have been randomly sampled from larger populations, and furthermore, (b) the error or within variance (σ_e^2) can be lumped with the triple interaction variance (σ_{pij}^2) and called the residual variance (σ_r^2).

In the illustrative example (Endler, *et al.*, 1962), while Ss represent a random effect, it is exceedingly difficult to justify the assumption that the situations and the modes of response represent random effects.

Logically, the Endler, *et al.* (1962) analysis is more congruent with a mixed model, with Ss random and both situations and modes of response fixed. However, in order to obtain unique solutions for each of the variance components of a mixed model, it is necessary to make an assumption about the triple interaction (e.g., $\sigma_{pij}^2 = 0$). This may be untenable because the triple interaction, in this case, has psychological meaning. It states that in a specific situation, a particular person has a particular mode of response. For example, one person may not need to urinate frequently or be especially concerned about automobiles, but when he is just starting off on a long automobile trip, he may exhibit this particular urinary response. This is an example of a real effect which is distinguished from a main effect, a simple interaction or error. One can hardly justify calling this triple interaction zero!

Another difficulty with the mixed model is with respect to the fixed effects factors where the entire *range* of possible levels may not be represented. (For random factors the entire range usually is represented.) Since the amount of variance is a function of the range, estimation of fixed effects factors may be biased if the range of all possible levels is not represented.

Therefore, both models have certain limitations; the random effects model is not always suitable, because E cannot always sample randomly for all factors; the mixed model does not allow unique solutions for each variance component to be obtained, unless the (usually unwarranted) assumption is made that the triple interaction is zero.

How can this dilemma be resolved? One possible solution for the mixed effects model, where there are eight equations and seven unknowns, is to compare the results under the assumptions of minimum and maximum triple interactions. Let us take the case of the mixed effects model using our illustrative example. The results for the variance components under the assumption of a *minimum* or zero triple interaction appear in Table 1 (see two middle columns). Since the residual variance is equal to triple interaction plus within (or error) variance, a *maximum* triple interaction variance is obtained when it is assumed that the within (or error) variance is zero. Letting $\sigma_e^2 = 0$ (i.e., maximizing the triple interaction) and solving Equations 15 to 21 for our illustrative example (mixed model), the results that appear in the last two columns of Table 1 are obtained.

Thus the middle two columns of Table 1 contain the results for the variance components under the assumptions of a *minimum* triple interaction

$(\sigma_{pij}{}^2 = 0)$;[10] and the last two columns contain the variance component results under the assumption of a *maximum* triple interaction ($\sigma_{pij}{}^2 = .660$ or $\sigma_e{}^2 = 0$). A comparison of the variance components under these two extreme sets of conditions (lower and upper limits or bounds of $\sigma_{pij}{}^2$) indicates that the results are practically identical. The total variation (or sum of the variance components) differs by only .115.[11] Therefore, in this particular empirical case it does not appear to make a difference. Assuming that the triple interaction is zero does not markedly affect the relative magnitude of the variance components.

However, in general, on what basis can the decision be made to assume a triple interaction of zero? Each E must compare his results under conditions where $\sigma_{pij}{}^2$ is both maximized and minimized. If there is no basic difference under these two sets of conditions, E can assume that the triple interaction is zero and obtain a unique solution for each component.

Another ostensibly workable solution for the mixed effects model is to have more than one observation per cell. This, however, would mean the re-administration of the inventory to the same Ss, an unsatisfactory solution since their responses may be more the reflection of negativism, boredom, etc. than of a true anxiety level.

The author proposes that the most practical solution when using the S-R Inventory is to have replications with *different* sample groups, and to use *different* forms of the inventory (each of which contains *different* situations and *different* modes of response). This may then justify the use of the random effects model (and would allow for the solution of each variance component without having to assume that the triple interaction was zero). If, using this procedure, the results from the different samples with different situations and different modes of response are comparable, then certain inferences can be made about the population parameters. Ideally, the use of the random effects model is theoretically justified only when levels and Ss have been randomly sampled, i.e., when all persons, situations, and modes of response have had the same possibility of being included in the sample. However, it is very difficult to define a universe of situations or of modes of response and to attempt to obtain random samples.[12]

Table 1 indicates that the results from the random and mixed effects models are nearly equivalent with respect to the percentage of variance contributed by

---

[10] The values under the random model in Table 1 do not involve the assumption of a minimum (zero) triple interaction.

[11] Note that these are differences in arithmetical values of our estimates of the components of variance. Whether these differences are significant will depend on the estimated sampling variances (or standard deviations) of these estimated variance components. Lindquist (1953) and Brownlee (1960) suggest procedures for determining sampling variances and confidence intervals for estimated variance components and for testing for significance of differences for independent samples. The present differences are *not* based upon independent samples and therefore the usual tests *cannot* be used.

[12] If a finite population of situations (or modes of response) were defined, it would be necessary to correct the variance components for sampling from a finite universe.

each component. In this particular case, it did not seem to make any real difference which model was used. Nevertheless, the random model seemed to be the least inappropriate for the S-R Inventory of Anxiousness.

In general, however, each *E* or research worker must make his own decision as to which model to use. He should realize that each model requires certain assumptions, some of which are usually completely untenable. But he must be prepared to defend his chosen assumptions and his decisions, on both theoretical and practical, as well as on statistical grounds.

A NOTE OF CAUTION

This paper uses a univariate component analysis procedure as an approximation to a multivariate problem. Because one of the factors is *S*s (on whom there are repeated measurements) there is no exact or unique solution unless one resorts to multivariate procedures. The use of a univariate procedure requires some assumptions that may not be completely tenable, but nevertheless provides us with a rough approximation of variance components which is better than chance and certainly better than no solution at all.

Gaito and Wiley (1963) discuss three types of analysis of variance structures: (a) Zero covariance: intercorrelations between treatments are zero; univariate analysis is the appropriate solution; (b) Constant covariance: intercorrelations are non-zero but are equal; univariate analysis may still be used but the $E(MS)$ of some sources are slightly modified by a coefficient which includes p (see Gaito & Wiley, 1963, p. 71-72); and (c) Unequal covariance: this is the general case in which intercorrelations may all be unequal and nonzero; multivariate analyses provide exact solutions.

The procedures presented in this paper are of zero covariance nature. Obviously these are most appropriate when those conditions hold. They should provide a suitable approximation also when constant covariance structure is involved, if one allows for p appearing in the $E(MS)$ of some sources. In the unequal covariance case the univariate procedures are least appropriate but would still provide a rough approximation. The exact distortion introduced by a univariate approximation to the multivariate case seems to depend on the differences between the covariances. When the differences are small, the approximation should be a reasonably good one; the approximation would be less adequate as the differences in covariances diverged. Likewise with a small number of tests or treatments separated by short time intervals if covariances are nonzero, it is reasonable to expect that they would not be too different.

The assumption of zero covariance introduces bias in that cross-products based on the fact that covariances are other than zero do not appear in the $E(MS)$ equations, and therefore the univariate model cannot be used as an exact solution. The multivariate model involves very laborious procedures which would not be recommended for the average investigator. In spite of the biases introduced by the univariate approximation, it may be useful for the empirical worker to have a *tool*, which is a first approximation rather than no solution at all. *Caveat Emptor!*

REFERENCES

Anderson, R. L., & Bancroft, T. A. *Statistical theory in research.* New York: McGraw-Hill, 1952.

Box, G. E. P. Some theorems on quadratic forms applied in the study of analysis of variance problems: II. Effects of inequality of variance and of correlation between errors in the two-way classification. *Ann. math. Statist.,* 1954, 25, 484-498.

Brownlee, K. A. *Statistical theory and methodology in science and engineering.* New York: Wiley, 1960.

Cornfield, J., & Tukey, J. W. Average values of mean squares in factorials. *Ann. math. Statist.,* 1956, 27, 907-949.

Danford, M. B., Hughes, H., & McNee, R. C. The analysis of repeated measurements experiments. *Biometrics,* 1960, 16, 547-565.

Edwards, A. L. *Experimental design in psychological research.* (Rev. ed.) New York: Holt, Rinehart & Winston, 1960.

Endler, N. S., Hunt, J. McV., & Rosenstein, A. J. An S-R Inventory of Anxiousness. *Psychol. Monogr.,* 1962, 76, No. 17 (Whole No. 536).

Endler, N. S., & Jobst, W. J. *Components of variance derived from mean squares for random, mixed and fixed effects analysis of variance models.* Technical Report: Project No. MH-08987; USPHS, Univer. of Illinois, October, 1964.

Gaito, J. The Bolles-Messick coefficient of utility. *Psychol. Rep.,* 1958, 4, 595-598.

Gaito, J. Expected mean squares in analysis of variance techniques. *Psychol. Rep.,* 1960, 7, 3-10.

Gaito, J., & Wiley, D. E. Univariate analysis of variance procedures in the measurement of change. In C. W. Harris (Ed.), *Problems in measuring change.* Madison: Univer. of Wisconsin Press, 1963. Pp. 60-84.

Gleser, G. C., Cronbach, L. J., & Rajaratnam, N. Generalizability of scores influenced by multiple sources of variance. *Psychometrika,* 1965, 30, 395-418.

Grant, D. A. Testing the null hypothesis and the strategy and tactics of investigating theoretical models. *Psychol. Bull.,* 1962, 69, 54-61.

Lindquist, E. F. *Design and analysis of experiments in psychology and education.* New York: Houghton-Mifflin, 1953.

McNemar, Q. *Psychological statistics.* (3rd ed.) New York: Wiley, 1963.

Medley, D. M., & Mitzel, H. E. Measureing classroom behaviour by systematic observation. In N. L. Gage (Ed.), *Handbook of research on teaching: a project of the American Educational Research Association.* Chicago: Rand McNally, 1963. Pp. 247-329.

Scheffé, H. *The analysis of variance.* New York: Wiley, 1959.

Schultz, E. F., Jr. Rules of thumb for determining expectations of mean squares. *Biometrics,* 1955, 11, 123-135.

Tukey, J. W. One degree of freedom for nonadditivity. *Biometrics,* 1949, 5, 232-242.

Winer, B. J. *Statistical principles in experimental design.* New York: McGraw-Hill, 1962.

22

Interaction Sequences

HAROLD L. RAUSH

Studies of interaction, whoever the subjects and whatever the situations, presume communication whereby the participants in an interchange influence one another. The fact of such influence permeates our daily lives. We greet someone and expect and most often get a greeting in return; we ask for directions and most often get a reasonable reply; we shop and expect that money will be accepted for our purchases. Our lives as social beings are premised on some degree of ability to change the behavior and attitudes of others by means of our own actions.

Social interaction as an influence or change-inducing process involves several features. First is the fact that interchanges occur in sequences over time. Second, the process of change presupposes variation and constraint. A third feature may be posed as an issue of balance between efficiency and flexibility.

1. Sequential aspects. Interchanges occur sequentially. A sequence may be confined to a single act by A followed by a single response by B. More often, it involves a chain of interchanges. By means of chaining, multiple contingencies may be taken into account, and, even for binary events, given a long enough chain, any level of complexity may be achieved (Ashby, 1958). The adaptive properties of such a chaining process have been noted by Bonner (1960). An effort to study the process of interchange and the chaining of interchanges, rather than single behavioral acts, gave rise to the studies discussed here.

2. Variation and constraint. Like chaining, variability allows for possibilities by which organisms can be sensitive to multiple contingencies (Beach, 1960;

From the *Journal of Personality and Social Psychology,* 1965, *2,* 487–499. Copyright 1965 by the American Psychological Association. Reprinted by permission.

Among those who have contributed most to the development of this paper, Richard A. Littman of the University of Oregon and Allen T. Dittmann of the Laboratory of Psychology at the National Institute of Mental Health deserve very special mention. Other major contributors to the work and ideas have been Josphine Arasteh, Donald S. Boomer, Robert G. Ryder, and my colleagues, noted later in the paper, from the Institute for Social Research in Oslo.

Campbell, 1959). Social interaction may be thought of as a process of constraint or modification of constraint on initial variability. That is, A's actions may be said to have an effect if they modify the distribution of actual responses from B's total potential repertory. A series of interchanges may thus be characterized by successive transitions over which the behavioral variation among participants undergoes modifications of constraint until a point of equilibrium is reached. The present studies investigate the extent of constraint produced by the action of one person on the immediately subsequent acts of another, the degree and manner in which some situational and personal factors constrain social interaction, and the nature of sequence chains and transitions as these appear in interactions of several different groups of children.

3. Efficiency and flexibility. The greater potential for variation and chaining in humans as contrasted with lower species contributes to the greater complexity and lower predictability of human behavior. So, even at the very simplest levels of perception in humans, there appears to be a residual "error" or uncertainty between stimulus and response (Brunswik, 1944; Garner, 1962), and more complex human transactions lack the efficiency that characterizes the spinning-off of a pattern of behavioral events in, for example, an insect mating ritual. However, since a system is modifiable only to the extent that some uncertainty exists between the classes of events, the inefficiency permits a flexibility which would not be possible if a given event a_1 always led to a given event b_1. That such flexibility has evolutionary adaptive advantages is suggested by Russell and Russell (1961) who contrast "exploratory" with "automatic" systems. The flexibility, associated with residual uncertainty between classes of events, allows diversity in forms of control and organization of behavior.

CONTROL AND ORGANIZATION

Human interaction can thus become sensitive to a variety of constraints. Some of these are considered below. More generally, however, two major modes of constraint may be distinguished. One is that of control; the other is that of organization or patterning.

Control

Participants, in interacting, generally exercise some degree of control on one another's behavior. That is, B's actions will vary somewhat according to what A does. For some behaviors B's responses to A tend to be complementary. Gellert (1962), for example, finds that a child's dominance tends to increase when he is paired with the less assertive of two peers; similarly, Raush, Dittmann, and Taylor (1959a) suggest a complementary relation between dominance by one child and submission by another. Other kinds of behavior tend to lead to similar rather than complementary responses. This appears to be so for affectional behavior, in which friendly action given is associated with friendly action received. This latter parallelism is illustrated in Figure 1, which summarizes a few results from observational studies of several groups (cf. Raush, Farbman, & Llewellyn, 1960). The figure suggests that the proportion of friendly or hostile behavior which children receive from their peers reflects rather closely the behavior they "send" to them. The studies, however, do not demonstrate directly the contingencies between the actions of one person and those of another, nor do they indicate their degree. In contrast, the present report deals with the contingencies through which the antecedent action of one child exerts control on the subsequent actions of another.

It is obvious, however, that the antecedent behavior of another is not the sole source of control on social behavior. For example, the potency of situational effects has been demonstrated in the ecological studies of Barker and his colleagues (Barker, 1963; Barker & Wright, 1954). Similarly, previous investigations with the subjects of the present studies showed the influence on social behavior exerted by both situational and individual factors (Raush, Dittmann, & Taylor, 1959b; Raush et al., 1960).

Each of the components mentioned—the action of others, the situation, individual factors—illustrate classes of constraint by control. In addition to its direct effects, such control may also have indirect effects. Control is direct in terms of its immediate influence. For example, as suggested in the earlier studies, a given situation α may increase the probability of social acts a_1 in contrast to a_2; similarly, a given individual A may in general tend to favor a_1 acts. So too, as shown in the information transmission analyses below, antecedent actions have an immediate effect; thus, antecedent act a_1 may increase the probability of responses $b_1 \ldots b_5$ and decrease the probability of responses $b_6 \ldots b_{10}$.

A class of events may, however, also have remote or indirect effects. That is, its effects may be mediated by intervening events. This would be the case if, for

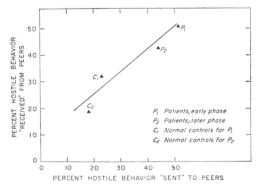

Fig. 1. Relation between "sent" and "received" acts with peers.

example, situation α increased the probability of act a_1, and a_1, in turn, increased the likelihood of response b_1. In this case, the situation would have a direct effect on a and an indirect effect on b. Similarly, an initial act may affect not only the immediately subsequent response, but, by this, may exert influence over more remote responses. The transition analyses below illustrate the chain of events, that is, the indirect effects, which may flow from the contingencies set by initial controls. Constraint by direct control thus refers to modifications of initial probabilities of certain actions out of the total repertory of possible actions; if the influence on initial probabilities then affects more remote events, we may speak of indirect control.

Organization

When more than two variables are present, possibilities for organization arise. Organization corresponds to statistical interaction. Thus, whereas control would be evidenced if Variable Z influenced the particular values of Variables X and/or Y, organization would be evidenced if Variable Z influenced the relationship between X and Y. An example of such organization may be referred to from previous studies (Raush et al., 1960). First, as noted above, the nature of the situation influenced the social behavior of children. But the relation between situational effects and social behavior was in part a function of a variable which might be thought of as reflecting the psychological status of the group. That is, the behavior of normal children was highly sensitive to situational variations, whereas the behavior of very disturbed children was much less sensitive to these variations; as the disturbed children improved in the course of residential treatment, their behavior became more sensitive to situational constraints. The connection between situation and behavior is thus not invariant, but rather is affected by a third component.

Although the present report is concerned with the contingencies between the antecedent social acts of one child and the subsequent acts of another, two other variables are considered. One is the nature of the situation—for example, whether it is that of a mealtime, or a structured game, or an unstructured social event; the other is the nature of the group—whether it consists of disturbed hyper-aggressive children (Redl & Wineman, 1957) or of matched well-adjusted children. We thus have conditions for exploring issues of both control and organization. According to our previous definitions, control is demonstrated if, for example, situation α increases the probability of a_1 acts (direct control), which may, in turn, be followed by an increase in the probability of b_1 acts (indirect control), whereas situation β is associated with greater likelihood of a_2 acts followed by increase in likelihood of b_2 acts. Organization is demonstrated if in situation α antecedent act a_1 is associated with greater likelihood of subsequent act b_1, whereas in situation β antecedent act a_1 yields a higher probability of b_2 acts. Control would thus affect the "level" of the variables, whereas organization would affect their patterning. The information transmission analyses consider issues of control and organization for immediate contingencies between antecedent and subsequent actions. The transition analyses consider issues of control and organization for chains of interactions.

GENERAL METHODS

Situations and Subjects

Each child, plus those with whom he interacted, was observed twice, systematically over six situations—breakfasts, other mealtimes, structured games, unstructured group activities, group instructional situations, and snack periods just before bedtimes. The children were in one of a number of groups: a group of hyperaggressive boys at two stages of residential treatment 1.5 years apart (Raush et al., 1959a, 1959b); groups of normal socially well-adjusted boys, who were matched to serve as controls (Raush et al., 1960); and more recently a group of Norwegian boys, studied in Norway. This latter group was matched in age and roughly in intelligence and socioeconomic status (lower to middle) with the younger American normal group. Like the American controls, the Norwegian children were selected by teachers as socially well-adjusted and the situations for observation were designed to be similar. The adult staffs were, however, quite different as was the general environment, the American subjects having been studied while living on a hospital ward for several weeks during the summer, the Norwegian sample having been studied in a rather isolated farm-resort for a period during the winter.[1] In all cases a group was composed of six boys. The early patient group and the Norwegian children were 9–11 years of age; the other groups were composed of 10.5–12.5 year olds. Because of some limitations in the earlier phases of data collection, together with the fact that the present analyses were not planned in the original design, the early patient group could not be used for all analyses. Apart from this, there were 12 observations for each child and 12 for each situation, which, with six children, made a total of 72 observations in each group.

Data Entry

Dictated raw protocols of observations were transcribed and then coded according to the interpersonal behavior categories devised by Freedman, Leary, Ossorio, and Coffey (1951), and elaborated by Leary (1957). The manner of data gathering and the coding scheme have been described in the previous papers.

[1] The author was a Fulbright scholar at the Institute for Social Research in Oslo in 1959–60. He and his Norwegian colleagues, Claus Fasting and Sissel Berggrav are indebted to the American Social Science Research Council for support of the study. We are grateful also to Ingrid Jacobsen, Jacob Nordland, Torild Skard, Berit Aas, and the Institute staff for their great help.

In order, however, to analyze sequences, a particular method is useful for entering codings. The technique is simply to record each interaction coding in the natural order in which it occurs, and to include in each code a notation of who does what to whom—A hits B, B hits A, A runs away, B shouts an insult at A, etc. The codes are entered onto lined data sheets. The rows of the sheet may be used for the successive acts in an observation, and a column may be assigned to each participant. For the analyses presented below, actions were classified dichotomously, as either friendly or unfriendly.

Sequencing

The previous studies employed frequencies irrespective of order. For the present studies it was necessary to refer back to both codings and the original raw protocols in order to determine sequences. A *sequence* was defined as occurring with any interchange in speech or action between two or more participants. The unit for a sequence was similar to one used by Barker and Wright (1954). A sequence continued so long as there was obvious continuity or contingency in the response of one subject to another; a break in the contingencies terminated a sequence. Farbman (1961) presents some further details and examples. Sequences occur within longer *episode* units (cf. Barker, 1963; Barker & Wright, 1954). For example, within a breakfast observation there might occur an episode of several minutes in which the children discuss a movie they had seen; within the episode may be several sequences, as when A, B, and C talk about a particular scene, or when A asks C to pass the milk, or when D comments to A about his favorite actors. Although such episodes might be treated as supersequences, we have not done so here. In the observations, sequences of interaction occurred between children and other children and between children and adults. This report focuses on the analyses of sequential interactions in affectional behavior among children.

Analytic Methods

Despite the temporal sequential aspects of behavior, noted cogently by Barker (1963), formal schemes for the analysis of the process have been, until recently, difficult to come by. Two such schemes are used here. Both derive from information and communication theory and deal with stochastic processes in which sequences of events are represented by probabilities. One technique, presented by Smith (1953), McGill (1954), and Garner (1958), is that of uncertainty or multivariate information analysis. A second scheme for analyzing sequential data is the transition probability model, described by Ashby (1958) and by Kemeny, Snell, and Thompson (1956).[2]

---

[2] Robert G. Ryder, of the Child Research Branch at the National Institute of Mental Health, has worked out generalized computer programs for both multivariate information and transition probability analyses.

MULTIVARIATE INFORMATION ANALYSES

Garner (1962) summarizes the experimental literature which uses multivariate information analysis, and he presents the theoretical implications of this mode of approach to psychological data. The application of the method is most clearly discussed by Attneave (1959). Since Attneave describes the analysis with sufficient examples so that it can be followed by the mathematically unsophisticated reader, it is not necessary to go into any detail here. A general comment by Ashby (1962) is perhaps appropriate:

[this approach] gives us a method for the treatment of conditionality that is not only completely rigorous but is also of extreme generality. Its great generality and suitability for application to complex behavior lies in the fact that it is applicable to any arbitrarily defined set of states. Its application requires neither linearity, nor continuity, nor a metric, nor even an ordering relation. By this calculus, the *degree* of conditionality can be measured, and analyzed, and apportioned to factors and interactions in a manner exactly parallel to Fisher's method of the analysis of variance; yet it requires no metric in the variables, only the frequencies with which the various combinations of states occur [p. 256].

Ashby looks forward to the time when these methods will become the accepted language for the quantitative treatment of complexities of relation in nonmetric variables of psychology and biology.

Multivariate information analyses were used previously for describing the relations among individual differences, situational influences, and behavioral change in treatment. Here, however, the method is used for analyzing contingencies between the behaviors of one person and another, and for describing how these contingencies are affected by the natures of the situation and the group. The findings may be considered from several perspectives. One is from the point of view of enhancing the predictability of behavior; another is from the point of view of studying communication processes; a third perspective, relevant here, comes from the question, raised earlier, of control and organization.[3]

Main Effects

Effect of the situation on antecedent acts. Table 1 presents results on information yielded about classification of antecedent acts from classification of

---

[3] Another perspective is noted by Stuart A. Altmann of the Department of Zoology of the University of Alberta (Altmann, 1965). Altmann suggests that information analysis of behavior sequences is relevant not only to issues of prediction and communication, but also to the issue of social memory. That is, the number of intervening events over which an act by A continues to influence B's behavior is an operational measure of B's social memory for such an act. This issue, which relates to the temporal extent of what is here called indirect control, cannot be studied by the present information analyses, since the data were sufficient to enable only an analysis of immediate contingencies. Although the transition analyses, since they involve predicting the ultimate fate of an initiating event, are related to this issue, one would need more complete data for tackling the question properly. It is worth noting that Altmann's suggestion of the social memory perspective introduces possibilities for comparative analyses across species, cultures, social classes, or personality types.

Table 1. Effect of the Situation on Antecedent Acts

Group	f	T [a]	% reduction of uncertainty of antecedent acts
Hyperaggressive (later group) plus American well-adjusted controls	854	.092	11
Norwegian well-adjusted	1,237	.081	13

[a] T is the information, in bits, transmitted between the classification of the six situations and antecedent friendly or unfriendly actions. Values are statistically significant, $p < .001$.

the situation. T, in this and in the tables which follow, is the information metric, in bits, from which an estimate of statistical significance can be derived. The last column in the table is the coefficient of constraint, D (cf. Attneave, 1959, pp. 35-36, 59-60), multiplied by 100 to yield the percentage of uncertainty—of, in this case, the antecedent act classification—accounted for—by, in this case, the situational classification. It represents the proportion of information shared between the two, and is analogous to the amount of variance accounted for. The table indicates that by distinguishing among the six situations we may reduce the uncertainty of antecedent affectional acts by some 12%. The values seem relatively consistent for the two analyses. An example from the data may illustrate the finding. For the American normal children, 42% of antecedent acts were unfriendly in game situations[4]; however, only 5% of antecedent acts were unfriendly at mealtimes. Thus, if we know the social situation, we can improve, considerably beyond chance, our guesses about the relative likelihood of friendly or unfriendly behavior.[5] From a communication viewpoint, the situation sets a tone, influencing the likelihood that certain acts will occur.

Effect of the group on antecedent acts. The group variable also related to antecedent acts. As one might indeed expect, hyperaggressive boys, as compared to normal boys, produced fewer friendly acts as stimuli for their peers. For the American normal children, antecedent acts were coded friendly in 89% of the instances; for the Norwegian boys, the value was 85%; the later patient sample produced only 58% antecedent friendly acts, and the earlier group, for whom only partial data were available, showed only 51% such acts.[6] As shown in Table 2, by distinguishing between the clinical group and their matched normals, we may account for about 10% of the variance of antecedent affectional behavior.

---

[4] Acts which were an intrinsic part of the games were eliminated from the analyses.

[5] This and following statements about statistical significance refer, it should be noted, to populations of *acts* rather than to populations of *children*; one may consequently argue that statistical requirements of independence are not met. I have therefore been cautious about interpreting results; unless the differences seem sizable, and unless they were in some way replicated, they are not commented on.

[6] Data on reliability of coding and on questions of rater bias are presented by Dittmann (1958) and by Raush et al. (1959a, 1960).

Table 2. Effect of Group on Antecedent Acts

Group	f	T[a]	% reduction of uncertainty of antecedent acts
Hyperaggressive (later group) plus American well-adjusted controls	854	.087	10
Hyperaggressive (both groups) plus American well-adjusted controls; incomplete but matched data	514	.061	7

[a] T is information yielded about antecedent actions from classifying children as to hyperaggressive or normal. Values are statistically significant, p <.001.

Like the situation, the nature of the group and/or its pathology sets a tone for the communication process.

Effect of antecedent on subsequent acts. Table 3 shows that the major determinant of an act was the immediately preceding act. That is, if you want to know what Child B will do, the best single predictor is what Child A did to B the moment before. For the three groups for which there were complete data, the results indicate that by classifying A's acts we can account for about 30% of the variance of B's immediately following behavior. The more limited sampling of data available for the younger, more disturbed patient group yields somewhat different results. The prior act was still the best single predictor, but in this case it accounted for only 7% of the variance of subsequent acts. Unfortunately, we cannot say here whether this difference is related to age, pathology, or to the nature of the data; the method, however, allows and suggests such investigations for studying development and psychopathology.

Table 3. Effect of Antecedent on Subsequent Acts

Group	f	T[a]	% reduction of uncertainty of subsequent acts
Hyperaggressive (later, after 2 years treatment)	472	.280	28
American well-adjusted	382	.192	31
Norwegian well-adjusted	1,237	.192	29
Hyperaggressive (early, after .5 year treatment; incomplete data)	181	.068	7

[a] T is the information, in bits, transmitted between antecedent acts and subsequent responses, both classified as friendly versus unfriendly. All values in the table are statistically significant, p <.001.

Control and Organization

Antecedent social acts thus exercise a measure of direct control on the subsequent behavior of others. Since the nature of ongoing situations and of particular social groups exert a degree of direct control on antecedent acts, they also indirectly control the behaviors which follow.

One advantage of multivariate information analysis is that it allows us, in examining the relation between two variables, to partial out either single or joint effects of other variables. The ability to hold variables statistically constant allows us to test for what has been called here organizational effects. Organization would exist, if, let us say, the situational variable exerted constraint on subsequent acts, when antecedent acts were partialed out. We would then have evidence that in situation α antecedent act a_1 has greater likelihood of leading to subsequent response b_1, whereas in situation β, antecedent act a_1 has greater likelihood of leading to subsequent response b_2, and this would meet our definition of organization.

Organizational effects of the situation. After eliminating the effect of antecedent acts, the situation had a reduced, but still statistically highly significant ($p <$ .001) effect on subsequent acts. The same was true when both group and antecedent act variables were partialed out. An example selected from the data may give concreteness to the finding. In game situations among the American normal boys, friendly acts led to unfriendly responses in 31% of instances, whereas at mealtimes, friendly acts led to unfriendly responses only 4% of the time; similarly, among the Norwegian children, friendly acts were followed by unfriendly responses 20% of the time at games and only 5% of the time at meals. Thus, the situation not only controlled the initiating events in interaction contingencies, but it modified the patterns of contingent relations.

Organizational effects of the group. The comparison between hyperaggressive boys later in treatment and matched socially adjusted children similarly illustrates not only control by the group or pathology variable, but also organization. Eliminating the influence of antecedent acts, or of both antecedent acts and situations, yielded a significant ($p <$ .001), though reduced, group variable influence on subsequent acts. The results thus indicate that the two groups of children reacted somewhat differently to the same stimuli. We may again turn to the data for concrete cues as to what goes on. The hyperaggressive and the normal boys responded rather similarly to unfriendly antecedent acts, with 80% and 77% unfriendly responses. Data for the early patient group, studied after 6 months of residential treatment, could not be submitted to an exactly comparable information analysis, but they were consistent in that this latter group responded to unfriendly acts with 75% unfriendly responses. Where the groups differed was in their responses to friendly antecedent acts. Among the normals, the friendly acts of one child were followed by unfriendly behavior on the part of the recipient in 8% of instances; the group later in treatment reacted to friendly acts in an unfriendly fashion in 19% of instances; and for the early patient group, this value is 45%. It is not clear to what extent the effects are due to differences in personality and pathology, or to differences in group formation, or, in the case of the earlier group, to age differences. It does, however, seem of clinical and practical significance that the groups differed not in their response to hostile gestures, but rather to friendly ones. There is the further implication that the disturbed children were less able to differentiate friendly from unfriendly acts. From the viewpoint of organization, it is apparent that the groups responded differently to antecedents which were coded as equivalent. The group variable thus exhibited an organizing effect. Like the situational variable, it not only controlled the initiating events, thus influencing subsequent acts, but it also modified the patterns of contingencies.

Relative Contributions of Components

Estimates of the relative contributions of each variable to behavior appear in Table 4. The table presents estimates of the proportion of remaining variance

Table 4. Estimated Contributions of Variables to Behavior

Classification (1)	Accounts for —% of the remaining variance (2)	Of (3)	In sample(s) (4)	When— is (are) partialed out (5)	Mode of constraint (6)
1. Antecedent act	23	Subsequent response	Hyperaggressive (later) plus American controls	Situation and group	Control
2. Antecedent act	25	Subsequent response	Norwegian	Situation	Control
3. Situation	15	Antecedent act	Hyperaggressive (later) plus American controls	Group	Control
4. Situation	13	Antecedent act	Norwegian	—	Control
5. Group	15	Antecedent act	Hyperaggressive (later) plus American controls	Situation	Control
6. Situation	10	Subsequent response	Hyperaggressive (later) plus American controls	Group and antecedent act	Organization
7. Situation	6	Subsequent response	Norwegian	Antecedent act	Organization
8. Group	7	Subsequent response	Hyperaggressive (later) plus American controls	Situation and antecedent act	Organization

Note.—The table is to be read across each row. Thus, Row 1 says that classification by antecedent act accounts for 23% of the potential remaining variance of immediately following responses in the hyperaggressive and well-adjusted children, after the effects of situational and group differences are removed. This illustrates control on subsequent responses by antecedent acts. Formulae for Column 2 are presented in the text.

that is accounted for by a particular variable, when the contribution of other components is removed.[7] Although the figures in the table cannot be evaluated for statistical significance, they suggest roughly how much of the possible variance is attributable to a given component independently. Both control and organizational effects are indicated. As noted earlier, the data were insufficient to examine organizing effects of antecedent acts, such as would occur, if, for example, act b_1, anteceded by act a_1, led to act c_1, whereas b_1, anteceded by a_2, led to c_2. But as determiners of immediately subsequent acts, antecedent acts play the predominant role. The situation and group variables contribute secondary independent effects. Other results indicate that, if all three components—antecedent acts, situations, and groups—are taken into consideration, some 40% of the variance of immediately subsequent behavior is accounted for. Individual difference factors, which could not be dealt with in these analyses, would, from indications of the earlier studies, increase this value.

Some further qualifications should be noted. One consideration involves the number of categories used. This is likely to affect specific values. A replication of an analysis, using eight categories for interactive behavior rather than the bivariate friendly versus unfriendly categorization, yielded somewhat different specific values. Nonetheless, the orderings discussed above were maintained. One should also note that for other kinds of interaction sequences than those involved in affectional relations among peers, the same ordering of results need not, and, indeed, does not hold. For example, children's friendly or unfriendly responses to *adult* behavior were determined relatively less by the specific antecedent acts of the adult, and relatively more by situational and group components. Nonetheless, similarities do appear. For example, as in the case of peer relations, the hyperaggressive children did not differ appreciably from the normals in reacting to unfriendly adult actions, but differed considerably in their responses to friendly actions. As compared to the data reported here on affectional behavior, studies of status behavior yielded, in general, a lower level of predictability and less consistency between American and Norwegian data. It was clear, however, that among all groups of children, submissive antecedent acts of one child were strongly associated with immediately subsequent dominant acts of another; dominant antecedent behavior tended to be followed by submissive subsequent acts, but at a much lower level of probability. Different kinds of behavior and different sources for, or recipients of behavior are thus likely to yield different orders of effects. What should be noted, however, is that the method enables us to study these orders and to infer from them the processes of communication as these relate to varied circumstances of interaction.

---

[7] The general formulae are: for three variables, $D_x(y{:}z)/1-D(x{:}z)$; for four variables, $D_{wx}(y{:}z)/\ 1 - D(w,x{:}z)$. The procedure was suggested to me, in personal communication, by Fred Attneave of the University of Oregon.

TRANSITION PROBABILITY ANALYSES

The information analyses consider contingencies between antecedent and consequent actions. In addition to furnishing information about sequential relations, the analyses yield precise measures of the contributions of other identified components. The transition analyses which follow do not yield such measures. But unlike the information approach, they do treat chains of interactions. In this way they can provide an insight into the process of interaction from its initiation to its natural termination.

The coding and entry of data are as discussed above. As a final notation, however, each chain of acts composing a sequence is listed. From the set of sequences one can then obtain initial probabilities and probabilities for each subsequent step along the series. Given two adjacent steps, we can determine the probability of any category of behavior on the part of one person leading to a given category of behavior on the part of another person. From this empirical relation, by making the assumption that these contingencies will continue, a subsequent course of events can be predicted. Finally, one can compare these probabilities, obtained from the assumptions of reiterated events, with the actual empirical probabilities. Thus, the method enables comparison between the events predicted from a given transition and the actual empirical probabilities. Thus, the method enables comparison between the events predicted from a given transition and the actual events as they occur. In a sense, then, we may compare the expected fate of a set of actions with the actual fate.

Early patient group. Figure 2 shows the results for the hyperaggressive boys early in treatment. We may note that in interactions among peers 70% of the first acts were friendly. By the second step, that is, the response by another to the first act, the proportion of friendly acts dropped to 48%. The hypothetical curve, represented by the dotted line, shows the theoretical continuation from the initial matrix of probabilities. If successive actions followed the hypothetical curve, the proportions would stabilize at the fourth step. At that point only 34% of the children's acts would be expected to be friendly. The actual data for successive actions are represented by the solid line. The frequencies of responses for the limited data from the early patient group are too small to warrant much confidence, but so far as the results are to be trusted they suggest two trends. The first is for hostile responses to increase in successive steps; the increase is quite sharp—by the second act less than half of the responses are friendly. More interesting is a suggested trend for hostility to increase beyond its expected theoretical course. A similar trend, not shown here, appeared in the interactions of these children with adults. It is as though in this group of very disturbed aggressive children, as interaction continues, the course of hostility is progressively accelerated.

Later patient group. The results for these same boys after an additional 1.5 years of residential treatment are shown in Figure 3. The figure shows that first acts in

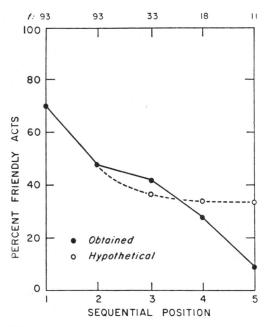

Fig. 2. Peer interactions of hyperaggressive boys early in treatment.

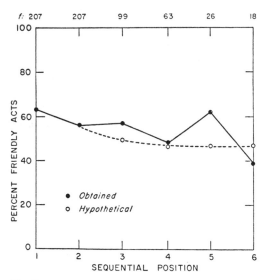

Fig. 3. Peer interactions of hyperaggressive boys later in treatment.

interaction chains were coded as friendly in 63% of instances; thus, in their initiations, the children were no friendlier toward their peers at this stage than they were at the earlier time. But the difference appears in the slope of the curve. The drop in the proportion of friendly acts at the second step was to 56%, considerably less sharp than occurred in the earlier period. The predicted course of events from the initial transition suggests that the process would stabilize at the fourth step with 47% friendly acts, as compared to the theoretical 34% for the earlier period. Comparing the obtained and hypothetical curves suggests another difference from the earlier phase. The obtained data—and here frequencies are somewhat more respectable—suggest that whereas hostility may increase as interaction continues, it does not, unlike the earlier situation, accelerate beyond its expected course as given by the theoretical curve. Successive acts are perhaps even somewhat less unfriendly than we would expect on the basis of the first transition. Data on the interactions with adults showed some differences from the above picture of interactions with peers: as compared to their earlier performance, the later group was considerably friendlier in initiations of sequences; furthermore, successive transitions became somewhat less friendly than was expected theoretically. But a major similarity held. As in the case of peer relations, the sharply progressive increase in hostility which characterized the earlier pattern of interaction was attenuated in the relations of the later group with adults.

Normal American children. As we may note from Figure 4, the control children showed a higher proportion of friendly initiations with peers than did either patient group (94%). As with the other groups, there was a decrease in friendliness at the second step. The matrix of probabilities from the initial transition indicates an expected stabilization by the fifth act in a chain with 63% friendly acts. Thus, in contrast with the patient groups, a chain of interactive events with these well-adjusted children would be expected to wind up in a friendly fashion more than half the time. A further difference between patients and controls occurs in the discrepancy between theoretical and obtained data. The obtained data for the early patients tended to show a higher proportion of hostile actions than theoretically expected; the later group showed proportions close to, or perhaps slightly less than expected; the control children deviated from expectations in a direction clearly opposite that of the early patients. At each successive step, the normal boys showed greater friendliness than would be expected from the hypothetical curve based on the initial transition matrix.[8] Relations with adults yielded similar indications, although high initial proportions of friendly acts limit the differences. For the control group, then, there is the suggestion of a corrective factor inhibiting the expected course of increase in hostility. In contrast to the acceleration of hostile actions found in the very

---

[8] Analysis indicated that these results are not an artifact of differences in the length of sequences.

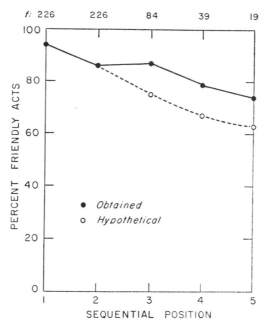

Fig. 4. Peer interactions of socially adjusted American boys.

disturbed boys, a kind of negative feedback on hostile responses seems to occur in the interaction stream of the well-adjusted boys.

Normal Norwegian children. A partial replication is found in the data for the Norwegian boys. Despite cultural differences and differences in the environments in which the studies were conducted, the two socially adjusted groups show similar processes in sequential chains of interactions (Figure 5). Both groups

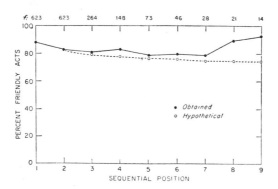

Fig. 5. Peer interactions of socially adjusted Norwegian boys.

started with a high proportion of friendly acts which dropped somewhat at the second act. For both groups the point of expected stabilization is on the friendly side of the ledger, although it is at a higher level for the Norwegians (75%). As with the American controls, the empirical data deviate consistently from the hypothetical curve, and the direction of deviation is the same for the two groups. That is, in the course of interaction the Norwegian boys also maintained a higher level of friendliness than was to be expected on the basis of the starting points. For this group too, then, a corrective factor seems to operate to inhibit the expected course of degradation of interaction toward greater hostility.

The results from the transition probability studies thus suggest an organizational component in the flow of social interaction. Interaction does not proceed in an automatic fashion based on its beginnings. The process of interaction appears rather to be modified systematically by a component which differs among the groups studied. From knowledge of the groups and of their selection, we would suggest that one variable organizing the sequential process of social interchange is what has been called ego control (Redl & Wineman, 1957).

DISCUSSION

We have demonstrated two methods, that of multivariate informational analysis and that of transition analysis, for studying the sequential aspects of social interaction. In a sense the findings tell us what we have always known: that among peers, affectional relations are strongly contingent—that is, what A does affects B's response; that the same kind of act will have different consequences, depending on the situation; and that the same kind of act is apt to be interpreted and reacted to somewhat differently by different groups. Nor would the patterns indicated by the transition analyses be particularly novel to anyone who spent much time with these groups of children. Those who worked with the disturbed children were indeed aware of the aptitude of these boys for moving rapidly from an atmosphere of friendliness to one of wildly chaotic aggression. And after working with hyperaggressive boys these same workers were impressed by the contrasting capacity of normal children to catch themselves up—to reorganize and correct for threats of disruption in group interaction.

The specificity of the methods allows us, however, to achieve something more than the clinically obvious. Given the situation, given the nature of the group, we can, knowing the actions of one child, predict rather well what another child will do. Even without considering individual differences—which on the basis of previous studies are a potent contributor to interaction—these three components yield a prediction of peer behavior corresponding to an R of more than .60. Specifically, we can detail which situations are likely to induce which behaviors and how particular situations are likely to modify the contingencies between stimulus and response acts. Furthermore, whereas earlier studies suggested that situations were not as discriminable for very disturbed children, the present data suggest additionally that behavioral events themselves are less differentiated by the very disturbed children. There was evidence that the groups of children differed rather little in their responses to unfriendly acts; rather it was acts thought by coders to be friendly which differentiated the groups, the disturbed children more often responding as though such acts had hostile meaning.

To fully confirm some of these suggestions would require more adequate data than were available, but what is clear is that the methods yield a lever for a more specific understanding of normal and pathological interaction processes. For example, an extension of the methods of analysis to the interactions of autistic children—or for that matter, to schizophrenic adults—suggests several alternative hypotheses: that contingencies between antecedent and response acts are highly fixed, albeit unusual and socially inappropriate (cf. Wallace, 1961); that contingencies are highly uncertain, fluctuating from moment to moment; that contingencies are fixed or uncertain, according to subgroups; that contingencies are primarily idiosyncratic; that it is not contingency relations which distinguish the interactions of these populations, but rather the range and/or nature of antecedent and consequent acts in themselves. The details of who and what are responded to and of modes of response might also provide more adequate bases for theory and clinical practice.

In a more general sense, the analyses point to two broad issues, one of differentiation or discrimination learning, the other of timing. Concerning differentiation, the data suggest that patterns of interaction are organized by contextual circumstances and by the psychological status of the child. Yarrow (1963) similarly notes that parent-child behaviors are likely to differ according to the situation, the developmental level of the child, the psychological state of the mother, etc., and she comments that few parents are uniformly nurturant or hostile; consequently, she suggests that the distribution of parental behaviors in relation to specific developmental stages and specific circumstances are likely to be more relevant for the child than are averaged occurrences. In this sense, a trait approach to personality and its learned aspects is, as we suggested earlier (Raush et al., 1959b) apt to be misleading. Children are, for example, no more taught not to be dependent than they are taught not to urinate. What they are taught are right and wrong times and places. For some parents and for some cultures, as compared to others, there are more wrong places, and in that sense one might speak of quantitatively greater or lesser amounts of expression or inhibition. But this is a rather different matter than presumed quantities of traits. On a research level, our data imply that it would be well for questionnaire and experimental, as well as observational studies to take into account the matter of sampling of situations called for by Brunswik (1947).[9]

Turning to the matter of timing, the transition probability analyses indicate that the position of an act in a sequence chain makes a difference. Experience

---

[9] This is true also for cross-cultural studies. For example, our data showed no differences *in general* between the peer behavior of Norwegian and matched American children, but there was a statistically significant difference in which settings produced which behaviors.

thus appears to be organized temporally. The data suggest that normal pre-adolescent children are able to foresee things going from bad to worse and are able to pull themselves up from the expected course of events. There is, to be sure, nothing magical about this "rescue" of the interaction process. On the basis of a purely clinical analysis, Blanche Sweet and I (Raush & Sweet, 1961) suggested the sensitivity of these children to the potentials of interaction and we illustrated some techniques by which healthy preadolescents foreclose and ameliorate the dangers in a potentially destructive course of events. A shift of topic, a recognition of the other's feelings, a conventional encouragement, for example, "nice try," convey a sensitivity to the potentials of the other and of the situation. In contrast, the very disturbed children not only failed to "rescue" the interaction process, but even failed to preserve its presumed course. I would suggest that this failure is less a matter of pleasure in malice, and more a matter of loss of already tenuous controls.

There is, however, another aspect to timing. As is familiar to every therapist-patient, parent-child, husband-wife pair, when something is done is often as important as what is done. For example, an interposition between quarreling children can come too early so that its relevance is lost, or it can come too late when the situation is past all except heavy-handed control. Given sufficient data, the transition probability model can enable us to understand the kinds of interventions and the timing of interventions which are effective in relation to specific goals. Finally, the present data suggested that chains of interaction sequences move toward stable equilibria. The achievement of such equilibria in interaction thus becomes a variable subject to study. Too little is known, but it is reasonable to suppose that time to reach equilibrium and the end points of equilibrium will vary with the character and the development of particular human relationships.

REFERENCES

Altmann, S. A. Sociobiology of rhesus monkeys: II. Stochastic of social communication. *Journal of Theoretical Biology*, 1965, **8**, 490–522.

Ashby, W. R. *An introduction to cybernetics.* New York: Wiley, 1958.

Ashby, W. R. Principles of the self-organizing system. In H. v. Foerster & G. W. Zopf, Jr. (Eds.), *Principles of self-organizations.* New York: Pergamon Press, 1962. Pp. 255–278.

Attneave, F. *Applications of information theory to psychology.* New York: Holt, 1959.

Barker, R. G. (Ed.) *The stream of behavior: Explorations of its structure and content.* New York: Appleton-Century-Crofts, 1963.

Barker, R. G., & Wright, H. F. *Midwest and its children.* Evanston, Ill.: Row, Peterson, 1954.

Beach, F. A. Experimental investigation of species-specific behavior. *American Psychologist*, 1960, **15**, 1–18.

Bonner, J. T. The unsolved problem of development: An appraisal of where we stand. *American Scientist*, 1960, **48**, 514–527.

Brunswik, E. Distal focussing of perception: Size-constancy in a representative sample of situations. *Psychological Monographs*, 1944, **56**(1, Whole No. 254).

Brunswik, E. *Systematic and representative design of psychological experiments.* Berkeley: Univer. California Press, 1947.

Campbell, D. T. Methodological suggestions from a comparative psychology of knowledge processes. *Inquiry,* 1959, **2**, 152–183.

Dittmann, A. T. Problems of reliability in observing and coding social interactions. *Journal of Consulting Psychology,* 1958, **22**, 430.

Farbman, I. Information transmission in the social interaction of hyperaggressive children. Unpublished master's thesis, University of Florida, 1961.

Freedman, M. B., Leary, T. F., Ossorio, A. G., & Coffey, H. S. The interpersonal dimension of personality. *Journal of Personality,* 1951, **20**, 143–161.

Garner, W. R. Symmetric uncertainty analysis and its implications for psychology. *Psychological Review,* 1958, **65**, 183–196.

Garner, W. R. *Uncertainty and structure as psychological concepts.* New York: Wiley, 1962.

Gellert, E. The effect of changes in group composition on the dominant behaviour of young children. *British Journal of Social and Clinical Psychology,* 1962, **1**, 168–181.

Kemeny, J. G., Snell, J. L., & Thompson, G. L. *Introduction to finite mathematics.* Englewood Cliffs, N. J.: Prentice-Hall, 1956.

Leary, T. *Interpersonal diagnosis of personality.* New York: Ronald Press, 1957.

McGill, W. J. Multivariate information transmission. *Psychometrika,* 1954, **19**, 97–116.

Raush, H. L., Dittmann, A. T., & Taylor, T. J. The interpersonal behavior of children in residential treatment. *Journal of Abnormal and Social Psychology,* 1959, **58**, 9–26. (a)

Raush, H. L., Dittmann, A. T., & Taylor, T. J. Person, setting and change in social interaction. *Human Relations,* 1959, **12**, 361–379. (b)

Raush, H. L., Farbman, I., & Llewellyn, L. G. Person, setting and change in social interaction: II. A normal-control study. *Human Relations,* 1960, **13**, 305–333.

Raush, H. L., & Sweet, Blanche. The preadolescent ego: Some observations of normal children. *Psychiatry,* 1961, **24**, 122–132.

Redl, F., & Wineman, D. *The aggressive child.* Glencoe, Ill.: Free Press, 1957.

Russell, Claire, & Russell, W. M. S. *Human behavior.* Boston: Little, Brown, 1961.

Smith, J. E. K. *Multivariate attribute analysis.* Ann Arbor: University of Michigan, Engineering Research Institute, 1953.

Wallace, A. F. C. The psychic unity of human groups. In B. Kaplan (Ed.), *Studying personality cross-culturally.* Evanston, Ill.: Row, Peterson, 1961. Pp. 129–165.

Yarrow, Marian R. Problems of methods in parent-child research. *Child Development,* 1963, **34**, 215–226.

23

Anxiety Profiles Based on Both Situational and Response Factors

DAVID MAGNUSSON and BO EKEHAMMAR

In recent anxiety research, there has been a growing interest in studying which types of stimuli or situations evoke anxiety in the individual. At the theoretical level, a conceptual distinction has been made between anxiety as a stable trait and anxiety as a transitory state (Spielberger, 1966), which would imply that situational characteristics have to be taken into account when describing and predicting the individual's anxiety state. At the applied level, there has been an increasing clinical practice of behavior therapy with a concurrent need for methods for the assessment of situationally conditioned fears in the individual. This increasing interest in situations within psychology is also reflected in recent attempts to study individuals' perceptions of situations (cf. Magnusson, 1971; Magnusson & Ekehammar, 1973; Ekehammar & Magnusson, 1973), and to conceptualize behavior in terms of individual by situation interactions (cf. Argyle & Little, 1972; Bowers, 1973; Endler, 1973).

The development mentioned has led to some new inventories of anxiety which take the situation into account in contrast to the previous "omnibus inventories." Some of the new inventories have been created primarily for research purposes (e.g., Hodges & Felling, 1970; Schalling, 1971), while others have been developed primarily for practical use (e.g., Geer, 1965; Wolpe & Lang, 1964; Scherer & Nakamura, 1968). With these inventories one can, compared to the "omnibus inventories," get a more differentiated picture of the individual's anxiety pattern by making a profile of the anxiety intensity across situations or types of situations. Comparing, for example, the sexes in this way situationally specific sex differences have been revealed (e.g., Ekehammar, 1974; Grossberg & Wilson, 1965; Hodges & Felling, 1970; Lawlis, 1971; Manosevitz & Lanyon, 1965; Scherer & Nakamura, 1968).

From *Multivariate Behavioral Research*, 1975, *10*, 27–43. Copyright 1975. Publication authorized by Multivariate Behavioral Research.

The study was supported by a grant to D. Magnusson from the Swedish Council for Social Science Research for a research program on person-by-situation interaction.

A further step in the direction toward a more detailed description of an individual's anxiety pattern is to incorporate different modes of response, chosen separately from the different situation. According to this strategy, the individual has to state, for example, the perceived intensity of different possible anxiety reactions for each of different possible anxiety evoking situations. Inventories constructed according to this approach have been presented by Endler, Hunt, and Rosenstein (1962) and Ekehammar, Magnusson, and Ricklander (1974). With such inventories, a more differentiated picture of the individual's anxiety pattern can be obtained, compared to the inventories mentioned earlier, by making a profile for each mode of response across situations.

Though the inventories taking both situations and modes of response into account have a potential advantage in permitting a comprehensive description of an individual's anxiety pattern, this advantage has not been completely utilized. The need for such analyses in personality research has clearly been stated by Hunt: "... for either understanding variations of behavior or making clinical predictions, we should be looking toward instruments that will classify people in terms of the kinds of responses they make in various categories of situations" (1965, p. 83). In the present context, this statement has two implications: (1) Since the number of responses and situations is usually rather large in these inventories, one should try to decrease the number by forming categories of similar situations, and categories of similar responses. In this way, one would obtain a perspicuous and manageable amount of information which would make it possible, for example, to depict individual data in profiles and make the inventory useful in applied contexts. (2) Classifying individuals with similar anxiety patterns across categories of situations might also have applications in clinical practice, and is relevant in the earlier mentioned interactionist context. Since the empirical interactionist studies using analysis of variance (cf. Bowers, 1973) have revealed important interaction components (Individual by Situation, Individual by Response, Individual by Situation by Response), it would be fruitful to try to classify individuals in the manner recommended by Hunt. This approach would be profitable in order to explain and illuminate the important interaction components reported in anxiety research (Endler & Hunt, 1966; Ekehammar, Magnusson & Ricklander, 1974).

The main aim of the present study was to compare anxiety profiles for subgroups of Ss homogeneous with regard to response pattern across situations. With reference to the points made above, this comparison involved two main steps: (a) reducing the total matrix by categorizing both situation and response variables on empirical ground, and (b) classifying the Ss in homogeneous groups on the basis of their anxiety profiles for different types of reactions across different categories of situations. In addition to a comparison of the anxiety profiles for these homogeneous groups, the profile for the total sample of Ss was studied as well as the profiles for each sex. The profile comparisons were made with a special emphasis on transsituational consistency which, in different contexts (cf. Campus, 1974), has begun to be regarded an important aspect of the individual's behavior.

All profile comparisons were made on data from the anxiety inventory presented in Ekehammar, Magnusson, and Ricklander (1974), where a detailed description of the inventory is given as well as the principles guiding its construction.

METHOD

The Inventory

The Inventory employed 17 situations and 18 modes of response. For each situation each S had to report the degree of experienced intensity of each mode of response, making up a total of 306 (17 x 18) items to respond to. The intensity ratings were given on a numerical five-point scale ranging from 1—"Not at all" to 5—"Very much." The order of presentation of the situations was randomized among Ss, whereas the order of presentation of the modes of response was the same for all situations. A written instruction was given to the Ss before the inventory was answered.

Subjects

Data from 116 Ss, 58 boys and 58 girls, were used for the present analyses. The Ss were 15—17 years of age, and were pupils from the six ninth-grade classes of a comprehensive school.

Data Reduction

To get a manageable amount of information and to obtain classifications of situations and modes of response, factor analysis was employed as data reduction method. The single situations and modes of response were primarily selected in order to permit such classifications. A priori groupings of situations had been formed using the method of similarity estimation; a priori groupings of modes of response had been formed on the basis of previous empirical findings. The response factors were obtained by collapsing data across situations and analyzing the Individual by Modes-of-Response matrix, and in a similar manner the situation factors were obtained by collapsing data across modes of response and analyzing the Individual by Situation matrix. In both cases, the same factor analytic methodology was employed, using an iterative procedure for estimating the communalities, and rotating factors with eigenvalues greater than unity to simple structure according to the varimax method. The data reduction procedure means a loss of information and thus the original interaction variances will be reduced. However, this must be weighed against the increase in generality that at the same time will be achieved. A detailed description of the factorial procedure and results is given in Ekehammar, Magnusson, and Ricklander (1974), and hence only the main findings will be recapitulated here.

The two main response factors were tentatively interpreted as "Psychic anxiety" and "Somatic anxiety." The character of the "Psychic anxiety" factor is indicated by the following short descriptions of the modes-of-response scales having their highest loadings for this factor: "Worried," "Feelings of insecurity," "Depressed," "Feelings of panic," and "Restless." The character of the "Somatic anxiety" factor is indicated by the following modes-of-response scales having their highest loadings for this factor: "Short of breath," "Hard time swallowing," "Hands shake," "Get in a sweat," "Heart beats faster," "Stomach trouble," "Mouth gets dry," "Tensions when speaking," and "Hands get cold." A third response factor was also obtained that contained only symptoms hardly ever reported by anyone in the present sample of Ss ("Pains in the neck," "Sensations of tingling," and "Headaches"). Since the distributions for these modes of response were highly positively skewed, the factor was excluded from the present analyses.

The three main situation factors were tentatively labeled "Threat of punishment," "Anticipation fear," and "Inanimate threat." The character of the "Threat of punishment" factor is indicated by the following short descriptions of the situation scales having their highest loadings on this factor: "Caught pilfering," "Discovered playing truant," "Called to the headmaster," "Discover a fire at home," "Get home too late," "Discovered gate-crashing (sports ground)," "Important examination." The following items had their highest loadings on the "Anticipation fear" factor: "Taking a blood test," "At the dentist's," "Having an injection," "Give an oral report," "Athletic contest," "Starting a new job," and "Having a wound sewed up." Three situations had their highest loadings on the "Inanimate threat" factor: "In the woods at night," "Alone at home," and "Alone in the woods."

Thus, the factor analyses reduced the original 18 modes of response to 2 response factors, and the original 17 situations to 3 situation factors. For each of the 6 combinations of situation and response factors, the unweighted factor scores were computed and averaged across items and Ss of current interest. On the basis of the mean factor scores, profiles were drawn for each response factor across each situation factor for each group of Ss of current interest.

Classification of Individuals

Individuals with similar types of anxiety responses across categories of situations were grouped together. For the purpose of isolating these homogeneous subgroups of Ss, the method of latent profile analysis (LPA, cf. Gibson, 1959; Lazarsfeld & Henry, 1968) was employed. In contrast to factor analysis, LPA has the advantages of being individual-oriented rather than variable-oriented, of structuring the data in terms of profiles, and also of utilizing non-linear relationships (cf. Mårdberg, 1973). Thus, LPA "permits us to construct a typology of respondents" (Lazarsfeld & Henry, 1968, p. 238), and seems well-suited for the present problem. A computer program worked out by Mårdberg (cf. Mårdberg, 1972) was used in the present case, and the choice of number of profiles was made according to two criteria: (a) the average distance between a theoretical profile and corresponding observed profile, and (b) the average theoretical discriminability (cf. Mårdberg, 1972).

Types of Analyses

The following descriptive analyses with regard to anxiety profiles were made:

(1) The average profile for the total sample of Ss was studied.
(2) A sex comparison was made. Sex can be regarded a most important "moderating variable" (cf. Bem, 1972), and the importance of studying sex differences in personality research has recently been stressed (Carlson, 1971; Sarason & Smith, 1971).
(3) The LPA groups containing Ss with similar anxiety profiles were separately compared for each sex. Analyses of the transsituational consistency of the profiles were especially emphasized. Campus (1974) has pointed out that transsituational consistency may be regarded as a personality characteristic per se, and she presented empirical support of the view that high-anxiety persons are situationally more inconsistent than low-anxiety persons.

In addition to the graphic descriptions of the anxiety profiles, complementary statistical analyses were made. For each situation-response combination, the differences between sexes, and LPA groups, were tested. An overall analysis was also made, including those factors treated in the present comparisons. This was accomplished through a five-way analysis of variance (ANOVA) with partially nested sets, thus comprising the following factors: Sex, Profiles (LPA) nested within Sex, Individuals nested within Profiles and Sex, Responses, and Situations. All factors, except Individuals, were treated as fixed. The overall analysis will be presented first, as a background to the specific profile comparisons.

RESULTS

Overall Statistical Analysis

The result of the five-way ANOVA, comprising those factors compared in the subsequent analyses, is given in Table 1.

Relevant parts of Table 1 will be commented upon in connection with the following profile comparisons.

Profile for Total Sample

In Fig. 1 is shown the average anxiety profile for the total sample of Ss, with the two response factors drawn separately against the three situation factors.

Table 1. Overall Statistical Analysis of the Present Effects

Source of variation	SS	df	MS	F	Denominator of F test (MS)
Sex	21.03	1	21.03	24.14	P and I pooled
Profiles (LPA) within sex (P)	70.18	4	17.55	66.21	I
Individuals within profiles and sex (I)	29.17	110	.27	7.50	Residual
Responses (R)	45.17	1	45.17	226.98	PxR and IxR pooled
Situations (S)	15.34	2	7.67	49.81	PxS and IxS pooled
Sex x R	1.05	1	1.05	5.28	PxR and IxR pooled
Sex x S	3.14	2	1.57	10.19	PxS and IxS pooled
P x R	8.86	4	2.22	17.18	I x R
P x S	7.33	8	.92	7.08	I x S
I x R	13.82	110	.13	3.61	Residual
I x S	27.78	220	.13	3.61	Residual
R x S	3.14	2	1.57	38.29	PxRxS and Residual pooled
Sex x R x S	1.00	2	.50	12.20	PxRxS and Residual pooled
P x R x S	1.48	8	.19	5.31	Residual
Residual	7.87	220	.04		

Note. All F-ratios, except for Sex x R, are significant at the .001 level. F for Sex x R is significant at the .05 level.

The mean anxiety profile depicted in Fig. 1 shows, in the first place, that the "Psychic" response factor has a systematically higher anxiety intensity than the "Somatic" response factor. The effect is statistically significant, as shown by the overall analysis in Table 1. This means that irrespective of type of situation, the Ss have reported a higher degree of "Psychic" anxiety than "Somatic" anxiety. It is plausible that this tendency is specific for the present category of Ss (adolescents), since somatic reaction patterns might take time to develop. In the second place, it is shown that the "Anticipation fear" situations have elicited the smallest amount of anxiety whereas the "Threat of punishment" situations have been reported as the most anxiety-evoking, with the "Inanimate threat"

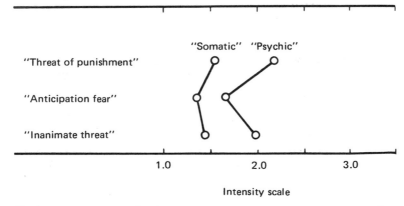

Fig. 1. Mean anxiety profile for the total sample based on two response and three situational factors.

situations in between. The overall test of the situational effect gave a significant result, as shown in Table 1. This table shows also that the Response by Situation interaction was significant. Fig. 1 demonstrates this fact and indicates a higher transsituational consistency for the "Somatic" than for the "Psychic" response factor.

Profiles for Each Sex

In Fig. 2 are shown the mean profiles for boys and girls, depicted in the same manner as in the earlier figure. Table 2 gives the relevant statistics for a sex comparison with regard to each situation-response combination. Table 3 gives a descriptive overview of how large proportions of each sex reported their highest intensity for each situation-response combination.

Sex differences with regard to anxiety pattern are readily apparent from Fig. 2, which primarily shows differences in anxiety level but also differences in profile shape. Girls have reported a significantly higher degree of anxiety than boys for each situation-response combination (see Table 2). Table 1 shows that the overall sex difference is highly significant, and that the interactions with sex are significant, too. Thus, the anxiety profiles for the sexes are not to be regarded as parallel. One profile difference is that girls have responded almost as strongly to "Inanimate threat" situations as to "Threat of punishment" situations which is not the case for the boys. This finding is also supported by Table 3, which shows that 55% of the girls reported "Threat of punishment" the most stressful situation, and 43% of the girls reported "Inanimate threat" the most stressful. For boys the corresponding figures were 72 and 14%, respectively. From Fig. 2 and Table 2 is seen that girls have a higher intensity than the boys in ratings of "Anticipation fear" situations. However, Table 3 shows that only 2% of the girls have their highest anxiety ratings for such situations, whereas this holds for 14% of the boys.

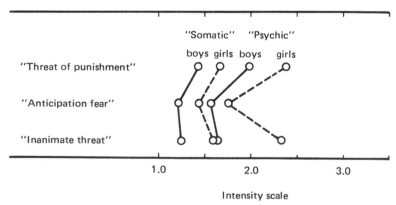

Fig. 2. Mean anxiety profiles for boys and girls.

Table 2. Sex Comparisons for Each Situation-Response Combination

Situation factors	"Psychic"					"Somatic"				
	Boys		Girls			Boys		Girls		
	M	SD	M	SD	t	M	SD	M	SD	t
"Threat of punishment"	1.98	.59	2.37	.66	3.36**	1.42	.35	1.65	.50	3.02**
"Anticipation fear"	1.56	.33	1.75	.49	2.43*	1.22	.18	1.44	.44	3.47***
"Inanimate threat"	1.63	.47	2.33	.80	5.75***	1.24	.31	1.59	.51	4.54***

Note: $*p \leq .05$; $**p \leq .01$; $***p \leq .001$; two-tailed test; $df = 114$

Profiles for Homogeneous Groups

The mean observed profiles for each LPA group of Ss, homogeneous with regard to anxiety profile, are shown separately for each sex in Fig. 3 (girls) and Fig. 4 (boys). Profiles with similar pattern across situations have been given the same labels across sexes. In contrast to the earlier figures, the "Psychic" response factor is presented above the "Somatic" response factor to increase clarity of exposition.

Tables 4 and 5 give the relevant statistics for a comparison of the LPA profiles with regard to each situation-response combination. A two-way ANOVA was applied to the 2 (Responses) x 3 (Situations) data matrix for each LPA group, in order to get an index of transsituational inconsistency (MS for Situations, MS_S), and an index of response inconsistency (MS for Responses, MS_R). These characteristics, as well as the mean overall anxiety score, are presented in Table 6 for each LPA group within each sex.

For each sex, three groups of Ss homogeneous with regard to anxiety profile were obtained with LPA. As indicated by Figs. 3 and 4, each profile in the female sample corresponds with regard to transsituational pattern rather well to a

Table 3. Percentages for Each Sex Reporting Their Highest Anxiety Intensity for Each Situation-Response Combination

Situation factors	Boys			Girls		
	"Psychic"	"Somatic"	Total	"Psychic"	"Somatic"	Total
"Threat of punishment"	69	3	72	52	3	55
"Anticipation fear"	12	2	14	2	0	2
"Inanimate threat"	12	2	14	41	2	43
Total	93	7	100	95	5	100

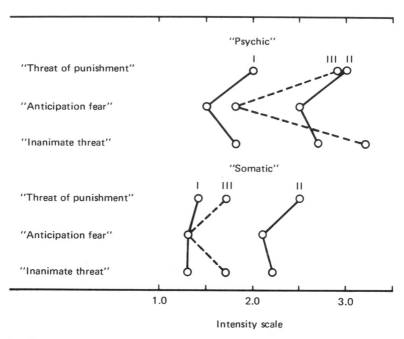

Fig. 3. Mean anxiety profiles for three homogeneous groups of girls obtained by LPA.

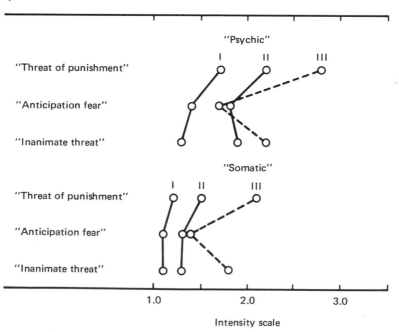

Fig. 4. Mean anxiety profiles for three homogeneous groups of boys obtained by LPA.

Table 4. Profile Comparisons for Each Situation-Response Combination for Girls

Situation factors	Response factors												
	"Psychic"							"Somatic"					
	Profile I		Profile II		Profile III		F	Profile I		Profile II		Profile III		F
	M	SD	M	SD	M	SD		M	SD	M	SD	M	SD	
"Threat of punishment"	1.95	.44	3.00	.56	2.94	.35	47.20	1.41	.26	2.47	.40	1.65	.35	79.49
"Anticipation fear"	1.50	.24	2.46	.53	1.85	.40	39.76	1.28	.20	2.12	.59	1.34	.23	36.40
"Inanimate threat"	1.85	.43	2.43	.74	3.20	.62	41.35	1.35	.29	2.20	.64	1.75	.42	24.91

Note: All F-ratios are significant ($p \leq .001$); $df = 2/55$

Table 5. Profile Comparisons for Each Situation-Response Combination for Boys

Situation factors	Response factors												
	"Psychic"							"Somatic"					
	Profile I		Profile II		Profile III		F	Profile I		Profile II		Profile III		F
	M	SD	M	SD	M	SD		M	SD	M	SD	M	SD	
"Threat of punishment"	1.65	.41	2.23	.50	2.79	.45	30.05	1.23	.18	1.49	.17	2.12	.48	64.47
"Anticipation fear"	1.35	.21	1.83	.29	1.69	.15	28.51	1.12	.11	1.32	.17	1.44	.14	58.47
"Inanimate threat"	1.31	.22	1.92	.45	2.23	.18	45.04	1.09	.09	1.31	.19	1.75	.64	28.61

Note: All F-ratios are significant ($p \leq .001$); $df = 2/55$

Table 6. Profile Characteristics of Each LPA Group for Each Sex

Profile Characteristic	Girls			Boys		
	Profile I	Profile II	Profile III	Profile I	Profile II	Profile III
Transsituational inconsistency (MS_S)	.05	.10	.44	.03	.05	.39
Response inconsistency (MS_R)	.27	.32	1.76	.13	.58	.33
Mean overall anxiety	1.56	2.50	2.12	1.29	1.68	2.01

group in the male sample, but there are sex differences in magnitude as noted before. That the classification of individuals was successful is sustained by the overall analysis in Table 1, which shows significant main and interaction effects for Profile as a variance source, and by Tables 4 and 5, which show highly significant differences between the LPA profiles for each situation-response combination. An inspection of Figs. 3 and 4, together with the indices given in Table 6, reveals the following tendencies:

For *girls;* Profile I is characterized by (a) a low anxiety level, (b) high transsituational consistency, and (c) high response consistency; Profile II by (a) a high anxiety level, (b) comparatively high transsituational consistency, and (c) low response consistency; Profile III by (a) a moderate anxiety level, (b) low transsituational consistency, and (c) low response consistency. Profile I comprised 59%, Profile II 17%, and Profile III 24% of the girls in the present sample. Thus, for girls, Profile I is the most frequent profile, Profile II is the high-anxiety group, and Profile III has the lowest consistency across both situations and reactions. The low response consistency means, in the present case, that the "gap" between the "Psychic" and "Somatic" response factors is large.

For *boys;* Profile I is characterized by (a) a low anxiety level, (b) high transitutational consistency, and (c) high response consistency; Profile II by (a) a moderate anxiety level, (b) comparatively high transsituational consistency, and (c) low response consistency; Profile III by (a) a high anxiety level, (b) low transsituational consistency, and (c) moderate response consistency. Profile I comprised 53%, Profile II 36%, and Profile III 11% of the boys in the present sample. Thus, for boys, Profile I is the most frequent profile, Profile II shows the greatest "gap" between the two reaction systems, and Profile III has the lowest transsituational consistency and highest anxiety level.

Thus, for both sexes Profile III was characterized by a low transsituational consistency. The main feature of this profile gives some preliminary support to the view of transsituational inconsistency as a characteristic of a certain personality type. Although not significant at the present low number of degrees of freedom (2/2), MS_S was 9.46 times greater for Profile III than for the most consistent group (Profile I) in the female sample, and 11.50 times greater in the male sample. The positive relationship between overall anxiety and transsituational inconsistency, suggested by Campus, (1974), is only partly supported here. For boys, the high-anxiety group (Profile III) is also the most inconsistent across situations, but this is not the case for the high-anxiety group for girls. On the other hand, for girls the most inconsistent group across situations is also the most inconsistent across responses, which is not the case for boys. These observations should, however, be interpreted with caution as long as scale properties and effects of response sets are not fully investigated, but they point to the necessity of making the present type of comparisons separately for each sex.

DISCUSSION

The present comparisons of anxiety profiles were made as a demonstration of the usefulness, with regard to description and analysis, of an anxiety inventory taking both situations and modes of response into account. The comparisons were made between different *groups* of Ss although the methodology proposed here naturally can be applied for the description of single individuals' anxiety profiles. In clinical contexts, for example, it would thus be possible to compare individual anxiety profiles in relation to those of relevant norm groups.

As cited earlier, there is a need for "instruments that will classify people in terms of the kinds of responses they make in various categories of situations." With LPA applied to data covering different modes of response in different situations, as in this study, it is possible to form groups of individuals which are homogeneous with respect to response pattern across situations. Such groupings of individuals may be valuable both in practical work and in research, for example, in studies of personality variables in relation to type of response pattern. In this study, a homogeneous group of individuals characterized by a high transsituational inconsistency was isolated. It might be profitable to make more intensive analyses of this type of individual, for example by applying measures of other variables, such as neuroticism and maladjustment. Moreover, the outcome of the LPA in the present study indicates that response inconsistency should also be taken more into account in order to illuminate the "gap" between individuals' different reaction systems.

Concerning the general methodological approach, other methods might have been used. Three-mode factor analysis (cf. Tucker, 1964) is one example. With this method applied to the present data, person factors would have been obtained in addition to the situation and response factors. However, the present investigation was broader in scope since the anxiety profiles for the total sample of Ss, as well as subgroups homogeneous with regard to an "external" variable (sex) were studied in essentially the same way. Further, a more distinguishing difference is that the present approach was categorical in character, whereas three-mode factor analysis is based on a dimensional model. In the present study, additional statistical analyses indicated that the categorical procedure was successful, and the present approach seems more straightforward and easily interpretable when, for example, comparisons are made with respect to transsituational and response consistency.

REFERENCES

Argyle, M., and Little, B. R. Do personality traits apply to social behaviour? *Journal for the Theory of Social Behaviour*, 1972, *2*, 1-35.

Bem, D. J. Constructing cross-situational consistencies in behavior: Some thoughts on Alker's critique of Mischel. *Journal of Personality*, 1972, *40*, 17-26.

Bowers, K. S. Situationism in psychology: An analysis and a critique. *Psychological Review*, 1973, *80*, 307-336.

Campus, N. Transsituational consistency as a dimension of personality. *Journal of Personality and Social Psychology*, 1974, *29*, 593-600.

Carlson, R. Where is the person in personality research? *Psychological Bulletin*, 1971, *75*, 203-219.

Ekehammar, B. Sex differences in self-reported anxiety for different situations and modes of response. *Scandinavian Journal of Psychology*, 1974, *15*, 154-160.

Ekehammar, B., and Magnusson, D. A method to study stressful situations. *Journal of Personality and Social Psychology*, 1973, *27*, 176-179.

Ekehammar, B., Magnusson, D., and Ricklander, L. An interactionist approach to the study of anxiety. *Scandinavian Journal of Psychology*, 1974, *15*, 4-14.

Endler, N. S. The person versus the situation—a pseudo issue? A response to Alker. *Journal of Personality*, 1973, *41*, 287-303.

Endler, N. S., and Hunt, J. McV. Sources of behavioral variance as measured by the S-R Inventory of Anxiousness. *Psychological Bulletin*, 1966, *65*, 338-346.

Endler, N. S., Hunt, J. McV., and Rosenstein, A. J. An S-R inventory of anxiousness. *Psychological Monographs*, 1962, *76*, (17, Whole No. 536).

Geer, J. The development of a scale to measure fear. *Behaviour Research and Therapy*, 1965, *3*, 45-53.

Gibson, W. A. Three multivariate models: Factor analysis, latent structure analysis and latent profile analysis. *Psychometrika*, 1959, *24*, 229-252.

Grossberg, J. M., and Wilson, H. K. A correlational comparison of the Wolpe-Lang fear survey schedule and Taylor manifest anxiety scale. *Behaviour Research and Therapy*, 1965, *3*, 125-128.

Hodges, W. F., and Felling, J. P. Types of stressful situations and their relation to trait anxiety and sex. *Journal of Consulting and Clinical Psychology*, 1970, *34*, 333-337.

Hunt, J. McV. Traditional personality theory in the light of recent evidence. *American Scientist*, 1965, *53*, 80-96.

Lawlis, G. F. Response styles of a patient population on the fear survey schedule. *Behaviour Research and Therapy*, 1971, *9*, 95-102.

Lazarsfeld, P. F., and Henry, N. W. *Latent Structure Analysis*. Boston: Houghton Mifflin, 1968.

Magnusson, D. An analysis of situational dimensions. *Perceptual and Motor Skills*, 1971, *32*, 851-867.

Magnusson, D., and Ekehammar, B. An analysis of situational dimensions: A replication. *Multivariate Behavioral Research*, 1973, *8*, 331-339.

Manosevitz, M., and Lanyon, R. I. Fear survey schedule: A normative study. *Psychological Reports*, 1965, *17*, 699-703.

Mårdberg, B. Clustering jobs to general requirement profiles. *The Swedish Council for Personnel Administration, Stockholm*, 1972, Report 43.

Mårdberg, B. A model for selection and classification in industrial psychology. *Reports from the Psychological Laboratories, The University of Stockholm*, 1973, Supplement 19.

Sarason, I. G., and Smith, R. E. Personality. *Annual Review of Psychology*, 1971, *22*, 393-446.

Schalling, D. Tolerance for experimentally induced pain as related to personality. *Scandinavian Journal of Psychology*, 1971, *12*, 271-281.

Scherer, M. W., and Nakamura, C. Y. A fear survey schedule for children (FSS-FC): A factor analytic comparison with manifest anxiety (CMAS). *Behaviour Research and Therapy,* 1968, *6,* 173-182.

Spielberger, C. D. Theory and research on anxiety. In C. D. Spielberger (Ed.), *Anxiety and Behavior.* New York: Academic Press, 1966, pp. 3-20.

Tucker, L. R. The extension of factor analysis to three-dimensional matrices. In N. Frederiksen & H. Gulliksen (Eds.), *Contributions to Mathematical Psychology.* New York: Holt, Rinehart & Winston, 1964, pp. 109–127,

Wolpe, J., and Lang, P. J. A fear survey schedule for use in behaviour therapy. *Behaviour Research and Therapy,* 1964, *2,* 27-30.

CHAPTER FIVE

THE ANALYSES OF SITUATIONS: STUDYING THE ENVIRONMENT

The fifth chapter contains seven papers, all concerned with the problems of systematizing the characteristics of the environment. The papers deal with the problem on different levels of generality, ranging from whole cultures as in the first paper by Arsenian and Arsenian [24], to specific situations as in the paper by Magnusson [28]. Three of the papers (by Arsenian and Arsenian [24], Chein [25], and Sells [27]) are primarily theoretical. The Frederiksen paper [26] presents a broad review of the problem of environmental descriptions on the basis of empirical results, and the remaining three papers report empirical studies based on the psychological significance of situations.

The Arsenian and Arsenian [24] paper presents a theoretical analysis of the environment, on a rather high level of generality. Mainly, their paper deals with the macro-social environment (see chap. 1). Their basic assumptions are that behavior is originated in tension-dominated "needs" and that the basic "goal" of behavior is tension-reduction. The techniques for reaching tension-reduction are called *paths*. Cultures are described along a dimension of "toughness"–"easiness." "Tough" cultures prohibit tension-reduction behavior, and "easy" cultures promote such behavior. Arsenian and Arsenian also discuss some behavioral indices of easy and tough cultures, such as suicides, crimes, "abnormalities," interpersonal relations, etc.

Starting from Koffka's distinction between the "geographical" and the "behavioral" environment (see chap. 1), Chein [25], in the second paper, argues for an analysis of what he calls the "ego behavioral" or "objective-behavioral" environment, i.e., the objective "outer world," as viewed by a psychologically sophisticated observer. The observer would presuppose psychological individuals with wants and desires, but would not at any moment be particularly concerned with any one person. The analysis is on the level of ecologies and situations (see Chap. 1). Among other things, Chein points to an important distinction between stimuli as *determinants* of behavior and stimuli as *initiators* of behavior.

In the third paper in this chapter, Frederiksen [26] starts his discussion on a taxonomy of situations from the problem of the prediction of behavior for individuals, and he uses the prediction of Mr. Krushchev's behavior at a diplomatic conference to illustrate the problem. He argues that it would be possible to predict, with some degree of certainty, whether Mr. Krushchev would be willing to compromise or not on an important issue. This would be based on an analysis of the situations in which he has compromised and not compromised in earlier negotiations. Frederiksen also provides a comprehensive overview of methods available for a useful description and classification of situations, and reports results from empirical studies on this issue.

Among modern interactionists, Sells is one of the few who has argued for a description of the objective environment in studies of the person by situation interaction (see chap. 1). In the fourth paper of this chapter, Sells [27] presents a comprehensive outline of aspects of the environment, which he hopes could serve as the starting point for the development of a taxonomy of situations. As a frame of reference, he uses four factors that were originally proposed by Sherif and Sherif (1956) as relevant to social situations: (a) factors related to individuals, (b) factors related to the problem or task, (c) factors related to the site and facilities, and (d) factors pertaining to relations of an individual to others, to the site, or to the problem or task.

In the fifth paper, Magnusson [28] discusses the fact that few, if any, systematic studies of how individuals perceive situations have been conducted. He reports the results of an empirical study of situational dimensions, based on situation perception data. He argues that situations should be studied as wholes, and proposes similarity ratings as one method for obtaining raw situation perception data. He uses a multidimensional approach to the analysis of data, with reference to a cognitive dimensional model of similarity. Subsequently, Magnusson (1974) has stated that cluster analysis techniques, with reference to a cognitive categorical model, would be more appropriate for the data treatment than the methods used in the paper presented here [28]. In the Magnusson study [28], judgments of perceived similarity were constant over time, and the dimensionality of the ratings showed great agreement for a homogeneous group. The five situation perception factors obtained (positive or pleasant, negative or unpleasant, active, passive, and social) have also been obtained in subsequent studies by Magnusson and his coworkers (e.g., Magnusson and Ekehammar, 1973). Magnusson [28] discusses the potential of the proposed methods for the study of person by situation interactions. He argues that studies of situation perception are also of interest in other areas of research such as interpersonal relationships, changes under psychological treatment, job evaluation, etc.

Moos and his coworkers have made important contributions to the study of person by situation interaction in different environmental settings, such as psychiatric ward settings and social settings. One such study is included in chap. 3 (Moos, [17]). In connection with these studies on person by situation interaction, Moos and his coworkers have developed inventories for the description of the environment in terms of their psychological significance. In the sixth paper in this chapter, Moos [29] reports the development of an inventory called the Community-Oriented Programs Environment Scale (COPES). The COPES provides a systematic assessment of the psychosocial environments of transitional community-oriented psychiatric treatment programs, such as halfway houses, rehabilitation centers, day care centers, and community care homes. The inventory has ten subscales. The psychometric properties of the subscales are reported, and profiles across subscales for both members (clients) and staff are compared for two different programs. The potential usefulness of the scale is discussed.

As discussed earlier (chap. 1) the psychological significance of situations can be studied in two main ways: by using situation *perception* data and by using situation *reaction* data. In the last paper in this chapter, Magnusson and Ekehammar [30] compare the outcomes of analyses using the two kinds of data. Perception and reaction data for a number of subjects were used for a multidimensional classification of 12 situations, which were selected so as to cover four different types of stressful situations. The outcomes for the two methods were similar for three of the four a priori groupings. After a discussion of the discrepancy in outcome for the fourth factor, the authors conclude that it is essential that we distinguish between situation *perception* factors and situation *reaction* factors in future research. They argue that the study of the relationship between a person's perception of and reactions to different situations is an important subject for research. They maintain that greater knowledge about this relationship would contribute to a better understanding and to a better prediction of behavior.

REFERENCES

Magnusson, D. The individual in the situation: Some studies on individuals, perception of situations. *Studia Psychologica*, 1974, *16*, 124–132.

Magnusson, D., & Ekehammar, B. An analysis of situational dimensions: A replication. *Multivariate Behavioral Research*, 1973, *8*, 331–339.

Sherif, M., & Sherif, C. W. *An outline of social psychology*. New York: Harper & Brothers, 1956.

24

Tough and Easy Cultures: A Conceptual Analysis

JOHN ARSENIAN and JEAN M. ARSENIAN

Attempts at systematic analyses of single cultures have proceeded apace since the early classic monographs of Malinowski, Radcliffe-Brown, Fortune, and others. Studies have long since become more preoccupied with people, less with artifacts, more concerned with the meaning of rituals than their bare recital. Recently exciting attempts have been made to further the understanding of cultures by studies of personality development. Culturally characteristic personalities are viewed as determined derivatives of different cultural practices and patterns. The terms "basic personality structure" and "character structure" have become common conceptual coinage for cultural anthropologists and social psychologists alike. Curiously enough these comparative analyses of people as end-and-sustaining products of a culture have advanced more rapidly than the comparative analyses of cultures as such. The analysis of cultures has suffered for want of specification of dimensions in which cultures may be meaningfully compared.

What has impaired thinking in this field? Perhaps the embarrassment and disdain of contemporary anthropologists for their predecessors' value pronouncements made in simple confidence that Christian norms were not merely ascendant but transcendental. Then the corrective idea of cultural relativity:[1] no practice can be evaluated apart from its cultural context, and the value placed upon a practice is valid since and only because it is found. These ideas have probably acted as deterrents prohibiting comparisons lest one seem provincial. Whatever the causes, somehow students have kept away from the following integration of ideas which will show how cultures can be compared and evaluated regardless of their vastly varying contents.

Reprinted by special permission of The William Alanson White Psychiatric Foundation, Inc. From *Psychiatry*, 1948, *11*, 377–385. Copyright 1948 by The William Alanson White Psychiatric Foundation.

[1] Curiously enough the two anthropologists most effective in documenting the value variability of specific cultural traits were neither of them without overdetermined middle class sentiments which constricted their capacity to understand certain social phenomena. See: W. G. Summer's writings on labor unionism, and E. A. Westermark on monogamy.

Obviously such an undertaking has general usefulness for the social sciences although we are here more interested in its applications to mental hygiene—the mental hygiene of cultures. We hope to show that and wherein some cultures are tough on their members while others are easy—an observation long since made by widely assorted groups: novelists, philosophers, cultural anthropologists, sociologists, psychiatrists, psychologists, and socialists.[2] But here a detailing of dimensions for comparison places the problem of tough and easy cultures beyond the realm of impression, sentiment, and argument.

With a set of motivational constructs and an analysis of the setting for social behavior, we shall proceed to derive the conditions requisite for tough and easy cultures, demonstrate a continuum by characterizing polar or extreme cases, and finally indicate how one may generally evaluate cultures for their toughness or easiness.

This type of analysis also has relevance to minority and class groups, for not all within a nation face the same field of forces: for example, with no more than the impression created by the contrasting words tough and easy, the reader will probably be able to entertain the question, "Is the U. S. A. tougher on Negroes than on whites?"

Before proceeding, a few postulates regarding behavior will be stated. They are in the nature of axioms which are rather generally accepted although often differently phrased. They are integral to the analysis, especially the postulates about tension.

1. In all cultures persons are the foci of actions and behavior.
2. Action or behavior is determined by forces from inside the person and from the outside. The term "need" will be used to describe the intraperson origin of behavior.
3. Some "needs" are rooted in limited physiologic systems such as thirst, hunger, sex; others are more generalized—for example, air, sleep. Other "needs" are residues of forces originally outside which have become differentiated as self-sustaining, action-inducing parts of the person—for example, taboos, habits, compulsions, sentiments, attitudes, and so on.
4. A "need" has as an essential property a variable quantum of tension which reaching a certain threshold induces action to reduce tension.[3]

---

[2] To cite a few: (*novelists*) Bellamy, Melville, Hudson, Huxley; (*philosophers*) Mill, Rousseau, Kropotkin, Russell; (*cultural anthropologists*) Linton, Benedict, Malinowski, Mead; (*psychiatrists*) Freud, Adler, Fromm, Horney, French; (*socialists*) Saint-Simon, Marx, Engels, Proudhon; (*sociologists*) Veblen, Tawney, Parsons, Merton, Davis, Lynd; (*psychologists*) Lewin, Brown, Frank.

The problem of intellectual indebtedness, but partly expressed by the above references, is one we would not evade. To all others who see their ideas here echoed unacknowledged we gratefully say *ex uno disce omnes*.

[3] This tension-reduction theory of behavior is almost a common denominator in motivational theories today. There is one important modification of a simple tension-reduction theory required by considering the organism so advantageously situated as to be interested in

5. Actions, being need *plus* tension initiated, are *goal directed*—they have terminals where the organism rests with a good feeling. This applies obviously to physiogenic needs such as hunger, thirst, sleep, and so on and equally though less obviously to culturally induced needs such as for prestige, security, and so on.

6. Historical processes find groups of people with more or less habitual sets of induced needs with apposite culturally defined goals. Cultures define all other than physiogenic needs and define the techniques for managing all needs—physiogenic as well as sociogenic. (For example, thirst is an organic or physiogenic need, but whether one drinks water or wine to satisfy the tension state may be decided by the habits of the group.)

7. Ways and means for managing needs, techniques of tension management in goal-directed action we shall call *paths*. "Culture" defines the paths a group uses to satisfy the needs biologically or sociologically inherited—that is, by virtue of birth into a group.

The analysis is to proceed by considering some relationships between paths and goals. We wish separately to specify certain properties of paths, irrespective of goals, and then goals, irrespective of paths. From an examination of these properties for their tension derivatives will emerge the concepts of tough and easy cultures.

PROPERTIES OF PATHS

We have premised that behavior is *goal-directed*. Persons not in goal regions are presumably moving in the direction of goal regions via *paths* having certain properties or dimensions of which the following seem meaningful—that is, they make a difference. Cultures are going to be easy or tough in part according to these qualities of paths.[4]

1. *Effectiveness:* Does the path actually communicate with the goal region? Does it lead one to the goal? For example, if "success" is the goal, does "work" as a path get one there?

2. *Efficiency:* Some paths are easier traversed than others. Let efficiency refer to the amount of *time* and/or *energy* necessary to get there. If the goal is riches, it is more efficient to win it in the stock market than obtain it by labor.

3. *Number:* Some groups possess as a part of their habit patterns (culture) a greater number of paths to a specific goal than others. Independently of goals, some cultures define more paths than others. (This number variable is

---

building up tension before it is reduced. This may well be called tension-eduction, as for example, fasting to sharpen one's appetite in contrast to tension-reduction.

[4] For the purpose of facilitating communication and due to our first-hand ignorance of the details of other cultures, examples will be chosen from the context of twentieth century U.S.A.

probably directly related to the *complexity* of a culture.) As an instance of multiple paths consider the goal of money-making in the U.S.A. Given the goal to amass wealth, there are many ways of doing it.

4. *Accessibility:* This term refers to the number of persons who can find a given path potentially effective, the number of persons who can get on a given path. A path which may be accessible for many may be effective for only one. To marry the boss' daughter is one way to get ahead, but only one person can do this. Similarly with "hard work" in an organization where a foreman is chosen from the ranks. But we have here in mind with accessibility of paths the limited idea of how many can get on it.

5. *Clarity:* Some paths are clearer than others. The perceptual clarity of a path makes a difference since some cultures define goals without indicating how or by what path they are to be achieved. For example, women are induced to value marriage, but what they should do to get a husband is not explicitly defined.

6. *Approval:* Where there exist more than one path to a goal it frequently happens that one is more honorific than another. The matter of comparative approval of paths is clearly seen again in the business of money-making. A patent medicine fortune is less honorific than a steel fortune.

7. *Substitutivity:* Once embarked upon, how possible is it to drop a path, reverse, or substitute other paths? Otherwise expressed, to what extent are paths mutually exclusive, though having the same direction. For example, to train for law is not to train for medicine. It would not be easy to shift (low substitutivity). But to train for medicine and to become a bacteriologist is relatively easy.

8. *Congruence:* Given a number of paths to what extent do they go in the same direction or converge upon goals or to what extent are there oppositions? For example, to follow the path of being generally charitable to the limit would be in opposition to the path toward the goal of being the good family provider.

9. *Cognizance:* To what extent is a population explicitly or inexplicitly acquainted with the properties of paths, their number, effectiveness, and so on? This is more than *clarity* which was limited to the perceptual level—that is, whether a path was discerned. It has to do with a people's generalized awareness of the qualities of paths as detailed above, though obviously ours is not folk language. Many young men in high schools aspire to professional positions and many seem generally unacquainted with the problems of "getting there"—that is, the properties of paths relating to their goals. In other cultures there is more cognizance of paths and possibly less chance of frustrated expectations.

From the above properties of paths, some derivations regarding degrees of toughness and easiness of cultures can be made. The essential argument is double-edged: *psychological tension depends upon and varies with the properties*

Easy	Approaches maximum	Dimension	Approaches minimum	Tough
	?	Number . . . . ?		
	. . . .	Approval		
	. . . .	Effectiveness.		
	. . . .	Efficiency		
	. . . .	Clarity		
	. . . .	Accessibility		
	. . . .	Substitutivity		
	. . . .	Congruence		
	?	Cognizance . . . . ?		

Fig. 1. Dimensions of paths related to easiness and toughness.

of paths as means of reducing tension; and where a culture's paths make for easy tension-reduction in its members the culture is easy. Conversely, where a culture's paths make for difficult tension-reduction the culture is tough. It is possible schematically both to represent polar or extreme cases of toughness or easiness by reference to tension-management problems posed by a culture's paths and to see all existing cultures as falling somewhere within the extremes.

In Fig. 1 the properties of paths are represented as dimensions or variables. That the paths of a given culture may vary in *number*, carry more or less *approval*, have greater or less *efficiency*, and so on, seems evident. At first glance *effectivensss* might seem to be an all or none variable (that is, the path terminates in a goal region or does not), but it may be considered a continuum in which more or less effectiveness refers to the number of people who, traveling the path, reach the goal. In competitive situations this percentage is low, or paths to certain goals have high accessibility but low effectiveness.

The toughness or easiness of cultures cannot be safely assessed from properties of paths taken singly. For example, in the derivation of our conceptual polar easy culture, a maximal rating on one path property must go with maximal ratings on at least six others in order to define the extremely easy or tension-reductive culture. This is to say, the paths of the polar easy culture are characterized by maximal *approval, effectiveness, efficiency, clarity, accessibility, substitutivity,* and *congruence.* In this conceptual paradise, it would seem to make little difference whether the paths were many or few or their properties fully cognized. The ambiguity of the *number* and *cognizance* dimensions is indicated in the diagram by question marks.[5]

---

[5] *Cognizance,* in particular, seems to be discordant with the other aspects of paths above specified: it is a sort of over-all variable embracing homo and his perception of the situation. Does it make it easier to know that a tough culture is tough? Widespread sophistication regarding path properties, or high cognizance, presumably makes a difference, but the tension-equivalents for degrees of cognizance are unknown.

In evaluating the toughness or easiness of real cultures, ratings of the several path properites will fall at variable points inside the polar extremes. Where tension-equivalents clearly cannot be inferred from one dimension alone it may be that taking two in conjunction plainly yields a necessary condition for toughness or easiness. Alone, *number* of paths tells nothing about toughness or easiness but, if given many putative paths, it happens that most if not all have low *efficiency* (that is, require great outlays of energy), it seems justifiable to speak of toughness. Or again, maximally *clear* paths are not indicative of an easy culture unless they are *also accessible, effective, approved,* and *efficient.* Thus, to rate a culture's easiness or toughness a *multidimensional* appraisal of its paths is required.

The next step is to detail some properties of goals as tension terminals. It will become evident that they are similar to the properties of paths, but as applied to goals the terms have a different reference.

PROPERTIES OF GOALS

Cultures are manifestly different in the number and kinds of artifacts, persons, attributes, positions, relationships, and so on, collectively seen as attractive. While instancing particular goals we shall attempt to extrapolate some essential properties of all goals and relate these to concepts of easiness and toughness by considering their meaning for tension levels and tension management.

1. *Number:* Some cultures specify a greater number of things as valuable than others—that is, discriminate with tension inducing-reducing of things as valuable than others—that is, discriminate with tension inducing-reducing possibilities more persons, positions, artifacts, titles, and so on. The U. S. A. defines more goals than Samoa.

2. *Approval:* Some goals are more valued by a group as tension terminals than others. Their possession or consumption binds more favorable feeling, gives more organismic or social gratification. Otherwise said, there exist in all cultures hierarchies of value or worth for persons, positions, possession, services, and so on.

3. *Distribution:* Some goals are more distributed, more commonly possessed and consumed than others. The proportion of a population in or having access to tension terminals is perhaps the most important single aspect of goals (and paths) bearing on the concept of tough and easy cultures.

4. *Clarity:* Goal regions may vary in clearness. An ascetic culture may ignore an organismic tension and its appropriate goal. Less obvious is the possibility that a culture induces tensions leaving unstructured the regions of tension-reduction. For example, a woman wants to get married, where there is no interested unengaged man about. Agreed here the goal is clear, the path wanting. Now take the same situation, including its tension complement and suppose that the woman is unhappy but does not know what she wants. Or

Easy	Approaches maximum	Dimension	Approaches minimum	Tough
	. . . .	Number	. . . .	
	. . . .	Approval	. . . .	
	. . . .	Distribution	. . . .	
	. . . .	Substitutivity	. . . .	
	. . . .	Congruence	. . . .	
	?	Cognizance	. . . . . . ?	

Fig. 2. Dimensions of goals related to easiness and toughness.

consider the clientele of counselors and psychiatrists, people emerging fuzzy from a socialization process, maybe because residuals of developed needs for support and unconditional love find no structured goal region in the culture.

5. *Substitutivity:* Given aspects of *number* and *approval* of goals, it is important to note the extent of substitutivity or equivalence among them. Thus at each level of approval there may be only one or a number of goals. It makes a difference if such equivalences exist, also to what extent and where in the hierarchy. Positions, titles and artifacts defining top status tend toward low substitutivity. There are only a few elite residential sections, more respectable ones; only a few "old families"; only one President, and so on.

6. *Congruence:* Being in one goal region may or may not prevent being in another. When conflicts of choice requiring abandonment of alternatives are evoked we shall speak of incongruity of goals; conversely where one may expect to have simultaneously or successively goal *a* and *z*, congruence is implied. Among professional people the goal of "enjoying life" may deploy time and energy from the goal of being productive or creative—low congruence.

7. *Cognizance:* In some cultures more than others people are explicitly or implicitly aware of the number, approval, substitutivity, distribution, and so on, of goals. By cognizance we mean general awareness of goals and their properties.

The purpose in specifying these properties of goals lies in their usefulness for the general thesis: tough and easy cultures can be conceptually defined. We may again summarize the argument in a diagram, where properties or dimensions of goals are represented as variables which can approximate a maximum and minimum and at these extremes define polar cases of tough and easy cultures.

Polar easy culture. The easy culture constellation as derived from a consideration of *goals* only would seem to require a *number* of goals sufficient to reduce all culturally and physiologically induced tensions: a *distribution* of goals such that all or practically all persons find themselves in and/or consuming goals; additionally, that the goals be *clear*; that the hierarchy of goals be such that all persons are in possession of goals at gratifying levels of the status hierarchy; that all have some highly valued objects, relations, properties (*approval* and *substitutivity*); and that having one goal does not preclude or make impossible having other goals (*congruence*).

Polar Tough Culture. The polar tough constellation can be described as follows: the *number* of goals is insufficient to reduce most all culturally and/or physiologically induced tensions; a *distribution* such that few persons find themselves with or consuming goals. (Obviously the ultimate limit of this is death!—a substantial proof of toughness.) The goals are *unclear*; the hierarchy of goals is such that a few persons are in possession of a narrow range of goals in the status hierarchy—for example, some have only of the best, others only of the worst the culture provides; that having one goal precludes the possession of another.

Briefly to consider the contributions of each dimension to the analysis, that of *distribution,* or extent of access to tension terminals, is clearly relevant for easiness-toughness. If goals are universally distributed, all persons can reduce tension, and the culture tends towards ease. Conversely, if goals are narrowly distributed, the culture tends towards toughness.

The dimensions of *congruence* and *substitutivity* are related to distribution. Absence of congruence between goal regions of a culture implies that access to certain goals imposes limitations upon the distribution of other goals. Substitutivity, or equivalences among goal regions, is itself a derivative of the categories of *number* and *approval*: several or more kinds of goals are equally honorific. Where, then, there exists a narrow distribution of certain goals, high substitutivity means that the distribution of satisfactions is potentially enlarged by equivalences.

The dimensions of *number* and *approval,* in themselves ambiguous tokens of easiness-toughness, become significant when viewed in relation to distribution. If the approved goals are few in number and these are narrowly distributed, the tension-level of the group may be presumed to be higher than where approved goals are many and are widely distributed.

Finally the over-all dimension of *cognizance* suggests that, for peoples informed about their goals, their properties, and interrelationships, matters are different from groups less knowing. It does not follow simply that a high cognizance level makes for easiness and low cognizance for toughness, but one would expect some increment in tension for those in a tough culture if they did not know about goals in terms of their properties. Knowing might reduce some tensions otherwise futilely sustained.

The analysis of goal properties and their tension-producing potentialities is not as contributory to the definition of easy or tough cultures as the analysis of paths. But this is not an error. Tension of the sort contributing to toughness is more related to *getting to* goals than *being in* goal regions where tension reduction is presumed to follow. Perhaps only the dimension of distribution of goals emerges singly and saliently related to the tension level of a group although other properties of goals taken in conjunction do describe situations potentially productive of tension.

It seems improbable that a culture could be easy in respect of paths and tough in respect of goals or vice versa. Yet perhaps variations of this sort can exist. For example, a culture may have an abundance of natural resources but also have cultural practices such that few people can get at them. Other things equal, one would expect easiness in respect of paths would go with easiness in respect of goals. Certainly a culture with tough path properties must result in a culture with a tough distribution of goals, so the argument could reasonably have been shortened. However, it is important to note that in rating cultures for easiness and toughness information on goal objects is often more readily and accurately obtainable than information on path properties. The number and distribution of camels, pigs, cows, automobiles, yachts, canoes, wives, incomes above $25,000, and so on, is a matter for simple enumeration, whereas the paths to these are often less accessible to observation and appraisal.

BEHAVIORAL INDICES OF TOUGHNESS

Throughout in discussing tough as tension-productive and easy as tension-reductive cultures we have assumed that human beings respond in a fairly similar manner to environmental and internal force fields—conceding but setting aside the idea of genetic differences in tension tolerance, and barring genetic differences yielding an allegedly "hardier" stock. Our immediate problem is to focus on some observable behaviors which may show that the cultures conceptually defined as tough are experienced so and conversely the cultures defined as easy are experienced so.

There is no simple way to demonstrate it, but for tough cultures with their tension-productive and tension-sustaining features, abortive and disorganized outlets for tension seem indicated. Tension activated or mobilized, yet unreleased at appropriate terminals, is somehow contained within the organism with feelings of discomfort and by one means or another the organism is compelled to do something to reduce, or avoid it—or will otherwise display it while attempting to contain it.

The following are tentatively cited as behavioral indices of toughness:

1. Accumulated tension seems connected with tenseness or *"nervousness"* as it is properly called; hence the inference that the tougher the culture the more "nervous" behavior.
2. Where tension becomes sufficiently unpleasant either because of an accumulation of unreducible bad feelings or because a situation is impossible *suicide* may occur. Barring institutionalization of suicide—although also it seems plausible that only a tough culture would institutionalize suicide—the tougher the culture the greater the number of suicides.

3. *Neurosis* and *psychosis* in so far as these disturbances are independent of constitutional factors may be taken as an indication of toughness. As Freud said, neurosis and psychosis evolve from a history of conflict and frustration and represent the individual's attempts to manage unresolved tensions. The tough culture provides inadequate opportunities for gratification and hence has a high incidence of "abnormality"—idiosyncratic modes of tension management. Contrawise the easy culture. We note here the same qualification regarding the institutionalization of abnormal patterns—for example, homosexuality, delusions, hallucinations, and so on—but prefer to entertain the argument that this too occurs within the framework of tough as contrasted to easy cultures.

4. *Crime* as an evidence of toughness requires that one see the forbidden activity as something which is tension-invested (a goal) or as a forbidden path leading to a goal. Easy cultures have paths such that people can get what they want within the framework of the *approved* established path-goal schemes. Hence persons in easy cultures are rarely induced to run counter to them—that is commit crime. Conversely, where people find goal-directed activities too difficult or tension-productive within the established framework, they may cut loose towards goals in ways designated as criminal. Thus it seems plausible to say that the tougher the culture the greater the incidence of crime (overt crime if suppressive techniques are inefficient; phantasied crime if "law and order" are firmly upheld). Perhaps the proportion of crimes against persons and property might index the toughness of a culture in these areas—for example, murder, assault, and rape are related to toughness with respect to management of interpersonal tensions; theft and larceny are related to toughness in acquiring goal objects (thing tensions). Here again we run into the possibility of institutionalization of an activity such as theft, homicide, and the like; however such activities not defined as criminal within the group would therefore not be "criminal," although there seems warrant for saying that such cultures are not easy, if the self may be the victim.

5. A less behavioral index of toughness is found in the discrepancy between a culture as it is, and as it projects its membership into an hereafter. It seems plausible that an easy culture would wish little difference between itself and its afterlife, whereas a tough culture would have a large discrepancy between itself and its next life projections. Essentially the argument is that easy cultures readily reduce tensions so members want for a *continuation of the same* in an afterlife, while difficult cultures build up and require sustaining of high levels of tension such that, thinking wishfully, its members are attracted to an afterlife which differs from their own in *the direction of easiness.*

6. *General malaise:* as reflected in non-ceremonial use of drugs; the number of people within a culture who do not have what they want and rate unsatisfactory their chances; the number of persons "in the culture but not of it": the hoboes, recluses, utopians, missing persons—possibly all these are products of toughness. Also they are examples chosen from the culture with

which the authors are most familiar; other cultures have other modes of expressing what is here called general malaise. The category, vague as it is, summarizes some residuals of experienced toughness in a population.

BEHAVIORAL INDICES OF EASINESS

Arguing that toughness and easiness are bipolar, it follows that behavioral indices of an easy culture are opposite to those described above. Thus an absence or near nullity of nervousness, neuroses, psychoses, suicide, crime, and general malaise would characterize an easy culture.

To state positive behavioral criteria of ease is curiously more difficult—but one could suppose that the amount of time given to nonritualistic song, dance, laughter, play, affectional activities, and nonmandatory work indexes the easiness of a culture. Within an easy culture biologic and socially induced tensions are easily reduced, therefore a group can be more at ease doing those things which produce pleasant tensions and simultaneously or soon reduce them.

Also one would expect relatively frictionless interpersonal relations because there would be no monopoly upon paths, positions, or possessions yielding pleasure, hence less occasion for rivalry, invidiousness, and revenge which characterize interpersonal relations in a tough culture.

Significantly enough, in trying to specify behavioral indices of an easy culture, one has recourse as much to the utopian constructions of dreaming or disgruntled members of tougher cultures as to functioning easy cultures. However vestiges of cultures approaching the polar easy type have been observed by anthropologists, and the above behavioral indices of easiness find some documentation.

TOWARD AN APPLICATION OF THE DIMENSIONAL ANALYSIS TO EXISTING CULTURES

The analysis of a given culture employing the above path-goal manifold and requiring ratings on the specified dimensions and entailed tensions is neither easy nor entirely objective. Judgments are required regarding degrees of presence or absence of variables and relationships, and these cannot approach objectivity without a frame of reference with which to make such judgments. The specification of polar cases (conceptual extremes) provides the basis for a systematic assessment scheme. But even with this conceptual continuum, the problem of rating existing cultures for easiness-toughness is not solved. How can one crystallize the complex totality of a culture to a point on a rating scale where only the extremes are defined?

Obviously the materials of a single culture are variable and not all of a piece or of the same weight for toughness and easiness. There seem instead to be *areas* of toughness or easiness. For example, within one and the same culture hunger tensions may be readily reduced, but not so for sexual tensions. Or a culture may be easy on certain age or class groups while tough on others.

For comparative purposes the notion of areas may be useful if major tension-involved areas of living can be delimited. Some such scheme as W. Lloyd Warner employs could possible serve here: the relation of persons to others—embracing everything from the family to political organizations; the relation of persons to things necessary for survival and comfort; and the relation of persons to the cosmos (ideology).[6]

Within these areas, the satisfaction of biologic needs could be evaluated reliably. Given the diversity of cultures, because of differences in socially induced needs, other material for evaluation will vary, although final ratings will be for constant areas. Comparison is hampered still by the fact that cultures differ in the importance ascribed to goals within these areas. A scale of weights is necessary to give to tension-involved matters a proportionally fitting contribution of a summary index. Such a scale could be derived by considering the hierarchy of values or goals in a culture, so one could compare first things with first things—regardless of content. Ultimately one could contrive a check list with some constants or constants variably weighted and some factors unique to each culture from which a single index of the degree of easiness or toughness could be obtained by the process of adding admittedly such diverse things as oranges, orgasms, and organizational status.

Observation, enumeration, discerning of relationships, and penetration of the value hierarchy of a group are all required. Participant observation seems the best way of becoming acquainted with the aspects or dimensions of goals and paths we have specified for rating. Maybe it follows that more complicated cultures, cultures differentiated into subparts, require participant observation at all levels before one can make an over-all statement. If these subcultures are sufficiently and consistently different from the total culture, even though geographically and nationally defined as the same, one would be required logically to make a separate report for them.

Pragmatically the procedure then seems to be systematic inquiry asking: (1) what do a people want (specification of goals)? (2) how do they go about getting what they want (paths), with what success? and finally, (3) what tensions result from discrepancies between desire and gratification?

As a rule anthropologists report some data on these particulars but not systematically. Still by processes of inference from published accounts of cultures one can make an assessment for easiness-toughness. With the scheme on hand it should be possible to make the relevant observations and extrapolations more surely. Ultimately one could look forward to a classification of all existing cultures for their easiness-toughness.

---

[6] W. L. Warner, and P. S. Lunt, *The Social Life of a Modern Community*; New Haven, Yale University Press, 1941; pp. 21-25 in chapter 2.

It should be noted that we do not state the easiest is the "best" culture, only that it is the least tension-producing-and-sustaining. We do say, however, that very tough cultures must be expected to be pathogenic. And we are not the first to note that a society can make sickness. We have tried to show wherein and how it is that some societies are more pathogenic than others.

25

The Environment as a Determinant of Behavior

ISIDOR CHEIN

A. INTRODUCTION

Perhaps one of the outstanding weaknesses of contemporary psychological theory is the relative neglect of the environment by many of the most influential theoretical viewpoints. Stimulus-response psychology, for instance, tends to assimilate the entire environment, insofar as it is relevant to behavior, into the term "stimulus" and perhaps also, as in the case of reinforcement theory, "goal objects"; for the most part, many environmental features tend simply to be taken for granted. Yet many aspects of the environment, when we single them out for attention, are not assimilable into any proper definition of either "stimulus" or "goal objects"; and, as for taking many of them for granted, it sometimes pays to take systematic account of even the obvious. Of course, not all theoretical viewpoints are equally neglectful of the environment. Tolman (7) and Lewin (6), for instance, have made important contributions in this regard; but even these contributions have tended to become obscured by the more challenging aspects of Tolman's and Lewin's systems, and it is likely that they are little known by those who are not thoroughly familiar with these systems.

It may be timely, therefore, to pull together a schema for taking better account of the environment than is customary. It is all the more timely inasmuch as psychology is coming to be called on more and more in connection with important personal and social problems. If, as I believe, a proper appreciation of the rôle of environmental factors is important to rat psychology, it is ever so much more so in a humanistic psychology—i.e., a psychology concerned with human beings in the conduct of the important affairs of their lives. Not only are human environments more complex, but the behaviors with which the rat psychologists are most concerned take place in the controlled environments of the laboratory, whereas the behaviors of greatest concern to the humanistic

From the *Journal of Social Psychology*, 1954, *39*, 115-127. Copyright 1954 by The Journal Press. Reprinted by permission of the author and the publisher.

psychologist take place in freely variable (from the viewpoint of the psychologist) environments. With the greater complexity of human environments they have perhaps more of a rôle to play, and with their free variability they have, so to speak, a more active rôle. Moreover, whereas one can perhaps afford to underestimate the importance of factors under one's control, it is an error of much graver consequence to underestimate the importance of factors beyond one's control.

I take as my point of departure Koffka's (5) distinction between the "geographical" and the "behavioral" environments. The former refers to the objective physical and social environment in which the individual is immersed. The latter refers to the environment as it is perceived and reacted to by the behaving individual; it may bear little resemblance to the geographical environment, being an organized "interpretation" of the latter based on recollections, anticipations, perceptual distortions and omissions, and upon reasonably correct perceptions. The behavioral environment deletes from and alters, as well as adds to the geographic environment. The point of Koffka's distinction is that behavior can be far more meaningfully understood if it is related to the behavioral rather than the geographic environment.

Important as the concept of the "behavioral" environment may be to a humanistic psychology, it calls for more or less intimate knowledge of the behaving individual before we can resort to it. Nor does it tell us what the objective environment does to the behaving individual. It is the latter problem that concerns me here. Moreover, there are factors in the geographic environment which influence behavior even though they do not belong in the behavioral environment as Koffka conceives of it. Thus, the chair I am sitting on and the desk I am using have an important facilitating rôle in the writing of this paper even—and perhaps especially—while I am not aware of them; but, in Koffka's usage, they belong in my behavioral environment only while I am aware of them.

Our starting point must be the "geographical" environment. Needless to say, however, the "geographical" environment can be looked at from many points of view. For my present purpose, I want to consider it from the viewpoint of a psychologically sophisticated observer who presupposes psychological individuals with wants and desires, but who is not at the moment particularly concerned with any one person. It seems desirable, therefore, to make an additional distinction to the one drawn by Koffka: the *geo-behavioral* or the *objective-behavioral* environment—i.e., the geographical environment looked at from a point of view that is concerned with understanding behavior.

The major features of the geo-behavioral environment, as I see them, will be outlined in the remainder of this paper.

I am primarily concerned with these features as they present themselves, rather than with how or why they came about. All of them are, of course, conditioned by factors of social organization and by one's place in the social order (in society at large and/or in some particular group) as well as by factors of the geo-physical environment. I am confident that our observation would be sharpened if we understood something of their genesis, but I do not feel called upon—in my rôle as a psychologist—to trace their origins; this may be left to fellow workers in other disciplines. Still, apart from the question of the origins of the patterns of stimuli, goal objects, etc., we must be prepared to take note of their significant correlations with various social variables. Thus, there are often important differences in the nature and distribution of stimuli acting upon, say, the two sexes or members of different social classes. Similarly with regard to the available goal objects, the unavoidable noxiants, the behavior supports and constraints, and directors. I am here, however, concerned only with the broad outlines of the schema and must content myself with calling attention to the existence of such correlations.

Let me take up these features of the geo-behavioral environment one at a time.

B. STIMULI

A stimulus is here regarded as whatever is capable of initiating a change in the stream of activity; it is, so to speak, a release or trigger mechanism. Although light and sound of certain wave lengths and other relatively simple forms of transmitted energy are stimuli, a "stimulus" as here defined is not necessarily reducible to such elementary components. A complex social situation, for instance, operating as a Gestalt, may function as a stimulus. Except for its initiation, the response is not viewed as a function of the stimulus;[1] the course of the response is seen as a function of physiological and motivational factors, but it is also viewed as a function of the other environmental factors outlined in this schema.

Consider for instance the case of a housewife who has been reading a "sexy" novel. That night her husband is surprised by the unprecedented fact that it is she who initiates amorous advances and that she turns out to be quite amorous indeed. It seems that "sexy" novels are often effective trigger mechanisms for sexual behavior; but, to account for the course of this particular response as distinguished from an alternative response of, say, lascivious phantasies, it seems relevant that factors other than the stimulus were operative, such as the fact that the husband was not away on a business trip and that he did not prove to be sexually impotent.

Or take the case of a man living in a generally frustrating environment. He comes home one evening to an unusually unsatisfying dinner. He sits about muttering to himself, suddenly announces, "God damn the Jews!" and takes himself off to join an anti-Semitic organization with headquarters in the neighborhood. To understand this behavior we must not only take into account the fact that the frustration of an unsatisfying dinner may set off seemingly irrelevant behaviors

---

[1] Cp. Holt's discussion of the "recession of the stimulus" (3, pp. 75-82) and also his definition of "behavior" (*ibid.*, pp. 153-171, esp. p. 164).

and the motivational and perceptual background into which this stimulus obtruded itself, but also that the course of the response is a function of such environmental factors as that there was an anti-Semitic organization in the neighborhood, that Jews constitute a convenient scapegoat in this man's social environment, that his wife would take no guff from him, etc.

To speak of a stimulus as something which can (i.e., as something which in the past has been observed to) set off a response is not to preclude the possibility that the same object (e.g., a pretty girl) or situation may sometimes function not only in the rôle of stimulus, but also as a goal or noxiant, as a support or constraint, and/or as a director. It is the sometimes concurrence of these various rôles in the same object that has led to what I believe is the common practice of overburdening the stimulus concept with the function of determining, as distinguished from initiating, responses. The important point is that these various rôles are always distinguishable and are often carried by distinct objects or situations.

It should not be supposed that relegating stimuli to the rôle of initiating responses makes them unimportant features of the environment. After all, responses still have to be initiated. But, apart from the rôle that stimuli play in relation to specific behavior, the over-all stimulus properties of an environment may have important psychological consequences. A relatively stimulusless environment, for instance, is, I believe, an important factor in neurasthenia: the individual is thrown upon his self-stimulating (although we have concentrated upon stimuli which emanate from the environment, we have not precluded stimuli which originate within the organism) resources which may prove insufficient for the initiation of activity. Conversely, an overstimulating environment often generates profound problems of self-management; one of the things we must learn, for instance, is not to respond to distracting stimuli. Less extremely, the stimulus characteristics of an environment may render certain motives more, or less, salient than they might otherwise be. Thus, environments differ in the relative number of stimuli evocative of, say, aggressive, fear, patriotic, religious, or sexual response tendencies.

Before leaving the subject of stimuli, I must note the partial circularity of the definition with respect to response. One important consequence of this circularity is an interaction between the individual and the potentially effective stimulus: whether a form of energy, or an object, or a situation stimulates a particular individual depends in part upon the characteristics of the individual and upon his momentary state. If we were to pursue this interaction, we would find ourselves in the "behavioral" environment in the full sense of the term. Since I have here limited myself to the geo-behavioral environment, however, I deliberately did not go the full circle in the definition of "stimulus" ("that which induces a response" rather than "that which can—has previously been observed to—induce a response"). The effect of the restraint is that we can identify a stimulus in the geo-behavioral environment, and do so without waiting until after the event when we have already noted that the "stimulus" actually stimulated. Still, we can take certain broad characteristics of individuals into account without leaving the geo-behavioral environment. Thus, if there are significant sex differences with respect to the way in which certain objects or situations act as stimuli, we can speak of the geo-behavioral stimulus environment of men as distinguished from the geo-behavioral stimulus environment of women. There is also much that we can discern of the stimulus world of any particular individual as contrasted with that of any other particular individual without making a thorough psychological analysis of either individual.[2]

C. GOAL OBJECTS AND NOXIANTS

"Goal objects" refers to objects or situations which can serve as need satisfiers and *"noxiants"* refers to objects or situations which can produce pain or unpleasantness.

Many psychologists, being almost exclusively concerned with such matters as the manner in which stimulus-response connections are established, tend to take goal objects for granted and have shown little interest in examining various environments, as such, from the point of view of what they have to offer by way of goal objects and/or noxiants. Yet this seems to me to be an important source of insight into behavior. Environments differ in the abundance or scarcity of goal objects and noxiants, and in the relative abundance of those related to certain needs as compared to others. Goal objects can, of course, be arranged along continua from the point of view of how well they satisfy particular needs; and environments differ in the relative availability of goal objects from different sections of these continua. The various patterns of availability of goal objects and unavoidability of noxiants have important consequences for behavior. They play a rôle, for instance, in determining the relative order of importance of different motives,[3] in establishing attitudes of withdrawal (as when there is little in life worth striving for), and in generating competitive social relationships.

---

[2] Needless to say, similar considerations apply to the other terms in the schema. The distinction between "behavioral" and "geo-behavioral" environments is, therefore, not rigid. Depending on how much we know about the correlation between types of environments and types of subjects and on our ability to select maximally differentiable types, the usage of the term "geo-behavioral environment" without detailed reference to any particular individual will run the gamut from the "average" geo-behavioral environment characteristic of a total society to that characteristic of a highly differentiated segment of that society. Similarly, with respect to any given individual, the more thoroughly we observe him in his environment (or the more complete our data are from other sources), the less distinguishable does what we observe as "geo-behavioral" environment become from the "behavioral" environment. But, on a conceptual level, the "geo-behavioral" environment never becomes equivalent to the "behavioral." The latter can only be observed through the eyes of the behaving individual, although it can often be reconstructed by the independent observer. The former can be observed directly by an independent observer; but the point is that the more he knows, the greater are his powers of observation.

[3] Many psychologists are interested in arranging motives in the order of their importance, but resort to non-psychological criteria of importance. Thus, they may work with the essentially sociological criteria of universality or dependability, or with biological criteria of

It may be noted that an individual's orientation to goal objects involves a future reference and, hence, that a given goal object need not actually exist and may indeed never come to be (as when one fails to bring about some desired situation). In such an event, we tend to get into the "behavioral" environment in the full sense of that term. The observer is, however, not limited to existing goal objects, but may also "discern" potential need satisfiers—e.g., in relation to Joe Doakes who is still going to school, a diploma inscribed "Joseph Doakes." The objectively observable environment offers—or fails to offer—potential as well as existing goal objects.

The present schema is concerned with goal objects that may be located in the observable environment, but this concern is not intended to preclude "ipsative" goals that refer only to the self—e.g., a change in one's personal characteristics. There are also goals which have both ipsative and environmental connections—e.g., a change in one's status—but these may usually be described as part of the environment, e.g., there is a status position in the environment the attainment of which can satisfy certain needs.

D. SUPPORTS AND CONSTRAINTS[4]

Supports refer to those features of the environment which make particular behaviors feasible. *Constraints* refer to those features of the environment which preclude particular behaviors, make their occurrences less likely, or limit their variability.

As Tolman (7, p. 85) has noted, the "fact that supports, and not merely stimuli, are needed for the actual going-off of any act . . . is a feature about behavior which orthodox psychologies, both stimulus-response psychologies and mentalisms, seem hitherto to have overlooked." Unhappily, since the publication of Tolman's book in 1932, this fact has continued to be overlooked.

1. Discriminanda

The properties of objects or situations whereby they can be discriminated from one another. A most important sub-class of discriminanda consists of *cues,* namely, discriminanda which offer relevant information—i.e., discriminanda which exist not in and of themselves but in systematic relationships to other

---

necessity for life and health or closeness to physiological processes. Relatively little attention has been paid in such listings to such psychological criteria of importance as how much of our behavior is devoted to given motives and what we are prepared to sacrifice in order to satisfy them. The need for air is certainly universal and essential for life; but it is certainly relatively unimportant, except in special cases, from the viewpoint of proportion of behavior devoted to it, precisely because of the availability of the goal object.

[4] For all the liberties I have taken with their concepts, my indebtedness in this section of the schema to Tolman (7) and Lewin (6) must be so obvious that I shall attempt no detailed annotation.

discriminanda, means-end paths, etc. Thus, an apple may be green; the color is a discriminandum. But inasmuch as the color of apples is also correlated with their taste and digestibility, their color is also a cue.

As used here, a "cue" is an objective feature of the environment; it may or may not be utilized as such by the behaving individual and does not depend for its existence (though it may for its use) on the learning process or on some immediate and direct inference. The utilization of cues may depend on learning and/or upon immediate and direct acts of inference; but this feature of the environment sets limits upon what may be learned or inferred, and it makes certain learnings and inferences more difficult than others. Whether the individual perceives the relation between the color and taste of certain types of apples, or not, the existence of this correlation presents him with a quite different environmental situation than would be the case if there were no visually perceptible correlates of the taste of apples. Environments differ in the number and variety of cues that they afford and behavior often goes astray, not because of the incapacities or contrariness of individuals, but simply because of the absence of sufficient cues, because cues are not sufficiently prominent to be discerned, because of misleading cues, or simply because what is conventionally supposed to be a cue does not correspond to an objective geo-behavioral environmental state of affairs (as when a parent's threats are not consistently followed through).

Note also that "cue" is commonly, but not here, used as a synonym of "stimulus" or, more precisely, as a composite concept of what are here separately defined as "stimulus" and "cue." All discriminanda, to be sure, are mediated by stimuli (the reflected light in the case of the green apple); but we are here interested in them, not because of this fact, but rather because of their rôle as supports.

2. Manipulanda

The properties of objects or situations whereby they can be handled in certain ways. These, of course, set limits as to what can be done or accomplished.

3. Means-End Paths

The steps one must take or things one must do in order to attain particular goals or avoid particular noxiants. An important class of means-end paths depends on instrumental and personal aids. By extension, the characteristic patterns of human interdependencies are of the utmost importance among the social aspects of any geo-behavioral environment. Means-end paths define conditions for attaining goals and may vary considerably from environment to environment. For instance, in some settings the routes to goal objects are individualistic and competitive whereas in other settings they are collective and coöperative.

Means-end paths also vary with respect to such characteristics as: (a) *Distance* (the number of intervening steps that must be taken), (b) *Quickness* (the time needed to reach the goal), (c) *Freedom from barriers or hurdles,* and (d) *Viscosity* (the degree of resistance to locomotion offered by a path apart from the specific barriers it contains). Thus, two paths to a goal (or to two equivalent goals) may be equally short, one may be (because of more or less automatic compensatory adjustments) no faster than the other, both may be free of specific barriers, and yet one may call for greater effort than the other. Where there are no clear-cut and separable goals, the concept of "viscosity" can also be applied to a total situation, there being more or less ease of locomotion in it; e.g., an informal setting is less viscous than a formal one.

The msot obvious type of constraint is *the absence or inadequacy of supports.*

4. Pseudo-Means-End Paths

What look to be means-end paths, but actually lead elsewhere than to the indicated goal or contain some impermeable barrier or insurmountable hurdle. I refer to the pseudo-means-end paths as constraints because their sheer presence may mislead the individual and hence lessen the likelihood that he will actually move toward his goals. The existence of pseudo-means-end paths accounts for much wasted effort. There is, of course, no sharp line of demarcation between true and pseudo-means-end paths.

5. The Concurrence of Contravaluant Properties in Goal Objects (or Means-End Paths to Goal Objects) and of Provaluant Properties in Noxiants (or Means-End Paths Away from Noxiants)

Objects, etc., may involve features which entail unpleasantness or pain for behaving individuals; we may refer to these as *contravaluants.* Other features are need-satisfying; we may refer to these as *provaluants.* The concurrence of contravaluant and provaluant properties in goal objects or noxiants and in means-end paths to or from them may be described as *incidental* rewards and punishments. However, it seems best to reserve "rewards" and "punishments" for that which is actually rewarding and punishing, something which depends on the reaction of the individual as well as on what the environment offers. The terms "contravaluants" and "provaluants" like the terms "goal objects" and "noxiants" are intended to be neutral with respect to any particular individual's actual reactions. They refer to environmental offerings.

The point is that "good" things may be more or less inseparably associated with "bad" and vice versa. Thus, medication may bring welcome relief, but nonetheless have a very bad taste in the taking; pie may be very palatable, but also highly calorific; and a young lady may be "beautiful but dumb" or vice versa. The effect of such concurrences is that they act as constraints with respect to behaviors that might otherwise take place.

E. DIRECTORS

Features of the environment which tend to induce specific directions of behavior.

1. The Spatio-Temporal Patterning of Stimuli, Goals, and Noxiants, Supports, and Constraints

Such patterning, which is to a variable extent under deliberate social control, acts as a director in a variety of ways. Thus: (a) The absence of means-end paths to particular goals at a particular time may tend to direct behavior to alternative goals. (b) Meeting up with a particular goal object at a particular time may divert the course of behavior into a new direction. (c) Objects and situations are often so ordered along means-end paths that they become goals and behavior is directed toward them; i.e., given certain ends, certain means-to-ends themselves become ends simply because of the structure of the environment. And so on. To explain why a certain individual became a psychologist, for example, we may have to take into account the fact that he could not get into medical school; the goal objects he encounters in the course of, or concurrently with, his career as a psychologist may make a medical career relatively less attractive even though an opportunity to enter medical school later opens up; and he may have studied French for no better reason than that this was required for the degree in psychology.

2. Physical and Social Currents

a. **Normative factors** which conceal possibilities of variant behaviors, control the availability and perceptibility of supports and constraints, control the patterns of concurrence of provaluants and contravaluants, limit the number of choice points and the number of possible choices, and define and structure environmental situations.

b. **Patterns of concurrence of social norms.** Most noteworthy are:

(1). Patterns of co-existing contradictory norms as elaborated, for instance, by Horney (4)–e.g., the coexistence in our society of the norms of "brotherly love" and of competition.

The individual who encounters such contradictory pressures must resolve them in some way, by withdrawal, by gravitating to those areas where the contradictory pressures are most unequal, by vacillation, by yielding to one of the pressures in one area and to the second in another area, etc. However he resolves them, it is obvious that an environment with such contradictory directors is more difficult in this respect than one without them.

(2). The hierarchization of social values which occurs in at least two ways: (a) Where conflict between norms arises, one is expected to take precedence over

the other and (*b*) where the individual cannot live up to the most valued norms, he is expected at least to live up to the next most valued, etc.—e.g., a club member is expected to participate in the committee work or at least come regularly to meetings, or at the very least pay his dues.

   (*3*). *The differentiation of rôle-defined behaviors in various contexts.* Bateson[5] (1, 2), for instance, has pointed to two important patterns: (*a*) Symmetrical rôle-defined behaviors, where *A* is expected to act toward *B* in the same manner as *B* is expected to act toward *A*—as in the case of two friends; (*b*) Complimentary rôle-defined behaviors, where *A* is expected to act toward *B* in a manner that is qualitatively different from, or opposite to, the way in which *B* is expected to act toward *A*—as in the case of employer and employee or a Negro and white in the South. From the viewpoint of the geo-behavioral environment of either *A* or *B*, it makes a difference whether the other individual actually acts in the rôle-defined way. The more important point, however, is that both *A* and *B* are subjected to pressures to act in their rôle-defined ways.

F. THE ENVIRONMENT AS A WHOLE;
GLOBAL FEATURES

   Up to this point I have broken up the geo-behavioral environment into various components; but there are also global properties of these environments, which are perhaps Gestaltish functions of these components. Some environments are discernibly more *difficult* than others, for example; some are discernibly more *secure,* etc. On another level, environments may be described as more or less *organized* or *disorganized* and as more or less *stable* or *unstable.* From still another point of view, the available goal objects, the unavoidable noxiants, the absence of goal objects, the supports and constraints and the directors, all of these taken together, determine the *number of degrees of freedom* available to the individual in the geo-behavioral environment. There are also psychological constraints[6] which limit the number of degrees of freedom, but I am here concerned with only the geo-behavioral environment. However, the concept of degrees of freedom, whether applied to the geo-behavioral or behavioral environments or to the individual-in-the-behavioral environment, has meaning only with reference to particular motives or sets of motives: the environment permits the individual to satisfy these motives in no, or one, or several, or many ways.

---

   [5] Bateson does not sharply distinguish between the environmental pressure to conform to rôle-defined behavior patterns and the actual patterns of behavior. For my present purpose, the distinction is an important one.

   [6] Misconstructions of the environment—due to limitations of intelligence, perceptual habits that obscure changes in the environment, the distorting influences of various motives, etc.—personal standards of behavior which may be more or less irrelevant to a particular geo-behavioral situation but are nonetheless operative within it, fears and doubts which may have little or no objective justification in the situation, interfering motives, defense mechanisms, etc.

G. CONCLUSION

I have outlined a comprehensive theoretical model of what I find to look at in the environment. That I find the schema useful in predicting as well as in understanding behavior which has already taken place should be obvious. That it is subject to theoretical improvement, I am, on general principle, certain. There are also many empirical questions the solution of which would greatly enhance its usefulness. Thus, to mention three lines of investigation: (a) The question of differentiable types of environment in relation to differentiable population types is a matter for empirical research. Then (b), there are problems of measurement and interaction between the factors. How, for instance, do you add the constraint of a quota system in college to the constraint of high fees when neither of these, by itself, constitutes an impermeable barrier? And how do you balance a constraint against a director or, for that matter, a drive? Finally, (c), there are questions of the relations of factors included in the schema to psychological phenomena of a higher order than specific behaviors. I have, for instance, already advanced the hypothesis that a relatively stimulusless environment is often a contributing factor in neurasthenia; I may add a similar hypothesis with regard to environments that are relatively impoverished in goal objects so that there is little worth striving for. Apart from the question of whether these hypotheses are sound, there are related questions as to how these two factors, a dearth of stimuli and a dearth of goal objects, interact with each other and with psychological factors in relation to neurasthenia.

But even while the schema is imperfect and many empirical questions are unanswered, I find that simply keeping it in mind enhances my sensitivity to the environments of my fellow human beings and is of material assistance in helping me to predict their behavior and to understand why they are what they are and why they do what they do, the commonplace as well as the unusual. Perhaps it will prove equally useful to others; and, even more important, perhaps it will stimulate some psychologists to improve upon it in the directions indicated or to provide a superior alternative so that we may take better and more systematic account of the environment in our day-to-day work and in the structure of psychological theory.

One further point should be made explicit. The anthropological and sociological literature is replete with materials relevant to the schema. This is especially true with respect to the sections on supports and constraints (as related, for instance, to social class differences) and on "directors." As a matter of fact, the whole notion (if not the terminology) of "directors" is largely borrowed from this literature. It may not be too much to hope, therefore, that some such schema as the present one may offer a bridge from these disciplines to psychology. The need for interdisciplinary unification has been evident for some time, but it has not always been clear how one disclipine can best utilize the materials of another with respect to its own problems. The psychology student, for example, may find that many topics in his social psychology course (particularly when the course is taught from a sociological point of view) have little connections with the "layout" of psychology as he learns the latter in his psychology courses; it often seems that social psychology involves a new world of psychology, not quite coordinate with the old. Perhaps the present schema points out one way in which psychology can enrich itself with certain anthropological and sociological findings without deviating from its own fundamental outlook or systematic structure.

REFERENCES

1. Bateson, G. Morale and national character. In Watson, G. (*Ed.*). *Civilian Morale.* New York: Houghton Mifflin, 1942.
2. ____. Naven. Cambridge: Cambridge University Press, 1946.
3. Holt, E. G. The Freudian Wish. New York: Holt, 1915.
4. Horney, K. The Neurotic Personality of Our Time. New York: Norton, 1937.
5. Koffka, K. Principles of Gestalt Psychology. New York: Harcourt Brace, 1935.
6. Lewin, K. Principles of Topological Psychology. New York: McGraw-Hill, 1936.
7. Tolman, E. C. Purposive behavior in animals and men. New York: Appleton-Century Crofts, 1932.

26

Toward a Taxonomy of Situations

NORMAN FREDERIKSEN

Several years ago a conference was held in Washington, D.C., to consider the question of how to predict the behavior of a single individual. The reason the government was concerned about the question was because a single individual's behavior might be of critical importance to the United States—if he happened to be someone like Nikita Krushchev, who, at that time, had the power to commit his nation to economic and military acts that could affect the welfare and security of Americans.

The fact that the question was posed and that a number of well-known behavioral scientists considered the question very seriously tells us something about the state of psychology as a science. Psychologists have developed a technology of prediction that depends almost wholly on individual differences, with heavy reliance on items of biographical history and measures of ability, attitude, and personality. The method works reasonably well when the problem is to make comparative statements about probable performance of many individuals—candidates for admission to college or applicants for a job. But the personnel psychologist, at least, is likely to be stumped when asked to make predictions about how a single individual's behavior will vary from one occasion to another over a period of time. Individual differences (at least as they are usually conceived) do not provide a solution to the problem, since they do not exist for a single individual.

The personnel psychologist's solution to the prediction problem requires that we have a measure of criterion performance, y (e.g., a rating of job performance), and at least one measure of a personal characteristic, x (e.g., aptitude or interest) that is correlated with y. The regression of y on x provides the basis for

From the *American Psychologist*, 1972, *27*, 114–123. Copyright 1972 by the American Psychological Association. Reprinted by permission.

This article was presented at the meeting of the American Psychological Association, Washington, D.C., September 5, 1971. The article is based on portions of a book entitled *Prediction of Organizational Behavior* by N. Frederiksen, A. Beaton, and O. Jensen, with a contribution by B. Bloxom, to be published by Pergamon Press.

predicting criterion performance. If one wished to follow an analogous procedure for predicting events in the life of a single individual, he would have to consider criterion behaviors as measured on many occasions, and the predictor variables would have to be personal characteristics that vary over time. If it were possible to obtain information about Mr. Krushchev's mood just prior to the occasions when the criterion behavior was exhibited, then one might compute a regression equation for prediction of his performance on the basis of his mood.

Another possibility is to employ a completely different class of predictor variables, that of situational variables. Let us suppose, for example, that the y we wish to predict is Mr. Krushchev's willingness to compromise in international conferences. Presumably there are, somewhere in Washington, many file drawers full of records of such conferences attended by Krushchev, and suitable ratings of the criterion variable "willingness to compromise" could be made. Similarly, ratings could be made of each conference with respect to various situational variables that might be predictive of performance (e.g., the extent to which the prestige of the USSR was involved). Given such data, it would be perfectly possible to obtain a regression equation that describes the relationship between y (Krushchev's willingness to compromise) and x (degree to which the prestige of the USSR is at stake). If the relationship were sufficiently high, one could "predict" the extent to which Krushchev would compromise at a new international conference, and perhaps one could have controlled to some degree Krushchev's behavior by managing the amount of stress placed on prestige.

Another approach to the problem is that of the clinician who, through careful study of the "dynamics" of an individual's behavior, achieves a degree of understanding that supposedly enables him to predict behavior even in circumstances where the performance has never been observed. Clinical psychologists are regularly called on to make predictions of how a patient will respond to a kind of therapy, how a prisoner will adjust to parole, or how a manager will perform in a new position. Such judgments are of interest because the clinician makes predictions that take into account the kind of situation in which the subject will be placed. He says, in effect, that a patient with a given set of personal characteristics will behave in a particular manner when placed in a certain kind of situation. Thus, the clinician's statements imply interactions between personal and situational variables.

From a scientific rather than a clinical point of view, psychologists are interested in generalizations that hold for a large number of people rather than for just one individual. There is the possibility that groups of people can be identified that are larger than one, but less than all mankind, whose behavior can be described in terms of particular kinds of relationships between performance and situational variables.

Interest in prediction models that involve precisely this kind of interaction between situations and personal characteristics has been increasing rapidly in recent years. Most notable are the efforts by educational psychologists to find evidence of aptitutde-treatment interaction and by organizational psychologists to find consistent differences in relationships between performance and predictor variables for organizations that differ with regard to organizational climates. Neither search has been particularly successful so far. The reason may be that we have a lot to learn about the strategy and methodology required for doing such research.

One of the methodological difficulties is that we lack a satisfactory classification of situations. We need a systematic way of conceptualizing the domain of situations and situational variables before we can make rapid progress in studying the role of situations in determining behavior.

We do have useful taxonomies in the domain of individual differences. Following Thurstone, many factorial studies of cognitive abilities have resulted in a classification of abilities into such categories as induction, deduction, perceptual speed, ideational fluency, and so forth. The *Kit of Reference Tests for Cognitive Factors* (French, Ekstrom, & Price, 1963) provides tests to measure such factors, and it has proved to be very useful. The availability of a common set of instruments has made it possible to integrate findings and to draw inferences based on studies by a number of different investigators. Guilford's structure of intellect model has also been influential in helping to introduce a degree of coordination into the research of many investigators. His distinction between convergent and divergent thinking, for example, has contributed to clarifying research problems in the area of creative behavior. Similarly, in the field of personality, factor studies by many investigators have helped to bring order into the field, even though we by no means have agreement on a list of personality dimensions.

TAXONOMIES OF SITUATIONS

We do not have a comparable toxonomy of situations. The lack of a taxonomy to represent the stimulus side of the S-R formula is interesting in view of the fact that the topic of individual differences was a relatively late arrival in psychology. The early behavioristic stimulus-response notion implied that all the variance in behavior was attributable to the various stimuli impinging on the organism; yet no systematic study of variation in stimuli was ever made, except in such limited domains as psychophysics where the relations between sensory experiences were related to aspects of the physical stimulus. Experimental psychologists of all stripes, including experimental social psychologists, have shown great ingenuity in devising situations for use as experimental conditions in their investigations. But the guiding principle in devising these experiments has, naturally enough, usually been the hypothesis or theory being tested. Such work has not led to the construction of a taxonomy of situations. Perhaps the development and testing of theories would have progressed more rapidly if a taxonomy of situations had been available to guide the work of various investigators and to facilitate the drawing of inferences based on studies by many independent investigators.

Sells (1963a) stated the problem very well:

The most obvious need in evaluating the manifold encounter of organism and environment is a more satisfactory and systematic conceptualization of the environment. This implies a taxonomic, dimensional analysis of stimulus variables comparable to the trait systems that have been developed for individual difference variables. . . . While work proceeds actively to extend the exploration of individual differences . . . the equally important frontier of situational dimensions is virtually ignored. . . . Experimenters must have systematic information about relevant dimensions of the environment beyond the piecemeal, concrete, immediate variables customarily observed on the basis of experience [p. 700] .

METHODS FOR DEVELOPING TAXONOMIES

How does one go about developing a taxonomy? The methods historically used in biology seem to have been based on careful observation and good judgment. They certainly cannot be characterized as "armchair" methods, since the field work must have been enormous. At the age of 25, Linnaeus, a student at Uppsala in Sweden, became interested in the classification of plants. He was sent to Lapland in 1732 as a collector of specimens, and in the next five months he traveled almost 5,000 miles in Lapland, Norway, and Sweden (at a total cost, we are told, of £25) observing, making notes and drawings, and collecting specimens. He developed a classification of plants based principally on characteristics of stamens and pistils. The method seems somewhat arbitrary, at least to a psychologist today. Why were stamens and pistils chosen rather than other morphological characteristics involving leaf, stem, roots, or fruit? What criteria *should* be employed in choosing a taxonomic system?

The aim of the plant taxonomist was then, and still is, to find a classification of plants that would accurately reflect their evolutionary development. The evaluation of taxonomies from that point of view requires information based on fossil remains, geographical distribution, immigration pathways, and chromosomal and biochemical relations as well as morphological features. The course of evolutionary development would seem to be an unlikely reason for seeking a taxonomy of situations. If we are to attempt to develop a taxonomy of situations for use in the behavioral sciences, what criteria can appropriately be used for choosing among the large number of classification systems that are possible?

A taxonomy is merely a useful way of classifying phenomena, whether they be books, plants, people, or ideas. It is a way of simplifying a complicated universe in order to make it easier to deal with, both conceptually and practically. Scientific advances are greatly facilitated by the availability of comprehensive and unambiguous classificatory systems.

Any classification system is to some degree arbitrary. One might sort the books in his library on the basis of size, so that they will fit on particular shelves; he might sort them on the basis of color in order to create aesthetic effects; or he might sort them into categories of books he might want to consult for particular purposes. Taxonomies can be purely descriptive, or they can to various degrees represent a theoretical orientation. The periodic table of the elements represents not only a classification but also a useful theory about the nature of matter.

In psychology we have few well-established taxonomies except in the domain of individual differences. We do not have accepted taxonomies of situations. What are some possible criteria for choosing one taxonomic system rather than another? And what empirical procedures might be employed in constructing taxonomies?

TAXONOMIES OF ATTRIBUTES AND TAXONOMIES OF INDIVIDUALS

In thinking about development of taxonomies, it is important to distinguish between taxonomies of *attributes* and taxonomies of *individuals*. The taxonomies used to describe individual differences in psychology are classifications of attributes of people, not classifications of the people themselves. The categories in the classifications are entities like *ideational fluency* and *extraversion*, not groups of people. In biological taxonomies, on the other hand, the elements are categories composed of the organisms themselves, such as oak, maple, pine, and hemlock trees. The difference is surely not accidental. The analog of *species* in biology would be *types* in psychology, and many attempts by psychologists to develop typological classifications of people have not survived, presumably because more people fall between the idealized types than fit them. Such is not the case in dendrology: oaks, maples, and pines can all be identified, even by a novice, and no individuals are found that fall between the oak and the maple. Such a claim cannot be made for distinctions between Jung's extraverts and introverts; among Spranger's theoretic, economic, aesthetic, social, political, and religious types; or among Freud's erotic, compulsive, and narcissistic types.

Both taxonomies of attributes and taxonomies of individuals would presumably be useful, but since the criteria and the procedures for developing classificatory schemes might differ, it will be well to discuss them separately.

DEVELOPMENT OF TAXONOMIES OF ATTRIBUTES

The empirical method most commonly used by psychologists for empirically developing a taxonomy of attributes would appear to be factor analysis. The procedure involves the following steps: (a) obtaining a list of variables that encompass the domain of investigation (e.g., cognitive abilities); (b) finding or developing a satisfactory method of measuring each variable (or a sample of the variables); (c) administering the resulting battery of tests to a sample of individuals representative of those possessing the attributes; (d) computing the intercorrelations of the tests; and (e) carrying out the various steps involved in the factor analysis, including rotation of axes. All these are familiar procedures except the first: How does one obtain a list of variables comprising the domain of investigation?

In his early work on personality, Cattell (1946) solved the problem by going to the dictionary. He assumed that any important aspect of human personality would have a name; on this reasonable assumption, he identified the words in the dictionary that were descriptive of personality and used this list to represent the domain. The Thurstones apparently used a variety of methods in assembling their batteries of cognitive tests. They chose items and item types that had previously been used by psychologists in tests of intellectual abilities, but they also made use of what Guttman would now call facet analysis and they were guided by a general hypothesis as to what the emerging factor structure might be. They put tests into the battery to represent such facets as verbal, numerical, and visual abilities, and they included tests that would help answer such specific questions as "whether reasoning involves a distinct mental ability which transcends the detailed form on which it is exercised [Thurstone, 1938, p. 11]," such as verbal, numerical, or spatial material.

There is no prescription that can be given to the would-be developer of a taxonomy of attributes of situations with regard to how to proceed. Sampling from a population of attributes would be desirable but impractical, since we do not have the necessary roster from which to draw a sample. One should certainly try to take advantage of any existing classification that can be found, and he should make as much use as he can of facet design. In the initial stages it would be prudent, one would think, to delimit the search to subtypes of situations, such as classrooms or typing pools, rather than situations in general. Classifying trees would be a far more feasible undertaking than classifying all living organisms. Ultimately, a taxonomy of situations, if we ever have one, will surely not be the work of any one investigator.

Sells (1963b) employed a scheme proposed by Sherif and Sherif (1956) to develop an "outline of basic aspects of the total stimulus situation" that should be consulted by anyone embarking on a project to develop a taxonomy of attributes of situations. The outline is quite extensive (occupying nearly five pages of small type), and it includes categories and subcategories concerned with weather, social institutions, socioeconomic status, informal group structure, regulation of group procedure, etc.

Krause (1970) proposed the following seven subclasses of social behavior settings: (a) joint working, which involves a mutual goal and some promise of compensation; (b) trading, which aims to compromise conflict of interest through exchange; (c) fighting, which is any means of settling a conflict without compromise; (d) sponsored teaching, which involves modification of a learner's behavior; (e) serving, in which one participant receives from another some satisfaction of a need for which the second participant receives some compensation; (f) self-disclosure, which is revelation of one's opinions to another; and (g) playing, which is a nonserious approximation of other situations merely for the pleasures of the performance. As Krause pointed out, wide ranges of variations within these categories are possible, involving physical environments, roles, institutional contexts, and other aspects of the setting as suggested by Sells' (1963b) outline.

One area of empirical investigation that has produced several classifications of attributes of situations is the measurement of college environments (Pace, 1968). Pace and Stern (1958) produced an instrument for measuring college environments, and since then a number of studies have yielded results that may be thought of as contributing to a taxonomy of situations. An instrument developed by Pace called *College and University Environment Scales* (CUES) is currently in use. The items are statements that might describe a particular college (e.g., "There is a lot of group spirit."). The items were administered to students, who responded by judging whether each statement is *true* or *not true*. A statement is assumed to be true about the college if two-thirds or more of the students endorse it, and a score for the institution is obtained by using this standard. A factor analysis of such scores obtained from 50 colleges and universities produced five factors that are the basis for the five scales employed in the current version of CUES. College environments can thus be described in terms of measures of five attributes named practicality, community, awareness, propriety, and scholarship.

Another factor-analytic study of college environments (Astin, 1962) was based on 33 items of information obtainable from public sources, such as size, proportion of men, number of fields in which degrees are offered, percentage of PhDs on the faculty, and budget. Data from 300 schools were obtained. The five factors obtained were named affluence, size, masculinity, homogeneity of offerings, and technical emphasis. The number of categories obtained from these studies seems quite small in relation to the diversity among American colleges. A beginning has been made toward the development of a taxonomy of attributes of situations, but we have a long way to go.

DEVELOPMENT OF TAXONOMIES OF SITUATIONS

We have shown that factor-analytic procedures might be useful in developing taxonomies of situational attributes, and examples have been cited of such applications of the method. What empirical methods are available for developing taxonomies of the situations themselves?

The simplest method is merely to define situational categories in terms of combinations of attributes. Given a list of attributes, it is possible to generate a classification of the situations themselves merely by taking all the possible combinations of attributes. A description of trees in terms of three dichotomous attributes would generate two cubed or eight categories of specimens. The three dichotomies might, for example, be broad leaves versus needle- or scalelike leaves, coniferous versus nonconiferous, and deciduous versus nondeciduous. One category defined by these attributes contains trees that are deciduous coniferous and have needle-shaped leaves and would include the larch and tamarack. The category formed by deciduous, nonconiferous, and broad-leaved would include the so-called hardwoods. An objection to such a procedure is that if there are a large number of attributes, the number of categories of indiviudals generated would become very large indeed. However, if many of these categories turn out to be empty cells, the method still might be feasible. In the tree example, the category defined by deciduous, coniferous, and broad-leaved would turn out to be an empty cell because there is no known tree possessing this combination of attributes.

Hoepfner and Klein (1970) at the Center for the Study of Evaluation at the University of California at Los Angeles have used this method of constructing a taxonomy in developing differentiated test norms for schools. The data came from the Coleman, Campbell, Hobson, McPartland, Mood, Weinfeld, and York (1966) study of equality of educational opportunity. Eight attributes of schools were employed, all of which are continuous measures; one was trichotomized, and the others were dichotomized. The eight attributes are based on the following questionnaire items:

1. What is the racial balance in your school?
2. How many families of your students are represented at a typical meeting of the PTA or similar parent group?
3. How many volumes do you have in your school library?
4. About what percentage of the students who attended your school last year are now attending a different school? Do not count those who moved because of graduation or promotion.
5. Which best describes the location of your school? (Small town, city, rural, etc.)
6. Which best describes the pupils served by your school? (Parents' occupations)
7. What percentage of the students in your school have mothers who are employed outside the home?
8. Which of the following indicates the area of the country in which your school is located?

Three hundred and eighty-four categories of schools are generated by this classification of attributes (3×2^7). A school principal could use the school-attribute classification to find which one of the 384 school categories his school belongs in, and by comparing the mean score for his school with the norms for that category, he could find out whether the mean for his school is low, middle, or high in comparison with other schools like his own.

With the large number of attributes that one would ordinarily expect to be associated with situations, the method would undoubtedly generate an astro-nomical number of categories, and it would be useful only if some further method of data reduction could be used.

There are, of course, a variety of statistical methods that might be used in searching for categories of situations. One of the earliest attempts to develop a measure of similarity was that of Pearson (1926), who developed a "coefficient of racial likeness." Fisher (1936) developed discriminant analysis for use in taxonomy. This approach is mainly useful, however, if the categories are already known and if one wants to minimize error in using variables in assigning individuals to those categories.

A method that is useful for exploratory studies is inverse factor analysis. In any factor study, one begins with a vector of attribute scores for each of a sample of individuals. In conventional factor analysis, correlations between all the pairs of *attributes* are computed and factored. In inverse factor analysis, one begins with the same kind of matrix but computes correlations between all the pairs of *individuals*. A high correlation means that two individuals are similar with respect to their scores on the attributes, and a factor then represents a cluster of individuals all of whom tend to be alike with regard to their attribute scores. Thus, an inverse factor analysis based on a matrix of morphological attributes for a population of trees would presumably yield factors interpretable as oaks, maples, pines, etc.

More generally, there are a variety of methods that are potentially useful in developing taxonomies that are called cluster analysis (e.g., McQuitty, 1956; Rubin, 1967; Tryon & Bailey, 1966). Such methods begin with a vector of attribute scores for individuals, as in inverse factor analysis, but the measure of similarity for a pair of individuals is not usually a correlation coefficient. It might be simply the number of characteristics shared by two individuals, a pooled judgment of the similarity of two objects, the Euclidean distance between two vectors (Cronbach & Gleser, 1953; Osgood & Suci, 1952), or a generalized distance measure of a more sophisticated sort (Mahalanobis, 1936). The cluster analysis methods have in common the identification of groups of similar individuals. The clusters themselves may be grouped hierarchically (Friedman & Rubin, 1967; Ward, 1963). Nonmetric multidimensional scaling methods (Kruskal, 1964; Shepard, 1962) may be used to search for clusters if one is unwilling to make metric assumptions about his data. The interpretation of a cluster or hierarchy of clusters (like the interpretation of a factor in conventional factor analysis) depends ultimately on a judgment regarding the characteristics common to the individuals that comprise the cluster.

The use of numerical methods in plant and animal taxonomy has been increasing in recent years (Sokal & Sneath, 1963), with applications in a wide variety of areas of biology and anthropology. An interesting application of cluster analysis was recently reported (True & Matson, 1970) that comes a little closer to our problem of classifying situations. Twenty archeological sites in Chile were described in terms of 74 characteristics, mainly based on bead and stone artifacts found at the sites. Similarity coefficients were computed for the pairs of sites, and a cluster analysis was carried out. Four main clusters were found; they tended to confirm grouping of sites that had previously been made judgmentally. One cluster, for example, contained artifacts suggesting use of vegetable foods and a minimum concern with hunting.

A more direct attempt to develop a taxonomy of situations was Hemphill's (1959) study of characteristics of executive positions. Hemphill developed a questionnaire containing a large number of statements that might be descriptive of aspects of an executive's position (e.g., "negotiate bank loans for the company"). The items were obtained from literature describing executive behavior, from interviews with executives, and from job descriptions. Each of several hundred executives responded to each item by rating the degree to which it was a part of his position. An inverse factor analysis was performed using the correlations between pairs of executives who responded to the questionnaire. Ten orthogonal factors were identified, and the interpretation of each factor was based on an investigation of the activities of the executives comprising that factor. The executive positions were classified as follows:

1. Providing a staff service
2. Supervision of work
3. Business control
4. Technical—markets and products
5. Human, community, and social affairs
6. Long-range planning
7. Exercise of broad power and authority
8. Business reputation
9. Personal demands
10. Preservation of assets

Since the interpretations of the factors were written in terms descriptive of the executive positions, the statements resemble attributes of jobs rather than the jobs themselves. But methodologically the study fits the cluster analysis rather than the factor analysis design. This classification would obviously be useful in studying the interactions of personal characteristics with executive positions in predicting performance.

Rock, Baird, and Linn (1972) generated classifications of colleges by using Ward's (1963) hierarchical clustering technique. Their data were based on students attending 95 different colleges. The basis of the clustering was similarity of colleges with respect to three regression parameters—intercepts, slopes, and mean predictor scores—of the regression of a Graduate Record Examination (GRE) score on a predictor test score. Separate classifications of colleges were developed based on GRE Humanities, Social Science, and Natural Science achievement test scores, using either the Verbal or Mathematical Scholastic Aptitude Test (SAT) score as the predictor. Rock et al. (1972) found five groups of colleges based on the Humanities criterion. One group of 17 colleges, for example, was characterized by steep regression lines, high intercepts, and high means for the predictor, Verbal SAT. Another group was characterized by flatter slopes and low predictor scores. Discriminant function analysis was employed in an effort to see if the groups could be described in terms of different college characteristics. Group 1 was found to have higher scores than the other groups on five college characteristics, including selectivity, budget, and percentage of students graduating in four years. The potential usefulness of such taxonomies in student guidance and educational research is apparent.

Sells (1964) proposed a somewhat similar basis for classifying organizations. His notion was that the differential patterns of predictive weights obtained for various combinations of factors be used as the basis for the clustering of organizations, using as the criterion the behavior of the organization with regard to some task or function.

Classification of Situations Based on Elicited Behavior

The criterion for determining taxonomic categories implied by the factor and cluster analysis methods is mutual similarity of the members of the factor or cluster. Such a criterion can be defended on such grounds as objectivity and empirical feasibility. But another criterion for classification could be proposed in the case of a taxonomy of situations. Instead of assigning situations to clusters on the basis of their mutual possession of various attributes, it is possible to group situations on the basis of their tendency to elicit similar behaviors. Such a criterion would seem to be especially appropriate when one's ultimate purpose is the investigation of person–situation interactions in predicting behavior.

The kind of data that is necessary for the empirical development of taxonomic categories by this criterion is rarely obtained. What is needed, for each of a large number of persons, is a record of which of many behaviors is displayed in response to each of many situations. In other words, a three-dimensional data matrix is required, the three dimensions representing subjects, behaviors, and situations. Given such a data matrix, our usual practice would be to collapse across situations to form a Subject X Performance matrix and to factor the matrix of intercorrelations of the behaviors. Such a procedure would yield a classification of behaviors. (We could also collapse across situations and factor the intercorrelations of subjects, an inverse factor analysis. This would yield clusters of people and possibly a basis for a typology.)

Still another possibility is to collapse the data matrix across people, yielding a Situation X Performance matrix. I am suggesting that the correlations between all the pairs of *situations* be computed and that a factor analysis of this inter-correlation matrix be performed. A high correlation between two situations means that they elicit similar behaviors. Thus, a factor represents a cluster of situations that tend to evoke the same responses. Such factors would constitute the categories in a taxonomy of situations, using the criterion of *similarity of behaviors elicited* rather than the criterion of similarity with respect to attributes.

The steps described so far are preliminary to a three-mode factor analysis (Tucker, 1966). Once factors in the domain of performance and in the domain of situations are obtained, one can go on to the computation of factors in the domain of the subjects. Subject factors may be interpreted on the basis of the relationships between performance factors and situation factors that characterize each person factor. Thus, the model provides a method for investigating Person X Situation interactions. The existence of person factors demonstrates an interaction between personal characteristics and situational variation.

Data that permit one to perform such an investigation are rare because we do not in one investigation ordinarily evaluate many aspects of performance in each of many situations. More typically, one or two dependent variables are recorded for one or two experimental conditions plus a control condition. Data reported by Endler, Hunt, and Rosenstein (1962) are relevant, although the basic datum is a self-report of what the subject *thought* his response would be to each hypothetical situation, rather than a record of actual behavior.

The data were obtained by administering an "S-R Inventory of Anxiousness" to 169 college students. The inventory required the respondent to report the probable intensity of each of 14 possible responses in each of 11 different situations. The responses included, for example, "heart beats faster," "perspire," "enjoy the challenge," "become immobilized"; and the situations included such things as "You are going to meet a new date," "You are starting out in a sailboat into a rough sea," and "You are going into an interview for an important job." A three-mode factor analysis of the data was done by Levin (1965) and reported by Tucker (1965).

The analysis revealed three factors in the domain of the responses reported. These factors are interpreted as (a) general distress (with high loadings on "get an uneasy feeling," "heart beats faster," "emotions disrupt actions"); (b) exhilaration (with high loadings on "enjoy the challenge," "seek experiences like this," "feel exhilarated and thrilled"); and (c) autonomic responses (with high loadings on "have loose bowels," "need to urinate frequently," "get full feeling in stomach").

The situation factors were also three in number and were interpreted as (a) interpersonal stress situations (with loadings on speech before a large group, interview for an important job, a competitive contest); (b) dangerous inanimate situations (on a ledge high on a mountainside, alone in the woods at night, sailboat on a rough sea); and (c) unknown situations (going into a psychological experiment, starting off on a long automobile trip, going to a counseling bureau to seek help in solving a personal problem). Thus, if one uses the criterion of similarity of responses elicited, the taxonomy for this very limited domain of situations would comprise the three categories of interpersonal stress situations, dangerous inanimate situations, and facing unknown situations.

The interpretation of the core matrix that resulted from the three-mode factor analysis showed that there are individual differences with respect to the relationship of response categories to the situational categories. Three person factors were found, each of which can be interpreted in terms of the responses characteristically made to the situation factors. The idealized person representing Person Factor 1 tended to report distress and autonomic responses to the interpersonal stress and dangerous inanimate situations, and he reported little exhilaration. The Person Factor 2 individual was likely to report exhilaration to all three types of situations, but particularly the inanimate danger situation. The Person Factor 3 individual reported exhilaration in the interpersonal stress situations and distress and autonomic responses to the inanimate danger situations. These are somewhat oversimplified interpretations of the person factors.

Another three-dimensional data matrix exists (Frederiksen, Jensen, & Beaton, in press) that permits one to search for situation factors, and the data represent actual behaviors rather than reports of how the subject thought he would behave. The data were obtained through the use of a realistic situational test that simulates the paper work of an executive.

Subjects were executives employed by the state of California in jobs varying from middle-management levels to department heads appointed by the governor. They were employed in a variety of fields from health and highways to accounting and law. During a two-day "research institute," each subject served as an executive in a simulated job, that of Chief of the Field Services Division of the Department of Commerce. His instructions were to deal with the items in his in-basket as though he were actually on the job. He was to take whatever action he deemed appropriate, such as writing letters or memoranda, asking for information, calling meetings, making appointments, making notes on his calendar, writing reminders to himself, or throwing things in the wastebasket. The in-basket items were identical for all subjects, and all subjects had the same opportunity to acquaint themselves with background materials describing the organization and the new job in which each subject found himself.

At the end of the exercise, each subject left behind a large envelope full of his written responses to the items. The scoring of these protocols was based on a list of about 60 categories of behavior, such as postpones decision, takes leading action, sets a deadline, gives directions to subordinates, follows lead by superior, makes plans only, shows courtesy to peers, and schedules work for a specific day. The score sheet provides a row for each in-basket item and a column for each category of behavior. The scorer recorded 1 or 0 in each cell to indicate presence or absence of the behavior defined by each behavior category. Thus, a stack of score sheets literally corresponds to the three-dimensional data matrix, the three dimensions representing the situations (the in-basket items), performance (the behavior categories), and subjects.

Collapsing the matrix across items, we get the customary Subject X Behavior matrix, and a factor analysis of the intercorrelations of the behavior categories resulted in 10 performance factors. They were given names like thoughtful analysis of problems, informality, controls subordinates, interacts with superiors, defers judgment and action, and productivity.

Collapsing the matrix across subjects gives us an Item X Behavior matrix, and factoring the intercorrelations of all the pairs of items results in six item factors. An item factor is a cluster of items that are alike in that they tend to elicit the same behaviors. If we adopt as our criterion for classifying items their similarity with regard to behaviors elicited, these six factors may be thought of as constituting a taxonomy of paper-work problems, at least for the sample of items employed in the study. The factors were quite easy to interpret on the basis of inspection of the items with the highest loadings. The factors were given the following names: (a) items requiring evaluation of procedures for accomplishing organizational goals; (b) items permitting a routine solution; (c) items requiring solution of interorganizational problems; (d) items requiring solution of personnel problems; (e) items recommending a change in policy; and (f) items presenting conflicting demands on staff time. These factors may tentatively be regarded as constituting a taxonomy of situations in a domain of the in-basket problems of state executives.

The final step in the three-mode factor analysis revealed that person factors do exist and that Person X Situation interactions are therefore demonstrated. There is not time to go into detail about the person factors, but they did appear to be interpretable in terms of the appropriate slices of the core matrix. Person Factor 1, for example, is characterized by tendencies to be orderly and to work through subordinates in responding to items that present problems involving personnel and relations with other organizations. This pattern recalls the stereotype of the low-level supervisor who deals with short-range, day-to-day operational problems. Person Factor 1 was named *systematic supervisor*.

The two examples show the feasibility of classifying situations on the basis of their similarity with regard to the behaviors they elicit. In both examples, the categories comprising the taxonomy were readily interpretable, and in both instances they proved to be useful in demonstrating Person X Situation interactions. In addition to cluster analysis and other methods for empirically developing taxonomic categories of situations, the method based on the criterion of "similarity with regard to behaviors elicited" seems worthy of further exploration and use, particularly for investigations of Person X Situation interactions.

If one wanted to go to the trouble, he might be able to get his hands on those file drawers full of proceedings of the many international conferences attended by Krushchev. After careful study of the contents, one might be able to develop a method of scoring the records of Krushchev's behavior, using categories like *agrees, compromises, denies, accuses, evades, attacks, yells,* and *pounds with shoe.* Then the protocol for each conference could be scored in terms of frequency of occurrence of each beahvior category. This procedure would produce a Situation X Performance matrix. It might then be possible to discover a set of conferences in which Krushchev's behavior was characterized by agreeing and compromising and another set characterized by attacking and shoe pounding. If one could then find what were the differentiating characteristics of the two sets of conferences, he would have discovered a possible way to predict and control Mr. Krushchev's behavior, although a little too late to be of much practical use.

A scientist seeking broader generalizations would want to extend the observations to a larger number of people, in order to see if the relationship between type of conference and behavior holds only for Krushchev, if it is true of everyone, or if it describes the behavior of a substantial subgroup of individuals. This would require the scientist to score the protocols of others who attended the same conferences in order to generate the three-mode data matrix that would be required. Our scientist would probably give up this particular enterprise quite soon because of a host of problems involving feasibility and experimental control. But the example perhaps illustrates three points: (a) Study of Person X Situation interactions would be facilitated by the existence of a suitable taxonomy of situations. (b) It is possible to develop such taxonomies empirically. And (c) a possible criterion for use in empirically developing a taxonomy of situations is the similarity of situations with regard to the behaviors they elicit.

REFERENCES

Astin, A. W. An empirical characterization of higher educational institutions. *Journal of Educational Psychology*, 1962, **53**, 224–235.

Cattell, R. B. *The description and measurement of personality.* New York: World, 1946.

Coleman, J. S., Campbell, E. Q., Hobson, C. J., McPartland, J., Mood, A. M., Weinfeld, F. D., & York, R. L. *Equality of educational opportunity.* Washington, D.C.: United States Government Printing Office, 1966.

Cronbach, L. J., & Gleser, G. C. Assessing similarity between profiles. *Psychological Bulletin*, 1953, **50**, 456–473.

Endler, N. S., Hunt, J. McV., & Rosenstein, A. J. An S–R inventory of anxiousness. *Psychological Monographs*, 1962, **76**(17, Whole No. 536).

Fisher, R. A. The use of multiple measurements in taxonomic problems. *Annals of Eugenics*, 1936, **7**, 179–188.

Frederiksen, N., Jensen, O., & Beaton, A. (With a contribution by B. Bloxom) *Prediction of organizational behavior.* Elmsford, N.Y.: Pergamon Press, in press.

French, J. W., Ekstrom, R., & Price, L. A. *Manual for kit of reference tests for cognitive factors.* Princeton, N.J.: Educational Testing Service, 1963.

Friedman, H. P., & Rubin, J. On some invariant criteria for grouping data. *Journal of the American Statistical Association*, 1967, **62**, 1159–1178.

Hemphill, J. K. Job descriptions for executives. *Harvard Business Review*, 1959, **37**, 55–67.

Hoepfner, R., & Klein, S. P. *Elementary school evaluation kit.* Booklet 4. *Collecting information.* Los Angeles: University of California, 1970.

Krause, M. S. Use of social situations for research purposes. *American Psychologist*, 1970, **25**, 748–753.

Kruskal, J. B. Multidimensional scaling by optimizing goodness of fit to a nonmetric hypothesis. *Psychometrika*, 1964, **29**, 1–27.

Levin, J. Three-mode factor analysis. *Psychological Bulletin*, 1965, **64**, 442–452.

Mahalanobis, P. C. On the generalized distance in statistics. *Proceedings of the National Institute for Science, India*, 1936, **12**, 48–58.

McQuitty, L. L. Agreement analysis: Classifying persons by predominant patterns of responses. *British Journal of Statistical Psychology*, 1956, **9**, 5–16.

Osgood, C. E., & Suci, G. A measure of relation determined by both mean difference and profile information. *Psychological Bulletin*, 1952, **49**, 251–262.

Pace, C. R. The measurement of college environments. In R. Tagiuri & G. H. Litwin (Eds.), *Organizational climate: Explorations of a concept.* Boston: Graduate School of Business Administration, Harvard University, 1968.

Pace, C. R., & Stern, G. G. An approach to the measurement of psychological characteristics of college environments. *Journal of Educational Psychology*, 1958, **49**, 269–277.

Pearson, K. On the coefficient of racial likeness. *Biometrika*, 1926, **18**, 105–117.

Rock, D. A., Baird, L. L., & Linn, R. L. Interaction between college effects and students' aptitudes. *American Educational Research Journal*, 1972, in press.

Rubin, J. Optimal classification into groups: An approach for solving the taxonomy problem. *Journal of Theoretical Biology*, 1967, **15**, 103–144.

Sells, S. B. An interactionist looks at the environment. *American Psychologist*, 1963, **18**, 696–702. (a)

Sells, S. B. (Ed.) *Stimulus determinants of behavior.* New York: Ronald, 1963. (b)

Sells, S. B. Toward a taxonomy of organizations. In W. W. Cooper, H. J. Leavitt, & M. W. Shelly (Eds.), *New perspectives in organizational research.* New York: Wiley, 1964.

Shepard, R. N. The analysis of proximities: Multidimensional scaling with an unknown distance function I. *Psychometrika*, 1962, **27**, 125–140.

Sherif, M., & Sherif, C. W. *An outline of social psychology.* (Rev. ed.) New York: Harper, 1956.

Sokal, R. R., & Sneath, P. H. A. *Principles of numerical taxonomy.* San Francisco: Freeman, 1963.

Thurstone, L. L. Primary mental abilities. *Psychometric Monographs*, 1938, No. 1.

True, D. L., & Matson, R. G. Cluster analysis and multidimensional scaling of archeological sites in northern Chile. *Science*, 1970, **169**, 1201–1203.

Tryon, R. C., & Bailey, D. E. The BC TRY computer system of cluster and factor analysis. *Multivariate Behavioral Research*, 1966, **1**, 95–111.

Tucker, L. R. Experiments in multi-mode factor analysis. In, *Proceedings of the 1964 Invitational Conference on Testing Problems.* Princeton, N.J.: Educational Testing Service, 1965.

Tucker, L. R. Some mathematical notes on three-mode factor analysis. *Psychometrika*, 1966, **31**, 279–311.

Ward, J. H., Jr. Hierarchial grouping to optimize an objective function. *Journal of the American Statistical Association*, 1963, **58**, 236–244.

27

Dimensions of Stimulus Situations Which Account for Behavior Variance

S. B. SELLS

Many psychologists, sociologists, and educators have at various times taken positions suggesting that either individual characteristics alone or situational stimulus factors alone account for most of the variability in behavior. However, sophisticated theorists have recognized that behavior is not accounted for by either inner or outer forces separately, but by their interaction. Representative *interaction* theorists, in the context of this discussion, are Lewin (9), Murphy (13), Brunswik (2), Sherif (19), and Helson (7).

The principle that behavior represents the interaction of the individual and the environmental situation implies that the total variance of any response can be accounted for only in part by individual differences in characteristics of the participating persons: It depends also on the stimulus characteristics of the environmental situation (both physical and social) and in part on the interactions between aspects of each. Full exploitation of this principle has not yet been achieved, largely because the methodological implications have not been systematically explored. Nevertheless, the principle receives widespread allegiance and important beginnings have been made toward clarification of the methodological issues (Sells and Trites, 18).

Recognition of the separate sources of variance in an *attitude* response is implicit in Green's (6) distinction of three kinds of attitude universe, corresponding to three different classes of individuals' responses to sets of social objects or situations: (a) elicited verbal attitudes, given in response to questions; (b) spontaneous verbal attitudes such as are usually expressed in casual conversation; and (c) action attitudes, which include both verbal and non-verbal behavior toward an object in the reference class. In terms of the foregoing principle, the differences in the same implicit attitude disposition, expressed in terms of these three types of attitude universe, represent variations in the

From S. B. Sells (Ed.) *Stimulus determinants of behavior*, Chapter 1, 1963, Pp. 3–15. Copyright © 1963. The Ronald Press Company, New York.

responses of the same individuals to different situational stimuli, and hence different interactions. Such analysis is relevant to the understanding of problems of reliability and validity, or what McClelland (10) has called *relational fertility,* the network of correlations with associated measures and criteria.

Festinger's (3) distinctions between real change of attitude and publicly expressed change without private acceptance (under threatening conditions) fit the frame of reference described. In a similar vein, Getzels (5) described a respondent's answer to questionnaire items as a suitable compromise between his *actual* opinion (which is inaccessible to study) and his perception of the requirements of the immediate situation. This is frequently referred to as test-taking set, faking, defensiveness, and the like, according to the nature of the social situation. Similarly, Suchman (20) found it necessary, in accounting for estimation of accuracy, to take into consideration the characteristics of the estimates and of the group situation, and the variables being estimated, as well as the characteristics of the estimator. Mausner (11) elaborated the schematic analysis of variance further by differentiating six types of determinants of social influence on attitudes: nature of stimulus being judged (situational variable), instructions given subjects (situational variable), history of contact between the subject and others present (interaction variable), reaction of others in the experimental situation (interaction variable), personality of subject (person variable), and subject's previous experience with the stimuli or class of judgments (person variable).

Blake and Helson (1), as part of an Air Force contract, carried out a series of laboratory experiments in which the effects of certain person and situational variables and their interactions were simultaneously evaluated. Using both attitude and perceptual judgments in a simulated group situation in which the responses of all but the experimental subject were presented over an "intercom" by tape recording, they demonstrated that responses of experimental subjects are predictable interactions reflecting identifiable person variables, group norms (as programed for the simulated group members), and stimulus characteristics. In one experiment students shifted generally from attitudes expressed when tested *alone,* on Thurstone attitude-toward-war items, to the center of clustered group expressions when tested in the simulated group. However, submissive subjects (measured on the Allport-Vernon ascendance-submission scale) shifted toward the group significantly more than ascendant subjects; and all subjects, in the particular University of Texas sample, shifted toward prowar more than toward items with neutral or antiwar scale values. In other experiments it was found that the influence of the group's norms was greater when subjects' identities were revealed than when responses were anonymous, when the difference between "group" and "alone" judgments was small rather than large, and when the stimuli were unstructured (e.g., involving attitude and opinion questions) rather than highly structured (e.g., in arithmetic problems). In the last-named case the ability to test objective reality tends to counteract group influence to some extent. This is only a partial recitation of the results of these highly significant experiments, but it serves to illustrate the isolation of a large number of sources of variance in the behavior of experimental subjects.

These experiments made it very clear that each separate attitude or perceptual judgment of the subjects tested was an interaction of individual and environmental situation in which the response could be represented as the resultant of all the factors operating. The discrepancies between "alone" and "group" responses do not impeach the reliability or consistency of the subjects or of the item scaling. They are in effect reproducible variations of responses to the same stimuli that may be expected in different individual-situation interaction settings.

Appropriate methodology for incorporating this interaction frame of reference in the scientific study of human behavior has not yet advanced very far. Certainly, the broad approach implied in the three independent systems of action, personality, and social system and culture, mentioned by Parsons and Shils (14), remains a grand strategy in search of implementation. The most obvious need is for the development of a taxonomy and measurement technology of variables describing the stimulus situation. However unsatisfactory they may be regarded, at least some generally accepted taxonomy and devices for measuring individual behavior characteristics have been produced by psychology. As a result it is possible, with varying degrees of accuracy, depending on the particular variables and measures employed, to account for individual differences in significant ability and personality dimensions. But no comparable dimensions of the stimulus situation have been systematically studied, and consequently only piecemeal and usually inadequate account can be taken of variance attributable to the situation.

In the absence of clear perception of the basic dimensions of the stimulus situation, either experimenters must be at a loss to know what factors should be controlled, as relevant to the behavior studied, or they must make such decisions without sufficient information. An example is an attempt to make an inventory of environmental factors which exercise some influence on the number of hours per week that students devote to study. It is easy to see that a lengthy list of factors could be produced, e.g., distance of residence from school, mode of transportation, hours of work or required chores, regularly scheduled extra-curricular activities, frequency of dating, amount of spending money received, number of age-mates residing nearby, disciplinary and other attitudes of parents, religious affiliation and behavior, nature and frequency of illness, illumination of home, air conditioning, availability of private room, number of courses carried, characteristics of teachers, class size, classroom practices, school policies re grading, and the like.

Some of these or others that might be added may appear more relevant or less relevant. Such variables may properly be regarded, however, not as basic dimensions, but rather as items contributing to dimensional scales, and may have factor loadings on one or more dimensions. Until a comprehensive, systematic analysis of situational dimensions is completed, this present state of technological ineptness of behavior science will continue. An excellent reference source for the initiation of such a study is the following list of "interrelated factors" relevant to social situations cited by Sherif and Sherif (19, p. 121):

1. Factors related to individuals involved—Number (size of aggregate); homogeneity or heterogeneity, in terms of backgrounds (e.g., sociocultural, economic, educational affiliations and ranks); age, sex, etc. Relationships to other participating individuals; previous acquaintance and the existence or non-existence of established relationship among all or some of the individuals. Particular motives related to participating in the situation, including the extent to which some motives are common to various individuals.

2. Factors related to the problem or task—Whether it is new or habitual; the degree of its structure (number of possible alternatives for attainment or solution); proportion of individuals present necessary for one activity; roles and capacities in which various individuals function. Special communication related to it, such as suggested lines of action or instructions; the content and source of communication.

3. Factors related to the site and facilities—Physical setting (laboratory, open space, auditorium, tavern, club, church, home, hotel lobby, etc.); tools and technological means available; the presence of non-participating individuals or groups in the surroundings, and their relation to the individuals and events taking place; opportunities the site affords for movement and contact with others.

4. Factors pertaining to relations of an individual to others, the site, or the problem or task—Relation of the problem or task to the individual, its significance to the individual and within any existing scheme of relationships among the individuals, the related abilities and talents of individuals; the individual's relation to the content and source of any special communication; the existence or non-existence of standards of conduct or social norms relevant to the locale, situation, problem or task, and other individuals.

Some noteworthy attempts have been made in the attack on this problem. In addition to Mausner's analysis of the types of determiners of social attitudes, mentioned earlier, and the Sherifs' exposition of the wide range of situational factors, just reviewed, a number of investigarors have taken positive steps to measure or otherwise account for large segments of situational variance.

Paterson (15), reviewed by Sells (17, 18), observed and manipulated both the behavior of leaders and relations among a number of different occupational and status groups at an RAF base in World War II, to reduce a threatening aircraft accident rate. His observations were not quantified, but were rich in substantive content describing a wide range of aspects of what is commonly referred to as "group dynamics" in the interrelations of pilots, radar comptrollers, and other personnel at that base.

Hemphill (8), working in the milieu of the Ohio State University Leadership Research Program, developed a set of variables which he described as dimensions of group performance and a measurement scale for them. His 14 dimensions include constructs such as the following, which fall quite easily in the Sherifs' outline:

Control—the degree to which the group regulates the behavior of individuals while they are functioning as group members

Stability—the degree to which the group persists over a period of time with essentially the same personnel, role relations, organization, and size

Intimacy—the degree to which members of the group are personally acquainted with one another in all areas of their lives

Although Hemphill's measurement scales are reliable and have been related to criteria of group productivity, they are noteworthy here primarily as a pioneering effort in an important new direction. They are deserving of further research attention in several respects; for instance, they are not factorially independent, and they are phenomenological in design rather than objective. The latter point will be developed in more detail below, but the position taken is that measurement of situational factors should be based on objective observation of the stimulus situation external to the participating individual. The individual's perception of the situation is considered to be reflected in the measure of his behavior. However, if important interaction effects, between individual and situational factors, are to be studied, the situational measures must be obtained independently of the individual's perception of them. For example, his perception of his teacher as overdemanding is a phenomenological datum, but the objective analysis of the teacher's demands of the students is an objective fact.

Another important contribution is Helen Sargent's (16) treatment of situational varibles in designing the research strategy of the Menninger Foundation Psychotherapy Research Project, in which a list of "psychosituational dimensions" was developed for the purpose of evaluating each recorded situational factor in the patients' lives. Briefly, these include

1. Degree of relevance in the individual life
2. Amount of stress to the individual (e.g., debt, death of a loved one)
3. Degree of support it provided him (e.g., education)
4. Degree to which the situational factor is a crucial conflict area (e.g., conflict instigator versus conflict resonator)
5. Extent of opportunity for self-realization, growth, autonomy, success, etc.
6. Congruence of situations with needs, interest, capacities, etc. (e.g., square peg in round hole versus round peg in round hole)
7. Degree of situational mutability

Sargent's list of major situational factors, obtained through a social history, is less general than that of the Sherifs, but was drawn up with particular reference to the psychotherapy research problem. It includes background factors (cultural, religious, ethical and value systems, and educational); interpersonal relations (family, etc.); marital-sexual relations; the living situation (house arrangements, financial situation and responsibilities); occupational stability, demands, and compensation; community and leisure-time factors (recreation and avocation, group participation, civil and cultural activities); and, finally, physical factors (appearance, physique, handicaps and somatic illnesses).

This is another highly significant pioneering effort and although it, too, depends unduly on the phenomenological life-space of the patient, as reflected in the social history, it points out the richness of the information that can be gathered and which accounts for the substantial amount of the behavioral variance observed. In personal conversations about this work, Helen Sargent acknowledged that, in planning the approach to data gathering and the evaluations by clinicians, the staff of the Psychotherapy Research Project was concerned about the lack of interest shown in this area of research, as reflected by literature.

The approach to measurement of situational influences which affect behavior by facilitating or preventing particular responses requires careful study. If behavior is truly an interaction of the myriad of inner and outer forces operating on the individual, then it appears clear that the phenomenological approach both obscures the nature of the external forces and confounds the interaction. Actually, the individual's perception of his world is largely included in the personality and motivational questionnaire items that are frequently used for measurement of personal traits. It is quite possible that a greater understanding of phenomenological data might result if they were investigated in relation to objectively measured stituational stimulus variables.

The objection has been raised that, since situational stimuli are unlimited, one could never hope to record all possible stimuli in any situation. Nevertheless, the following preliminary outline, classified according to the Sherifs' scheme, suggests an imposing but manageable system of variables that can be adapted to empirical measurement in relation to strategically selected dependent variables and ordered by multivariate analytic techniques. It is possible that special purpose measurement scales, adapting the principal dimensions obtained to the requirements of particular types of situations, might be developed. This outline may be regarded as a preliminary step toward the development of taxonomic dimensions of the stimulus situation in behavior:

Outline of Basic Aspects of the Total Stimulus Situation

100.000	Natural aspects of the environment
110.000	Gravity
120.000	Weather
121.000	Temperature
122.000	Humidity
123.000	Oxygen
124.000	Atmospheric pressure
125.000	Climate
126.000	Atmospheric changes (storms, rain, showers, hurricanes, typhoons)

130.000	Terrain	
131.000	Rivers	
132.000	Lakes	
133.000	Mountains	
134.000	Valleys	
135.000	Deserts	
136.000	Altitude	
137.000	Erosion	
138.000	Stability (earthquakes)	
140.000	Natural resources	
141.000	Sources of food	
141.100	Fish and game	
141.200	Vegetation	
141.300	Crops	
142.000	Sources of shelter	
142.100	Wood	
142.200	Minerals	
142.300	Rocks	
143.000	Sources of clothing	
144.000	Minerals	
145.000	Timber	
200.000	Man-made aspects of the environment	
210.000	Social organization (a structuring or grouping of any sort in which there is a systematic differentiation of parts or functions)	
211.000	Formal vs. informal	
212.000	Group vs. collective	
213.000	Incorporated vs. unincorporated	
220.000	Social institutions	
221.000	Family	
222.000	Religion	
223.000	Language	
224.000	Music	
225.000	Law	
226.000	Education	
227.000	Politics	
228.000	Government	
229.000	Art	
230.000	Transitory social norms (a standard, pattern, or representative value for a group)	
300.000	Description of task-problem, situation, and setting	
310.000	Factors defined by the focal task situation	
311.000	Area and level of knowledge and skills required	
312.000	Hazards and risks involved	
313.000	Novelty of situation in relation to prior experiences	
314.000	Procedures permitted	
315.000	Information required and available	
316.000	Number of participants present or available	
317.000	Material and facilities required and available	
318.000	Degree of personal contact involved	
319.000	Role expectations of other persons concerning the individual	
320.000	Factors defined by the individual's relation to the situation	
321.000	Degree of freedom vs. restriction in group activities	

322.000	Degree of competition vs. cooperation required
323.000	Degree of friendliness vs. hostility required
324.000	Status hierarchy position required
330.000	Factors defined by other persons in the situation
331.000	Social and cultural normative characteristics and homogeneity of participants in terms of backgrounds
331.100	Background characteristics
331.110	Age
331.120	Sex
331.130	Social
331.140	Economic
331.200	Skill characteristics
331.210	Abilities
331.220	Experiences
331.230	Training
331.300	Motivation
332.000	Relationship of persons in situation
332.100	New or previous acquaintances
332.200	Pre-existing relationships
340.000	Factors defined by situational setting
341.000	Physical restraints
342.000	Remoteness
342.100	Communication
342.200	Traveling conditions
343.000	Physical characteristics of site location
344.000	Comfort and satisfaction or habitability
400.000	External reference characteristics of the individual
410.000	Biologically defined factors
411.000	Factors defined by sex
412.000	Factors defined by age
413.000	Factors defined by height
414.000	Factors defined by weight
415.000	Factors defined by physique
416.000	Factors defined by physical abnormalities or injuries
417.000	Factors defined by race
420.000	Socially defined factors
421.000	Factors defined by education
422.000	Factors defined by marital status
422.100	Duties
422.200	Responsibilities
423.000	Factors defined by individual's special duties, responsibilities, and commitments
424.000	Factors defined by citizenship
425.000	Factors defined by legal restraints, military service, etc.
426.000	Factors defined by geographic position
426.100	Rural vs. urban
426.200	National
426.300	Personal habits
427.000	Socioeconomic status
427.100	Social status
427.200	Economic status
427.210	Income
427.220	Residence

427.230	Transportation
427.240	Occupational classification
427.250	Debts
427.260	Savings
427.270	Employment status
427.280	Number of dependents
427.290	Education
428.000	Background factors
428.100	Family group
428.110	Social status of family group
428.120	Role in family group
428.130	Status in family group
428.140	Parents
428.141	Legal status
428.142	Age
428.143	Religion
428.144	Health
428.145	Language
428.146	Education
428.147	Parents' group memberships
428.150	Siblings
428.151	Age and sex
428.152	Ordinal position
428.153	Type (adopted, stepchildren)
428.200	Primary or marriage group
428.210	Social status
428.220	Family role
428.230	Status in family
428.240	Legal status
428.250	Education
428.260	Religion
428.270	Language
428.280	Children
428.281	Number
428.282	Age and ordinal position
428.283	Sex
428.284	Type
429.000	Group memberships
429.100	Number of group memberships
429.200	Type of groups
429.300	Social status of groups
429.400	Social status in groups
429.500	Roles in groups
429.600	Group structures (formal vs. informal, group goals, membership requirements, control of memberships)
500.000	Individuals performing relative to others
510.000	Togetherness situations
520.000	Group situation
521.000	Intragroup
521.100	Factors defined by required pattern
521.110	Formal group structure
521.111	Group goals
521.1111	Definiteness

521.2133	Regulations of group procedure
521.21331	Degree to which group is informal
521.21332	Regulations concerning meetings
521.21333	Regulations concerning staffing
521.21334	Regulations to guide group activities
521.21335	Regulations covering group participation
521.21336	Regulations covering daily contact
521.21337	Regulations concerning absences
521.214	Group's social status
521.2141	Degree of dependency on other groups
521.2142	Degree of cooperation with other groups
521.2143	Group's social status
521.220	Factors defined by role responsibility
521.221	Role requirements
521.222	Role responsibility for what, to whom, from whom
521.223	Role power, privileges, prestige
521.230	Factors defined by the group's relation to the site
521.231	Space required and available
521.232	Site location requirements
521.233	Facilities required
521.240	Factors defined by the group's significance to its members
521.250	Factors defined by group cohesion
521.2501	Belief on the part of members that the group functions as a unit
521.2502	Absence of personal conflicts
522.000	Intergroup
530.000	Collective situations (e.g., theater audience, street crowd, etc.)

The usefulness of scales for measurement of the stimulus situations that might be derived from systematic analysis of data based on the preceding outline appears to lie in the following areas:

First, in the study of group and organizational behavior, they would clarify the effects of individual (inner) and situational (external) factors which account for significant variance in behavior. Such scales may reflect such factors as those referred to above in reference to the work of Hemphill, Sargent, and the Sherifs.

Second, for purposes of prediction, it might be possible to think of predictor data in terms of a two-dimensional profile, with person variables on one axis and situational variables on the other. The scores entered would reflect the variations of person measures in terms of the situational dimensions (which would of course not be possible in advance of extensive research). Predictions using values of the predictor scales corresponding to the situational variables identified in the criterion situation might be expected to be considerably more accurate than those used at present which either assume a particular aspect for a particular criterion (inaccurately, at best) or ignore the problem completely.

Third, the availability of measures of the stimulus situation and analysis of total variance for any behavioral measurements into variance attributable to individual differences and variance attributable to situational factors (plus error, of course) would bring about a better understanding of the limitations of many currently accepted concepts. For example, validities of tests which are often thought to be fixed at the levels reported in the publishers' manuals would be found to be values fluctuating from situation to situation according to the structural variations involved. Of greatest value, perhaps, would be the new knowledge assigning proportions of variance for many familiar behaviors, now capable of only marginally accurate prediction, to many factors presently overlooked.

REFERENCES

1. Blake, R. R., and Helson, H. *Adaptability screening of flying personnel: Situational and personal factors in conforming behavior.* San Antonio: USAF, Sch. aviation Med., Rep. Nos. 56–86, 1956.
2. Brunswik, E. *Perception and the representative design of psychological experiments.* Berkeley: University of California Press, 1956.
3. Festinger, L. An analysis of complaint behavior. In M. Sherif and M. O. Wilson (eds.), *Group relations at the crossroads.* New York: Harper & Row, 1953. Pp. 232–256.
4. French, J. R. P., Jr. A formal theory of social power. In L. von Bertalanffy and A. Rapoport (eds.), *General systems.* Ann Arbor, Mich.: Braun-Brumfeld, 1957. Vol. 2. Pp. 92–101.
5. Getzels, J. W. The question-answer process: A conceptualization and some derived hypotheses for empirical examination. *Publ. Opin. Quart.,* 1954, **18,** 80–91.
6. Green, B. F. Attitude measurement. Chapter 9 in G. Lindzey (ed.), *Handbook of social psychology.* Vol. 1. Reading, Mass.: Addison-Wesley, 1954.
7. Helson, H. Adaptation level theory. In S. Koch (ed.), *Psychology: A study of science.* Vol. 1. New York: McGraw-Hill, 1959. Pp. 565–621.
8. Hemphill, J. K. *Group dimensions: A manual for their measurement.* Columbus, Ohio: Bureau of Business Research. Ohio State University, 1956.
9. Lewin, K. Field theory and experiment in social psychology: Concepts and methods. *Amer. J. Sociol.,* 1939, **44,** 868–896.
10. McClelland, D. C. Methods of measuring human motivation. Chapter 1 in J. W. Atkinson (ed.), *Motives in fantasy, action and society.* Princeton, N.J.: Van Nostrand, 1958.
11. Mausner, B. Studies in social interaction: I. A conceptual scheme. *J. soc. Psychol.,* 1955, **41,** 259–270.
12. Menninger, K. A. Psychological aspects of the organism under stress. In L. von Bertalanffy, and A. Rapoport (eds.), *General systems.* Vol. 2. Ann Arbor, Mich.: Braun-Brumfeld, 1957. Pp. 142–172.
13. Murphy, G. *Personality: A biosocial approach to its origins and structures.* New York: Harper & Row, 1947.
14. Parsons, T., and Shils, E. A. (eds.). *Toward a general theory of action.* Cambridge, Mass.: Harvard University Press, 1951.
15. Paterson, T. T. *Morale in war and work: An experiment in the management of men.* London: Parrish, 1955.
16. Sargent, Helen D., Madlin, H. C., Paris, Mildred T., and Voth, H. W. The research strategy and tactics of the psychotherapy research project of the Menninger Foundation. III. Situational variables. *Bull. Menninger Clinic,* 1958, **22,** 148–166.

17. Sells, S. B. Human behavior in groups. *U.S. Armed Forces Med. J.*, 1959, **10**, 926–944.
18. Sells, S. B., and Trites, D. K. Attitudes. In C. W. Harris (ed.), *Encyclopedia of educational research*. (3d ed.) New York: Macmillan, 1960. Pp. 102–115.
19. Sherif, M., and Sherif, C. W. *An outline of social psychology*. Rev. ed. New York: Harper & Row, 1956.
20. Suchman, J. R. Social sensitivity in the small task-oriented group. *J. abnorm. soc. Psychol.*, 1955, **31**, 3–12.

28

An Analysis of Situational Dimensions

DAVID MAGNUSSON

This report presents an attempt to describe the dimensionality of individual judgments of situations. There is an extensive and well documented need for such an analysis.

The major conclusion from some recent experiments on the generality of behavioral data was that individuals differ not mainly with regard to certain stable aspects of behavior but particularly regarding their specific, characteristic ways of adjusting to the varying characteristics of different situations (Magnusson, Gerzén, & Nyman, 1968; Magnusson, Heffler, & Nyman, 1968; Magnusson & Heffler, 1969[1]). The results confirm the interactionistic views of psychological research advocated by researchers using different forms of approach (cf. e.g., Abelson, 1962; Brunswik, 1955; Carson, 1969; Cronbach, 1957; Endler & Hunt, 1966; Fiske, 1963; Helson, 1964; Hunt, 1965; Lewin, 1951; Meltzer, 1961; Miller, 1963; Mischel, 1968; Murphy, 1947; Sells, 1963b; Shibutani, 1961). Knowledge of the interaction between individual and situation is essential to an adequate description and understanding of behavior. Psychological research has to date almost exclusively studied one aspect of this interaction system, the *individual,* whereas systematic analyses of *situations* have been almost entirely lacking (cf. Miller, 1963, p. 700). "While work proceeds actively to extend the explorations of individual differences, however, the equally important frontier of situational dimensions is virtually ignored" (Sells, 1963b). It is urgent then that in the same way as we have for

Magnusson, D. An analysis of situational dimensions. *Perceptual and Motor Skills,* 1971, *32,* 851–867. Reprinted by permission.

Great assistance in the carrying out of this experiment was given by the late Bjoern Ryder. The investigation was supported by the Swedish Council for Social Science Research.

The matrix of mean similarity judgments has been deposited with the American Society for Information Science. Order Document NAPS-01417 from ASIS National Auxiliary Publications Service, c/o CCM Information Corp., 909 Third Ave., 21st Floor, New York, N.Y. 10022. Remit $2.00 for microfiche or $7.70 for photocopy.

[1] D. Magnusson & B. Heffler. The generality of behavioral data: IV. Cross-situational invariance in an objectively measured behavior. (Unpublished manuscript, Univer. of Stockholm: Applied Psychology Unit, 1968)

decades devoted our attention to systematic analysis of individual variations we now more systematically devote time and resources to a similar analysis of situations.

The task of determining psychologically relevant dimensions, which could be used for a description and classification of situations, is a difficult one. Only limited attempts have been made to develop a methodology suitable for this type of analysis (cf. e.g., Cattell, 1963; Sells, 1963a) and scarcely any empirical results are available. Concerning the study of situational variation, we find ourselves at the same stage as that concerning the study of individual differences at the initial development period of differential psychology. It is probable that the task of determining individual dimensions was at that time regarded as being as full of difficulties as we now regard the task of attacking the dimensionality of situations. During 50 to 60 yr. of systematic individual studies, we have, however, made conspicuous advances in research on dimensionality on the individual side. We may assume that the investigation of situations and the description of their relevant dimensions cannot be made without a considerable period for systematic, empirical studies and theoretical model construction, in the same way that it proved impossible to find immediate solutions and adequate methodology for the study of dimensions of individual differences.

Empirical studies of situation variables deal almost without exception with the effect on behavior of variation of one or several specific features within the framework of a given total situation, which is often laboratory-like. One of the weaknesses of this approach, as has been pointed out by Brunswik (1955) among others, is that the effect of variation of one or a few features of a situation while holding all others constant, does not correspond to the reality which we normally experience. There is a continuous interaction among all of the components in a real-life situation. Another deficiency is that the situations studied have a very limited range of variation.

A situation can be described in two different ways; by describing in objective terms the physical and social stimulus features, the situation as it actually is [cf. for example, Murray's "alpha press" (1938) and Koffka's "geographical environment" (1935)] or by describing in terms of different aspects of the psychological significance of the situation, how it is perceived and reacted to ("beta press," "behavioral environment," see above).

This report deals with the dimensionality of individuals' perception of situations. Empirical results from three individuals are presented as a basis for a cognitively oriented discussion of this matter. The data were collected and analyzed with the assumption that it is possible and fruitful to use situations as a whole as stimuli when studying the dimensionality of an individual's judgments of situations.

METHOD

A General Cognitive Model

Objects in the external world can, for every individual, be regarded as being represented in a cognitive space, defined by their internal cognitive relationships.

The position of each object is then determined in relation to the cognitive dimensions used by the individual when he discriminates among objects. The psychological content of the objects is determined by their projections on these dimensions. The number and characteristics of cognitive dimensions for individuals has been the subject of extensive research (cf. e.g., Bieri, *et al.*, 1966).

The above description contains the basic elements of a general cognitive model which is used explicitly or implicitly not only for studying cognitive organization of objects and events, but also in other connections, e.g., by Osgood, Suci, and Tannenbaum (1957) for the study of the concepts of meaning, by Kelly (1955) in his theory of personal constructs, and by Sarbin, Taft, and Bailey (1960) for the study of the cognitive processes in person perception. The psychophysical, multidimensional scaling methods are based on the same basic model (cf. e.g., Ekman, 1970; Torgerson, 1958).

The present experiment was planned by assuming that the same general model can be used to study the structure of an individual's perception of situations. We assume, thus, that individuals discriminate among situations along cognitive dimensions and that situations can be regarded as related to each other in a cognitive space in the same way as objects, events, concepts, individuals, tones, colors, etc. Applying terms used by Sarbin, *et al.* (1960), we regard situations as modules in a modular organization. The psychological content of a situation is then determined by its projection on the cognitive dimensions applied by the individual in order to discriminate among situations. The task is to determine these dimensions.

The cognitive organization with respect to the number and nature of dimensions is not necessarily the same for different individuals. Individuals have varying degrees of cognitive complexity. An important task for research on the dimensionality of situation perception is, therefore, to analyze individual data (cf. Cronbach, 1958). Bearing in mind results from other areas, it is, however, reasonable to assume that if enough of the dimensionality is shared it would be meaningful to study also aggregates of individuals (cf. Bieri, *et al.*, 1966, pp. 191-193).

Cognitive Similarity

When the structure of the cognitive organization of objects, concepts, individuals, etc., is studied within the general model presented, it is assumed that distances in the cognitive space define the psychological relationships of the objects, concepts, individuals, etc., to each other. The more psychologically similar they are, the nearer they are assumed to be to each other in the cognitive organization. Different methods have been used to determine distances between objects in a cognitive space (cf. Attneave, 1950; Coombs, 1964; Ekman, 1970; Gulliksen & Messick, 1960; Kelly, 1955; Osgood, *et al.*, 1957; Shepard, 1962; Torgerson, 1958).

As an expression for the psychological similarity of situations, i.e., their proximity in the cognitive organization, similarity judgments were used. Similarity judgments as a basis for dimensional analyses have the advantage that it is not necessary to determine in advance the features of the situations to be measured.

Multidimensional Analysis

The analysis of the dimensionality of the similarity judgments was done using factor analysis. Previous studies have successfully used factor analysis of similarity judgments for the determination of the dimensionality of similarity ratings of colors (Ekman, 1954, 1961), odors (Ekman & Engen, 1962; Engen, 1962), emotions (Ekman, 1955; Ekman & Lindman, 1961), geometric figures (Kuennapas, Maelhammar, & Svenson, 1964), letters of the alphabet (Kuennapas, 1966, 1967, 1968), and words (Tolman, Jarret, & Bailey, 1959). Interesting in this connection is a study by Magnusson and Ekman (1970) in which factor analyses of a correlation matrix and a similarity rating matrix with respect to an array of behavior gave identical primary dimensions.

EXPERIMENTS

Situations

One problem common to the study of the dimensionality of individual perception and the dimensionality of other cognitive organizations is that of stimulus sampling. The problem is a difficult one and no systematic attempt has been made to solve it in this study.

Descriptions of 36 situations were formulated. These were chosen subjectively so as (a) to represent a definite domain of situations, namely, those which are common for students in connection with their academic studies, and (b) to cover different types of situations within this domain. Preliminary judgments showed that the situations ought to be defined as specifically and unequivocally as possible. Examples of situations are as follows. "You are sitting and listening carefully to a lecture but do not understand a thing."—"You are sitting at home alone preparing an oral report."

Judgmental Procedure

The degree of perceived similarity between situations was judged on a scale from 0 to 4, the different scale values being given the following general definitions: 0, Not at all similar; 1, Somewhat similar; 2, Rather similar; 3, Very similar; and 4, Identical.

The total matrix containing 36 X 36 situation descriptions was divided up into three submatrices. Each of them was judged without a break. Breaks of 30 min. were taken between the judgments of the submatrices.

The order of the situations in the matrix was determined using random tables and the order in which the submatrices were judged was also randomized among the judges.

The instructions called upon the judges to think very carefully about each situation and thereafter to judge the perceived similarity between the situations.

Subjects

Three students rated the similarity of the situations. Two of them gave judgments on more than one occasion, which gave a basis for the study of the constancy of the perception of situations.

RESULTS

Analysis of Group Data

Dimensionality analysis.—The individual similarity ratings were transformed into a scale ranging from 0 (no similarity at all) to 1 (identity) by dividing by 4. Mean estimates of similarity of situations over subjects were computed from these transformed values. The similarity matrix was factor analyzed by the method of principal components and the obtained factor matrix was rotated to a varimax solution. After plotting the eigenvalues, the number of factors chosen to be rotated was five. The rotated factor matrix is shown in Table 1.

Even a cursory inspection of the values in Table 1 provides a picture of very clear structure. This is readily apparent from Fig. 1, where adjacent factor columns have been plotted against each other.

Variables with factor loadings higher than 0.50 were chosen to describe the character of each factor. With that criterion the following variables represent Factor I:

13 Receive praise for a report during group work
19 Able to answer a difficult question during a lecture
15 Have passed an examination with top marks
22 A statistical problem becomes clear
 8 Get exactly the questions expected in an examination
21 Listen to a lecture about a subject which has been mastered
29 Undergo an oral examination
24 Listen to an interesting lecture
34 Sit together with fellow students and cross-examine before an examination
 9 Present a report during group work

The basic content of Factor I is very clear. The feature common to the situations which determine the dimension is their positive and rewarding character. None of the situations has a factor loading higher than 0.50 on any other dimension.

The following variables have factor loadings higher than 0.50 on Factor II:

12 Have just been returned a laboratory report with negative criticism
30 Cannot answer a simple question during a lecture

Table 1. Rotated Factor Matrix for Group Data

Variable	Factor					h^2
	I	II	III	IV	V	
1	.371	.293	.147	.286	.191	.36
2	.011	.294	.742	−.162	.244	.72
3	.420	.384	.028	.032	.571	.65
4	.278	.174	.132	.181	.758	.73
5	.304	.170	.034	.609	.114	.50
6	.154	.110	.026	.811	.336	.80
7	.171	.081	.137	.109	.851	.79
8	.743	−.051	.028	.084	.309	.65
9	.515	.361	−.005	.169	.270	.49
10	.059	.200	.370	−.018	.427	.36
11	.135	.009	.164	.779	−.177	.68
12	.003	.848	.047	.013	.102	.73
13	.907	−.038	.059	.064	−.086	.84
14	.024	.046	.774	.137	−.062	.62
15	.794	−.077	.084	.108	−.081	.66
16	.191	.045	.538	.394	.034	.48
17	.021	.533	.184	.360	.011	.44
18	−.090	.688	.105	.025	.308	.58
19	.909	.000	.011	.161	.170	.88
20	−.097	.733	.353	.143	.123	.70
21	.664	−.070	.474	.181	.100	.71
22	.753	−.079	.068	.116	.289	.67
23	.421	.266	.246	.168	.233	.39
24	.557	−.063	.167	.472	.080	.57
25	−.004	.291	.753	−.055	.272	.72
26	.218	−.081	.574	.387	−.024	.53
27	.050	.691	.105	.064	.113	.50
28	.040	.155	.831	.066	.153	.74
29	.599	.486	−.032	.012	.282	.67
30	.043	.810	.043	.108	−.005	.67
31	.052	.760	.067	−.070	−.009	.59
32	.086	−.025	.538	.405	.053	.46
33	.212	.071	.150	.202	.866	.86
34	.541	.223	.004	.387	.249	.55
35	.098	.123	.743	−.042	.053	.58
36	.147	.138	.020	.796	.292	.76

31 Have just failed an examination
20 Do not understand a thing about a lecture
18 Have unsuccessfully attempted to solve a numerical problem
27 Have forgotten to prepare a report
17 Unprepared for seminar and do not participate in the discussion

Factor II is also very pure and easy to interpret. All of the situations are of a negative nature. No loading on any other dimension is greater than 0.40 for these situations.

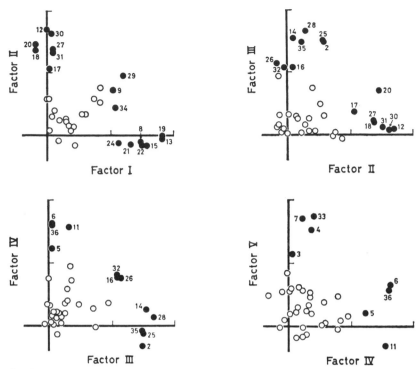

Fig. 1. Plots of factor loadings for group data. Filled circles represent factor loadings higher than 0.50.

Factor III is characterized by the following variables:

28 Wait on laboratory subjects completing questionnaire
14 Rest during a break in lectures
25 Wait for the others before group work
35 Sit after an examination and wait for a fellow student
 2 Adjust to darkness prior to an experiment
26 Sit in the Student Union and read a paper
32 Listen to lectures during external study visit
16 Casual study before an examination knowing that there is plenty of time

The highest loadings suggest that Factor III should be interpreted as passiveness. It is interesting to note that lectures during external study visits are included in this group of situations. The highest loading on any other dimension for any of these situations is 0.41 (situation 32).

Four variables have factor loadings higher than 0.50 on Factor IV:

 6 Carry out a joint group task together with fellow students
36 Plan a laboratory experiment together with some fellow students

11 Eat lunch with some fellow students
 5 Discuss politics with fellow students

The common feature of the situations representing Factor IV appears to be the social interaction. Situations where one is together with others without this interaction (see, e.g., situations 8, 9, 17, 20, 21) belong to other factors than Factor IV.

Factor V can be characterized by the following four variables:

33 Sit alone at home and do homework
 7 Sit alone at home and write a laboratory report
 4 Sit alone at home and prepare an oral report
 3 Undergo a written examination

The feature common to the four situations which determine Factor V is the activity of the individual, irrespective of whether he is together with others or not.

Three situations have no loadings which exceed 0.50. These are situation 1 (Interview a freshman student), 10 (Participate as a subject in an experiment), and 23 (Administer an intelligence test to a subject). It can be seen from Table 1 that these three situations have the lowest communalities. However, an analysis of the individual similarity matrices showed that the low communalities for group data is a result of the fact that these situations belong to different factors for individuals A, B, and C.

The interpretations given above of the factors are of course only very tentative and hold for the present only for the structure of these data.

Comments.—Analysis of group data shows a clear, concise and easily interpreted structure. None of the situations has a loading higher than 0.50 on more than one dimension. It is clearly possible at the data level to assign the variation in similarity ratings of situations to a limited number of factors. One interpretation of this result is that it is possible to identify common cognitive dimensions used by individuals to discriminate between situations.

DIMENSIONALITY ANALYSIS OF INDIVIDUAL DATA

Factoring

A principal component analysis was carried out for each of the individual similarity matrices in exactly the same way as for group data. The rotations were also performed using the same program as for group data and rotating for five factors. As an example of an individual factor matrix the rotated matrix obtained for Judge A is shown in Table 2.

Table 2. Rotated Factor Matrix for Judge A

Variable	I	II	III	IV	V	h^2
1	.479	.106	−.006	.434	.136	.44
2	−.002	.111	.965	−.066	.005	.94
3	.328	−.025	−.065	.194	.650	.57
4	.241	−.034	.037	.115	.893	.87
5	.177	.018	.008	.775	.128	.64
6	.052	.063	.009	.876	.248	.83
7	−.042	.014	.038	.102	.833	.70
8	.595	−.056	−.011	.084	.664	.80
9	.590	.071	−.019	.428	.046	.53
10	.087	.122	−.055	.031	.645	.44
11	.029	.041	.149	.821	−.094	.70
12	.059	.975	−.053	−.112	.076	.97
13	.901	.015	.024	−.112	−.098	.83
14	−.009	.003	.920	−.042	−.024	.85
15	.837	−.007	−.000	−.045	−.190	.74
16	.147	.140	.386	.197	.423	.40
17	.008	.456	.173	.223	.017	.28
18	−.079	.807	−.020	−.135	.477	.90
19	.927	.133	.037	.105	.102	.90
20	−.103	.713	.276	.181	.104	.64
21	.575	−.080	.481	.235	.189	.66
22	.821	−.076	.108	.010	.432	.87
23	.466	−.011	.059	.368	.249	.41
24	.485	−.078	.258	.395	.376	.60
25	−.015	.049	.892	−.053	.008	.80
26	.125	−.103	.495	.317	.080	.37
27	.075	.550	.071	.082	−.062	.32
28	−.052	.065	.864	.105	−.054	.76
29	.677	.174	−.064	.406	.239	.71
30	.113	.809	−.039	.152	−.069	.69
31	.013	.536	−.039	−.035	−.027	.29
32	.031	−.005	.447	.281	.296	.36
33	.031	.035	.097	.070	.999	1.00
34	.663	.036	−.024	.535	.270	.80
35	.108	.154	.870	−.061	−.048	.79
36	.040	.229	.025	.841	.111	.77

Structure

An inspection of the three rotated factor matrices showed a clear structure for all the judges. This is indicated by the fact that it occurred only twice for Judge A that a situation had two factor loadings higher than 0.50. The same thing happened only twice for Judge B and three times for Judge C. A representative picture of the clearness of structure at the individual level is shown in Fig. 2, where adjacent columns of Judge A's factor matrix have been plotted against each other.

Table 3 shows the individual factor loadings for the situations used previously to characterize the principal dimensions for individual data. The table shows that the five main dimensions can be given the same basic interpretations for each of the three judges as for the group data.

A rough estimate of the degree of agreement in structure among the judges was obtained by computing product-moment coefficients of correlation between factor loadings for the factors most nearly corresponding to each other. The obtained correlations are shown in Table 4. With few exceptions the values show a high level of agreement in structure among the individual factor matrices. This is another way of illustrating that all three judges have the same basic structure for their ratings as that obtained at group level.

An inspection of the individual factor matrices showed, however, differences that can be of some interest in judging the implications of this methodology for the study of individual ways of interpreting situations. For Judge A situations 1 (Interviewing a freshman student) and 23 (Administer an intelligence test to a subject) have high loadings on Factor I (tentatively interpreted as "positive") and on Factor IV ("social"). For Judges B and C the same situations have high factor loadings on Factor III ("passive"). Another example is situation 10 (Participate

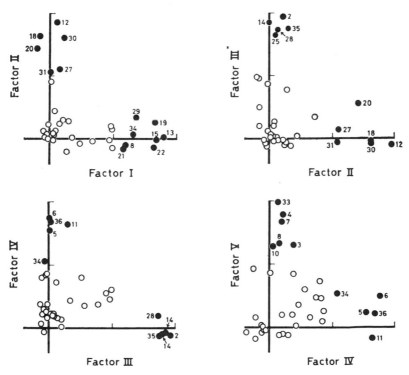

Fig. 2. Plots of factor loadings for Judge A on occasion 1. Filled circles represent factor loadings higher than 0.50.

Table 3. Individual Factor Loadings for Situations at Group Level

Factor		Variable	Judge			Group
			A	B	C	
I.	"Positive"	13	.90	.95	.87	.91
		19	.93	.99	.92	.91
		15	.84	.63	.88	.79
		22	.82	.67	.79	.75
		8	.60	.71	.94	.74
		21	.58	.79	.58	.66
		29	.68	.54	.43	.60
		24	.49	.55	.47	.56
		34	.66	.48	.45	.54
		9	.59	.41	.41	.52
II.	"Negative"	12	.98	.87	.89	.85
		30	.81	.97	.70	.81
		31	.54	.82	.93	.76
		20	.71	.70	.76	.73
		18	.81	.65	.86	.69
		27	.55	.73	.65	.69
		17	.46	.63	.55	.53
III.	"Passive"	28	.86	.73	.82	.83
		14	.92	.43	.83	.77
		25	.89	.87	.54	.75
		35	.87	.83	.58	.74
		2	.97	.49	.73	.74
		26	.50	.40	.61	.57
		32	.45	.62	.61	.54
		16	.39	.27	.82	.54
IV.	"Social"	6	.88	.74	.76	.81
		36	.84	.66	.76	.80
		11	.82	.80	.75	.78
		5	.78	.42	.64	.61
V.	"Active"	33	.99	.84	.51	.87
		7	.83	.74	.47	.85
		4	.89	.79	.52	.76
		3	.65	.56	.58	.57

Table 4. Correlation Coefficients between Factor Loadings for Principal Factors for Individual Judges

Factor	r_{AB}	r_{AC}	r_{BC}
I	0.90	0.83	0.86
II	0.82	0.87	0.86
III	0.65	0.81	0.59
IV	0.53	0.82	0.73
V	0.69	0.34	0.43

as a subject in an experiment) which has its highest loading on Factor V ("active") for Judge A but on Factor III ("passive") for B and C. Such differences among the judges may be interpreted in terms of the cognitive model; the judges differ with respect to the dimensions along which they discriminate certain situations.

Comments

The fact that the main dimensions were the same for the three judges in this study cannot, of course, be used as the basis for the conclusion that the same main dimensions would be found for any group of individuals whatsoever. The judges were an extremely homogeneous group in certain important respects. All three had concrete experience of the situations and this experience was relatively recent. There is, in fact, reason to believe that the structure of situational perception differs between groups of individuals. This is in all probability a fruitful problem for further research.

Differences among individual factor matrices may be interpreted to reflect the well-known fact that a situation can have a different psychological relevance for different individuals. Previous findings mentioned in the introduction suggest that the important characteristics of an individual are to be found in his specific manner of adjusting to different situations. The method used here may provide a possibility to study this problem in a more systematic way than has hitherto been possible.

STABILITY OF JUDGMENTS

Analyses and Results

One of the requirements for the meaningful study of the structure of situational perception is that this structure has some degree of stability. Two of the three judges who participated on the first judgmental occasion were able to provide further judgments on a later occasion under varying conditions, and this has permitted the following analyses of the stability of the similarity judgments and their structure.

Judge B performed new similarity judgments for half of the situations a fortnight after the first rating. An estimate of the stability of the judgments was obtained by computing a product-moment correlation coefficient for the relationship between the judgments on the two occasions. Its value was 0.68. Still another week later he performed similarity ratings for the remaining situations. The correlation coefficient for the relationship between the judgments on the two occasions for this part of the similarity judgments was 0.62.

Judge A carried out new similarity judgments of the complete array of situations 3 wk. after the first judgment under experimental conditions similar to those on the first occasion. The correlation between judgments for the two occasions was 0.77.

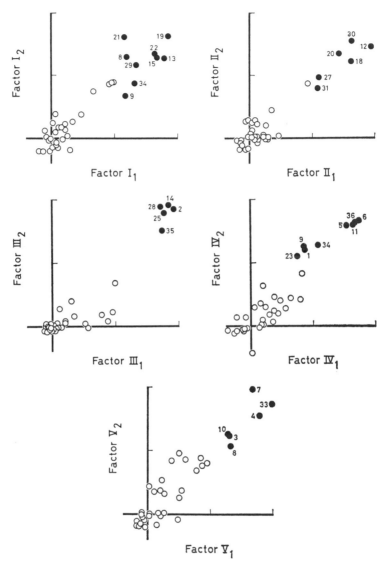

Fig. 3. Factor loadings from occasion 1 plotted against factor loadings from occasion 2 for Judge A. Filled circles represent factor loadings higher than 0.50 for both factors.

Judge A thus provided a new complete judgment matrix with judgments given at a single setting. This matrix was factored in exactly the same way as the earlier matrices.

A study of the factor matrix shows the same clear structure as on the first judgment occasion. Plotting the factor loadings from the two factor matrices against each other for Judge A suggests a remarkably great stability in the structure from the one occasion to the other (see Fig. 3). The correlations between the factor loadings for congruent principal factors from the two occasions expressed by product-moment correlation coefficients are 0.94 (I), 0.97 (II), 0.93 (III), 0.92 (IV), and 0.97 (V).

Comments

It is hard to believe that the constancy in structure between the judgment occasions is the result of memory from the first occasion. Although caution should be shown in drawing conclusions based on a single case, the outcome of the analysis supported the assumption that we are dealing with a cognitive structure with a considerable degree of stability over time.

CONCLUSIONS

The main findings were (a) that judgments of perceived similarity between situations have a considerable degree of consistency over time, (b) that the dimensionality of these judgments shows great agreement among individuals in a homogeneous group, and (c) that dimensional analysis both of average and individual similarity judgment matrices provides a clear and psychologically interpretable structure.

The results suggest that the methodology applied here can be used to study the structure of individual and group perception of situations and to express this structure in psychologically relevant dimensions. This result may be of importance for further research on the relationship between individual and environment, seen both from the interactionistic and transactionistic viewpoints (see Pervin, 1968). It should now, for example, be possible to relate changes in individual *behavior* from situation to situation to information about how the individual himself *perceives* these situations.

The individual's interpretation of different situations plays an essential part in his adjustment to reality, i.e., for his satisfaction and social relationships. There is in research and practice a need for systematic analyses of these interpretations *per se,* both for groups and for individuals. Some examples will be given of the possibilities of attacking these problems by means of individual and group analysis using the methodology outlined here.

With the methodology used here, it should be possible to obtain measures of the structure of the situational perception of different clinical groups and compare them with measures from relevant control groups. This type of comparison might be useful both in construct validation studies and in clinical diagnostic work. One could, for example, test the prediction that individuals with specific symptoms, say claustrophobia, would discriminate situations in closed and narrow spaces along other dimensions than individuals in general.

As a rule, clinical treatment aims at producing greater adjustment to reality on the part of the patient. The effect of the treatment can be studied by means of the extent and nature of changes during treatment, both in the structure of situational perceptions, and in the perception of specific situations which may be of special interest in the individual case (cf. Kelly, 1955; Osgood & Luria, 1967).

At the group level, opportunities are opened for the study of social psychological problems. The method could, for example, be used to study differences between politically, religiously, socio-economically homogeneous groups with respect to attitudes to situation—specific questions such as problems of interpersonal relationships, conflict research, etc.

It is possible that the method can also be used within a further area, where suitable methodology has long been the subject of research, namely, that of job evaluation. It should be possible to use similarity judgments for job positions and work duties in order to empirically determine the relevant dimensions. The judgments could be performed by individuals at different levels of proximity to the duties and positions.

All research concerning the dimensionality of cognitive organization presents some form of sampling problem. Here the problem is, however, scarcely greater than or different from that involved when studying cognitive structure within other areas. Only one consideration on sampling situations will be mentioned in this connection. The total cognitive organization of an individual can be assumed to be flexible and elastic, so that the internal relationships of the objects are variable under varying circumstances. It is probable that the organization changes both over time according to a more general trend, as well as between situations as a result of the specific domain which is focused upon. It may be assumed, for example, that if the focus is changed, this will also change the internal relationships between the objects in the cognitive organization. This means that the sampling of situations ought to be limited to some specific domain of situations, e.g., interpersonal relationships, leisure activities, studies, work duties, job positions, etc., as was the case in this study.

REFERENCES

Abelson, R. P. Situational variables in personality research. In S. Messick & J. Ross (Eds.), *Measurement in personality and cognition.* New York: Wiley, 1962. Pp. 241-248.

Attneave, F. Dimensions of similarity. *American Journal of Psychology,* 1950, 63, 516-556.

Bieri, J., Atkins, A. L., Briar, S., Leaman, R. L., Miller, H., & Tripodi, T. *Clinical and social judgment: The discrimination of behavioral information.* New York: Wiley, 1966.

Brunswik, E. Representative design and probabilistic theory in a functional psychology. *Psychological Review,* 1955, 62, 193-218.

Carson, R. C. *Interaction concepts of personality.* Chicago: Aldine, 1969.

Cattell, R. B. Formulating the environmental situation and its perception in behavior theory. In S. B. Sells (Ed.), *Stimulus determinants of behavior.* New York: Ronald, 1963. Pp. 46-75.

Coombs, C. A. *A theory of data.* New York: Wiley, 1964.

Cronbach, L. J. The two disciplines of scientific psychology. *American Psychologist,* 1957, 12, 671-684.

Cronbach, L. J. Proposals leading to analytic treatment of social perception scores. In R. Tagiuri & L. Petrullo (Eds.), *Person perception and interpersonal behavior.* Stanford: Stanford Univer. Press, 1958. Pp. 353-380.

Ekman, G. Dimensions of color vision. *Journal of Psychology,* 1954, 38, 467-474.

Ekman, G. Dimensions of emotion. *Acta Psychologica,* 1955, 11, 279-288.

Ekman, G. Multidimensional ratio scaling applied to color vision. *Report Psychological Laboratories, Univer. of Stockholm,* 1961, No. 92.

Ekman, G. Comparative studies on multidimensional scaling and related techniques. *Report Psychological Laboratories, Univer. of Stockholm,* 1970, Supplement 3.

Ekman, G., & Engen, T. Multidimensional ratio scaling and multidimensional similarity in olfactory perception. *Report Psychological Laboratories, Univer. of Stockholm,* 1962, No. 126.

Ekman, G., & Lindman, R. Multidimensional ratio scaling and multidimensional similarity. *Report Psychological Laboratories, Univer. of Stockholm,* 1961, No. 103.

Endler, N. S., & Hunt, J. McV. Sources of variance in reported anxiousness as measured by the S-R Inventory. *Psychological Bulletin,* 1966, 65, 336-346.

Engen, T. Psychophysical similarity of the odors of aliphatic alcohols. *Report Psychological Laboratories, Univer. of Stockholm,* 1962, No. 127.

Fiske, D. W. Problems in measuring personality. In J. W. Wepman & R. W. Heine (Eds.), *Concept of personality.* Chicago: Aldine, 1963. Pp. 449-473.

Gulliksen, H., & Messick, S. (Eds.) *Psychological scaling: Theory and applications.* New York: Wiley, 1960.

Helson, H. *Adaptation-level theory: An experimental and systematic approach to behavior.* New York: Harper & Row, 1964.

Hunt, J. McV. Traditional personality theory in the light of recent evidence. *American Scientist,* 1965, 53, 80-96.

Kelly, G. A. *The psychology of personal constructs.* New York: Norton, 1955.

Koffka, K. *Principles of Gestalt psychology.* New York: Harcourt, 1935.

Kuennapas, T. Visual perception of capital letters: Multidimensional ratio scaling and multidimensional similarity. *Scandinavian Journal of Psychology,* 1966, 7, 189-196.

Kuennapas, T. Visual memory of capital letters: Multidimensional ratio scaling and multidimensional similarity. *Perceptual and Motor Skills,* 1967, 25, 345-350.

Kuennapas, T. Acoustic perception and acoustic memory of letters: Multidimensional ratio scaling and multidimensional similarity. *Acta Psychologica,* 1968, 28, 161-170.

Kuennapas, T., Maelhammar, G., & Svenson, O. Multidimensional ratio scaling and multidimensional similarity of simple geometric figures. *Scandinavian Journal of Psychology,* 1964, 5, 249-256.

Lewin, K. *Field theory in social science.* New York: Harper & Row, 1951.

Magnusson, D., & Ekman, G. A psychophysical approach to the study of personality traits. *Multivariate Behavioral Research,* 1970, 5, 255-274.

Magnusson, D., Gerzen, M., & Nyman, B. The generality of behavioral data: I. Generalization from observation on one occasion. *Multivariate Behaviroal Research,* 1968, 3, 295–320.

Magnusson, D., & Heffler, B. The generality of behavioral data: III. Generalization as a function of the number of observational situations. *Multivariate Behavioral Research,* 1969, 4, 29-42.

Magnusson, D., Heffler, B., & Nyman, B. The generality of behavioral data: II. Replication of an experiment on generalization from observation on one occasion. *Multivariate Behavioral Research,* 1968, 3, 415-422.

Meltzer, L. The need for a dual orientation in social psychology. *Journal of Social Psychology,* 1961, 55, 43-47.

Miller, D. R. The study of social relationships: Situation identity, and social interaction. In S. Koch (Ed.), *Psychology: a study of a science.* New York: McGraw-Hill, 1963. Pp. 639-737.

Mischel, W. *Personality and assessment.* New York: Wiley, 1968

Murphy, G. *Personality: A biosocial interpretation.* New York: Harper, 1947.

Murray, H. A. *Explorations in personality.* New York: Oxford, 1938.

Osgood, C. E., & Luria, Z. A blind analysis of a case of multiple personality using the semantic differential. In. D. N. Jackson & S. Messick (Eds.), *Problems in human assessment.* New York: McGraw-Hill, 1967. Pp. 600-615.

Osgood, C. E., Suci, G. J., & Tannenbaum, P. H. *The measurement of meaning.* Urbana, Ill.: Univer. of Illinois Press, 1957.

Pervin, L. A. Performance and satisfaction as a function of individual-environment fit. *Psychological Bulletin,* 1968, 69, 56-68.

Sarbin, T. R., Taft, R., & Bailey, D. E. *Clinical inference and cognitive theory.* New York: Holt, Rinehart & Winston, 1960.

Sells, S. B. Dimensions of stimulus situations which account for behavior variance. In S. B. Sells (Ed.), *Stimulus determinants of behavior.* New York: Ronald, 1963. Pp. 3-15. (a)

Sells, S. B. An interactionist looks at the environment. *American Psychologist,* 1963, 18, 696-702. (b)

Shepard, R. N. The analysis of proximities: Multidimensional scaling with an unknown distance function: I and II. *Psychometrika,* 1962, 27, 125-140, 219, 246.

Shibutani, T. *Society and personality: An interactional approach to social psychology.* Englewood Cliffs, N.J.: Prentice-Hall, 1961.

Tolman, E. C., Jarret, R. F., & Bailey, D. E. Degree of similarity and the ease of learning paired adjectives (1959). In T. R. Sarbin, R. Taft, & D. E. Bailey (Eds.), *Clinical inference and cognitive theory.* New York: Holt, Rinehart & Winston, 1960. Pp. 108–111.

Torgerson, W. S. *Theory and methods of scaling.* New York: Wiley, 1958.

29

Assessment of the Psychosocial Environments of Community-Oriented Psychiatric Treatment Programs

RUDOLF MOOS

The assumption that the immediate psychological environment in which patients and staff function is an important if not the crucial, aspect of the overall treatment process is reflected in many descriptions of both inpatient ward and community-oriented psychiatric programs (e.g. Jones, 1953; Stanton & Schwartz, 1954). More recently, others (e.g., Cumming & Cumming, 1962; Fairweather, 1963) have extended this logic and have attempted to experiment with different ways of structuring the ward environment to improve its therapeutic impact on patients. Raush and Raush (1968) made an extensive survey of 40 transitional programs in which they explored the concept of the therapeutic effect of the milieu on the residents. Apte (1968), using a 65-item scale to classify 25 halfway houses in England and Wales, found a higher return rate to the community in permissive than in restrictive houses, but he made no definite conclusions about the actual effects of the therapeutic milieu because he was unable to use matched groups of patients

The descriptions of Elm City Rehabilitation Center by Moses (1969), of Woodley House by Doniger, Rothwell, and Cohen (1963), of day hospitals in Great Britain by Farndale (1961), of day–night services in the United States by Conwell, Rosen, Hench, and Bahn (1964), and of halfway houses by Glasscote, Gudeman, and Elpers (1971) give information about history, funding, therapy, staffing, and resident characteristics. While some idea of the type of treatment

From the *Journal of Abnormal Psychology*, 1972, *79*, 9–18. Copyright 1972 by the American Psychological Association. Reprinted by permission.

This research was supported in part by the Veterans Administration Research Funds and National Institute of Mental Health Grants MH16026 and MH10976. Appreciation is due to Robert Shelton and Marguerite Kaufman for statistical computation and programming and to Bernice Moos, Jean Otto, Charles Petty, and Penny Smail for help in data collecting and analysis.

environment provided may be inferred from these published accounts, there is clearly a need for a more systematic method for the description and comparison of the environments provided by these programs.

In addition, many investigators have become more interested in attempting to specify the importance of situational and environmental influences on the determination of individual behavior, for example, Mischel, 1968. Work by Endler and Hunt (1968), Magnussen, Gerzen, and Nyman (1968), and Moos (1969) has contributed to this trend, the evidence from which generally suggests that environmental influences may play a much more important part in the determination of individual behavior than had previously been thought.

Systematic measures by which to assess the social environments of a number of different kinds of institutions have been developed. Much of the initial work was concentrated in educational and industrial organizations (e.g., Likert, 1967; Pace, 1969), but recently attempts have been made to measure various aspects of psychiatric ward environments (e.g. Ellsworth, Maroney, Klett, Gordon, & Gunn, 1969; Kellam, Schmelzer, & Berman, 1966).

Moos and Houts (1968) have developed a Ward Atmosphere Scale (WAS) which assesses a psychiatric ward's social environment as perceived by patients and staff on 10 different dimensions reflecting relationship variables (e.g. Involvement, Support), treatment program variables (e.g., Autonomy, Practical Orientation, Personal Problem Orientation), and administrative structure variables (e.g., Order and Organization, Program Clarity). The WAS empirically differentiates between different inpatient psychiatric wards, shows high profile stability over a period of several months, and has recently been standardized on a national sample of 160 psychiatric wards (Moos, 1971).

This paper reports the development of a Community-Oriented Programs Environment Scale (COPES)[1] which assesses the psychosocial environments of transitional community-oriented psychiatric treatment programs in a manner which is parallel to the WAS, thus making it possible to directly compare the perceived environmental characteristics of in-hospital and out-of-hospital psychiatric programs.

METHOD

Most of the items in the initial form of COPES were adapted from the WAS by both patients and staff who were particularly familiar with the characteristics of the social environments of a variety of community-oriented psychiatric programs, particularly day hospitals and halfway houses. The items for the WAS had originally been obtained from several different sources, for example, observations of ward differences made by trained Os, popular and professional books about psychiatric wards, and interviews of patients and staff

---

[1] Copies of COPES, scoring key, and preliminary norms are available on request from the author.

who had spent time on different wards. Additional items were also formulated.

The choice of items was guided by the general conceptualization of environmental press (Murray, 1938). The press of the environment as the individual in the environment perceives it, tends to define what he must adapt to and cope with and indicates the direction his behavior should take if he is to be adequately satisfied within the environment. "Press" may refer either to the objective ecological aspects of the environment (alpha press) or to the subjective perception which each person has of the events in which he takes part (beta press). There is a point at which the individual's private world tends to merge with the private world of others; that is, to some extent at least, people tend to share a common interpretation of those events in which they directly participate. This common interpretation might be called a mutually shared consensual beta press. The COPES developed in this study measures this consensual beta press. This logic closely follows that of Murray (1938) and of Stern (1970).

For example, an emphasis on program involvement would be inferred from the following items: "Members put a lot of energy into what they do around here," "This is a lively place." An emphasis on autonomy would be inferred from these items: "Members are expected to take leadership here" and "Members here are very strongly encouraged to be independent." An emphasis on order and organization would be inferred from still other items: "Members here follow a regular schedule every day" and "Members' activities are carefully planned." Operationally "press" are the characteristic demands or features of the environment as perceived by those who live or function in it. To each statement in COPES, the person who takes the questionnaire answers true if he believes it is generally characteristic of his program and false if he believes it is not generally characteristic of the program.

The resulting 130-item Form B of COPES was administered to both members and staff in 21 different community-oriented treatment programs. These programs were picked in order to obtain a sample of a wide variety and broad range of different kinds of programs. The 21 programs included nine day care centers, two mixed-sex residential centers, one men's and one women's residential program, two rehabilitation center programs, a community care home, a residents' workshop, and two adolescent residential centers.

About half of the houses tested were established to serve as transitional residences for ex-mental patients, whereas the other half were designed to serve those in the community as an alternative to hospitalization. Some of these were residential and some were day care centers. While most of the programs were open to both men and women, three of the houses served only men and one only women. The members in general were able to function fairly normally and were at least eligible for full-time employment; one of the programs did deal with men having a chronic history of illness and was attached to a sheltered workshop. There was a very wide range of structure in the programs. The adolescent centers and the home for men were fairly structured and kept close control over their members, whereas most of the other programs allowed members to be as autonomous as possible.

RESULTS

The total numbers of members and staff tested in the 21 programs were 373 and 203, respectively. Over 80% of the members and essentially all of the staff approached were both willing and able to take COPES adequately. Items were initially sorted, by agreement between three independent judges, into 12 rationally derived press subscales which paralleled the WAS subscales used in assessing the social environment of psychiatric wards (Moos & Houts, 1968).

The 102-item, 10-subscale revised Form C of COPES was derived by using the following criteria:

1. Each subscale should have acceptable internal consistency and each item should correlate more highly with its own than with any other subscale. Two of the original 12 subscales were dropped because they did not meet these criteria. The original variety subscale had low item-subscale correlations and showed poor internal consistency, and most of the items in the original affiliation subscale correlated as highly with other subscales (particularly involvement) as they did with affiliation. Form C has only two items for members and two items for staff which show a correlation of less than .25 with their appropriate subscales. Over 90% of the items for members and over 95% for staff correlated above .30 with their appropriate subscales. Table 1 summarizes, separately for members and staff, the internal consistencies for the 10 subscales, the average correlations between the items and their own subscales, and the average correlations between the item and the other 9 subscales. Internal consistencies were calculated, following Stern (1970), using Cronbach's alpha and average within program item variances. The results indicate that all of the subscales have acceptable internal consistency and moderate to high item-subscale correlations. In addition, the items tend to correlate much more highly with one another than with other subscales.

Table 1. Internal Consistencies and Average Item-Subscale Correlations for COPES Form C Subscales

Subscale	Alpha		Average item-subscale correlation		Average item-other subscale correlation	
	Members	Staff	Members	Staff	Members	Staff
Program Involvement	.79	.82	.48	.46	.16	.16
Support	.67	.64	.44	.42	.15	.14
Spontaneity	.63	.75	.43	.46	.16	.14
Autonomy	.62	.89	.38	.49	.11	.15
Practical Orientation	.64	.64	.44	.43	.12	.10
Personal Problem Orientation	.78	.84	.52	.50	.13	.16
Anger and Aggression	.82	.86	.51	.52	.10	.13
Order and Organization	.81	.87	.53	.53	.15	.15
Program Clarity	.68	.77	.45	.44	.15	.13
Staff Control	.67	.76	.40	.45	.10	.12

2. Insofar as possible, not more than 80% nor less than 20% of Ss should answer an item in one direction. This criterion was used in order to avoid items which were characteristic only of extreme programs. Ninety-five of the 102 COPES Form C items had item splits which were between 20 and 80 for either members and/or staff; that is, there were only 7 items which showed an item split that was more extreme than 20–80 for both members and staff.
3. There should be approximately the same number of items scored true as scored false within each subscale so as to control for acquiescence response set.
4. Items should not correlate significantly with a halo response set scale, which assessed both positive and negative halo in program perceptions, and which was also given to members and staff.

The use of these four criteria resulted in a 102-item, 10-subscale Form C of COPES. The 10 subscales of COPES, brief definitions of each, and examples of items included in each are as follows:

1. Program Involvement: measures how active members are in the day-to-day functioning of their program.
   Members put a lot of energy into what they do around here.
   Members here really try to improve and get better.
2. Support: measures the extent to which members are encouraged and supported by staff and other members.
   The healthier members here help take care of the less healthy ones.
   "Staff" [members] go out of their way to help members.
3. Spontaneity: measures the extent to which the program encourages members to act openly and express their feelings openly.
   Members say anything they want to the staff.
   Members are encouraged to show their feelings.
4. Autonomy: assesses how self-sufficient and independent members are encouraged to be in making their own decisions.
   The staff act on members' suggestions.
   Members are expected to take leadership here.
5. Practical Orientation: assesses the extent to which the member's environment orients him towards preparing himself for release from the program.
   This program emphasizes training for new kinds of jobs.
   Members are encouraged to plan for the future.
6. Personal Problem Orientation: measures the extent to which members are encouraged to be concerned with their personal problems and feelings and to seek to understand them.
   Members tell each other about their personal problems.
   Staff are mainly interested in learning about members' feelings.
7. Anger and Aggression: measures the extent to which a member is allowed and encouraged to argue with members and staff, to become openly angry, and to display other aggressive behavior.
   Members often gripe.
   Staff here think it is a healthy thing to argue.

8. Order and Organization: measures how important activity planning and neatness is in the program.
   Members' activities are carefully planned.
   The staff make sure that this place is always neat.
9. Program Clarity: measures the clarity of goal expectations and rules.
   If a member breaks a rule, he knows what will happen to him.
   Staff tell members when they are getting better.
10. Staff Control: assesses the extent to which the staff determines rules.
    Once a schedule is arranged for a member, the member must follow it.
    Everyone knows who's in charge here.

The Program Involvement, Support, and Spontaneity subscales are conceptualized as measuring *relationship* variables. These three dimensions assess the extent to which members tend to become involved in the program, the extent to which staff support members and members tend to support and help each other, and the extent to which there is spontaneity and free and open expression within all these relationships. Thus, these variables essentially assess the types and intensity of personal relationships between members and among members and staff which exist in the program.

The next four subscales, that is, Autonomy, Practical Orientation, Personal Problem Orientation, and Anger and Aggression are conceptualized as *program* variables. Each of these subscales assesses a dimension which is particularly relevant to the types of treatment program which have been initiated and developed. Autonomy assesses the extent to which members are encouraged to be self-sufficient and independent and to take responsibility for their own decisions. The subscales of Practical Orientation and Personal Problem Orientation reflect two of the major types of psychotherapeutic treatment orientations which are currently in use in psychiatric programs. The Anger and Aggression subscale is also conceptualized as assessing a program variable since the amount and extent of emphasis on the expression of aggression is usually related to psychotherapeutic values of staff, for example, whether or not it is perceived as beneficial to openly express angry feelings. These four subscales appear to assess the major treatment dimensions along which psychiatric programs vary.

The last three subscales of Order and Organization, Program Clarity, and Staff Control are conceptualized as assessing *administrative structure* variables. These subscales are system oriented in that they assess dimensions related to the goal of keeping the program functioning in an orderly, organized, clear, and coherent manner.

The next step was to obtain the 10 subscale scores for each S. Means and standard deviations of subscale scores were calculated for each program separately for members and staff for each of the 10 subscales. The results of one-way analyses of variance indicated that all 10 subscales significantly ($p < .01$ for all 10 subscales for members and for 9 of the 10 subscales for staff) differentiated among the 21 programs for both member and staff responses. Thus the major

Table 2. Percentages of Total Variance Attributable
Between-program Differences

Subscale	Members	Staff
Program Involvement	12	15
Support	12	12
Spontaneity	6	15
Autonomy	36	53
Practical Orientation	10	5
Personal Problem Orientation	29	38
Anger and Aggression	36	30
Order and Organization	28	51
Program Clarity	11	20
Staff Control	21	28

purpose of the research, which was to develop a scale, the dimensions of which would significantly discriminate among the average perceptions of members and the average perceptions of staff on different types of programs, was achieved.

Estimated omega-squared (Hays, 1963) was used to calculate, separately for members and staff, the percentages of each subscale's "total variance" which was accounted for by differences among the 21 programs. Table 2 indicates that these percentages vary from a low of 5% on the Practical Orientation subscale for staff to a high of over 50% on both the Autonomy and Order and Organization subscales for staff. These percentages may of course vary greatly depending upon the particular sample of programs studied; however, the present results indicate that the percentages of variance accounted for by program differences may be quite substantial.

The 10 subscale scores were intercorrelated, separately for the 373 members and the 203 staff, in order to discover whether it might be fruitful to conceptualize a smaller number of dimensions. The intercorrelations among the subscales are shown in Table 3. These intercorrelations were not considered high enough to justify the collapsing of any set of two or more subscales. The highest intercorrelation is exactly .50 (accounting for only 25% of the variance), and the only cluster of subscales which shows even moderate intercorrelations in both the member and the staff samples was composed of the relationship dimensions of Involvement, Support, and Spontaneity. The average correlations among the subscales were .23 for member sample and .24 for the staff sample. Thus it appears that the 10 dimensions measure rather distinct, albeit correlated characteristics of member and staff perceptions of program atmospheres.

Sample Profiles and Interpretations

Figure 1 shows the COPES profile for the members and staff in Program 113, a small residential center for men and women 16 yr. of age and over who are returning to the community after hospitalization, who might otherwise have to be hospitalized, or who are coming from a crisis situation. Members are expected

Table 3. COPES Form C Subscale Intercorrelations for Members ($N = 373$) and Staff ($N = 203$)

Subscale	Program Involvement	Support	Spontaneity	Autonomy	Practical Orientation	Personal Problem Orientation	Anger and Aggression	Order and Organization	Program Clarity	Staff Control
Program Involvement		.50	.34	.13	.44	.27	−.08	.49	.32	.06
Support	.39		.44	.31	.39	.27	−.12	.44	.47	−.08
Spontaneity	.43	.40		.28	.21	.39	.13	.17	.34	−.27
Autonomy	.19	.28	.24		.16	.25	.00	.04	.34	−.27
Practical Orientation	.30	.34	.14	.19		.14	.01	.26	.27	.04
Personal Problem Orientation	.36	.27	.42	.46	.22		.30	.03	.19	.00
Anger and Aggression	.10	−.12	.11	.24	.02	.46		−.47	−.18	.04
Order and Organization	.07	.29	.01	−.30	.16	−.29	−.49		.38	.10
Program Clarity	.28	.32	.23	.20	.25	.06	−.21	.37		−.01
Staff Control	−.12	−.19	−.26	−.40	−.06	−.30	−.13	.28	.07	

Note.—Member correlations are above the diagonal, and staff correlations below.

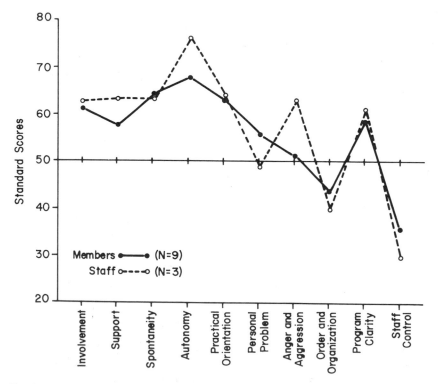

Fig. 1. Comparison of COPES From C scale profiles for members and staff on Program 113 based on member norms for 21 programs.

to be involved in regular daytime activities and have responsibility for housework and cooking. Other than attending a management meeting and a group therapy meeting, they are encouraged to be as independent as possible. Rules and restrictions are kept to a minimum. The house is staffed by a resident manager, a part-time student manager, and a program director. The staff also consult with visiting social workers.

Members and staff showed high agreement on the characteristics of their treatment environment. Both agreed that the emphasis on the three relationship variables was moderately above average. For example, eight of the nine members and all three of the staff agreed that members often did things together on weekends, and six of the nine members and all three of the staff also agreed that discussions in the house were very interesting (Involvement). All members and staff felt that members were strongly encouraged to express their feelings (Spontaneity).

The treatment program variables were also seen in similar ways by members and staff, with the exception that staff perceived about an average emphasis on Aggression whereas members perceived it as only average. The empahsis on Autonomy and Practical Orientation was seen as moderately to substantially above average, whereas average emphasis was perceived on encouraging members to be concerned about their personal problems. In the area of Autonomy, eight of the nine members and all three of the staff agreed that members were encouraged to take leadership and be independent, and everyone agreed that members had to demonstrate continual progress toward their goals (Practical Orientation) and that members told each other about their personal problems (Personal Problem Orientation).

Members and staff also agreed on the degree of emphasis on the administrative structure variables, with both groups perceiving the emphasis on Order and Organization and Staff Control to be moderately to substantially below average, and the emphasis on Program Clarity to be moderately above average. For example, two-thirds of the members and all staff agreed that things were sometimes disorganized, but all agreed that members followed a regular schedule. None of the staff and only two of the members felt that staff made and enforced all the rules.

Thus, this program was characterized by a moderately high emphasis on the relationship dimensions and on facilitating independence and practical planning. The program did not strongly emphasize understanding personal problems, nor did it particularly encourage members to openly express their anger. The program rules and procedures were perceived to be clear and explicit, but there was relatively little emphasis either on having a highly organized and structured program or on having the staff control the program decisions.

Figure 2 presents the COPES profile for Program 108, which is a residential women's quarters located in a comfortable home in a city residential area. The program serves women who are making a transition from hospital to community living. The women may go to work, school, or a day care center during the day

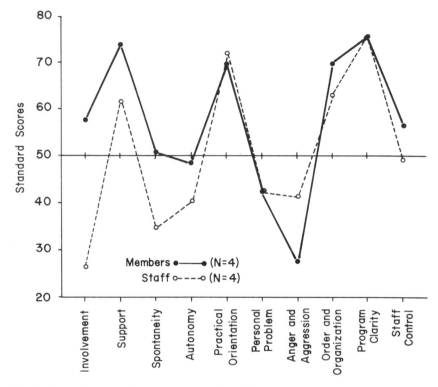

Fig. 2. Comparison of COPES Form C scale profiles for members and staff on Program 108 based on member norms for 21 programs.

time. The house is managed by two women who act as housemothers to the residents and who encourage the women to participate in community activities, and there are two additional part-time staff.

This profile illustrates a different type of treatment environment and also shows greater disagreements among members and staff, particularly on the relationship variables. Members rated Involvement and Spontaneity as about average, whereas staff perceived the emphasis on those variables to be substantially below average. For example, all four members felt that they put a lot of energy into what they did in the program, but all four staff members disagreed. Only one of the four members felt that members hid their feelings from staff, but three of the four staff felt this statement was true. Members rated Support as very strongly emphasized, while staff saw it as moderately above average.

There was more agreement between members and staff on the treatment program variables. Both felt that Practical Orientation was strongly emphasized and that Autonomy and Personal Problem Orientation were slightly below average. All members and staff agreed that members had to demonstrate continued concrete progress toward their goals and that they had to make specific plans for the future. Members and staff also agreed that while members were encouraged to be independent, staff rarely gave in to pressures from a member. Both members and staff perceived relatively little emphasis on Aggression; for example, they agreed that members rarely argued openly.

Both members and staff viewed the program as an orderly and organized one, with clear rules and expectations. All members and staff agreed that members knew both the program rules and the consequences of breaking them. Both felt there was above-average emphasis on the extent to which staff used measures to keep members under necessary controls. For example, both agreed that once a schedule was arranged for a member she had to follow it, but both also agreed that the staff rarely punished members by taking away their privileges.

In summary, this program places high emphasis on members and staff supporting a member, as did the first program, but places somewhat less emphasis on members being involved in program activities and openly expressing their feelings. Both this program and Program 113 strongly emphasize a practical orientation, but Program 113 also stresses member autonomy and allows for the open expression of anger whereas Program 108 does not. The members and staff in both programs perceived program rules and expectations to be clear, but Program 108 places considerably more emphasis on both Staff Control and Order and Organization than does Program 113.

Thus, the treatment environments of the two programs as assessed by both member and staff perceptions on COPES are quite different. The extremely wide range of differences among the 21 programs used in this study is further illustrated by the fact that on most items at least 80% of the members in one or more programs responded in one direction, whereas at least 80% of the members in one or more other programs responded in the opposite direction; for example, this was true for 8 of the 12 items on the Program Involvement subscale and for 9 of the 10 items on the Anger and Aggression subscale.

DISCUSSION

These results suggest that COPES may be a potentially useful test. Usually, transitional community-oriented psychiatric programs, much like inpatient psychiatric wards, have been compared in terms of readily observable indexes such as the number of patients, the number of staff, whether the program is residential or not, whether or not there are group therapy meetings, etc. The present results indicate that there is a whole range of additional dimensions which differentiate between treatment environments and thus should be taken into account in program descriptions. COPES may provide investigators with important psychosocial dimensions on which psychiatric treatment programs can be systematically assessed and compared. In addition, since the 10 dimensions assessed by COPES are conceptually similar to the 10 dimensions assessed by the Ward Atmosphere Scale, it becomes potentially possible to directly compare the treatment environments of hospital-based and community-based programs.

There are several possible applications of this type of "social systems analysis." The methodology makes it possible to directly compare the perceived characteristics of treatment environments with themselves over time (Grant & Saslow, 1971). with each other (Kish, 1971; Moos & Daniels, 1971), and cross-culturally (Moos, 1972). When the psychosocial elements of treatment environments are adequately dimensionalized, the differential impact of different social atmospheres upon different types of members and staff can be more adequately studied.

Social systems analysis can also be utilized to identify those environmental factors which relate to favorable or unfavorable treatment outcomes and possibly to predict outcome based on the differential impact of milieu settings on specific groups of patients. For example, Moos and Schwartz (1972) and Moos and Petty (1971) have shown that the dimensions are related to objective indexes of treatment outcome such as drop-out rate, release rate, and community tenure. Knowledge of social systems components may allow one to determine the effects of different environments upon patients and subsequently to match patient types more adequately with those treatment settings which meet their needs and hence facilitate recovery. In this way, maximum fit between patient and treatment environment may be obtained. For instance, Manasse (1965) showed that self-regard was related to the degree to which chronic schizophrenics were able to meet the demands and expectations of their ward or day treatment setting. Similarly, staff members might be placed in programs which emphasize those treatment dimensions which are consonant with their personal preferences.

Regular social systems assessment can also serve a valuable monitoring or "quality control" function. Congruence between idealized views of a treatment program and perceptions of its actual operation can be determined. A second form of COPES (Form I) which asks members and staff about their conceptions of an ideal treatment program has been developed for this purpose. The extent of agreement between members and staff and/or among various groups of staff can also be determined. Congruence between group and/or between the actual and ideal program treatment environment may be an important factor in effective system operation, whereas incongruence may point up specific directions in which change could occur (Moos & Otto, 1972).

Repeated measures of social system process over time provided the opportunity for self-analysis at the individual program and institution levels. They thus can be used to help direct planned social program change and system design. Regular feedback of process data provides a way to monitor the evolution and function of a system over time. Hence, it may assist in identifying oscillations in performance, including the spotting of crises, and in helping to bring about desired changes in program goals. In this connection Pierce, Trickett, and Moos (1972) have successfully used the WAS in helping staff to change the treatment environment of an inpatient psychiatric ward in ways which were more consonant with their own goals.

Finally, COPES may identify those individuals, both members and staff who show deviant perceptions of their environment. These individuals generally are less satisfied with the environment and thus may be more likely to drop out or become failures in the program (e.g. Pervin, 1967; Trickett & Moos, 1971). Thus, the systematic assessment of the psychosocial treatment environment of different types of psychiatric programs has a variety of practical implications for the specification and change of ongoing social systems and for furthering research aimed toward enhancing the person–environment fit.

REFERENCES

Apte, R. *Halfway houses.* London: Bell and Sons, Ltd., 1968.

Conwell, M., Rosen, B., Hench, C., & Bahn, A. The first national survey of psychiatric day-night services. In R. Epps & L. Hanes, (Eds.), *Day care of psychiatric patients.* Springfield, Ill.: Charles C. Thomas, 1964.

Cumming, J., & Cumming, E. *Ego & milieu.* New York: Atherton Press, 1962.

Doniger, J., Rothwell, N., & Cohen, R. Case study of a halfway house. *Mental Hospitals,* 1963, **14,** 191-199.

Ellsworth, R., Maroney, R., Klett, W., Gordon, H., & Gunn, R. Milieu characteristics of successful psychiatric treatment programs. Paper presented at the 14th Annual Veterans Administration Conference on Cooperative Studies in Psychiatry, Houston, April 1969.

Endler, N., & Hunt, J. S-R inventories of hostility and comparisons of the proportions of variance from persons, responses, and situations for hostility and anxiousness. *Journal of Personality and Social Psychiatry,* 1968, **9,** 309-315.

Fairweather, G. W. *Social psychology in treatment mental illness.* New York: Macmillan, 1963.

Farndale, J. *The day hospital movement in Great Britain.* London: Pergamon Press, 1961.

Glasscote, R., Gudeman, J., & Elpers, R. *Halfway houses for the mentally ill.* Washington, D. C.: The Joint Information Service of the American Psychiatric Association, 1971.

Grant, R., & Saslow, G. Maximizing responsible decision making, or how do we get out of here? In G. M. Abroms & N. S. Greenfields (Eds.), *The new hospital psychiatry.* New York: Academic Press, 1971.

Hays, W. L. *Statistics for psychologists.* New York: Holt, Rinehart and Winston, 1963.

Jones, M. *The therapeutic community: A new treatment method in psychiatry.* New York: Basic Books, 1953.

Kellam, S., Schmelzer, J., & Berman, A. Variations in the atmospheres of psychiatric wards. *Archives of General Psychiatry,* 1966, **14,** 561-570.

Kish, G. Evaluation of ward atmosphere. *Hospital and Community Psychiatry,* 1971, **22,** 159-161.

Likert, R. *The human organization: Its management and value.* New York: McGraw-Hill, 1967.

Magnusson, D., Gerzen, M., & Nyman, B. The generality of behavioral data. I. Generalization from observations on one occasion. *Multivariate Behavioral Research,* 1968, **3,** 295-320.

Manasse, G. Self-regard as a function of environmental demands in chronic schizophrenics. *Journal of Abnormal Psychology,* 1965, **70,** 210-213.

Mischel, W. *Personality and assessment.* New York: Wiley, 1968.

Moos, R. Sources of variance in responses to questionnaires and in behavior. *Journal of Abnormal Psychology,* 1969, **74,** 405-412.

Moos, R. *Revision of the Ward Atmosphere Scale* (WAS). (Tech. Rep.) Palo Alto, Calif.: Stanford University, Department of Psychiatry, Social Ecology Laboratory, 1971.

Moos, R. British psychiatric ward treatment environments. *British Journal of Psychiatry,* 1972, in press.

Moos, R., & Daniels, R. A social systems analysis of the treatment environments of two psychiatric wards. Palo Alto, Calif.: Stanford University, Department of Psychiatry, Social Ecology Laboratory, 1971.

Moos, R., & Houts, P. Assessment of the social atmospheres of psychiatric wards. *Journal of Abnormal Psychology,* 1968, 73, 595–604.

Moos, R., & Otto, J. The Community-Oriented Programs Environment Scale: A methodology for the facilitation and evaluation of social change. *Community Mental Health Journal,* 1972, in press.

Moos, R., & Petty, C. Treatment environment and treatment outcome: A replication. Palo Alto, Calif.: Stanford University, Department of Psychiatry, Social Ecology Laboratory, 1971.

Moos, R., & Schwartz, J. Treatment environment and treatment outcome. *Journal of Nervous and Mental Disease,* 1972, in press.

Moses, H. A. Halfway or more? *Rehabilitation Record,* 1969, 10, 35–37.

Murray, H. *Explorations in personality.* New York: Oxford University Press, 1938.

Pace, R. *College and University Environment Scales (CUES) Technical Manual.* (2nd ed.) Princeton, N. J.: Educational Testing Service, Institutional Research Program for Higher Education, 1969.

Pervin, L. Satisfaction and perceived self-environment similarity: A semantic differential study of student-college interaction. *Journal of Personality,* 1967, 35, 623–634.

Pierce, W., Trickett, E., & Moos, R. Changing ward atmosphere through staff discussion of the perceived ward environment. *Archives of General Psychiatry,* 1972, 26, 35–41.

Raush, H., & Raush, C. *The halfway house movement: A search for sanity.* New York: Appleton-Century-Crofts, 1968.

Stanton, A., & Schwartz, M. *The mental hospital.* New York: Basic Books, 1954.

Stern, G. *People in context.* New York: Wiley, 1970.

Trickett, E., & Moos, R. Satisfaction with the correctional institution environment: An instance of perceived self-environment similarity. *Journal of Personality,* 1971, in press.

30

Perceptions of and Reactions to Stressful Situations

DAVID MAGNUSSON and BO EKEHAMMAR

There is an implicit need for systematic analyses of situations in some well-known psychological theories, for example, in Murray's (1938) need-press theory and in Lewin's (e.g., 1951) field theory. The importance of situational analyses was clearly expressed on different grounds during the early 60s by Abelson (1962), Miller (1963), and Sells (1963a) among others. The emphasis on situational analyses increased in connection with the rapidly developing theoretical and empirical interest in the Person X Situation interaction (see Argyle & Little, 1972; Bowers, 1973; Endler, 1973; Endler & Hunt, 1968, 1969; Magnusson, Gerzén, & Nyman, 1968; Magnusson & Heffler, 1969; Pervin, 1968). From different standpoints researchers have recently advocated that the systematic study of situations is urgent (e.g., Endler, 1975b; Magnusson, 1971, 1974; Mischel, 1973; Schneider, 1973).

As was early stated by Kantor (1924), Koffka (1935), and Murray (1938), among others, a situation can be described in two main ways: by describing in *objective* terms the physical and social characteristics of the situation "as it is," and by describing it in terms of the *psychological* significance for the individual. The first of these approaches for empirically classifying situations has been advocated by Sells (1963b) and Sherif and Sherif (1969). However, most of the researchers mentioned above underline the importance of using the second approach, that is, studying the psychological significance of situations.

Systematic analyses of situations with regard to their psychological significance for individuals have two purposes: (a) the classification of situations (see Frederiksen, 1972; Moos, 1973; Sells, 1963b), and (b) the use of the Person X Situation interaction in the description and prediction of behavior (see

From the *Journal of Personality and Social Psychology,* 1975, *31,* 1147–1154. Copyright 1975 by the American Psychological Association. Reprinted by permission.

The study was supported by a research grant from the Swedish Council for Social Science Research to D. Magnusson for a research program on situation perception.

Professor Norman S. Endler, York University, Toronto, Canada, who was visiting professor at the laboratories during 1973–1974, has contributed with valuable comments on the manuscript.

Magnusson, 1971). According to the interactional view of behavior "individuals differ not mainly with regard to certain stable aspects of behavior but particularly regarding their specific, characteristic ways of adjusting to the varying characterisitcs of different situations" (Magnusson, 1971, p. 851). Thus the behavioral pattern of different reactions of individuals across situations of varying significance should be an important object for psychological research. Knowledge about the significance of the situations for the individual is a necessary condition for understanding and predicting individual behavior.

Two main approaches can be used for the empirical study of the psychological significance of situations, one based on individuals' *reactions* to the situations, the other based on individuals' *perceptions* of the situations.

In the reaction approach the individual might be instructed to rate his reaction, say the experienced degree of apprehensiveness (Hodges & Felling, 1970) or his degree of unpleasantness (Schalling, 1971) to a set of situations which are verbally presented to him. The data give individual reaction patterns across situations for the variable rated. For the classification of the situations, the correlations between situations are calculated and the correlation matrix can be treated with factor or cluster analysis.

A more subtle variation of this approach was first proposed by Endler, Hunt, and Rosenstein (1962) and was used in the construction of their S-R Inventory of Anxiousness. According to that technique the subjects rate their own reactions on a number of scales for each of a number of situations, thus yielding a three-dimensional data matrix. In addition to main effects these data contain information about the Person X Reaction X Situation interaction, as well as simple interactions between two main variables at a time. For the classification of situations, the correlations between situations can be calculated on the basis of the summed individual reaction scores for each situation and the matrix can be treated with factor or cluster analysis. This technique for classification has been used in studies on the Person X Situation interaction (see e.g., Ekehammar, Magnusson, & Ricklander, 1974; Endler et al., 1962). It was also employed in the present study.

The *perception* approach, using measures of individuals' perceptions of situations as raw data, was discussed by Magnusson (1971) who also proposed a method for the empirical study of situation perception. According to this method subjects are presented short, concrete descriptions of situations two at a time and instructed to judge the perceived similarity between the situations. For classifications of situations the obtained similarity matrix can be treated with multidimensional scaling techniques or cluster analytic methods, which are linked to a dimensional or a categorical model for cognitive functioning, respectively (see Bieri et al., 1966). A few studies which support the potentiality of the method have been made (Ekehammar & Magnusson, 1973; Magnusson, 1971; Magnusson & Ekehammar, 1973). It was also used in the present study. A study on the same problem, using different groups of subjects for perception and reaction data, was reported by Ekehammar, Schalling, and Magnusson (1975).

According to the interactional model actual behavior of an individual in a situation is the result of an interaction between the individual and the situation. It is reasonable to assume that it is the meaning or significance which the individual gives to the situation which is of importance for his behavior (see e.g., Raush, Dittmann, & Taylor, 1959). Furthermore, individuals differ with regard to the meaning they give to the same situation (Magnusson, 1974; Mischel, 1973). Data for situational meaning are treated in the perception approach. The reaction approach treats reactions to situations, that is, data refer to situational behavior. According to the assumptions made above, the individual's reaction in a certain situation is dependent upon his perception of the situation. Thus, a systematic relation can be expected between data for individuals' perceptions of a set of situations and data for their reactions to the same situations. Such a prediction was empirically tested in the present study. With the reasoning above in mind, *perception* data should be regarded as independent variables and *reaction* data as dependent variables in studies of the relation between the two kinds of data.

The Present Study

The main purpose of the present study was to investigate the relationship between situation perception data and situation reaction data. This was attained by comparing the outcomes of a classification of the same stressful situations using the two approaches discussed above.

For perception data the classification of situations was made by dimensional analysis of the mean similarity matrix, and for reaction data by factor analysis of the matrix for the correlations among situations. According to the assumptions made about the dependence of individual behavior on individual perception of the situations, the individual mean reaction scores should be more similar for situations which are perceived as similar than for situations which are perceived as less similar or not at all similar. Consequently, the matrix for the correlations between situations, based on individual mean reaction scores, should have the same main structure as the similarity matrix for perception data. Thus, the reaction and perception data were expected to give the same main grouping of the situations.

METHOD

Experimental Procedure

Inventory ratings and similarity estimates were collected during 2 hours of group testing. Two groups of subjects made their ratings separately but simultaneously. One group completed the inventory ratings (reactions) before giving the similarity ratings (perceptions), with an unrelated task (distractor) performed between these two ratings. For the second group the order of presentation was reversed. The time interval between the two types of ratings was about 30 minutes for both groups.

The Reaction Approach

Subjects. The subjects were 40 adolescents, 25 girls and 15 boys, from two ninth-grade classes of the compulsory unselected school system. The subjects had a mean age of about 16 years and can be regarded as fairly representative of their age group.

Inventory. A modified version of an "S-R inventory of anxiety" constructed by Magnusson and Ricklander and presented by Ekehammar et al. (1974) was employed. The present version comprised 12 situations and 10 reaction scales, selected on the basis of previous analyses of the inventory. The situations used here were chosen so as to cover four types of stressful situations, tentatively denoted "Threat of punishment," "Ego threat," "Threat of pain," and "Inanimate threat" in the earlier report. The reaction scales were selected so as to cover two types of anxiety reactions, tentatively denoted "Psychic anxiety" and "Somatic anxiety." In addition to the instruction page, the inventory consisted of 12 pages. At the top of each page a situation was formulated, and below were printed the 10 reactions, with their 5-point intensity scales.

Situations. The 12 verbally described situations of the inventory, grouped according to the a priori classification, are presented in Table 1. The order of presentation of situations was randomized among subjects.

Ratings. For each situation, the subjects were instructed to rate the intensity of their reactions on each of the 10 reaction scales. The ratings were given on a numerical 5-point scale ranging from "1—not at all" to "5—very much." The order of presentation of reaction scales was the same for each situation. The reactions assumed to indicate "Psychic anxiety" were: "1—Become nervous," "4—Get worried," "6—Get feelings of insecurity," "8—Get depressed," "10—Get feelings of panic." The reactions assumed to indicate "Somatic anxiety" were "2—Hands begin to shake," "3—Swallowing difficulties," "5—Heart beats faster," "7—Get in a sweat," "9—Get stomach trouble."

Method of analysis. Data were collapsed across reaction scales, and the Person X Situation matrix was analyzed. Product moment correlation coefficients were computed among the situation scales across subjects, and the correlation matrix was treated with principal components analysis. The factor matrix was orthogonally rotated to simple structure according to the varimax procedure. The number of factors to be rotated was chosen according to two criteria: (a) factors with eigenvalues greater than unity, and (b) the number of factors (four) expected from the a priori grouping were rotated. The eigenvalue criterion gave three factors which accounted for 72% of the total variance. The four-factor solution accounted for 78% of the total variance.

Table 1. Situations Grouped According to A Priori Classification

---

"Threat of punishment"

---

1. Have just been caught pilfering
2. Called to the headmaster for doing something forbidden
3. Discovered by a teacher when playing truant

"Threat of pain"

---

4. Going to have an injection that will hurt
5. Going to have a wound sewed up at the hospital
6. Wait at the dentist's to have a tooth pulled

"Inanimate threat"

---

7. Alone at home hearing someone try to get in
8. Got lost in the woods at nightfall
9. Alone in a desert cottage during a violent thunderstorm

"Ego threat"

---

10. Give an oral report before the class
11. Starting a summer job for the first time
12. Entering an athletic contest

The Perception Approach

Subjects. Similarity estimates were obtained from the same 40 subjects who took the reaction inventory.

Situations. The same 12 stressful situations used in the inventory approach were employed (see Table 1).

Ratings. The subjects were instructed to rate the degree of perceived similarity for each pair of situations on a numerical 5-point rating scale, ranging from "0—not at all similar" to "4—completely similar" (see Magnusson, 1971). The order of presentation of stimulus pairs was randomized among subjects.

Methods of analysis. Mean similarity estimates among situations across subjects were computed as arithmetic means of the individual similarity matrices. The mean similarity matrix was analyzed according to a multidimensional scaling methodology proposed by Ekman (e.g., 1965). The simplest variant of this method (cf. Ekehammar, 1972) was used here, by which the similarity estimates after linear transformation to a scale ranging from 0 to 1 are treated, in principle, as correlation coefficients. The same factorial procedure as described under the inventory approach was employed. The eigenvalue criterion (greater than 1) gave four factors in accordance with the expectations based on the a priori grouping (see Table 1). The four factors accounted for 67% of the total variance.

Overall Comparison of the Approaches

The main comparison between the two approaches was made by estimating the degree of congruence among corresponding situational factors obtained by the two kinds of data. This was accomplished by rotating the two factor structures to a common space according to a method proposed by Veldman (1967), which may be regarded as a target rotation procedure. In this case the four-factor solution based on the similarity estimation approach was used as the target in accordance with the view that the perception data is regarded as the independent variable in relation to the reaction data, as explained in the introduction. After rotation, two different measures were computed for the agreement between the loadings of corresponding factors in the two matrices: (a) product moment correlation coefficients and (b) coefficients of congruence (cf. Harman, 1967).

Comparison of Single Situations

More detailed comparisons between perception and reaction data were made for one situation at a time. Two different indices were employed for indicating the agreement of each situation's position in the perception and reaction spaces, respectively. The first index was based on the mean *similarity* matrix for perception data and the *correlation* matrix for reaction data. For each situation a correlation was calculated between the values of its row in the similarity matrix and the values of its row in the correlation matrix. Such a coefficient, for a certain situation, gives a rough indication of the similarity between the perception and the reaction matrices with respect to the target situation's distance from the other situations. Second, product moment correlation coefficients were calculated between corresponding rows (situations) of the *factor* matrices for perception and reaction data, respectively. The last index was computed on the factors after rotation to a common space.

RESULTS

The mean similarity matrix for perception data and the correlation matrix for reaction data are shown in Table 2. The similarity estimates are presented above the main diagonal and the correlation coefficients below.

Since the perception data were regarded as the independent variable, the factor matrix for the similarity data is reported first. The four situational perception factors, chosen on the basis of the eigenvalue criterion and rotated to

Table 2. Mean Similarity Estimates and Correlation Coefficients among Situations

Situation	1	2	3	4	5	6	7	8	9	10	11	12
1		57	46	21	24	20	24	21	19	26	24	27
2	70		62	24	23	23	26	26	19	30	26	29
3	62	70		22	23	20	22	19	19	30	21	26
4	40	38	31		58	59	26	24	26	32	18	26
5	62	56	46	72		63	29	25	23	30	23	31
6	38	46	49	46	50		25	23	16	28	19	25
7	66	52	44	47	62	25		43	41	19	16	19
8	56	55	35	32	51	18	62		53	21	14	24
9	42	42	08	31	54	11	49	61		23	15	24
10	42	50	44	40	51	47	36	33	12		41	34
11	67	78	57	54	64	40	50	52	50	43		33
12	58	45	49	41	65	36	58	42	41	36	58	

Note. Zeros and decimal points omitted. Mean similarity estimates are above the diagonal and correlation coefficients are below the diagonal.

varimax simple structure, are shown in Table 3. Using similarity data, the situations were distributed on factors according to the expectations based on the a priori grouping of the situations (see Table 1).

The three factors for reaction data chosen on the basis of the eigenvalue criterion and rotated to simple structure are reported in Table 4. The highest loadings of the situations for the first three a priori groupings were distributed on factors according to the expectations. However, the situations for the fourth a priori grouping (Situations 10, 11, and 12) did not form a factor of their own.

Table 3. Situational Factors Based on the Perception Approach Rotated to Simple Structure

	Factor				
Situation	I	II	III	IV	h^2
1. Caught pilfering	.76	.11	.13	.15	.63
2. Called to the headmaster	.85	.11	.14	.16	.77
3. Discovered playing truant	.81	.11	.10	.14	.69
4. Having an injection	.12	.80	.17	.14	.71
5. Having a wound sewed up	.12	.81	.16	.19	.74
6. At the dentist's	.11	.85	.09	.12	.76
7. Alone at home	.19	.20	.69	.04	.55
8. Got lost in the woods	.11	.11	.81	.11	.69
9. Alone in a desert cottage	.06	.07	.81	.16	.70
10. Give an oral report	.19	.21	.11	.71	.59
11. Starting a new job	.13	.05	.04	.82	.68
12. Athletics contest	.19	.18	.19	.61	.48

Note. Highest loading for each situation is italicized.

Table 4. Situational Factors Based on the Reaction Approach Rotated to Simple Structure

Situation	Factor			
	I	II	III	b^2
1. Caught pilfering	.64	.21	.55	.76
2. Called to the headmaster	.77	.20	.43	.81
3. Discovered playing truant	.88	.21	.12	.83
4. Having an injection	.05	.84	.32	.80
5. Having a wound sewed up	.24	.70	55	.86
6. At the dentist's	.46	.68	—.08	.69
7. Alone at home	32	.26	.70	.66
8. Got lost in the woods	.30	.05	.78	.70
9. Alone in a desert cottage	—.05	.13	.87	.77
10. Give an oral report	.50	.54	.06	.54
11. Starting a new job	.55	.35	.53	.71
12. Athletics contest	.36	.40	.51	.55

Note. Highest loading for each situation is italicized.

Situation 10 had its highest loading on Factor II, Situation 11 on Factor I, and Situation 12 on Factor III, and all these three situations had two loadings higher than .40.

In order to examine the congruence between the factor structures of perceptions and reaction data, the four-factor solutions were rotated to a common space with the similarity matrix as the target (see the Overall

Table 5. Situational Factors Based on the Reaction Approach Rotated to Maximum Agreement with the Factors from the Perception Approach

Situation	Factor				
	I	II	III	IV	b^2
1. Caught pilfering	.67	.22	.42	.31	.77
2. Called to the headmaster	.60	.08	.29	.65	.87
3. Discovered playing truant	.84	.21	—.04	34	.87
4. Having an injection	—.01	.80	.26	.31	.80
5. Having a wound sewed up	.23	.68	.46	.35	.85
6. At the dentist's	.27	.57	—.20	.51	.70
7. Alone at home	.44	.33	.62	.12	.70
8. Got lost in the woods	.24	—.02	.72	44	.77
9. Alone in a desert cottage	—.05	.08	.85	.29	.82
10. Give an oral report	.21	.35	—.05	.72	.69
11. Starting a new job	.47	.29	.42	.49	.72
12. Athletics contest	.55	.54	.42	—.05	.77

Note. Highest loading for each situation is italicized.

Table 6. Indices of Factorial Agreement between Corresponding Factors of the Perception and Reaction Data, Respectively

| | Agreement index | |
Factor	Coefficient of congruence	Product moment coefficient
I	.90	.78
II	.92	.84
III	.89	.76
IV	.69	.15

Comparison of the Approaches section above). The four-factor solution for reaction data rotated in this way is reported in Table 5.

Two different quantitative measures of the agreement between the two factor matrices rotated to maximum possible agreement were calculated as described in the Overall Comparison of the Approaches section above. The obtained indices are presented in Table 6. These results plus an inspection of Tables 4 and 5 indicate that the congruence between the two matrices was good for the first three factors, "Threat of punishment," "Threat of pain," and "Inanimate threat." For the fourth factor, containing situations which were supposed to be ego threatening in the a priori grouping, the congruence was lower. The correlation coefficient, mainly expressing the agreement between the two rank orders of factor loadings disregarding magnitude, was very low for the fourth factor. The two indices gave the same rank order of the factors with respect to agreement between the two types of data.

Two indices for the agreement of each situation's position in the perception and reaction space, respectively, were computed as described previously. The indices are presented in Table 7. For most of the situations the measures indicate a high agreement in positions in the two situational spaces. There are, however, some situations for which this does not hold. For Situations 11 ("Entering an athletic contest") and 12 ("Starting a summer job for the first time"), both measures show the poorest agreement. These two situations belong to the fourth a priori grouping of situations, supposed to be ego threatening, and they contribute heavily to the low agreement for the fourth situational factor (see Table 6) in the two kinds of data.

DISCUSSION

The expectations were that the situations should be distributed on factors in the same main way for situation *reaction* data as for situation *perception* data. For the first three factors, tentatively denoted "Threat of punishment," "Threat of pain," and "Inanimate threat," the congruence was very clear and the

Table 7. Product Moment Coefficietns for the Agreement between each Situation's Position in the Perception and Reaction Space, Respectively

Situation	Similarity matrix vs. correlation matrix	Factor matrix for perception data vs. factor matrix for reaction data
1	.56	.91
2	.59	.81
3	.67	.96
4	.59	.97
5	.20	.91
6	.46	.77
7	.27	.93
8	.51	.90
9	.50	.98
10	.43	.97
11	.06	.69
12	.06	.41

grouping of situations was as expected from the a priori groupings. These results support the use of the first three groupings of stressful situations in further research on anxiety. Especially in research on the Person X Situation interaction, empirically verified situational factors are of great importance.

The clear distribution of stressful situations on different factors both for situation perception data and for situation reaction data supports the conclusion that anxiety cannot be considered as one general factor but should be studied in a multidimensional space (Endler, 1975a).

For one of the a priori groupings, containing situations which were supposed to be ego threatening, the two kinds of data did not yield the same result. In the analysis of situation perception data these situations formed a separate factor as expected. When the eigenvalue criterion was applied in the analysis of situation reaction data only three factors were obtained, corresponding to the first three a priori groupings. The situations in the fourth a priori group were distributed on different factors, with rather high loadings on more than one factor. It is interesting to note that a similar difference in structure between situation perception and situation reaction data was obtained in the earlier study from which the situations for this study were selected (see Ekehammar et al., 1974). The situations for that study were initially selected on the basis of an analysis of situation perception data, which gave four main, expected situation factors. In the main study, which yielded only situation reaction data, three factors were obtained corresponding rather well to the ones in the present study for the same kind of data.

What then is the character of the situations in the fourth a priori grouping of situations, which were obtained in the analysis of the perception data but not in the analysis of the reaction data? A reasonable interpretation is that they all involve demand of achievement from the individual. In this respect they differ from all the other situations. If this is the most obvious similarity between these situations, and a characteristic feature not shared with the other ones, it seems reasonable that they form a homogeneous group in the analysis of situation perception data. This *situation perception factor* could be relabeled "Demands of Achievement."

In the introduction of this article reasons were given why we might expect a systematic relation between situation perception data and situation reaction data. Such a systematic relation data was also found for the first three a priori groupings of situations. The less clear factor structure for reaction data and the discrepancy in outcome for the fourth a priori grouping of situations lead, however, to a more nuanced view on the relation between the two kinds of data.

The discrepancy in outcomes for the fourth a priori grouping of situations may serve as a starting point for a tentative discussion on the relation between situation perception and situation reaction. From the reasons given above, it seems natural that the situations which have the common feature of demanding achievement, as distinguished from the other situations, formed one separate factor when the analysis was based on situation perception data. However, individuals obviously differ in their *reactions* to achievement demands. To some individuals such demands are challenging, to others anxiety provoking. The first kind of individual would probably seek achievement demanding situations and react actively and perhaps aggressively to them, while the second kind would react with avoidance and withdrawal. Thus, individuals' reactions may be different to a situation which they perceive similarly. This reasoning can explain the fact that we obtained a clear situation factor for perception data, which was not obtained for reaction data. It can also explain the generally less clear factor structure for reaction data than for perception data in the present study. The point is clearly seen for the achievement demanding situations but the same kind of reasoning also holds for other types of situations, to an extent which is dependent upon the character of the situations.

The basic conclusion of this discussion is that there is no necessary general systematic relationship between situation perception data and situation reaction data which is valid across individuals and across situations of different character. The consequence of this is that we have to proceed with research on both kinds of data. This conclusion has implications for the two kinds of problems which are crucial in the study of the psychological significance of situations: for the classification of situations and for the understanding and prediction of individual behavior in an interactionist frame of reference. (a) Even if there is a substantial agreement in factor structure between the two kinds of data, we have to distinguish clearly between situation *perception* factors and situation *reaction* factors in further research. Each of these factor structures needs to be investigated. The relationship between the two kinds of situational factors may be a fruitful subject for further research. (b) Obviously it is not always possible to predict an individual's reaction to a situation only from knowledge about perception of it. Individuals differ in reactions to a situation which they perceive similarly. These interindividual differences per se are of interest for further research. According to the interactionist view, what is characteristic for an individual is the specific multivariate pattern of reactions across situations that have different meanings for him. From the standpoint that the meaning of situations determines an individual's behavior, the specific, individual relationship between perception of and reaction to different situations should be an important subject for further research. A better knowledge about that relationship would contribute to a better understanding and a better prediction of individual behavior.

REFERENCES

Abelson, R. P. Situational variables in personality research. In S. Messick & J. Ross (Eds.), *Measurement in personality and cognition*. New York: Wiley, 1962.

Argyle, M., & Little, B. R. Do personality traits apply to social behaviour? *Journal for the Theory of Social Behaviour*, 1972, *2*, 1–35.

Bieri, J., Atkins, A. L., Briar, S. Leaman, R. L., Miller, H., & Tripodi, T. *Clinical and social judgment: The discrimination of behavioral information*. New York: Wiley, 1966.

Bowers, K. S. Situationism in psychology: An analysis and a critique. *Psychological Review*, 1973, *80*, 307–336.

Ekehammar, B. Multidimensional scaling according to different vector models for subjective similarity. *Acta Psychologica*, 1972, *36*, 79–84.

Ekehammar, B., & Magnusson, D. A method to study stressful situations. *Journal of Personality and Social Psychology*, 1973, *27*, 176–179.

Ekehammar, B., Magnusson, D., & Ricklander, L. An interactionist approach to the study of anxiety. *Scandinavian Journal of Psychology*, 1974, *15*, 4–14.

Ekehammar, B., Schalling, D., & Magnusson, D. Dimensions of stressful situations: A comparison between a response analytical and a stimulus analytical approach. *Multivariate Behavioral Research*, 1975, *10*, 155–164.

Ekman, G. Two methods for the analysis of perceptual dimensionality. *Perceptual and Motor Skills*, 1965, *20*, 557–572.

Endler, N. S. The person versus the situation—a pseudo issue? A response to Alker. *Journal of Personality*, 1973, *41*, 287–303.

Endler, N. S. A person-situation interaction model for anxiety. In C. D. Spielberger & I. G. Sarason (Eds.), *Stress and anxiety* (Vol. 1). Washington, D. C.: Hemisphere, 1975. (a)

Endler, N. S. The case for person-situation interactions. *Canadian Psychological Review*, 1975, *16*, 12–21. (b)

Endler, N. S., & Hunt, J. McV. S-R Inventories of Hostility and comparisons of the proportions of variance from persons, responses, and situations for hostility and anxiousness. *Journal of Personality and Social Psychology*, 1969, *9*, 309–315.

Endler, N. S., & Hunt, J. McV. Generalizability of contributions from sources of variance in the S-R Inventory of Anxiousness. *Journal of Personality*, 1969, *37*, 1–24.

Endler, N. S., Hunt, J. McV., & Rosenstein, A. J. An S-R Inventory of Anxiousness. *Psychological Monographs*, 1962, *76*, No. 17 (Whole No. 536).

Frederiksen, N. Toward a taxonomy of situations. *American Psychologist*, 1972, *27*, 114–123.

Harman, H. H. *Modern factor analysis* (2nd ed.). Chicago: University of Chicago Press, 1967.

Hodges, W. F., & Felling, J. P. Types of stressful situations and their relation to trait anxiety and sex. *Journal of Consulting and Clinical Psychology,* 1970, *34,* 333–337.

Kantor, J. R. *Principles of psychology* (Vol. 1). Bloomington, Ill.: Principia Press, 1924.

Koffka, K. *Principles of Gestalt psychology.* New York: Harcourt, 1935.

Lewin, K. *Field theory in social science.* New York: Harper & Row, 1951.

Magnusson, D. An analysis of situational dimensions. *Perceptual and Motor Skills,* 1971, *32,* 851–867.

Magnusson, D. The individual in the situation: Some studies on individuals' perception of situations. *Studia Psychologica,* 1974, *16,* 124–132.

Magnusson, D., & Ekehammar, B. An analysis of situational dimensions: A replication. *Multivariate Behavioral Research,* 1973, *8,* 331–339.

Magnusson, D., Gerzén, M., & Nyman, B. The generality of behavioral data: I. Generalization from observations on one occasion. *Multivariate Behavioral Research,* 1968, *3,* 295–320.

Magnusson, D., & Heffler, B. The generality of behavioral data: III. Generalization potential as a function of the number of observation instances. *Multivariate Behavioral Research,* 1969, *4,* 29–42.

Miller, D. R. The study of social relationships: Situation, identity, and social interaction. In S. Koch (Ed.), *Psychology: A study of a science* (Vol. 5). New York: McGraw-Hill, 1963.

Mischel, W. Toward a cognitive social learning reconceptualization of personality. *Psychological Review,* 1973, *80,* 252–283.

Moos, R. H. Conceptualizations of human environments. *American Psychologist,* 1973, *28,* 652–665.

Murray, H. A. *Explorations in personality.* New York: Oxford, 1938.

Pervin, L. A. Performance and satisfaction as a function of individual-environment fit. *Psychological Bulletin,* 1968, *69,* 56–68.

Raush, H. L., Dittmann, A. T., & Taylor, T. J. Person, setting, and change in social interaction. *Human Relations,* 1959, *12,* 361–378.

Schalling, D. Tolerance for experimentally induced pain as related to personality. *Scandinavian Journal of Psychology,* 1971, *12,* 271–281.

Schneider, D. J. Implicit personality theory: A review. *Psychological Bulletin,* 1973, *79,* 294–309.

Sells, S. B. An interactionist looks at the environment. *American Psychologist,* 1963, *18,* 696–702. (a)

Sells, S. B. Dimensions of stimulus situations which account for behavior variance. In S. B. Sells (Ed.), *Stimulus determinants of behavior.* New York: Ronald, 1963. (b)

Sherif, M., & Sherif, C. W. *Social psychology.* New York: Harper, 1969.

Veldman, D. J. *Fortran programming for the behavioral sciences.* New York: Holt, 1967.

CHAPTER SIX

CONTROVERSIES

This final chapter includes six papers that are concerned with some recent controversies in interactional psychology. These papers have implications with respect to theory, method, and research strategy for the field of personality. While providing no conclusive results, it is hoped that the issues raised by these papers will stimulate further personality research and theory.

The first selection, by Alker [31], emphasizes the importance of personality variables in explaining people's behavior, even though the behavior varies from situation to situation. He criticizes Mischel's emphasis on situations and suggests that individual differences are more important for behavior than situations. Furthermore, Alker suggests that individual difference variances are much more important for abnormal people than for normal people. Alker states that Mischel (1968, 1969) has underestimated the consistency of personality across different situations because he has ignored alternative measurement procedures. Alker claims that Mischel is biased in favor of social learning theory and against psychodynamic theory. Finally, Alker stresses that the moderator variable approach (see also Bem [32] and Endler [33]) represents a new paradigm for personality research and suggests that investigators attempt to determine person–situation interactions.

In the second selection, Bem [32] presents a conceptual reply to Alker and defends Mischel. Bem states that Alker's contention that Mischel has ignored factors that attenuate correlation coefficients is erroneous. Bem reiterates Mischel's (1968) position that although personality theories have been dominated by the assumption of cross-situational consistencies in behavior, i.e., the trait position, there is little empirical support for this position. The empirical results with respect to cross-situational consistencies have rarely yielded correlation coefficients above .30, i.e., accounting for about 10 percent or less of the variance in behavior. Bem suggests that perhaps we should start with the assumption that cross-situational correlations are zero (rather than one) until we can demonstrate otherwise. Finally, Bem emphasizes the importance of the moderator variable strategy and suggests how this might be used in studying person–situation interactions.

Endler [33], in the third selection, examines the issue of cross-situational consistency versus situational specificity. After reviewing the controversy historically and examining some of the empirical evidence, he rejects Alker's claim that personality variables are a major source of behavioral variance. Endler suggests that the person versus situation issue has been phrased in such a way so as to make it a pseudo-issue. He examines Alker's claim that abnormal and normal people constitute two distinct populations and provides empirical evidence to disprove this and to indicate that the person–situation interaction is an important source of variance. Finally, Endler discusses various research strategies with respect to personality and suggests why he believes an interactionist approach is preferable to other strategies.

Wallach and Leggett [34], the fourth selection, criticize the moderator variable approach, indicate the inconsistent results it has produced, and point out that most of the predictions using this approach have been *post hoc*. They suggest that one should look for consistency in behavior and its products, and present evidence that they interpret as supporting the consistency position. However, Endler, in his paper [33] contends that the Wallach and Leggett study neither supports the consistency position nor the situational specificity position.

The Wachtel [35] and the Mischel [36] papers, the fifth and sixth selections, are concerned with the person–situation controversy as it applies to psychodynamic theories. Wachtel, supporting the psychodynamic viewpoint, proposes that inconsistent phenotypic responses can be explained by underlying genotypic personality structures. He also suggests that a person influences and selects his situational encounters *and* that situations influence persons. Wachtel also states that behavioral theorists (situationists) have been primarily concerned with normal populations and experimental methods, whereas psychodynamic (trait) theorists have been primarily concerned with abnormal populations, and observational and clinical methods. Furthermore, he criticizes the experimental strategy because it structures the situation for the subject, and therefore limits the manner in which the person may structure his environment prior to responding. Wachtel believes that it is possible to integrate the psychodynamic and behavioral approaches.

Mischel [36] rejects Wachtel's contention about a possible integration. He accuses Wachtel of diverting attention from the basic issues confronting psychodynamic theorists and behaviorists, and of focusing on irrelevant theoretical issues. Mischel believes that psychodynamic and behavior theories differ in several fundamental ways, including methods, techniques, criteria, data they attempt to interpret, and the content they focus on. Finally, Mischel suggests some possible links between behavioral approaches and existential–phenomenological approaches.

Wachtel (1973) has subsequently answered Mischel's [36] charges. Citing Mischel's own research as evidence, Wachtel has indicated that it is not perpetuating "inaccurate stereotypes" to distinguish between the ambiguous interpersonal and affective events, which have been the major concern of psychodynamic theorists, and the more clear-cut and readily identifiable stimuli and responses, which have been prominent in social learning research. Wachtel cites research to indicate that there is no clear basis for concluding that behavioral methods of treatment or assessment are superior to psychodynamic methods when one is concerned with complex clinical problems or interpersonal events. He suggests that in lumping psychodynamic and trait approaches under the "trait–state" label, Mischel had earlier (1968) implied that behavioral specificity was damaging to psychodynamic theories. Wachtel is gratified that "Mischel now feels that data indicative of situational specificity in behavior presents no problems for psychodynamic theories" (p. 539). Mischel (1973), in answering Wachtel's reply, denies that his views on this topic have changed. Mischel both earlier (1968) and in 1973 has not claimed that the basic challenge to psychodynamic theories derives from the research data on situational specificity. Instead, Mischel stresses that "the most important challenge to psychodynamic clinical applications comes from the failure of psychodynamic clinicians to show convincingly the utility of their own diagnostic and therapeutic work (see Mischel, 1968, Chapter 5)" (p. 541, 1973). Wachtel (1973) states that the question as to whether the psychodynamic and behavioral approaches can be integrated is primarily an empirical question. Mischel (1973) states that efforts to integrate the two approaches will not succeed unless "the empirical issues are faced without distortion" (p. 541).

REFERENCES

Mischel, W. *Personality and assessment.* New York: Wiley, 1968.

Mischel, W. Continuity and change in personality. *American Psychologist,* 1969, *24,* 1012–1018.

Mischel, W. Facing the issues. *Journal of Abnormal Psychology,* 1973, *82,* 541–542.

Wachtel, P. L. On fact, hunch and stereotype: A reply to Mischel. *Journal of Abnormal Psychology,* 1973, *82,* 537–540.

31

Is Personality Situationally Specific or Intrapsychically Consistent?

HENRY A. ALKER

This paper advances the claim that personality variables can explain peoples' behavior even though that behavior varies from situation to situation. The argument is developed in the course of a critique of several interpretative reviews of personality research (Mischel, 1968, 1969). Mischel asserts that the hypothesis that persons exhibit large trans-situational consistencies in their behavior is simply and generally not supported by the available data. According to Mischel, the unenlightened proponents of trans-situational personality consistency include nonprofessional users of ordinary language trait names such as "aggressive," "honest" and "friendly" who reify these attributions. Dynamic personality theorists who speak of some "inner" or intrapsychic features of personality such as "ego strength" or "defensiveness," are likewise void of convincing empirical support. Both of Mischel's opponents are purportedly committed to the view that response constancies will emerge in spite of situational variation.

In the course of the argument presented here the claim will be made that situational specificity of response itself is a personality variable. Mischel's assertion is thus regarded as a proposition that ultimately is a misleading summary of previous findings and an abortive guide for future personality research. The near-sighted misuse of certain standards of measurement validity has obscured this point. Judgments about the worth of "intrapsychic" theories have also been biased in the process.

From H. A. Alker, "Is Personality Situationally Specific or Intrapsychically Consistent?" *Journal of Personality*, 1972, *40*, 1–16. Reprinted by permission of the Publisher. Copyright 1972, Duke University Press, Durham, North Carolina.

Gratitude must be expressed to Kenneth Craik and Judy Regan for their extensive and constructive reviews of earlier drafts of this paper. Remaining errors in the argument reflect only the obdurate perseveration of the author.

THE RELEVANCE OF PERSONALITY COEFFICIENTS

The evidence of situational specificity comes according to Mischel from a variety of sources. Each of these sources provides data which demonstrate that the same person makes different responses in different situations. Among these sources of evidence for situational specificity is the abundance in the literature of what Mischel calls "personality coefficients." These coefficients are correlations between responses made in different situations by the same person and are typically in the .2 or .3 range. As such these coefficients constitute very weak evidence for response constancy. The resulting proportion of variance explained by the personality characteristic exhibited by these response constancies is simply trivial. Even these minimal correlations often reflect shared method rather than shared trait variance. Response sets and other artifacts inflate these correlations. Among such artifacts are the intuitive personality theories of raters who make clinical judgments to the effect that the same trait is exemplified by behaviors in different settings. These ratings constitute invalid evidence for response constancy and only obscure the variation in behavior due to situational factors. Mischel's perspective is extended to the multivariate case.

Patterns of intercorrelations among a set of responses frequently provide no comfort, in Mischel's view, for the proponent of personality psychology. Factor analytic studies such as that of Vannoy (1965) on measures of cognitive complexity and Burton (1963) on measures of honesty have shown, for example, response constancies specific to only a few highly similar assessment situations. General factors, if any are found, account for small amounts of observed variance. Inspecting raw correlation matrices renders this outcome unsurprising. There is little initial common variance to be explained. Slovic (1962) has commented, for example, on the paucity of intercorrelation among measures of "risk taking." Weinstein (1969) tells the same story about various measures in the domain of achievement orientation. If measures of a presumed common trait are virtually specific to a particular assessment situation, no convincing argument could be given, it would seem to Mischel, that that trait will be of any general explanatory or predictive value.

The most directly relevant data concerning the situational specificity versus the trans-situational generality of personality come from well designed comparative studies of these two classes of variables. Obviously this evidence is superior to that which shows only that the same kind of person makes different kinds of responses in different situations. Mischel's argument, in so far as it is based on the multitude of small "personality coefficients," does not allow generalization to result from a full factorial design of personality and situational variables. Specifically, it might be discovered that even though situation effects are stronger than personality effects, interaction effects may be stronger than both.

COMPARATIVE STUDIES OF PERSON
VERSUS SITUATION

Some studies are available that fit these specifications. Endler, Hunt and Rosenstein (1962) in a study of variance in responses to an anxiety questionnaire find 11 times the amount of variance attributable to situation effects as is accounted for by individuals. Mischel, who cites this study, does not mention a reanalysis of the data (Endler and Hunt, 1966) which suggests that the interaction between individuals and situations is a larger source of variance than either considered separately. Endler and Hunt in this and a later publication (1968) develop the argument that interactions such as this one as well as interactions with modes of response constitute the bulk of the variance in the assessment of behavior. Modes of response involve such variables as sweating in a threatening situation rather than feeling uneasy. This study hardly can provide any conclusive data on the matter, however, because its data is all from self reports.

Moos (1969) overcomes this defect in what must qualify as the most definitive study to date on the problem of personality and situationally specific responses. He collected both paper and pencil self reports and observational data. Moos used questionnaire self rating measures covering aspects of perceived worth, affiliation and mood. He also measured simple observed behaviors such as smiling, nodding yes, smoking and body movements. Setting differences included lunch, therapy, free time and intake interview. Personality differences and situation differences each account for less variance than personality-situation interactions. In the Moos study no case can be made for the interaction term being an artifact of self report procedures. Comparable results are obtained with descriptive observational data.

The use of a hospitalized psychiatric population in this study may limit the generality of its findings. One might obtain systematically different results with other (equally atypical) subjects such as college sophomores. A tantalizing clue in this connection is the replication in the study by Moos of his findings on subjects judged ready to leave the mental hospital. These subjects again confirmed the superiority of personality-situation interactions as the largest single source of variance. Situation effects, however, are clearly larger for this nearer to "normal" subject population than simple personality effects. Further consistent evidence is provided by a study of psychiatric staff (Moos & Daniels, 1967). For this population, setting effects were larger than person differences. Person-setting interaction is, again, the single largest source of variance. Mischel does not qualify his thesis concerning situational specificity in terms of any other individual difference variable. That such a distinction is warranted and perhaps even crucial for personality theory will be argued below.

At this point we might reconsider the issue of situation versus individual difference variance as it bears on the larger issue of situational specificity vs. intrapsychic consistency. The data from Moos suggest that two general hypotheses are tenable. Firstly, the comparison of situation-determined variance with individual difference variance is not invariably a victory for situation effects. Secondly, it is not the case, as Endler and Hunt (1966) have argued, that a contest between personologists and experimental social psychologists on this simple matter is lacking in substantive importance. Differences in the outcome of this comparison may correspond to differences in two distinct populations that have served historically to generate personality theory and research. The first population includes hospitalized or severely disturbed individuals who most likely would be seen in clinical contexts that generated the classical dynamic theories of Freud, Erikson and their followers. The second population, admittedly an overlapping one with the first, includes individuals more basically sensitive to situational variation. Such individuals more probably correspond to the subjects in sophomore psychology classes who have generated much of the data on situational specificity Mischel cites. These populations may be said to differ on rather basic personality variables.

The data from these studies also suggest that arguments about intrapsychic consistency might be more fruitful if they are conducted in terms of personality-situation interactions. Contrasts between "dynamic" intrapsychic theories and their social learning counterparts may turn on their relative effectiveness in explaining these interactions. Some elaboration of the distinctive advantages of the dynamic theories, in this connection, will be discussed below. Firstly, some comments on more productive ways of delineating the size of personality and situation main effects must be considered. Without some accuracy on this significant matter, arguments concerning the resulting interactions may be singularly inconclusive.

MEASURING PERSONALITY VARIABLES ACROSS SITUATIONS

In the process of arguing that personality coefficients are somehow too small, Mischel ignores many factors attenuating the size of these coefficients. Our attention will be limited to considerations which follow from an attempt to take the notion of intrapsychic consistency seriously. Firstly, personality coefficients are obviously severely limited by the restriction of range. Carlson (1971) has documented the poverty of subject populations employed in current personality research. She does not point out, however, that virtually no studies employ heterogeneous populations deliberately selected to yield a proper estimate of the magnitude of effect resulting from personality variables. Such restrictions may affect the size of personality effects as compared with situation effects. Our consideration of different populations who may vary in the degree of their psychopathology comprises a case in point. No studies estimating situation versus personality effects have ever combined disturbed and "normal" samples, for instance, in the same design for the explicit purpose of overcoming this under-estimation problem. Anyone taking seriously the importance of intrapsychic organization and disorganization would obviously want to see the full range of variation in this individual difference variable included in research that supposedly demonstrates intrapsychic features of personality are of negligible empirical significance. Even Moos might profitably have included both patients and staff in the same analyses.

A further approach to the detection of substantial variance attributable to the intrapsychic organization of personality is found in a paper by Opton and Lazarus (1967). They report a series of personality coefficients above the .2–.3 range. These values are found by using ipsative rather than normative measurement of response to two different stress situations. Normative measures of heart rate, skin conductance and anxiety yielded in this study no more significant correlations with a large set of personality test items than would be expected by chance. Ipsative analyses, however, were markedly more successful. Determining whether the same person responded, for example, with a faster heart rate to the first stressor (a harrowing accident film) than to a second stressor (threat of electric shock) yielded many significant personality coefficients. Here the importance of intrapsychic organization, that is the relation between responses of the same individual, is no longer underestimated. Many of the individual items in these analyses, of course, were in the .2 or .3 range of magnitude. Opton and Lazarus, however, combine the items into composite scales that easily exceed this range.

The combination of different responses of the same individuals is a time honored method of incrementing the magnitude of predictions about those individuals. For some reason Mischel does not consider this approach. In particular the complete neglect of multiple regression techniques for predicting socially significant behaviors with a magnitude of more than .2 or .3 is surprising. Gough (1966) is one of many practitioners in this area. The use of personality inventories rather than individual personality tests measuring one trait naturally lends itself to this method of analysis—a point also overlooked in Mischel's review. One cannot fault personality researchers concerned with intrapsychic organization for using measures of more than one feature of personality for predicting behavior. Their focus, by definition, must be multivariate. Admittedly, such analyses are normative rather than ipsative. Intrapsychic analysis need not be limited to the ipsative perspective. The focus is rather on the total personality.

Meltzer, Hayes, and Shellenberger (1967) illustrate another productive approach to the problem of prediction with individual differences. Their data, physically defined parameters of speech amplitude, interruption, and silence, exemplify those preferred by Mischel for behavioral assessment. These variables measured in a series of group discussions with changing participants and changing topics failed to show any simple trans-situational generality. The same individual in one situation might talk loudly while in another he would almost whisper. Meltzer, et al., did a further analysis, however, in which the *relative* position of each person in his initial group discussion was used as the measure of interest. The resultant score exhibited consistencies of a .5 magnitude across situations. This relative score was defined by simply computing the ratio of the person's amplitude, for instance, to the sum of amplitudes for every person (including himself) in the group. Interpersonal perspectives on personality can discover useful invariances across situations with the same data others might use only to document situational specificity.

At this point the reader may insist that a distinction must be drawn between problems of personality trait designation and problems of trans-situational response constancy. One might insist that trans-situational trait constancy is demonstrated only by the same concretely specified response occurring in different situations. The personality psychologist concerned with the "intra-psychic consistency" of personality thinks differently. He develops concepts that involve aggregations of numerous person X situation interactions. When forced to argue only about specific responses, his point is that interactions are prevalent. A soldier, for example, ordinarily expresses his aggressiveness towards the enemy differently than he would be aggressive with his wife. Only a probably deranged individual in such circumstances would booby trap his wife's hairbrush. If one demands, however, that concrete response constancy in this form must occur if trait psychology is to avoid reliance on intuitive personality theory, nothing more than a metaphysical bias has been shown.

It is the latitude in defining what constitutes the same response which also determines one's evaluation of the situational specificity thesis. Flexibility on this matter, which certainly is the rule for trait concepts in ordinary language, allows a simple conclusion. Personality characteristics may be revealed in a variety of situations by different behaviors exemplifying the same trait. One can be conscientious, for example, by reading all assignments twice in the library but not by listening to all remarks twice in the same classroom. In such terms personality consistency would be demonstrated by making different responses in different situations. If, on the other hand, one narrowly defines a class of same response, then interaction is the order of the day. Moos exemplifies this approach with smiling and talking, for example, being categorized as different responses. In appropriate situations either smiling or talking could constitute legitimate aspects of an attribution that one was, for instance, friendly. Precluding any latitude of definition must bias the outcome of comparisons of personality versus situation. Such a prohibition is accomplished by misapplying a standard of convergent validity.

CONVERGENT VALIDITY AND RESPONSE GENERALITY

Mischel confuses the issue of convergent validity with the issue of the generality of personality traits. "Validity . . . requires convergence between responses to maximally different independent stimulus condition or measures

(1968, pp. 13—14)." This statement is tantamount to asserting a direct antithesis between trait psychology and any instance of limited response generalization. Personality psychology does not need this pseudoconflict. The conceptual equivalence of two measures is not the same as their functional equivalence (Stephens and Crowne, 1965). Strong correlations between two measures may establish their functional equivalence or substitutability in a particular setting. This is a simple problem of convergent validity. Conceptual equivalence of measures in widely dissimilar settings does not require such correlations. Both particular responses may be logically appropriate instantiations of a given construct and in that sense be conceptually equivalent. A deductive relation from a higher order concept to a particular instantiation would not, on the other hand, be a matter of convergent validity. One would not claim, for instance, that a personality inventory measure of neuroticism was subject to a failure of convergent validity if it correlated only in the .2 or .3 range with forgetting a word dealing with a purported conflict area such as sex, dependency or aggression. A correlation between hostility expressed on a sociometric rating and in interview might be more appropriate for convergent validation. The point expressed here is that in the obvious case of deduction from a more aggregated concept to the situationally specific instance, construct validation rather than convergent validation is at issue. Even Campbell and Fiske (1959) in their classic paper on construct validity obscure this point. Convergent validity does not merit methodological primacy when convergent invalidity is demonstrated by the presence of negligible correlations between several measures that somebody thinks for no good reason at all are functionally equivalent. In this manner one rotten measure of a given trait must ruin a barrel of acceptable measures.

Even in the case of measures at the same level of aggregation, no demand for convergent validation is always or even frequently logically warranted. Block (1968) has pointed out a number of constructs qualifying any simple prediction of personality consistency. Assuming the prevalence of personality-situation interaction, one cannot conclude that the same personality trait is being measured in different assessment situations by apparently similar responses. This question should be settled before the issue of measure substitutability in either or both situations arises. Creativity, for example, could hardly be demonstrated by monotonously indicating divergent thinking on any and all occasions with any and all materials. Intercorrelational studies such as that of Slovic (1962) and Weinstein (1969) are perhaps equally insensitive to this point. Factor analytic studies not based on an assumption of logical comparability, as might be provided by Guttman's facet analysis (1959), are equally negligent.

Gulliksen (1968) has discussed a number of multidimensional approaches to measure equivalence. For concepts lacking logically explicit comment on expected situational interaction, these inductive approaches may have some heuristic value. For personality traits embodying interaction or situational implications, convergent validation is not lacking simply because some workers have labelled different measures obtained in different situations with different samples as measures of the same trait. A full-blown example of this argument will be provided below in the discussion of a new paradigm for personality research. Now we shall turn to the last of the arguments against Mischel's situational specificity thesis.

BIASED COMPETITION BETWEEN PERSONALITY THEORIES

Taft (1960) analyzed the issue by theorist matrix taken from the first edition of Hall and Lindzey's classic personality text (1957). The most prominent dimension of personality theorist dispute identified pitted learning approaches versus dynamic-purposive theorists. This dimension was defined with a loading of .97 for the issue of purposive organization of personality. The argument about this competition advanced here is that Mischel's methodological concerns tend to prejudge this issue in favor of (social) learning approaches. As the exposition of substantive behavior modification approaches occupies the latter portion of the monograph (1968) in which the methodological views discussed here occur, this claim should not be surprising.

Winter (1968) provides a typical and useful illustration of consistency from the dynamic or purposive point of view. Two clusters of correlated indices are reported for a construct, the need for power. One cluster represents realized social power. Persons high in the motive for power tend to join more organizations and to become officers of these organizations. The other cluster describes a "stud" syndrome consisting of such variables as reading Playboy, watching Mission Impossible, displaying many credit cards, and owning a well stocked bar. These two clusters themselves are uncorrelated with each other.

My claim is that we have no evidence here for either the merely situational specificity of personality or the absence of convergent validity. Goals such as power may be striven for in different ways. Situational conditions certainly will influence the extent and success of goal directed activity. But these variables, which are not specifically included in Winter's analyses, interact with the motive at issue. A factor or other multidimensional analysis would not discredit this claim simply because different dimensions emerge. Nor does the total lack of correlations between two relevant indicators support a claim concerning convergent *in*validity. In fact one could claim the presence of genuinely alternative paths to the gratification of a given motive constituted construct validation for a basic feature of a purposively organized response system. Brunswick's representation of purposively organized response (1955), cited by Winter, argues this point in a more elaborate manner that explicitly requires situational variation. A fundamental antithesis of S-R units as units of analysis is developed in Brunswick's classic analysis.

A NEW PARADIGM FOR PERSONALITY RESEARCH

Following Kuhn (1962) one can raise at this point the question whether a new paradigm for personality research is available. Such a paradigm would put issues of situational specificity, trans-situational consistency, and convergent validity in a new, concrete perspective. Paradigms serving this purpose must combine methodological innovation to counter the strictures of older paradigms obscuring substantive discoveries. It is suggested here that the work of Kogan and Wallach (1964, 1967) on rational versus irrational risk taking constitutes just such a paradigmatic example.

This work features an apparently flagrant violation of Mischel's version of convergent validity. Kogan and Wallach commenced their investigation of risk taking with intercorrelations of miscellaneous risk taking measures. Results conformed to an expectation following from Slovic's work (1962) in this area. Intercorrelations of what might be taken to be measures of the same trait, namely, risk taking, were negligible. However, using a complex moderator analysis Kogan and Wallach exposed the folly of this conclusion. Test-taking anxiety and a defensive need for social approval were used as moderator variables. Persons exhibiting large amounts of both these characteristics were analyzed as a separate subpopulation from persons exhibiting both minimal test-taking anxiety and defensive need for social approval. Convergent "validity" correlations of various risk taking measures were then computed for each subpopulation separately. This multivariate approach based on two patterns of interrelated "intrapsychic" traits produced a surprising result. For the high anxiety-high defensive individuals (called irrational risk takers) substantial inter-correlations emerged. These individuals were consistently risky or consistently conservative regardless of the tasks at hand. For the low anxiety-low defensive individuals (called rational risk takers), on the other hand, typically minute or nonexistent correlations between risk taking measures emerged. Surely one does not want to conclude from this analysis that the notion of irrational risk taking possesses convergent validity while the notion of rational risk taking does not.

The paradigmatic features of this finding include, firstly, a demonstration of rich person-situation interaction. In this case it is purported situational specificity of personality that is itself the dependent variable. Persons fitting the specificity view comprise the less disturbed subpopulation—low anxiety and low de-fensiveness. Persons disconfirming this view are more motivationally disturbed. The independent variables explaining the varying situational specificity are personality variables.[1]

One might speculate here that the disturbed group resembles persons seen in therapy who provided the original data for dynamic theorists such as Freud, Jung, Fromm, Erikson and others. These theorists have derived from their experience with clinical populations concepts referring to subtle forms of personality consistency. Such populations, to be sure, might plausibly be assumed

---

[1] No denial is offered of the claim that situational variables also affect the emission of response consistency. Placing persons in a stressful evaluative setting might have a powerful effect in this connection. My claim is only that such a manipulation would probably interact with characteristics of the population studied.

to have exhibited high-self-perceived anxiety and a tendency to seek social reassurance in a way that is ordinarily self-defeating or defensive. In such circumstances psychotherapists might be particularly sought after instead of one's ordinary circle of friends. Persons with more minimal conflict might typify somewhat more closely the subject population drawn from introductory psychology classes. Such populations, as has been noted, are often used to generate evidence for situational specificity. Of particular note here also is the range of persons included in the same analysis. With such a range, personality variables are seen as antecedents of whether or not one makes situationally specific responses. Apparently the irrational risk takers ignore situational differences in their troubled and self-defeating search for approval. Rational risk takers on the contrary are most responsive to cognitive features of particular tasks. The parallel with Moos's (1969) report of diminished personality effects and increased situation effects in hospitalized patients judged ready for reentry to society, and in psychiatric staff as compared with patients, may not be accidental.

Additionally paradigmatic in this research is the conceptualization that does not demand meaningless interresponse correlation. In the tradition of Jessor and Hammond (1957), logical analysis of the personality variables involved determines the conceptual relevance of these findings to the related higher-order constructs. Prior to the question of convergent validity one must ask why similar responses are expected on dissimilar risk-taking tasks. Irrational risk takers seeking desperately to vindicate their choices as desirably cautious or desirably daring might be expected to generalize their aspirational strategy across a set of superficially similar tasks. Rational risk takers with their cognitive orientation towards successful outcomes regardless of risk strategy are different. Calling for a generalized risky or conservative strategy from these individuals on a variety of tasks is simply unreasonable. Such a strategy could easily be self-defeating as the tasks vary in their familiarity, difficulty and subjective pay off expectations.

Further aspects of the Kogan-Wallach research illustrate the points developed in the preceding arguments. The systematic regularities in these data are observed by a multivariate strategy in which considering only one personality variable such as defensiveness or anxiety in isolation is not illuminating. In addition the shift from a highly aggregated form of behavior sampled by the paper and pencil questionnaires to a set of concrete behavioral responses does not discredit the utility of the former approach. In Kogan and Wallach's data there is, in fact, essentially no correlation between the paper and pencil defined personality types and concrete riskiness or specific conservatism. Patterns of correlation among the behavioral measures constitute construct validation.

The fact, in conclusion, that the rational group exhibits a purposively organized, reason-determined choice of different responses, as the situation warrants, adds to the appeal of this paradigm. Responses in the service of the same goal need not be intercorrelated. Their communality resides in having the same consequences, not the same antecedent. Irrational risk takers' behavior on the other hand appears more purposively disorganized. They exhibit the rigid response generalization across situations that Mischel regards as an acceptable instance of convergent validity of a trait concept. This contrast between purposively organized and purposively disorganized behavior is central to dynamic personality theories. Freud's distinction between primary and secondary process is another paradigmatic instance of this point. This contrast between purposive organization and disorganization is obscured in most social learning approaches. Without such a contrast dynamic personality psychology is robbed of its potentially most valuable contribution to humanistic psychology. A focus on matters such as who one really is, i.e., matters of intrapsychic consistency, loses its meaning. It is precisely the sense of personal identity resulting from one's purposeful interactions with the environment over time that gives empirical meaning to identity questions. Personality variables have status as independent variables interacting with environmental change in spite of Mischel's preoccupation with their status as dependent variables. To be is certainly not to be merely a consequence of a manipulated situational change.

One might agree, as a concession to Mischel, that speaking of these two kinds of risk takers simply in terms of two different traits obfuscates the importance of situational factors. Tyler in the conclusion of her book (1965) on individual differences and personality suggests that "strategies" replace "traits" as units of analysis in personality psychology. Such a conceptual innovation renders the Kogan-Wallach approach even more paradigmatic as an example of a constructive approach to the problem of personality and situational specificity. An even more salutary effect of Mischel's critique would be a redirection of attention away from monotrait approaches. That attention should go not to the study of particular responses but rather to the study of persons.

SUMMARY

Mischel's claims concerning the situational specificity of personality (1968, 1969) are examined and rejected. The facts of situational specificity used to support Mischel's argument supported only the claim that the same person or the same kind of person makes different responses in different situations. This generalization (a) ignores the interaction of persons and situations, (b) under-estimates personality consistency across situations by ignoring alternative measurement procedures, (c) begs questions concerning what constitutes the same response in studies of convergent validity, and (d) biases a comparison between social learning and dynamic purposive approaches to personality in favor of the former view. A new paradigm for personality research is suggested which overcomes these objections. This framework incorporates facts of situational specificity into a more general contrast between purposively organized and purposively disorganized personalities.

REFERENCES

Block, J. Some reasons for the apparent inconsistency of personality. *Psychological Bulletin,* 1968, **70,** 210-212.

Brunswick, E. Representative design & probabilistic theory in functional psychology. *Psychological Review,* 1955, **62,** 193-217.

Burton, R. V. Generality of honesty reconsidered. *Psychological Review,* 1963, **78,** 481-499.

Campbell, D. T., & Fiske, D. W. Convergent and discriminant validation by the multi-trait multi-method matrix. *Psychological Bulletin,* 1959, **56,** 81-105.

Carlson, Rae. Where is the person in personality research? *Psychological Bulletin,* 1971, **75,** 203-219.

Endler, N. S., Hunt, J. McV., & Rosenstein, A. J. An S-R inventory of anxiousness. *Psychological Monographs,* 1962, **76,** (Whole No. 356).

Endler, N. S., & Hunt, J. McV. Sources of behavioral variance as measured S-R Inventory of Anxiousness. *Psychological Bulletin,* 1966, **65,** 336-346.

Endler, N. S., & Hunt, J. McV. S-R inventories of hostility and comparisons of the proportions of variance from persons, responses, and situations for hostility and anxiousness. *Journal of Personality and Social Psychology,* 1968, **9,** 309-315.

Gough, H. G. Appraisal of social maturity by means of the CPI. *Journal of Abnormal Psychology,* 1966, **71,** 189-195.

Gulliksen, H. Methods for determining equivalence of measures. *Psychological Bulletin,* 1968, **70,** 534-544.

Guttman, L. Introduction to facet design and analysis. In *Proceedings of fifteenth international congress of psychology* [Brussels, 1957]. Amsterdam: North Holland Publishing, 1959.

Hall, C. S., & Lindzey, G. *Theories of personality.* New York: Wiley, 1957.

Jessor, R., & Hammond, K. R. Construct validity and the Taylor anxiety scale. *Psychological Bulletin,* 1957, **54,** 161-170.

Kogan, N., & Wallach, M. A. *Risk taking.* New York: Holt, Rinehart, and Winston, 1964.

Kogan, N., & Wallach, M. A. Risk taking as a function of the situation, the person, and the group. In *New directions in psychology III.* New York: Holt, Rinehart, and Winston, 1967.

Kuhn, T. S. *The structure of scientific revolutions.* Chicago: University of Chicago Press, 1962.

Meltzer, L., Hayes, D. T., & Shellenberger, O. Consistency of vocal behavior in discussion. Paper presented at meetings of the American Psychological Association, 1967, Washington, D.C.

Mischel, W. *Personality and assessment.* New York: Wiley, 1968.

Mischel, W. Continuity and change in personality. *American Psychologist,* 1969, **24,** 1012-1018.

Moos, R. H. Sources of variance in responses to questionnaires and in behavior. *Journal of Abnormal Psychology,* 1969, **74,** 405-412.

Moos, R. H., & Daniels, D. Differential effects of ward settings on psychiatric staff. *Archives of General Psychiatry,* 1967, **17,** 75-83.

Opton, E. M., Jr., & Lazarus, R. S. Personality determinants of psychophysiological response to stress: A theoretical analysis and an experiment. *Journal of Personality and Social Psychology,* 1967, **65,** 291-303.

Slovic, P. Convergent validation of risk taking measures. *Journal of Abnormal and Social Psychology,* 1962, **65,** 68-70.

Stephens, M. W., & Crowne, D. P. Correction for attenuation and the equivalence of tests. *Psychological Bulletin,* 1965, **62,** 210-213.

Taft, R. A statistical analysis of personality theories. *Acta Psychologica,* 1960, **17**, 8–88.

Tyler, L. *The psychology of human differences.* (3rd ed.) New York: Appleton-Century-Crofts, 1965.

Vannoy, J. S. Generality of cognitive complexity-simplicity as a personality construct. *Journal of Personality and Social Psychology,* 1965, **2**, 385–396.

Weinstein, M. S. Achievement orientation and risk preference. *Journal of Personality and Social Psychology,* 1969, **13**, 153–172.

Winter, D. G. Need for power in thought and action. *Proceedings of the 76th American Psychological Association,* 1968, 429–430.

32

Constructing Cross-Situational Consistencies in Behavior: Some Thoughts on Alker's Critique of Mischel

DARYL J. BEM

For years personality theorizing has been dominated by the "trait" assumption that there are pervasive cross-situational consistencies in an individual's behavior. After reviewing the literature, however, Mischel (1968) concludes that despite the plausibility of the assumption and the ingenuity of many competent researchers over the years, the empirical search for the anticipated consistencies has rarely generated a correlation coefficient above +.30, a finding of some disappointment for those of us who had hoped that personality variables might account for more than 10 percent of the variance in behavior.

But it is clear from his critique of Mischel that Alker (1972) remains optimistic. In particular, Alker believes that the "moderating variable" strategy utilized by Kogan and Wallach (1964) might contain the seeds of a more promising approach for detecting (constructing?) personality differences which display trans-situational generality. Alker is, I believe, correct.

Alker claims, moreover, that Mischel has not only overlooked this particular strategy in his review, but that he fails to consider factors which attenuate correlation coefficients and ignores research employing alternative measurement and combinatorial procedures (e.g., ipsative measures, multiscale personality inventories, and regression-compounded indices). Here Alker is simply wrong. Mischel not only comments favorably on the promise of the Kogan-Wallach moderating-variable approach (pp. 32–33), but he mentions factors which attenuate correlation coefficients (p. 37), and discusses in detail the failure to achieve predictive utility of nearly every trait-based methodology to be found in the literature, including multiscale personality inventories and regression-compounded indices (pp. 103–146). There is even a three-page presentation (pp. 135–137) of a CPI-MMPI multiple-regression study by Gough (Gough, Wenk, & Rozynko, 1965) whom Alker specifically accuses Mischel of ignoring.

But more important than Alker's simple misreading of the empirical review is his erroneous charge that Mischel misunderstands construct validation, for this reveals that Alker has misapprehended the logical status of Mischel's arguments and conclusions. Contrary to Alker's implication, Mischel in no way restricts on a priori grounds the phenotypically dissimilar responses an investigator may include as "indices" of an underlying genotype. Nor does he in any way prejudge the inferential or combinatorial processes by which the equivalence classes of phenotypic behaviors are constructed. All that Mischel asks is that "the results of construct-validation research . . . provide evidence for the *utility* of categorizing behavior in accord with the particular construct" (p. 100). Thus, if Alker's haruspex secretly informs him that certain phenotypic measures of altruism, aggression, authoritarianism and aardvark-like gait are in fact separate indices of the "A" genotype, Mischel is perfectly willing to consider the results section of the subsequent experimental report—just as he did with not dissimilar methodologies in his review. And if these separate indices permit Alker to predict behavior across situations better than +.30, Mischel will fold up his tent and steal away.

Even if "traits" are constructed post hoc from empirical results, all Mischel requires is that they cross-validate and have some utility in predicting behavior trans-situationally. It is Mischel's conclusion that no set of traits has yet met this empirical criterion. For example, Mischel's only expressed reservation about the Kogan-Wallach moderating-variable analysis of risk-taking is that many of the "interactions are obtained post hoc rather than predicted [and hence] considerable interpretative caution must be observed" (p. 33). Similarly, Alker cites favorably an experiment by Opton and Lazarus (1967) which employed ipsative measures of behavior and combined an enormous set of personality items into composite scales. This combination of strategies did indeed yield correlations above +.30 between observed behavior and some of the resulting "personality" indices. But Alker should have withheld his enthusiasm pending cross-validation, for Lazarus himself has now published the second of two failures to replicate these results (Averill, Olbrich, & Lazarus, 1972), and he ends the article with an explicit bow to Mischel.

In sum, Mischel agrees that the attempt to predict behavior cross-situationally by inferring underlying personality traits from phenotypic "signs" was a plausible thing to try, but the empirical vindication for the strategy has simply not been forthcoming. He also recognizes that he cannot possibly state with finality that it can't be done, only that it hasn't been done. Contrary to Alker's implication, the burden of proof has not shifted: Any broad set of cross-situational consistencies will force Mischel to reverse his conclusion. On the other hand, no a priori strategy for raising the magnitude of the correlation coefficients, no matter how plausible, can be used to counter Mischel in the absence of data. For example, it is quite reasonable for Alker to suggest that combining normal and deviant populations in the same design would overcome the restriction of range problem and thus raise the variance accounted for by personality factors. But it must be tried first. As Mischel has pointed out, most of the strategies for increasing the correlations have been reasonable—personologists are not stupid—but they have simply not worked in practice. Nor, it appears, will this strategy, according to one of Alker's own references (Endler & Hunt, 1969, p. 14). Thus the logic of Mischel's position does not lend itself to purely theoretical attack, for he does not have to carry the burden of proof. Unfair of him perhaps, but he's right.[1]

Ordinarily a misreading of an empirical review would not warrant a response in an archival journal. But ironically, the full heuristic potential of the moderating-variable strategy is likely to be realized only if Mischel's conclusions and warnings are taken seriously. In fact, the strategy expands into a fresh and promising idea precisely when it is animated by Mischel's more radical implication that we change our initial premise and assume cross-situational correlations to be zero until proved (or explicitly constructed) to be otherwise.

MODERATING VARIABLES, IMAGE MAINTENANCE, AND CONSISTENCY

Any variable which affects the relationship between two other variables can be called a moderating variable. For example, the correlation between authoritarianism and influenceability is positive for subjects with high self-esteem, but negative for those with low self-esteem (Berkowitz & Lundy, 1957); self-esteem "moderates" the relationship between the other two variables. Psychologists unfamiliar with the term itself should not be surprised to discover that they have been "speaking prose" all of their lives, for any investigator who has ever analyzed the results of a study for male and female subjects separately has ipso facto performed a "moderating variable analysis." Similarly, any investigator who has ever uncovered a non-zero interaction term between two independent variables has found a "moderating-variable effect."

As utilized by Kogan and Wallach (1964), the strategy consists of first separating the population of subjects into subgroups on the basis of particular moderating variables and then examining the correlations among other variables within each of the defined subgroups. Using this approach, Kogan and Wallach uncovered strong positive correlations among risk-taking behaviors for certain subgroups and zero or negative correlations for others. Note that if correlational or factor analytic techniques had been used on the sample as a whole, these

---

[1] In the second half of his book, Mischel presents his own view that a strategy based upon social behavior theory can meet the empirical challenge. Here one could conceivably criticize Mischel on conceptual grounds, argue that a trait-based strategy will still prove to be better, and challenge the empricial findings generated by that research tradition. But this is not the thrust of Alker's critique.

strong differential correlations would have been masked, yielding spurious negative results instead.

Although Kogan and Wallach cast personality variables into the moderator role, situational variables can also be conceptualized this way. For example, individuals high in "machiavelianism" outmaneuver their "low Mach" counterparts only if the situation (1) permits face-to-face interaction, (2) contains latitude for improvisation and (3) contains distracting affect-arousing elements (Christie & Geis, 1970). These three situational variables can thus be said to "moderate" the relationship between machiavellianism and behavior. Since experimental social psychologists have characteristically investigated personality variables in this way, that is, by dividing their population on the basis of some personality dimension and then predicting that highs and lows will behave differently in different experimental settings, they too have been performing moderating-variable analyses without so labeling them. Similarly, Mischel's observation that behavior consistencies are situation-specific can be translated into the assertion that individual differences are themselves a function of situational moderators.

The moderating-variable strategy becomes more than an empty analytic or linguistic convention, however, only when one can begin to predict on a priori grounds which moderators are likely to divide up the world into useful equivalence classes: What kinds of people might display trait-like consistency? What responses should covary for these people? What kinds of situations might be functionally equivalent for these people? The important point to note here is that such questions reverse the usual assumption of consistency as given and inconsistency as problematic. Instead, we implicitly adopt Mischel's position that inconsistency is the norm and that it is the phenomenon of consistency which must be explained (or constructed). Such an approach commits the theorist not only to identifying possible personality moderators, but also to giving more explicit attention than heretofore to the relevant equivalence classes of responses and situations he expects to cohere.

Consider, for example, the personality moderator of defensiveness as measured by the need-for-approval scale (Crowne & Marlowe, 1964). The individual who has a high "need for approval" might be expected to give socially desirable responses in any situation where interpersonal evaluation is present. And in fact research shows that defensive individuals conform more than nondefensive individuals in an Asch situation; they verbally condition better; and they do not show overt hostility when provoked (Crowne & Marlowe, 1964). Thus for these individuals, "socially desirable responses" form an equivalence class of behaviors and "interpersonally evaluative settings" form an equivalence class of situations. For nondefensive individuals, on the other hand, these responses and situations may have nothing in common and hence their behavior cannot be predicted from one of these situations to the other.

The moderator of defensiveness is of special importance in the present context because it provides on important answer to the question, "What kinds of people might display trait-like consistency?" In particular, because the defensive individual appears to monitor his behavior in order to maintain a particular self-presentation, he may be unwilling or motivationally unable to alter his behavior to take advantage of shifting situational contingencies beyond social approval. Accordingly, he will display cross-situational consistency. Thus the defensive subjects in the Kogan-Wallach study of risk-taking (1964) would not abandon a conservative or risky strategy even when it was not paying off, whereas nondefensive subjects could not be characterized as risky or conservative because they were more sensitive to subtle alterations in the situational requirements.

The defensive image-maintenance process also has implications for the response consistency within a single situation. The individual who is attempting to present or maintain a particular image probably monitors only those overt behaviors whose connotations are known to him and which are under his functional control. Expressive behaviors, projective behaviors, and physiological responses probably escape the monitoring process. Accordingly, even when more monitorable behaviors are being suppressed, these "covert" indices may still occur. This suggests that within a single situation, the defensive individual may show inconsistency across those response modes which are differentially subject to monitoring. In contrast, the nondefensive individual will show consistency across response modes. Evidence consistent with this hypothesis has appeared in studies which show that covert and overt measures of extroversion/introversion are negatively correlated for defensive or anxious subjects, but positively correlated for nondefensive or nonanxious subjects (Taft, 1967; Wallach & Brantley, 1968; Wallach & Gahm, 1960; Wallach, Green, Lipsitt, & Minehart, 1962; Wallach & Thomas, 1963). (Several of these articles provide alternative interpretations of the findings, however.) In general, then, image-maintaining subjects should show cross-situational consistency but cross-modality inconsistency, whereas non-image-maintaining subjects should show cross-situational inconsistency but cross-modality consistency.

So far this analysis has implied that there are two kinds of people, those with traits and those without. If we take Mischel's conclusions concerning behavioral specificity seriously, however, then we should anticipate that the global trait of "defensive image-maintenance" is itself too broad. Although some individuals may monitor their entire behavioral repertoires in order to obtain social approval generally, most individuals probably monitor only selected portions of their repertoires in order to maintain self-images of particularly central self-concepts. For example, the highly sex-typed individual may be consistently masculine or feminine because he or she actively defends against displaying behaviors which are considered sex inappropriate. Thus some women may show "feminine" passivity and dependence even in situations where more assertive, independent behaviors are called for, and certain men may guard against open emotional expression like crying even in settings where it is situationally appropriate. (Such trait-like consistency could also result from simple learning deficits; in our society many individuals are socialized so that they do not even learn the responses appropriate to the other sex role.) Individuals who are low in sex typing, on the other hand, will appear "androgynous," that is, they will alter their behavior, not capriciously, but in appropriate accord with shifting situational requirements. For them the "trait" of masculinity or feminity simply does not exist.

It should be noted that individuals who are "defensive" about their sex-role images may well not be monitoring their behavior with respect to "honesty," "generosity," or other traits not definitional of a particular sex role, and hence, they may still show behavioral inconsistency on these other dimensions. They might also obtain low scores on the global need-for-approval scale, which does not even sample sex-role behaviors among its items.[2]

We should also guard against the assumption that the image-maintenance process should always be considered "defensive" or indicative of "motivational disturbance." Such a classification might be appropriate when the image-maintenance process is indiscriminate across all behavioral domains, as might be the case for high scorers on the need-for-approval scale. But what of those of us whose self-concepts revolve strongly around political liberalism, for example? We are undoubtedly more predictable across certain broad ranges of situational contexts than are those for whom a guiding political ideology is not important. In other words, we do display trait-like consistency across a particular situational domain. Perhaps it is only a matter of semantics to say that we are "defending" against politically conservative behaviors and attitudes, but for reasons of parsimony, the motivational construct is probably unnecessary (not to say unflattering).

The image-maintenance process, then, may be more important for dealing with individual differences in personality than it first appeared. Future research in this area might well utilize an instrument which obtains from the individual himself those "traits" which have phenomenological reality for him and are central for his self-concept. (Kelly's 1955 Role Construct Repertory Test is a likely place to begin.) This, in turn, would permit us to construct for any given individual the equivalence class of responses and situations across which his behavior could be predicted.

It should be clear that the strategy outlined here, if successful, would permit us to predict (1) certain behaviors (2) across certain situations (3) for certain people. But we will not be able to predict beyond the intersections of the particular three-part sets of equivalence classes we have been able to construct in this way. Insofar as one's scientific interest is truly individual differences ("What differential predictions can I make about this individual as opposed to other individuals?"), this strategy is promising. But insofar as one is interested in predicting particular behaviors across people and situations ("Who is likely to

---

[2] This discussion of sex roles is drawn from S. Bem (1971), whose research is currently examining many of these larger personality issues within that specific context; many of these more general points have evolved from our joint discussions.

survive which assignments in the Peace Corps?"), the strategy is not a likely candidate. No legerdemain with personality differences can predict behavior from variables which do not contain significant amounts of the variance to begin with, and those interested primarily in problems of placement would do better to turn to the "large-variance absorbers" at the cheapest cost, whether they be situational variables, demographic characteristics of the individual, or simple base rates.

As noted earlier, there was nothing silly about the initial assumption of personologists that everything was glued together until proved otherwise. But since it has now proved otherwise, it seems only fair to give a sporting chance to the counter-assumption that nothing is glued together until proved otherwise. Instead of assuming cross-situation correlations to be +1.00, let us begin by supposing them to be 0.00 until we can explicitly construct them to be otherwise. The heuristic value of this assumption and the strategy here outlined is not guaranteed of course. But the real world will bite back soon enough. Besides, the change in morale if +.30 correlations continue to come in is itself worth considering.

REFERENCES

Alker, H. A. Is personality situationally specific or intraphysically consistent? *Journal of Personality*, 1972, **40**, 1-16.

Averill, J. R., Olbrich, E., & Lazarus, R. S. Personality correlates of differential responsiveness to direct and vicarious threat: A failure to replicate previous findings. *Journal of Personality and Social Psychology*, 1972, in press.

Bem, S. L. Sex roles: The behavioral consequences of androgyny. Unpublished manuscript, Stanford University, 1971.

Berkowitz, L., & Lundy, R. M. Personality characteristics related to susceptibility to influence by peers or authority figures. *Journal of Personality*, 1957, **25**, 385-397.

Christie, R., & Geis, F. L. *Studies in machiavellianism.* New York: Academic Press, 1970.

Crowne, D. P., & Marlowe, D. *The approval motive.* New York: Wiley, 1964.

Endler, N. S., & Hunt, J. McV. Generalizability of contributions from sources of variance in the S-R inventories of anxiousness. *Journal of Personality*, 1969, **37**, 1-24.

Gough, H. G., Wenk, E. A., & Rozynko, V. V. Parole outcome as predicted from the CPI, the MMPI, and a base expectancy table. *Journal of Abnormal and Social Psychology*, 1965, **70**, 432-441.

Kelly, G. A. *The psychology of personal constructs.* Vols. 1 & 2. New York: Norton, 1955.

Kogan, N., & Wallach, M. A. *Risk taking: A study in cognition and personality.* New York: Holt, Rinehart, & Winston, 1964.

Mischel, W. *Personality and assessment.* New York: Wiley, 1968.

Opton, E. M., Jr., & Lazarus, R. S. Personality determinants of psychophysiological response to stress: A theoretical analysis and an experiment. *Journal of Personality and Social Psychology*, 1967, **6**, 291-303.

Taft, R. Extraversion, neuroticism, and expressive behavior: An application of Wallach's moderator effect to handwriting analysis. *Journal of Personality*, 1967, **35**, 570-584.

Wallach, M. A., & Brantley, H. T. Relative graphic expansiveness as a function of gross bodily activity and level of psychological disturbance. *Journal of Personality*, 1968, **36**, 246-258.

Wallach, M. A., & Gahm, R. C. Personality functions of graphic constriction and expansiveness. *Journal of Personality,* 1960, **28**, 73–88.

Wallach, M. A., Green, L. R., Lipsitt, P. D., & Minehart, J. B. Contradiction between overt and projective personality indicators as a function of defensiveness. *Psychological Monographs,* 1962, **76** (1, Whole No. 520).

Wallach, M. A., & Thomas, H. L. Graphic constriction and expansiveness as a function of induced social isolation and social interaction: Experimental manipulations and personality effects. *Journal of Personality,* 1963, **31**, 491–509.

33

The Person Versus the Situation-a Pseudo Issue? A Response to Alker

NORMAN S. ENDLER

Most personologists (e.g. Cattell, 1946, 1950; Cattell & Scheier, 1961; McClelland, 1951; Murray, 1938) and clinicians (e.g. Rapaport, Gill & Schafer, 1945) have assumed that personality variables are the major source of behavioral variance and are expressed in a relatively consistent manner across different situations. Social psychologists and sociologists (e.g. Cooley, 1902; G. H. Mead, 1934) have suggested that situational factors are more important than individual differences as sources of behavioral variance. Mischel (1968, 1969) suggests that the empirical evidence does not support the personologists' viewpoint and that situational factors are important. Alker (1972), despite the absence of supporting empirical evidence, claims "that personality variables can explain people's behavior even though that behavior varies from situation to situation" (p. 1). Bem (1972) has defended Mischel's position and has presented a conceptual reply to Alker, and Wallach and Leggett (1972) in discussing the issue of cross-situational consistency versus situational specificity have provided some data which they interpret as supporting the consistency position.

Mischel (1968) has indicated that until recently much of our theorizing about personality has been dominated by trait theories and by psychodynamic or state theories, which have assumed the existence of trans-situational consistency. These theories have assumed that personality is basically stable and continuous regardless of the situation. However, social behavior theory emphasizes situational specificity and states "that a person will behave consistently across situations only to the extent that similar behavior leads, or is expected to lead, to similar consequences across those conditions" (Mischel, 1971, p. 74).

From *Journal of Personality*, 1973, *41*, 287–303. © 1973 by the Duke University Press Reprinted by permission.

The study was assisted under Grant No. 391 of the Ontario Mental Health Foundation. The comments and suggestions of Morris Eagle, John Holmes and Marilyn Okada regarding this paper are appreciated.

The issue of consistency (continuity) versus specificity (change) is a complex one as Mischel (1969) has indicated. No one would be sufficiently foolhardy to deny the existence of continuity and stability. But there is substantial evidence (e.g. Mischel, 1968, 1969, 1971) to indicate that there are both significant longitudinal personality changes over time, and cross-situational differences at any particular time.

As Mischel (1969) has indicated "it may be useful to distinguish between consistency in various types of human activity" (p. 1012). There is evidence for cognitive and intellectual cross-situation consistency and stability over time. However, with respect to social behavior and noncognitive personality dimensions the trans-situational consistency is not very high. Mischel (1968) in reviewing the literature has provided evidence for behavioral *specificity* for such character traits as dependency, aggression, social conformity, rigidity, attitudes to authority and many other noncognitive personality variables. Mischel (1969) believes, on the basis of both theoretical and empirical grounds, that "the observed inconsistency so regularly found in studies of noncognitive personality dimensions often reflects the state of nature and not merely the noise of measurement" (p. 1014).

Validity coefficients for measures of personality traits usually range from .20 to .50 and are typically about .30. A correlation of .30 accounts for 10 percent of the relevant variance, a trivial amount (see Endler & Hunt, 1969; Hunt, 1965; Mischel, 1968, 1969). It is true that validity coefficients are attenuated by reliability coefficients and by other errors of measurement, and that self-report measures create additional statistical and methodological problems. However, it is equally evident that behaviors presumed to be indicators of stable personality traits are quite specific, and are dependent on both the evocative situations and modes of response used to assess these behaviors.

Mischel (1969) has indicated that those favoring the consistency position have attempted to explain diversity of behavior in different situations by assuming underlying genotypes of consistent personality traits which may manifest themselves in phenotypically dissimilar behaviors. Alternatively Mischel (1969) has suggested that "seeming inconsistencies, rather than serving one underlying motive, actually may be under the control of relatively separate causal variables" (p. 1015). This appears to be an empirical question and those advocating consistency have not yet empirically demonstrated an underlying genotypic consistency. The issue is a complex one and perhaps new research strategies are needed. We will return to the question of research strategies in the last section of this paper but let us first of all, however, examine Alker's (1972) contention that personality variables can adequately explain a person's behavior that varies from one situation to another.

THE PERSON VERSUS THE SITUATION

Endler and Hunt (1966) on the basis of a reanalysis of their anxiety questionnaire data (Endler, Hunt & Rosenstein, 1962) assert that "the question of whether individual differences or situations are the major source of behavioral variance, like many issues in the history of science, turns out to be a pseudo issue" (p. 344, Endler & Hunt, 1966). They do *not* suggest, as Alker (p. 4, 1972) has claimed, that the contest between personologists and social psychologists is not substantial. In fact, the first sentence of their paper (Endler & Hunt, 1966) states that this is an important recurrent issue. Rather, it is the manner in which the question has been raised (e.g. which one, or how much is due to situations and how much to persons) that makes it a pseudo issue. Asking whether behavioral variance is due to either situations *or* to persons, or how much variation is contributed by persons and how much by situations (an additive approach) is analogous to asking whether air *or* blood is more essential to life or asking one to define the area of a rectangle in terms of length *or* width. The more sensible question is *"How* do individual differences and situations interact in evoking behavior?"

Endler and Hunt (1969), in a paper which Alker (1972) mysteriously does not cite, analyzed self-report anxiety data for 22 samples of males and 21 samples of female subjects. Samples of "disturbed" and normal populations *were* included. Six different forms of the S-R Inventory of Anxiousness, with differing samples of situations and modes of response were used. The samples of subjects varied in age, social class, geographical location and mental health. Individual differences contribute on the average 4 to 5 percent of the total variance, and situations only about 4 percent for males and about 8 percent for females. Each of the two-way interactions (Subjects by Situations, Subjects by Modes of Response, and Situations by Modes of Response) contributes on the average about 10 percent. Obviously the interactions explain more of the variance than either persons or situations.

It is true that the Endler and Hunt anxiety data are based on self-reports, and it would be desirable to have in addition behavioral as well as physiological measures. However, one cannot dismiss these results as inconclusive, as Alker (1972) suggests. He should indicate *why* he believes that self-report data are inconclusive. To dismiss self-reports as invalid, is to ignore a great deal of important psychological data and to invalidate most of the clinical data derived from psychotherapy. Denying the importance of data derived from clinical settings could mean the exclusion of much of the information presently obtained from hospitalized or severely disturbed individuals—the very populations for whom, according to Alker (1972), individual differences are an important source of variance. Furthermore, self-reports may very well maximize the effects of intrapsychic factors since the individual is in fact "removed" from the impact of the actual situation.

ARE NORMALS AND ABNORMALS DISTINCT POPULATIONS?

Alker (1972) suggests that differences in results obtained by personologists or clinicians and social psychologists "correspond to differences in two distinct populations that have served historically to generate personality theory and research" (p. 4). He suggests that for the first population, consisting of hospitalized or severely disturbed individuals (abnormals or disorganized personalities), individual differences or intrapsychic consistency can explain people's behavior, and for the second population, consisting of normal people or organized personalities (primarily college sophomores according to Alker), situational factors may be important as a source of variance. To suggest that normals and abnormals are qualitatively different may be a naive assumption. If there were in fact a qualitative difference, the available evidence (Endler & Hunt, 1969) would suggest that this difference may possibly be in the direction of the increased importance of interactive components rather than in terms of intrapsychic factors. To suggest that the behavior of disorganized people can be best explained by intrapsychic consistencies seems like a contradiction in terms. In some instances disorganized people are more sensitive to situational factors as is the case with phobias for example. The onus is obviously on Alker to demonstrate that individual differences are an important source of behavioral variance for abnormal behavior.

The Endler and Hunt (1969) paper (not cited by Alker) bears on this issue as does some data recently collected by the present author. Not only does the Endler and Hunt (1969) paper report data on both normals and abnormals, but the normal samples in addition to sophomores include data from children and adults, as well as data from different social classes and data from diverse geographical regions in both Canada and the U.S.A. A summary of the samples on which anxiety data were collected appears in Table 2, p. 7, Endler and Hunt, 1969.

Table 3, p. 8 (Endler & Hunt, 1969) reports the median data for 22 male and 21 female samples, including one male abnormal sample and one female abnormal sample. Because of space limitations it was not possible to present the variance components for the sources of anxiety variance for each of the samples separately but these data were and are available from the American Documentation Institute. The data for both male and female samples from the Mental Health Clinic, consisting of disturbed neurotic adolescents referred for psychotherapy, appear in Table 1.

Note that the variance attributable to both individual differences and situations is trivial. This is for a population for which Alker insists individual differences are an important source of behavioral variance. In footnote 5, p. 9, Endler and Hunt (1969) report data on psychotic patients and here the variance due to individual differences for females was 6.58 percent and for males it was 14.50 percent. The variance due to situations was 5.77 percent for females, and 2.63 percent for males. However, the data for these psychotic patients were considered unreliable because as Endler and Hunt (1969) state "contact with these patients was so poor, however, that we have no assurance that their reports were discriminating with any consistency among either situations or modes of response" (p. 9). Nevertheless, one can conclude from the Endler and Hunt

Table 1. Variance Components and Percentages for Each Component of Reported Responses to Situations in the S-R Inventory of Anxiousness from East York Mental Health Clinic, Males and Females

| | Neurotic adolescents | | | |
| | Males (N = 49) | | Females (N = 34) | |
Source	Variance component	Percent	Variance component	Percent
Subject (S)	.075	2.93	.175	6.54
Situations (Sit)	.068	2.67	.100	3.76
Mode of response (M-R)	.703	27.46	.627	23.49
S × Sit	.240	9.38	.283	10.59
S × M-R	.253	9.88	.245	9.17
Sit × M-R	.194	7.57	.134	5.03
Residual	1.027	40.11	1.106	41.42
Total variation	2.561	100.00	2.670	100.00

(1969) study, a study which combined both normals and abnormals, that neither situations nor individual differences are an important source of anxiety variance.

Let us now turn to the data recently collected by the present author. In connection with some research on trait versus state anxiety, we are in the process of developing a measure of trait anxiety. We had hoped to develop a general scale that would consistently measure anxiety across situations, maximizing the effects of individual differences and minimizing the effects of situations. Using the Endler, Hunt and Rosenstein (1962) S-R Inventory of Anxiousness (Inventory of Attitudes Toward Specific Situations) format we devised an S-R Inventory of General or Trait Anxiousness (Inventory of Attitudes Toward General Situations) consisting of four general situations, the first three of which were based on the three situational anxiety factors (interpersonal, physical danger and ambiguous) found by Endler et al. (1962). The fourth general situation was designed to measure anxiety in routine or generally innocuous situations. There were nine modes of response.

This inventory was administered to a sample of high school students, a sample of university students and a sample of adults attending an evening college. We had expected that the individual differences would be a major source of general anxiety variance. The results are serendipitous and are reported in Table 2. Note that for this presumed measure of trait anxiety, individual differences account for less than 5 percent of the variance for normal people.

After reading Alker's (1972) paper and Bem's (1972) reply, we decided to administer the same inventory to neurotic (including those diagnosed as depressive reaction, anxiety reaction, phobia, and suicidal attempts) and psychotic

Table 2. Percentages of Variance Components of Reported Responses to General Situations on the S-R Inventory of General Trait Anxiousness from High School, University, Evening College, Toronto East General Hospital (Neurotic) and Lakeshore Psychiatric Hospital (Psychotic) Samples

	Percentage of variance components				
	Normals			Neurotic	Psychotic
Source	High school (N = 56)	University (N = 81)	Evening college (N = 72)	East General (N = 60)	Lakeshore (N = 39)
Subject (S)	.93	3.65	4.20	12.13	18.78
Situation (Sit)	17.88	28.71	24.20	5.78	5.25
Mode of response (M-R)	10.43	5.55	2.39	.87	2.89
S × Sit	16.86	17.74	20.40	22.09	8.28
S × M-R	9.39	6.57	5.98	10.18	12.71
Sit × M-R	9.59	6.28	6.25	3.53	.98
Residual	34.92	31.50	36.59	45.42	51.11
Total variation (components sum)	99.99	100.00	100.00	100.00	100.00

psychiatric patients (disorganized personalities).[1] According to Alker's thesis, individual differences should be a major source of variance for disorganized personalities. The results for these samples are also reported in Table 2 with the same serendipitous findings. For neurotic patients, individual differences contributed about 12 percent of the variance and for psychotic patients about 18 to 19 percent.[2] These results are comparable to those found for normals by Endler and Hunt (1968) with respect to the trait of hostility. Even for disorganized personalities, individual differences are not a major source of behavioral variance.

Alker (1972) suggests that the effects of individual differences as a source of variance are underestimated because no studies employ heterogeneous populations. "No studies estimating situation versus personality effects have ever combined disturbed and 'normal samples' for instance, in the same design for the explicit purpose of overcoming this underestimation problem" (p. 5). To remedy this situation we combined the results of the disturbed and normal samples reported in Table 2. These results appear in Table 3. The results are quite unambiguous. Individual differences are not a major source of anxiety variance. In fact, for this heterogeneous sample of abnormal and normal subjects, situations (16.11 percent) contribute more to behavioral variance than individual differences (9.66 percent). The interaction between persons and situations

---

[1] We wish to thank the staff and patients of the Department of Psychiatry, Toronto East General Hospital and Lakeshore Psychiatric Hospital for their cooperation and participation.

[2] The variance due to individual differences was higher for psychotic patients than it was for neurotics or for normals. However, the validity of the data for psychotic patients is questionable since we had to discard data for some patients because they did not complete the questionnaire. Contact with many of the psychotic patients was poor. The residual variance (error plus triple interaction) for the psychotic sample was 51.11 percent.

Table 3. Variance Components and Percentages for Each Component of Reported Responses to Situations in the S-R Inventory of General Trait Anxiousness from Normal and Abnormal Samples Combined (Derived from Table 2) ($N = 308$)

Source	Variance component	Percent
Subject (S)	.19	9.66
Situation (Sit)	.32	16.11
Mode of response (M-R)	.07	3.64
S × Sit	.36	18.14
S × M-R	.18	9.06
Sit × M-R	.09	4.35
Residual	.78	39.04
Total variation (components sum)	1.99	100.00

contributes 18.14 percent and is the largest source of variance next to the residual component.

To assume as Alker does that situational factors are a personality variable is to beg the question. A more fruitful approach is to determine *how* personality and situational factors interact in determining behavior. Of course Alker can dismiss the data reported above as being inconclusive since they are based on self-reports. However, the onus is still on him to demonstrate via both behavioral and physiological measures that individual differences are a major source of behavioral variance for disorganized personalities.

RESEARCH STRATEGIES

It is obvious that both our theorizing and research strategies with respect to the area of personality are still at a very primitive stage. And it may be that the problems are insoluble, but hope springs eternal.

Correlation Measures

The typical strategy has been to correlate measures (usually responses to questionnaires or rating forms) that are indicators of some underlying hypothesized personality trait. The low correlations (about .30) that this strategy usually yields can be interpreted to indicate the importance of situational factors. That is, a failure to obtain construct validation using this strategy has been used as support for the situational-specificity model. Alker (1972) has erroneously accused Mischel (1968) of ignoring some of the factors that reduce the size of the correlation coefficients. However, as Bem (1972) has indicated Mischel has discussed factors that attenuate correlation coefficients (e.g. criteria selected, reliability, methodological problems, etc.) and has discussed and evaluated many trait-based methodologies (e.g. regression-compounded indices, multiscale personality inventories). Despite the limitations of the various approaches there is no empirical support for the trait position nor is there any evidence for any genotypic consistency underlying the phenotypic diversity. However, the dilemma with the correlational approach is that while empirically it does not support the trait position, it does not offer direct support for the situational viewpoint. One might wish to argue by the process of elimination of alternative hypotheses, but this is a risky undertaking, since there are a number of possible alternatives (e.g. interactionist viewpoint, methodological and statistical problems, etc.).

Moderator Variables

Advocates of the situational specificity position (e.g. Mischel, 1968, 1969; Bem, 1972) as well as advocates of the trait position (Alker, 1972) have suggested that the "moderator" variable strategy is useful for seeking trans-situational consistency. Bem (1972) defines a moderating variable as "any variable which affects the relationship between two other variables ..." (p. 20). For example, Grooms and Endler (1960) found that anxiety moderated or modified the relationship between predicted grade point average and academic achievement, such that the correlation was high (.63) for high anxious subjects and negligible (.19) for low anxious subjects. Zedeck (1971) has questioned the utility of the moderator variable approach on statistical and methodological grounds and in terms of the difficulties inherent in identifying moderators. Zedeck also points out that the moderator variable concept has been used ambiguously (e.g. "to control or population variables, or interactions, and/or differences in predictability," p. 308). Wallach, one of the early proponents of the moderator variable strategy (e.g. Kogan & Wallach, 1964, 1967; Wallach & Brantley, 1968), has recently (Wallach & Leggett, 1972) questioned the use-fulness of this strategy. Wallach and Leggett (1972) suggest that the moderator variable approach (based on selected subsamples) does not consistently yield higher correlations than the approach using unselected samples.

There is no logical or a priori basis for identifying moderator variables and often investigations have been on a "hunting expedition" looking for elusive moderator variables. Often they are found on the basis of post hoc analyses and the cross-validation attempts have not been successful. Alker (1972) suggests that the moderator variable approach represents a new paradigm (see Kuhn, 1962) for personality research yet Wallach (Wallach & Leggett, 1972), one of the early proponents of this approach, indicates that Alker (1972) and Bem (1972) both of whom favor the moderator variable strategy, use the Kogan and Wallach (1964, 1967) results on risk taking and present contradictory interpretations about the kinds of people that manifest the greatest consistencies in risk taking. For Bem consistencies are presumed to be greatest for people who are high on defensive and low on anxiety, while for Alker consistencies are presumed to be greatest for people high on both variables. Wallach and Leggett (1972) state that the Kogan-Wallach results do not clearly support either interpretation, and that attempts at replication have not been very successful.

Wallach and Leggett (1972) point out that the moderator variable approach, using selected subsamples, is essentially the same as the correlation approach using total samples, in that it attempts to determine consistency by seeking evidence for traits or disposition. Wallach and Leggett believe that one should look for consistency in behavior and its products—a topic we will discuss in the next section. The moderator variable approach has the same problems as the ones we discussed in connection with the search for consistency among traits by correlating various test measures. One can attempt to obtain evidence for consistency with this approach but there is no direct way to confirm the specificity hypothesis.

Bem (1972) has suggested that in addition to treating personality variables as moderators, one can treat situational variables in the same way. However, because of the confusion and ambiguity with respect to the concept of the moderator variable (Zedeck, 1971) it would be more fruitful to think in terms of the interaction of situational and personal factors, and their relative contribution to behavior.

Behavioral Measures

Wallach and Leggett (1972) have made an important contribution in emphasizing the importance of behavioral measures and their products, rather than looking for consistency in response indicators (test measures) of traits or constructs. Since psychologists are ultimately interested in predicting behavior this seems to be a commendable approach.

Wallach and Leggett (1972) presented some evidence of consistency in competence or achievement and then conducted an experiment in which they attempted to demonstrate stylistic consistency in size of children's drawings. Briefly they attempted a partial replication of Sechrest and Wallace's (1964) study. Sechrest and Wallace found that the size of children's drawings of a Santa Claus figure was greater during the Christmas season than it was either before or after the Christmas season—an inverted U-curve of the size of Santa Claus drawings was obtained as a function of time. The situational factor of the Christmas season was presumed to be an important determinant of the size of the drawing. Wallach and Leggett (1972) had kindergarten children draw pictures of a Santa Claus figure and of a man on three separate occasions—about three weeks before Christmas, about a week before Christmas and about two weeks after Christmas. They used two measures (height of drawing, and area of drawing) and found that children consistently drew the Santa Claus figure larger than the man figure, but that there were no differences as a function of time or occasions. They also found a significant conditions (man vs. Santa Claus) X occasions interaction. They also correlated the size of the children's drawings across occasions and found that the correlations ranged from .47 to .68. Wallach and Leggett (1972) interpret their results to indicate that there is transsituational consistency, and that there is no evidence for situational specificity.

It is our contention that the Wallach and Leggett (1972) study neither supports the consistency position nor the situational specificity position. Alternative interpretations to theirs are possible. A failure to obtain a significant effect due to occasions does not mean that there is consistency. One cannot prove the null hypothesis! Possibly the measures used were not very reliable, and this would preclude obtaining differences. The extremely large and non-homogeneous variances (for the various means) could conceal possible effects.[3] The Sechrest and Wallach (1964) theory of expected differences may be incorrect. One could also attempt to interpret the Wallach and Leggett interaction[4] (not interpreted by Wallach & Leggett) but the most obvious interpretation would seem to be that the findings of Sechrest and Wallace were unstable and were not replicated by Wallach and Leggett because the Christmas season per se has no situational effect on size of Santa Claus drawings, and the behavioral measures used were not reliable. Inconsistent results from two different experiments do not mean consistency in behavior!

Wallach and Leggett (1972) emphasize that psychologists should focus on behaviors that are of intrinsic interest to them rather than on test responses that are indices of some hypothetical trait. Nevertheless, these behavioral measures must also be assessed reliably. The correlation between the second and third occasions for the drawing of the man figure (which can be interpreted in terms of "test-retest" reliability) was .68—the highest correlation obtained. This correlation accounts for 46 percent of the variance (the square of .68) but still leaves 54 percent of the variance unaccounted for. In general the correlations of drawings on different occasions suggest that the "behavioral responses" (drawings) used were not highly reliable. But, Wallach and Leggett offer the correlational data as support for the consistency position. However the failure to obtain differences as a function of occasions may be due to the test-retest (behavior 1 vs. behavior 2) unreliability of the measures used rather than due to the absence of any real effect.

We therefore have two studies: one (Sechrest & Wallace, 1964) showing a significant effect on size of the "Santa Claus" figure due to occasions, and the other (Wallach & Leggett, 1972) showing a nonsignificant effect due to occasions, but indicating significant correlations (ranging from .465 to .681)

---

[3] The author wishes to thank Michael A. Wallach for providing the raw data from the Wallach and Leggett (1972) study. We reanalyzed their data using sex as one of the independent variables (since they mention sex differences on p. 322) in addition to conditions and occasions. The variances for the two sexes are different and non-homogeneous; e.g. on occasion one, the SD for the boys for the "Santa Claus" condition was 90.88 and for girls for the "Man condition" it was 67.05. We did not find a conditions by occasions interaction, but did find a significant sex by condition interaction for the area measure. Any possible meaningful and consistent effects are probably obscured by the heterogeneity of the variances and the possible unreliability of the measures used.

[4] We would be reluctant to do this since in reanalyzing their data we were unable to replicate the interaction they obtained. There may well be computational errors in their Table 3 and Table 4 results or computational differences in the format of their analysis and ours.

between occasions. The most reasonable interpretation at present (regarding the Santa Claus data) is that the results are inconclusive with respect to the consistency-specificity issue.

In principle the Wallach and Leggett (1972) emphasis on behavioral measures is a valid one and is potentially fruitful. However, their paradigmatic approach seems to be inappropriate in that it treats the issue of situational specificity versus trans-situational consistency as either situations *or* persons propositions. As indicated earlier in this paper this does not seem to be a fruitful approach.

An Interactionist Approach

Because of the complexity of human behavior it is our belief that a useful paradigm (Kuhn, 1962) for the trait versus situation issue in personality research is one that examines the relative contribution of situations and individual differences to behavioral variances, and determines how situations and individuals interact in evoking behavior. The methodology one uses often influences the results one obtains. For example, with respect to the nature-nurture issue in intelligence, those favoring the nature (heredity) position have used correlational techniques to prove their point, while those favoring the nurture (environment) position have used mean differences to prove their point.

As indicated before the low correlations of personality traits neither proves nor disproves the existence of consistency, and similarly differences across situations would not conclusively prove the primacy of situational effects. The question in the past has been inappropriately phrased. It is obvious to everyone that both situational and personal factors are important determinants of behavior yet the question has frequently been phrased as an either-or proposition. Mischel (1971) who mentions interactions has placed too much emphasis on social learning and situational factors and personologists have tended to ignore situational components.

While it is true that the ultimate aim has to be with respect to behavioral measures as Wallach and Leggett (1972) suggest, we need a paradigm that can examine the interaction of personal and situational factors within the same experimental design. Endler and Hunt (1969) have done this with respect to self-report measures and have indicated the importance of interactions with respect to anxiety variance. Obviously the next step has to be with respect to behavioral measures and with respect to additional personality variables.

Bowers (1972) has summarized nine articles, published since 1959, that deal directly with the person versus the situation issue. The studies were classified into three major categories: (a) those using S-R self-report inventories (of anxiousness and hostility) for specific situations, which most people have experienced personally or vicariously; (b) those concerned with self-ratings, based on real situations (measuring affect, feelings of trust, affiliation, etc.); and (c) those based on actual behavior or on observation of behavior in specific situations (e.g. hyperaggressive behavior, honesty, talking, smoking). The results of these studies indicate that the person by situation *interaction* accounts for more variance than either person or situation in 13 of 16 possible comparisons, and for more variance than the sum of the main effects for 8 out of 16 comparisons. The mean variance due to persons was 12.69 percent, that due to situations 7.86 percent, and that due to the person by situation interaction 19.72 percent (Bowers, 1972). Argyle and Little (1972) have reviewed evidence with respect to social behavior, social response questionnaire studies, and person perception studies and have concluded that "Person X Situation Interaction accounts for more variance than either Situations or Persons alone. With the passage of time and in more adequately functioning groups, Situations are relatively more important sources of variation than are Persons" (p. 16, Argyle & Little, 1972).

McGuire (1968) has indicated the complexity of the relationships between personality and susceptibility to social influence and has pointed out that we have still not isolated the basic parameters. He has stated that even if we were aware of the parameters "the interactional approach would still be more attractive from the theoretical viewpoint, since multifactorial designs would offer the economy of testing predictions and specifying parameters not only on main effects of the separate variables but on the interaction between them" (p. 1176, McGuire, 1968).

SUMMARY

The issue of cross-situational consistency (stability) versus situational specificity (change) with respect to personality was discussed. Alker's (1972) claim concerning the importance of personality variables as a major source of behavioral variance was examined and rejected. It was proposed that the personality vs. situation issue was a pseudo-issue because it was usually conceptualized in terms of which is more important rather than in terms of how personality variables and situational factors interact in affecting behavior. It was suggested that self-reports can contribute important information regarding this issue. Alker's claim that abnormal and normal people constitute two distinct populations and that individual differences were a much more important source of variance for abnormal people was examined and rejected. Empirical evidence from two separate studies indicated that individual differences are *equally unimportant* for both normals and abnormals. The person by situation interaction appears to be an important source of variance. If Alker wishes to question these findings, clearly the onus is on him to provide evidence to the contrary. Finally, various research strategies with respect to personality research were examined, and the advantages of an interactional approach were discussed.

REFERENCES

Alker, H. A. Is personality situationally specific or intrapsychically consistent? *Journal of Personality,* 1972, **40,** 1–16.

Argyle, M., & Little, B. R. Do personality traits apply to social behaviour? *Journal for the Theory of Social Behaviour,* 1972, **2,** 1–35.

Bem, D. J. Constructing cross-situational consistencies in behavior: Some thoughts on Alker's critique of Mischel. *Journal of Personality*, 1972, **40**, 17–26.

Bowers, K. S. Situationism in Psychology: On making reality disappear. Department of Psychology Research Report No. 37, University of Waterloo (Waterloo, Ontario), September, 1972.

Cattell, R. B. *The description and measurement of personality.* New York: World Book, 1946.

Cattell, R. B. *Personality: A systematic, theoretical and factual study.* New York: McGraw-Hill, 1950.

Cattell, R. B., & Scheier, I. H. *The meaning and measurement of neuroticism and anxiety.* New York: Ronald, 1961.

Cooley, C. H. *Human nature and the social order.* New York: Scribner's, 1902.

Endler, N. S., & Hunt, J. McV. Sources of behavioral variance as measured by the S-R Inventory of Anxiousness. *Psychological Bulletin*, 1966, **65**, 336–346.

Endler, N. S., & Hunt, J. McV. S-R Inventories of Hostility and comparisons of the proportions of variance from persons, responses, and situations for hostility and anxiousness. *Journal of Personality and Social Psychology*, 1968, **9**, 309–315.

Endler, N. S., & Hunt, J. McV. Generalizability of contributions from sources of variance in S-R Inventories of Anxiousness. *Journal of Personality*, 1969, **37**, 1–24.

Endler, N. S., Hunt, J. McV., & Rosenstein, A. J. An S-R Inventory of Anxiousness. *Psychological Monographs*, 1962, **76**, No. 17 (Whole No. 536).

Grooms, R. R., & Endler, N. S. The effect of anxiety on academic achievement. *Journal of Educational Psychology*, 1960, **51**, 299–304.

Hunt, J. McV. Traditional personality theory in the light of recent evidence. *American Scientist*, 1965, **53**, 80–96.

Kogan, N., & Wallach, M. A. *Risk taking: A study in cognition and personality.* New York: Holt, Rinehart and Winston, 1964.

Kogan, N., & Wallach, M. A. Risk taking as a function of the situation, the person and the group. In *New directions in Psychology III.* New York: Holt, Rinehart and Winston, 1967.

Kuhn, T. S. *The structure of scientific revolutions.* Chicago: University of Chicago Press, 1962.

McClelland, D. C. *Personality.* New York: Wm. Sloane Association, 1951.

McGuire, W. J. Personality and susceptibility to social influence. In E. F. Borgatta & W. W. Lambert (Eds.) *Handbook of personality theory and research.* Chicago: Rand McNally, 1968.

Mead, G. H. *Mind, self and society.* Chicago: University of Chicago Press, 1934.

Mischel, W. *Personality and assessment.* New York: Wiley, 1968.

Mischel, W. Continuity and change in personality. *American Psychologist*, 1969, **24**, 1012–1018.

Mischel, W. *Introduction to personality.* New York: Holt, Rinehart and Winston, 1971.

Murray, H. A. *Explorations in personality.* New York: Oxford University Press, 1938.

Rapaport, D., Gill, M., & Schafer, R. *Diagnostic psychological testing.* Chicago: Year Book, 1945, 2 Vols.

Sechrest, L., & Wallace, J. Figure drawings and naturally occurring events: Elimination of the expansive euphoria hypothesis. *Journal of Educational Psychology*, 1964, **55**, 42–44.

Wallach, M. A., & Brantley, H. T. Relative graphic expansiveness as a function of gross bodily activity and level of psychological disturbance. *Journal of Personality*, 1968, **36**, 246–258.

Wallach, M. A., & Leggett, M. I. Testing the hypothesis that a person will be consistent: Stylistic consistency versus situational specificity in size of children's drawings. *Journal of Personality*, 1972, **40**, 209–330.

Zedeck, S. Problems with the use of "moderator" variables. *Psychological Bulletin*, 1971, **76**, 295–310.

34

Testing the Hypothesis that a Person Will Be Consistent: Stylistic Consistency Versus Situational Specificity in Size of Children's Drawings

MICHAEL A. WALLACH and MARGARET I. LEGGETT

Whether at least some behavior shows cross-situational consistency—in contrast to the claim that behavior can be best understood as situationally specific—is a controversy of considerable proportions in personality and social psychology. In the controversy's most recent phase, those who seem more friendly (Bem, 1972) as well as those who seem more hostile (Alker, 1972) to the situational specificity thesis as advanced, for example, by Mischel (1968, 1969) appear to be in agreement that the most promising way to seek trans-situational consistency is through the search for "moderator variables"—variables which are thought to influence whether other measures are interrelated. Alker, in fact, goes so far as to ascribe to the moderator variable approach the status of a "new paradigm," in the sense meant by Kuhn (1962), for personality research. While one of us has been a party to work which is viewed by Alker, Bem, and others as supporting the viability of this moderator variable approach (for example, Wallach & Gahm, 1960; Wallach & Greenberg, 1960; Wallach, 1962; Wallach, Green, Lipsitt, & Minehart, 1962; Wallach & Thomas, 1963; Kogan & Wallach, 1964; Kogan & Wallach, 1967; Wallach, 1967; Wallach & Brantley, 1968), our present belief is that moderator variables do not in fact offer a useful strategy for finding consistency in behavior. We also believe, however, that there is consistency aplenty. In this paper we shall spell out why, in our estimation, moderator variables are not the answer—and, on the other hand, how to find consistency, together with an empirical demonstration attesting to its existence.

Why Moderator Variables Are Not the Key to the Search for Consistency

Consider the following definition of the term "personality" offered by Child (1968). This definition provides, on the one hand, the essence of the consistency idea and, on the other, includes some excess baggage which, as we see it, leads those who search for consistency astray. According to Child, personality refers to "... those more or less stable internal factors that make one person's behavior consistent from one time to another, and different from the behavior other people would manifest in comparable situations" (p. 83). Quite simply, then, a person behaves consistently if his behavior on different occasions shows similarity, while also being different from the behavior of others on such occasions. Situational specificity, by contrast, refers to the power of a given occasion, by virtue of its properties, to control a person's behavior to such an extent that it is better predicted from knowing the nature of the occasion than knowing how that person behaves at other times.

But note that Child's definition also includes a reference to what produces consistency—namely, "more or less stable internal factors." This must be true in some sense, of course, in order for consistency to be found—it can have no other source in the person than factors internal to him or her. One can determine whether or not behavioral consistencies exist, however, without having to solve the intractable and complex problem of what causes them—of the nature of those internal factors. Speculations concerning these internal factors lead to the galaxy of "constructs," "traits," and "dispositions" for which Mischel claims, correctly we believe, that there is little by way of convincing evidence. Attempts at "construct validation"—at finding functionally equivalent signs of a hypothetical conceptual entity such as a trait or disposition—can fail without doubt being cast thereby on the hypothesis of behavioral consistency. The mistake, then, is to throw out the consistency notion because of having found that the enterprise of construct validation comes to grief.

The trouble with construct validation as a research strategy is that it encourages the investigator to use as the criterion for what to study not whether a particular type of behavior is intrinsically meaningful—is of interest in its own right—but rather whether it can be taken on theoretical grounds as a sign or "test response" for indexing some presumed underlying trait or disposition. The search for such dispositions, as inferred from clues which are expected to intercorrelate, then ensues, with the disappointing results that Mischel documents. To answer this negative evidence by proposing that moderator variables will indicate where consistency is to be found seems, rather than constituting a "new paradigm," actually to offer only a small, conservative modification in viewpoint. The assumption is kept that it is appropriate to seek evidence for consistency by inferring traits or dispositions from the intercorrelating of behavioral signs. The difference is in the proposal that people only of a particular type, rather than all people, will show these correlations.

Before exploring how the consistency thesis fares when we stop looking for evidence of traits or dispositions and focus instead on behavioral phenomena that we want to learn about per se, we must consider what the evidence for the moderator variable approach looks like. Does it really warrant the faith that Alker and Bem have placed in it or is its appeal illusory?

Two major sources of empirical support are cited by Alker (1972) and Bem (1972) as bases for their advocacy of the moderator variable approach—research on risk taking and research on expressive behavior. We shall take up each of these lines of work in turn. Neither, in our present estimation, has about it the kind of stability or replicability of findings that is essential if moderator variables are to be judged useful.

The work using moderator variables to isolate subsamples of persons who might reveal presumed dispositions toward risk or conservatism as indexed by various "tests" was conducted by Kogan and Wallach (1964; 1967). The ambiguity of the actual results obtained in this research is nicely indicated by the fact that Alker and Bem, both of whom rely on it heavily, use it to document contradictory generalizations concerning which kinds of people show the greatest consistencies among putative indicators of risk taking. To Bem, consistencies should be greatest for those simultaneously scoring high on a defensiveness moderator and low on a test anxiety moderator. They are maximally defensive—their high defensiveness belies their claim of low test anxiety—and hence they are trying to maintain what they view as a socially desirable image of a particular sort. To Alker, consistencies should be greatest for those simultaneously scoring high on both the defensiveness and the test anxiety moderators, rather than high on the first and low on the second. The former persons are maximally disturbed—both defensive in general and also admittedly upset by tests—and hence a risky or conservative posture for them is in the service of overriding need states rather than tuned to the specifics of reality.

The Kogan-Wallach findings, in turn, support neither of these suppositions with real clarity. The evidence against both views seems at least as convincing as the evidence favoring either one of them, sex differences are found for no apparent reason, and effects do not replicate in the way that they should if the moderators were really illuminating what was going on. Subsequent attempts at replication have not been marked by success in any clear way either.

Research on expressive behavior by Wallach and Gahm (1960), Wallach, Green, Lipsitt, and Minehart (1962), Wallach and Thomas (1963), Taft (1967), and Wallach and Brantley (1968) is cited by Bem as further evidence of the fruitfulness of the moderator variable approach. In this work the construct under consideration was "introversion-extraversion," and the assumption was made that different "test performances" were reflections of such a trait and also were tapping into it at more overt or covert—i.e., more recognizable or disguised—levels. The argument then was advanced that by defining subsamples of individuals who were homogeneous with respect to a relevant moderator, intercorrelations among these different tests could be found that would be absent from the sample as a whole. Bem here takes the position that consistencies will be stronger for those low in defensiveness. On this view, those high in defensiveness will, by monitoring and controlling the behavior whose meaning is recognizable to them, render it inconsistent with behavior that, because it is more covert, escapes their censorship. He might just as well, however, have proposed that, more in line with the interpretation he advanced for the risk taking research, those who are most defensive will be most consistent—by virtue of drawing a wider range of performances, and hence less obvious ones as well, into a unified system that functions to maintain the self-image of being introverted or extraverted.

When we ask again what the empirical findings turn out to show, the evidence once more is disappointing. Some of it looks, in fact, as if it supports the second rather than the first interpretation, since consistency seemed greater among low manifest anxiety scorers than high, and low manifest anxiety scores—because they correlate inversely with defensiveness measures and indicate an unwillingness to admit the occurrence of socially undesirable symptoms—may be more indicative of defensiveness than of an absence of anxiety. But there also is some evidence that, by finding consistency to be greater among low defensiveness scorers than high, seems congruent with the first rather than the second interpretation. Evidence on each side, however, once again fails to replicate in a clear way. Further analyses and additional data collection by us and others suggest that not only are findings ungeneralizable from one sex to the other, but even when, within sex, one simply tries to duplicate the results of a given study, such attempts do not pan out. For expressive behavior too, then, we cannot say that use of moderators has successfully pinpointed subgroups for whom consistency among diverse tests will be predictable.

The empirical basis for recommending moderators as the answer to the search for consistency thus seems more apparent than real. Why should the effects of applying moderators be so unstable? First, because internal processes are sufficiently subtle to defy capture by the kinds of theorizing that have been advanced. We have seen, for example, how possible it is to come up with contradictory construct-level interpretations as to how moderators should act in each of the two lines of work we considered. To unravel such complexities in a way that leads to repeatable empirical demonstrations may not be a practical undertaking. Second, moderator effects are statistically complex—they involve statistical interactions such that the members of one part of a sample are expected to exhibit a relationship between two indicators while this relationship should not be found among the members of another part of that sample. Statistical interactions of the aforementioned kind are rather notorious for their lack of stability. Even under the best of circumstances they depend, for example, on sampling constancy regarding the ways in which the subsamples are to be constituted in replication attempts. In addition, however, the unfortunate fact seems to be that a statistically significant interaction can appear for reasons that are not really understood and that go far beyond the elements in one's theorizing. The consequence of such a state of affairs is that replication will not work.

Where Consistency Should Be Sought

With constructs thus turning out to be as difficult to validate within moderator-defined subgroups as they were in samples as a whole, it seems time to emphasize that the search for consistency does not stand or fall with the finding of evidence for traits or dispositions. The demonstrated elusiveness of such evidence tells us not that people are inconsistent but rather that constructs of the kind considered don't seem to be useful conceptual entities. Whether people manifest consistency remains to be seen—by focusing not on test responses which are of interest only if they function as signs of some hypothetical trait or other, but rather on behaviors and effects of behavior that are of interest in their own right. In the case of such behaviors and behavioral effects we can ask, quite straightforwardly, whether persons exhibit relative constancy in producing them across varying occasions. This is not the mere study of test-retest reliability, because test responses do not carry inherent meaning— their meaning depends on whether they serve as a clue to something else. We are talking, by contrast, about performances and products that do not call for a justification beyond themselves in order to qualify as objects of study.

As an example of evidence which bears on the consistency question as we have just formulated it, take the following study by Richards, Holland, and Lutz (1967). Intrinsically meaningful achievements by students in each of various domains of talented nonacademic activity were considered as manifested outside the classroom during the high school years. It then was determined whether a student's exhibiting talented attainments in a given line of endeavor in his extracurricular life during the high school years offered a useful basis for predicting whether that student would manifest comparable extracurricular accomplishments when in college. Predictability turned out to be substantial— quality of attainment in a type of activity such as art, music, or creative writing maintained itself from high school to college. Such attainment, moreover, had little to do at either point in time with traditionally defined intellective skills as reflected in academic grades. Presumably, abilities, capacities, and motives were at issue which are quite different from those implicated in the conventional forms of academic achievement. The student samples were extensive and covered a considerable range as far as intellective skills were concerned.

To illustrate the ways in which quality of contribution within a given domain of nonacademic accomplishment was evaluated in this work, consider the field of music, where the attainments noted included the following: "composed or arranged music which was publicly performed, publicly performed on two or more musical instruments, attained a first-division rating in a state or regional solo music contest" (Richards, et al., p. 345). What has been shown, then, is consistency across different situations of accomplishments like these, not only in the arts but in literature and the sciences as well, together with their unpredictability from the usual information about academic proficiency. Demonstrations of this kind, which are discussed at greater length by Wing and Wallach (1971), testify to the consistency over time of performances and products that seem to possess considerable inherent interest-value and meaning. Their ecological validity as real-life manifestations of excellence has, in fact, led Wing and Wallach to propose them as offering more suitable ways of defining talent and competence for educational selection purposes than the "test response" yardsticks currently in use.

It is possible at this point to offer the rejoinder, however, that talk about consistency regarding inherently meaningful forms of behavior and effects of behavior is all very well when capacities or skills and the motivation to exercise them are at issue. While consistency may be demonstrable in those realms, consistency in matters of personal style is something else again. Our answer, however, is that precisely the same points apply in the case of stylistic consistency. To refer to "style" is to describe kinds of differences in behavior or its effects where evaluations as to quality distinctions do not apply in any clear way. Demonstrated skill or competence in an activity can be comparable among people and yet the style with which it is carried out can vary. To seek evidence for stylistic consistency, just as for consistency in the exhibiting of competences, the requirement simply is to study behaviors and products of behavior that are meaningful per se—that tell us directly about something we want to know.

Regarding art, for example, while the preceding discussion suggests that individual differences in quality of work produced show consistency from occasion to occasion, is the same true for individual differences in style? To answer this we must consider attributes in art products which don't contribute to judgments of the product's quality but nevertheless offer information of interest to us concerning what the product is like. One such characteristic is the size of the image that is drawn on the paper. Assuming a drawing's size is not being determined by differences in the specific content of what is drawn—an elephant will, on the average, tend to be drawn larger than an ant—or by differences in the size of the paper itself, the possibility is present that ordering drawings by size on one occasion gives you a powerful basis for predicting what the ordering will be for new sets of drawings made by the same individuals on other occasions. Larger images are not better or worse than smaller images—the differences in question pertain not to skill but to the style of executing the drawing. The question posed, then, is one of learning about a stylistic aspect of drawings, and that is precisely what we look at empirically. By so doing we can be quite confident about the ecological validity or direct meaningfulness of the kind of data collected.

Size of image in drawings offers what may perhaps be a particularly intriguing arena in which to investigate evidence for stylistic consistency, because research has been reported which supports the view that drawing size is responsive to situational determinants—that it varies predictably from one situation to another. As a demonstration concerning how to look for consistency, therefore, we conducted research on a stylistic variable—size of drawing image—for which control by situational factors had been claimed on the basis of previously reported evidence. The approach we followed was to carry out our investigation in a way that, according to the earlier work, should be conducive to a predictable form of situational control, and to examine under these circumstances what could be learned concerning stylistic consistency versus situational specificity for the behavioral product in question.

A Demonstrational Study: Size of Children's Drawings of Santa Claus and of a Man on Occasions Varying in Temporal Distance from Christmas

Research by Sechrest and Wallace (1964) suggests that the situational factor of amount of time before and after Christmas exerts control over the size of drawings of Santa Claus made by children. The type of situational specificity supported by this evidence is an inverted U-curve when plotting size of Santa Claus drawings against time, such that the drawings are larger as Christmas approaches than they are when made either earlier or after Christmas is over. A control condition also was included of children who drew pictures of a man rather than of Santa Claus on the occasions in question, with the result that man drawings did not show the inverted U-curve found for Santa Claus drawings. It was concluded from these findings that the approach of Christmas has an effect on the size of drawings of Christmas-related images (such as Santa Claus) in particular, rather than a nonspecific effect on the size of any drawings. The implication was that Santa Claus drawings are largest at Christmastime not because of an "expansive euphoria" effect which would influence the size of Christmas-irrelevant drawings as well, but rather because of enhanced value and/or strengthened expectancy concerning the Santa Claus image as Christmas comes nearer in time. The Sechrest-Wallace research further suggested that the inverted U-curve effect for Santa Claus drawings was stronger for children in kindergarten and the early elementary years of school than for children in the later elementary years. The drawings—of either Santa Claus or a man in the case of different samples of children—were obtained on each of three occasions in this work: the first occasion was December 6, 7, or 8, the second occasion was December 20, 21, or 22, and the third occasion was January 12.

As a study which seemed to provide systematic support for earlier, more informal work that in general had also indicated situational specificity effects for children's drawings of Santa Claus in relation to Christmas (Solley & Haigh, 1957; Craddick, 1961), the Sechrest-Wallace research appeared to offer a suitable paradigm within which it would be informative to look for evidence of stylistic consistency. That is what our investigation undertook to do, working with an age group of children—kindergarteners—for whom we could expect on the basis of the Sechrest-Wallace evidence that situational control should be particularly strong. Given the rather massive "naturally occurring" environmental manipulation constituted by the arrival of Christmas, would we find that the size of the Santa Claus drawings that are made reflects situational control exercised by the environmental event in question? The prediction, based on the Sechrest-Wallace evidence, would be for Santa Claus drawings to be larger right before Christmas than they are either earlier or after Christmas is past—while drawings of a man should not show this inverted U-curve effect. Or, on the other hand, would we find a quite different sort of fact emerging as the dominant phenomenon—namely, a demonstration of stylistic consistency? The prediction, based on the consistency hypothesis, would be that, regardless of occasion, drawings made on any given topic have a size that is characteristic for the person in question. We might note finally that both types of hypotheses, stylistic consistency and situational specificity, should apply equally to children of both sexes.

METHOD

Task and Instructions

Children in kindergarten classes were given a drawing task by a female experimenter on each of three occasions. The schools containing the classes were assigned at random to one of two conditions—"Santa Claus" or "man." In the former condition, the children were asked to draw a picture of Santa Claus on each of the three occasions. In the latter condition, they were asked on each of those occasions to draw a picture of a man. All drawings were made without time limits on 12 inch by 18 inch sheets of drawing paper. Each child on every occastion had a box of sharpened crayons in 8 different colors to use for the task.

For every class, two weeks elapsed between the first and second drawing occasions, while three weeks elapsed between the second and third drawing occasions. The first occasion took place, for different classes, on December 1, 2, 3, 6, and 7; the second occasion, on December 15, 16, 17, 20, and 21; and the third occasion, on January 5, 6, 7, 10, and 11. The five dates comprising each occasion fell on Wednesday, Thursday, Friday, Monday, and Tuesday, respectively. Any given class made its drawings for all three occasions on the same day of the week, thus maintaining the constancy of the time interval between a given pair of occasions for all classes in the study.

For the "Santa Claus" condition, instructions on each occasion were as follows:

First occasion. Hello. My name is ___. I have been to visit a lot of boys and girls your age. At the schools I visit, I ask the children to draw pictures for me. Today, I would like everybody to draw a picture of Santa Claus for me. (At this point materials were distributed.) Does everyone know who Santa Claus is? As soon as you get your paper and crayons, you may begin.

Second occasion. Hi. Do you remember who I am? What did we do the last time I came? What did we draw? Well, today I would like you to draw another picture of Santa Claus for me.

Third occasion. Hello again. Today, we are going to do some more Santa Claus drawings. I know Christmas is over, but for the study I'm doing, I need some more pictures of Santa Claus.

For the "man" condition, instructions on each occasion were the following:

First occasion. Hello. My name is ___. I have been to visit a lot of boys and girls your age. At the schools I visit, I ask the children to draw pictures for me. Today, I would like you to draw a picture of a man for me. (At this point materials were distributed and questions were answered to indicate that the children should draw any man they would like to draw.) As soon as you get your paper and crayons, you may begin.

Second occasion. Hi. Do you remember who I am? What did we do the last time I came? What did we draw? Well, today, I would like you to draw another picture of a man for me.

Third occasion. Hello again. Did you have a nice Christmas? Today, I'd like you to make some more man drawings for me. For the study I'm doing, I need some more pictures of men.

Samples of Children

The final sample sizes for the study, consisting of all children who were present and drew a human figure upon all three drawing occasions, were 129 for the "Santa Claus" condition (68 boys, 61 girls) and 106 for the "man" condition (49 boys, 57 girls). The children were distributed among all of the kindergarten classes taught in 6 private schools—9 classes at 3 schools for the "Santa Claus" condition and 6 classes at the other 3 schools for the "man" condition. Five to 6 years in age, all children were middle class in socio-economic background, and most were white. To indicate the amount of attrition taking place because of absences on one or two of the three occasions or failure to draw a human figure on all three occasions, the largest number of children present on any one of the three occasions was 162 for the "Santa Claus" condition and 126 for the "man" condition. Attrition rates were comparable for the two sexes.

Scoring of Drawings

Size of drawn figures was evaluated in each of two ways, which were expected to yield parallel results as means of testing the hypotheses of the study: the two kinds of measures used concerned height and area. *Height,* a one-dimensional index of size based on the approach taken by Sechrest and Wallace (1964), was defined as the height of the figure, measured along the axis of the figure, to the nearest millimeter. *Area*, a two-dimensional index of size deriving from the method used by Wallach and Gahm (1960), Wallach, Green, Lipsitt, and Minehart (1962), Wallach and Thomas (1963), Wallach and Brantley (1968), and Wallach and Martin (1970), was defined in the following way. A 12 inch by 18 inch sheet of clear lucite, ruled off into 1 inch squares, was placed on the figure in such an orientation as to minimize the number of squares falling on any part of the figure's area. Unlike the earlier applications of such a grid in the studies just cited, which did not concern representational drawings, any empty squares were included in the count if they fell within the outline of the figure. The measure was the number of squares covering the figure or any part of it.

In scoring the drawings for height and area, any naturally attached items of clothing worn by the figure were included in defining the figure's extent. For example, if a hat was attached to the head of the Santa Claus or the man drawings, it was included in the definition of the figure. If a hat was present but not attached to a figure's head, however, it was not included in the scoring. Additional items of paraphernalia, such as Santa Claus's bag of presents, were not included in the scoring. It should be noted that the scoring convention just described concerning clothing has the consequence that figures in the "Santa Claus" condition should turn out to be larger than those in the "man" condition, for the mere reason that a hat is part of the conventional image of Santa Claus while its presence on the figure of a man is much less predictable. The conventional images of "Santa Claus" versus "man" differ in other ways too that can be expected to yield larger drawings of the former than the latter—such as the stereotype of Santa as on the chubby side. Santa Claus drawings were expected to be larger in general than man drawings, therefore, simply because of predictable differences in the conventional image for the two kinds of figures.

While the instructions requested that only one figure be drawn, occasionally a child made more than one. Only one figure was scored in those cases, however, and it was chosen by the following rules: (1) If the drawing was from the "Santa Claus" condition and one figure looked more or most like Santa Claus, it was scored. (2) If the first rule did not apply, that figure which was more or most complex was scored, with complexity defined by counting the number of features present (hair, eyes, ears, nose, etc.) and the number of colors used—any tie in the total being broken by giving precedence to features over colors.

RESULTS AND DISCUSSION

Since the hypotheses under consideration make no differential predictions as a function of sex of child, the results that follow are presented for both sexes combined—as also was the case, by the way, for the results reported by Sechrest and Wallace. To check, however, we did take a preliminary look at the results separately by sex before combining them. The outcome, in brief, of considering the data for boys and girls separately was as follows. Strong support was forthcoming for the stylistic consistency prediction because the correlations bearing upon this prediction (see Tables 5 and 6 below) were of the same order of magnitude for the sexes separately as for the sexes combined. The situational specificity prediction, on the other hand, failed to receive clear support because one of the two sexes actually showed, by both height and area measues, a mean *decrease* in size from first to second occasions.

The Situational Specificity Prediction: Children's Drawings of Santa Claus, But Not of a Man, Will Become Larger from First to Second, and Smaller from Second to Third Occasions

Turning first to the evidence bearing upon the situational specificity hypothesis, Tables 1 and 2 present the relevant means and standard deviations for the height and area measures, respectively, of figure size. It is apparent from the large magnitudes of the standard deviations relative to the means in the case of each measure that individual variation in size of figure on any occasion is considerable. We nevertheless can ask whether, despite these substantial amounts of variability, the predicted form of statistical interaction between "Santa Claus" versus "man" conditions, on the one hand, and the three occasions of measurement, on the other, is obtained. The means indicate a negative answer to this question since, for both the height and the area measures, while size of Santa Claus drawings goes up from first to second occasions, it also goes up—rather than decreasing—from second to third occasions. Instead of an inverted U-curve effect for the Santa Claus figures, therefore, something more like a continuously rising trend is found. The drawings in the "man" condition do not share in this trend, becoming if anything smaller across the three occasions—an outcome that would be congruent per se with the situational specificity prediction had the inverted U-curve been found in the "Santa Claus" condition.

Repeated measures analyses of variance for these data, using the unweighted means solution for unequal group size (Winer, 1971), are presented in Tables 3 and 4, respectively, for height and area. That the interaction between conditions and occasions turns out in both analyses to be statistically significant must be viewed as an ambiguous outcome since, as just noted, the mean sizes for Santa Claus drawings did not fall into the inverted U-curve pattern that had been predicted on the basis of the Sechrest-Wallace research. Recall as well that, when examining the results separately by sex, the means for one sex in the "Santa Claus" condition had actually become smaller rather than larger from first to second occasions.

Returning to the height and area means in Tables 1 and 2 we find, in fact, that they span only a small range within each of the two conditions—for height, about 14 millimeters in one condition and about 8 millimeters in the other; for area, about 4 square inches in one condition and about 2 square inches in the

Table 1. Means and Standard Deviations for Figure Height (Millimeters) in the "Santa Claus" and "Man" Conditions on Each of the Three Occasions

	First occasion	Second occasion	Third occasion
"Santa Claus" condition (N = 129)	216.4 (mean) 89.94 (SD)	220.9 (mean) 95.27 (SD)	230.2 (mean) 93.33 (SD)
"Man" condition (N = 106)	178.2 (mean) 74.27 (SD)	175.1 (mean) 77.66 (SD)	170.3 (mean) 68.55 (SD)

Table 2. Means and Standard Deviations for Figure Area (Square Inches) in the "Santa Claus" and "Man" Conditions on Each of the Three Occasions

	First occasion	Second occasion	Third occasion
"Santa Claus" condition (N = 129)	38.6 (mean) 29.59 (SD)	41.1 (mean) 33.56 (SD)	42.8 (mean) 32.10 (SD)
"Man" condition (N = 106)	28.0 (mean) 20.42 (SD)	27.7 (mean) 22.87 (SD)	26.0 (mean) 23.47 (SD)

Table 3. Repeated Measures Analysis of Variance for the Figure Height Data in Table 1

Source	df	MS	F	p
Between subjects	234			
Conditions	1	401,675.047	27.214	<.001
Subjects within groups	233	14,759.493		
Within subjects	470			
Occasions	2	553.071	0.162	n.s.
Conditions × occasions	2	20,822.972	6.064	<.01
Occasions × subjects within groups	466	3,433.763		

Table 4. Repeated Measures Analysis of Variance for the Figure Area Data in Table 2

Source	df	MS	F	p
Between subjects	234			
Conditions	1	32,290.409	19.286	<.001
Subjects within groups	233	1,674.257		
Within subjects	470			
Occasions	2	93.924	0.283	n.s.
Conditions × occasions	2	2,001.274	6.036	<.01
Occasions × subjects within groups	466	331.554		

other. That differences of such small magnitudes can yield a statistically significant interaction of a form that was not predicted beforehand seems best understood as offering yet another example of the way, as discussed in the introduction, statistically significant interactions can be obtained that do not replicate. This one, after all, failed to replicate the interaction effect pattern that had been found—at a statistically significant level—by Sechrest and Wallace. Our conclusion, therefore, is that the prediction made on the basis of the situational specificity hypothesis was not supported by the results. Furthermore, even if one wants to argue on a post hoc basis that a different type of situational control than what had been predicted was manifested in the results, it must be admitted that the effect at best is quite small in magnitude.

There is, on the other hand, another kind of effect revealed in Tables 1 through 4 that is substantial in its magnitude—although theoretically un-interesting. As expected on the mere basis of differences in the conventional images of "Santa Claus" and a "man," as discussed before—such as the greater likelihood that figures of the former kind will wear a hat—we find in Tables 1 and 2 that, by both height and area measures, Santa Claus figures are considerably larger across the board than figures of a man. The substantial magnitudes of these size differences—something on the order of 46 millimeters for height and 13 square inches for area—are reflected in the large F values found for conditions in Tables 3 and 4.

In sum—and contrary to what Sechrest and Wallace had suggested—the situational specificity hypothesis fares rather poorly as a means of accounting for variation in size of children's drawings. This is the case even at an age level which the Sechrest-Wallace evidence suggested should be particularly conducive to supporting that hypothesis. We must next ask whether the stylistic consistency hypothesis does any better.

The Stylistic Consistency Prediction: Children's Drawings of Santa Claus or of a Man Will Show Consistency of Size Across All Occasions

Recalling the extensive individual variation in size of drawing found in Tables 1 and 2 for any occasion, it is clear that there is plenty of opportunity, in principle, for stylistic consistency to manifest itself. But does it? Tables 5 and 6

Table 5. Product Moment Correlations for Figure Height between Each Pair of Occasions within the "Santa Claus" and "Man" Conditions

	First and second occasions	First and third occasions	Second and third occasions
"Santa Claus" condition (N = 129)	.628	.507	.540
"Man" condition (N = 106)	.500	.465	.563

Table 6. Product Moment Correlations for Figure Area between Each Pair of Occasions within the "Santa Claus" and "Man" Conditions

	First and second occasions	First and third occasions	Second and third occasions
"Santa Claus" condition (N = 129)	.576	.528	.616
"Man" condition (N = 106)	.514	.533	.681

answer this question for the figure height and figure area measures, respectively, reporting product moment correlations between each pair of the three occasions for the children in each of the two drawing task conditions. For either measure of size, stylistic consistency is found to be considerable indeed. It is equally substantial, furthermore, for children asked to draw Santa Claus on the various occasions and for children asked to draw a man each time. And this high degree of consistency maintains itself not only across the two weeks from first to second occasion and the three weeks from second to third, but also across the five-week period from first to third. The consistency results thus turn out to replicate across the different pairs of measurement occasions and also across the two drawing topics that comprised the task for different groups of children.

Regarding their specific magnitudes, all 12 of the correlations in Tables 5 and 6 are sufficiently large not only to be significant well beyond the .001 level by two-tailed tests but also to account for substantial proportions of the variance in the measures. The correlations fall, by and large, in the area of .5−.6, with one even up toward .7. This means that they are accounting for something on the order of 25 to 36 percent of the variance. Such consistency correlations are considerably higher, of course, than those in the personality literature reviewed by Mischel (1968), on the basis of which he found himself concluding in favor of the situational specificity idea.

It seems evident, then, that drawing size as a stylistic aspect or effect of behavior shows a high degree of consistency from one occasion to another. By contrast, the thesis that drawing size is controlled by environmental events received no clear support in our research, and would seem at best—even if it ultimately proves to be valid in some sense—to account for only a small portion of the size variation that is found in drawings. We have provided through these data a demonstration that size of children's drawings is very much a matter of stylistic consistency. Here is one respect in which a person will be quite consistent. It concerns a characteristic of art products that is of intrinsic interest as such, and one for which, moreover, situational specificity had been claimed on the basis of previous work—even in language so strong as to refer to the connection between Christmas and the size of Santa Claus drawings as an "intimate relationship" (Solley & Murphy, 1960, p. 165).

The place to look for consistency thus is in behaviors and behavioral effects that provide us with inherently meaningful information about people—not in relationships, whether for unselected samples or moderator-defined subsamples, among "test responses" whose claim to our attention is that they supposedly refer to some hypothetical trait or disposition. That humans do in fact show consistency across occasions for a wide range of their activities and behavioral products seems fairly clear and can, as we have seen here for size of children's drawings, be evaluated as an hypothesis in regard to any realm of phenomena in which we find ourselves interested. It may be noticed that there is in all of this a leaf that we advise taking from the behaviorists, but it is not their inclination toward the situational specificity hypothesis. Rather, it is their tendency to choose as objects of study behaviors which they care about as such, instead of focusing on presumptive signs of hypothetical entities.

SUMMARY

This paper argued that the controversy over the extent to which behavior is cross-situationally consistent versus situationally specific has been led astray by an erroneous assumption. The error consists in assuming that the case for consistency rests upon finding evidence for constructs, traits, or dispositions—an enterprise that gets carried out by seeking correlations among measures that are not of interest in their own right but only as presumptive indicators of an underlying hypothetical entity of some kind. The low correlations typically found as the result of this enterprise of "construct validation" have been viewed by situational specificity advocates as support for their position. Most recently, advocates of the consistency position have responded to such low correlations by proposing that the correlations should be run not on unselected samples but on subsamples selected by other measures—"moderator variables"—that are thought to yield groups for whom the constructs, traits, or dispositions are more relevant than they were for the unselected samples. We discovered, however, that the correlational evidence resulting from this moderator variable approach in fact is no more promising than it was for unselected samples, and we pointed out that the moderator approach really is not very different from the method it tried to improve upon because it too assumes that to document consistency you must find evidence for traits or dispositions.

We asserted rather that the place to look for consistency is in behavior itself and its products. A person is consistent in a particular respect to the extent that he manifests behavior or effects of behavior that are similar across different occasions, and that differ from the behavior or behavioral effects produced by others under these same circumstances. Finding a person to be consistent is noteworthy, therefore, to the extent that the *way in which* he manifests consistency is of direct interest to us as an object of study—rather than a "test response" of meaning only as a possible sign of a construct. Some behavioral phenomena which have this kind of inherent interest-value and which can in principle be examined for possible evidence of consistency then were considered. Two kinds of potential consistency were distinguished—consistency in the exhibiting of competences and in the style with which performances are carried out or products made. Because critics of the consistency thesis may be particularly skeptical about the existence of stylistic forms of consistency, we then proceeded to an empirical demonstration which tested the consistency hypothesis in regard to a matter of style—namely, the sizes of drawings of figures made by kindergarten children. As a particularly stringent test of the stylistic consistency claim, moreover, we chose an experimental paradigm which had provided earlier results that seemed to support the situational specificity view.

Drawings of Santa Claus and of a man were collected from different groups of kindergarten children at various points in time before and after Christmas. The situational specificity prediction, as derived from earlier work within the same paradigm, was that Santa Claus drawings should be larger right before Christmas than they are when made earlier or when made after Christmas is over, while this kind of inverted U-curve effect should not be found for drawings of a man. The stylistic consistency prediction, on the other hand, was that drawings made on any given topic should have a size that is characteristic for each person regardless of the occasion on which the drawings are produced. With data for a total of 235 kindergarten children and drawing size evaluated in terms both of figure height and figure area, strong support was found for the stylistic consistency prediction (consistency correlations on the order of .5–.6), while no clear support was found for the situational specificity prediction.

REFERENCES

Alker, H. A. Is personality situationally specific or intrapsychically consistent? *Journal of Personality,* 1972, **40,** 1–16.

Bem, D. J. Constructing cross-situational consistencies in behavior: Some thoughts on Alker's critique of Mischel. *Journal of Personality,* 1972, **40,** 17–26.

Child, I. L. Personality in culture. In E. F. Borgatta and W. W. Lambert (Eds.), *Handbook of personality theory and research.* Chicago: Rand McNally, 1968.

Craddick, R. A. Size of Santa Claus drawings as a function of time before and after Christmas. *Journal of Psychological Studies,* 1961, **12,** 121–125.

Kogan, N., & Wallach, M. A. *Risk taking: A Study in cognition and personality.* New York: Holt, Rinehart and Winston, 1964.

Kogan, N., & Wallach, M. A. Risk taking as a function of the situation, the person, and the group. In *New directions in psychology III.* New York: Holt, Rinehart and Winston, 1967.

Kuhn, T. S. *The structure of scientific revolutions.* Chicago: University of Chicago Press, 1962.

Mischel, W. *Personality and assessment.* New York: Wiley, 1968.

Mischel, W. Continuity and change in personality. *American Psychologist,* 1969, **24,** 1012–1018.

Richards, J. M., Jr., Holland, J. L., & Lutz, S. W. Prediction of student accomplishment in college. *Journal of Educational Psychology,* 1967, **58,** 343–355.

Sechrest, L., & Wallace, J. Figure drawings and naturally occurring events: Elimination of the expansive euphoria hypothesis. *Journal of Educational Psychology,* 1964, **55,** 42–44.

Solley, C. M., & Haigh, G. A. A note to Santa Claus. *Topeka Research Papers, The Menninger Foundation,* 1957, **18,** 4–5.

Solley, C. M., & Murphy, G. *Development of the perceptual world.* New York: Basic Books, 1960.

Taft, R. Extraversion, neuroticism, and expressive behavior: An application of Wallach's moderator effect to handwriting analysis. *Journal of Personality,* 1967, **35,** 570–584.

Wallach, M. A. Active-analytical vs. passive-global cognitive functioning. In S. Messick and J. Ross (Eds.), *Measurement in personality and cognition.* New York: Wiley, 1962.

Wallach, M. A. Thinking, feeling, and expressing: Toward understanding the person. In R. Jessor and S. Feshbach (Eds.), *Cognition, personality, and clinical psychology.* San Francisco: Jossey-Bass, 1967.

Wallach, M. A., & Brantley, H. T. Relative graphic expansiveness as a function of gross bodily activity and level of psychological disturbance. *Journal of Personality,* 1968, **36,** 246–258.

Wallach, M. A., & Gahm, R. C. Personality functions of graphic constriction and expansiveness. *Journal of Personality,* 1960, **28,** 73–83.

Wallach, M. A., Green, L. R., Lipsitt, P. D., & Minehart, J. B. Contradiction between overt and projective personality indicators as a function of defensiveness. *Psychological Monographs,* 1962, **76,** No. 1 (Whole No. 520).

Wallach, M. A., & Greenberg, C. Personality functions of symbolic sexual arousal to music. *Psychological Monographs,* 1960, **74,** No. 7 (Whole No. 494).

Wallach, M. A., & Martin, M. L. Effects of social class on children's motoric expression. *Developmental Psychology,* 1970, **3,** 106–113.

Wallach, M. A., & Thomas, H. L. Graphic constriction and expansiveness as a function of induced social isolation and social interaction: Experimental manipulations and personality effects. *Journal of Personality,* 1963, **31,** 491–509.

Winer, B. J. *Statistical principles in experimental design.* (2nd ed.) New York: McGraw-Hill, 1971.

Wing, C. W., Jr., & Wallach, M. A. *College admissions and the psychology of talent.* New York: Holt, Rinehart and Winston, 1971.

35

Psychodynamics, Behavior Therapy, and the Implacable Experimenter: An Inquiry into the Consistency of Personality

PAUL L. WACHTEL

One of the central points of contention between behavior therapists and those theorists and clinicians with a psychodynamic viewpoint is the degree of consistency and generality evident in personality functioning. Dynamic therapists tend to view personality as an organized system. Many diverse events are viewed as functionally related, and the person's individuality is expected to show itself in a wide variety of situations. Even where seemingly inconsistent behaviors appear, the viewpoint of most psychodynamic thinkers points toward a search for underlying organizational principles that can account for the phenotypic behavioral differences in terms of a genotypic description of that person's psychic structure.

Such a characterization of psychodynamic approaches as seeking coherence in people's behavior may at first glance seem inconsistent with the strong emphasis of psychodynamicists on conflict. But an examination of the explanatory role of conflict in most psychodynamic theories reveals that often *conflict itself* is the organizing principle providing coherence in the seeming diversity of everyday behavior. For example, excessive timidity in one context and extreme aggressiveness in another may both be seen as manifestations of a strong conflict over aggression. Both kinds of behavior may be seen as bearing the stamp of the person who is readily aroused to act hostilely and who is also afraid of this tendency in himself. Such divergent extremes are viewed from a psychodynamic perspective, especially one that emphasizes the analysis of character, with an eye

From the *Journal of Abnormal Psychology,* 1973, *82,* 324–334. Copyright 1973 by the American Psychological Association. Reprinted by permission.

Much of the work on this paper was accomplished while the author was at the Research Center for Mental Health at New York University and was supported by Grant 5-P01-MH17545 from the National Institute of Mental Health.

toward finding underlying unities, though these unities lie in the organizing role of conflict or apparent *dis*unity.

In contrast, the theoretical underpinnings of behavior therapy have tended to stress specificity in behavior and the relative independence of an individual's various response dispositions. Little emphasis is placed on the relation among the responses made by a person in different situations or between these responses and any organizing personality structure. As Mischel (1968) pointed out, low response-response correlations are expected by social behavior theory, and the focus of investigation by workers in this framework is on how particular behaviors are independently related to particular stimulus situations. Mischel's influential brief for a social behaviorist approach to personality assessment and therapy begins with and is largely based upon a critical examination of the research on consistency of personality. The meager yield of efforts to demonstrate consistency is one of the central issues in Mischel's argument against the psychodynamic approach.

Mischel's arguments are cogent and his analysis thoughtful and perceptive. But before psychodynamic concepts are forever consigned to that scientific Valhalla flowing bountifully with phlogiston, ether, and the four humors, it may be of value to take another look both at the kind of consistency in fact predicted by psychodynamic theories and the kind of studies that have supported the case for specificity. The present paper argues (*a*) that modern psychodynamic theories are far more able to deal with the facts of man's responsiveness to variations in stimulus conditions than the model of psychoanalysis typically described by proponents of behavior therapy; and (*b*) that the particular way of framing questions in much experimental personality research tends to underestimate the degree of consistency that does exist in the everyday behavior of individuals. Consequently, there is far more possibility of convergence between the theories and techniques of behavior therapists and dynamic therapists than is generally recognized. The worker from either perspective who dismisses the work of the "opposing" approach risks diminishing his efficacy in aiding men of flesh and blood for the pleasures of slaying men of straw.

VARIETIES OF PSYCHODYNAMIC APPROACHES

Typically, when proponents of behavioral approaches discuss psychodynamic theories, it is Freudian psychoanalysis of the early twentieth century that is their focus. Little attention is paid to the later developments in Freud's own work, much less to those contributions of later writers within the psychoanalytic and interpersonal traditions. For example, Bandura and Walters (1963) stated:

the psychodynamic "disease" model thus leads one to seek determinants of deviant behavior in terms of relatively autonomous internal agents and processes in the form of "unconscious psychic forces," "dammed-up energies," "cathexes," "countercathexes," "defenses," "complexes," and other hypothetical conditions or states having only a tenuous relationship to the social stimuli that precede them or even to the behavioral "symptoms" or "symbols" that they supposedly explain [p. 30].

In a later volume, Bandura (1969) again suggested that psychodynamic theories posit "an organism that is impelled from within but is relatively insensitive to environmental stimuli or to the immediate consequences of its actions [p. 19]."

Were such characterizations written before World War I, they might have been cogent and important. For a variety of reasons, discussed elsewhere, Freud did for a time emphasize internal, "instinctual" processes almost to the exclusion of environmental and learning factors. Even in his later writings, despite the introduction of important conceptual changes pointing toward concern with environmental events (e.g., Freud, orig. publ. 1923, 1926), Freud's theorizing showed an imbalance in favor of the inner and automatic. And it is unfortunately the case that many psychodynamic thinkers continue to operate on the basis of this inadequate early model.

But more sophisticated modern varieties of psychodynamic thinking are quite different from this early model. An important example of the development in psychodynamic models is provided by recent psychoanalytic discussions of the energy concepts in psychoanalysis. Critics of psychoanalysis have often, with considerable cogency, pointed particularly to the circular and pseudoscientific way in which terms and concepts such as cathexis, countercathexis, and dammed-up libido are used. Within the psychoanalytic community as well, such criticisms were at times voiced (e.g., Kubie, 1947), and Erikson (1950), in his highly influential *Childhood and Society,* commented that Freud's use of the thermodynamic language of his day, with its emphasis on the conservation and transformation of energy, was an analogy or working hypothesis that "appeared to be making concrete claims which neither observation nor experiment could even attempt to substantiate [p. 59]." But despite Erikson's clear illustration by example that the important insights of psychoanalysis could be expressed more clearly without resort to the confusing and vulnerable energy formulations, such "metapsychological" theorizing continued to abound in psychoanalytic writing.

Within the past few years, however, a number of authors writing from a perspective within the psychoanalytic point of view have provided not only serious criticism of the energy constructs but demonstrations that *such constructs are not at all essential to the main points of psychoanalysis* (e.g., Holt, 1967; Klein, 1966, 1969; Loevinger, 1966; Schafer, 1970; Wachtel, 1969). Thus criticisms of psychoanalysis as positing a closed energy system within which blind energies build up and discharge, oblivious to the world outside, address themselves to an outmoded and inessential feature of the psychoanalytic approach.

Other developments in psychoanalytic theory in recent years also distinguish it from the model usually discussed by behavior therapists, and render it more able to handle the data indicative of behavioral specificity. Although earlier versions of psychoanalytic theory paid inadequate attention to adaptation and response to real situations, the psychoanalytic ego psychology that has developed from the work of Hartmann (1939), Erikson (1950), and others has led to a far greater concern with how the developing human being learns to adapt to the real demands, opportunities, and dangers that his ever-widening world presents to him. To be sure, psychoanalytic workers do attribute greater organization and consistency to personality than stimulus-response theorists, and posit greater residual influence of psychic structures formed by the early interaction of biological givens with environmental contingencies. But these integrating structures are not independent entities driving people to predetermined behaviors regardless of the stimulus conditions that prevail. They are, rather, persistent proclivities to perceive particular classes of stimulus configurations in particular idiosyncratic fashion, and to behave in accordance with these perceptions.

Accordingly, selectivity of perception has become a central concern of modern psychoanalytic researchers, who far from being indifferent to how stimuli influence and guide our behavior, have intensively studied precisely how we do register, interpret, and respond to environmental stimulation. Thus psychoanalytically oriented researchers have in recent years been studying processes of selective attention and inattention (Luborsky, Blinder, & Schimek, 1965; Shapiro, 1965; Wachtel, 1967), styles of perceiving and thinking (e.g., Gardner, Holzman, Klein, Linton, & Spence, 1959), the effects of weak or ambiguous stimuli (Pine, 1964), and the effects of the *absence* of environmental stimulation (e.g., Goldberger, 1966; Holt, 1965). Psychoanalytic thinkers guided by such models would hardly be embarrassed by observations of different behavior in different situations.

Even more explicitly attentive to situational influences and the occurrence of different behavior in different situations is the interpersonal school of psychodynamic thought (e.g., Sullivan, 1953). Sullivan has in fact questioned the very concept of a "personality" as an entity independent of the interpersonal situation in which a person exists. In place of the older, more static model of the analyst as a blank screen upon which the patient's transference distortions are projected, Sullivan emphasized the analyst's role as a *participant* observer. The blank screen model did stem largely from a conception of personality that paid little attention to stimulus determinants of a person's thoughts, feelings, and actions. The underlying structure was sought in a way that implied it could be described independently of the situations in which the person found himself. In the absence of external distractions, the true personality was expected to be revealed. In contrast, the model of the participant observer implies not only that the analyst cannot be a blank screen (after all, a person upon whom one is relying for relief from suffering, who does not permit himself to be looked at, rarely answers questions, and requests a good portion of one's income is hardly a "neutral" stimulus) but also that to even attempt to observe the "personality" free from the "distorting" effects of one's own influence upon the person's behavior is to seek after an illusion. For the person is always responding to some situation, and a silent, unresponsive analyst is no less "real" a stimulus than a warm, energetic, or humorous one.[1]

---

[1] It should be clear, however, that when the therapist does not reveal his reactions to the patient's behavior, he makes more likely the observation of hidden assumptions and strivings

The contrast between the "blank screen" and "participant observer" models raises a number of therapeutic issues that cannot be discussed in detail in this presentation. Among them are (a) the importance of the therapist knowing clearly what kind of stimulus he in fact is. (The "myth of therapist homogeneity" is apparent not only in outcome research, where Kiesler [1966] first labeled it, but also in much theoretical writing on technique in the psychoanalytic literature); (b) the advisability of the therapist *intentionally* being a different stimulus at different times (cf. Alexander, 1956; Wolf, 1966); (c) the role of group therapy in eliciting a wider range of the patient's responses to various interpersonal situations; and (d) the relation between interpersonal assessments and behavioral assessments as ways of sampling response to a variety of situations (cf. below and Goldfried & Kent, 1972).

It may also be noted that in some sense experimenters are now going through a reorientation similar to that which occurred in psychoanalysis. The work of writers such as Rosenthal (1966) and Orne (1962) points to the limits of a "blank screen" conception of the experimenter, and the importance of recognizing that the experimenter too is a *participant* observer. Parts of the discussion below suggest that, rather than being merely a nuisance to be corrected for, the experimenter's influence as a participating human other may be an untapped source of richer knowledge of personality functioning.

FRAMING OF QUESTIONS BY ANALYSTS AND EXPERIMENTERS

It should now be clear that the picture of psychodynamic theories as necessarily describing people as moved solely by inner urges and as inattentive to environmental demands is a portrait in straw. The mere fact that behavior varies from situation to situation is in no way a refutation of the psychodynamic approach. Equally fallacious is the view, held by many dynamic thinkers, that all behavior therapists are unaware of individual differences, blind to the role of language and cognition, and uninterested in how a person's history has led to idiosyncratic patterns of equating situations and developing preferences (see, e.g., Mischel, 1968, or Bandura, 1969). Tenable theories converge as their range of inquiry begins to expand and overlap. Nonetheless, it hardly needs to be pointed out that Mischel's conclusions from the data he cited do differ considerably from the view of man evident in the writings of even modern psychodynamic thinkers. This article now considers how in some respects both views may be seen as correct, as a step toward guidelines for theoretical integration and practical innovation.

---

which might not emerge were clearer clues as to "expected" or "appropriate" behavior to homogenize patient response. Stone (1961) and Greenson (1967) have presented sophisticated discussions of these issues from a Freudian point of view. The present author's differences from their view center on the degree to which psychodynamic descriptions can and should consider evoking situations.

"Neurotics" and "Normals"

Psychodynamic theories developed originally to account for primarily maladaptive behavior. Learning theories, in contrast, have tended to start with observations of successful alteration of behavior in response to situational demands. (Learning curves are typically monotonically increasing.) Though both broad theoretical perspectives have subsequently developed to encompass detailed consideration of both adaptive and maladaptive behavior, each still bears the stamp of its origin. Learning theorists prefer to examine how even behavior that is troublesome is in some way in tune with current environmental contingencies. Dynamically oriented thinkers, on the other hand, frequently are most interested in how a person's behavior is *out of touch* with the current situation, how he *fails* to adapt to changing situations.

In a sense, the defining property of neurotic behavior is its rigidity, its inflexibility in the face of changed conditions. Psychodynamic theories, which originated as theories of neurosis, heavily emphasize concepts that account for lack of change and are particularly designed to describe the persistence of past patterns into the present. Among the most prominent of these concepts is that of transference, the tendency to react to persons in the present as though they were important figures from one's past.[2] Transference is viewed by psychodynamic thinkers as a phenomenon evident in all people, but one whose influence may be expected to be greater in more severely neurotic persons than in the general population. When one considers the difference between the population of severe neurotics who constitute the observational base for psychodynamic theories, and the less psychologically handicapped groups who form the population for most of the studies Mischel cited as evidence for specificity, at least some of the difference in theoretical perspective becomes understandable.[3] It is likely that the neurotic patients seen by psychoanalysts are considerably less able to alter their behavior appropriately from situation to situation and person to person than a typical group of children or adults. That inability is a major reason why the former are in therapy.

Ambiguity and Affect

Mischel noted in passing, but did not emphasize, that when stimulus conditions are ambiguous, individual differences arising from past history are more noticeable. Here lies another important source of difference in the observations

---

[2] Here again it should be clear that transference need not be viewed as a completely autonomous inner disposition but rather as a particular way of organizing new stimulus input, biased but not completely unresponsive to the actual situation (cf. Alexander, 1956; Sullivan, 1953; Wolf, 1966).

[3] Alker (1972) has made a similar point in an important recent paper that may be seen as complementing the present contribution. Several sections which appeared in earlier drafts of this paper have been shortened or omitted because they are excellently dealt with by Alker.

and theorizing of analysts and social behaviorist researchers. In addition to focusing their efforts on somewhat different populations, workers from these differing orientations also concentrate on different phenomena.

The data generated and examined by most behaviorally oriented students of normal and abnormal behavior involve changes in clearly denotable behaviors in response to clear, unambiguous changes in environmental events. The subject, or the model in some studies, is given money or has it taken away, he is shocked or he escapes from shock, he is allowed privileges or they are denied him, etc. Under such circumstances, a kind of lawfulness tends to emerge in which the ʻcomplicated formulations of psychodynamic theorists seem very much beside the point. Behavior varies closely with changes in environmental events. The individual's "learning history with similar stimuli" is, of course, relevant, but one hardly needs to conceptualize complex personality structures with considerable cross-situational application. Change the situation and you change the behavior.

To the analyst, however, such studies are likely to seem irrelevant to the phenomena of interest to him. The data he observes consist largely of statements such as: "I feel angry at my girlfriend because she smiled in a condescending way. She said it was a warm smile, but it didn't feel that way to me." Or, "My boss criticized me for being so insistent with him, but I could tell from his tone of voice he was really proud of my assertiveness, and I had a good feeling that he supports me." Or, "It seemed to me that you were more silent this hour. I felt you were angry with me because I complained about the fee, and I was afraid you'd say we should stop therapy. I know you'll think *I'm* the angry one, and *I* want to stop, but I think you're wrong, and I resent your distortion of my feelings."

Such reports do describe behavior in response to environmental events. In principle, a girlfriend's smile, a boss' tone of voice, or an analyst's silence are events that can be observed just as the administration of a food pellet to a rat or a token to a back-ward patient. But whereas the latter two events are specifically chosen to be clear and unequivocal, the interpersonal events scrutinized by the analyst are often exceedingly ambiguous. The experimenter, no less than the subject, must judge on largely idiosyncratic grounds whether a smile is warm or condescending, and observer reliability regarding a tone of voice is unlikely to be impressive. Views may and do differ as to whether it is a wise *strategy* to study such ambiguous events at this point in the development of our discipline, but it must be acknowledged that we all spend a good portion of each day responding more or less adequately to just such ambiguous "stimuli."

The events focused on by analysts, then, tend to be those in which their patients' ability to discriminate is most challenged. Finely articulated alteration of response with stimulus changes, evident in studies where environmental events are readily discriminable, is not so evident where affective, interpersonal events are concerned. In the latter realm, early global and generalized predispositions may less readily become differentiated, and assumptions and reaction tendencies may apply to a wider range of situations. In Piagetian terms, analysts are likely

observing phenomena where difficulties in perceptual discrimination make assimilation predominant, whereas Mischel's emphasis on specificity applies to
situations where a greater degree of accommodation and differentiation is
possible.

It should also be noted that in the examples of psychoanalytic data noted
above, the patient's *response* is complicated and ambiguous, as well as the
situation to which the response is made. The man who claimed his analyst was
more silent during the hour stressed that he (the patient) was not angry, that it
was the analyst who was angry at him. But he ended up saying he *resented* the
analyst's distortion, and he earlier *complained* about the fee. One may well
wonder whether this man was in fact angry, or framed differently, at what point
in the session he first became angry, or from a slightly different perspective,
which situations evoke in him a tendency to attack or hurt and which to
experience and label his response as "anger." However one wishes to frame the
question, it would seem that how best to conceptualize and describe his affective
response to the situation he perceives is exceedingly difficult, and that a great
deal of interpretation and inference is necessary to decide fully just how he did
respond.

Many researchers, faced with such ambiguity, have decided it is best to study
simply the overt behaviors that can be reliably and consistently identified and
that to worry about whether or not the patient is really "angry" is a fruitless
endeavor. Such a strategy does yield clearer curves and a greater sense of having
discerned a repeatable pattern. But it must also be noted that the dilemma faced
by the researcher is also faced by each of us in our everyday lives. We are all
frequently faced with the task of understanding and identifying our own
affective responses to the events of our lives, and as Dollard and Miller (1950)
have pointed out, failure to label accurately one's own drive states has very
serious consequences. Further, the personal experience of feeling and wishing, no
matter how difficult to study, remains an exceedingly important psychological
phenomenon, and changes in experienced feeling states are often the implicit
hidden criteria of avowedly behavioral programs of therapy (Locke, 1971).

The difficulty in accurately identifying ambiguous affective and motivational
phenomena renders perception of these events, whether one's own feelings and
wishes or those of others, peculiarly susceptible to the distorting effects of
anxiety; hence the particular emphasis on anxiety and defense by psychoanalytic
authors. In attempting to study defensive processes experimentally, researchers
have frequently focused on distortions of perception of *external* stimuli and have
been forced to introduce ambiguity through artificial means, such as tachistoscopic
presentation. Such procedures correctly take into account that the concept of defensive distortion depends on ambiguity and does not imply an arbitrary and un-
checked intrusion upon perception of clearly discriminable events. The study of defense via perceptual experiments has, however, typically involved a number of other
difficulties (Wachtel, 1972; Wolitzky & Wachtel, 1972). Psychodynamic concepts of
defense are concerned primarily with phenomena of *self*-perception, particularly

perception of one's own affective and motivational states. As with other aspects of psychoanalytic thinking, defensive phenomena too are now seen as responsive to environmental, as well as organismic, events, but their relation to environmental occurrences is seen as far more complex than is the case with the behavioral phenomena typically studied in social learning experiments (see Silverman, 1972, for an interesting and lucid discussion of clinical and experimental data bearing on the psychoanalytic conceptualization of this relationship).

The preference of behaviorally oriented investigators for seeking simple stimulus-response relationships, and for focusing on clearly discernible events, may lead to an underestimation of the importance of complex anxiety-distorted mediating processes. In turn, the particularly strong interest of psychoanalytic investigators in the murky subtleties of wish and feeling has likely led to an underestimation of how directly their patients might respond to environmental contingencies when they are up off the couch and taking clearly visible steps. Results of efforts to alter directly psychotic behaviors (e.g., Ayllon & Azrin, 1968; Ullmann & Krasner, 1966) or particular behavioral deficits in children (e.g., Allen, Hart, Buell, Harris, & Wolf, 1964) suggest that this may be the case. As Davison (1969) has pointed out, however, such alterations of overt behavior do not necessarily imply an alteration of the ideas and feelings that accompany them.

The "Implacable Experimenter"

Still another way in which differing strategies of investigation may lead dynamic and behavioral investigators to differing conclusions is illuminated by an interpersonal perspective on human behavior. If each person's behavior is largely a function of the interpersonal situation in which he is engaged, then when two or more people interact, they are each not only influenced by the behavior of the other (in the familiar sense of a response to a stimulus); each also influences the behavior of the other, by virtue of the stimulus properties of his own behavior. Person A responds to the stimulus properties of Person B, but Person B in turn is responsive to the behavior of Person A which he has in part determined. Further, these are both continuous adaptations, not simply sequential. From such a systems orientation, the understanding of any one person's behavior in an interpersonal situation solely in terms of the stimuli *presented to* him gives only a partial and misleading picture. For to a very large extent, these stimuli are *created by* him. They are responses to his own behaviors, events he has played a role in bringing about, rather than occurrences independent of who he is and over which he has no control. The seductive, hysterical woman who is annoyed at having to face the aggressive amorous advances of numbers of men has much to learn about the origin of the stimuli she complains she must cope with. So too does the man who complains about the problems in dealing with his wife's nagging, but fails to understand how this situation, which presents itself to him, derives in turn from his own procrastinating, unresponsible behavior.

From the above considerations we may see that the postulation of consistency of personality need not be incompatible with the view that people may be acutely sensitive to changes in the stimulus situation. For consistency need not be the result of a static structure that moves from situation to situation and pays no heed to stimuli. Much of the rigidity and persistence of human behavior can be accounted for without conceiving of an id, cut off from the perceiving, adapting aspect of the personality; and the striking tendency, observed by Freud and many others, for human beings to persist in beating their heads against countless proverbial walls does not require the postulation of a repetition compulsion (Freud, orig. publ. 1920). Rather, one can in many cases view consistency as a result of being in particular situations frequently, but situations largely of one's own making and themselves describable as a characteristic of one's personality.[4]

These considerations suggest that the finding in many experiments of rather minimal consistency in behavior from situation to situation (Mischel, 1968) may be in part an artifact of the conceptual model and research strategy that has typically guided American personality research. Mischel noted the discrepancy between these research findings and the persistent impression that people are characterizable by their typical way of acting. He attributed the discrepancy largely to a documented tendency for observers to *falsely* construe consistency when diversity is the fact. But genuine consistency may also occur in most life situations and yet not be evident in the laboratory. For the typical experiment, with its emphasis on standardized independent variables as antecedents of the behavior to be studied, may short-circuit the mutual influence process described above, which is importantly involved in the generation of consistency.

In most experiments, some stimulus event is designated as the independent variable, and every effort is made to assure that this independent variable is presented to each subject in the same fashion. Research assistants are trained to behave similarly with each subject, and if they do vary their behavior in response to some feature of the subject's interpersonal style, this is generally viewed as a failure of the experimental method; the "independent variable" is supposed to be standardized. Such a model of research, with the behavior of the experimenter preprogrammed to occur independently of the myriad interpersonal cues of the subject may be designated as the model of the "implacable experimenter."[5]

Such a model is well suited for testing the isolated effect of a particular independent variable, for it assures, if proper controls are included, that that

---

[4] Millon (1969, Ch. 5) has also pointed to ways in which the principles of social learning theory may be consistent with the expectation of considerable generality in important aspects of personality.

[5] Of course, some behavior of the experimenter may be *contingent* on the subject's behavior, but it should be clear that this is a far cry from the kind of interpersonal processes discussed in this section (see Carson [1969] for descriptions of research that comes closer to the model discussed here; see also Laing, Phillipson, & Lee, 1966).

variable is what accounts for the differing behaviors in the various experimental groups. Mischel's survey suggests that in experiments conducted in this fashion, the behavior of individuals will vary considerably when the "independent variable" is varied (subject, of course, to the limiting parameters discussed above, e.g., degree of psychopathology and ambiguity of the situation encountered).

But let us note what such a research procedure does *not* examine. Although the highly practiced and routinized behavior of the experimenter does not rule out all opportunity for observing individual differences in the subjects of the study—differences in perception or interpretation of events, or in response to the same situation, may be noted—it does effectively prevent the subject from recreating familiar stimulus situations by evoking typical complementary behavior by the experimenter in response to the subject's behavior. In most life situations, whether someone is nice to us or nasty, attentive or bored, seductive or straightlaced is in good part a function of our own behavior. But in the typical experiment the subject has little control over the interpersonal situation he encounters. It has been determined even before he enters the room. Borrowing the language of the existentialists, such experiments reveal a person in his "thrownness," but do not make clear his responsibility for his situation.

Mischel (1968) suggested that the impression of identity or constancy in personality may be reinforced by regularities in the environmental contexts in which a person is observed. Mischel's focus is on the occasions when the regularity is a function of the conditions of observation rather than of the person's life, as when we only see someone in a particular context, though he in fact operates in a wide variety of situations. But what if the person is *usually* in a particular situation? In such a case it may be true that his behavior is describable as a function of his situation, and perhaps also that he could act differently if the situation were different. But then we must ask why for some people the situation is so rarely different. How do we understand the man who is constantly in the presence of overbearing women, or constantly immersed in his work, or constantly with weaker men who are cowed by him but offer little honest feedback? Further, how do we understand the man who seems to bring out the bitchy side of *whatever* woman he encounters, or ends up turning almost all social encounters into work sessions, or intimidates even men who usually are honest and direct?

Certainly we need a good deal more data before we are sure just how general such phenomena are, how characterizable people are by the situations they "just happen" to run into. What should be clear, however, is that piecemeal observation of "stimuli" and "responses" or "independent" and "dependent" variables, divorced from the temporal context of mutually influencing events, can shed little light on these questions. If experiments in the implacable experimenter model are the central source of data for one's view of man, it is understandable that conceptions of man as constructing his life or his world, or of personality as a self-maintaining system, would have little appeal.

Bem (1972), in a recent defense of Mischel's critique, has argued that the burden of proof lies with those who would posit considerable consistency in personality to demonstrate it empirically. But empirical studies may get different answers depending on how they ask their questions. A conceptual understanding of the limits of the implacable experimenter model, as well as of the other issues discussed above, may prevent a premature judgment of failure.

To ask whether behavior is best describable in terms of global traits or as responses to particular situations is to misleadingly dichotomize a very complex and important question. We have seen that modern psychodynamic thinkers do indeed consider how an individual responds to the situations he encounters. The difference between psychodynamic and social behaviorist positions lies not in whether the role of environmental events is considered, but rather in the nature of the relationship between environmental and behavioral events. To the psychodynamic theorist, this relationship is more complex and less direct than it tends to be in social learning accounts. Psychodynamic investigators have been particularly impressed with the complicating effects of anxiety and efforts learned to avoid it. The protracted helplessness of the human young, his need to rely on seemingly all-powerful giants for many years, and his almost inevitable fear of displeasing these enigmatic authorities are seen by psychodynamic thinkers as making anxiety and defense a regularly important feature in the development of personality and psychopathology.

It follows from the considerations advanced in this article that recent efforts to invalidate the psychodynamic viewpoint on the basis of currently available data on specificity and generality are based on misconceptions both of what modern psychodynamic theories are like and of the bearing of most research studies on the critical issues addressed by psychodynamic thinkers. The present arguments do not imply, however, that this is a time for psychodynamic workers to breathe easy and conduct business as usual. Mischel, for example, has based his case against psychodynamic theories not only on the observations of behavioral variability considered above but also on what he views as a failure of psychodynamic clinicians to demonstrate the utility of their judgments. In his more recent writings (e.g., Mischel, 1971) this issue has become the central focus of Mischel's critique of the psychodynamic approach, and his earlier work (Mischel, 1968), like that of Meehl (1954), Sawyer (1966), and others, reviews considerable evidence that may be construed as casting doubt on the utility of psychodynamically derived assessment methods. Holt's (1970) recent paper is in many respects a cogent and effective reply to such critiques; but it is consistent with the arguments of the present paper, and with Holt's paper as well, to suggest that psychodynamic theories might well benefit from further consideration of specificity in human behavior, and to consider as well ways in which clinical assessment methods may have lagged behind the theoretical developments in psychodynamic theory discussed earlier.

Psychodynamic theories are still based largely on a body of clinical observation. Work such as that of Chapman and Chapman (1967), which illustrates the pitfalls in such observational methods, presents another serious challenge to psychodynamic workers. Whether psychodynamic ideas can or should be examined by strictly experimental methods is a controversial question.[6] Although a great many experiments have been inspired by psychoanalytic concepts, the bearing of experimental findings on psychoanalytic theory is far from clear (cf. Hilgard, 1968; Horwitz, 1963; Rapaport, 1959). The present discussion has pointed to ways in which current experimental studies tend to focus on different phenomena than those traditionally of central interest to psychoanalytic investigators. Unless experiments can be devised that adequately deal with the problem of man's behavior as both chosen and caused (Wachtel, 1969), with disavowed intentionality (Schafer, in press), with freedom and inhibition of affective experience, and with the perpetuation of old patterns and expectations by the evocation of "countertransferential" behavior (cf. Laing et al., 1966; Wolf, 1966), some form of naturalistic clinical observation will probably continue to be an important means of exploring key psychological questions. The need for such efforts to be more systematic (e.g., by examination of tape-recorded clinical data, open to alternative interpretations and checks of reliability) is obvious. Some of the work reviewed by Luborsky and Spence (1971, especially pp. 423–430) represents important steps in this direction. It is likely that some of Freud's more baroque formulations will prove casualties of such refined observation. But the conviction of many social behaviorist writers that almost all of psychodynamic thought will prove to be merely a time-wasting detour on the road to a purely situational theory (see Bowers, in press) seems to this writer to be a product of the failure to recognize that psychodynamic theories have developed from observations of phenomena that experimentally derived theories have hardly considered.

Developments in behavior therapy are likely to prove a corrective to the zealots of both dynamic and behavioral persuasion. Already, the impressive results reported by behavior therapists are forcing psychodynamic thinkers to reconsider a number of their basic premises and their limitations. On the other hand, contact with the more complex problems of neurosis and "real life" joy and suffering is likely to bring more to the fore the phenomena that until now behavioral theories have dealt with only by analogy. In observations of behavior therapists at work, the present author has noted a good deal more interviewing and efforts to grasp ambiguous occurrences interpretively than one would expect from the literature (see also Klein, Dittmann, Parloff, & Gill, 1969). Recent writings by practicing behavior therapists (e.g., Lazarus, 1971) have stressed the primacy of careful clinical observation over strict adherence to a stimulus-response faith. In future communications, guidelines for the integration of dynamic and behavioral approaches will be examined in detail. It is hoped that the present contribution will aid in diminishing the resistance to such efforts.

---

[6] The too ready assumption by many psychologists that the experimental method is the only path to truth has been critically examined by Bowers (in press) in a valuable paper that is in many respects complementary to the present one.

REFERENCES

Alexander, F. *Psychoanalysis and psychotherapy*. New York: Norton, 1956.

Alker, H. A. Is personality situationally specific or intrapsychically consistent? *Journal of Personality*, 1972, **40**, 1-16.

Allen, E. K., Hart, B. M., Buell, J. S., Harris, F. R., & Wolf, M. M. Effects of social reinforcement on isolate behavior of a nursery school child. *Child Development*, 1964, **34**, 511-518.

Ayllon, T., & Azrin, N. *The token economy*. New York: Appleton-Century-Crofts, 1968.

Bandura, A. *Principles of behavior modification*. New York: Holt, Rinehart & Winston, 1969.

Bandura, A., & Walters, R. *Social learning and personality development*. New York: Holt, Rinehart & Winston, 1963.

Bem, D. Constructing cross-situational consistencies in behavior: Some thoughts on Alker's critique of Mischel. *Journal of Personality*, 1972, **40**, 17-26.

Bowers, K. S. Situationism in psychology: An analysis and a critique. *Psychological Review*, 1973, **80**, 307-336.

Carson, R. C. *Interaction concepts of personality*. Chicago: Aldine, 1969.

Chapman, L. J., & Chapman, J. Genesis of popular but erroneous psychodiagnostic observations. *Journal of Abnormal Psychology*, 1967, **72**, 193-204.

Davison, G. C. Appraisal of behavior modification techniques with adults in institutional settings. In C. Franks (Ed.), *Behavior therapy: Appraisal and status*. New York: McGraw-Hill, 1969.

Dollard, J., & Miller, N. E. *Personality and psychotherapy*. New York: McGraw-Hill, 1950.

Erikson, E. H. *Childhood and society*. New York: Norton, 1950.

Freud, S. Beyond the pleasure principle. In J. Strachey (Ed.), *The standard edition of the complete psychological works of Sigmund Freud*. Vol. 18. London: Hogarth, 1955. (Originally published: 1920).

Freud, S. The ego and the id. In J. Strachey (Ed.), *The standard edition of the complete psychological works of Sigmund Freud*. Vol. 19. London: Hogarth, 1961. (Originally published: 1923).

Freud, S. Inhibitions, symptoms and anxiety. In J. Strachey (Ed.), *The standard edition of the complete psychological works of Sigmund Freud*. Vol. 20. London: Hogarth, 1959. (Originally published: 1926).

Gardner, R. W., Holzman, P. S., Klein, G. S., Linton, H. B., & Spence, D. P. Cognitive control: A study of individual consistencies in cognitive behavior. *Psychological Issues*, 1959, 1(4), 1-185.

Goldberger, L. Experimental isolation: An overview. *American Journal of Psychiatry*, 1966, **122**, 774-782.

Goldfried, M. R., & Kent, R. N. Traditional versus behavioral personality assessment: A comparison of methodological and theoretical assumptions. *Psychological Bulletin*, 1972, **77**, 409-420.

Greenson, R. *The technique and practice of psychoanalysis*. New York: International Universities Press, 1967.

Hartmann, H. *Ego psychology and the problem of adaptation*. New York: International Universities Press, 1958. (Orig. publ. 1939).

Hilgard, E. R. Psychoanalysis: Experimental studies. In D. L. Sills (Ed.), *International encyclopedia of the social sciences*. Vol. 13. New York: Macmillan, 1968.

Holt, R. R. Ego autonomy re-evaluated. *International Journal of Psychoanalysis*, 1965, **46**, 151-167.

Holt, R. R. Beyond vitalism and mechanism: Freud's concept of psychic energy. In J. Masserman (Ed.), *Science and psychoanalysis*. Vol. 11. New York: Grune and Stratton, 1967.

Holt, R. R. Yet another look at clinical and statistical prediction: Or, is clinical psychology worthwhile? *American Psychologist,* 1970, **25,** 337–349.

Horwitz, L. Theory construction and validation in psychoanalysis. In M. H. Marx (Ed.), *Theories in contemporary psychology.* New York: Macmillan, 1963.

Kiesler, D. J. Some myths of psychotherapy research and the search for a paradigm. *Psychological Bulletin,* 1966, **65,** 110–136.

Klein, G. S. Two theories or one? Perspectives to change in psychoanalytic theory. Paper presented at the Conference of Psychoanalysts of the Southwest, Galveston, Texas, March 1966.

Klein, G. S. Freud's two theories of sexuality. In L. Breger (Ed.), *Clinical-cognitive psychology.* Englewood Cliffs, N. J.: Prentice-Hall, 1969.

Klein, M. H., Dittmann, A. T., Parloff, M. B., & Gill, M. M. Behavior therapy: Observations and reflections. *Journal of Consulting and Clinical Psychology,* 1969, 33, 259–269.

Kubie, L. S. The fallacious use of quantitative concepts in dynamic psychology. *Psychoanalytic Quarterly,* 1947, **16,** 507–518.

Laing, R. D., Phillipson, H., & Lee, A. R. *Interpersonal perception.* New York: Springer, 1966.

Lazarus, A. A. *Behavior therapy and beyond.* New York: McGraw-Hill, 1971.

Locke, E. A. Is "behavior therapy" behavioristic? (An analysis of Wolpe's psychotherapeutic methods). *Psychological Bulletin,* 1971, **76,** 318–327.

Loevinger, J. Three principles for a psychoanalytic psychology. *Journal of Abnormal Psychology,* 1966, **71,** 432–443.

Luborsky, L., Blinder, B., & Schimek, J. G. Looking, recalling, and GSR as a function of defense. *Journal of Abnormal Psychology,* 1965, **70,** 270–280.

Luborsky, L., & Spence, D. P. Quantitative research on psychoanalytic therapy. In A. Bergin & S. Garfield (Eds.), *Handbook of psychotherapy and behavior change.* New York: Wiley, 1971.

Meehl, P. E. *Clinical versus statistical prediction: A theoretical analysis and a review of the evidence.* Minneapolis: University of Minnesota Press, 1954.

Millon, T. *Psychopathology.* Philadelphia: Saunders, 1969.

Mischel, W. *Personality and assessment.* New York: Wiley, 1968.

Mischel, W. Specificity theory and the construction of personality. Paper presented at the annual meeting of the American Psychological Association, Washington, D. C., September 3, 1971.

Orne, M. T. On the social psychology of the psychological experiment: With particular reference to demand characteristics and their implications. *American Psychologist,* 1962, **17,** 776–783.

Pine, F. The bearing of psychoanalytic theory on selected issues in research on marginal stimuli. *Journal of Nervous and Mental Disease,* 1964, 13, 205–222.

Rapaport, D. The structure of psychoanalytic theory: A systematizing attempt. In S. Koch (Ed.), *Psychology: A study of a science.* Vol. 3. New York: McGraw-Hill, 1959.

Rosenthal, R. *Experimenter effects in behavioral Research.* New York: Appleton-Century-Crofts, 1966.

Sawyer, J. Measurement *and* prediction, clinical *and* statistical. *Psychological Bulletin,* 1966, **66,** 178–200.

Schafer, R. An overview of Heinz Hartmann's contributions to psychoanalysis. *International Journal of Psychoanalysis,* 1970, **51,** 425–446.

Schafer, R. Action: Its place in psychoanalytic interpretation and theory. *The Annual of Psychoanalysis,* Vol. 1, in press.

Shapiro, D. *Neurotic styles.* New York: Basic Books, 1965.

Silverman, L. H. Drive stimulation and psychopathology: On the conditions under which drive related external events trigger pathological reactions. *Psychoanalysis and contemporary science.* Vol. 1, New York: International Universities Press, 1972.

Stone, L. *The psychoanalytic situation.* New York: International Universities Press, 1961.

Sullivan, H. S. *The interpersonal theory of psychiatry.* New York: Norton, 1953.

Ullmann, L. P., & Krasner, L. *Case studies in behavior modification.* New York: Holt, Rinehart & Winston, 1966.

Wachtel, P. L. Conceptions of broad and narrow attention. *Psychological Bulletin,* 1967, **68,** 417–429.

Wachtel, P. L. Psychology, metapsychology, and psychoanalysis. *Journal of Abnormal Psychology,* 1969, **74,** 651–660.

Wachtel, P. L. Cognitive style and style of adaptation. *Perceptual and Motor Skills,* 1972, **35,** 779–785.

Wolf, E. Learning theory and psychoanalysis. *British Journal of Medical Psychology,* 1966, **39,** 1–10.

Wolitzky, D. L., & Wachtel, P. L. Personality and perception. In B. Wolman (Ed.), *Handbook of general psychology.* Englewood Cliffs, N. J.: Prentice-Hall, 1972.

36

On the Empirical Dilemmas of Psychodynamic Approaches: Issues and Alternatives

WALTER MISCHEL

Since its inception at the turn of the century, psychodynamic theory has been subjected to almost continuous conceptual attacks (sometimes justified, often spurious), and it has withstood them with great vigor, as its long survival attests. My purpose here is to try to clarify some of the main dilemmas that currently face psychodynamic approaches, to separate any genuine crises from pseudoissues which obscure them, and to consider the nature and implications of any basic (as opposed to stereotypic) differences between psychodynamic and social behavior approaches to abnormal psychology.

PSEUDOISSUES AND GENUINE CRISES

Psychodynamic theory and its variations have been accused at differnt times of paying too much or too little attention to one construct and phenomenon or another (sex, aggression, the id, ego functions, mature and creative behavior, psychopathology, the present, the past, etc.). These abstract assaults have not generated any serious crises for psychodynamic theory: its formulations have been robust enough to withstand such criticisms with little difficulty.

Pseudoissues

At a theoretical level, there is also no need to defend psychodynamic theories on the specificity-generality issue. Wachtel (1973) asserted, "the mere fact that

From the *Journal of Abnormal Psychology*, 1973, *82*, 335-344. Copyright 1973 by the American Psychological Association. Reprinted by permission.

Preparation of this manuscript was facilitated by National Institute of Mental Health Research Grant M6830 to the author. Portions of this paper are based on the author's address to Section III (Development of Clinical Psychology as an Experimental-Behavioral Science) Division 12, American Psychological Association, Washington, D. C., September 3, 1971.

behavior varies from situation to situation is in no way a refutation of the psychodynamic approach [p. 327]." I thoroughly agree. While traditional trait approaches have paid inadequate attention to the role of situational varibles, psychodynamic approaches have long recognized both the specificity and complexity of behavior and have rejected the idea of broad overt behavioral consistencies across situations, as has been repeatedly emphasized (Mischel, 1968, 1969, 1971a, 1971b). For example:

> Psychodynamic theorists clearly recognized the inconsistencies among a person's overt behaviors across seemingly similar situations. Thus the "behavioral specificity" found in trait measures . . . was no surprise to many of them. They felt, however, that the observed inconsistencies in the individual's behavior could be understood as merely superficial diversities that masked the fundamentally consistent, underlying motives that acutally drove him enduringly. Recall in this regard Freud's focus on the vicissitudes of impulses. According to psychodynamic theory, the basic motives persist and press for discharge across diverse settings, but their overt manifestations or "symptoms" are transformed defensively. Hence the psychodynamic assessor's task is to find the person's fundamental motives and enduring dynamics behind the defensive facade and surface distortions of his overt behavior [Mischel, 1971a, p. 153].

Psychodynamic theories thus are totally explicit in their recognition that "overt" behavior varies depending upon specific conditions, but they construe diverse behavioral patterns as serving the same stable, relatively generalized *underlying* dynamic (motivational) dispositions. This distinction between surface behaviors ("signs" or "symptoms") and the motives that they serve is similar to the well-known distinction between the "phenotypic" and the "genotypic" and leads to an indirect, rather than a direct measurement model, as previously discussed (Mischel, 1968, 1969). Granting that overt behavior is not highly consistent, psychodynamic theorists posit genotypic personality dispositons that endure, although their overt response forms may change (Mischel, 1971b, 1972).

Psychodynamic approaches hypothesize motives, needs, conflicts, complexes, basic attitudes, and other underlying but not directly observable dispositions that produce many diverse overt manifestations, similar to a physical disease which generates a multitude of clinical symptoms. The clinician must try to infer hypothesized underlying consistent dispositions from the diverse, often misleading events he observes (Mischel, 1972). The relation between the observed behaviors and the underlying disposition is apt to be extremely indirect because defenses are hypothesized which may distort and disguise the real meaning of the observed behaviors. To charge (as Wachtel, 1973, p. 324, does) that psychodynamic theories are being questioned by behavioral ctitics mainly for a failure to recognize "variability in behavior from situation to situation" is to divert attention from their real dilemma while focusing on a pseudoissue.

In sum, psychodynamic theories at an abstract level have no difficulty dealing with overt behavioral inconsistencies. The current dilemma confronting psychodynamic theory, however, is not primarily conceptual: it is, rather, empirical. Because the crux of the current dilemma is not that psychodynamic theory forgot or misinterpreted some phenomenon, or overemphasized others, but that it has not proved to be useful for most clinical purposes.

Beginnings of Disillusionment with Psychodynamic Approaches

Disillusionment with psychodynamic approaches began to arise primarily from the clinical experiences of the 1950s and early 1960s with clients seeking help, not from experimental studies with animals, children, or college sophomores. It was in that clinical context, not in the laboratory, that clinicians became increasingly dubious about the value of the psychodynamic and trait-dispositional portraits to which they were devoting most of their time (e.g., Peterson, 1968; Vernon, 1964). Skepticism about the utility of such assessments arose not from a disinterest in the client's inner states nor from a neglect of individual differences. On the contrary, it arose from a growing worry that psychodynamic and trait "personality diagnostics," too often formulated with little regard for the client's own construction of his life and his specific behaviors, might be exercises in stereotyping that miss the uniqueness of the individual and pin him instead on a continuum of clinician-supplied labels (e.g., Kelly, 1955; Rotter, 1954).

Guided by the view that test responses are merely "indirect signs" of underlying psychodynamics, assessors elicited signs such as picture drawings, or associations to inkblots, or global self-characterizations, whose demonstrable relations to the individual's important life behaviors tended to be tenuous and remote (Mischel, 1968). Some clinicians began to feel that their "diagnostic reports" were used more to call the client interesting names than to help him. But a focus on the immediate behavioral problems of the client was widely regarded as naive and hazardous, because these problems were construed merely as "symptoms" and even as manifestations of "resistances." Traditionally, the clinician's task was to go beyond behavioral complaints to underlying psychodynamics, and the fear of symptom substitution led many to eschew direct behavior intervention. As a result, clients often may have remained crippled by their disadvantageous behaviors while waiting (how long?) for insight-based relief from psychodynamic treatments.

Empirical Dilemmas of Psychodynamic Approaches

Although the psychodynamic indirect "sign" approach to dispositions is inherently logical, its utility for the clinician depends on the value of the inferences provided by the psychodynamically oriented clinical judge. While modern versions of psychodynamic theory have given increasing theoretical attention to the role of the environment and the person's current psychological situation, their clinical applications remain fully based on a search for generalized cross-situational predispositions inferred intuitively by the clinician from highly indirect behavioral signs (e.g., Erikson, 1958). Therefore, the reliability and validity of clinician's judgments become crucially important.

In the last two decades, many empirical studies have investigated carefully the utility of clinicians' efforts to infer broad dispositions indirectly from specific symptomatic signs and to unravel disguises in order to uncover the hypothetical dispositions that might be their roots. The results have indicated that the disillusionment beginning to be expressed by skeptical clinicians was fully justified empirically. The total findings undermined the utility of clinical judgments even when the judges are well-trained, expert psychodynamicists, working with clients in clinical contexts and using their own preferred techniques. Surveys of the relevant research generally showed that clinicians guided by concepts about underlying genotypic dispositions have not been able to predict behavior better than have the person's own direct self-report, simple indexes of directly relevant past behavior, demographic variables, or, in some cases, their secretaries (e.g., Mischel, 1968, 1971a, 1972; Peterson, 1968). Moreover, dispositional labels and the psychodynamic "portraits" formulated often may be based more on illusory correlations perpetuated by shared semantic organizations and belief systems than by valid data (e.g., Chapman & Chapman, 1969; D'Andrade, 1970; Shweder, 1972). Increasingly, it appeared that the intriguing hypothesized psychic structures and dynamics that clinicians weaved at case conferences may have added more to the weight of the client's diagnostic folder than to the design of treatments tailored to his specific needs and circumstances (Mischel, 1968).

As distressing as the failure to demonstrate the utility of the inferences and predictions of psychodynamically oriented clinicians is the evidence on the utility of psychodynamic treatment efforts. Detailed reviews of the data on this topic indicate that psychodynamic psychotherapy lacks efficacy when compared to more parsimonious alternatives (e.g., Bandura, 1969; Bergin, 1966); moreover, it may provide an ideological conversion to the belief system of the therapist more than a cure for the client's problems (e.g., Bandura, 1971). The fears of "symptom substitution" turned out to be largely unjustified (e.g., Grossberg, 1964). Clients whose maladaptive behaviors were directly alleviated, rather than becoming victimized by substituted symptoms, appeared more likely to show generalized gains from overcoming their original handicaps (e.g., Bandura, 1969).

It is these failures to demonstrate utility in clinical applications that are the basic dilemmas which clinically oriented proponents of psychodynamic approaches need to face. Progress in our field will not be achieved by professing dismay at polemics while at the same time dwelling on irrelevant arguments which deflect attention from the genuine challenges (Wachtel, 1973).

BASIC DIFFERENCES BETWEEN PSYCHODYNAMIC AND BEHAVIORAL APPROACHES

In part, differences between approaches undoubtedly arise from differences in the phenomena on which they concentrate. But that truism should not obscure any basic differences that do exist. Because an integration and rapproachement between different viewpoints is always attractive, it is tempting to believe that the differences between psychodynamic and behavioral approaches to clinical psychology reside primarily in their concentrating on different populations and different phenomena, as Wachtel (1973) proposed. In his comparisons, the psychodynamically oriented clinician is depicted as focusing on the complex maladaptive interpersonal problems and subjective feelings of troubled individuals studied intensively in the single case. In contrast, the behaviorally oriented psychologist is characterized as an "implacable experimenter," who gives or gets money, shocks subjects or lets them escape shock, seeking "simple stimulus–response relationships [Wachtel, p. 329]," impervious to the ways in which people construct their own life situations.

This comparison between approaches, while offered as a step toward constructive integration, unfortunately perpetuates inaccurate stereotypes. It is certainly true that candy pellets have been foolishly hurled by radical behaviorists at subjects who were uninterested in them, that trivial experiments with silly manipulations occur too often, and that simplistic conceptions and narrow technologies have been offered naively as panaceas under the preemptive banner of "behaviorism." Indeed, such phrases as "behaviorism" and "experimental approaches" have so often been associated either with silly research or with antihumanistic, Orwellian imagery that they may evoke an almost automatic aversion in many of us. But the strong passions that exist on this topic should not separate the clinician from a broader social behavior framework that extends well beyond partisan conceptions put forth by any single theorist. It is time to forego the old clichés about how behaviorally oriented psychologists avoid cognition, affect, and complexity. In current social behavior research, human choices, subjective expectancies, observational and vicarious experiences, cognitions and affect, self-control, and complex interactions—not bar presses and monotonic learning curves for motor responses and twitches in animals—are the phenomena of concern (e.g., Bandura, 1971; Mischel, 1971a, 1973).

It is especially misleading to suggest that the challenge to psychodynamic approaches rests on experimental studies which demonstrate behavioral "specificity" with relatively normal children and adults whose behavior is relatively easy to modify (Wachtel, 1973, p. 328). In fact, the negative data on the utility of psychodynamic clinical applications come from the failure of psychodynamic clinicians to demonstrate the value of their own daily diagnostic and therapeutic activities (e.g., Mischel, 1968, ch. 5). Likewise, the positive challenges to psychodynamic treatments in the form of alternative behavioral therapies come to a large extent from therapeutic improvements in people so severely disturbed (e.g., self-annihilating schizophrenic youngsters) that they had been abandoned as hopeless by traditional methods (e.g., Lovaas, 1967).

While the dilemmas of psychodynamic theory are empirical, conceptual differences between it and social behavior approaches (broadly construed) do exist. The most basic of these differences between the approaches reflect not merely a focus on different phenomena, or a preference for different specific methods, but two fundamentally different, and sometimes directly opposite, orientations.

Focus on Behavior–Condition Relations versus Focus on Behaviors as Signs

Contemporary social behavior approaches focus specifically on what the person does cognitively and behaviorally instead of trying to infer what dispositions he has, and they concentrate on the functional relations (the specific interactions) between what he does and the psychological conditions of his life (e.g., Bandura, 1969; Kanfer & Phillips, 1970; Mischel, 1968; Peterson, 1968). Instead of attempting to infer global underlying dispositions, they focus on problematic behavior in relation to the conditions that covary with it. This requires sampling the particular behaviors directly, rather than trying to use them as signs of broad underlying dispositions. The definition of "behavior," of course, includes much more than motor acts and requires us to consider what people do cognitively and emotionally.

In a comprehensive social behavior approach, one analyzes the relations between changes in selected behavior patterns (samples of "impulsivity," for example) and changes in conditions, either in the single case or in the multiple-groups study. In such an approach, attention shifts from inferences about dispositions and correlations between the signs of those dispositions to an analysis of behavior patterns in relation to the conditions that evoke, maintain, and modify those patterns. Attention shifts from attempting to generalize about what an individual "is like" to an assessment of what he does cognitively and behaviorally in relationship to the conditions in which he does it. The "conditions" studied, however, are by no means confined to the physical environment: they encompass the individual's interpersonal relations and his own cognitive as well as behavioral activities (e.g., Mischel, 1973). Thus the person's self-instructions, coding schemes, cognitive rehearsals, cognitive stimulus transformations, and other self-regulatory processes (e.g., Bandura, 1971; Mischel & Moore, 1973a, 1973b) are phenomena of central interest, and objective methods are available for studying them systematically. Moreover, in the analysis of such phenomena, the person who "does things" to behavior is not merely the psychologist: it is also (and sometimes, primarily) the individual himself who engages in new self-instructions or other cognitive operations whose impact on behavior is then assessed.[1]

---

[1] A focus on behavior–condition interactions by no means prevents attention to person variables. But such variables are conceptualized in terms of specific cognitive social learning processes rather than as generalized trait characteristics (Mischel, 1973). Such person variables (e.g., coding operations, specific expectancies, stimulus values, self-regulatory

As Heider (1958) has stressed, people quickly leap from behavior to inferences about dispositions and readily attribute personality characteristics and motives to themselves and each other. In a behavioral approach to clinical problems, that quick trip from behavior to disposition has to be temporarily reversed. In that reversal, the assessor helps the client to *externalize* the behavioral referents for the problematic personality constructs that the latter has attributed to himself (e.g., "I'm too shy," "I'm not enough of a mustard cutter") so that one can discover the conditions that control them and, if necessary, proceed to alter those conditions therapeutically.

Skepticism about the utility of psychodynamic constructs regarding dispositions in no way requires us to ignore the person's own constructs. Psychologists are not the only people who are personality theorists: a distinctive feature of all humans is that they also generate theories about themselves, and even about the psychologists who study them. They invoke motives, traits, and other dispositions as ways of describing and explaining their experience and themselves, just as professional psychologists do, and it would be strange if one tried to define out of existence the personal constructs and other concepts, perceptions, and experiences of our clients. Indeed, these phenomena can be studied like any other complex phenomena by finding appropriate observable referents for them (Mischel, 1968). A large part of the clinician's task (and perhaps the most challenging) is to help the client in the search for such referents for his own constructs, instead of supplying him with the clinician's favorite dispositional labels. Rather than leading the client to repackage his problems in our terms, with our constructs, we need to help him to objectify *his* constructs into behavioral terms, so that the relevant behaviors can be changed by helping him to achieve more judicious arrangements of the conditions of his life.

A comprehensive social behavior assessment includes detailed exploration of the unique or idiographic qualities of the individual (e.g., Mischel, 1968; Peterson, 1968). This focus on the idiosyncratic organization of behavior strikingly contradicts the "mechanistic stimulus–response" stereotypes and the images of "implacable experimenters" often invoked by critics of behavioral analyses. The essence of social behavior assessment is the exploration of the acquired meaning of stimuli, and that exploration is inextricably linked with behavior change. A comprehensive behavior change program attempts to modify what stimuli do to the individual (and what he does to them) by rearranging with the person the relevant conditions, including the ways in which he reacts to himself and controls his own behavior.

It is becoming fashionable to depict the experimental method as a strait-jacket

---

systems) may be assessed and systematically varied as independent variables (e.g., through instructions and self-instructions or selectively focused attention). Thus their contribution to behavior can be analyzed directly, rather than requiring more indirect sign inferences (as in clinical judgments about behavioral meanings).

technique imposed on unwilling subjects who busily try to outwit an ex-perimeter who is exploiting them. This view misses the essence of an ex-perimental attempt to analyze complex human behavior. The crux of such analyses in clinical contexts is the systematic exploration of "If___, then ___" relationships. In such exploration, the "if" consists of person-supplied variations in behavior, and the "then" consists of the consequences that covary with those changes. Applied with flexibility and ingenuity, this method provides a chance to assess the relations between what an individual does and what happens to him. In clinical applications the hypotheses about these "if___, then ___" relations need to come from the client at least as much as from the clinician, and the consequences of alterations in behavior are both created and experienced by the client in interaction with the conditions of his life rather than being arbitrarily manipulated by the clinician. In a sense, it is the client who learns to become an experimenter and who is helped to assess and control more effectively the relations between actions and their consequences.

An emphasis on the role of stimulus conditions (or in other terms on the role of situational moderator variables and interactions) in the regulation of behavior is easily misconstrued to imply a passive view of man and distorted into an image of an empty organism filled at most by psychological glue that binds response bundles automatically to stimuli impinging from the outside world. It is true that behavioral analyses focus on the exact covariations between changing conditions and the indiviudal's changing behavior. But while conditions may come to regulate behavior to a large degree, they do so only insofar as they have acquired meaning for the individual (Mischel, 1973). It is the individual (not the stimulus, or the situation, or the moderator) that is alive and does the construing and the acting. Only organisms, not stimuli or conditions, are capable of generating—indeed, con-structing—behavior. A focus on stimuli is interesting only insofar as it helps us to understand the person and to help him change, hopefully for the better and in accord with his goals rather than ours.

Focus on Ongoing Interaction Analysis versus Focus on Recall-Based Dispositions

In abstract discussion, "situations" and "conditions" are easily treated as if they were inanimate entities. Yet the functional analysis of interpersonal behavior (e.g., Peterson, 1968; Patterson & Cobb, 1971) immediately reminds us that the most important psychological "stimuli" and "situations" are alive (e.g., your best friend, your lover, your parents) and that a person continuously influences the situations of his life as well as being affected by them in an ongoing, mutual, organic interaction (Mischel, 1973). Caricatures of behavioral psychology tend to focus on an "implacable experimenter" who rigidly adheres to standard manipulations. Such portraits should not distract us from the fact that the functional analysis of in vivo interpersonal behavior is one of the most important methodological contributions of modern behavioral psychology.

Fortunately, behavioral psychology does not lack methods for systematically studying complex interpersonal interactions and the manner in which individuals construct and select the conditions of their lives. Classic behavioral analyses of interaction, like the studies of Rausch and his colleagues (e.g., Raush, 1965; Raush, Dittmann, & Taylor, 1959), dramatically illustrate the reciprocal relations of persons with conditions and with each other and show in elegant detail how people generate their own situations. And in a similar vein, functional analyses illuminate the specific conditions that evoke and maintain these complex interactions. It is precisely such analyses, not simplistic laboratory studies of artificial or trivial phenomena, that have cast further doubt on psychodynamic approaches that rest on verbal reconstructions of relationships rather than on direct observation of ongoing interactions.

In most psychodynamic assessments the client tells the clinician about himself, relying heavily on memories about what he "was like" in various past situations. To the extent that psychodynamic approaches continue to rely on the client's recall-based descriptions of perceived attributes and relationships, they are subject to some hazards whose scope has only recently begun to be realized. These hazards arise from the fact that a person's judgments about human attributes based on memory (especially long-term memory) tend to become distorted in the direction of his preexisting cognitive structure. For example, D'Andrade (1970) found that correlations between ratings based on long-term memory were "similar to judgments about how much alike the terms for these traits are in *meaning*—but quite different than correlations for these same behaviors which are based on data using the immediate recording of ongoing interaction [p. 1]." Similar conclusions come from anthropological studies by Shweder (1971, 1972) and, in the clinical context, from the research of Chapman and Chapman (1969) on illusory correlations in clinical judgments. These findings are congruent with the earlier research on verbal personality factors which suggested that:

the covariation which gave rise to these factors could be determined as much by the meaning systems and perceptual tendencies of observers as by the behavioral characteristics of the people under observation . . . [Peterson, 1968, p. 23].

Once formed, such personality attributions tend to become extremely difficult to disconfirm, thereby further perpetuating stereotypic assessments. For example, initial observations easily lead to the attribution of "deep" or motivating traits in the observed person (Hayden & Mischel, 1972). Later, these inferred motivating traits bias the observer's subsequent attributions toward consistency. Thus, after an observer has diagnosed another person as "aggressive" (and he does that very quickly and on the basis of few facts), if he is confronted by new inconsistent behavior he is likely to dismiss it as due to external or situational variables and to factors other than the person's "real" or "true" self. The layman thus shares the psychoanalyst's phenotypic–genotypic motivational analysis. Like the analyst, he can reconstrue and negate all sorts of discrepant behaviors from the person as if they were merely "superficially" incongruent but "basically" compatible with his true self. And, like the analyst, his judgments may become biased toward the perpetuation of consistent stereotypes. He puts his labels on the other person and then construes the other's behavior to make it fit. The cost of such procrustean cognitive neatness, unfortunately, may be a more tenacious adherence to rigid stereotypes. In this manner, through post hoc analyses and postdiction, we may be sacrificing accuracy and specific prediction while achieving a gratifying sense of order.[2]

Moreover, the tendency to overattribute consistency may be greater when describing other people than when describing oneself. When explaining other people's behavior, we tend to invoke their consistent personality dispositions, but when we have to explain our own behavior we focus on specific conditions (Jones & Nisbett, 1971). Thus Jack fell because he's clumsy, but I fell because it was dark. Jones and Nisbett proposed that "Actors tend to attribute the causes of their behavior to stimuli inherent in the situation while observers tend to attribute behavior to stable dispositions of the actor [p. 93]." This discrepancy may be due partly to the tendency to treat every sample of behavior displayed by another person as if it were typical. Perhaps we function more like dispositional theorists when analyzing other people but more like social behaviorists when we try to understand ourselves. That might occur because we have more information about ourselves and the multiplicity of the situations in our own experiences, but we know other people in only limited situations and overgeneralize from them. If so, the clinician needs to be forewarned lest he pin his clients with consistent dispositional labels more than he does himself.

A recognition that memory-based human constructions about dispositions are *constructions* that do not necessarily accurately describe the behaviors on which they are based is easily misunderstood to mean that observers "*falsely* construe consistency when diversity is the fact [Wachtel, 1973, p. 330]." But as I have stressed (Mischel, 1971b) and as Vaihinger said in 1924 in his book *The Philosophy of "As If,"* to prevent drowning in a world of facts men invent fictions about each other, and then behave "as if" they were real. These fictions, like most good fiction, are *not* sheer fantasies unrelated to the events and behaviors of real life; on the contrary, they are rooted in life but go far beyond the facts. The implication is not that these constructions are "false" but that people may proceed quickly beyond the observation of *some* consistency which does exist in behavior to the attribution of greater perceived consistencies which they construct (see also Mischel, 1973).

The main implication for the present discussion is that no matter how much psychodynamically oriented clinicians may *talk* with their clients about interpersonal relationships, their data will remain highly limited (and subject to

---

[2] As stressed elsewhere (Mischel, 1968, 1973), such data may be highly informative about the cognitive constructions of the observer, but they should not be confused with (or substituted for) a comprehensive analysis of the specific conditions and behaviors to which they refer.

serious distortions), unless they venture out of their chairs to observe the ongoing relationships as they unfold. Of course the clinician may reply that the crucial relationship is the ongoing one with the client facing him at the moment in the office. But to make the client–therapist relationship (i.e., the "transference") the central focus and to assume that it mirrors most other important relations is to assume again the very high degree of "underlying" cross-situational generality which clinicians have not been able to demonstrate (Mischel, 1968).

A central message of the social behavior approach to assessment and therapy is not that the "specificity of behavior" implies a capricious world but that it dictates a much more specific, discriminative approach to behavior sampling than has been traditional:

> The implications of the relative specificity of treatments are similar to those found for the specificity of predictors and of criteria. Predictions tend to be best when the predictor behavior is sampled in situations that approximate the criterion situation as much as possible. Likewise, behavior change in a given situation generalizes most to the most closely similar situations. Consequently, therapists should structure situations that approximate and sample as much as possible the criterion situations in which behavioral improvements are intended. The ultimate goal of most behavior therapies is to help the client to function well in naturalistic life contexts outside the clinic or hospital rather than to remain subject to external contingencies in artificial or special environments. To achieve this aim the critical conditions in the treatment environment should evoke and develop behaviors similar to those desired in the life environment, thus minimizing the transition from the therapy program to the settings in which the client functions naturally [Mischel, 1968, p. 278].

The above considerations suggest that the structure of treatment has to be much more specific than has been assumed by traditional therapies. If, for example, a person can think calmly about public speaking but panics when he does it, treatment might focus on developing the desired behavior in vivo rather than on relaxation to imagined stimuli alone. Or if a client is able to achieve effectively in school but devalues and derogates his own accomplishments, treatment might be directed at helping him to reconstrue and to reevaluate his achievement goals and standards, rather than to strengthen his academic skills. Alternatively, if his school failure reflects learning deficits, treatment might be directed at the acquisition of basic skills rather than at the elaboration of feelings. And if a client suffers from obsessive, bizarre ideation, treatment might be aimed at helping him gain better control of his cognitive processes rather than at modifying his overt actions.

Some Unexpected Links

Although often labeled as "behavioristic," a rejection of the search for global dispositions is not unique to a behavioral position. Surprisingly, the same rejection occurs in most existentially oriented and phenomenological positions (Mischel, 1971). This seems like an unexpected conceptual union. Yet the empirical lack of utility found for traditional dispositional constructs and the resulting specific focus on what the person is doing rather than on his attributes or motives, supports fully the existential doctrine; as Sartre (1956) phrased it, "existence precedes essence:"

man first of all exists, encounters himself, surges up in the world—and defines himself afterwards. If man as the existentialist sees him is not definable, it is because to begin with he is nothing. He will not be anything until later, and then he will be what he makes of himself. Thus, there is no human nature . . . Man simply is [Sartre, pp. 290-291].

Kelly (1955) in the same vein declared "I am what I do" and said that to know what a man is we must look at what he does. Dispositional constructs about dynamics, agencies of the mind, fundamental complexes, conflicts, and sexual and aggressive drives as foundations of later development—all these and similar constructs about the a priori nature of personality—are eschewed by existentialism as much as they are by current social behavior theories. Moreover, it is not just behaviorally oriented psychologists who have been disillusioned by diagnostic personality testing and dispositional assessments: Rogerians for the last two decades have disavowed trait tests and the constructs that guided them in the first place.

This unexpected similarity between social behavior theory and the existential-phenomenological orientation seems to hinge on several common qualities. Both share an emphasis on the current situation—on the "here and now"—a reluctance to posit generalized dispositional constructs, a focus on what the individual is doing ("where he is at" psychologically) rather than on the theoretical constructs of the psychologist who is assessing him. They also may share a disinterest in the historical reconstruction of events from the distant past and a concern instead with new action alternatives available now.

The similarities between a behavioral and an existential-phenomenological orientation are provocative, but the degree of their overlap has limits. The two approaches suffer from one basic incompatibility. As Sartre (1956) put it, man "is what he wills to be [p. 291]." While sharing Sartre's wish to put "every man in possession of himself," a behavioral analysis of causation cannot end with the person's will as the final explanatory construct. A behavioral approach requires more specific causal analyses that link what the person does and construes to the psychological conditions in which he does it.

CONCLUSIONS

In sum, the dilemmas of psychodynamic approaches concern their relative lack of efficacy for assessment, prediction, and therapeutic change when compared to more parsimonious alternatives. An adequate defense of the psychodynamic paradigm needs to face those issues. To suggest that the primary challenge to psychodynamic theory has been the criticism that it fails to recognize "different behavior in different situations [Wachtel, 1973, p. 326]" is to obscure the genuine problems. Our field is sorely in need of a thoughtful integration of its most promising elements, but such a synthesis will not be achieved by diverting attention from the challenges that face us.

When confronted with the evidence on the lack of utility of psychodynamically oriented assessment and treatment, one can question the methodological adequacy of the research, criticize (usually with good reasons) the techniques and criteria that were used, and look forward to the development of better methods in the hope that ultimately they will prove the usefulness of the psychodynamic paradigm. For years, sophisticated researchers sympathetic to psychodynamic approaches have called for improvements in the methods and quality of psychoanalytic research and have offered constructive suggestions (e.g., Janis, 1958). One keeps hoping that the message will have beneficial effects. But, while acknowledging the fallibility of the existing research and recognizing the need for better methods, one could also accept the thrust of the general findings and take seriously the implications, thus questioning deeply the basic paradigm and not merely the available methods and seeking more useful alternatives in both theory and practice.

REFERENCES

Bandura, A. *Principles of behavior modification.* New York: Holt, Rinehart & Winston, 1969.

Bandura, A. *Social learning theory.* New York: General Learning Press, 1971.

Bergin, A. E. Some implications of psychotherapy research for therapeutic practice. *Journal of Abnormal Psychology,* 1966, 71, 235–246.

Chapman, L. J., & Chapman, J. P. Illusory correlations as an obstacle to the use of valid psychodiagnostic signs. *Journal of Abnormal Psychology,* 1969, 74, 271–280.

D'Andrade, R. G. Cognitive structures and judgment. Paper prepared for Research Workshop on Cognitive Organization and Psychological Processes, Huntington Beach, California, August 16–21, 1970. Unpublished manuscript, Department of Anthropology, University of California at San Diego.

Erikson, E. H. The nature of clinical evidence. *Daedalus,* 1958, Fall, 65–87.

Grossberg, J. M. Behavioral therapy: A review. *Psychological Bulletin,* 1964, 62, 73–88.

Hayden, T., & Mischel, W. Maintaining trait consistency in the resolution of behavioral inconsistency: The wolf in sheep's clothing. Unpublished manuscript, Stanford University, 1972.

Heider, F. *The psychology of interpersonal relations.* New York: Wiley, 1958.

Janis, I. L. The psychoanalytic interview as an observational method. In G. Lindzey (Ed.), *Assessment of human motives.* New York: Rinehart, 1958.

Jones, E. E., & Nisbett, R. E. The actor and the observer: Divergent perceptions of the causes of behavior. In E. E. Jones et al. (Eds.), *Attribution: Perceiving the causes of behavior.* Morrestown, N.J.: General Learning Press, 1971.

Kanfer, F. H., & Phillips, J. S. *Learning foundations of behavior therapy.* New York: Wiley, 1970.

Kelly, G. A. *The psychology of personal constructs.* New York: Norton, 1955.

Lovaas, O. I. A behavior therapy approach to the treatment of childhood schizophrenia. In J. P. Hill (Ed.), *Minnesota symposia on child psychology.* Vol. 1. Minneapolis: University of Minnesota Press, 1967.

Mischel, W. *Personality and assessment.* New York: Wiley, 1968.

Mischel, W. Continuity and change in personality. *American Psychologist,* 1969, 24, 1012–1018.

Mischel, W. *Introduction to personality.* New York: Holt, Rinehart & Winston, 1971. (a)

Mischel, W. The construction of personality. Address of the Chairman, Section III (Development of Clinical Psychology as an Experimental-Behavioral Science) Division 12, at the annual meeting of the American Psychological Association, Washington, D. C., September 3, 1971. (b)

Mischel, W. Direct versus indirect personality assessment: Evidence and implications. *Journal of Consulting and Clinical Psychology*, 1972, **38**, 319–324.

Mischel, W. Toward a cognitive social learning reconceptualization of personality. *Psychological Review*, 1973, **80**, 252–283.

Mischel, W., & Moore, B. Effects of attention to symbolically presented rewards upon self-control. *Journal of Personality and Social Psychology*, 1973, in press. (a)

Mischel, W., & Moore, B. Cognitive transformations of the stimulus in delay of gratification. Unpublished manuscript, Stanford University, 1973. (b)

Patterson, G. R., & Cobb, J. A. Stimulus control for classes of noxious behaviors. In J. F. Knutson (Ed.), *The control of aggression: Implications from basic research*. Chicago: Aldine, 1971.

Peterson, D. R. *The clinical study of social behavior*. New York: Appleton-Century-Crofts, 1968.

Raush, H. L. Interaction sequences. *Journal of Personality and Social Psychology*, 1965, **2**, 487–499.

Raush, H. L., Dittman, A. L., & Taylor, T. J. The interpersonal behavior of children in residential treatment. *Journal of Abnormal and Social Psychology*, 1959, **58**, 9–26.

Rotter, J. B. *Social learning and clinical psychology*. Englewood Cliffs, N. J.: Prentice Hall, 1954.

Sartre, J. P. Existentialism. In W. Kaufmann (Ed.), *Existentialism from Dostoevsky to Sartre*. New York: Meridian, 1956.

Shweder, R. A. Is a culture a situation? Unpublished manuscript, Department of Social Relations, Harvard University, 1971.

Shweder, R. A. Semantic structures and personality assessment. Unpublished doctoral dissertation, Harvard University, Department of Social Relations, March 1972.

Vaihinger, H. *The philosophy of "as if."* New York: Harcourt, Brace, 1924.

Vernon, P. E. *Personality assessment: A critical survey*. New York: Wiley, 1964.

Wachtel, P. L. Psychodynamics, behavior therapy, and the implacable experimenter: An inquiry into the consistency of personality. *Journal of Abnormal Psychology*, 1973, **82**, 324–334.

AUTHOR INDEX

Numbers in italics refer to the pages on which the complete references are cited.

SUBJECT INDEX